SEED & GROWTH

The Story of the Dominican Sisters of Mission San Jose

Mary Thomas Lillis, O.P.

**Congregation of the
Queen of the Holy Rosary**

©2012 Dominican Sisters of Mission San Jose, Congregation of the Queen of the Holy Rosary

All rights reserved. No part of this book may be reproduced or transmitted in any form or by any means, electronic or mechanical, including photocopying, recording, or by any information storage and retrieval system without the written permission of the publisher, except where permitted by law.

>Dominican Sisters of Mission San Jose
>43326 Mission Blvd.
>Fremont, California 94539-5829
>
>www.msjdominicans.org

Published by Dominican Sisters of Mission San Jose

Cover photo by Dominique Mintz
Typesetting by Select Press
Printing by Lightning Source

ISBN 978-1-890777-50-0 (hard cover)
ISBN 978-1-890777-51-7 (soft cover)

10 9 8 7 6 5 4 3 2 1

Printed in the United States of America

*My thanks to my sisters who wrote
this story long before
I ever set pen to paper.*

Sister Mary Thomas Lillis, O.P.

SEED & GROWTH

Contents

	Foreword	vii
	Acknowledgments	ix
	Prologue	1
1	Roots	3
2	Pioneer Days	27
3	Growing Pains	61
4	Coping with the Albatross	93
5	Separation	101
6	Northwest Venture	125
7	Southern California Beckons	147
8	Affiliation to the Order	183
9	Mission San Jose	211
10	Working with the Friars	233
11	The Fox Catcher	261
12	Crisis in Community	279
13	Mission to Ukiah	287
14	Mother Antonina Fischer	309
15	Catastrophe!	321
16	Foundational Work	339
17	La Palmera	349
18	Mission to Mexico	377
19	Looking South Again	393
20	Altenberg and Rome Revisited	413
21	Altenhohenau	427
22	Mission to Marin	455

23	God Alone	473
24	Ministry Under Fire	497
25	The Legacy Continues	525
26	Dominican Collaboration	553
27	Native Daughter	563
28	Good Measure	579

Epilogue 617

Community Lore 623

Appendices
    A - Ministry Sites before 1963   629
    B - Maps   633

Glossary of Monastic and Church Terms 637

Works Cited and Consulted 645

Index 649

FOREWORD

You are holding a *labor of love* crafted by our Sister Mary Thomas Lillis. It was born of her hearing, living and witnessing the stories of the Dominican Sisters of the Queen of the Holy Rosary for some 70 years. It was the work of the last 10 years of her life as day in and day out she poured over annals, letters, pictures and any reference she could find that might elucidate the journey that has shaped our Congregation these past 135 years.

Sister Mary Thomas was scholar and storyteller *par excellance*. She was assiduous in her study and knew the power of stories to teach, inspire and shape the heart and spirit of those who follow. She knew the significance of stories as described by Robert N. Bella in *Habits of the Heart:*

> Communities have a history—in an important sense they are constituted by their past and for this reason we can speak of a real community as a "community of memory," one that does not forget its past. In order not to forget that past, a community is involved in retelling its story, its constitutive narrative and in so doing, it offers examples of the men and women who have embodied and exemplified the meaning of the community. These stories of collective history and exemplary individuals are an important part of the tradition that is so central to a community of memory. (p. 153)

Through this labor of love, Sister Mary Thomas draws us more deeply into the stories that gave shape to our life, our spirit and our values as Dominican women from our founding in 1876 to the opening of the Second Vatican Council. She weaves the tale of those years that we might be inspired and challenged in our efforts to face the reality of this historical moment and respond with similar clarity of vision, rootedness in God and courage.

This labor of love becomes gift of love in the reading. May we, her Sisters, make real our heartfelt gratitude to our Sister Mary Thomas for this gift through our fidelity and passion for the mission captured in these pages. May our lives be faithful to our past while giving birth to new stories yet to be shared and treasured!

Sister Gloria Marie Jones, OP
Congregational Prioress
April 29, 2011

This work of love by our Sister Mary Thomas Lillis was completed by our Sisters Evangela Balde, Mary Brennan, Katherine Jean Cowan, Veronica Lonergan, Mary Paul Mehegan, and Mary Peter Traviss, Chairman. We are indebted to them for their commitment to honor our Sister Mary Thomas's work and bring it to completion in her spirit.

ACKNOWLEDGMENTS

The publication of *Seed and Growth,* Sister Mary Thomas Lillis's story of the Dominican Sisters of Mission San Jose, written during the last years of her life, would not have been possible without the special assistance of others. Sister Donna Maria Moses, O.P., Judy Archer and Sister Elizabeth O'Donnell, O.P., contributed to the creation of a digitized version of the original manuscript, and Sister Lisa Marie Anthony, O.P., of the photographs. The maps were produced by Floyd Nabonne in collaboration with Sister Rosaleen Stoiber Kubitzki, O.P.

The occasional need for translation of German script was generously supplied by Sister Assunta Vorndran, O.P., Richard A. Schenk, O.P., and Monika Klein. Verónica Moreno Díaz and Sister Martha García, O.P., edited Spanish personal and location names in the English edition, and Sister Noreen Coleman, O.P., translated editorial comments for the Spanish edition.

Sister Frances Mary Pierson served as proofreader of the final English copy.

All pictures and primary sources not otherwise identified are from the archives of the Dominican Sisters of Mission San Jose.

Rick and Carolynn Crandall of Select Press prepared the manuscript and pictures for publication, patiently respecting the preferences of the Editing Committee, and providing advice on the publication process.

For the expertise and generous assistance of all of these individuals the Editing Committee is deeply grateful.

Special gratitude is due to Sister Gloria Marie Jones, O.P., Congregational Prioress, for her support of this project.

Editorial Committee:
    Sister Evangela Balde, O.P., Archivist
    Sister Mary Brennan, O.P.
    Sister Katherine Jean Cowan, O.P.
    Sister Veronica Lonergan, O.P.
    Sister Mary Paul Mehegan, O.P.
    Sister Mary Peter Traviss, O.P., Chair

PROLOGUE

November 11, 1876. A ripple of excitement ran through the crowd gathered on the Benicia platform as the *Overland* from the East, its brakes screeching and engineers slowing, ground to a jarring halt. Friends and relatives surged forward, crowding the car doors as weary passengers began their slow descent from the dust-covered coaches.

Among the last to emerge were three black-clad and bonneted figures who stood apart, gazing uneasily into the sea of strange faces before them. Anxiety gave way to relief at sight of a priest elbowing his way through the happily chattering groups. The Reverend Julius Herde, pastor of St. Boniface Church, San Francisco, welcomed the trio warmly and, carpet bags in tow, escorted them to the ferry for the picturesque ride across the bay.

San Francisco at last! With a prayer of fervent thanks, the travelers entered the waiting carriage for the last lap of the long journey that had begun ten days before in Brooklyn, New York. The nuns drew the carriage curtains discreetly; they had endeavored to adhere conscientiously to their Rule on the trip west; they would admit no exception on the streets of San Francisco.

CHAPTER ONE

ROOTS

The three young women who made the cross-country trip from Brooklyn to San Francisco were lineal descendants of an old and distinguished line. Some six centuries earlier, Dominic de Guzman had founded the Dominican Order in providential response to a crisis then threatening the Church. Castilian by birth, Dominic had been a canon of the Cathedral of Osma for nine years when called from his cloister to accompany Bishop Diego de Acebes on a diplomatic mission to Denmark involving the negotiation of marriage between the King of Castile's son and a Danish princess.[1]

En route, the royal emissaries were appalled at what they saw; southern France had become a stronghold of Albigensianism, a particularly oppressive brand of heresy heavily shaded with Manichean dualism.[2] In Toulouse where the party stopped for the night, the innkeeper proved a member of the notorious sect. Although tired from the day's travel, Dominic sat up all night in discussion with his host until in the early morning hours when the latter capitulated and was reconciled to the Church. For Dominic the encounter was to mark a turning point in his life.

Their mission accomplished, Diego and Dominic returned home, only to be sent back after two years to escort the princess to her waiting bridegroom. Unfortunately, the royal mission was destined to disappointment. According to one version, the bride had meantime died; according to another, she had chosen the cloister! In either case, the bride was missing, and the negotiators were relieved of further responsibility.

But the expedition was not without consequence, for

Providence has a way of turning apparent failure to Divine purpose. The travelers' experience in southern France and the ravages they heard of wrought by the pagan Cumans in Eastern Europe had made a profound impression on both clerics. So much so that they set out at once for Rome where Diego sought permission from Innocent III to resign his episcopal see in order to work for the salvation of the pagans to the north. The request met with refusal; there was enough to be done at home, said the Pope.

On their way back from Rome, Diego and Dominic were met at Montpellier by the little band of Cistercian legates whom the Pope had appointed preachers to the heretics. Despite the monks' efforts, however, the Albigensians continued to gain ground, their inroads attributable in large part to the convincing power of example. Their preachers were models of austere Gospel living, a style of life distinguished from the worldly Catholic clergy of the time. Discouraged by the meager results of their labors, the legates were on the verge of abandoning the mission, and they appealed their case to Diego who, though sympathetic, used the opportunity to call the situation as he saw it. To be effective, he told the legates, they must rid themselves of all pomp and trappings, travel about on foot and beg their bread; in a word, they must be poor men of the Gospel. Unenthusiastically the legates agreed—on condition that Diego lead the way.

Accepting his own challenge, Diego sent his retinue back to Osma and with Dominic as companion began a preaching crusade. During the weeks that followed, the two crisscrossed the countryside, taking on the heretics in public disputation and supporting their preaching by the witness of radical poverty and simplicity of life. No longer could the heretics present themselves as sole exemplars of authentic Gospel living; the preachers' message had the incontrovertible support of rigor of life. "Holy preaching" would henceforth be inseparably linked to Gospel witness—a life-restoring antidote to heretical error.

Be that as it may, the two did not immediately take the Midi by storm. An event of some promise occurred, however, toward the end of 1206 when a group of well-born women, confused by the heretics and graced by the missionaries, approached the latter, asking to be instructed in the truth. For some time the plight of the women of the area had weighed heavily on the two preachers. The heretics had established hostels where women and even children were trained in a monastic lifestyle firmly established in heretical teaching. Aware of the women's vulnerability at the hands of the Cathari leaders, Diego and Dominic gathered the little group of inquirers at an abandoned church site in Prouille, a Languedoc village situated at the foot of the Pyrenees; there Dominic went almost daily to instruct the women in the faith and to encourage them in the same disciplined life that he demanded of himself. Thus, without fanfare or deliberate measure of intent, the little convent at Prouille became the cradle of the future Dominican Order.

Gradually the idea of a permanent body of men committed to the preaching of sacred Truth began to take shape in Diego's mind; and in Dominic, his trusted friend and coworker, he found a ready ally in his thinking. But their shared persuasions suffered a serious setback when Diego died on December 30, 1207, while on a visit to his diocese in Osma. The Bishop's death left Dominic alone, except for the few companions he and Diego had managed to gather around them. As matters now stood, the future of the preaching mission would rest henceforth on the shoulders of Dominic.

Nine years would elapse, however, before the dream became a reality—years of devastating civil war that swept southern France in the wake of the assassination of the Cistercian missionary, Peter of Castlenau. Despite such adverse conditions, Dominic continued to preach, gaining the interest and admiration of Bishop Fulk of the Diocese of Toulouse. Impressed by what he saw and heard, the Bishop issued a charter formalizing Dominic's little band into a "preaching," that is, into a permanent company of itinerant preachers, authorized to preach anywhere in his diocese and obligated by no other parochial commitments. According to Tugwell, "This meant that Dominic was now free to accept recruits on a stable, institutional basis,"[3] although his was not yet a formal religious community.

When Fulk was called to Rome in 1215 to attend the Fourth Lateran Council, he took Dominic with him for the purpose of obtaining papal confirmation of the new institute. Innocent III's response was more than they had bargained for; the Pope proposed that Dominic return to Toulouse and, in consultation with his followers, choose an already existing Rule as a way of life.[4] The papal intent was ambitious: Seeing in Dominic's request exactly what the larger Church desperately needed at the time, Innocent wished the little institute to become a full-blown religious order, worldwide in its mission of preaching the Gospel.

Dominic might have found the absurdity of the notion amusing had he not been expected to act upon it. One night while praying in St. Peter's in Rome, the troubled preacher had a vision in which the Prince of the Apostles presented him with a staff, and St. Paul, with a book of the Gospels. "Go and preach," they told him. "You have been chosen by the Lord." Protesting the small number of his followers, Dominic was reassured when he saw in vision the brothers setting out by two's to preach throughout the world.[5]

An Order of Preachers

Returning to Toulouse, Dominic conferred with his followers. Their unanimous choice was the Rule of Saint Augustine,[6] which they fleshed out with details drawn from the Customary of the Premonstratensian monks,[7] a surprising choice in view of the active character of the brothers' preaching mission. Dominic's influence in the decision is unquestionable; he yielded to no one in his conviction that "holy preaching" is validated in Gospel living, exemplified and supported by a monastic way of life. As radical and demanding as the choice was, it would ever remain a distinguishing characteristic of the Order.

Innocent's death on July 16, 1216, was a severe blow to Dominic's plans; it meant that he had to begin all over again with the new pope, Honorius III. Patiently he set about winning the papal confidence, succeeding to the degree that Honorius, too, became his staunch supporter. On a wintry day in December, 1216, the Pope approved the little band, addressing to Dominic, his "dear son," the following bull of approval:[8]

> Considering that the brethren of your Order will be the champions of the faith and the true lights of the world, we confirm your Order, with all its lands and possessions, present and future, and we take under our care and protection the Order itself, together with all its possessions and privileges. Given at Rome at Santa Sabina, the eleventh day before the Kalends of January, one thousand two hundred and sixteen in the first year of our pontificate.[9]

This was routine fare, however; it confirmed the brothers as religious, but said nothing about them as preachers. Dominic bided his time and did not have long to wait. On January 21, 1217, he received a second bull that referred to the brothers as "preachers in the territory of Toulouse."[10] Dominic had his wish; their official duty, recognized as such by the Pope, was to spread the Gospel by preaching. In this second of four bulls addressed to the brothers between December 22, 1216, and February 7, 1217, the Church gave official confirmation to the Order of Preachers as we know it in broad outline today.

Scarcely had Dominic received approbation for his fledgling band than he dispersed it across the face of Europe to preach and to study at the leading universities. From the outset, the Founder's strong emphasis on the place of study in the Order was the outgrowth of his conviction that "the best protection against heresy... [is] a properly instructed Christian people, and this... [cannot] be achieved without a better educated clergy."[11] So daring a move did not meet with universal approval, the brothers greeting the announcement with reluctance and Bishop Fulk with protest; in their thinking, a brilliant concept was being ruined by premature action.

"It seemed to their worldly prudence," wrote Jordan of Saxony, Dominic's successor as Master General of the Order, "that he

Statue of St. Dominic de Guzman sculpted by Thomas McGlynn, O.P., erected at the Motherhouse, Mission San Jose, 1996

[Dominic] was tearing down rather than raising up the building that he had started."[12]

"On the contrary," was Dominic's response to his critics, "seed when scattered fructifies, when hoarded rots."[13]

Subsequent developments through the centuries have given the lie to Dominic's critics. When he died in 1221, the Order was sufficiently well established to carry on without him. Under his successors in governance, it enjoyed remarkable periods of growth and expansion, survived a variety of crises threatening its very existence, and produced an impressive roster of saintly women and men, brilliant scholars, and occasional rogues. Its durability to the present gives credence to Dominic's dying promise to be even more helpful to his brothers and sisters after death than he had been in life.

Holy Cross Priory, Ratisbon, Bavaria

Twelve years after Dominic's death, a little company of pious women approached the Dominican Friars in Ratisbon (now Regensburg), Bavaria, asking to live a cloistered life according to Dominican rule. Siegfried, Bishop of Ratisbon, gave enthusiastic endorsement to the project and persuaded the townsfolk to provide a land grant for the women on which a monastery could be built. The Convent of the Holy Cross, as it would henceforth be known, thereupon began its long, unbroken history of religious life.[14] Papal confirmation, obtained in 1244, was the final step in the process of the nuns' approval.

Through the years Holy Cross Convent flourished in both sanctity and numbers, so much so that at times it became necessary to refuse applicants—or at least to postpone their entry until the death of members provided choir stalls for the newcomers. But despite the monastery's admirable reputation, survival was sometimes doubtful. Dissolution seemed inevitable when, in 1803, the secularization of religious houses in Bavaria began to empty out the cloisters. Helpless in the face of events, the nuns packed their few belongings and awaited eviction. With commendable foresight the prioress distributed among them what convent funds were to be had. Came the fateful day when the emperor's commissary stood at the gate, demanding to see the community. Fearing the worst, the

Chapter 1 / ROOTS

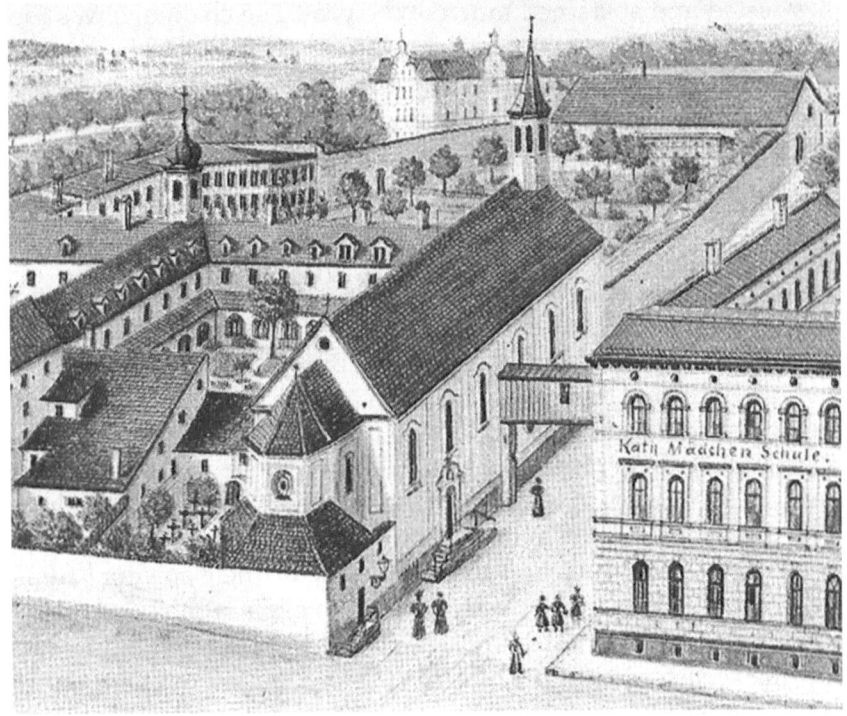

Holy Cross Priory, Ratisbon (Regensberg), with the enclosed bridge joining the convent to the school

nuns assembled in the refectory where, to their astonishment, they were offered an alternative: Return to the world or remain in their cloister—subject to the Prince-Bishop of Ratisbon, Karl Theodore von Dahlberg, to whom the convents of the city had been given in compensation for property losses in France.

One by one, the nuns came forward and solemnly avowed their intention of remaining. But non-suppression came at a price; they would have to open an elementary school in the monastery! Inspection of the premises convinced the Prince-Bishop that the nuns' storerooms would do quite nicely as classrooms. Teaching school was, of course, in dire conflict with the nuns' way of life. As Second Order Dominicans they were not permitted to leave the enclosure without the Bishop's permission; they could speak to seculars only through the grille, they rose at midnight to pray, and they fasted and abstained much of the year. The challenge was formidable, but they were determined to keep their Rule! They would give the lay sisters responsibility for escorting the children to and from the classrooms, for supervising the playground, and for taking care of all business with parents. The grille alone would have to go unresolved.

The Teaching Nuns

Little did they realize the impact of their decision; all unwittingly they had taken the initial step toward the founding of a teaching mission in distant America. That such a significant modification of their purpose demanded sacrifice on the part of the community can scarcely be exaggerated, but that the nuns were able to reconcile cloistered contemplative life with the activity of classroom teaching is testimony to the flexibility of the women who at the time comprised the community and to the solidity of their spiritual foundation. The Prince-Bishop's demands also explain the nuns' ready acceptance of the American mission some 50 years later—they had become accustomed to the idea of cloistered religious doing Third Order ministry!

Nonetheless, over the years modification in lifestyle to accommodate the demands of the classroom made gradual inroads in the religious discipline of the house—that is, until 1845, when the community elected Sister Benedicta Bauer as prioress.[15] Born Maria Anna Bauer on June 17, 1803, in the village of Pielenhofen, Bavaria, Anna grew up and entered Holy Cross Convent, Ratisbon, on July 2, 1820. At the time of her election as prioress, she engaged in teaching the younger pupils. In her the nuns found a woman who

Mother Maria Benedicta Bauer, O.S.D.

would make her mark in Holy Cross history as a resolute reformer bent on restoring religious discipline regardless of the cost to herself. Deviations, such as independent use of money and the ordering and serving meals in the nuns' rooms, struck a discordant note in the harmony of common life. Mother Benedicta had her task laid out for her, and she set about it with determination and gusto.

Mission to America

While thus busily occupied, she was summoned one day to meet a visitor who would affect significantly the future of Dominican life in the United States. Dom Boniface Wimmer, founder and abbot of the Benedictine Abbey of St. Vincent in Latrobe, Pennsylvania, himself a native of Bavaria and frequent visitor to his homeland, called at Holy Cross in 1851 to see Sister Elizabeth Kissel, a cousin. His description of the urgent need for nuns to safeguard the faith and culture of immigrant German girls in America fired the missionary spirit in Mother Benedicta, a spirit needing little enough enkindling in the first place. Her appeal for volunteers elicited a generous response, and from their number she selected four: Sisters Augustine Neuhierl; Josepha Witzlhofer, superior; Jacobina Riederer; and Francesca Ritter, the latter two lay sisters. Two years would elapse, however, before the mission to America materialized, as the Bishop of Ratisbon, the right Reverend Valentiene Riedel, was slow in granting permission.

In the interim, enthusiastic letters crossed the Atlantic between Mother Benedicta and the Dom, the latter assuring her of his willingness to assist the nuns. They were to come to St. Vincent's Abbey and remain for some time in order to learn the English language. At the Abbey they would be able to fulfill their religious obligations undisturbed. Dom Wimmer would himself assume all other responsibilities; at least, such was Mother Benedicta's understanding. That the Dom had a different perception may be concluded from a letter he wrote to a fellow Benedictine in Germany on July 29, 1853:

> In the near future I shall have to go to New York again to meet six [sic] Dominican Sisters that the Convent of the Holy Cross of Ratisbon is sending me as a cross (as if I did not as yet have enough crosses). I am to look for a suitable

place for them. Already letters for that purpose have been sent East and West. Perhaps I shall be able to locate them in Williamsburg, a suburb of New York City, where the German pastor and Vicar General Raffeiner is disposed to take them if the Archbishop permits it....I really should not have burdened myself with this affair; but the Prioress did not cease to beg me and so I agreed, or rather promised to help as much as I could to find a place for them outside of our diocese. I hoped thereby that Saint Dominic would put in a good word for me when I needed it.[16]

That the Dom's peevish attitude would move Dominic to "put in a good word" for him seems dubious at best, and later events would seem to render the saint even less receptive!

Armed with the Bishop of Ratisbon's dimissorial letter sending them forth in God's name, Sister Josepha and her three companions bade a tearful farewell to their beloved Holy Cross community and set out for Bremerhaven. From there, on August 1, 1853, they sailed on the steamer *Germania*, bound for a land whose customs and language would be completely foreign to them. With them went twenty chests of chapel furnishings, household goods and sundry necessities. Twenty-six days after embarking, the *Germania* docked in New York harbor, and the nuns followed their fellow travelers down the gangplank, setting foot for the first time on American soil.

Their reception was bleak. No one was at the Franklin Street pier to meet them! In mounting panic they searched the crowd for Dom Wimmer, finally admitting to themselves the inadmissible: He was not there! In fairness to the Dom, it must be said that when he realized he would not be able to meet the nuns, he arranged for a priest friend, Father Nicholas Balleis, O.S.B., to take his place. The latter's failure to show accounts for the desperate straits in which the travelers, none of whom spoke English, except Sister Augustine who knew a few words, now found themselves.

Fortunately for all concerned, the crisis was averted when Sister Josepha remembered a letter given her before leaving Germany by the Reverend Joseph Mueller, C.SS.R., court chaplain and spiritual director of the *Ludwig Missionsverein* in Munich.[17] Addressed to the Redemptorist pastor of the Church of the Most Holy Redeemer in New York City, the letter was to be used in the unlikely event that the nuns would need it. At this point it proved a godsend. Aided by a friendly stevedore, the nuns took a carriage to the Redemptorist rectory, where the priests spoke German and welcomed the travelers most cordially.

Temporary quarters were arranged for Sisters Josepha and Augustine with the Ziegler family in New York City, while Sisters Jacobina and Francesca were sent off to the Blaggi's across the Hudson in Newark, New Jersey. Exhausted from the strain, the nuns must have longed for the peace and dear familiarity of their convent home in Bavaria or at least the security of the Pennsylvania mission where they could settle in and begin in earnest their work for souls.

Williamsburg, New York

But Carrolltown, Pennsylvania, was not to be their destination. The Very Reverend Stephan Raffeiner, vicar general of the Archdiocese of New York and pastor of the Church of the Most Holy Trinity, Williamsburg (soon to be incorporated into Brooklyn, New York), whom Dom Wimmer had apprised of the nuns' coming, saw in the travelers' predicament a heaven-sent opportunity too good to miss, for in Williamsburg he had a school filled with children of German immigrant truck farmers. Losing no time, he invited the nuns to take charge of his school. However shocking the abrupt change of plan, the nuns saw in their predicament God's holy Will; after all, they had come to a mission country, and missionaries were expected to be prepared to adapt. They accepted the new situation, therefore, sight unseen! And so it happened that through a providential oversight they were destined to dedicate their apostolic energies to the children of Williamsburg, New York, rather than Carrolltown, Pennsylvania.

That the arrangement was a happy solution to his problem Dom Wimmer never doubted. On his arrival in Williamsburg five days later, he was relieved to find the nuns somewhat settled and wrote Mother Benedicta a letter intended to allay her anxieties and absolve himself from guilt:

> Latrobe, Westmoreland County, Pennsylvania
> September 18, 1853
>
> Venerable dear Mother Prioress:

That your daughters arrived safely in America, you are already aware. As well as I could, I provided that they should be immediately received by my co-frater, P. Nicolas Balleis, in New York. I could come to see them and to provide for them only on the fifth day after their arrival. Because for the time being I knew of no place for them in the country, I agreed with the Reverend Vicar General of New York, Father Raffeiner, that he take the Sisters to his parish church in Williamsburg, a suburb of New York, which numbers 30,000 inhabitants, nearly 15,000 of whom are German Catholics. The place is excellent in location and as a field of activity. Oh, how the girls and mothers rejoiced as they heard that they had Sisters and especially when they saw them! Also the Rt. Rev. Archbishop gladly received them. Because no convent is there, we were obliged to lodge the Sisters in the rectory which adjoins the old church. Do not be alarmed at this. The pastor, the above-named Vicar General, is an old Father, a holy priest, and has only one curate. The rectory is spacious. I remained four days with him to arrange everything. The four Sisters already after the first week have a complete enclosure as regards the outside—the people; and also interiorly with regard to the priests. Naturally they are in considerably close quarters, but it is satisfactory. They have a kitchen; next to it is a study room; on the other side is a dormitory large enough for four. At the same time I bought four iron, very comfortable bedsteads, so that I might see whether there was sufficient room; we found that there was additional space for a table and a chest or bureau. The pastor who lives on the upper floor has access only to the kitchen. I arranged to make even this a part of the enclosure by locking the door to his quarters....A large garden surrounds the church which gives them space in which to recreate and to work. The school also adjoins the church. Their future convent will either be built on that same spot, if the old pastor so desires, or on the west side of the large new church which would be still better. Here the pastor has three lots or places for buildings; between these, however, in the center, there are two small houses which would have to be purchased.

They would cost from $5,000 to $6,000. This amount must not alarm or frighten you. $6,000 here is a trifle. By means of school activities and an institute, that amount would soon be paid—the real burden for your children is this: that they must cook for both priests, i.e., that these will share the food with them.

We have arranged that the Sisters will send the meals upstairs by means of a dumb-waiter....Nevertheless this, we realize, is somewhat annoying and troublesome. Alas, nothing else could be done. The old priest purposely took the Sisters so that he would not be obliged to have a cook and also to save money. He is rich, but he is very close. ...Perhaps in return he will some day will the Sisters his money. If he grants them only the lot for the building as he promised, he will be donating the equivalent of $1,000....In order that the Sisters will not be obliged to arrange the beds and rooms of the priests, the Father engaged the services of a pious widow and I told the Sisters to pay the salary to her for this service because they, too, would often be in need of her services; in this way the old priest may more easily be satisfied....

The two exchangeable notes of 6,000 gulden and 1,000 gulden, 4,000 of which was in my name, I collected. The Reverend old gentleman wonders if the Sisters could not lend him the money until they need it. He would give them five per cent interest. I urged the Sisters to accept the offer. The old Father does not need the money personally but he will re-invest it in a so-called Savings Bank which will give him six per cent interest; thus he will gain one per cent. Thereby the Sisters will be worth more to him materially; at the same time the Sisters will benefit for they do not need the money now....The money earned by teaching will support them otherwise. Naturally I am not in a position to discuss the building of a new convent. We must see how everything develops—at any rate just now there is no need therefore.

But there is something which needs immediate attention; ie., you *must* admit one or two postulants who are well versed in English. You may not object to this because the nature of the case demands such....You are at liberty to send us German teachers or postulants but we ourselves must admit and train English postulants here....Since you yourself confided your daughters to me, and also the Rt. Rev. Bishop in his testimonials and Rt. Rev. Archbishop of New York, also his Vicar General, consider me the spiritual director of your Sisters, I have, therefore, assumed a definite responsibility for them. I believe that I have the necessary authority to direct the Sisters in this matter—hence I have ordered Mother Josepha to admit promptly any worthy English postulant who might apply for admission. I told her that I would be responsible to you for such action and I hope that you will trust me for I am better acquainted in America and I know better what must be done here, than you at Holy Cross, in Regensburg. I certainly mean well in your regard and that of your Sisters....

Whether I have performed my task well or badly, I do not know—I certainly did mean well—of that I am certain. I cannot often travel to Williamsburg because it is 400 miles from here and requires at least 60 florins. But if there is need, I will come in spite of that fact. Furthermore I wish to keep in touch with my adopted children by letter writing and wish to direct them until they are better acquainted and can direct themselves. Every beginning is hard. Much must be endured. But whoever means well with God and possesses good will, God will be helpful to the end. The Sisters were all very well; they served me well, entertained me as long as they could. Please reprove them because they would not accept anything from me for the chest or trunk which cost 34 florins. At the beginning they were somewhat depressed and anxious but when I left they were full of hope and courage (Sept. 7), and I hope all will be well. Everything was so well ordered that one cannot help feeling that the Will of God is being done. Pray for me and write an answer soon. I greet you all in the Lord and remain with utmost respect.

Yours sincerely,

P. Boniface Wimmer, O.S.B.

P.S. I regret that I have been compelled to write you so frankly concerning the character of the Rev. Fr. Raffeiner. But it was necessary that you should know in order to clarify the situation as far as you, your Sisters, and my dealings with the priest were concerned. Nevertheless I must add that the same priest has been in America almost 20 years. At the beginning he had to endure many hardships and privations, yet he founded many churches and parishes. Now of course he is well-to-do because he has a large parish with a good income.[18] I doubt not in the least that some day he will use all his money for the good of the church—we dare not judge him in this matter. Please do not reveal the contents of my letter *in extenso*. You may allow the Rt. Rev. Bishop and the confessor to read the letter. But both should also read these added lines so that they may not through my fault become prejudiced against the worthy priest. Greet both for me heartily....[19]

To absolve the Dom from all responsibility for the depressing situation in which the nuns found themselves would be to disdain the truth. The fact is that however "spacious" the rectory was, the nuns were confined to the basement, and Dom Wimmer's attempts to portray conditions so positively must have seemed to them an exercise in clerical fantasy.

Almost immediately Mother Josepha and Sister Augustine assumed responsibility for the school. "School" was the church basement, where the nuns divided the 140 pupils into two groups of 70 each, with no particular disposition as to grade. In December, at the urging of his bishop, Father Raffeiner offered the nuns a classroom under the old church as residence. Although larger, the new quarters still left much to be desired. Winter brought its own problems; the wind howled through the cracks in the walls, and rain or snow on the nuns' beds was no novelty. That within two years of their arrival Sister Francesca developed tuberculosis and died soon after should come as no surprise. But despite such adverse conditions the mission succeeded, for the nuns were highly skilled teachers and their reputation spread. By their first Christmas in Williamsburg, enrollment at St. Alphonsus Female School (named in honor of the Redemptorists who had first welcomed them) had increased to 225. Tuition was 25 cents per week, an income that netted, roughly, $50 weekly. From this amount the nuns were expected to feed and clothe themselves, heat and maintain the school, pay the housekeeper's salary and set aside something for a future convent—no mean challenge even in those far-off days. The Ratisbon Motherhouse had given the nuns $1,600 to help them get started. Of this they used $1,200 for the purchase of a lot for a future convent; the $400 remaining was quickly spent on furniture and classroom benches.

Growth of the Community

Gradually conditions improved for the pioneer community. On May 9, 1855, reinforcements arrived from Ratisbon in the persons of Sisters Michaela Braun, Seraphina Staimer, and Emilia Barth. Financial aid also appeared. The Most Reverend John Loughlin, first bishop of the newly erected Diocese of Brooklyn, lent the nuns funds ($4,000) for the purchase of a small house adjacent to the new church; King Ludwig I of Bavaria sent them $2,400 toward a convent; and the *Ludwig Missionsverein* promised an annual donation of $600 for a period of five or six years. The windfall made possible the erection of a "real" convent, located on the corner of Montrose and Graham Avenues. Begun in June 1857, it was dedicated in November of the same year.

Meanwhile, across the Atlantic the convent in Ratisbon was involved in its own problems. Two members of the community, disenchanted with Mother Benedicta's efforts at reform, were spreading discontent within the cloister. Duly penanced, the malcontents appealed to the new Bishop of Ratisbon, Ignatius von Synestry, for support. He made no attempt to hear the other side of the story and simply ordered Mother Benedicta to resign. Her compliance provided a long-desired opportunity for her to join the missions in America. Accordingly, in 1858 the last nuns to make the trip from Ratisbon arrived in New York: Mother Benedicta Bauer, Sister Thomasina Ginker, Sister Cunigunda Schell, and Crescentia Traubinger, a candidate.

In the interim since the first group of Dominican nuns had arrived in America, Father Ambrose Buchmeier, O.F.M.Cap., had been patiently biding his time. Pastor of St. Nicholas Church in lower Manhattan, he had long dreamed of German-speaking religious for his school and was decidedly frustrated when he learned that nuns from Ratisbon had been available in 1853, but no one had notified him. With an eye to keeping in contact, he agreed to accept appointment as the nuns' extraordinary confessor, and in a matter of time came to be recognized as a loyal and faithful friend of the little community. When, therefore, the nuns received their first postulant in 1858, Father Buchmeier decided the time had come; he spoke up, earnestly pleading for nuns for the girls of his school. Moreover, he had a house—not a basement—ready for them!

Mother Josepha was faced with a dilemma. Here was a genuine need voiced by one who had befriended the nuns in their difficulties, often at personal inconvenience. Over against this was the eventuality of excommunication threatening a religious who had the temerity to open a new convent without the consent of the Ratisbon Motherhouse and the permission of both bishops concerned. In her predicament Mother Josepha very likely took counsel with Bishop Loughlin who, as a missionary bishop, enjoyed "vast discretionary powers"[20] when dealing with local situations in which communication difficulties presented crucial problems. Since even under the best of circumstances a lapse of three months could be anticipated before an answer to a letter arrived from Ratisbon, the issue of communication was judged valid; in consequence, Bishop Loughlin felt free to take authority into his own hands and grant the requisite permission. Father Buchmeier was a happy man!

Word of the new foundation, however, was not received with enthusiasm in Ratisbon, where the American *filiale*[21] was thought to be acting in much too independent a manner. The growing resentment at the autonomy exercised by the nuns in America is evident in a letter from the frustrated prioress of Ratisbon, Mother Agnes Rosenloehner, Mother Benedicta's successor. Replying to her predecessor's request for authorization to establish a new foundation in the Midwest, she wrote somewhat testily:

> Ratisbon, May 12, 1860
>
> Dear Mother Benedicta:
>
> Your circumstances I can understand in a measure, but it is impossible for me to help you. You declare that it would be an aid to you if you received my permission to go elsewhere. The following is the bishop's reply:

"Those in America must become independent. But before taking that step they must declare if it be their intention to stay in America or to return to the Motherhouse. They need not come immediately, but they must declare their intention."

Perhaps the best thing for me would be to add no further remarks of my own because, after all, I can only say, "become independent and then do what you consider best." The Rev. Spiritual Director Schoettle told me there was a decision of the Holy Father to the effect that branch houses must become independent. Whether this applied to all convents I cannot say.

I have informed Sister Josepha that Williamsburg must comply with this order, and I have written to her several times to this effect. But the letters, it seems, do not reach their destination. The first one, however, was received. I am certain of that, for the Sisters acted as if they were insane and declared that they would not agree to any separation from the Motherhouse. They even stated that they would all return to Europe. It is most singular—these people may found convents in America without our permission—may appoint subjects to these houses without asking us—and may leave them at will. Most singular dependence on the Motherhouse! I have already told Sister Josepha that she can no longer claim subjects or financial aid from the Motherhouse. What new tricks will these American Sisters be up to when they hear again that they must become independent?

In as far as you are concerned, you are the best judge of your own case. You do not want to come back to us, and no good will come of your staying with those Sisters....In the first place the prioress of Holy Cross Convent cannot give you this permission. Secondly, it is equivalent to the Motherhouse opening a new foundation through you, and we should be under obligations to supply a sufficient number of subjects and be responsible for the support of the foundation....If you know that a Dominican nun would be allowed to work as a missionary and found a new house as you, or rather Sister Thomasina writes, then certainly we would have no objections. Indeed, every one of us would wish to be of service to you, so that you might obtain your goal. I wrote to Sister Josepha that she must pay back the one thousand francs belonging to Sister Jacobina, because my subjects are not willing to make a gift of that sum to Williamsburg. In case you find a little place of your own in America, then Sister Josepha is to turn over the thousand francs to you....I would so much like to help you, but every aid I could offer you would be contrary to our *Constitutions*....

You may do as you wish as long as I will not be concerned in any transaction. Therefore, you people in America should become independent, and then you could adjust yourselves according to the regulations which exist in America. You could spread out and work in the missions as the Lord provides occasions. I cannot give a more definite decision than this, and it may probably grieve you....God will surely help you as He has always helped in the past. Let these be the words of comfort.

From your,

Mother Agnes[22]

Cloistered Ratisbon could hardly be expected to understand conditions in the missionary church of the United States in the mid-1800s. Clearly, the American community was becoming a burden to its parent, and Bishop von Synestry's judgment of the case brought neither comfort to Mother Josepha nor appeasement to Mother Agnes.[23] There could be no mistaking the meaning of the following communication from the Ratisbon Chancery Office on October 26, 1860:

> A convent in which there are only 3 professed sisters and 4 novices is in all things in a condition of defect. It is not possible to observe the Holy Rule in all its entirety nor is it possible to make the convent self-subsisting. The affiliated Convent in Williamsburg has gone against the spirit of the Order and the Rule of St. Dominic and even against the

obedience which it is obliged to render the Motherhouse. You neglected to get in connection with the Motherhouse. It is possible for newly founded convents to become independent if it is done according to the spirit of the Order and according to Rome, but you have, through the founding of new affiliations in New York and Somerset [sic] without the consent of the Motherhouse to whom you are subject, blamably worked against your own independence.

Such conduct against the rule and obedience for which no authority, no privilege from Rome can be shown, caused the high authority to inform Rome and in the meantime all former acts by means of which new affiliations from the yet dependent affiliated Convent in Williamsburg could be founded are to be considered null and void.

(Signed) J. V. Regar, Vicar General[24]

In reality, the shift in canonical status of the Williamsburg community from a *filiale* to an independent convent had in all probability become official three years earlier when Bishop Loughlin canonically erected the nuns' new convent at Montrose and Graham as the Brooklyn Motherhouse. Supporting this line of thought is the fact that Rome, even though informed of the distressing state of affairs in New York, made no move to censure the long-suffering Mother Josepha.

Mother Josepha Witzlhofer died on April 9, 1864, a victim of tuberculosis. She was 46 years of age and had been professed for 24 years. In the words of Father Crawford, she set for her sisters an example of "wonderful perseverance in the face of disheartening obstacles. The spirit of this sorely tried woman was never broken....She was a highly talented woman and a very capable teacher. ...the embodiment of refinement and religious decorum, a woman of prayer and sacrifice."[25]

The pain that separation from the Ratisbon Motherhouse brought with it was real, but from the historical perspective of the American Dominican sisterhoods, it proved both providential and life-giving. Today, twelve congregations of American women religious—the Dominican Sisters of Mission San Jose among them—look to the cloistered community of Holy Cross Convent, New York, the direct descendant of Holy Cross Priory, Ratisbon, as their parent group. With love, respect and enduring gratitude they acknowledge their immense debt to the New York and Ratisbon Motherhouses, the source and inspiration of the Mission San Jose story that follows.

Notes

[1] William A. Hinnebusch, O.P., *The History of the Dominican Order: Origins and Growth to 1500* (Staten Island, New York: Alba House, 1966) 20–21.

[2] Catharism was a dualistic heresy of Eastern origin that gained footing in the West, particularly in southern France around 1150 A.D., where it was known as Albigensianism, after the town of Albi. In its Albigensian form, the heresy supported absolute dualism, i.e., the existence of two supreme principles, one good, one evil. The latter was the source of material things; hence, the body is evil, as is marriage, also the eating of meat and animal products, etc. Salvation was reserved for the elite or "Perfect," who achieved perfection by rigorous asceticism and strict poverty, i.e., by liberation from material things. The majority could live pretty much as they pleased, being saved on their deathbed by receiving the *consolamentum* or baptism of the Spirit. Meanwhile, the holiness of the perfect "utterly discredited the worldly clergy of the Catholic Church." Benedict Ashley, O.P., *The Dominicans* (Collegeville: Liturgical Press, 1990) 4 and Guy Bedouelle, O.P., *Saint Dominic and the Grace of the Word* (San Francisco: Ignatian Press, 1987) 171–174.

[3] Simon Tugwell, O.P., *Saint Dominic* (Strasbourg: Editions du Signe, 1991) 20.

[4] The Fourth Lateran Council had decreed that only Rules already approved by the Church could be adopted by new groups. To conform to the decree the Pope advised Dominic to choose an already existing Rule, such as that of St. Augustine, as the rule of life to be followed by the brothers.

[5] Tugwell 23.

[6] A rule of life based on a letter from Saint Augustine to a community of nuns and adopted by Saint Dominic to be followed by the brothers.

[7] Premonstratensians, also called Norbertines or Canons Regular of Premontre, an order founded by St. Norbert at Premontre, France, in

1120 A.D. Their customary was the strictest in its monastic observances among the existing orders. St. Dominic mitigated it for the purposes of his order by omitting those elements that would impede its mission and adding the principle of dispensation.

[8] A papal letter distinguished by significance of subject and sealed with a special seal or *bulla*.

[9] Honorius III, *Religiosam vitam*, December 22, 1216 as found in Hinnebusch 48.

[10] Honorius III, *Gratiarum omnium*, January 21, 1217 as found in Hinnesbusch 48–49.

[11] Tugwell 26.

[12] Hinnebusch 51.

[13] Hinnebusch 51.

[14] Holy Cross Convent continues today its more than 700 years of unbroken existence. During World War II the convent was bombed and a sister killed, but the community remained together.

[15] Prioress from 1845 to 1858, Mother Benedicta was responsible for three foundations: Niederviebach; Mintraching which failed after Mother Benedicta came to America; and Williamsburg, Long Island. When Bishop Ignatius von Synestry of Ratisbon ordered Mother Benedicta to resign, she and her companions left for Williamsburg. She later founded the Congregation of St. Catherine of Siena in Racine, Wisconsin. This valiant woman died on October 13, 1865. Mary Hortense Kohler, O.P., *The Life and Work of Mother Benedicta Bauer* (Milwaukee: Bruce Publishing, 1937).

[16] Dom Wimmer, O.S.B., letter to Gregory Scherr in Eugene J. Crawford, *The Daughters of Dominic on Long Island: the History of the Congregation of the Holy Cross:* Sisters of the Third Order of St. Dominic of the Diocese of Brooklyn (New York: Benziger Brothers, 1938) 42.

[17] The *Ludwig Missionsverein* was founded in Munich in 1838 under the patronage of King Ludwig I of Bavaria for the express purpose of providing financial assistance to the Catholic missions of America.

[18] Eugene J. Crawford maintained that Dom Wimmer was misinformed regarding Father Raffeiner's personal wealth: "At the time he probably did not possess much money, for he had given considerable away in the course of his priestly career. Whatever material goods he possessed were not obtained from a lucrative parochial career as Dom Wimmer insinuates, for most of his missionary labors were undergone under

extreme poverty....He undoubtedly was free-spending in regard to works of religion; on the contrary there is no doubt that he was stingy in small things, and somewhat callous in his treatment of the pioneer sisters." Crawford *The Daughters of Dominic on Long Island: the History of the Congregation of the Holy Cross Sisters of Saint Dominic of the Diocese of Brooklyn* (New York: Benziger Brothers, 1938) 58–59.

[19] Dom Wimmer, O.S.B., letter to Bauer in Crawford 18 September 1853, 53–58.

[20] Crawford 81.

[21] *Filiale:* A monastery dependent on the Motherhouse, not an independent foundation.

[22] Crawford 85–87.

[23] Crawford 91. Father Crawford added a lengthy footnote, which reads in part: "Bishop von Synestry's hasty decision in 1858 to depose Mother Benedicta and reinstate the two disaffected sisters was most unfortunate. Both of them later were expelled from the Convent. The Bishop's decision in regard to Williamsburg was undoubtedly made hastily and without an accurate knowledge of conditions. Bishop Loughlin should have been consulted by him."

[24] Regor , J. V. letter to Mother Josepha Witzlhofer, O.S.D., 26 October, 1860 in Crawford 88–89.

[25] Crawford 100.

CHAPTER TWO

PIONEER DAYS

1876. California is 26 years into the Union as the nation's thirty-first state; Ulysses S. Grant is the country's eighteenth president. San Francisco is one generation removed from the wildly incredible days of the Gold Rush, not yet two decades away from the Vigilantes, and a mere seven years from the linking of the Atlantic and Pacific coasts by rail. On Telegraph Hill the semaphore is still announcing the arrival by boat of passengers, mail, and cargo. Emperor Norton I, genial in his self-delusion, is still walking the streets of his "kingdom" in uniform, epaulettes, and cocked hat.

Pioneer Sisters

To the City by the Golden Gate came the three Dominican Sisters from Holy Cross, Brooklyn, their arrival causing little stir outside the parochial boundaries of St. Boniface Church. In appropriate anonymity the San Francisco *Daily Examiner* chronicled their arrival simply as "3 Sisters of St. Dominick" [sic] on the passenger list published daily as part of the local newspaper service.[1]

Sister Pia (Mary) Backes, daughter of Mathias and Margaretha Schram Backes, was born on October 11, 1852, in Neukirchen, Germany, near the historic city of Treves. At the age of four she moved with her parents and only sister, Elizabeth, to the eastern seaboard of the United States. Mathias Backes settled his family in another historic city, Philadelphia, where Mary was enrolled in St. Peter's Parochial School under the direction of the School Sisters of Notre Dame. Philadelphia made a deep impression on the youthful Mary. She delighted in visiting the old Revolutionary sites, and years later still enjoyed describing them in detail for her California sisters. Her recollections of the slave platform on which she saw men and women sold like chattel aroused her deepest sympathy, so much so that throughout her life she retained a special place in her heart for black children. It was, in fact, upon a black playmate that she determined to exercise her first recorded act of ministerial zeal. Providing herself with an oyster shell, Mary took her little friend to a nearby creek, intent on turning him from a devout Baptist into an enthusiastic Catholic. Fortunately for all concerned, her father discovered her in the act and put an end to his daughter's proselytizing.

In the early 1860s the Backes family moved again, this time to Brooklyn, New York, where Mary continued her education at Holy Trinity School, her first contact with the Dominican Sisters of Holy Cross Monastery, Brooklyn. Impressed though she was by the sisters' religious spirit and teaching skills, she never forgot her beloved School Sisters and, when time came for her First Communion, persuaded her parents to allow her to rejoin her former classmates in Philadelphia for this special occasion.

Mary's leadership qualities were early apparent. Frequently she would gather her peers and lead them to the parish church for a visit to the Blessed Sacrament. On one occasion, during the octave of Christmas, she organized a procession to the crib. Singing lustily, the children marched down the aisle behind their leader just as the Redemptorist Fathers were entering the church for their customary noonday prayer. Breaking ranks hurriedly, the children fled—all except Mary who stood her ground sturdily before the startled priests, who had not been forewarned of the extra-liturgical observance.

The untimely death of Mary's father on her seventeenth birthday cast a heavy pall over the hitherto happy Backes household. In deference to her widowed mother, Mary waited a year before voicing her desire to enter religious life with her former teachers in Philadelphia. Maternal consent, however, carried with it a condition—ironic in view of future events: "If you wish to be a sister, all right; but you may not go so far away. Join the sisters across the street." This Mary did joyfully, entering Holy Cross Convent, Brooklyn, on August 14, 1870. She received the Dominican habit and her new name, Sister Maria Pia, on September 14, 1871, and pronounced her first and final vows on September 17, 1872.

As Sister Pia she was assigned a large class in Holy Trinity School and, in addition, entrusted with the supervision of boys in the orphanage attached to the Motherhouse. Later she served as assistant in the pharmacy of St. Catherine's Hospital, Brooklyn, and superior of Our Lady of Sorrows Convent, New York City, a responsibility she exercised until selected from the sisters who volunteered for the California mission.

Those who knew Sister Pia early in her religious life described her as "deeply pious, strict in observance, and capable of shouldering responsibility."[2] They would go on to say later that:

> Her continual prayer was for the grace to know and to fulfill God's Holy Will....Human respect never deterred her from working out her plans according to the dictates of her conscience. Firm in her convictions, she courageously bore contradictions and bravely faced opposition when there was question of sustaining her religious principles. On the other hand, she never swerved in her loyal submission to the Rule and to the laws and decrees of Holy Mother Church.[3]

Like Sister Pia her companions were made of the stuff of pioneers. Sister Salesia (Anna) Fichtner was born in Buchenau, Bavaria, on September 11, 1855. As a young girl Anna gave serious thought to joining the Servite nuns in Munich where her aunt, Mother Johanna, was superior. An enclosed community, the Servites accepted only a set quota of postulants each year, and Anna found herself obliged to wait her turn. This did not satisfy the enthusiastic applicant. Having made up her mind, she had her heart set on entering at once. On the nuns' recommendation, Anna was admitted—sight unseen—into the postulancy of Holy Cross, Brooklyn, on May 11, 1875. Across the ocean with her went a statue of the Infant of Prague, a parting gift from Mother Johanna. After a four-month postulancy Anna was clothed in the Dominican habit on September 8, 1875, and made final profession a year later on October 28, 1876—six days before leaving for California—accompanied by the Infant of Prague, her faithful traveling companion.

The third member of the trio, Sister Amanda (Rosalia) Bednartz, a native of New York City, was born on April 19, 1859, the daughter of Wenzel and Louise Arendt Bednartz. She received her early education at Our Lady of the Assumption School conducted by the School Sisters of Notre Dame, and became acquainted with the Dominicans of Holy Cross when her family moved from New York City to Brooklyn. There she attended the newly founded St. Michael's School taught by the Dominican Sisters. On May 8, 1873, Rosalia was accepted into the Dominican community at the age of 14. The following January she received the habit of the Order and her new name, and pronounced final vows on November 25, 1875. Before her assignment to California Sister Amanda taught at All Saints School, Brooklyn, and Our Lady of Sorrows School, New York City. Love for the missions urged her to volunteer herself in response to the San Francisco Archbishop's request for sisters.

At the time of their missioning to the West, Sister Pia was 24 years of age; Sister Salesia, 21; and Sister Amanda, 17. To their inexperience they brought a faith and a courage that would serve them well in the challenging years ahead.

Mission to California

The events leading to the western mission had begun in 1850, when Joseph Sadoc Alemany,[4] a Dominican priest of Catalonian birth, was named to the Diocese of Monterey, California, and consecrated in Rome on June 30, of the same year. On the following December 6, he sailed through the Golden Gate on the steamer Columbus with two companions, Father Francis Vilarrasa, O.P., and a Dominican Sister, Sister Mary Goemaere, foundress of the Dominican Sisters of Benicia (later San Rafael). Arriving in Santa Barbara on Christmas Day the new Bishop presented his credentials to the Vicar

Joseph Sadoc Alemany, O.P., Archbishop of San Francisco, 1853–1885

General and thereupon took formal possession of his diocese. His was a providential appointment. Ten years on the missions in Ohio, Kentucky, and Tennessee had given him a fluency in English and a familiarity with United States customs that would work to his advantage in the days to come.

Three years later, Pope Pius IX established the Province of San Francisco, consisting of the Diocese of Monterey and the Archdiocese of San Francisco. It was as San Francisco's first archbishop that Joseph Sadoc Alemany wrote to Mother Seraphina Staimer,[5] second Mother Superior or Mother Prioress of the Dominican Sisters of Brooklyn, New York, earnestly requesting sisters to teach the children of German-speaking immigrant parents in St. Boniface Parish, San Francisco.

> Would it be possible for you to send a few of your Sisters to work among my people? I must tell you that I have nothing to offer in the way of materialities. But I can promise you a harvest ready for the picking, souls clamoring for the message of the Gospel. But, dearest Mother, please send me zealous young ladies, ones who love their vocation and reflect its virtues. The vineyard here is worthy of the ultimate in dedication. If you and your advisers, with the grace of God, answer my request, I can promise your community many blessings. In a hundred years from now, your successors will be able to point with great satisfaction to their accomplishments for God and nation.[6]

In spite of its eloquence, the Archbishop's plea was refused on the dual grounds of distance and the pressing demand for sisters to staff the community's rapidly expanding foundations closer to home. But the "little Archbishop" was not easily put off. When a second letter brought a second negative response, he went personally to the New York Motherhouse to plead his cause. Persistence won the day; Mother Seraphina found it impossible to resist the appeal of "souls clamoring for the message of the Gospel."

Hoping to forestall the possibility of a change of heart on the part of the Brooklyn superior, Archbishop Alemany went into immediate action. Within four months of his visit to the East Coast, he wrote again to Mother Seraphina:

> San Francisco, Aug. 28/76
>
> Dear in Christ Sister,
>
> You will be surprised to learn that the Sisters' new Home is far advanced and it will likely be finished soon. It seems that the work has been done with much zeal, and yet well....
>
> Before the building is finished I will write again. In the meantime I would say, that I suppose three or four Sisters might be enough at the beginning, and probably two able to teach, out of the three or four, might be sufficient, while I would deem it most useful that one at least would understand English, though perhaps all know it.
>
> Yours truly in Our Holy Father,
> Joseph Sadoc, O.P. A.S.F.
> Mother Seraphina Staimer, O.S.D. Superior[7]

October saw the sisters' house completed. It was now time to make good the promise. Mother Seraphina Staimer summoned Sister Pia to the Motherhouse for the purpose of discussing her appointment. "I arrived there at 2:30 p.m.," she wrote in her Diary, "leaving the Sisters behind me on the verge of tears. Without betraying the least emotion, I broke the news to my people."[8] But her calm was short-lived.

> On the first day of retreat, however, I nearly succumbed. It seemed extremely hard, and had I not been ashamed of myself I...would have declined. The next day, however, my heart was much lighter, though there was little progress in the making of my retreat. My thoughts kept wandering to San Francisco, or dwelling on the leave-taking from my dear sisters and relatives.[9]

The announcement of the California mission to the sisters in New York could not be accused of embellishment: "Following the invitation of the Most Reverend Joseph Sadoc Alemany, O.P., Archbishop of San Francisco, California, Sister M. Pia Backes, Sister M. Amanda Bednartz, and Sister M. Salesia Fichtner shall leave the Motherhouse, Holy Cross, Williamsburg, to take up missionary work among the German Catholics of California."[10]

The sisters, however, regarded their colleagues' assignment as akin to joining the foreign missions. Africa or California—what difference did it make? In tears they accompanied the departing missionaries to the cloister door. "In our little convent parlor," recorded Sister Pia in the Diary, "my sister and brother-in-law were waiting to take us to the train. Our dear Mother Superior Seraphina Staimer, Mother Assistant Emilia Barth, and Mother Mistress Cunigunda Schell remained at the front door waving an affectionate and tearful 'Farewell.' My mother bade me goodbye at the carriage door with a handshake."[11]

Sister Maria Pia Backes, 1876

Escorted by parishioners, the carriage with the sisters stopped first at the rectory, where the missionaries took leave of Father Michael May, pastor of Holy Trinity Church and spiritual director of the Holy Cross Congregation; Fathers Peter Schwarz and Joseph Hauber, assistant pastors; and a number of other priests who had gathered in the parlor to bid the travelers Godspeed. Meantime, a swelling crowd of well-wishers had overflowed the rectory porch, jamming the stairs and making passageway well nigh impossible.

But at last there was nothing left to say, and the conveyance carrying the sisters, followed by an entourage of three carriages of parishioners, set out for the Jersey City depot. To the travelers' surprise Father May awaited them at the ferry. In an effort to conceal his emotion he kept repeating nervously, "Have courage, have courage."[12] Arrived at the depot, the sisters took leave of the parishioners and boarded the train, Father May and Sister Pia's sister and brother-in-law remaining at the coach window until departure time. Promptly at 9:00 p.m. the whistle sounded a hoarse warning, and the train rumbled slowly out of the station until lost to the tear-dimmed eyes of the three on the platform. It was All Souls evening, November 2, 1876.

In spite of Archbishop Alemany's thoughtful gift of $500 to provide the sisters with comfort on their cross-continental journey, the travelers found themselves on the short end of anything remotely resembling well-being. Judging from an account left by a fellow traveler of the period, the seven-day trip was a harrowing ordeal.

> Cinders flew in at the window; the drinking water was alkaline. The atmosphere reeked of smoke and the odor of food, for those with foresight carried well-stocked lunch baskets with them. Since a dining car was non-existent, the passengers descended three times a day to satisfy their hunger in eating houses where flies swarmed, table-cloths were spotted, the crockery none too clean, and the cups as likely as not without handles. Fried steak and potatoes swimming in grease constituted the basic menu.[13]

But despite the general discomfort of the journey, the sisters courageously maintained the Motherhouse schedule, praying the Breviary and rosary at the designated times, fulfilling the prescribed spiritual reading, and faithfully spending time in contemplation—a major feat, given the circumstances.

Arrival in Chicago on November 4 provided a welcome respite. There, at Archbishop Alemany's request, the sisters were met by the ubiquitous Dom Wimmer and taken to the Benedictine Convent of St. Scholastica. For the next two days Mother Theresa and her community hosted the travelers cordially, reviving their spirits by numerous acts of kindness. About to resume their journey, the three found awaiting them a basket of provisions which the sisters had thoughtfully prepared.

At Ogden, Utah, the train stopped to allow the passengers opportunity to explore the offerings of the local cafe. Famished as the sisters were—the lunch basket having long since been emptied—their timidity prevailed, confining them to the stuffy coach while their fellow travelers filed out. And lo! A gentleman, whom the sisters had neither seen before nor were to see after, appeared before them with a basket containing two deliciously prepared wild ducks, fresh fruit, and nuts. Before the surprised sisters could express their gratitude, the gentleman vanished, and a community tradition was born. The travelers were convinced that their gracious benefactor was none other than that good provider, St. Joseph!

Journey's end at last, the weary trio were met at Benicia, California, by Father Julius Herde, pastor of St. Boniface Church, San Francisco, and ferried across the Bay to The City. There they caught their first glimpse of the neat little house on Tyler Street (name changed to Golden Gate Avenue in 1880) that they would call "home" for the next 11 years. Newly built and completely furnished, Queen of the Holy Rosary Convent stood to the east of a modest two-story frame building, whose upper floor served as parish church and whose lower floor housed temporary clergy quarters and the school. In startling contrast to the home they had left behind in Brooklyn, the sisters noted uneasily that the only breaks in the monotony of the sand dunes stretching in all directions around them were a small Methodist church across the road and a solitary cottage around the corner on Jones Street. Aching from exhaustion, the travelers were relieved when Father Herde declined in their name an invitation to meet a welcoming committee of eager parishioners. Tomorrow would be soon enough.

The next morning, face veils carefully lowered, the trio bowed their way graciously through the long line awaiting them outside St. Boniface Church after Sunday Mass, their hearts cheered by the cries of *"Willkommen"* that rose from the smiling parishioners. Standing shyly with her parents on that eventful day was little four-year-old Louise Michel. The sisters had no way of knowing then that in the grave little girl clutching her parents' hands they were meeting for the first time the one destined to become the third Prioress General of the Mission San Jose Dominicans, the future Mother Bernardina Michel.

St. Boniface School, San Francisco

The era of pre-registration and entrance tests being far in the future, the sisters stood ready to teach the following morning in the little school conducted previously by a layman. Forty children greeted them on their first day, enrollment increasing to 105 by the end of the school year. "School" consisted of a single classroom located on the first floor of the church building, and thus it remained until

Saint Boniface Church, school on the first floor (right), the convent (left) c. 1880

a partition was erected six years later. Sisters Pia and Amanda divided the children between them without reference to grade level. English was the language of the school day, religion and German excepted. In deference to parental wishes religion was taught bilingually. To Sister Salesia was assigned responsibility for the little convent, where she busied herself with household tasks when not engaged in perfecting her English.

The day after school opened, a knock at the convent door announced the presence of a little priest, who introduced himself as Archbishop Alemany—come, he said, to welcome the sisters and to apologize for his absence on their arrival. Unaware of the sisters' stopover in Chicago, he had gone to Sacramento to meet them on November 9, two days too early. A Confirmation appointment at a distance had prevented his awaiting them. But now here he was, pleasantly surprised to find the school already in operation and happy to initiate a friendship that would continue unbroken until his death in Spain 12 years later. Rarely did a month pass that Archbishop Alemany did not visit the little community.

Convent Life

Immediately upon arrival, the sisters set up an oratory in the convent, where they lovingly enshrined a picture of the Queen of the Holy Rosary, a memento they had carried with them from Brooklyn. Here they gathered daily for community prayer and the nightly singing of the *Salve Regina (Hail Holy Queen)*, the beloved hymn to Our Lady with which Dominicans traditionally close their day. Gradually the trio settled into the familiar rhythm they had known in their New York convent and had learned to love. Of necessity they were early risers, the bell summoning them to a new day at five o'clock. Meditation, Office, and Mass preceded a simple breakfast of black coffee and dry bread, which was followed by household chores and classroom preparation. Morning classes were taught from nine o'clock until noon. After dinner at noon the teachers returned to their classrooms until three. Vespers, Compline, and rosary were prayed at 4:30 p.m. with supper at six. Matins and Lauds followed, with an hour's recreation, beginning about 7:30 p.m. Night Prayer was the concluding exercise of the day, with "Lights out" at 9:15 p.m.

Eagerly the sisters awaited word from home, and Mother Seraphina did not fail them. The familiar handwriting on the envelope from New York, postmarked November 9, 1876, brought excited smiles to their faces as the three gathered in the little community room to share the contents of that first letter. Sister Pia's voice broke as she read aloud the words of greeting:

> My dear, precious Children,
>
> When you receive this letter you will, with God's help, have happily completed your difficult trip. Oh, how often I think of you and recommend you with all my heart to the most sweet Heart of Jesus. Last night I woke up at least a dozen times; every time my first thought was of you and I said a prayer for you. Oh, how happy I shall be when we receive the news of your arrival in San Francisco.
>
> I hope, too, that you will have reached your destination by

Sunday and a good reception will be your reward for all the difficulties you encountered during your long trip.

Take up your school work in the name of God and with great endeavor. The Divine Heart of Jesus will grant you the grace to work much for His honor, and our glorious Father St. Dominic will take you under his protective mantle to preserve you from every harm of body and soul. We all pray much for you and place great hopes in you.

Yesterday morning, Wednesday, I told Sister Imelda that she would receive a holy card when she brought me Sister Pia's first letter. A few hours later she joyfully arrived with the letter you had written in Chicago. I am very glad that you were received well there and could rest a little. I gave the letter to Father May to read; he sends you heartfelt greetings. All the Sisters here are still well and happy and greet you lovingly....

Now, write to me often and in great detail. I am very much interested in everything I hear from you—every little thing. When we exchange letters often, you will scarcely notice or be aware of the great distance that is between us now, so far from New York.

In the Heart of Jesus I greet you a thousand fold.

Your worrying about you Mother,

Seraphina[14]

A week later the Brooklyn superior's concern had increased to such a degree that she was unable to contain her anxiety and sent a telegram to Father Herde. His prompt response delighted and relieved her.

My dear, precious Children,

You cannot imagine how worried we are about you since we have not yet received a single word from you. As I was unable to suppress these worrisome feelings any longer, I sent a telegram this afternoon to your Reverend Pastor. To my surprise and that of all of us here, I just now (3:30 p.m.) received an answer, informing me that you have already started teaching and that all of you are well. I cannot tell you how excited and grateful I was to our dear God for this news. I went straight to the chapel right away to pray the *Te Deum*.

God, who gave you the grace to endure happily this difficult trip, will also enable you to do much for His honor and the expansion of our holy Order. Oh, have great recourse to the Sacred Heart of Jesus. This sweet Heart will wondrously help you. I commend you almost hourly to His dear Heart, and when I wake during the night, my first thought is always a prayer for you, my dearly loved Children. The good God has chosen you to help extend His holy Kingdom and our holy Order. God has given you a marvelous lot. Show your appreciation daily by trying to avoid even the slightest fault.

Now all of us here are waiting with great anticipation for letters from you. I hope you will have only good things to report to us.

Friendly greetings to your Reverend Pastor, and thank him in my name for the telegram. I sent it immediately to Father May and to the Berges [Sister Pia's sister and brother-in-law] who also enjoyed the news very much. Here and in the branch houses everyone is healthy and happy. On November 30, the convent in Amityville will be dedicated.

Let me hear from you at least once a week. Loving greetings!

In the holy Heart of Jesus,
Your loving Mother,
Seraphina[15]

The first Christmas in the West passed unmentioned in Sister Pia's Diary, too painful perhaps to bear recording. Though the little house was fragrant with the scent of pine boughs—the sisters having decorated bravely for the feast—their courageous efforts could not compensate for the reality of the continent that separated them from their loved ones.

True to her word, Mother Seraphina tried valiantly to help the young community "scarcely notice...the great distance that is between us." The frequency of her letters containing news from home and the efforts she made to direct the little band as conscientiously as she did her sisters in New York witness to her loving concern. She advised Sister Pia to listen as little as possible to complaints about the parish priests, to collect the tuition herself, and to make earnest effort to have the Blessed Sacrament reserved in the convent; "then all things will go well."[16] She approved Sister Pia's request for permission to conduct afternoon sewing classes and recommended advertising in the local newspapers—though she had little enough use for the San Francisco press of the 1800s. Sister Pia's well-intentioned effort to convey the "flavor" of the West by sending her superior a copy of the local daily had met with little success. "The newspaper is terribly coarse," Mother Seraphina wrote. "I do not know what to say about it. These are hellish inventions."[17] Her bias was not simply geographical, however, for the New York press did not fare much better, the Brooklyn superior regarding it with an equally jaundiced eye: "The two newspapers [I sent], you may keep," she wrote; "only do not read the stories which are published in them"[18] —an intriguing restriction that encourages diverting speculation.

Sister Pia's efforts to follow her superior's recommendations were soon evident. On February 24, she rejoiced in the Diary: "Jesus deigned to take up His abode in our convent chapel, one too small for a tall Sister to make the prostration."[19] Size, however, did not diminish the sisters' joy on the memorable day of the Lord's entry; from early morning until nightfall they knelt in prayer and loving welcome before the Blessed Sacrament. Membership in the little community was now complete.

For Mother Seraphina the news that the sisters had the Blessed Sacrament reserved in their convent chapel was both comfort and joy:

> My anxieties and concern for you have now lessened considerably. Your divine Bridegroom, now in your midst day and night, will not permit His faithful brides, who out of love for Him and to increase His honor, have left parents, relatives and friends, to sustain harm from evil people....
>
> Oh, how relieved and pleased it makes me to know that you are happy and content. You are right; your last letter was for my suffering heart like a health-restoring balm and was

better for me than receiving a large amount of money from you. Let me know each time how many children you have. How about the Young Ladies Circle? Did Father Dominicus hear your confessions already? I think he is a man whom you can consult in difficult and doubtful situations, is it not true? Did the Archbishop not visit you again? Am I right in thinking that you haven't left the house yet, except to go to church?[20]

This last was probably a tactful reminder that life in the "Wild West" did not preclude cloister.

Sewing classes—with or without the assistance of the San Francisco press—were introduced also and scheduled to follow the school day. So successful was their addition that at the end of the term an exhibit of sewing and fancy work was held, including a display of the omnipresent samplers.

During that first spring, preparation of the children for reception of the Sacraments of Penance and Holy Eucharist claimed a good part of the sisters' time and energy. Limited as were their accommodations, they managed to make room in the little convent for children from the country in need of sacramental instruction. Parents and parishioners expressed their satisfaction at the thoroughness of the children's preparation and enthusiastically commended the sisters' efforts when for the first time they witnessed Solemn Holy Communion.

Sister Pia's Health

But all too soon a shadow cast itself over the young community. Early in 1877, the first warning of what was to plague the California mission throughout Sister Pia's life was sounded in the Diary. "My health declined so," she wrote, "that for a time there was danger of consumption."[21] The increasingly frequent bouts of illness left Sister Pia vulnerable to discouragement and bouts of homesickness. That at such times her letters home reflected a need for reassurance can only be surmised, for Sister Pia's letters to her superior in Brooklyn are no longer extant, a deprivation for her sisters and other readers only partially compensated by the preservation of the Diary.

Mother Seraphina sought to bolster her ailing sister's spirits, though on occasion a degree of frustration is evident in her responses to the youthful outpourings.

> Concerning your not feeling well, I will daily ask the dear God in earnest prayer to restore your health soon, if this is His holy Will. Then you will be of good cheer again.
>
> What does it matter if you cannot work in the garden? I did not send you to San Francisco for that!...Besides, it is not necessary for you yourselves to bother so much about work in the garden. Hire a man to do it for you. For so few dollars you should not work yourself up so that you cannot move any more. I am not that stingy....It bothers me to the depth of my soul when you write as if I thought that you spend money unnecessarily, etc. At the end of your financial account, you remarked, "Now you will see that we have not wasted a single cent."...Don't you remember that a few months ago I wrote you that you should eat and drink well and should not lack anything? I would prefer to send you $20 or $30 each month to make you happy than to hear again and again such complaints that in reality are unfounded. I requested an expense account from you—and informed you of it earlier—only to gain some insight into your situation....Your account I have now, and it is such a good report, much better than I would have dared to dream of. Within half a year, you have saved $300. Is that not enough for three Sisters? You should not be ungrateful to our dear God; that would be a sin. So be satisfied—every beginning is difficult.[22]

Five months later, another letter from New York outlined conditions for settling the question of Sister Pia's future once and for all.

> You must consider and decide if you will remain in San Francisco for several years or return home with me. The main decision will rest on the condition of your health and on the climate's proving beneficial for you. If you decide to come home, I will have to bring someone to take your place....If you remain, you must make up your mind that under all circumstances—even if God should send much suffering and many crosses, you will remain another four years, counting from 1878. I do not tell you to come home or to remain. Pray much to know the Holy Will of God. I write this to you early so that you will have time to talk

it all over with God in prayer. If you remain, you must offer your whole self for the aforementioned four years—even should you become very ill, you must offer all up as a sacrifice. This is what I mean: Should a serious sickness befall you, you must be ready to die in California. A trip home would be an impossibility.[23]

Growth of the Community

Undoubtedly Sister Pia's precarious health reinforced the plea she now made for additional personnel to support the western mission. To her request Archbishop Alemany added the weight of episcopal urging. Mother Seraphina's reply was generous: "You can imagine how short help is. Yet, in spite of this shortage, I will write to let you know when two sisters start their trip to you....Pray earnestly that God will protect them on the trip. Sister Victoria has some experience. She was formerly in Chicago."[24]

The following month (October 1878) Mother Seraphina wrote again:

> I just want to inform you that the two Sisters leave this evening, will remain over Sunday in Racine and continue the trip on Monday. If all goes well, they should be with you by Saturday. What a joyous meeting it will be. Oh, could I but share it with you!
>
> I need not assure you that the Sisters are good and useful. You know them. Sister Seraphina is a thousand fold artist in painting and drawing. I believe that as much as is possible in human life the hard and sorrowful days are behind. You five are of one mind and heart and will work in unity and love for one another and for God; what more beautiful life could there be! God grant that the Sisters arrive safely among you.[25]

To make sure her California sisters appreciated the sacrifice involved in sending additional personnel to the West, Mother Seraphina appended a postscript: "Sending you these sisters meant a great sacrifice on my part. This will give you an idea of what the success of your foundation means to me."[26]

A letter from Father Michael May, the New York community's

spiritual director, reinforced Mother Seraphina's wish to support the western foundation.

> You may be certain [he wrote] that Mother Superior will do all that is possible for her. You must not expect the impossible....In proportion your place is better taken care of than we out here....I wanted to tell you this in order that you can see that Mother Superior is doing her best, but cannot grant all your requests immediately.[27]

The two recruits were welcome additions to the Tyler Street community. Sister Victoria (Magdalena) Kine or Kena, born in Selz, Alsace, Germany, had emigrated to the United States at some time in her youth. She entered the Brooklyn monastery as a lay sister on July 23, 1874, at the age of 40. From childhood she had felt called to religious life, but care for her invalid mother had prevented her from realizing her long-cherished desire until her mother's death. She made first and final profession on November 25, 1875, and three years later was assigned to the California mission. As an extern sister, Sister Victoria rendered invaluable service to the little community. To her fell the responsibility of transacting business, delivering messages (The telephone, patented in 1876, was not yet a household item.), and doing the weekly shopping. She died at the age of 67 after a devout and faithful life, the only sister in the Congregation to die as a lay sister before that status was altered.

Sister Seraphina (Crescentia) Maerz, a native of Brooklyn, was born on June 15, 1855, the daughter of John and Barbara Geutel Maerz. She was baptized Crescentia in the Church of the Most Holy Trinity, Brooklyn, two days after her birth. Her father, a jeweler by profession, had left Europe in 1834, to make his fortune in America and had arrived in New York in April of the same year. Little is known of the family's early history, except for the tragic death of the mother from tuberculosis, which left six motherless children to the grief-stricken father's care. Crescentia, the youngest, was just four years old.

Crescentia attended Holy Trinity School conducted by the Dominican Sisters of Brooklyn. When she was 10, a Franciscan missionary visited the school and held the children spellbound with stories of his work among the Indians. At the conclusion he asked who would come and help him. Immediately Crescentia's hand shot up. After lunch she and two like-minded little friends appeared at the rectory door to present themselves for mission duty. Solemnly Father accepted their offer—with the tactful suggestion that perhaps they should wait until a little older. The plight of the Indians would never after be far from Crescentia's thoughts and sensitive heart.

Her contact with the Dominican Sisters at Holy Trinity School nurtured in her a desire for religious life, and on February 1, 1872 at the age of 16, she sought admission to Holy Cross Convent. She received the habit on August 4, 1873, and pronounced perpetual vows on February 2, 1875. Sister Seraphina never forgot the missionary's visit, and when the call went forth for volunteers for the California mission, she offered herself at once. But her father would not hear of his "dear Crestl's" joining the mission band; she was entirely too young and the distance too great. His resistance was a severe disappointment to Mother Seraphina Staimer, who had her young namesake singled out as first choice for superior of the mission band. The lapse of two years, however, produced a change of heart in the anxious father, and he gave his blessing to his daughter's missionary aspirations, even though she was only 21. Kissing him goodbye, Sister Seraphina left for the West to work, so she thought, among the California Indians. Her disappointment was keen when on arrival she discovered that the Indians were not roaming the streets of San Francisco and that she would be living too far away from them for her ministrations.

The presence of Sister Seraphina, gifted in art as well as music, enabled the sisters of St. Boniface to add painting and piano to their daily offerings. The newcomer's greatest delight, however, was in teaching religion. Her arrival also marked the beginning of a long and faithful working relationship with Sister Pia; through the years ahead she would be the latter's "right hand" and loyal and trusted friend, and would be called on to guide the Congregation through the desolate years following Mother Pia's death.

In New York, reports following the two sisters' arrival in California pleased the Brooklyn superior.

> It is a great joy for me [she wrote] to know that you are all happy, living together in peace and fulfilling your duties.

> Truly, such a life is already a foretaste of the happy life in heaven. I have no worry that it will not remain this way; you five fit well together.[28]

The reader is tempted, however, to speculate whether the five in question would have described their life in terms as sanguine as did their superior. The "discontented decade" of the 1870s was not the bonanza days of the '50s and '60s, and the economic slump had repercussions felt even in the cloister. Times were hard; drought caused extensive crop failure, and banks and businesses tottered. The malaise that had settled over the East in 1875 reached the West Coast the following year, and to the general complaints California added its own variety. Unrest mounted as the unemployed poured into San Francisco looking for work. A scapegoat was needed, and The City found one in the Chinese laborer.

Onto the political scene just at this time strode a young and fiery nuisance named Denis Kearney. An orator of no mean ability, he targeted with his eloquence the Chinese workers and the wealthy "Nabobs" of Nob Hill. Resentment against the Orientals who were willing to work for lower wages than their Anglo counterparts was building steadily throughout The City, and the unemployed became a receptive audience for the flamboyant Kearney, who night after night harangued the mobs that gathered in a sand lot near City Hall. Kearney's fierce denunciations delighted the crowd, and their frenzied shouts of "The Chinese must go; Denis Kearney says so,"[29] coupled with sporadic acts of violence, terrified the sisters in their nearby convent. The situation became even more threatening for them when they were served notice to discontinue patronizing the Chinese fruit and vegetable vendors who trotted past the convent, baskets bobbing in rhythm to their swinging gait. Although the sisters suffered no actual harm, conditions remained menacing until around 1880, when Kearney's influence began to wane. Two years later a federal law drastically limiting Chinese immigration brought to a close this sorry chapter in San Francisco history.

On the east coast concern of a different nature was once again occupying the attention of the Brooklyn superior, to whom news of Sister Pia's deteriorating health was "like a bolt out of the blue." Mother Seraphina wrote at once to Sisters Pia and Seraphina:

> I hope to God that this spitting of blood is just a passing occurrence and that by the time this letter reaches you, good Sister Pia will be well again....What I tell you now is in Holy Obedience....All that Sister Seraphina finds best for your health you must do and what she finds harmful, you must omit. If she thinks that the praying of the Divine Office is too exhausting (She can ask the doctor's opinion.), then do not say it and pray instead a rosary. Eat meat as often as it is good for you—also on Wednesdays and Saturdays [days of abstinence observed by the sisters]....Do not forego morning and afternoon lunch; this is absolutely necessary for you, and your good Dominican Father cannot judge that as we can....I prefer that you remain healthy rather than that you try to save so and so much money.[30]

Archbishop Alemany couched a similar concern in good Dominican theological persuasion with an Ignatian turn.

> San Francisco, Jan. 9/79
>
> Dear in Christ Sister,
>
> The will of God is the law in heaven and on earth, which has to guide us. In doing that we are never wrong, and we are ever wrong in not doing that. Now you know, as well as myself that the will of God is shown to us in our Superior and Spiritual Director, and He likes that beautiful faith on our part very much, so that when St. Ignatius thought he should not eat meat on Good Friday and the physician ordered him to eat it and he ate it, God was pleased with his humble and holy submission. I do not infer from that, that Sister Pia is as holy as St. Ignatius, but that she should imitate his holy docility, and do what the bishop is bound to prescribe for her as follows:
>
> Until you be perfectly cured with sound lungs, you must not teach, but simply superintend and very little of that also for some weeks or months as the Doctor may point out. Secondly, you must not get up from bed until the sun is fairly up. Thirdly, you must neither abstain nor fast; but when you think you are fairly restored must apply to me for

modifications. *Und Sie wie einer guten Tochter werden bleiben mit meinen Briefe, ich hoffe.* [And you, I hope, will like a good daughter keep to my letter.] And God will bless you.

Yours truly in P.N.S.D.,
Joseph Sadoc Alemany, O.P., A.S.F.

Sr. Pia, O.S.D., Supr.[31]

By late spring Sister Pia's return to New York for reasons of health had become a foregone conclusion in Mother Seraphina's mind, and in May 1879 she wrote in encouragement. The sisters will "all pray for you and beg God to grant you enough strength to make the trip here. In Amityville your health will improve so much that in a little while you can do some light school work. But all as God wills. You have been in San Francisco almost three years and have worked hard. You may return home."[32]

But of a different mind, presumably, was Sister Pia, for in June Mother Seraphina wrote in some surprise:

> Concerning the letter before your last, I wish to remark that I am not forcing you to come home. I did not know that it is the same to you whether you die in San Francisco or here. This means a great change in the matter. Remain where you are and in future I will judge the matter differently. The contract—but this is not the right expression—would not give you any great scruples of conscience and you would come back anyway if you knew you would get well in Amityville. But, sad to say, there is no herb growing, neither in Amityville or anywhere in the world, for the prevention of death![33]

On this philosophical note correspondence regarding Sister Pia's return to the East for reasons of health seems to have reached an amicable conclusion.

Experience early taught the young community an appreciation of friendship. Not long after arriving in California, Sister Pia noted: "The Most Reverend Archbishop Alemany came with Reverend Father Dominicus Lentz, O.P., whom he appointed as our extraordinary confessor. This zealous priest was exiled from Germany at the time of Bismarck's Kulturkampf. He had been the Vicar General of the Austrian Province."[34] Father Lentz had been a key figure in reestablishing the Dominican Order in Germany in the '50s and '60s after it had been suppressed for many years. Strictly speaking, he was not a provincial, as none of the regions in Germany could qualify as provinces at the time because of their small numbers. Sometime after the sisters' arrival on the West Coast, Mother Seraphina, pleased when she learned that the San Francisco community had celebrated Father Lentz's Jubilee with appropriate solemnity, advised Sister Pia: "Keep hold of this good old Father, who is suitable for you and can in some way replace Father May [as spiritual director of the sisters in the West]. If you are in need of any counsel, go to him for it."[35] By then, the "good old Father" had become a frequent visitor at the little house on Tyler Street, and the sisters knew themselves blessed in a staunch friend and trusted counselor.

In addition to Father Dominicus, Archbishop Alemany, and Father Francis Sadoc Vilarrasa, first Vicar General and founder of the Western Dominican Province, other Dominicans who befriended the community in those early days included: Fathers Pius Murphy, superior of the western Dominicans and pastor of St. Dominic's, San Francisco; Mannes Doogan, first pastor of St. Dominic's; Albert Lawler, pastor and prior of Holy Rosary, Portland, Oregon; Benedict McGovern, from St. Joseph's Province, a transfer for reasons of health and later first superior of Holy Rosary; and William Dempflin, exiled from Guatemala in 1872, ordained by Archbishop Alemany in 1875, and missionary to the Indians in California as their beloved "Padre Blanco" until his death in 1912. A Diary entry for October 1880, is typical:

> During the octave of Rosary Sunday, we felt honored by having our good Father Provincial [sic] Vilarrasa, O.P., celebrate High Mass for us, after which we sang the *Te Deum*. At 5:00 p.m., dinner was served to Father Vilarrasa, Father Pius Murphy, O.P., and Father Dominicus Lentz, O.P. They remained until 7:15. Father Provincial remarked: "That was a fine day. I enjoyed it so much."[36]

Holy Cross Convent, Brooklyn, was Sister Pia's model and first love as she struggled to meet the challenges of fidelity to the Rule she had brought with her from the East while adapting it to conditions in the Far West, but the Dominican Fathers, both on the

West Coast and in Europe, would figure prominently as friends and advisers to whom Sister Pia would often turn as she sought to establish the young community on a firm Dominican foundation.

Among the sisters' communities mentioned gratefully in the Diary and the early annals of the Congregation are the Dominican Sisters of Benicia (San Rafael), the Sisters of the Holy Family, the Sisters of the Holy Names, and the Sisters of Mercy. Sister Pia was especially indebted to the Dominican Sisters of Benicia, who on several occasions received her graciously as patient in their hospital in Stockton.

The first intimation that the California missionaries were thinking of a second foundation is contained in a letter from Mother Seraphina, dated February 22, 1879. Replying to a letter from Sister Pia, she is somewhat noncommittal, stating simply that the plan to make a foundation in North Beach (northeast section of San Francisco fronting on the Bay) might be all right if Sister Pia's health were better. But the following month the Brooklyn superior was less encouraging: "I do not recall having given you a definite answer concerning North Beach and could not do so because there is not even a priest there. What were you going to do there?"[37] Sister Pia's youthful enthusiasm for new foundations was becoming a concern to Mother Seraphina. Although the foundation failed to materialize, it is of interest as an indication that the western community was already entertaining ambitions of expansion. Other doors would open soon.

In February 1880, Father Sebastian Wolf succeeded Father Julius Herde as pastor of St. Boniface Church, with Father John Meiler as assistant. Mother Seraphina's comment on the clerical change is puzzling, as no explanation accompanies it: "It will be better now than it was with Father Herde."[38] But such was not to be the case. Trouble, needing little encouragement to reach explosive proportions, announced itself when a parishioner brought word that disgruntled members of the *Kolping Verein*[39] were spreading spiteful talk because of a play that the young girls of the parish were planning to present for the sisters' benefit. The well-intentioned actresses were members of a sodality begun earlier by Sister Pia.

The idea of a dramatic production—a popular form of entertainment in those days of neither radio nor television—was inspired by the sisters' wish to enlarge the convent, a necessity since the community had now increased in membership to five, with sometime boarders. A week later, the affair ballooned. "We are in great trouble," wrote Sister Pia. "It seems as though the whole parish... [is] working against our little community. No help is to be given us. I offer to God all the annoyances of the past month."[40] Whether or not the play ever reached the boards, the gossip eventually subsided and the sisters managed to realize their plan. The Diary was mildly triumphant: A "new dormitory...was added to the little convent in spite of opposition by parishioners; we even acquired a new refectory located on the first floor."[41] Unpleasant as the incident was, the end result proved a welcome addition to the little house.

Meantime, the public examinations customary at the time in both public and private schools, the literary and musical programs which regularly accompanied them, and the popular sewing and fancy work displays drew enthusiastic praise from the children's parents. Encouraged by the approval, the sisters organized a children's choir and established a circulating library in the school. First Holy Communion became each year more impressive, lighted candles in the hands of the communicants adding a degree of solemnity to the renewal of baptismal promises. Mother Seraphina was generous in her praise:

> I am happy to hear that all of you are very well and eagerly striving ahead. When one reads the program of your Exhibition [closing exercise], one thinks that you have an academy instead of a parish school. And the music professor [Sister Seraphina] did especially well....All is for the greater honor and glory of God![42]

As 1880 drew to a close, an event of some significance occurred in the young community, even though Sister Pia's Diary entry is so low-keyed that it could be passed over with little attention: "Our first postulant arrived—Miss Magdalena Waechter."[43] A native of Alsace, Magdalena had resided in California for a number of years before applying for entrance into the community at the age of 21.

Despite the hope generated by Magdalena's presence, the year ended sadly for Sister Pia: "I could not go to school. Everything seemed to be going wrong. Money lacking, children lacking—O God, this has been a hard year. Only five months did You bless me with health; the other seven, illness, crosses, dereliction. *Fiat voluntas tua*....I close the year in the Name of the Lord."[44]

And the New Year dawned just as somberly. In her distress Sister Pia confided to the Diary:

> January 1, 1881 – Never before have I begun a year with so heavy and troubled a heart. Is it because the past year brought so much sadness? I cannot master a certain fear, a timidity which seems to hold me in its grip. Come what may, joy or sorrow, happiness or distress, health or illness—be it my last hour—in all things may God's Holy Will be done. Grant, O God, that in this New Year, I may seek Thee alone, find Thee alone and do only Thy Holy Will![45]

But as the year progressed, Sister Pia's outlook became more positive, and she began to look afield. By spring she was discussing her hope of opening a hospital with Father Pius Murphy. It was a hope well into the future, if at all, for the little quintet had their hands full at the time. *"Deo gratias!"* exclaimed the Diary. "The school exhibition was remarkably successful. Father Meiler praised Sister Seraphina publicly. We were fatigued from the numerous preparations demanded of us during the preceding days."[46] Nevertheless, the following morning the sisters opened the children's retreat in preparation for First Communion. Unfortunately Sister Pia's physical vigor proved no match for her aspirations: "Several hemorrhages these days. I thought that I was feeling pretty well, but—O my God, forgive me my disobedience. Although I felt the attacks coming on, I did not spare myself. All day in bed on the 24th. On the next day, I felt better but still very weak."[47]

Sister Pia's condition prompted a blunt note from Archbishop Alemany to Mother Seraphina in New York:

> May 21, 1881
>
> Our dear Sister Pia is getting on nicely but the occasional bad attacks show that she should not teach else she might have a fatal hemorrhage. Send some Sisters because Sister Pia should not teach and another Sister is kept busy with music scholars.
>
> Alemany[48]

The Archbishop's forthright approach accomplished its purpose, as the ensuing months would prove.

Visitors from Brooklyn

As early as a year after the sisters' arrival in the West, Mother Seraphina had written that Archbishop Alemany had invited her to visit "beautiful California...[and] bring a few sisters along."[49] Hardly subtle, the invitation nevertheless pleased Mother Seraphina. "I am very proud that the Archbishop gave me such an invitation," she wrote. "Please God. I will come next year [1878]."[50] Brooklyn's first visitor to the West, however, was not Mother Seraphina but Father Peter Schwarz, chaplain to the sisters of Holy Cross Convent, Brooklyn, and, in Mother Seraphina's opinion, "a very good priest and, after Father May, our best friend."[51]

Because Father Schwarz's first-hand account of his visit brought so much comfort to her, Mother Seraphina decided that she could postpone her trip to California. But she assured the little band that the Lord would direct all so that she would see them once more before she died. And she was delighted with the sisters' frugality when she learned that they had managed to save $150 toward her trip. "For heaven's sake," she wrote, "from where are you getting so much money? Have you become gold-diggers?"[52] Despite her assurances, more than three years would elapse before she realized her desire. At last, on January 8, 1881, she informed her "Franciscans," as she teasingly called her San Francisco sisters, that she would definitely come during the year unless something unforeseen interfered with her plans.

April brought another promise of "meeting you in the Gold-land and of looking into your loyal eyes"[53]; and as late as May 10, she wrote that if her health remained good, she would see them on the eve of Saint Dominic's day, i.e., August 3. Hence, her abrupt change in travel plans is somewhat baffling, occurring as it does without explanation. Mother Seraphina's diary records simply:

> May 23, 1881—Today I began my trip to California in company with Sister Brigitta Seitz. We left the Penn R.R. Station at 8 p.m. to visit our Sisters in San Francisco. We arrived in Chicago on the 25th and went from there to Racine, 66 miles from Chicago. We arrived there at 1 p.m. The Sisters received us very graciously and the convent pleased me very much. In the evening at 5 we visited the cemetery where M. Benedicta and Sr. Thomasina are

buried. Their graves were marked with a little iron cross without inscription and I had to weep. May 27—We continued our trip back to Chicago and thence to Omaha via the Burlington Quincy Railroad. We arrived safely in San Francisco June 1 at 12 noon.[54]

Despite the sisters' joyful anticipation of Mother Seraphina's visit, her early arrival caught them by surprise.

I was in the garden with a group of children, when Sister Victoria, pale with excitement, announced the arrival of two Sisters....On reaching the parlor, I beheld the good, honest face of my spiritual mother. I fainted in her embrace. Then we went together to the chapel to thank God for this great joy.[55]

In Mother Seraphina's account of the meeting, "The joy of reunion was indescribable. We all wept for joy. I found all the sisters happy and contented."[56]

The next day in a diverting exception to the rule of enclosure Sister Pia took Mother Seraphina and Sister Brigitta to the San Francisco Cliff House, where they had their first glimpse of the Pacific. Observing also the German custom of an outing on Pentecost Monday, the trio went by carriage to Santa Clara, delighting in the seemingly endless orange groves along the way.

The New York superior's arrival occasioned a steady flow of visitors to the Golden Gate Avenue convent. Archbishop Alemany renewed his acquaintance by calling on Mother Seraphina at least twice. Others who came to welcome her included Fathers Sebastian Wolf, Father Herde's successor as pastor of St. Boniface; Telesphore Demasini, S.J.; and Benedict McGovern, O.P., prior of St. Dominic's Convent, San Francisco. Mother Seraphina elected to do a little visiting herself, calling on the Dominican Fathers and Sisters in Benicia and making note of their friendliness.

In between visitors Mother Seraphina managed to hold a personal interview with each sister, encouraging her to continue her good work. For Sister Pia she had, in addition, a mild reprimand: The sisters' guimpes were entirely too modish, i.e., too long! There was a caution also not to be too hasty in her judgments. In general, however, the New York superior was pleased with the progress and spirit of the California mission and found both priests and Archbishop devoted to the sisters. She also learned that in the summer another school in a distant part of The City (Mission District) would be given them. In consequence, she took time to go with Sister Pia to look at lots on Twenty-first Street as possible sites for a new convent, an initiative compelled by necessity since the arrival of Miss Magdalena and the on-and-off presence of boarders were at times taxing the little Golden Gate Avenue house past endurance. But the *piece de resistance* of Mother Seraphina's visit was her promise to send two additional sisters in the near future.

The day of the travelers' departure found the community shedding tears in anticipation. Sister Pia recounted the leave-taking simply:

> At 2:00 p.m. Mother appeared in her black attire for traveling. At 2:30 she gave us her blessing—sobbing. The rest of us were in tears. It was a heart-rending farewell. Her last admonition was: "Be more thoughtful. Pray daily to the Holy Ghost." Her departing words: "Remain loyal to me."
>
> Sister Salesia and I accompanied Mother and Sister Brigitta to the depot. Father Meiler followed. A short but heartfelt goodbye. The train started moving. For some time Mother Superior kept waving her handkerchief. We returned at 5:30 and found the Sisters in tears.[57]

Although the visit brought joy to the little community, it served also to reopen the old wounds of homesickness. For Sister Pia, Mother Seraphina's departure meant further the loss of ready accessibility to a wise and trusted adviser.

One of the consequences of the Brooklyn superior's visit was the initiating of a supplemental means of support for the community. To Sister Victoria's other responsibilities as extern sister was now added that of procuring funds. Accompanied by Miss Magdalena, she began door-to-door solicitation. The community rejoiced when the pair brought home $20 the first day, and "$25,...and half a ton of coal, a piece of cotton flannel, and some dry goods to make dresses for our poor children [the next]. *Deo gratias* for this blessing."[58] But their efforts were not always so impressive. "Forty-one houses gave ten cents each,"[59] Sister Pia noted somewhat dispiritedly. Some days later, however, their fortune improved and the day's collection totaled $35. While grateful for the additional income, Sister Pia confided to the Diary her aversion for begging: "O my God, if only I were as mortified as Sister Victoria. How this good Sister overcomes her feeling of repugnance!"[60]

On her part Mother Seraphina was delighted in a mildly "told-you-so" way. "Did I not tell you that the collecting would be met with success? Who of you could by teaching school and music earn as much as Sister Victoria? Therefore, three cheers for [her]."[61] And she foresaw even better results when Sister became more familiar with The City; but she should remember to be careful when she went out.[62] Caution not-withstanding, fund-raising was on its way, and the mortified Sister Victoria was the community's first, if modest, development director!

Notes

[1] *Examiner,* [San Francisco], 11 November 1876.

[2] *Historical Sketch of the Dominican Sisters of the Congregation of the Queen of the Holy Rosary.* (Mission San Jose, CA: Dominican Sisters, 1926) 42.

[3] *Historical Sketch of the Dominican Sisters of the Congregation of the Queen of the Holy Rosary.* (Mission San Jose, CA: Dominican Sisters, 1926) 42.

[4] Joseph Sadoc Alemany, O.P. was born in Vich, Spain, on July 3, 1814, the third of 12 children. At the age of 16, he entered the Dominican Order in the priory of Vich and pronounced solemn vows on September 23, 1831. When his studies were interrupted by the closure of religious houses in Spain, the Master General invited him to Rome to continue his studies, an invitation he eagerly accepted. He was ordained to the priesthood on March 11, 1837, and three years later was sent to the United States. For seven years he labored in the missions of Ohio, Kentucky, and Tennessee, and in 1845, became an American citizen. At the Provincial Chapter of 1847, Alemany was made master of novices for St. Rose Priory, Kentucky, and shortly thereafter, was elected provincial of the Dominicans in the United States. Returning to Rome the following spring, Alemany attended the 1849 General Chapter of the Order. While in attendance, he was appointed Bishop of Monterey, which comprised all of Upper and Lower California. Three years later, Pius IX named him first Archbishop of the new Provincial See of San Francisco, which included Utah and Nevada. After serving as archbishop for 31 years, he returned to his native Spain and died

there in 1888. The final document in Archbishop Alemany's file in the Mission San Jose Archives is a letter from his brother, Miguel Alemany, addressed to Mother Pia on June 30, 1888. The letter tells how he was able to "assist Brother in his last hour and convey his remains to our birthplace and inter them in the sepulcher of our father in the Church of the Rev. Dominicans of Vich where he received the Holy Habit." Miguel Alemany signed himself "Slyl Chaplain."

5. Seraphina Staimer, O.S.D. was born on February 8, 1830 at Upfkofen near Ratisbon. An excellent student, she pursued the teachers' course and, on completion, applied for entrance in the Dominican Convent in Ratisbon, pronouncing her first vows on November 30, 1851, and making final vows on March 7, 1855. Two months later on May 9, she arrived in Brooklyn in the second group of volunteers from Holy Cross, Ratisbon. In 1864, Mother Josepha died, and Sister Seraphina was appointed Mother Prioress of the New York community by Bishop John Loughlin, first Bishop of the recently established new diocese of Brooklyn. He appointed her for life and changed her title from "Mother Prioress" to "Mother Superior." During her term of office Mother Seraphina founded 20 convents, and the congregation grew from nine members to 300. She died on January 14, 1889. *Golden Jubilee, Fiftieth Anniversary of the Holy Cross Convent* (Brooklyn, N.Y: 1903).

6. Joseph Sadoc Alemany, O.P. letter to Seraphina Staimer, O.S.D., 3 May 1876. All letters cited are contained in the Archives of the Dominican Sisters of Mission San Jose.

7. Alemany, letter to Staimer 28 August 1876.

8. Maria Pia Backes, O.P., *Her Days Unfolded: Woman of the Word*, Trans. Bernardina Michel, O.P. Ed. Julie Distel, O.P. (Mission San Jose, CA: Dominican Sisters, 1991). (Hereafter referred to as the Diary in the text and listed as Backes followed by a page number in the endnotes.)

9. Backes 1.

10. Backes 1.

11. Backes 1.

12. Backes 1.

13. For this description of early transcontinental travel the writer is indebted to Madame Matilda Barreda, a socially prominent woman of the time who was cited in Atherton, Gertrude, *Golden Gate Country* (New York: Duell, 1945) 206.

14. Seraphina Staimer, O.S.D., letters to Sisters in California, 9 November 1876. Mother Seraphina Staimer's diary and all letters from her cited

in the text are contained in the Dominican Sisters of Mission San Jose Archives.

[15] Staimer, letter to Sisters in California, 16 November 1876.

[16] Staimer, letter to Sisters in California, 2 January 1877.

[17] Staimer, letter to Seraphina Maerz, O.P. and Backes, 24 December 1877.

[18] Staimer, letter to Maerz and Backes, 29 October 1878.

[19] Backes 4.

[20] Staimer, letter to Backes, 9 March 1877.

[21] Backes 4.

[22] Staimer, letter to Backes, 16 July 1877.

[23] Staimer, letter to Backes, 24 December 1877.

[24] Staimer, letter to Backes, 20 September 1878.

[25] Staimer, letter to Backes, 4 October 1878.

[26] Staimer, letter to Backes, 4 October 1878.

[27] Michael May, letter to Sisters in California, 5 August 1881.

[28] Staimer, letter to Backes, 30 November 1878.

[29] John B. McGloin, S.J., *California's First Archbishop* (New York: Herder and Herder, 1966) 293.

[30] Staimer, letter to Backes and Maerz, 14 January 1879.

[31] Alemany, letter to Backes, 9 January 1879.

[32] Staimer, letter to Backes, 17 May 1879.

[33] Staimer, letter to Backes, 17 June 1879.

[34] Backes 4.

[35] Staimer, letter to Backes, 29 October 1879.

[36] Backes 9.

[37] Staimer, letter to Backes, 19 March 1879.

[38] Staimer, letter to Backes, 30 March 1880.

[39] The *Kolping Verein* is a socio-religious society for young men, founded in Cologne, Germany in 1849. By means of Kolping Houses the society provides adult education programs with emphases on Christian Living. H. A. Krewitt, "The Kolping Society," *New Catholic Encyclopedia*, 2nd ed. 2003, 231.

[40] Backes 7.

[41] Backes 7.

[42] Staimer, letter to Backes, 20 June 1880.
[43] Backes 9.
[44] Backes 9.
[45] Backes 10.
[46] Backes 11.
[47] Backes 12.
[48] Alemany, letter to Staimer, 21 May 1881.
[49] Staimer, letter to Backes, 24 December 1877.
[50] Staimer, letter to Backes, 24 December 1877.
[51] Staimer, letter to Backes, 17 June 1879.
[52] Staimer, letter to Backes, 9 February 1879.
[53] Staimer, letter to Backes, 26 April 1881.
[54] Staimer 27.
[55] Backes 13.
[56] Staimer 28.
[57] Backes 14.
[58] Backes 14.
[59] Backes 15.
[60] Backes 15.
[61] Staimer, letter to Backes, 11 August 1881.
[62] Staimer, letter to Backes, 11 August 1881.

CHAPTER THREE

GROWING PAINS

Word of the sisters' success at St. Boniface spread rapidly, and children came from all parts of San Francisco to attend school. Frank and Mary Ruegg, residents of the City's historic Mission District and parents of seven, were among the St. Boniface supporters, but soon found the daily trek from Twenty-first Street and Valencia to Golden Gate Avenue too long and tiresome for their children, especially the younger ones. Supported by other German-speaking parents of the Mission District, Frank Ruegg made a proposal that Sister Pia found too tempting to refuse: He offered the basement of his house on Twenty-first and Valencia streets for a school.

The thought of an affiliated school had the community in a ferment. Opening day was set for July 11, 1881, with Sister Amanda in the roles of principal, teacher, nurse, and all-around handywoman. Cloister to the contrary, the appointment necessitated her traveling daily, on foot or by horse-car, the two miles out to the school site—a far cry from the simple overpass in Ratisbon! With her for the next two years dutifully walked/rode the postulant, Miss Magdalena.

Sister Pia's enthusiasm for the affiliate did not long endure, however, especially after she realized that the parents expected the school to be tuition-free. Nor was Mother Seraphina happier when she received the first report of the new undertaking.

> Before all, I must tell you that I am terribly disappointed in the income of 21st Street. If you did not make a mistake and wrote $8.00 as the monthly income instead of $38 or $48, I do not know what to say. If this is the case, the sisters who go there every day do not even earn their car fare and

Frank Ruegg, his wife and students

shoes. How does $8.00 fit 46 children?...You cannot live on air and neither can you build a house.¹

The school had opened with 23 pupils, boys and girls. The following day the number had increased to 31 and gradually climbed to 46. Compared with St. Boniface, however,—"Here at St. Boniface there are 152"²—the Mission School was a disappointment, enrollment never going much above 40. What it did do, however, was solidify in Sister Pia's mind the idea of locating definitely in the Mission District as a more proper location for a school than the business section rapidly developing around St. Boniface.

New Additions to the Community

Meantime, true to her word, Mother Seraphina was "breaking... [her] head about which Sisters to send."³ Finally, confirmation of additional personnel arrived in a letter from Brooklyn on August 1, 1881:

> Before all, I must tell you two sisters have now volunteered for San Francisco: Sister Bonifacia and Sister Gonzaga. The first named is a model religious. Her knowledge is medium; she is equally acquainted with English and German. She speaks English very well. Sister Gonzaga is much better and, since she is only 19 years old, she can acquire still more education. She also has very good handwriting. Her principal accomplishment is playing the organ and piano very well. She is also very industrious...I think she will be of great help to you. Write soon so that the two sisters can leave soon. I cannot send three for the time being. Anyway, you do not have much room. Should one or two candidates come, your house would be overcrowded. Further, the cost of the trip would be too much for me at one time.⁴

Announcement of the sisters' arrival on September 6, 1881, sent Sister Pia to the recently completed Oakland Mole, the terminal where trains met the ferries, to meet the travelers. To her great surprise there was no Sister Bonifacia, but in her place Sister Felicitas Weiss, O.P. (Louise Breitenbach)! No explanation was given for the change, though a letter from Father Michael May, the spiritual director of the New York community, mentioned that Sister Bonifacia

San Francisco Transportation c. 1880

would be missed too much. In New York Mother Seraphina noted simply in her diary: "On the feast of St. Rose, August 30, Sisters Felicitas and Gonzaga left on the Erie R.R. for San Francisco. Now they will have seven sisters and a postulant who will soon receive the habit."[5]

Youth still favored the California mission. Sister Gonzaga (Catherine) Buehler was born in Brooklyn, New York, on September 19, 1862. She received her early education from the sisters at Holy Cross and at the age of 14 entered the postulancy, receiving the habit on June 13, 1877, and making Final Profession on May 3, 1879. Although young in years, she early displayed the predilection that would characterize her throughout life—a love for the orphans entrusted to her care. Two years after Profession, Sister Gonzaga volunteered for distant California.

Sister Felicitas (Louisa) Weiss, Bavarian by birth, was born on April 27, 1855. When 17 years of age, she came to New York and the following year entered Holy Cross Convent (September 20, 1873). She received the habit and her religious name on January 10, 1874, and was finally professed on February 2, 1875. An enthusiastic teacher, Sister Felicitas would devote many years to the teaching of younger children in the West.

Weary though they were, the travelers enjoyed the ferry ride across the San Francisco Bay, but were unprepared for the bedlam that greeted them as they stepped off the boat. To Sister Felicitas it was little short of an attack. "Carriage, lady?" the hack drivers shouted in the sisters' faces, vying for patronage. "Hack here, lady! Hack!"[6]

Hardly had they set out for St. Boniface than Sister Felicitas suffered another jolt. "We were shocked,"[7] she said, recalling their arrival years later, "when we saw the sidewalks of thick, rough planks and when our carriage rolled, not over a smooth street, but over bumpy cobblestones."[8] There was more to come. The little convent on Golden Gate Avenue was partly hidden from view by the wooden fence that surrounded it. Sister Felicitas could not conceal her surprise. "Oh my," she exclaimed in some dismay, "is this really the convent?"[9] Admittedly, it was not the five-story structure they had left in Brooklyn on the corner of Montrose and Graham Avenues. This was the West; an adjustment of sights would be definitely in order.

It did not take the travelers long to explore their new quarters. On the first floor of the convent they found the community room, which also doubled as a refectory; the parlor, which did double duty as music room; and the tiny kitchen, which the sisters had not yet been creative enough to put to an alternate use. The upper floor contained the chapel, "...so small," Sister Felicitas observed, "that the distance from the door to the altar could be covered in three steps!"; a second small room which doubled as sacristy and infirmary; and a dormitory which boasted five cots. Since the household of eight now presented a problem in logistics, Sister Pia moved her bed to the sacristy-infirmary, and Sister Gonzaga set hers up in a narrow hallway that served also as wardrobe. Not long after the new sleeping arrangements were settled, Sister Pia was awakened one night by a loud noise. Thinking burglar, she rushed to the dormitory and summoned Sister Salesia. "Where is this fellow?" cried the fearless Salesia. "Let me at him!" Matters returned to normal when it was discovered that the "intruder" was Sister Gonzaga, placidly snoring her way through the crisis.

Shortly after arrival, Sister Felicitas began teaching. St. Boniface's two classrooms were divided simply: Primary and

The sisters in Queen of the Holy Rosary Convent garden: (l to r) *Back row:* Sisters Victoria Kine (lay sister), Salesia Fichtner, Felicitas Weiss, and Gonzaga Buehler. *Front row:* Seraphina Maerz, Maria Pia Backes, and Amanda Bednartz

Other. In the former, Sister Felicitas taught and mothered the children of the first, second and third grades, and in the "Other," Sister Seraphina taught the fourth to the eighth grades. Frances Klein[10] (the future Sister Dominica) assisted Sister Seraphina in the upper grades.

The following month (October 15, 1881) the community rejoiced when its first postulant received the habit and her new name, Sister Maria Rosa of the Sacred Heart. Father Dominicus Lentz, O.P., presided at the ceremony. A few days later, Sister Pia wrote in her Diary: "Miss Maggie Mulligan will probably enter this week. It seems God is hearing our prayers for postulants. We thank Thee, O God."[11]

Growing Tensions

Mother Seraphina, however, was of a different mind. When news of the candidate reached New York, she fired off a letter to Sister Pia expressing her displeasure at the turn of events:

> Your report from November I received a few days ago. The news that you have a candidate surprised me very much. You did not ask me about it and you have no right to accept one. Did the Most Reverend Archbishop give you perhaps the right to do it?
>
> As long as you belong to us you must ask here, and without permission from here such a reception has no value and we do not consider the girl in question as one of our candidates. Should she remain with you, we will not, under the present conditions, acknowledge her; she does not belong to us.
>
> Why did you not ask first since you always did before? My God, I do not know why there is no more understanding between us now!! When I think that one trouble is settled, another is right there. It was better before my visit than now. For this reason, I am almost sorry that I undertook that difficult trip. It seems I did not accomplish anything; only made things worse. May God help us. In Him I place all my trust and lay all my worries. Without Him I really could not carry the burden.
>
> Believe me, since the last two sisters are with you I have worried much about you; have prayed and wept much.[12]

It is fervently hoped that Miss Maggie was unaware of the stir she had created by entering the Golden Gate Avenue convent. Mother Seraphina's letter reached Sister Pia on December 19, and she answered the next day, asking to be relieved of office. The Brooklyn superior's response to this new development was to appoint Sister Pia novice director! On the day word of the appointment reached San Francisco, Father Dominicus happened—providentially—to visit the sisters. To him, Sister Pia took her troubles:

> He told me to trust in God [wrote the distraught Sister Pia]. Troubles will come. Mother wrote that I was...to train the novices....The next day, after much prayer, I answered Mother's letter telling her that I felt sure that I was morally and spiritually unfit to train novices. I recommended Sister Seraphina [Maerz] for that responsible office.[13]

Meantime, a mollified Mother Seraphina wrote again, this time to the professed community:

> My dear Children,

> Before these lines reach you Christmas time will be here.... May the dear Christ Child, the Divine King of Peace, help us with His grace so that between you and me love, openness and trust may always abide. In a word, may no such serious misunderstandings happen again as during the past months. Through these your old Mother felt just as hurt and sad as you. Yes, these were hard times, and I would not want to live through anything like that again; it was the most bitter time I had to battle through this year. [It is] peculiar that the greatest joy—the joy of meeting one another—and the greatest sorrow for me came from the West....In spirit I place myself in your midst, stretching out my hand to each one in motherly love and saying, "My Child, we are again good to each other from our hearts and have nothing but the same trust and love as we had for one another in June when we bade each other goodbye." We will not think any longer of what has happened, and we will do our best that it will not happen again.[14]

What other sources of misunderstanding were creating tension between the two superiors remain a mystery, but some light is derived from a letter about the same time from Mother Cunigunda Schell,[15] the sisters' highly revered novice director in New York. A champion of peace, Mother Cunigunda stood ever ready to explain one to the other across the miles that separated the Brooklyn superior from her young representative in California. Referring to a letter from Mother Seraphina "that hurt very much and that you will have to offer up to God with all your other worries as a sacrifice,"[16] Mother Cunigunda admonished her former novice to be more circumspect:

> Another good advice I wish to give you. In the future, leave all the appointments of the sisters to Mother Superior. Ask for none and refuse nobody; for this always works out best. As to the sad misunderstandings, all of them caused by your letters, let it be a personal humiliation for you which God permits for your own sanctification. Never insist on your opinion, but leave the final decision always to Mother. In case of doubt, always wait and see if you can straighten out the trouble by yourself. Pray much to the Holy Spirit to guide your hand and not allow you to be excited. If you use severe colors in your letters, then Mother Superior's answer will be a reflection of yours.
>
> Oh! How happy and pleased Mother Superior was when she returned from San Francisco and also how she still trusts you all, but your letters, dear Sister, do not please her as well as your personal contact with her. It is a great trial when one has to rely entirely on letters, as you have to do. All one can do then is bear it patiently and beg the Holy Spirit to give you all the needed strength to accept whatever comes with a willing heart. Otherwise, there is nothing else you can do in this matter.[17]

In Mother Cunigunda's mind Sister Pia's letters were the Gordian knot that needed immediate cutting. Never one to circumvent the truth as she saw it, her language left no room for doubt: "And then, dear Sister Pia," she wrote about the same time, "it seems to me your letters are too forceful. You sometimes use expressions too strong, which give the impression of being domineering."[18] Sister Pia was growing in wisdom; she was not offended by Mother Cunigunda's counsel, but received it as "loving."

Affairs seem to have simmered down sufficiently to forestall a change of superior. Mother Seraphina settled matters to her own satisfaction by appointing the five professed sisters in the convent as a house council:

> When in future something of importance has to be discussed if any trouble arises—in a word, all the happenings in the community shall be arranged and fixed or straightened out by the Council. Assemble for such an occasion in the chapel and pray the *Veni Creator* or the Litany of the Holy Spirit....

Three votes will be decisive. Sister Pia should send me the result and mention that it is the opinion of the Council. Act in the same way with regard to the acceptance of a candidate. A candidate may never enter before four weeks have passed after her application. During this period my opinion can be secured.

You five must hold together like steel and iron....Only courage and trust in God; away with all these womanish and sentimental stories of so-called homesickness.[19]

Sister Pia greeted the solution with approval; the onus of responsibility could now be shared. In January 1882, she noted in the Diary that the community spent the Feast of the Epiphany:

> ...pleasantly—playing dominoes and other games. We shall sing every evening several verses of the hymn *Ave Maris Stella* with the oration. May the Queen of Heaven bless us in spiritual and temporal affairs and remove all misunderstanding which might arise between East and West. I pray the Litany of the Holy Ghost frequently. We often speak lovingly of our Motherhouse in Brooklyn.[20]

Mother Seraphina Staimer, O.S.D.

It would be gratifying to record that affairs ran "happily ever after," but history writes with a free hand. In Brooklyn Mother Seraphina was experiencing the difficulties involved in governing a community 3,000 miles away, and in San Francisco Sister Pia was suffering the frustrations of awaiting permissions, despite the fact that Mother Seraphina was usually a prompt correspondent. Up to this point it had been relatively simple for the Brooklyn superior to instruct Sister Pia "...to get some Karlsbader water for Sister Seraphina if, as you wrote, her complexion is yellow and she has no appetite....Have her drink about six bottles and soon she will be better."[21] As for the purchase of a piano, "I have nothing against it, if you can get one for $300. But to help you out with money, even as a loan, is impossible....The traveling expenses for the two sisters [Sisters Gonzaga and Felicitas] I had to pay entirely."[22] Nor did she hesitate to advise Sister Pia to deposit the community savings in a local bank, where interest would probably be double that of New York. And with a blend of astuteness and naiveté she counseled: "Perhaps one of the bank employees will come [to the convent] if they know that you are not allowed to go out. But I would give the money neither to the Archbishop nor any priest. Should you have to go to the bank, write me first and I will ask Father May what to do." [23]

Three Decisions of Consequence

In the five years since the sisters' arrival in California, it was evident that conditions had changed significantly and decisions of far greater complexity were clamoring for Mother Seraphina's attention. Three were of immediate consequence: The Kaiser Property; the orphanage, and a new convent and school.

The first was the Kaiser Property. On Rosary Sunday 1881, Father Peter Kaiser, one-time rector of St. Boniface, San Francisco, and, since 1878, pastor of St. Joseph Church, Mission San Jose, died in the hospital of the Franciscan Sisters in Jersey City, New Jersey, while on his way to Germany for reasons of health treatments. In his will he left 165 acres just outside of Benicia, California to Archbishop Alemany:

> ...with the view of seeing some pious work carried out, which does not exist yet on this Pacific Coast, to my best knowledge. I mean a Convent of Dominican Sisters of

the Second Order, who would dedicate themselves to a life of exclusive contemplation and prayer and make it their principal duty to offer their good works before the Throne of the High Priest in Heaven in behalf of their own Archbishop, Bishop and Priests of this Ecclesiastical Province, extending their charity in the second place to all Bishops and Priests of the United States, all of the Missionary Countries and all Priests of [the] Holy Roman Catholic Church.

My intention in desiring such a good work realized, is the result of a long observation of priestly life and living. The stupendous hardships and difficulties and privations of all kinds, to which we poor Priests are exposed, throw down and discouraged [sic] many times the missionary and he believes that he cannot find time for prayer and meditation and the recital of his office and in many instances indeed their belief is justified, when they have been traveling, fasting for many miles day and night, or night and a great part of the day, as it has happened to me and most of my fellow Priests in this Country.

Besides in the life of the church there must be a mystical basis and continual current of prayer, contemplation and mortification, and Sisters like those of the Second Order of St. Dominick [sic] can fill the vacuum left in our Province of California and make up for our own deficiencies. For these reasons holy souls have to dedicate themselves exclusively to the holy office of atoning for our sins to God's justice and imploring his mercy on Bishops and Priests in every part of the world. Let the holy Dominican Sisters of the Second Order pray for us on *Kaiserheim* [Kaiserhome] which is far enough from the turmoil of the world and near enough to the Dominican Fathers in Benicia to be Spiritual Directors of the Sisters.

It is therefore my desire that Your Grace or Your Successors may accept my *Kaiserheim* as a free gift for the purpose above mentioned and take possession thereof immediately after my death.

> Let all movable effects in *Kaiserheim,* such as, Furniture, Wagons, Buggies, Harness, Agricultural Implements, Horses and all the necessary machinery and pipes for the purposes of making wine be the exclusive property of the Dominican Sisters of the Second Order in *Kaiserheim*.[24]

In accordance with Father Kaiser's wishes Archbishop Alemany immediately notified Sister Pia of the deceased's intentions. When apprised of the conditions, she wrote in the Diary that "His intention will in future be kept in mind by the Sisters of our Congregation in the offering of all their prayers and other works every Friday for the Archbishop and the priests of the Archdiocese."[25] The Archbishop further informed Sister Pia that it was Father Kaiser's wish that:

> five hundred dollars...be given to your community for your personal comfort and to pray for him; but it is his very express desire that this be kept secret, lest those who contribute a pittance towards your support, might partially withdraw even that.[26]

The deceased need not have worried. Archbishop Alemany wrote a second time, telling Sister Pia that the "$500 (five hundred dollars) left to the German Dominican Sisters, which, owing to the court expenses, etc., and there not being as much as he [Father Kaiser] supposed, is reduced to $350 by a *pro rata* division, or equalization."[27] Moreover, Father Kaiser's sister, whom he had brought from Germany some years previously, had a large family and now desired to go back to her native land. The Archbishop wished to know if Mother Pia would forego her claim [$350] in favor of Father Kaiser's sister. If not, would she be willing to forego a part of it? Not surprisingly, Sister Pia's answer to the request was a disclaimer for the full amount—whatever it turned out to be.

In December 1881, Archbishop Alemany wrote to Mother Seraphina in New York concerning the disposition of the ranch. She immediately alerted Sister Pia:

> He wants to turn the property over to us with complete certainty for the future. I did not answer his second letter as yet. Please ask him to give you permission to look at the place with Sister Seraphina and Sister Salesia, who knows something about farming. Afterwards, each one should write to me separately her opinion of the place....Give me

an idea as to what the house looks like and if it can be used for an indefinite time as a home for four or five sisters.[28]

Accordingly, Sister Pia asked and received the Archbishop's permission for the three so designated to visit the Benicia site. Dominican Fathers Dominicus Lentz and Hyacinth Derham elected to be party to the mission also. To the surprise of all, the "ranch" proved to be a vineyard, with some 3,000 gallons of wine and a few hundred gallons of vinegar stored in the wine cellar. Without warning Sister Pia found herself cast in the role of vintner, and she was not at all sure that she liked the idea.

In New York, the acquisition of a ranch was viewed in a more favorable light. The question of a suitable novitiate house for the California community had long been weighing on Mother Seraphina. Was the Kaiser property perhaps the answer? Archbishop Alemany was guarded in his response when next he visited the sisters. Providing a priest to celebrate daily Mass for the sisters would be difficult. Perhaps the property could be sold for a more advantageous site. To relocate would not, in his opinion, violate Father Kaiser's wishes. In any case, nothing should be done until the disposition of the ranch was settled, an event that the Archbishop optimistically judged would occur soon. Meantime, he wished the sisters to accept no postulants until they had adequate accommodations for them.

Despite Archbishop Alemany's reassurances, the settlement of Father Kaiser's affairs dragged on. The following year he advised Sister Pia to send a few sisters to live on the property; consequently, on August 21, 1883, Sisters Pia, Agnes, and Rosa left San Francisco by boat for Benicia. "Oh, in what condition we found the place," wrote a shocked Sister Pia. "What dirt!"[29] Returning in haste to the City, she enlisted reinforcements in the persons of Sisters Amanda and Gonzaga. Back to the ranch they went where they cleaned with Teutonic thoroughness. Although the premises were scrubbed to antiseptic perfection, Sister Pia found little to comfort her. She did not trust the two men who took care of the ranch. Jim, the overseer, told her the harvest would not be good that year. Under the circumstances, she could expect little yield from the ranch for the present.

The sisters' sojourn was brief. In September 1883, a troubled Mother Seraphina wrote Archbishop Alemany urgently from New York:

> I beg leave to appeal to your paternal heart on account of my sisters at the Kaiser home as I have no rest day or night since I know they are there. The reason for my anxiety is not the fear that the farm may not bring in as much as is sufficient for the livelihood of the sisters, although the reports I get are not encouraging,...But the most important reason to me is the spiritual welfare of my sisters....What could happen if tramps were to visit there?...This danger is increased by the [fact] that my sisters, not being able to have their own priest, particularly in the approaching time of winter when the roads will be impassable, cannot have regular opportunities for confession, Communion, and even Mass on Sundays, and their spiritual life must go downwards.
>
> For this reason, dearest Father, I must humbly pray that my sisters be recalled at once from the Kaiserhome in order that you may sell the place and buy from the money obtained therefrom a suitable place for the sisters, where the intention of Father Kaiser may be carried out as well as in the *Kaiserhome*.[30]

The appeal drew an immediate response from the Archbishop, who sent Mother Seraphina's letter to Sister Pia with a personal note added: "Recall the Sisters from the farm. I suppose they feel lonesome."[31] "Lonesome" was hardly an accurate description for Mother Seraphina's concern.

The second piece of property of concern was the orphanage. In January 1882, Miss Catherine Gross, who conducted an orphanage in San Francisco, became ill and contacted the convent with a vague message. Apparently she had intentions of willing her property to the sisters. Sister Pia spoke to Father Wolf concerning the orphanage, but he dismissed it as of no consequence, saying that the lady constantly changed her mind. The next afternoon Miss Gross did, indeed, seem of a different disposition, giving substance to Father Wolf's opinion; but some days later, she was again definite about leaving the orphanage to the sisters. For practical reasons Mother Seraphina Staimer did not support the project. She had only two sisters to send for the Kaiserhome—and none for the orphanage.

Meantime, a concerned Father May wrote to Sister Pia from New York cautioning her not to act prematurely in the business of the orphanage. He feared for the California foundation if so many new places were taken, as the sisters would have to employ their new candidates for the increased work. When would they have opportunity to acquire a good foundation in religious life? In the same letter he admonished Sister Pia for her zeal and reminded her of the need for prudence. Mother Seraphina might approve an idea, but not be in a position to act as rapidly as Sister Pia would wish. She should always ask first and wait for an answer. Should it be a refusal, she should drop the affair, leaving it in God's Hands.

Right Reverend Michael May, Spiritual Director of the Brooklyn community

In the end, the orphanage lost its appeal when the Archbishop confirmed a report of indebtedness ($8,000 or $9,000) on the property. On Easter Sunday, April 9, Mother Seraphina settled the affair by dispatch from New York bidding Sister Pia not to accept the orphanage.

The third property was a new convent and school. Throughout her lifetime Sister Pia's forte was faith, not finance. In this she differed from her superior who, although a woman of faith in her own right, was endowed also with an admirable business sense. On her visit to the West Mother Seraphina had seen for herself the sisters' urgent need for a larger convent, as well as a novitiate, and had returned to New York open to the idea. But she suffered a shock on learning the cost of San Francisco property. "From where...[will] you get the money that you are thinking of building right away?" she asked in a letter to Sister Pia. "Pray fervently and God will help us find a cheaper piece of land."[32]

The more she thought about the matter the more determined Mother Seraphina became in her opposition to acquiring property in San Francisco at the time, especially since the Mission School income continued well below that of the "worst of our [other] places."[33] Her letter left little room for doubt:

> We cannot do more for the next five or seven years. This is my firm conviction, and nobody can convince me differently....I write all this to you to convince you that we cannot buy the lot for $10,000; this is an impossibility. We would have to add another $15,000 to put a decent building on it. From what would you pay the interest, the taxes, and from what would you live? Try, therefore, to increase the income so that we can think of buying the Schmitz home [first mention]. Then for now the most important thing [a novitiate] would be accomplished. Later we can think of something larger. You are now eight. Everyone has a good will and can work. If you are good, God will see that you get a larger home; of this I have no doubt. But you cannot think of an empty lot costing $10,000.[34]

Despite her "firm conviction" to the contrary, spring brought an upsurge of optimism, and Mother Seraphina found herself again thinking "convent" for her sisters in the West. "I hope," she wrote in April 1882, "that this year I will get rid of all our debts. In the year 1883 I hope with the help of God to do all in my power to prepare a nice home for you in California."[35]

In San Francisco meanwhile, Sisters Pia and Seraphina went house-hunting for a rental more suitable as a school site than the Ruegg basement. To the sisters' disappointment, the managers of the Twenty-first Street School Society reneged on their promise to provide financial assistance. Small wonder that Sister Pia recorded in her Diary:

> I wrote to Mother Superior: "I wish you were here; we would then surely be further ahead. You would be at liberty to act; we, however, cannot say either yes or no to any alternative. It would be a different matter if Twenty-

first Street [Frank Ruegg's home] belonged to a parish. This not being the case, the school there cannot be considered a parish school."[36]

Back in New York Mother Seraphina's desire to have a nice home for the sisters betrayed her resolve to be debt-free first. "A letter from Mother Superior," reads an entry in Sister Pia's Diary just four months later, "grants permission for a convent in connection with the school at Twenty-first Street at a cost of $12,000. She will provide...$10,000 and see to the interest paid on the loan...."[37]

Fortified by the permission, Sister Pia once again went in search of property, her enthusiasm for specific sites tempered by obstacles, such as faulty land titles, mortgages, and missing deeds. To further complicate matters the Archbishop turned uncooperative. He did not support her plan to rent a house for the novices. She should wait, he again insisted, until the settlement of the Kaiser property. As for a new convent, he was unwilling to approve the purchase of the proposed lot on Valencia Street. "He wishes to see the location, and then he will refer the matter to his council," Sister Pia wrote in the Diary. "The title of the property must be examined. O God, unless You help, the plan cannot be carried out."[38] The next day she admitted: "I am depressed. Here I am young and inexperienced. Now the Archbishop disapproves, but what will Mother Superior's final decision be?"[39] Her depression did not lift, and on September 20 she reflected wearily that for two years they had been discussing the purchase of property and had nothing to show for it. "I have overcome my impatience as well as I could. O Lord, do not let me needlessly come to shame."[40]

A few days later her emotions roller-coastered. She was elated to receive a telegram from Mother Seraphina approving the purchase. But the afternoon mail brought frustration. From an unexpected quarter came another block: Father May did not approve the sisters' buying property at this time. Discomfited by the turn of events, Mother Seraphina reluctantly admitted the validity of the spiritual director's reasoning:

> He said to wait until we have the Kaiserhome [Benicia] as our own. He himself believes that we will have to build soon, but that if we build now on 21st Street, no other building can be done....He also said that if we have the

> Kaiserhome, four or five sisters will be needed right away. The same number of sisters would be needed for 21st Street, and St. Boniface School has to keep at least six sisters....I told him that unless we do something about 21st Street, the school will have to be closed. He answered that this is the business of the Archbishop and of the people who live there. If they want a school there, then it is their duty to furnish a suitable place. It is an unheard of thing that the sisters will have to build a school. Other sisters take a place after the parish has built the school and convent for the sisters. In this I also had to agree with him.[41]

Sister Pia's reaction to the setback was less receptive: "What a disgrace now that the matter has become public."[42]

But the matter was not yet laid to rest. A few days later Archbishop Alemany reversed his opinion; the new development did nothing to cheer Sister Pia. "Archbishop Alemany finally gave his permission today", she wrote in the Diary. "O God, in what darkness dost Thou leave me. What shall I do? I am supposed to buy—and then again I should not buy!"[43] Her distress was compounded by a letter from the realtor informing her that he had a buyer for the lot; was she still interested? A long and sleepless night brought her to a decision:

> After a great deal of deliberation and discussion with God and my Sisters, I have decided to buy rather than recall my decision after having troubled the Archbishop with the affair. Otherwise, it will be disgraceful. Mother Superior authorized me to transact the business. Then the permission was revoked by Father May's letter. This is not my fault. We need a convent. We cannot find a better or a cheaper place; therefore, I consider it my duty to proceed with the purchase. I am sure Mother Superior would agree if she could see the place.[44]

The sympathetic reader will surely cheer the decision, circuitous as the logic was. Two days later Sister Pia's reasoning was validated when the anxiously awaited letter arrived. Before opening it, she placed it near the Tabernacle. Mother Seraphina had also come to a decision. "Good news!" rejoiced Sister Pia. "We may purchase the property. Praise and honor to God."[45] Mother Seraphina had also come to a decision. Since the lot is 171 feet in length, she would purchase it and explain her decision to Father May. Further, she reassured Sister Pia:

> You will receive...besides the $878 which you sent here in cash another $10,000 little by little for the building of a new home in California. In all, you will have $12,239, which is a great sum of money and I think will help you have a nice home. You may not make any debts; I will make those here. The whole may not cost more than $12,200.[46]

But there was a limit to her generosity, and Mother Seraphina felt obliged to warn Sister Pia that she should not expect additional financial aid for building on the ranch site.

Unfortunately, Sister Pia's concerns were not yet over, for the title to the Valencia Street lot, the better and cheaper place, proved to be flawed. Further, the property was encumbered with a lawsuit, and so, in November Sister Pia went lot-hunting again. Mother Seraphina chided her gently: "In future you must be more careful; otherwise I will not know what to do. I want to be able to depend on you, especially in such important matters....If everything is in order with the new lot, then buy it for $3,600"[47] [Actual cost: $3,500].

This time Sister Pia was more circumspect, and a deal was closed only after title, street improvements, and mortgage releases had been checked. The deed for the 60 x 125 foot lot, situated on Guerrero Street near Twenty-fourth, was signed on November 21, 1882. A grateful Sister Pia received the deed on December 27.

It was high time. Five new applicants were about to be received into the community—undoubtedly with Mother Seraphina's permission: Clara Romkowski Wilson, 33, a native of Danzig, Prussia; Maria Sailor, 34, a native of Bohemia and resident of Portland, Oregon; Appollonia Schneider, 24, a native of Bavaria and resident of California; Anne Hocker, 24, a native of Weaverville, California; and Catherine Powers, 23, a native of Benicia, California. Sister Seraphina Maerz was appointed novice director.

On the little house on Tyler Street (now Golden Gate Avenue), built originally for the pioneer group of three and enlarged to accommodate five or at most seven, was now thrust the task of housing 14, not to mention orphans, whose plight Sister Pia could not refuse, and boarders, who came and went seasonally according to sacramental instructional need (First Holy Communion and

Confirmation). Mother Seraphina thought it time to intervene; accordingly, a letter from New York gave Sister Pia explicit orders regarding the acceptance of orphans in the future:

> I did not mean for you to have five orphans, but only three. This is really too much! I know that for the love of God we must show mercy, but as long as we cannot help ourselves yet we must not go too far. Do not say that Sister Victoria collects for them. This I approve only half way. The children have also to be taken care of, taught, etc. It is easy to be generous if I can step in for you in the end. And how narrow are the quarters you have to live in? All this is not in order. I tell you in obedience not to take another child free unless you get my permission beforehand.[48]

Immaculate Conception Convent and Academy

A new convent would prove a blessed relief to the growing community.

With her considerable building experience, Mother Seraphina decided to direct the project herself. "I want Mr. Schickel [New York architect] to draw the plan," she wrote; "he will know best what we need. For this I will pay extra."[49] Nevertheless, she encouraged Sister Pia to submit a description of projected needs as she saw them, despite the likely prospect that Mr. Schickel's thinking would prevail. Substantiating the latter view, Mother Seraphina wrote in answer to Sister Pia's proposed schema: "He [Mr. Schickel] thinks four classrooms are too many; the building will be too large. We will plan on three and later, if necessary, one more can be added....I think that one dormitory should be sufficient for the boarders."[50] As plans evolved, school and convent were to be housed under one roof.

The following month Mother Seraphina sent a description of the new building that was ingenious in its proposed dual uses of the various rooms:

> It will be a nice, comfortable convent; a better one you could not ask for. The basement will be a regular floor by itself and will be nine feet high....In the laundry for now will be six wash tubs. The room marked as the children's playroom can also be used for sewing and mending....The

parlor to the right on the first floor is large and should also be used as a music room. The music room on the left can be used as living quarters for a guest....Out of the two classrooms and the children's sitting room, a visitor's room can also be made....The chapel will be roomy and will be 18 feet high. It will have painted windows. There will also be a sliding door so that the children are enabled to hear Holy Mass from the classroom. About the second floor I need not explain anything. From the infirmary you will be able to look into the chapel....There will be two spacious dormitories for the children; the other half [of the third floor] remains an attic.[51]

As letters concerning the building traveled back and forth between coasts, Mother Seraphina admitted that directing construction from such a distance was not easy. Furthermore, building costs and conditions differed substantially from East to West Coast. James Klein, San Francisco contractor (and father of our future Sister Dominica), was awarded the contract, and he was emphatic. New York specifications simply could not be met. "The cost would be too high," he declared. "There is no house in San Francisco built so well."[52] Consequently, plans had to be modified to accommodate to western building standards. Eventually East and West came to common agreement, and on April 8, 1883, a jubilant Sister Pia noted in her Diary that she had received a telegram from Mother Seraphina telling her to accept Mr. Klein's last estimate and start work immediately. She would send the contract by mail. Four days later work began, and Sister Pia wrote gratefully:

> Mother Superior kindly promised as a gift to pay for carpentry and painting the sum of $14,880. At last the day has arrived that a convent home is to be erected for us. I resolved daily to pray Mary's Psalter until the building is completed. My soul renders thanks to Thee, O Jesus, for this unmerited boon.[53]

Though the bid exceeded the limit Mother Seraphina had originally set ($12,200), she did not protest the difference because she wished the sisters to have a comfortable and attractive home.

Once begun, construction of the new convent progressed so rapidly that by late October the building was declared ready for occupancy. The announcement signaled buckets and mops for the sisters, who went to work with enthusiasm, readying their new home for entry. For Sister Pia, emotions were mixed. On October 29, she recorded in the Diary that the community would soon be separated. This would be the last night that all the sisters would be together in their little "Tyler Street" convent.

Dedication of the new building was set for November 29, and the intervening days were spent in a flurry of activity. Stoves had to be bought, chapel windows installed, and the newly arrived altar erected. A week prior to the event Sister Pia purchased the tower bell, the gift of Mr. Klein. Christened "James" in honor of its donor, it was blessed and hoisted to its place of dignity the day after purchase in time to ring the noon Angelus.

In her generosity Mother Seraphina not only underwrote the building costs, but also contributed statues of St. Dominic and St. Catherine for the altar, crucifixes for the sisters' rooms and stained glass windows for the chapel. The New York sisters were most gracious in their gifts. Mother Cunigunda Schell provided the chapel priedieux; Sister Emilia Barth, six candlesticks (purchased with her feastday money); and Sister Angela Roth, a ciborium.

An event that normally would have generated excitement within the community was greeted with dismay by the members. Four days before the dedication, the Right Reverend Patrick Riordan, who in July had been appointed Coadjutor Archbishop of San Francisco with right of succession, announced his intention of visiting St. Boniface School the following day. A redirection of activity was immediately called for; classrooms had to be decorated, a program prepared, and the convent parlor set with the best china. Miraculously, all was in readiness when the Archbishop arrived: the sisters were most gracious, the children most welcoming, and the program was most enjoyable. Immediately following the guest of honor's departure, the sisters went into high gear, packing and moving the last remaining items. "How hard it was to see my bed carried out,"[54] lamented Sister Pia. The diversion of the Archbishop's visit accounted for the sisters having to work until midnight on the eve of the dedication.

Regrettably the one who had directed and underwritten the entire project was not present for the joyous occasion. Mother Seraphina's thoughts drifted westward frequently as the day of dedication approached. "Next Thursday," she wrote, "I myself and

Immaculate Conception Convent and Academy 1883, the Motherhouse until 1907

many more will be with you in spirit and praying that the new convent under the protection of the Immaculate Conception will become a nursery of piety and virtue."[55]

Thanksgiving Day, November 29, 1883. Archbishop Alemany arrived at 9:15 a.m. to celebrate the Eucharist and dedicate the building. In his homily for the occasion he voiced the hope that the new convent would be "a nursery of saints."[56] Charmed with the sisters' chapel, "he exclaimed: 'A gem of Gothic architecture.' He left at 3:45 p.m. How dear and fatherly of him to stay so long with us, and how we appreciated his kindness,"[57] was Sister Pia's summation of the day—followed by the comment, undoubtedly germane: "All were very tired."[58]

San Francisco's weekly, *The Monitor*, ran an account of the dedication, laudatory in its approval of the site.

> The building was especially erected for a school and dwelling, and from basement to attic it has been laid out so as to utilize every inch of space for some useful purpose. The Sisters have accommodations for boarders, as well as for day scholars, and the healthy location of the building will doubtless attract a large number of interested people.[59]

On December 8, the feast of the Immaculate Conception, the five sisters from St. Boniface joined the Guerrero Street community of eight in a solemn Act of Consecration, placing the new convent under the patronage of Our Lady. Sometime in the same month the Twenty-first Street School moved from Mr. Ruegg's basement to the new location and was re-christened Immaculate Conception Academy. The project was now complete.

By January all available space in the new building had been converted into classrooms. Reviewing the situation, Sister Pia reflected gratefully on the goodness of God Who had sent them so many new pupils. Later she had even more reason for thanksgiving, when enrollment increased to 92 in July and 116 in August.

That the sisters were grateful for their new home may be inferred from Mother Seraphina's letter some six weeks after the dedication: "For your new convent you [have] thanked me enough and need not continue to do it in the future. All gratitude is due to God, for without HIM I would not have been able to do anything."[60]

Early in the planning stages of the building, Mr. Herbring, a benefactor, had offered to donate an oil painting of the Immaculate Conception for the chapel. Mother Seraphina was not impressed.

> If you received an oil painting as picture for the altar, that is not to be undervalued; but it seems strange to me that in San Francisco they think first of the object which one needs last. It would be much more pleasing if this benefactor would have thought of the altar first, because without an altar you cannot use the picture; you do not yet know how large the picture should be even if one knows the height of the chapel.[61]

When the disparaged painting arrived from Dusseldorf on November 25, 1884—four days short of the first anniversary of the dedication of the convent—there was general rejoicing in the community. Approximately six by three feet in dimension, it proved an excellent copy of Murillo's "Immaculate Conception," its hand-carved frame matching the main altar above which it was hung. There it held honored place until the convent was razed many years later in favor of a new home for the sisters.

Although there was reason for rejoicing as they watched the new building taking shape, the sisters' happiness was tempered by the reality of other events. Even the unexpected visit of their beloved Father May from New York had its bittersweet moments. In June 1883, the astonished community received an early morning dispatch announcing that he would be with them at 1:00 p.m. that afternoon! "Joy in the community!" exulted Sister Pia. "After seven long years we shall once again behold the loving countenance of our esteemed spiritual Father. On his arrival, we knelt with him before the Blessed Sacrament and sang the *Te Deum* in thanksgiving. We sat together and talked until 3 p.m."[62]

The next day Father May spoke at length with Sister Pia concerning Mother Seraphina's wishes, adding that, if on occasion, her letters seemed somewhat sharp, Sister Pia should remember that she is often weighed down by worry. The visit was a blessing for the young superior; on-site contact gave the spiritual director a much better perspective henceforth in understanding the problems and challenges facing the California mission, and on his return to New York, his report was so positive that Mother Seraphina cried for joy. Notwithstanding, Sister Pia's comment following his departure reveals that with the blessing came pain: "Bitter nostalgia. I have no more desire for visitors from home. The leave-taking is too hard."[63]

July brought a new sadness in its wake. Father Thomas Dyson, O.P., called at the convent to inform the sisters of the illness of their good friend, Father Dominicus Lentz. They were totally unprepared, then, for the sick priest's appearance at the convent door the following afternoon! "He told us," wrote Sister Pia, "that he had had a heart attack. Said he: 'I am feeling pretty well this afternoon, so I thought I would run over to my Sisters.' He heard our confessions remarking: 'It will be the last time. I had a great desire to see you once again.'"[64] Three days later, the sisters were shocked to learn of their beloved friend and counselor's death. "What a blow!" grieved Sister Pia. "It seems impossible. All of us shed tears."[65] The grief-stricken community prayed the Office for the Dead, and Mother Pia sent a telegram at once to Mother Seraphina announcing the sorrowful news. She followed with a letter telling her superior that she felt abandoned so far from home.

July also bore the news that Archbishop Alemany had been assigned a coadjutor—the Right Reverend Patrick J. Riordan from the Archdiocese of Chicago. December held an even more depressing announcement: Archbishop Alemany informed the sisters that in the future they should refer their needs to Archbishop Riordan who had agreed to be responsible for the sisters' interests. "Another link broken,"[66] was Sister Pia's terse comment in her Diary.

There was more to come. January 28, 1885, brought word of Archbishop Alemany's resignation, a source of dismay to Sister Pia. At once she sent Sister Victoria to the Archbishop's Office to convey the sisters' regrets and to propose that he be their chaplain. His reply impressed her. "A pleasant home for me would be the Kaiser estate, but I will go wherever I am told. I have no wish."[67] Sister Pia marveled at her friend's humility. The "pleasant home" did not come to be, however, and the sisters learned of the Archbishop's impending retirement to his native Vich in Spain. In a farewell gesture to the community, Archbishop Alemany offered to preside at the ceremony of the Reception of the Habit on April 20. According to Sister Pia the Archbishop was wonderfully kind; he told her that he would leave for Spain in May. As a farewell gift, the sisters made him a new habit, which they told his attendant to hide in the bottom of his trunk.

Three years later the longstanding friendship with Archbishop Alemany came to an end when he died in Valencia in his native Spain on April 14, 1888. At his own request he was buried in Vich where he had been born and where he had entered the Dominican Order. Three-quarters of a century later, his remains were exhumed and returned to San Francisco for interment in Holy Cross Cemetery, where he rests today.

Concluding the chapter on a happier note: Immaculate Conception Convent took on a distinguished, albeit temporary, role early in its history. St. James Parish came into existence on Sunday, April 29, 1888, in the classrooms of the Academy. Sister Pia offered their use to the first pastor, Father Patrick Lynch, until a church could be built. The day preceding the opening Mass the sisters worked diligently, setting up an altar and arranging desks to serve as pews. "April 29 – Sunday. At 9 a.m. the spiritual child of Archbishop Riordan, Saint James Parish—named for the parish he left in Chicago—came into existence in our classrooms,"[68] wrote Mother Pia. Here in the Academy, Mass was celebrated each Sunday and holyday for the Catholics of San Francisco's Mission District until July 6, 1890, when the new St. James Church at 23rd and Guerrero Streets was dedicated. "For two years," the San Francisco Chancery records read, "in the quiet retreat of the Dominican Sisters' classroom chapel, at the hours of 8:00 and 10:00 o'clock, the faithful of the parish were accorded the opportunity of hearing Mass."[69] For Mother Pia, Mass in the Academy classrooms was a special grace.

Meanwhile, the school was becoming so overcrowded by 1893 that the sisters judged an annex an absolute necessity. As soon as school was out, work on an extension began. The addition joining the Oughin's and Berge's houses, (three-story frame buildings on Fair Oaks Street purchased in 1887) would satisfy the demand for more classrooms. On September 10, Father Lynch blessed the completed addition, and the following Saturday Mother Pia wrote that the sisters were working putting the final touches on the building in preparation for the open house that would take place the next day. "Great excitement in the air," she noted in her Diary. "About 700 people visited the new building. Father Leo [Bruener, O.F.M.] made an announcement at Saint Boniface. $180 was donated."[70] In the years ahead, the additional classrooms would prove a boon.

Notes

[1] Staimer, letter to Backes, 17 September 1881.

[2] Backes 16.

[3] Staimer, letter to Backes, 4 July 1881.

4 Staimer, letter to Backes, 1 August 1881.

5 Staimer 29.

6 Felicitas Weiss (Breitenbach) O.P., Unpublished Memoirs, n. d.

7 Weiss, Unpublished Memoirs, n. d.

8 Weiss, Unpublished Memoirs, n. d.

9 Weiss, Unpublished Memoirs, n. d.

10 Frances Klein, daughter of Jacob Klein and Margaret Schafer, was born on September 3, 1860, in Speyer, Bavaria. At the age of four, she accompanied her mother to the United States, where her father had preceded them to settle the family. Sister grew up with San Francisco and always showed a great interest in its progress. The Kleins were among the pioneer members of St. Boniface Parish, and Frances was one of the group that welcomed the sisters to the parish and became one of the first members of the Young Ladies Sodality organized by Sister Pia. She applied for entrance to our community on June 21, 1884, and received the habit on April 20, 1885, and was professed on June 15, 1886. A superb educator, especially in the field of secondary education, Sister Dominica was gifted with a brilliant mind. Her last accomplishment was the building of Immaculate Conception Academy, which she enjoyed only a few short months, as she died after a brief illness of five days, on February 21, 1929. For her funeral St. James Church was crowded, and San Francisco Mayor James Rolph was an honorary pallbearer.

11 Backes 19. (Cf. Sisters' File and Necrology). Margaret "Maggie" Mulligan was a likely candidate. Born in Lionsden, Ireland, on November 16, 1852, she came to California when 29 years of age to be near her sister, Mother Agnes Mulligan, S.M., a pioneer worker in the Diocese of Sacramento. Although she felt called to religious life, Maggie was undetermined as to congregation. A friend described our community to Mother Agnes as a "flower garden," and after visiting our convent, she encouraged her sister to apply. Maggie called on Sister Pia and the result of the interview was her entrance on November 10, 1881. She received the habit and her name Sister Agnes on August 30, 1882, made profession on June 10, 1884 and pronounced her final vows on St. Dominic's Day, August 4, 1896. Sister Agnes spent over 30 years teaching in the primary grades. She died at Mission San Jose on February 20, 1927. (Cf. Necrology).

12 Staimer, letter to Backes, 12 December 1881.

13 Backes 21.

[14] Staimer, letter to Professed Sisters in California, 19 December 1881.

[15] According to Crawford, Mother Cunigunda Schell "was an ideal Mistress of Novices, motherly yet firm, understanding, and allowing for the gaucheries of immature beginners. She was well versed in the spiritual life, devoted to convent discipline and religious observance. Knowledge learned from...Mother Benedicta in Ratisbon was handed down to her...[novices]. She was a vital link between Europe and America." Crawford 146.

[16] Cunigunda Schell, O.S.D., letter to Backes, 28 November 1881.

[17] Schell, letter to Backes, 28 November 1881.

[18] Backes 20.

[19] Staimer, letter to Professed Sisters in California, 19 December 1881.

[20] Backes 21.

[21] Staimer, letter to Backes, 17 June 1879.

[22] Staimer, letter to Backes, 30 November 1878.

[23] Staimer, letter to Backes, 28 August 1880.

[24] Peter Kaiser, "Testament," n.d.

[25] Backes 18.

[26] Alemany, letter to Backes, 4 October 1881.

[27] Alemany, letter to Backes, 9 May 1883.

[28] Staimer, letter to Backes, 12 December 1881.

[29] Backes 42.

[30] Staimer, letter to Alemany, 7 September 1883.

[31] Backes 44.

[32] Staimer, letter to Backes, 11 August 1881.

[33] Staimer, letter to Backes, 17 September 1881.

[34] Staimer, letter to Backes, 17 September 1881.

[35] Staimer, letter to Backes, 30 April 1882.

[36] Backes 26–27.

[37] Backes 27.

[38] Backes 28.

39 Backes 28.

40 Backes 28.

41 Staimer, letter to Backes, 16 September 1882.

42 Backes 28.

43 Backes 29.

44 Backes 29.

45 Backes 29.

46 Staimer, letter to Backes, 22 September 1882.

47 Staimer, letter to Backes, 11 November 1882.

48 Staimer, letter to Backes, 11 May 1883.

49 Staimer, letter to Backes, 22 September 1882.

50 Staimer, letter to Backes, 21 December 1882.

51 Staimer, letter to Backes, 20 January 1883.

52 Backes 33.

53 Backes 36.

54 Backes 46.

55 Staimer, letter to Backes 24 November 1883.

56 Caldwell, Aquinas Marie, O.P., "The Spirit of the Centuries." [Term Paper]. (Mission San Jose, CA: Queen of the Holy Rosary College, 1961) 10.

57 Backes 46.

58 Backes 46.

59 The Monitor, 5 December 1883 [San Francisco]

60 Staimer, letter to Sisters 9 January 1884.

61 Staimer, letter to Backes 11 November 1882.

62 Backes 38.

63 Backes 39.

64 Backes 40.

65 Backes 40.

[66] Backes 49.
[67] Backes 61.
[68] Backes 104.
[69] San Francisco Chancery Records in Backes 127.
[70] Backes 148.

CHAPTER FOUR

COPING WITH THE ALBATROSS

The Kaiser ranch was becoming an albatross around Sister Pia's neck. By bequest it was the property of the Archbishop of San Francisco, but by expressed wish of the decedent its use was reserved to the Dominican Sisters of the Second Order. Despite the goodwill exhibited by the interested parties, the resultant situation was awkward at best. From all quarters, advice—sought or unsought—came freely. Father May counseled that responsibility for the Kaiserheim should be accepted only if it were debt free. Father Hyacinth Derham, O.P., advised Sister Pia to supervise the ranch herself. Father Joseph Bucholzer, longtime friend of the community, warned of possible mismanagement by the overseers. Archbishop Alemany opted for leaving the sisters to their "knees and Archbishop Riordan,"[1] who favored neither a community nor a novitiate at the ranch because of the difficulty in providing daily Mass and the fear that the sisters "would feel too lonesome having no girls to teach."[2]

Next came the disquieting news that the ranch had an indebtedness of $1,617.34. In panic, Sister Pia wired Mother Seraphina Staimer, who granted permission to pay the debt on condition that the sisters be given a clear title and deed to the property. But the condition could not be met, as Archbishop Alemany explained in a letter to Sister Pia:

> ...I fear the property cannot [be] passed over from me to you since it is held in trust for a specific object....As to the administration of it, that can be transferred to you if you wish, but I do not know whether you could manage it better than it is being done. Father Grey has a good man

there planting it in vines, which are a little expense now, but will [yield] good returns soon.³

Only Mother Seraphina's outlook continued positive. Although she had written Sister Pia earlier (July 22, 1884) that she was leaving decisions regarding the ranch to her—"One can judge rightly only if one is on the place"—news of the vineyard had sparked fresh interest on the East Coast. The tonic qualities of the grape yield would be excellent for the Brooklyn sisters' hospital patients, she wrote, as well as for their ailing sisters, and the community could provide altar wine—at a small profit to themselves—for neighboring pastors. Moreover, the New York market would be a boon to the California community. With a shrewd eye to prospective sales, the Brooklyn superior critiqued the wine shipped from the West: "Of the last three barrels of wine, the...red wine is exceptionally fine; the other, medium; and the white wine deserves no praise."⁴ Fortunately for the latter, its quality improved with maturity and it, too, came to be recognized as "exceptionally fine." In time, sales became so brisk (300 gallons sold in four weeks!) that the New York sisters had not only to rearrange their cellar to accommodate additional barrels, but also to answer the charges of a neighboring wine merchant who complained to the New York Board of Excise that the sisters were ruining his business. "Our wine sales are a thorn in his eye,"⁵ wrote Mother Seraphina.

Marketing possibilities notwithstanding, the ranch was still a liability; taxes were high, expenses many, and lay management of the ranch was frequently suspect. Mother Seraphina's perplexity was evident. "As to the matter of selling the farm," she wrote, "I cannot make the final decision. I do not know what is profitable and best, since I am not there. Neither do I understand all about it. Do as you think best."⁶

To add to her problems, Sister Pia now had to deal with the new Archbishop on matters of ranch concern. However important to her, the settling of the *Kaiserheim* was not Archbishop Riordan's foremost responsibility. "I will arrange the property transfer or at least the administration in a few days,"⁷ he promised. Well meant as his intentions were, a note in Sister Pia's handwriting on the back of a letter dated four years later reveals that she was still without the administration papers.

In the intervening years the disposition of the Kaiser property moved no nearer solution. On occasion, sections of the ranch were leased to neighboring farmers, and from time to time inquiries indicated interest in its acquisition, but without result. In consultation with Father May, Mother Seraphina finally concluded that the best course would be to keep the ranch and build the novitiate on site, but Archbishop Riordan would not hear of it:

> It would be much better to dispose of *Kaiserheim* entirely, and secure a location in the country in some parish where a school is needed and where a priest resides. I have two or three very beautiful places in my mind at present and probably I shall be able to locate you in one of them. But have patience and give me time to arrange some matters first.[8]

Affairs remained at a standstill until August 28, 1886, when Sister Pia made note in the Diary of a buyer: "Mr. Lille bought the ranch today for $9,000—$2,000 cash. Mortgage—$7,000 at five per cent for five years."[9] Her report of the sale to Mother Seraphina was received without enthusiasm.

> ...I must say that this news was not joyful for me. How much trouble and unpleasantness we had until we were able to sell your wine you do not know; and now after things have been straightened out and have met with success, all at once the farm has been sold. Sold without asking my opinion first and if the selling price was acceptable to me. Could you not have asked by way of telegram? Now everything is over, and it must have been God's Holy Will. This is my consolation.[10]

But affairs involving the ranch could never be simple, and a letter from Father George Montgomery, Vicar General of the Archdiocese of San Francisco, signaled another hurdle to be cleared. "Mr. Comte, an attorney, thinks there is some legal difficulty in the way of your selling of the property in Solano [County]....He speaks of an abstract of title. I doubt whether we ever had one or not, and in fact I do not think we had."[11] Until the title was cleared, the sale could not be completed. Mr. Lille withdrew his bid.

Sister Pia's concerns, however, were not simply financial. The non-fulfillment of the condition of Father Kaiser's will regarding the establishment at the ranch of "a Convent of Dominican Sisters of the Second Order, who would dedicate themselves to a life of exclusive contemplation and prayer and make it their principal duty to offer their good works...in behalf of their own Archbishop, Bishop and Priests of this Ecclesiastical Province"[12] continued to trouble her. For whatever reason, the Archbishop did not favor Sister Pia's long-cherished desire of a contemplative branch of the Congregation, and the disposition of the ranch remained at an impasse. Possibly the reason for the episcopal reluctance lay in the fact that Archbishop Riordan was at the time corresponding with a group of cloistered nuns in Mexico regarding the establishment of a convent in the Archdiocese of San Francisco. Two such convents in close proximity might be overdoing it. As late as 1901, Sister Pia was still sharing her anxieties with Archbishop Riordan.

Dominican Convent, Guerrero St.

January 7, 1901

Most Reverend and dear Archbishop,

The enclosed copy of the last will and testament of the late Rev. P. J. Kaiser, by which [the] Kaiserheim is bequeathed to Sisters of the Second Order of St. Dominic for purposes therein set forth, will explain to Your Grace the object of my writing. Your Grace is aware that, until now, the terms of this will have not been fulfilled. We tried to correspond in some measure by offering the prayers, works and mortifications of the whole Congregation on every Friday for our dear Archbishop and his priests.

However, this does not fulfill the wishes of the deceased and the matter is a source of considerable anxiety to me, the more so, since my last visit, some time ago, to Your Grace when you were so sore and worried. Your words and the will of the Rev. P. Kaiser seem constantly before me as reminders of a duty unfulfilled. Only Your Grace can take the weight from me and give me peace and therefore I most humbly beg of Your Grace to decide the matter definitely.

Should Your Grace desire to have the wishes of the deceased carried out, I propose the following plan: By degrees I would establish a Community of Sisters to the number of fifteen, who would lead the contemplative life and live according to the strict rule of the Second Order of St. Dominic. I would prepare a home for them at Mission

San Jose where they would form a separate Community, and gain their livelihood by sewing for the orphans. These contemplatives would then devote their whole lives to praying for the Archbishop and the Archdiocese of San Francisco.

Although the accomplishment of this will take several years, I nevertheless beg of Your Grace to give this matter attention and...decide.

I feel that I can no longer shoulder the responsibility of having accepted the property of the deceased without having fulfilled the obligations imposed.

Humbly begging your blessing, I am most respectfully,

S. M. Pia [13]

The last mention of the Kaiser property in the Diary occurs under date of January 7, 1901, and refers to the above letter: "Wrote to Archbishop Riordan concerning Father Kaiser's last will that a contemplative branch take over in Benicia. We have prayed much to know God's design in this matter. I shall accept the Archbishop's answer as decisive."[14] Whatever his answer, a note dated September, 1904, from Father Mulligan of the San Francisco Chancery Office was probably the final word:

Dear Sister Superior:

I beg to notify you that we have received here the sum of $5021.70 for the sale of the Kaiser Ranch, which sum has been credited to your account in this office.

Yours truly,

F. Mulligan[15]

With the above, information relating to the ranch closes down, though the sisters attempted to satisfy Father Kaiser's wishes regarding prayer for priests as best they could. Each Friday the sacristan hung a placard at the door of the Motherhouse chapel reminding the sisters to offer their prayers, works, and sufferings of the day for the archbishop and priests of the archdiocese. The albatross had flown its nest!

Meantime, Sister Pia's horizons were broadening, and the Kaiser property was not her sole preoccupation. New foundations held a magnetic appeal for the young superior. "The more souls can be saved, the better," she wrote, "...O Jesus, give us souls."[16] Opportunities were indeed multiplying. North Beach in San Francisco was still under consideration, attention focusing on St. Brigid's parish, and Archbishop Riordan was urging a foundation in the capital city of Sacramento. Father Bucholzer wished sisters for his new school in St. Helena. Mother Seraphina decided in favor of prudence; she would make no decisions until she had an opportunity to discuss with Sister Pia the troublesome matter of new houses. With this in mind she decided to call Sister to New York. On April 8, 1885, a dispatch arrived from Brooklyn: "Start journey to New York May 17." The day before she left, Sister Pia wrote to Archbishop Alemany:

> Tomorrow I shall leave for New York. How much I should like to see you and receive your blessing before my going. Your Grace's departure from California is also drawing near. May the good God give us strength to bring this sacrifice. How keenly do we feel our great loss! I feel that we shall never again have such a good father. Please, dearly beloved Father, permit me to express sincere thanks for all your kindness towards me.[17]

In reply, the Archbishop assured Sister Pia that he would never forget her in his prayers.

On the trip, Sister Pia traveled alone. Fortunately she met a woman on board, bound for Cleveland, with whom she felt comfortable. Nine years after her departure from New York, Sister Pia returned for the first time to her beloved Holy Cross. At Grand Central Station she was met by Mother Assistant Emilia Barth and Sister Augustina Fleck. "Mother Superior had remained in the coach, still quite weak from her recent illness. Oh, what a joyful welcome. Father May was also at the depot."[18]

Sister Pia's heart rejoiced to see once again the dear faces of her family, and Mother Seraphina thoughtfully provided occasions for her to visit the convents in the area where she renewed ties with the sisters. En route, business was often conducted in the carriage. Mother Seraphina informed Sister Pia that it was time now to allow the California mission some latitude in regard to its affairs.

She therefore authorized the incorporation of the community, delegated the choice of location of the novitiate house to Archbishop Riordan and Sister Pia, and gave the sisters their financial independence, explaining that as she had just built four convents in New York, she was unable to promise the California foundation further financial aid. Moreover, they seemed to be managing nicely. But she did not approve of her engaging a male Latin teacher for the sisters. Oddly enough, Sister Pia makes no mention of any discussion of new foundations in the West, even though such ostensibly was the main reason for the trip.

Returning from a visit to Amityville, where the Holy Cross Congregation had bought property and moved the novitiate, Sister Pia learned that Archbishop Alemany had called on her in Brooklyn en route to Spain. "How sorry I felt! Missed him! Here I am, sitting in the cell and feeling as if my heart would break—I know not why....For Thee, O my God!"[19]

All too soon the long-anticipated visit was over, and Sister Pia found herself bidding farewell to family members and dear friends. Leave-taking saw tears shed by both superiors, and there is something inexpressibly sad about the Diary entry: "My mother, standing at her window across the street, bade me a silent farewell as I stepped into the carriage." [20]

An immediate outcome of the visit concerned personnel. Sister Pia offered to bring Sister Bartholomea (Mary) Deckert to California in the hope that the change of climate would restore her failing health. A native of New York, Mary Deckert had entered Holy Cross Convent as a lay sister in 1877 at the age of 16. She had received the habit on June 13, 1878, and made her first and final profession on May 3, 1880. Early in her religious life, she was sent to St. Catherine's Hospital in Brooklyn where she became proficient in nursing skills. At the time of Sister Pia's visit, Sister Bartholomea had contracted tuberculosis; hence, Sister Pia's offer. So beneficial did the change prove that Sister Bartholomea was allowed to remain permanently in the West.

In California Sister Bartholomea gave valuable service as practical nurse and outgoing sister, providing faithfully for the community's physical and material needs, as well as the orphans' and the poor. Among the first to minister to the injured brought to the Mechanics' Pavilion in downtown San Francisco following the 1906 earthquake, Sister Bartholomea was one of the last volunteers to leave the Pavilion when it was engulfed in flames that wracked the City. During the 1918 influenza epidemic she served beyond the call of duty at Mission San Jose, caring for the stricken sisters by day and often by night, as well as the ill gathered in the church hall in the nearby town of Centerville. As extern sister, Sister made many friends, Catholic and Protestant alike. Sister Bartholomea died on August 21, 1940, at the Motherhouse, just one week after her Diamond Jubilee of Profession. The last sister from Holy Cross, Brooklyn, to join the California mission, Sister Bartholomea made a significant contribution to the community in the years that followed her transfer.

Notes

[1] Alemany, letter to Backes, 17 March 1885.

[2] Alemany, letter to Backes, 17 March 1885.

[3] Alemany, letter to Backes, 26 December 1884.

[4] Staimer, letter to Backes, 10 September 1885.

[5] Staimer, letter to Backes, 11 August 1886.

[6] Staimer, letter to Backes, 4 May 1886.

[7] Patrick W. Riordan, letter to Backes, 11 March 1885.

[8] Riordan, letter to Backes, 10 March 1885.

[9] Backes 79.

[10] Staimer, letter to Backes, 24 September 1886.

[11] George Montgomery, letter to Backes, 4 September 1886.

[12] Peter Kaiser, "Testament," n. d.

[13] Backes, letter to Riordan, 7 January 1901.

[14] Backes 247.

[15] F. Mulligan, letter to Backes, 26 September 1904.

[16] Backes 54.

[17] Backes 66.

[18] Backes 67.

[19] Backes 68.

[20] Backes 69.

CHAPTER FIVE

SEPARATION

Mother Seraphina was not enthusiastic when she learned that Sister Pia had asked a bishop for a new mission. In her opinion, to ask for a mission was to lower the Congregation in the episcopal esteem; it made the sisters too available. Nevertheless, she supported Sister Pia's ambition to spread the Order and its mission throughout the West.

Verboort, Oregon

As early as 1882, Archbishop Charles Seghers of the Archdiocese of Oregon City (changed to the Archdiocese of Portland in Oregon in 1928) visited Sister Pia in San Francisco and discussed with her the desirability of an Oregon foundation, thereby sparking her interest in the Great Northwest. Nothing came of the conversation, however, until three years later when the Most Reverend William Gross, C.SS.R., succeeded to the Metropolitan See of Oregon City on the death of Archbishop Seghers. The new prelate lost no time in writing to Sister Pia concerning a foundation in Our Lady of the Visitation parish in Verboort, Oregon, a small farming community with Dutch roots about ten miles northwest of the city of Portland. Seen through the Archbishop's eyes, Father Edward Hermann, pastor, was:

> ...one of the most pious and zealous and hard-working priests that I know of. The place where he wishes you to open a school has a most pious congregation....I am of the

opinion that you can have a large school in Verboort [sic]; and can easily find support for three sisters. I shall be most pleased if you can accept.[1]

The Archbishop's superlatives had the desired effect; the mission was accepted.

With her customary prudence, Mother Seraphina advised Sister Pia to visit the Oregon site to determine if the sisters would have a suitable home and a sufficient income before answering Father Hermann, but changed her mind when she learned that Verboort was three days distant by boat from San Francisco. "Since the convent for the sisters has to be built yet, it would not pay to spend so much time and money just to see the surrounding countryside. The main thing is that you will select a good sister as leader and one on whom you can depend."[2]

In a letter to Sister Cunigunda Schell, New York novice director, Mother Seraphina commented favorably, if not exuberantly:

> Sister Pia wrote. It seems that the place in the Archdiocese of Oregon is acceptable. The priest is German and already has a nice Church dedicated to Our Lady of the Visitation and also a parish school with 60 children. His name is Rev. Edward Hermann. In Sadlier's Almanac of 1885 you will find this settlement on p.118 and it is named the Village of Verboort. It is about ten miles out of Portland. From San Francisco it is a three days' trip by water.[3]

Mid-January, 1886, brought a letter from Father Hermann requesting the sisters to open his school the following September. With high hopes and youthful enthusiasm Sisters Amanda Bednartz, Hyacintha Schneider, Vincentia Powers, and Miss Belle (Moore?), a postulant, boarded the steamer for Portland on September 8, 1886. Alas, from Day One the Verboort mission was a disaster. No pastor was on hand to welcome the sisters; as Father Hermann had gone to Europe on a fund-raising quest for a convent—an endeavor praiseworthy in intent, but regrettable in its consequences. No house was available to receive the newcomers. The situation called for an immediate solution, and the sisters found one by asking the acting pastor to vacate the rectory—which he did, after a fashion—for he continued to come and go as he wished, entertaining his friends without regard for the sisters' privacy or convenience. This state of affairs elicited a swift reaction from Mother Seraphina:

> You should have been absolutely sure that the sisters had a house to live in before you sent them....It was a mistake that you sent Sisters without first going to look at the place. This was only done to save money....[Father Hermann] may be a holy man, but I cannot see wisdom in this action [going to Europe at the time]....Your zeal is only to be praised when it is joined with wisdom. Pray each day to the Holy Spirit to enlighten you to do only that which is for the greater honor of God, for your own sanctification, and the welfare of your neighbors.[4]

Moreover, although Archbishop Gross was of the opinion that three sisters could "easily find support" in the Verboort mission, such did not prove to be the case. The first month's tuition for 57 children grossed $5.50, as most parents opted to pay in produce, an option that guaranteed an adequate table, but a critically limited cash flow.

Letters from Verboort to New York and San Francisco to New York arrived one after the other until Mother Seraphina concluded that the interim pastor was either mentally ill or an alcoholic! For one thing, the sisters had no access to the church, which was kept locked; and for another, they had not been able to receive Holy Communion or the Sacrament of Penance since their arrival six weeks earlier. "You are too credulous," wrote Mother Seraphina to her young superior, "and too easily influenced in favor of an undertaking. In the future be more discreet. Your present day experiences are of some value. You young people must sow some wild oats."[5]

Then, as if matters weren't bad enough, gossip reared its ugly head and set the rural community buzzing. Miss Belle, the postulant, left ("ran off," it was noised abroad) to marry the bread man after a whirlwind courtship conducted presumably at the sisters' back door on occasion of the young man's regular deliveries. And romance had its moment in the sun when the acting pastor, with benign approval and full community support, married the pair at the Sunday High Mass attended by the village. This could well have been the last straw, but Mother Seraphina was determined to salvage the mission, come what may. A telegram to Archbishop Gross brought the immediate removal of the priest and the appointment of an "older" man (42!) to the immense satisfaction of Mother Seraphina. It was now her hope that there would be no further "hair-raising" experiences[6] and that the situation would settle down. She would make no decision regarding the sisters' future in Verboort until Father Hermann's return from Europe in January; nevertheless, a "return trip [was] always open to them."[7]

Affairs, however, continued their downward trend, Sister Amanda complaining that the priests came and went in the house as they pleased, stayed as long as they liked, and created general havoc in the cloister. To this Mother Seraphina replied that since the house was theirs, she could not forbid them entry, but that this state of affairs would never do. Finally, the last ray of hope vanished, she ordered the sisters home, trusting that Sister Pia had learned a lesson for life.

At Mother Seraphina's behest, Sister Amanda went to Portland to see the Archbishop, who, unfortunately, was out of town for an extended period. Complying with Mother Seraphina's wishes, Sister Pia sent a telegram to Sister Amanda: "If Archbishop does not come home this week telegraph to him; in the meantime get ready so that you may come home. S. Pia."[8] A letter of apology followed, explaining the situation in detail to the absentee Archbishop. How bad it really was may be gleaned from the Diary: "Conditions were unendurable there. The trouble in Oregon was so profound and so sharp that I could confide it only to Jesus in the tabernacle. Yes, Oregon has taught me how circumspect one must be in making foundations."[9]

Not surprisingly, the Archbishop was not pleased on learning of the sisters' untoward departure. Nevertheless, he confided to a friend of the community, "Though I scolded the poor Sisters a little for leaving so soon, still I could not blame them. Father Hermann is to be blamed for all the trouble, since he did not return from Europe by September as he should have done."[10] The lamentable saga of Verboort was over—after a duration of three demoralizing months!

Loss of the Convent at St. Boniface

Meantime, happenings much closer to home had begun to occupy Sister Pia's attention. Prompted by concern for the German-speaking families who worshipped at Saint Boniface, she had long been hoping for clergy fluent in the German language and conversant with the German culture. Hence, she had been delighted when, the previous year, Redemptorist Fathers had made their appearance in St. Boniface parish. "What an agreeable surprise!" she wrote. German-speaking "Redemptorist Fathers are visiting here. They will probably take charge of Saint Boniface Church. I thank Thee with my whole heart, O Lord! Finally, after nine years of prayer, we are to be heard!"[11] For whatever reason, the plan failed to materialize, and her disappointment was keen until word began to circulate of a possible Franciscan take-over. Rumor became fact when Fathers Gerard Becker, pastor-superior, Paulinus Tolksdorf, and Victor Aertker of the German Franciscan Fathers in St. Louis, Missouri, arrived at the parish on February 10, 1887, and took official possession of St. Boniface Church on February 18. On the same day Father Gerard opened the sisters' retreat prior to Reception of the Habit. A supportive and enduring association between the Franciscan Fathers and the Dominican Sisters had begun.

But the advent of the Friars had a far more significant effect on the sisters' immediate lives than they had bargained for. Within a week of arrival they asked the sisters to vacate their convent in favor of the Friars. The request elicited a negative response from Mother Seraphina:

> As regards your little convent at Saint Boniface, I am really surprised that you take all so quietly that they wish to take it away from you. According to my and others' opinion, no one has a right to do that. You were sent to San Francisco on one condition a house would be built for you. You know that as well as I do and, therefore, you should hold on to it. Tell them to get in touch with me. To give up the right to the house just like this is not the right thing.
>
> Other Sisters, before they go to a place, have the parish build a house for them. I am sure the Franciscans know that and will not take it amiss if you hold on to it. As regards the Franciscan Fathers, they have a very high reputation; I have inquired about that.[12]

Before her letter reached its destination, however, the deed was done! For Sister Pia personally, the surrender of the little house was painful:

> After lunch I went with Sister Salesia to Saint Boniface's little convent to pray once again before the tabernacle

> where I passed through periods of joy and trial. Farewell! Sister Amanda, Sister Salesia, and I, we three who began our work here under difficult circumstances, prayed the *Te Deum* in thanksgiving for all benefits received and the *Miserere* as a penance for faults committed. On leaving this sacred spot, I felt as though I were losing a part of my heart. Today Sister Gonzaga and Sister Dominica came to Guerrero Street and the first load of the Sisters' belongings was brought. All for Thee, O Lord! Help me to love, love, love Thee![13]

The next day she recorded simply, "The little convent connected with Saint Boniface school was handed over today to the Franciscan Fathers. The Sisters came to live at Guerrero Street. It was a great sacrifice to leave the house which was the cradle of our community here on the Pacific Coast."[14]

And the pain was compounded by Mother Seraphina's disappointment at the turn of events:

> The first part of your letter evoked sad feelings in me. Do you not think it would have been your duty to await an answer from me instead of simply withdrawing? The Franciscans are religious themselves, and know, therefore, the duties of subjects. Well, in God's Holy Name, it is your business. Did you ask for some remuneration for the addition to the house which you yourself paid for, or did you give it to them?
>
> Yes, if it would be for a short time only, then it could be. But you have no assurance that this bad situation will be changed. Should you get a horse and carriage, you would need a man to look out for it. This would cost you as much as you take in from school in St. Boniface.
>
> I remember...that you informed me in the beginning that the Most Rev. Archbishop wished you to turn over your Convent to the priests at St. Boniface. So he must feel satisfied that you will have to go back and forth each day. Since he is your Superior, all responsibility on my part is removed.[15]

To his credit (from the sisters' perspective) Father Gerard expressed regret on more than one occasion that the sisters had been obliged to vacate the convent.

Tensions Mount

In mid-April came startling news from New York. Mother Emilia Barth, Mother Seraphina Staimer's assistant, wrote to inform Sister Pia that the Brooklyn superior had been ill for two weeks and that Sister Pia's letters were responsible. "It made me heartsick," confided Sister Pia to the Diary, "because I have been accused of causing this illness. O my God, let me suffer but spare my spiritual mother."[16]

In a letter to her beloved novice director, Mother Cunigunda Schell, Sister Pia asked: "Can I help that my letters are a cause of excitement to her [Mother Seraphina]? I now ask, shall I write or not? Gladly would I embrace this cross if only our dearly beloved Mother Superior were relieved of worry."[17]

Although Mother Cunigunda denied Sister Pia's responsibility for her superior's illness, she was forthright in her observations, and, as tensions mounted, she assumed increasingly the role of Chorus in the East Coast-West Coast drama, her letters offering incisive comment on the actions of the principals. Earlier, Mother Cunigunda had cautioned her former novice not to allow past experiences to disturb her and had drawn an interesting conclusion for the growing strain between the two superiors: "Moreover, we have concluded that unrestrained high spirits are part of the San Francisco air....We have a living proof of that in our dear Rev. Father Schwarz who is so lively and fiery since he was in California."[18]

Sometime later Mother Cunigunda wrote in a happier vein:

> It is such a consolation for me to know that my novices in the distant West are making progress in all directions. As a mother takes pride in her children, I as your spiritual mother also rejoice at the God-given success....At the closing I would like to state that it makes me very happy that Mother Superior's attitude toward you has changed. So, dear Sister Pia, be more careful when writing because Mother Superior does not accept any suggestions.[19]

Entrance to Brooklyn convent: (l to r) Mothers Emilia Barth, Seraphina Staimer and Cunigunda Schell

That the western foundation had been a source of anxiety to Mother Seraphina from its inception is gathered from a letter from Mother Cunigunda, written early in 1885:

> God is blessing your work and by doing so proves again that the branch which eight years ago was transplanted from the East to the distant West was the direct Will of God. This thought is for me always a very consoling one and makes me feel that I too was an instrument in His hand—that this foundation was made. Of course, God did not ask my advice, or if I was for or against the sisters being

allowed to go so far West. Still, it is a comfort to think back on the time when almost everyone was against sending sisters to California ad even Mother Superior became timid and discouraged. Yet her final decision was not to give Archbishop Alemany a direct and final "No" as answer. Yes, I felt at that time especially that God was using me, unworthy as I was, as a tool to bring His holy Will to final completion.[20]

The sisters' disapproval of the distant mission may account, in part at least, for Mother Seraphina's desire to make sure things were "right" in California. In addition, she was finding increasingly burdensome all the plans and possibilities that Sister Pia's fertile imagination continued to generate. Even while approving Verboort, Mother Seraphina had admonished Sister Pia for her mission fervor:

> That you would pray right away for so many new branch houses without having sufficient sisters to staff them I would never have dreamed. You do not know whom to send to Oregon and now you want to start another place already. Truly this goes beyond my comprehension. I also must say to my own shame I have never yet offered a bishop or priest my sisters; for that I am too proud. Until now we were always asked to take a place and it shall remain thus also in the future. But that it shall not give the impression that I am trying to hinder you and lack your holy zeal, I tell you that you may take the last two places if you put Sister Amanda in one and...Sister Salesia in charge of the second....We cannot send you any help, for we have not enough sisters ourselves.[21]

Just how serious the problem had become was made painfully clear when separation from the parent community was expressed in a letter from Mother Cunigunda to Sister Seraphina, who immediately shared its contents with Sister Pia. The latter recorded her fears in the Diary: "Sooner or later, thinks Mother Superior, the question of our separation must be considered. What worrisome thoughts this idea of Mother Superior arouses in me. Have I not always been obedient? O my God, hear my prayer. Let me not be a cause of anxiety to our dear Mother."[22]

The situation had been further aggravated the previous year when Sister Pia's family—mother, sister, brother-in-law, and nephew Tommy—moved West from New York to San Francisco. Mother Seraphina did not approve the move and, as time went on, became convinced that Sister Pia's relatives were influencing her decisions. "That is the reason she gives for saying that you have become more independent from the Motherhouse of late,"[23] wrote Mother Cunigunda in an attempt to interpret the reserve which had begun to mark Mother Serphina's correspondence with the Western community. The novice director's advice was discreet:

> Conduct yourself toward her as a good candid child and ask permission for everything in advance as much as possible. You see, my dear Sister, that Mother Superior is perfectly right in saying that you as a subject must request permission before acting for instance, leaving the house at St. Boniface and going every day to and from school by [horse] car. This is an important matter and it was one of the conditions when the sisters came to St. Boniface that they would have living quarters.
>
> Now, my dear Sister Pia, you will tearfully think and say, 'Oh, dear Sister Mistress, you do not understand that the Bishop and the priests will not wait patiently until I finally receive an answer.'
>
> If this, dear Sister, is really the case then I am convinced it will really be the best for you to become independent from the Motherhouse. This disagreeableness which continually arises from the impossibility of reaching an agreement in less than twelve days is wearing you out; for Mother Superior it is only a well of worries and unrest because in this way she cannot have any responsibility for you all. You must admit that the saying, 'The German Dominicans belong to Brooklyn,' cannot be true when we have nothing to say there anymore.
>
> My dear Sister,…Do not take this letter amiss. Nobody asked me to write, but I know that Rev. Father May often made the statement that it is impossible to direct a convent at such great distance for any length of time.

And so we will pray that God may guide everything in ways that are best for all of us. On the other hand, if you become independent there will no longer be a chance for me for a sea voyage to San Francisco. These are dreams with open eyes and so tell nobody about them...[24]

A month later Mother Seraphina herself wrote in some frustration:

May 8, 1887

My dear Sister Pia,

In your last three letters, you have placed before me so many plans that I am at a loss how to answer regarding them. The first was the extension of your present property by acquiring a piece of land at the cost of $12,000....I had given you the required permission.

Regarding the hospital project, I must tell you frankly that I am opposed to it. You have no idea of the difficulties connected with such an undertaking....We sent you to San Francisco to conduct schools for the German Catholics there. Carry out this purpose with zeal and prudence, and then you will have accomplished your task.

Regarding Anaheim, I shall be pleased to have you open a branch house there under the following conditions:

1. A house must be provided for you there so that you may be able to lead a true convent life.

2. This house should be located near the church.

3. Your spiritual needs must be properly attended to...

You may think Mother Superior cannot judge conditions here correctly; were she here, she would agree with my opinion, etc. Under existing circumstances you may be right. Personally, I have already felt that by reason of the great distance it is impossible for me to attain a clear insight into your problems. In addition, it is the Archbishop or his representative who is your Superior. It has happened that my wish conflicted with the orders of the Archbishop. I could not complain in the matter. It will be much better, therefore, that in future you submit entirely to the Archbishop's wishes. He knows best how to solve your problems.

Propose to the Archbishop that I think it might be better to form a separate community under the following conditions:

1. Our convent here will donate to you all the money advanced so far for the erection of your building.

2. The Sisters who made their profession here will always have the privilege of returning to their Motherhouse...

3. I shall be willing to help you in future as best I can. Your financial affairs, however, you must manage entirely yourself. The property recorded in my name may be transferred to your name and Sister Seraphina's. In short, all your affairs should be taken over by the Archbishop.

I am growing old and feeble, and I have plenty to do with the convents and branch houses here.

As soon as you will have discussed this matter with the Archbishop, inform me and then I will send you the deed of your convent. In reality you will not be separated from us in spirit....I shall answer your letters as regularly as heretofore. The Sisters may return at any time. If you wish to visit here, you will be welcome. If God grants me health, it will not be at all improbable for me to make my appearance some day at Guerrero Street. You are and you will always remain my beloved children until death.

The above mentioned changes are meant for the advancement of your welfare. I hope that you realize my good intentions. Inform all your Sisters of the contents of this letter. Likewise extend to them my cordial greetings.

In sincere affection,

Your spiritual mother,

M. Seraphina Staimer[25]

Well intended as the letter was, it shocked the western community. In answer, Sister Pia sent a telegram asking permission for Sister Seraphina and herself to come home to settle matters. The Diary revealed her distress: "Offered Holy Communion for Mother Superior's serious proposal. What sorrow her idea of separation has caused me! I shed tears of regret."[26]

Mother Seraphina did not think the trip East necessary, however, and urged Sister Pia to read her letter once again and give the matter serious thought. "Then you will see that I am right. Should the matter remain as it has been until now, then you must be patient if I let you go ahead slowly. You are young and zealous; I am old and act according to my experience."[27]

Three weeks later, Mother Seraphina wrote again in answer to a letter which Sister Pia had spent days in composing. The letter was addressed to Sisters Pia and Seraphina.

> Because you wish so much to belong to us we will begin to be totally united. I had the best intention when I told you that from now on you should look out for your own temporal affairs. I thought that by so doing you could make more rapid progress and not be hampered in spreading our Holy Order. For instance, I do not allow you to begin a hospital, but when you are independent you can do it.
>
> As for branch houses, I give the permission only if the requirements are fulfilled, which I set down in the letter when you asked about Los Angeles. Well, we will remain the Old Ones, but then you must also take your Old Mother the way she is. You must not be dissatisfied and even get sick when she tries to hold back your zeal on account of the experiences she has lived through. I also wish that you no longer undertake anything without waiting for my answer. If it is in a hurry, then send a telegram. You must report the matter to me, even if I cannot change anything anymore. I hope that you are ready to abide by this arrangement and so I welcome you again from my heart, just as at the time of your first entrance into the holy walls of our convent.[28]

Despite the conciliatory tone of Mother Seraphina's letter, the calm was of short duration. On July 3, 1887, Sister Pia wrote to

Father May in protest: "I do not understand why Mother Superior requires more of us here than of the houses in Brooklyn. She does not allow us to accept a school unless the pastor provides the Sisters' house. This prohibition forms an obstacle to our advancement."[29]

As might be expected, Father May took the complaint to Mother Seraphina, who wrote to Sister Pia on July 24, 1887:

> Oh, dear Sister Pia, this is again a misunderstanding. I wrote to you that you should insist in Anaheim and anywhere else where you would start that the parish should provide a convent for the sisters in case you yourselves have not yet the means to do it. If you have the money, I gladly give you the permission with the greatest joy to build, not only a small convent, but one as large as Amityville. The more, the better.[30]

A second letter followed shortly, reemphasizing the point:

> That you will know for always that I do not want to hinder your progress whether in the North or in the South, I tell you now definitely that you may go ahead as much as you like, provided only that you need no money or sisters from us. On property which is in my name you may not contract any debts.
>
> I counsel you not to make too many debts or you will not have a quiet hour any more. Do not depend on me because I cannot help you. I tell you my intention seriously and earnestly in advance.[31]

The relationship between East and West was becoming increasingly tenuous. A convent in California, claiming to belong to a Motherhouse in New York, but exercising independence in regard to new foundations, personnel, and finance seems something of an anomaly. In addition, and not without reason, there was still uneasiness in New York and, in consequence, Mother Seraphina decided that a trip East would, after all, be in the best interests of both parties. On September 19, 1887, she wrote:

> I have thought much about you in these last weeks, especially with the starting of new branch houses.
>
> I have come to the conclusion that this matter should be well thought over and not discussed by writing but by word of mouth. Yes, I put so much importance on that and

so call you and Sister Seraphina here and will pay your trip. In case that both of you would not be able to get away on account of the school year having already started, then Sister Amanda shall be your companion instead of Sister Seraphina....Two weeks will be sufficient to complete our business....The way of making foundations in California has caused me many a headache. Gladly I do offer some hundreds of dollars if only this matter will be settled to the mutual satisfaction of both parties, and of this I have not the least doubt. Pray much to the Holy Spirit that all will be done for the greater honor and glory of God and the spread of our Holy Order.[32]

On October 5, 1887, Sisters Pia, Seraphina, and Amanda left for New York. (Although Mother Seraphina had appointed Sister Amanda as an alternate traveling companion to Sister Seraphina Maerz, no explanation is given for the three sisters making the trip.) The visit was not without pain. On the first day Sister Pia described an interview with her superior as grueling. The next day Father May would not listen to her. In the evening, she "missed the devotional exercises in order again to listen to the whole array of misinterpretations. The cause of this new trouble is to be attributed to a misunderstanding in the purchase price of the property [a lot on Guerrero Street with two three-story houses costing $12,500]. God alone knows how I passed the night."[33]

Invited to visit St. Catherine's hospital the following day, Sister Pia asked to remain home, where she poured out her troubles before a statue of the Sacred Heart. At the Hospital, the sisters met Mother Cunigunda Schell, their former novice director. She did not mince words. "Why did you not separate?" she asked. "I would have done it."[34]

Separation Formalized

Two weeks after their arrival the travelers returned to San Francisco. The long trip home gave them opportunity to become accustomed to a proposal that had at first appeared outrageous; then, possible; and finally, reasonable—a course of action that had come to term not only for them, but also for Holy Cross and Mother Seraphina, on whom the challenges of decision-making, coupled with Sister Pia's lively planning, were placing an unreasonable burden. Consultation with the western community, now 28 in number, brought the sisters to a unanimous decision that simply seemed inevitable. They would become independent.

Mother Seraphina's letter (November 26, 1887) in reply to their petition to separate specified the conditions:

> Dear Sister Pia and Sister Seraphina,
>
> If you wish to separate from us, I put no hindrance in your way. But the circumstances are much different than they were in May. Then I myself offered your independence and now you are asking for it. The trip and all your trouble for a renewal of the matter are wasted because the proposals will not even be tried.
>
> The first thing you will have to get for me is a written declaration from your Archbishop that he agrees with the matter.
>
> The second is that each professed sister writes on a separate piece of paper the following declaration: "I, Sister N.N., ask for the independence of our convent from the Mother Convent at Montrose and Graham Aves., Brooklyn, and renounce hereby all claims on it." Then follows the signature. Each sister must send this to me individually.
>
> Should a sister not sign it, then she is free to return to the Motherhouse. This permission will hold for a year. She shall also write to me herself and inform me that she wishes to return. Then I will send her the fare. Naturally this counts only for the sisters who made their profession here.
>
> The newly bought property remains in your name; also the old one you have for free use. The deed for it I will send you after I see that you are making progress. God be with you!
>
> Your sincere,
>
> Mother Seraphina[35]

The conditions stated in the letter were fair, as well as generous. The sisters would have an entire year to consider their options.

All eight sisters originally from Brooklyn wrote individual

letters requesting independence as specified by Mother Seraphina. With her petition Sister Seraphina enclosed a note that conveys an idea of the emotional impact of the break on her:

> Dear Mother Superior:
>
> Please do not think that my conduct in this matter is due to malice, lack of gratitude and too little attachment to the Motherhouse, although it may appear so. The good God knows I have a pure intention.
>
> I feel keenly the loss of your affection and that you cannot think of me any longer as "your little Crescentia." Nevertheless, I shall not permit my love, attachment and childlike affection to diminish in the least, and never will I forget your maternal love and exceptional kindness toward me. (These are no empty words.) Daily will I unite with you in the Heart of Jesus; then we are never separated. Enough of this my good Mother—I am unable to express myself any further because I cannot overcome my emotions. In Jesus I remain
>
> Your ever grateful child,
>
> Sister M. Seraphina[36]

The document from Archbishop Riordan, which Sister Pia procured and sent to New York, was brief and to the point:

> Dec. 15, 1887
>
> I herewith grant my permission for the separation of the Dominican Sisters from the Motherhouse in Brooklyn, and consent to their independent existence under the authority of the Archbishop of San Francisco.
>
> The property of the Community now situated in the Diocese should be transferred to me. The title should be "Patrick William Riordan" and nothing more. I will apply to Court to grant the sisters the privilege of a corporation and when obtained, will transfer the property to said corporation.
>
> P.W. Riordan[37]

For Mother Seraphina the decision to separate had overtones of disloyalty. Her diary tells the story from her perspective.

During the past year I had a presentiment that all was not well with our Sisters in San Francisco. Sister Pia acted so independent, self-willed, etc. That the finances were not in good order was as clear as day. In the beginning of September Reverend Father Wolf stopped off with us on his way to Germany and told me that Sister Pia is conducting matters with a high hand, etc. We sent for Sister M. Pia, M. Seraphina and M. Amanda to discuss matters and paid their fare, $500. Very Reverend Father May made new suggestions to them and gave them good advice. They appeared to accept all with good will. But when they returned to San Francisco they wrote that they desired to become independent because the Sisters who entered from San Francisco (about 20) clamored for it.

Since I had already suggested on May 10 of this year, that they become independent under conditions most advantageous to them and they then begged to remain connected with us, their changed sentiments grieved us deeply. However, we acceded to their desires. The San Francisco Sisters then obtained a statement from the Very Reverend Archbishop in which he declared that they, under his protection, might organize an independent Congregation in San Francisco. The deed of the Convent that all in all cost $27,000 was in my name because our Convent sent $22,000 for the building of it. I promised the Sisters to have this property deeded over to them, if I learned that they would conduct all their work like true Daughters of St. Dominic and good religious. In the middle of April, 1887, the Sisters of San Francisco bought more property adjoining their convent for $12,000. The deeds for this were put in the names of Sister M. Pia Backes and Sister M. Seraphina Maerz. The Most Reverend Archbishop Riordan wished, at the time of separation, that all should be put in his name and perhaps that is how it will be done. The Sisters who made their profession here (8 in number) had to declare in writing that they wished to remain in San Francisco and would make no further claims on our Congregation. These papers are all preserved in our archives.[38]

Chapter 5 / SEPARATION

As was her custom, Sister Pia also entrusted her feelings to her Diary on December 31, 1887:

> My heart has been so full and so weighed down by the many trials I have experienced that I have had no energy to write save what was absolutely necessary.
>
> This evening at table the following was read from the *Life of Pere Bresson, O.P.*, 'There are trials harder to bear than death: things which wound one's heart and soul.' Pere Bresson was under the impression that his Superiors had no longer their original confidence in him....I passed through a similar trial with this difference, however, that I was not simply under the impression, but was told by my Superioress that she no longer had confidence in me. My God, without Your aid, at present, I do not see how I can stand this trial. I was certainly innocent of the accusation, but you have kindly let me know how often I have failed in other matters. I will offer up all—all for the progress, spiritual and temporal, of our dear California mission. And then, O God, do You in return bless our beloved California foundation.[39]

Separation caused hurt on both sides of the continent. Writing the history of the Holy Cross Congregation, the Reverend Eugene Crawford summarizes the situation succinctly:

> The western foundation prospered, but as time went on the distance and lack of communication resurrected the old difficulties so painful in the early years of the Brooklyn Community with

Patrick William Riordan, Archbishop of San Francisco, 1884–1914

Brooklyn now enacting the role of the pained Motherhouse, indignant at the apparent independence of the far distant *filiale*.[40]

Legally, the separation was now complete, but ties were still strong, and one suspects that the feeling of loss exceeded any feeling of exhilaration when one reads Sister Pia's Diary entry shortly after the separation: "Homesick—no letter from our Motherhouse in Brooklyn, New York."[41] There is a certain naiveté, however, in Sister Pia's expectation that affairs will go on as if nothing had occurred. At the end of the month she was still waiting and, however unwarranted, was feeling a little piqued: "I made up my mind not to worry about delay of letters from New York. If they do not write, neither will I."[42] But Mother Seraphina did write, and the letters, though fewer in number, remained cordial; she was still their "sincere and loving spiritual Mother."[43] Four months after the separation she decided that it was time now to live with their feelings and stop trying to explain matters to one another:

> But let us now stop discussing this matter. I will forget everything and will be as good to you as we were in our former happy days; I will help you as much as I can, and then you are again my dear children. We are united in God and also your convent belongs to the East and so before the eyes of outsiders we are not separated. The sisters here do not know that a separation has taken place.[44]

In March, Father Gerard, O.S.F., St. Boniface superior, suggested that, in view of the break, it would be advisable for the community to elect a prioress so that the sisters could renew their vows. With the Archbishop's approval, an election took place on April 6 during Easter Week. The formality of the occasion is concluded from the document witnessing to the event.

Election of the First Prioress of the Convent of the Immaculate Conception,

> Dominican Sisters, San Francisco, California

>> I, the undersigned, Gerard Becher, of the Order of St. Francis, being appointed by His Grace, P.W. Riordan, Archbishop of San Francisco, California, to preside at the

Election of the first Prioress of the Dominican Sisters of the Convent of the Immaculate Conception, hereby certify that Sister Mary Pia Backes was duly elected, April Sixth (6), A.D. 1888, as the First Prioress of the above mentioned Convent, for three (3) years or until her successor will be appointed: in my presence and that of Rev. Clementinus Deymann, O.S.F., and of Rev. Paulinus Tolksdorf, O.S.F., who acted as *Scrutatores;* and that she was duly installed on the same day in presence of the whole Community of the Sisters of said Convent.

In witness whereof I have set my name and affixed the seal of the aforesaid Convent this Sixth (6) day of April, A.D. 1888.

Frater Gherardus Becher, O.S.F.[45]

Delegate of his Grace, P.W. Riordan,

Archb. of San Francisco

Frater Clementinus Deymann, O.S.F

Scrutatores, Fr. Paulinus Tolksdorf, O.S.F.

P.W. Riordan

The Archbishop's signature, added at a later date, signified his approval of the election. In contrast, Sister Pia wrote simply:

> Today this house was raised to a priory. Father Superior presided at the election in place of Archbishop Riordan. Father Paulinus and Father Clement were the scrutineers. What I went through at the thought of Mother Superior; for now, no longer is she our head.[46]

The election brought the new prioress no elation; the sense of loss was too acute. With the election Sister Pia became Mother Pia, and from this time until 1907, the Convent of the Immaculate Conception, San Francisco, served as the Motherhouse of the fledgling Congregation.

The painful course of events notwithstanding, Mother Seraphina's generosity to the California community continued. On December 11, 1888, she included with her letter and best wishes a check for $300 for the new foundation in Anaheim (Cf. Chapter VI).

Just one month later, on January 14, 1889, Mother Pia was shocked and saddened to receive a dispatch from New York telling of Mother Seraphina's sudden death. "My God, is it possible?" she wrote in the Diary, "Mother Superior dead! 'Departed in the Lord at 4 a.m.' We owe our dear Mother all that we possess in property and in a solid religious foundation. May she rest in peace."[47] The deceased's last letter to Mother Pia was written on January 9, 1889, and arrived in San Francisco two days after her death. It acknowledged receipt of the Dominican *Ordos*, which Mother Pia sent annually to New York, and told of the death of Sister Christina [Harth] of Amityville. For the final time she signed herself, "Your devoted spiritual Mother."[48]

On the last day of her life Mother Seraphina remarked to Mother Cunigunda: "I have lately written to Sister Pia and also to Sister Seraphina. I am now quiet and at peace about the San Francisco situation. Am also glad to have no longer any responsibility for them. Most of all, there is again a friendly understanding."[49]

Despite their strained relations on occasion, the two women had a profound respect and love for each other that managed to surmount their difficulties. Mother Seraphina Staimer was a deeply religious, staunchly Dominican woman—gifted with a keen intelligence, a generous spirit, a sharp business sense, and a sincere love for her sisters. The Dominican Sisters of Mission San Jose remain greatly in her debt.

Notes

[1] William H. Gross, C.SS.R., November 22, 1885. The arrival of six Dutch families from Wisconsin in 1875 marked the beginning of the settlement known as "the Catholic colony of Forest Grove." Father William Verboort, a member of one of the six families, arrived a little later in September, 1875. He did not long survive his parents. At his funeral Archbishop Blanchet announced that the name of the little community would henceforth be Verboort.. (*The Catholic Sentinel*, 7 May 1999, Vol. 130, No. 19. 10 & 12).

[2] Staimer, letter to Backes, 27 January 1886.

[3] Staimer, letter to Schell, 27 January 1886.

[4] Staimer, letter to Backes, 11 October 1886.

[5] Backes 80.

[6] Staimer, letter to Backes, 19 November 1886.

[7] Staimer, letter to Backes, 19 November 1886.

[8] Backes 80.

[9] Backes 81.

[10] Backes 82.

[11] Backes 65.

[12] Staimer, letter to Backes, 13 March 1887.

[13] Backes 87.

[14] Backes 87.

[15] Staimer, letter to Backes, 20 March 1887.

[16] Backes 88.

[17] Backes 89.

[18] Schell, letter to Backes, Feast of St. Augustine, 1879.

[19] Schell, letter to Backes, 24 July 1884.

[20] Schell, letter to Backes, February 1885. Although the letter is dated February 1885, it contains Christmas and New Year greetings and was more likely written toward the end of 1884..

[21] Staimer, letter to Backes, 24 July 1886.

[22] Backes 90.

[23] Schell, letter to Backes, 1 April 1887.

[24] Schell, letter to Backes, 1 April 1887.

[25] Staimer, letter to Backes, 8 May 1887 in Backes 91–92.

[26] Backes 93.

[27] Staimer, letter to Backes, 24 May 1887.

[28] Staimer, letter to Backes and Maerz, 10 June 1887.

[29] Backes, letter to May in Backes 93.

[30] Staimer, letter to Backes, 24 July 1887.

[31] Staimer, letter to Backes, 6 August 1887.

[32] Staimer, letter to Backes, 19 September 1887.

[33] Backes 95–96

[34] Backes 96.

[35] Staimer, letter to Backes, 26 November 1887 in Backes 97.

[36] Maerz, letter to Staimer, n.d.

[37] Riordan, letter to Dominican Sisters, n.d.

[38] Staimer 44.

[39] Backes 98

[40] Crawford 125.

[41] Backes 100.

[42] Backes 100.

[43] Staimer, letter to Backes, 1 May 1888.

[44] Staimer, letter to Backes, 1 May 1888.

[45] Gherardus Becher, O.S.F., (Document of Election of First Prioress), 6 April 1888 "General Chapter Minutes", 1888.

[46] Backes 103.

[47] Backes 112.

[48] Staimer, letter to Backes, 9 January 1889.

[49] Schell, letter to Backes, 14 May 1889.

CHAPTER SIX

NORTHWEST VENTURE

Mother Pia's generous heart resonated to St. Dominic's passion for the salvation of souls. For her, the broader the arena of mission activity the better; hence, she welcomed the opportunities for new foundations that were multiplying in the West.

Nor had Archbishop William Gross given up on Dominican Sisters, despite his disappointment at their abrupt departure from Verboort. Consequently, when Father Alois Sommers, pastor of the newly established St. Joseph Parish on Portland's West Side, invited Sister Pia to staff a school for the children of German-speaking parents, the Archbishop was prompt in adding his approval, "I learn with very great pleasure that Rev. Dr. Sommers has invited you to send a colony of your community to take charge of the school belonging to his parish: I hereby give my most hearty approval and consent to the foundation."[1]

Not one to ignore opportunity when it was apparently knocking, the Archbishop decided to push his good fortune a little further and added:

> There is a very flourishing town in Oregon called Roseburg—it is on the line of railway between Portland and San Francisco. The people—Protestants and Jews as well as Catholics—are most anxious to have a Sisters' School. The Rev. Pastor has not yet invited any of our communities to take charge of the school and has requested me to provide for it. Now I shall be very much pleased if you will also accept this foundation.[2]

But the Archbishop's invitation was evidently a bit much even for Mother Pia. Roseburg never became a mission of the Congregation.

St. Joseph School, Portland, Oregon

The cornerstone for St. Joseph Church was laid on March 20, 1887, and on May 12, 1888, Mother Pia noted in her Diary: "Today we accepted the new school, Saint Joseph's, in Portland, Oregon. My Jesus, give Thy blessing."[3]

On Sister Seraphina Maerz fell the dual responsibility of superior and principal of the new mission. Pioneering with her were Sisters Dominica Klein, Hyacintha Schneider, Ambrosia Niedermeier, and Francisca McCarthy. St. Joseph's was to prove a challenging assignment. A lengthy undated entry appended to the end of Sister Seraphina Maerz's diary speaks for itself:

> We arrived at Portland on Tuesday, August 28 [1888], at 10:30 a.m. Two ladies were at the railroad station to pick us up. By carriage we traveled to St. Joseph's Church.
>
> The two Reverend Mothers, as the ladies called...[us] entered the church and knelt down at the communion rail where each was engulfed in her own thoughts and asked God's blessing upon the work to be undertaken. The church made a good impression on the sisters and was much better than they had expected.
>
> After finishing their business with the dear Lord, the sisters and ladies went to the living quarters intended for the sisters. At the door, they met the pastor, Reverend Doctor Alois Sommer, who welcomed them and led them into their quarters. One could easily see how embarrassed he was at being unable to offer them something better....Five rooms were placed at the sisters' use: first, the parlor with one window; next to it, a bedroom with one window; the refectory with one window; a kitchen with one window; and one additional room to be used as laundry, pantry, bathroom and whatever else was needed. The rooms were very low and dark, and inhabited by thousands of flies and cockroaches. The awful heat here during the summer months brings them out of their hiding places. The first night

the two...[sisters] stood there, motionless and shocked, watching the creatures' actions. Mother Prioress then said with a deep sigh, "It's enough to kill your appetite."

On August 29, we attended...[our] first Mass in Portland. A feeling of gratitude to God and the realization that it is the same dear God who reigns everywhere with His treasures and graces overcame us.

In the evening after Vespers on September 2, the pastor requested a piece of bread. Just as it should be, out of courtesy we prepared a good snack for him. But no pastor was around. What we suspected proved to be true. He had asked only for a piece of bread, and when he realized that we were preparing something more for him, he walked off. The next morning when he showed up, one could immediately read from his face that he was in a very bad humor....My courage started to fail. "In God's name", I thought, "it's going to get worse."

Mass was at 8:30 a.m. Songs to the Blessed Mother were sung. Then the pastor said special prayers, asking God's blessings most fervently and cordially. After that, school opened with 49 children. (They appeared most poor.) The children were examined and grouped, and soon children and teachers became good friends.

The next day Father requested to have a Requiem sung. The children, certainly, were unable to sing and the sisters unable to play. During the sermon, Father remarked that he had wanted a Requiem sung, but that the inability of the venerable sisters stood in his way. One can imagine how we felt. What a humiliation! Thus began our work in the Northwest, seasoned with difficulties right from the beginning. But the affection of the children sweetened all difficulties, and with God's help, everyone fulfilled her obligations as best she could. Besides, good Mother Prioress was still here and her presence made everything easier. Also, the visit of Bishop Junger [of Vancouver] who came to see the poor daughters of St. Dominic...was an occasion to lift the spirits of the sisters.

But soon the hour arrived when our Mother Prioress had to leave….We received her blessing and with tears…said goodbye…our eyes followed the carriage until it turned the corner and disappeared. After that we cried awhile, each took her needlework and sat silently around the table in the parlor. No one felt like talking…

One day followed the other with many trials, which I cannot mention here, but we also had peaceful, pleasing hours. The situation was especially difficult for our cook as she was still unskilled in the art [...] Further, she had to cook for the pastor, too. Poor Sister Francisca, how many tears she shed in her primitive kitchen! But, God stood by her and she overcame all the difficulties.[4]

The sisters' second venture in the Northwest was proving as discouraging as the first! One cause of difficulty was the sisters' request for an oratory. Having no chapel in the convent, they petitioned the pastor for a small private room for prayer in the church. Father Sommer could not make up his mind. Finally, after a five-month delay, he agreed, and on February 10, the sisters used the room for the first time. Sister Seraphina's description of access to the oratory suggests it was a hazardous undertaking. Entry was up a narrow stairway without handrail and involved lifting a heavy trapdoor above one's head in order to climb through. Bumps and bruises quickly taught the sisters to balance the door carefully. Arriving above, the climber was rewarded an unobstructed view of the Tabernacle below–if she happened to be among the first arrivals. Latecomers had to be satisfied with kneeling behind a plank wall! Praying the Office together must have been a challenge.

In what seems to have been prevailing practice at the time, school opened in the basement of the church. Eight days into the school year, the "swapping" began. A room in the sisters' quarters was vacated in favor of a second classroom, and by December the increase in enrollment warranted an even more dramatic change. The sisters moved into the church basement, and the school took over the convent. With the onset of winter, the basement provided little protection from the Northwest cold and dampness. Disheartened, Sister Seraphina wrote, "This morning I knocked on the Tabernacle and asked God to remember us and help us. It hurt me so much that Sister Hyacintha had put a piece of carpet on her bed [for additional covering] and that the sisters were suffering from the cold."[5]

Mother Pia was not pleased when she learned of the sisters' shift in living arrangements. The depth of her displeasure may be gathered from her reference to their new quarters as a "hole." Father Sommer, however, remained stubbornly unreceptive to the idea of a new school and convent building for which Mother Pia began to press. Sister Seraphina went out to look at lots, but had little success in borrowing money. Four hundred dollars was the best offer she could elicit. Nor was Father Sommer any help; he informed her that he could pay nothing toward a new site, much less a new building–a statement in all probability true. With matters at an impasse, Mother Pia resolved to visit Portland and settle affairs herself. As she had suspected, her presence proved more effective than her letters, the pastor falling prey to her persuasion. "We parted friends,"[6] she wrote with satisfaction, pardonable in view of her accomplished mission: an architect's completed plans for a combined school and convent at a cost of $4,000, the work to begin shortly. It was not much of a triumph, however, as the debt would belong to the sisters!

Immaculate Heart of Mary School, Albina

While negotiating with Father Sommer, Mother Pia entertained a visitor, Father Gerard Van Lin, who came in quest of sisters for the newly established parish of Immaculate Heart of Mary in Albina. Located across the Willamette River from Portland, the town of Albina, named after the town planner's daughter, had been laid out in 1872. By 1886, thirty-five Catholic families had moved into the area. Sunday Mass was celebrated in the Hill Building on the corner of Russell and Goldsmith streets by priests from nearby St. Francis Parish. Unhappy with this arrangement, several members of the burgeoning congregation began clamoring for a church of their own; as a result, a meeting was called in the home of one John Kelly. Only five men appeared, host included.

A discussion of ways and means of raising money for the project yielding no action plan, the meeting sputtered to an inconclusive end. On the point of adjourning, the men had not reckoned with the redoubtable Mrs. Kelly. Arms folded, feet apart, she blocked the doorway and announced, "You'll not be leaving my house without making some plans for our church. This is no laughing matter; we need a Catholic Church here, and it's up to you to start it."[7] Faced with this ultimatum, the men somewhat shamefacedly sat down again and organized themselves into a fund-raising committee. Success followed their efforts, non-Catholics as well as Catholics contributing to the appeal. Mrs. J. B. Montgomery, herself a non-Catholic, donated the land for the new church, which was completed in time for dedication in June 1887 by Archbishop Gross. At the time of Mother Pia's arrival in Portland, Father Van Lin had a church; he now wanted a school!

Mother Pia's visit to Albina two days after Father Van Lin's request for sisters decided the issue. "We were well pleased with conditions there," she reported in the Diary on August 23, 1889, "one hundred and nine families in the parish, seventy children. Father Van Lin guarantees fifty dollars a month for the Sisters' maintenance for the first year."[8]

Things moved at high speed after that. Though her heart bled "to give up these two Sisters at such cost of sacrifice,"[9] Mother Pia's telegram brought Sisters Alberta Hocker and Emilia Moore from San Francisco to Portland on August 28. Shortly after arriving, the sisters held open house in order to become acquainted with the people of Albina (September 2) and two days later welcomed 67 children to St. Mary's School. "Classrooms" were the rectory parlor and church.

Before Mother Pia left Portland, Father Van Lin called on her a second time to inform her that he was ordering pews for the church. He was quite pleased with the idea. The pews would serve the dual purpose: as benches on Sundays and as "desks" on schooldays.

Tragedy struck early in the Northwest. At St. Joseph's Sister Hyacintha's deteriorating health led Mother Pia to recall her from Portland. On November 28, 1889, the ailing sister, accompanied by a young Indian woman, left for San Francisco by steamer. When her trunk arrived at the Guerrero Street without Sister, the sisters became apprehensive. A call from the San Francisco Chancery Office revealed the devastating news that Sister had died on board ship the previous night. "O God, give me strength to bear this trial," prayed Mother Pia in the Diary. "The precious remains of Sister Hyacintha were brought to the convent this evening. I am worked up—dreadfully."[10]

On December 2, a Requiem Mass was sung at nine o'clock, with burial following at Holy Cross cemetery, where Mother Pia, with unwitting foresight, had purchased a plot the preceding month. "The first flower has been plucked," she mourned. "Who will be the next to follow? Yet, Lord, Thy Will be done!"[11] The first member of the Congregation to die, Sister Hyacintha had been professed only four years. Her death was a crushing blow to the young community.

Oregon was proving a difficult mission, "a continuous Good Friday,"[12] as far as Sister Seraphina was concerned, and the death of Sister Hyacintha had come as a grievous shock to the discouraged superior. On the last day of 1889, she assessed the year with little hope for the future: "My God, with You I will end this year. O, what a terrible year this…has been for me!!! My God, my heart almost breaks…I thank You for everything, especially for the wrongful accusations and spiritual sufferings.[13]

At the time the sisters from Immaculate Heart were living at St. Joseph's across the river and commuting to school by free ferry. But on November 8, 1890, Sisters Alberta Hocker, Emilia Moore and Francisca McCarthy moved into a little rented house behind the church in Albina. "May God bless the mustard seed," wrote Mother Pia. "The sisters now have a school of one hundred pupils, dedicated to the Immaculate Heart of Mary."[14] Later in the month Sister Agnes Mulligan joined the staff in order to meet the needs of the growing enrollment. In November also the new convent-school building at St. Joseph's was ready for occupancy, much to the relief of Mother Pia, a relief somewhat diminished by the ever present debts. The Diary bore witness:

> Today I found in the hand of Saint Joseph a petition which I placed there on December 2, 1888. At that time the sisters lived in the basement at Saint Joseph's, Portland. I begged Saint Joseph to provide a decent, healthful dwelling for the sisters. The prayer was heard, for we have been able to build a house for them which is now ready. Debts, however, are resting upon it heavily. Undoubtedly, Saint Joseph will take care that they be liquidated.[15]

To accommodate the number of Catholics who had moved into Albina, a new and more spacious Immaculate Heart of Mary Church was designed, and the cornerstone laid in 1890. The original church was then moved around the corner and relocated to Stanton Street to serve the needs of the school which was continuing to grow.

The sisters' solution to the enrollment problem at Immaculate Heart (or St. Mary's as the school was popularly known) might be described as somewhat irregular. On August 27, 1892, they simply withdrew from St. Joseph's. A temporary measure to bolster the teaching staff of St. Mary's, it was justified in the sisters' minds by the rapidly increasing enrollment at the Albina school. Not everyone was in accord, however; and a change of pastor at St. Joseph's altered the course of events more quickly than had been anticipated. Father James Rauw, who succeeded Father Sommer as pastor of St. Joseph's, demanded the immediate reopening of the school. After a hiatus of six months, St. Joseph's opened again in March!

By 1894, the foundations in Oregon had become a problem of such dimension to Mother Pia that she determined to withdraw her sisters from the Northwest.

> I fear that Oregon must be given up to save our name. I am about to inform Archbishop Gross that I intend to withdraw the sisters...My God, I tremble in fear. Is it thy Will, O God? Holy Father Saint Dominic, are you not satisfied with this decision? I believe I am acting with the best intentions.[16]

But Archbishop Gross was of a different mind. He would not be caught unaware a second time. The sisters were not to leave the archdiocese! He sent as his representative the Dominican superior of Holy Rosary Convent in Portland, Father Benedict McGovern, to negotiate with Mother Pia for the retention of the sisters. Determined to accomplish his mission successfully, Father McGovern proved a mild and conciliatory advocate, allaying Mother Pia's fears and misgivings quite effectively. Whether by coincidence or strategy, Father Rauw from St. Joseph's also visited the Motherhouse about the same time (July 25, 1894), settling school affairs and agreeing that his teachers would live with the sisters in Albina. He further consented to an annual stipend of $250 for the sisters.

Partial source of the trouble surrounding the Oregon schools seems to have been the then pastor of Immaculate Heart, Father Charles O'Reilly; the pastor and Mother Pia were in disagreement over the status of the school–whether parochial or community-owned. Father O'Reilly maintained that Saint Mary's School was parochial, while Mother Pia held out for community ownership. Ultimately, it required the Archbishop's intervention to settle the difference. In a formal notice sent to Mother Pia, the Archbishop cited the Third Plenary Council of Baltimore (1884):

> June 13, 1894
>
> With a view to make the schools of the Dominican Sisters in the Archdiocese of Oregon parochial schools in the sense of the Plenary Council of Baltimore, it is agreed upon that the Sisters provide their own residence and the rector of the church will pay each teaching Sister.
>
> The decrees of the Plenary Council of Baltimore will regulate the relations existing between the rector of the mission and the school. The undersigned Archbishop of Oregon—trusting to the good judgment and prudence of Rev. F. McGovern, O.P., sends him as his representative to negotiate on these pieces of business.
>
> In witness whereof
>
> Wm. H. Gross
>
> Archbp. Oregon[17]

A second episcopal letter was needed, however, to settle the still troubled waters. This time Mother Pia's concerns seemed legitimate—quality of instruction was addressed.

> Portland: July 11, 1894
>
> Rev. M. Pia, Prioress
>
> Rev. Dear Mother:
>
> Before writing to you on the written conditions brought me by Rev. B. McGovern, I waited to see Rev. C. O'Reilly, pastor of the church of our Lady's Immaculate Heart in Albina. I see no difficulty on his part to your continuing in charge. He says that all he wants is that the Sisters' School be made to reach the standard of the public schools. I have no doubt that you and your good sisters wish to make your schools even superior to the public schools. I have ordered

the priests to refuse absolution to parents who will not send their children to the Catholic Schools, and hence the remark of Rev. C. O'Reilly that the Catholic School should always be up to the standard of the public school.

I would like also that the Rev. Pastor give twice in the week a catechetical instruction to the children—at some hour convenient to the school exercises. For while the catechism is learned by the children in the school every day, the proper one by reason of his office, etc., to give the thorough explanation so needed by the children, is the priest. The Rev. C. O'Reilly and his assistant have made a thorough census of the parish and inform me that they expect to have at least three hundred children attending the school when it reopens.

Now in regard to the new convent: 1. You will please let me know how much money you require for it. 2. Rev. C. O'Reilly will build to the present schoolhouse an addition which will amply supply for all the classrooms which the school may need. 3. In borrowing money to build the Sisters' Convent on your own property, a mortgage to secure the loan is always required by the parties lending.

I shall, I assure you, do all in my power to promote the spiritual and temporal welfare of your esteemed community. And pray that God and His Immaculate Mother may make it flourish in great piety and holiness. I wish that you would reconsider—and if at all possible—keep the school of St. Joseph's parish in Portland....Sending you my blessing, I am in Xto. Jesu

Yours truly,

Wm. H. Gross
Archbp. Oregon[18]

Mother Pia did not abandon the Oregon foundations. In May 1898 she signed a contract for a convent in Albina. The following month the first bricks were laid for the foundation, beginning with the chapel. The sisters made a ceremony of the occasion. Sister Dominica

Klein, superior, laid the first brick in Mother Pia's name; the second, in her own. Sister Agnes Mulligan, Sister Clara Irwin, Sister Aloysia McSweeney, Sister Ignatia Mullally and Sister Aloysia (for Sister Antonia Callahan, who was ill at the time) followed in ceremonial order. The bricklayers then reclaimed their trowel and went about their task.

Work progressed at such a pace that the sisters moved into the completed convent on October 15, 1898. Father Lawrence Breen, O.P., a founding member of the Dominican Fathers community in adjacent Holy Rosary Parish (Cf. Below), celebrated the first Mass offered in the sisters' chapel. When Mother Pia arrived for a visit in November, she had the convent privately blessed on Thanksgiving Day and dedicated to St. Dominic. The following September the sisters from St. Joseph's, who had meantime moved back to Portland's West Side, crossed the river once more to become part of St. Dominic's community.

Enrollment at both Portland schools gradually fell into a pattern. St. Mary's regularly began the scholastic year with a registration of 190 that increased to 300 or 350 by Christmas. St. Joseph's opened the year with some sixty pupils and later increased to a little over one hundred by the end of the hop-picking season. At the behest of Father William A. Daly, third pastor of St. Mary's, the Albina school was made tuition-free. Later, because of the confusion of so many "St. Mary's" in the Portland area, Father Daly decided that the church and school should once again be known as "Immaculate Heart of Mary."

St. Dominic's Convent—fulfilling the necessary conditions[19]—was elevated to priory status at the General Chapter of the Congregation in 1900, with Sister Dominica Klein as the first prioress. For 64 years the Convent of St. Dominic was occupied continuously by the sisters until they moved to the Marycrest High School campus on N.E. 132nd Avenue.

By the mid-1940s the Immaculate Heart Elementary School building was in urgent need of replacement, and Father John Laidlaw, pastor, assumed responsibility for the erection of a one-story, four-classroom, brick structure fronting on Morris Street. Archbishop Edward D. Howard dedicated the new building on September 6, 1949. But despite the new school, enrollment continued to drop. Commercialization of the area and subsequent demographic changes accounted for the sisters' eventual withdrawal from Immaculate Heart in 1974. The school continued to operate, however, under a tri-parish arrangement.

Suffering a fate similar to that of many early institutions, St. Joseph's School succumbed to the residential shift in population from the West Side of Portland to the rapidly expanding East Side and closed permanently in 1918. The spanning of the Willamette by a series of bridges that eliminated the ferries influenced the population shift.

Archbishop Gross was recruiting again! Painstaking in providing for the spiritual needs of his people, he was convinced of the blessings a religious order of priests would bring to his archdiocese. He chose, therefore, as early as 1885, to approach "the zealous sons of St. Dominic"[20] in a letter to Father Vincent Vilarrasa in San Francisco appealing for assistance. Though the response was negative, the Archbishop was not discouraged, but bided his time patiently. After a lapse of three years, he wrote again, this time to Father Thomas Dyson, O.P., Father Vilarrasa being now deceased.

> My request is to have a foundation of the Reverend Dominican Fathers for the Archdiocese of which I am the unworthy Archbishop. Being myself a member of a religious Congregation, I deeply appreciate the immense value—and necessity of religious orders to a diocese.[21]

Although the second appeal went unanswered, the Archbishop was not one to give up easily, for in a letter to Mother Pia, dated December 23, 1888, he confided:

> I can tell you *sub rosa* that I have applied to the V. Rev. F. Provincial to procure a foundation of the Sons of St. Dominic for my diocese; they will have plenty to do. Please do not mention this to others; only pray our Immaculate Queen to obtain from her Divine Son this favor for my diocese.[22]

A third time, the Archbishop wrote to the Dominican Fathers for help. This letter was answered—and favorably, but it would be another three years before formalities were concluded and a church and rectory built. Holy Rosary Church at Third and Clackamas streets in East Portland was formally dedicated on January 28, 1894, the fruit of nine years of the Archbishop's steadfast perseverance!

Under the first superior, Irish-born Father Benedict McGovern, O.P., the community of six were busily engaged in retreat work and establishing such Dominican devotions as the Holy Name Society, the Confraternity of the Rosary and the Lay Dominicans.

New status was proposed for Holy Rosary Church when Archbishop Alexander Christie, successor to Archbishop Gross who had died in November 1898, wrote to the Dominican Vicar General, Father Pius Murphy, informing him that because of the growth in the Catholic population in the area, he wished to establish another parish and school in Portland and to designate Holy Rosary as his choice. Further, he would like the Fathers to take charge. Cautious in their response, the Dominicans were determined to safeguard their rights and privileges as an exempt religious order while remaining attentive to the needs of the people of the archdiocese. But, finally, on February 15, 1908, an agreement satisfactory to both parties was reached, and Holy Rosary became the first Dominican parish in the Archdiocese of Portland.

As was often the case, catechetical teaching preceded the opening of the school. The *Parish Digest* states:

> To Father Breen goes the credit for organizing the first Sunday School almost immediately after the dedication of the church... Some of the teachers called at the children's homes to take them to the instructions. When the number of children increased, the Sisters from Stanton Street at St. Dominic's Convent took charge until Holy Rosary School was opened.[23]

Holy Rosary School, Portland

Four years after the establishment of the parish, Mother Pia responded to the Father's invitation to open another elementary school in Portland at Holy Rosary. Sister Amanda Meyer and Sister Amata Morris, the latter a native of Oregon, began classes in a private residence known as the "Noon House," a three-story frame structure on N.E. Weidler Street, not far from the church. Sister Aloysia McSweeney joined them in the role of music teacher. Forty-three pupils spread throughout the first four grades, awaited the sisters on opening day. The following year, Sister Seraphica Behm taught third and fourth grades, and a year later Sister Loretto Schafer was added to the staff to teach the fifth and sixth grades.

For six years, the sisters walked rain or shine, from St. Dominic's Convent on Stanton Street in Immaculate Heart Parish to Holy Rosary School on Weidler, a distance of almost a mile. In rain, they arrived with habit hems soaked; in cold, numb! Brother John Leo Haggerty, O.P., proved a blessing; without fail, he would have a crackling fire burning in a classroom stove so that the sisters could dry their clothing in inclement weather and warm themselves in winter before the school day began.

But more serious problems than weather soon faced them. Oregon Catholics were suffering the consequences of growing prejudice fanned by the Ku Klux Klan, an organization designed to maintain the political supremacy of native-born, white, Protestant citizens. Fiery crosses burning on lawns and parades of hooded, white-garbed figures threatening dire consequences generated fear among the 60,000 Catholics of Oregon, who, though a minority, were becoming strong enough to constitute a threat in the minds of their anti-Catholic neighbors. Using the initiative process, the opponents of Catholic schools managed to have the Compulsory School Act added to the November 1922 ballot. Aimed at destroying private schools (read Catholic) the Act compelled all students between the ages of eight and sixteen to attend public schools. Its passage would affect some 6,000 children and sound the death knell for Catholic schools in Oregon, and more than likely, the nation. The sisters stormed heaven with their children, but Oregon voters, swayed by the propaganda circulated by the proponents of the act, passed the bill—115,506 for, 103,685 against.

The Sisters of the Holy Names filed an appeal with the United States District Court in Portland whose judges declared the law unconstitutional, but the matter was not yet settled. In *Pierce vs. Society of the Sisters of Holy Names of Jesus and Mary*, the case went to the United States Supreme Court where, on June 1, 1925, the Justices handed down a unanimous decision declaring once and for all time the Compulsory School Act unconstitutional:

> The fundamental theory of liberty upon which all governments of this Union repose excludes any general power of the State to standardize its children by forcing

them to accept instruction from public school teachers only. *The child is not the mere creation of the State* [italics mine]; those who nurture him and direct his destiny have the right, coupled with the high duty, to recognize and prepare him for additional duties.[24]

A landmark decision, it proved a happy day for Oregon Catholics!

With the school controversy at white heat, Father Stanislaus Olsen, O.P., pastor of Holy Rosary, sought and received permission to build a new school and parish hall. It was an act of faith rather than defiance. Archbishop Christie presided at the laying of the cornerstone on Sunday, August 26, 1923, with an impressive number of clergy and laity attending the ceremony. With the school completed, the second and third floors of the Noon House became the sisters' convent, the first floor serving as music studio. Gone without regret were the days of the daily walk from St. Dominic's Convent to Weidler Street. The first resident community of Dominican Sisters in Holy Rosary Parish consisted of Sister Amanda Meyer, superior, and Sisters Amata Morris, Seraphica Behm, Cyrilla Poschmann, Afra Jagar and Dolores Stopper.

The contract drawn up between parish and sisters specified that the latter would receive a stipend of $30 per month for 10 months; or $25 per month for 12 months. Stipends would be paid quarterly. Tuition would be given to the pastor, but monies received from "extras" such as music and painting would accrue to the sisters. In addition, the sisters would be expected "to teach Sunday school and take charge of the Sodalities, if desired to do so by the Pastor."[25] It was a clear and cordial arrangement, and the Dominican Sisters enjoyed a 43-year working relationship of prayer and ministry with the Friars in Portland.

A memoir, written by a 1941 graduate of Holy Rosary, Jim Bobzien, sheds light on the early years of the school from a student's perspective:

> Holy Rosary Parish School was a wonderfully small institution when I entered the fifth grade in 1937. There were about 75 students. I remember Sister Mary Dominic [Engelhard] as our principal....There were two grades in each room. I'm sure this was an interesting challenge for the nuns.

> Our football-baseball athletic field was a block south of the church....This was a challenge for Sister Mary Dominic. She came out to the corner of Third and Halsey and rang a big brass bell at 1:00 p.m. to summon us back from lunch play a block away. When the bases were loaded, we were not too prompt in returning to school. Then we heard from one of the priests on a very threatening note.
>
> We had a large gym/auditorium which was used day and night during rainy times. This was also a bone of contention because of the added electric bill for our late night basketball. Father was pressed for funds in those times [the middle of the Great Depression]. But he thought the higher costs worth it to keep us off the streets. He was, of course, right....
>
> The devoted and saintly Dominican Sisters at Holy Rosary School gave me the basic building blocks to enter and be successful in other schools and career paths. Moreover, they helped infuse in me a rock-solid faith. I shall always be in their debt.[26]

In the early 1940s, Holy Rosary Parish underwent a demographic change. World War II years brought a dramatic shift in population from white to black. Many of the old families began to relocate in newer neighborhoods. Reflecting the change, the school population ceased to represent only children from the parish. In addition, other parishes were building schools and sending their children to Holy Rosary temporarily while their schools were under construction. In 1947, thirty students were bussed daily from the little town of Vanport, lying northeast of Portland on the Columbia River. The next year 65 children were brought in from St. Rita's Parish in Parkrose. But despite the increase, enrollment at Holy Rosary dropped to 147, including the children from St. Rita's. The following year only 120 students were registered when St. Rita's Elementary School opened with five grades, leaving only two students at Holy Rosary. The enrollment pattern demonstrated clearly that the school was being sustained by temporary infusions of students outside parochial borders. By 1953, after the war, the ethnic

Holy Rosary Community: (l to r) seated, Sisters Brendan Bonney, Emilia Techtman; standing, Kathleen Corbett, Celeste Gardner and Geraldine Kelly

mix in the school represented 62% black and 38% white, with 62% of the students non-Catholic.

The handwriting was on the wall when a new series of events impacted the future of Holy Rosary. Shortly after school opened in the fall of 1954, Sister Callista Stopper, superior of the convent, and Sister Redempta Prose, prioress of St. Dominic's, wrote to the Motherhouse asking permission to discuss with the Dominican Fathers of Holy Rosary, the Archbishop, and Father Martin Thielen,

Portland superintendent of Catholic schools, the possibility of eliminating the first and second grades at Holy Rosary, beginning in September 1955. Stating their reasons for the request, the sisters set forth the following:

1. The rapid industrialization of the areas around Holy Rosary and Immaculate Heart.

2. The opening of eight grades at St. Anthony Elementary School, thereby reducing Holy Rosary's enrollment.

3. The location of the new St. Therese Elementary School within the parish where the sisters had purchased land for their new high school (Marycrest).

4. The rapid development of that area and the fact that St. Therese Parish included seven public schools with 13 first grades within its boundaries, a compelling statistic guaranteeing students.

5. Plans being currently made for the development of the area. Unless the opportunity is taken advantage of, the district will be lost to others. This would be unfortunate for Marycrest. Further, it does not seem good planning to remain in two dying parishes and lose the opportunity to begin in a developing area.

6. St. Therese pastor's plan to begin with only two grades, allowing time to staff the school gradually.[27]

If permission were granted, the sisters expressed willingness to accommodate themselves to the number of sisters then assigned to Oregon—for the time being! Permission was given, and subsequently, all parties involved agreed to the closing of Holy Rosary School the following June. Encroaching industrialization and the significant decline in parishioners with school-age children, as well as the opening of new parochial schools in surrounding districts, sounded the death knell of the parish school. Before the end of the school year, the sisters made sure that the Catholic students enrolled at Holy Rosary were all accepted at Immaculate Heart, and that the non-Catholic students enrolled at Holy Rosary were absorbed by the public schools of the area. As the last principal of Holy Rosary,

Sister Jerome Delsman was responsible for the transfer of students, and in September of the new school year, Sister Jerome assumed the principalship of Immaculate Heart, thereby providing continuity for the students and their families formerly associated with Holy Rosary.

Immaculata Academy, Portland

For some time the thought of a girls' high school on Portland's East Side had been stirring in Sister Dominica Klein's mind; when she believed the time right, she moved to put her plan into action. Inaugurated without fanfare, the high school began in 1911 as a part of the already existing Immaculate Heart Elementary School and consisted of a ninth grade and a commercial department. Four pupils, Immaculate Heart graduates from the previous June, formed the nucleus of the new enterprise. Classes were held in St. Dominic's Convent and were taught by a faculty of two. Sister

St. Dominic Priory (left), Immaculata Academy (right) on Stanton Street

Dominica Klein taught commercial and served as principal, and Sister Carmelita Keogh assumed responsibility for the academic ninth grade. By the third year the high school was in need of additional space and Father Daly generously offered the original church building for high school use. The sisters had the building moved east of the grade school and renovated. They also added a wing to house the blossoming music department.

In its new quarters, the Academy opened its doors to nineteen high school and eleven commercial pupils. Blessing of the refurbished building took place on Sunday, November 13, with the Most Reverend James Morrison, visiting Bishop of Nova Scotia, presiding. Tours of the expanded building were conducted following the ceremony. The following year the high school received an identity of its own when it was christened Immaculata Academy and on June 18, 1914, proudly conferred high school diplomas on the first graduates, two in number. By 1916, the Academy was fully accredited to the University of Oregon and affiliated to the Catholic University of America, Washington, D.C.

Eventually the pressures of the growing student body made the former church building no longer adequate. A one-story brick structure facing on Morris Street was erected in 1929. Designed to contain auditorium, library, cafeteria, and five classrooms, it relieved much of the congestion in the old church-turned-school.

In the mid-1940s the convent annalist exulted, "School reopens with a record-breaking enrollment of almost 200 in the high school."[28] The growth in numbers and offerings necessitated further adjustments, and the sisters decided that a simple addition to the Morris Street building was in order. One large classroom and an extension to the library were added.

Notes

[1] William H. Gross, C.SS.R., letter to Backes, 14 March 1888.

[2] Gross, letter to Backes, 15 March 1888.

[3] Backes 104.

[4] Maerz, letter appended to the end of her diary, 1888.

[5] Maerz, letter appended to the end of her diary, 1888.

[6] Backes 118.

[7] *The Catholic Sentinel Centenary Edition*. (Supplement to *Catholic Sentinel* 4 May 1939) 14.

[8] Backes 118.

[9] Backes 118.

[10] Backes 121.

[11] Backes 121.

[12] Maerz, diary, 31 December 1889.

[13] Maerz, diary, 31 December 1889.

[14] Backes 130.

[15] Backes 130.

[16] Backes 157.

[17] Gross, letter to Backes, 13 June 1894.

[18] Gross, letter to Backes, 11 July 1894.

[19] Conditions for a priory: Priories must be the property of the Congregation with at least 10 sisters regularly assigned (Art. 165, *Constitutions*). Permission of the Ordinary is required if the foundation is a new one.

[20] Gross, letter to Vilarrasa 28 September 1885 in Fabian Stan Parmisano, O.P., in *Mission West: the Western Dominican Province: 1850–1966* (Oakland, CA: Western Dominican Province, 1995) 191.

[21] Gross, letter to Dyson, 30 October 1888 in Parmisano 192.

[22] Gross, letter to Backes, 23 December 1888.

[23] *Parish Digest* (March 1944) in Joseph F. Foye, *A Treasure of Promises Kept: A Centenary History of the Queen of the Most Holy Rosary Priory and Parish* (Paducah, Kentucky: Turner Publishers, 1999) 31.

[24] United States Supreme Court, "Compulsory School Act," in Foye 81.

[25] Foye 52.

[26] Foye 54–55.

[27] Callista Stopper, O.P. and Redempta Prose, O.P., letter to Pius Marbaise,

O.P., September/October 1954.

[28] Annals of Saint Dominic Convent, Portland, September mid-40s.

CHAPTER SEVEN

SOUTHERN CALIFORNIA BECKONS

The Northwest was not the only new area of Sister Pia's attention. Southern California was also sending up signals and she was disposed to respond.

The town of Anaheim, located some thirty miles southeast of Los Angeles on the site of *Rancho San Juan Cajon de Santa Ana,* an early Mexican land grant, was founded in 1857 by a group of German settlers from San Francisco. For nearly twenty years, the Catholic settlers from Anaheim were without a resident priest until Bishop Thaddeus Amat, C.M., bishop of Monterey-Los Angeles (1853–1878), established St. Boniface Parish in 1875, with Father Victor Foran as first pastor. Ten years later he was succeeded by Father Patrick Hawe, who remained only one year. His replacement, Father Peter Stoetters, was bitterly disappointed when he arrived in Anaheim and found his parish without a Catholic school. Determined to remedy the situation, he applied to Sister Pia for teaching sisters. Although his request struck a responsive chord in her heart, Verboort had left its mark, and she resolved that this time she would see for herself before resorting to Mother Seraphina for approval.

Accompanied by Sister Hyacintha Schneider, Sister Pia took *The Owl,* the night train for Los Angeles, on September 2, 1887. On arrival, the sisters went directly to the Chancery, where they presented themselves to the Most Reverend Francis Mora, Bishop Amat's successor. The bishop received them cordially and was particularly pleased to learn of their interest in making a foundation in the diocese. Following an overnight stay at the Cathedral residence of the Sisters of Charity, who received them most hospitably, they toured the city by coach. Sister Pia's impression was positive: "... one can easily imagine oneself in Mexico....Most of the houses, one-story. Many built in strict Mexican style; a personality all its own with... a large atrium."[1]

In the late afternoon, the travelers boarded the train for Anaheim, where they were met by Father Stoetters, "tall and stiff,"[2] and members of the Rimpau family, the sisters' host for the night. The next morning the sisters on their way to Mass at St. Boniface Church had their first glimpse of the town, and Sister Pia liked what she saw: "A delightful place with about 1,300 inhabitants."[3]

At lunch at the hospitable Rimpaus, Father Stoetters and Mother Pia discussed the details involved in establishing a school. The conversation ending to both parties' satisfaction, Sister Pia sent a report of her impressions to Mother Seraphina in New York. Among the latter's conditions for acceptance was the erection of a convent by the parish. Reasonable though it was, the condition proved frustrating for Sister Pia, who protested it in a letter to Father [Michael] May. He, of course, shared the contents with Mother Seraphina, prompting her earlier instruction to Sister Pia on July 24, 1887. (c.f. Ch. Five, page 114).

St. Catherine's Academy, Anaheim

Sometime after the separation from Holy Cross Convent, Sister Pia, now Mother Pia, purchased a three-acre tract on Palm Street (presently Harbor Boulevard) and approved plans for the construction of a three-story brick building, containing two classrooms and accommodations for sisters and boarders. By the spring of 1889, the building was pronounced ready for occupancy, a signal for Sisters Amanda Bednartz, Emilia Moore, Catharina Wilson and six resident pupils to board a San Francisco steamer for the south. They were followed four days later by Mother Pia and Sister Vincentia Powers who arrived to assist in the preparations for the "dedication of the first foundation made by our Motherhouse in California"[4] That they were needed is evident from Mother Pia's Diary entry: "So taken up were we with preparations for the coming event... that we had breakfast only at one o'clock."[5]

On March 19, the morning of the Dedication, the sisters were still putting the finishing touches on their preparations when they were notified that Bishop Mora, who had arrived the previous evening with his Vicar General, the Reverend Joachim Adams, was ready to celebrate Mass! The announcement caused a flutter of excitement. Hurrying off to change from work aprons into habits, the sisters arrived in chapel just as the episcopal Mass was ending. A second Mass, celebrated by Father Adams, followed immediately, allowing the sisters no time to withdraw. Eying the clock, the captive congregation responded literally to the celebrant's "*Ite, Missa est*" by rushing off to complete their last minute touch ups. All was restored to calm by nine o'clock when the dedication ceremonies began with a *Missa cantata* sung by Father A. Reithaar. Father Adams rendered dual service as homilist for the occasion by preaching in both English and Spanish.

Following Mass, Bishop Mora dedicated the building, placing it under the patronage of the great 13th century Dominican saint, St. Catherine of Siena. An unidentified sister, writing to Sister Seraphina Maerz in San Francisco, described the event:

> Many people were there; more than we had expected. The sisters sang very well, and Mother was on the platform with them. Mrs. Rimpau took care of the clergy's lunch, and her daughters, Mathilda and Sophie, took up the collection. A good German lady, Eberhard by name, whose two great aunts were sisters in Ratisbon, brought us cake, fruit, and butter....The whole meal did not cost Mother a cent. On the contrary, she had a balance of $1.75. We had enough to eat for the next week, and on Sunday we ate turkey![6]

In weary contrast, the analyst summed up the day from her perspective: "How many inconveniences we had to put up with today!" [7]

School opened on March 25, 1889, under the principalship of Sister Amanda Bednartz, assisted by Sister Emilia Moore. Nineteen day-pupils, the six resident students from San Francisco, and five from Los Angeles comprised the enrollment. In July Sisters Augustina O'Connor and Teresa Meyer arrived as additions to the faculty, the latter to teach music. Registration for the new term, which began in September, boasted an increase to 43 day students and fifteen resident pupils from Anaheim and the nearby town of Fullerton. Since Catholic families in Anaheim numbered only twenty-five at the time, the sisters pronounced themselves satisfied.

December brought Sister Felicitas Weiss to St. Catherine's as replacement for Sister Amanda. She traveled by steamer from San Francisco with Sister Walburga Muller's aunt, Barbara Bruttig, whose place in early congregational history is assured by her generous support of the struggling young community and her willingness on multiple occasions to be the canonically required companion when a sister traveled. Arriving in Los Angeles, the travelers found that a violent storm had left the city flooded and bridges washed out. Anaheim was out of the question that afternoon.

Since Mrs. Bruttig had received specific instructions restricting her companion's overnight stay to a convent—should such prove necessary, she accompanied Sister Felicitas to the Bishop's residence to inquire if a night's lodging might be available in a nearby convent. By then it was after eight o'clock. Bishop Mora met the emergency by summoning a priest to serve Sister a warm supper and then escort her to the Daughters of Charity's residence at the Cathedral, leaving the long-suffering Mrs. Bruttig to fend for herself with relatives.

Having arrived at the convent after the sisters had retired for the night, Sister Felicitas followed the portress to the dormitory, where she was shown a bed. Despite the hospitality, the visitor could not sleep, and in the early morning darkness ventured out of her cubicle, there to encounter a young sister on her way to chapel. Thinking the white apparition coming toward her was a ghost, the frightened sister threw up her hands and retreated toward the wall, calling for help in a lusty crescendo. The more Sister Felicitas tried to reassure her, the more she cried for assistance. Finally Sister succeeded in convincing her that she was a real-life Dominican and actually quite harmless—though not before the entire household had been roused. Fortunately for all, Mrs. Bruttig arrived at the convent early, and the two left on the 8 a.m. train for Anaheim.

Sister Felicitas's "green thumb" was given a great opportunity at St. Catherine's. The entire "expanse of sand" had to be landscaped, a formidable challenge even for one with her horticultural abilities. To her aid came Timothy Carroll, an Irish-born Anaheim farmer who had developed a nursery specializing in orange and walnut trees. He arrived at the convent one morning with a working crew of six volunteers, some sixty orange trees, and a generous variety of other fruit trees. Sister Felicitas was in her glory. She happily directed Mr. Carroll and his men in laying out the grass and garden areas and in planting the trees. The Anaheim Gazette was generous in its praise: "The grounds...[are] elegantly laid out with trees, flowers and shrubbery."[8] But the grounds were not the reporter's sole interest:

> The faculty was selected from the College [term synonymous with grade school at the time] of Dominican Sisters at San Francisco, which had acquired a most enviable reputation as an institution of learning....The work is done in a masterly manner and reflects great credit upon our townsman [Charles Schindler].... The College is a standing advertisement of Anaheim and should be aided by our citizens to the fullest extent of their power. It is to be hoped that the Sisters shall have no cause to regret their selection of our city as the scene of their operations and that the College may wield the same power for good as the Dominican College in San Francisco, which has a reputation second to no institution of learning on the Pacific Coast.[9]

High hopes and glowing praise for the little schools on Palm and Guerrero Streets!

Sometime in the 1870s Count Karol Bonzenta Clapowski and his wife, Madame Helena Modjeska, the famous Polish tragedienne, had established residence near Anaheim. At the suggestion of Clementine Langenberger, the sisters' neighbor and gracious benefactor, the actress gave a performance in Los Angeles for the benefit of the school that netted $2,000 and provided a generous boost to St. Catherine's dubious financial stability.

St. Catherine's Orphanage

From the outset, St. Catherine's, Anaheim, had struggled to maintain itself financially, but it soon became apparent that it was a losing battle. The feasibility of an orphanage in place of the boarding and day school began to appear more and more appealing to the sisters and led to conversations with the Daughters of Charity at their Boyle Heights orphanage in East Los Angeles. The talks re-

Mother Maria Pia Backes and Sister Gonzaga Buehler at St. Catherine's Orphanage

sulted in the transfer of the orphan boys from Boyle Heights to St. Catherine's as the original intent of the Sisters of Charity had been the care of orphan girls only. Accordingly, on July 20, 1894, thirty boys—the youngest, three months—arrived at Anaheim to take up residence there.

Unfortunately, the orphans' building was not ready when the boys arrived—clothes neatly packed but unlabeled! The sisters were hard put to meet the challenge of matching clothing with boy. To add to the general misery, the sisters were new to the children, who spent a good part of the day crying. "Never in my life will I forget our first Holy Father St. Dominic's Day at Anaheim,"[10] wrote Sister Salesia of her first August 4th. Mercifully, affairs took a turn for the better at the end of the month when the orphans, now 43 in number, moved from their temporary classroom dormitories into new and more identifiable quarters. But finances continued a problem, and the sale of two cows netting $70 and an old piano bringing in $50 more in supplemental income brought only short-term relief. Sister Gonzaga sent $31 in alms, probably more than she could well afford, and neighboring farmers contributed produce whenever they could to help provide food for the children. On Christmas

Eve, the sisters rose at 2 a.m. to decorate the orphanage and arrange the wagonloads of toys contributed by generous benefactors and organizations. The next year brought welcome relief when for the first time State Aid arrived in a check from San Francisco for $953.32 and another from San Bernadino for $563.

That conditions were improving was noted by *The Tidings*, the Los Angeles diocesan weekly newspaper:

> There are now 108 boys at St. Catherine's Orphan Asylum, quite an increase over last year's best total. An addition to the orphanage is projected and will need to be made in the near future in order to accommodate the increasing demands for admission. St. Catherine's School for day pupils affords an opportunity for the parents of the district to give their children a thorough Catholic education.[11]

The following year the projected addition to the orphanage was begun, and on April 30, 1897, Father John Bannon of St. Boniface Parish, Anaheim, blessed the new frame building which provided accommodations for 200.

Gradually life in the orphanage settled into a pattern. The orphans ranged from two to ten years of age. Boys over ten were not admitted; and when a boy turned ten, he was transferred to the Franciscan Fathers in Watsonville, where he learned a trade. Occasionally, infants were placed in the sisters' care, and at times a child died, usually from previous malnutrition or some other form of prior neglect that the doctors and sisters were unable to counteract. Outbreaks of measles or smallpox taxed the sisters' strength, demanding round-the-clock duty. Registration was often informal; children were brought in from the street, no questions asked, as in the case of a little boy abandoned outside St. Boniface Rectory and turned over to the sisters for care. Judged to be about three years old, he was weak and sickly and, despite the sisters' caring efforts, died after a few months. The death of a child was always a cause of sadness to the sisters who cared for him.

On August 8, 1900, the annalist recorded that St. Catherine's had been raised to a priory, the conditions having been met. Sister Raymunda Wilson was the first prioress and Sister Ambrosia Niedermeyer, her sub-prioress assistant.

By 1903, the orphanage was at capacity, housing 200 orphans or "half-orphans," i.e., one parent living. Again it was found necessary to enlarge the orphanage and arrange a chapel in the attic that would accommodate the boys. The additions were blessed by Bishop Conaty of Los Angeles. Meantime, in March of the following year, Mother Gonzaga* and three sisters from St. Catherines' were invited to open Sunday School classes in nearby Santa Ana for approximately 40 children.

State Aid brought with it State inspection and new friends. The Hon. Edward F. Hyatt, state superintendent of public instruction, and his wife became frequent visitors in the classrooms of St. Catherine's. The *Anaheim Gazette* made note of one such visit on September 19, 1912, as quoted in the convent Annals:

> Edward Hyatt... was a visitor at the Orphanage school in this city this week, accompanied by his wife. He pronounces the school one of the very best in the State, and commends the management in the highest terms. This coming from an educator like Hyatt, who is not given to flattery, speaks as nothing else could speak for the Anaheim Orphanage.[12]

But despite the evident success, Mother Pia was forced to conclude that the orphanage must be closed; the Congregation simply could not support it. Moreover, a client was waiting in the wings. Owners of an Eastern-based shoe factory were seeking a suitable location on the West Coast and had discovered St. Catherine's. Would the Reverend Mother be willing to sell? Reluctantly Mother Pia agreed. As she and a companion were on her way to the bank to sign the papers closing the transaction, her companion noticed a swarm of bees following the carriage. "Mother," she pleaded, "please don't think of selling St. Catherine's; bees bring good luck. God will surely bless us."[13] Taking the unsuspecting bees as a sign from above, Mother Pia ordered the carriage turned around and headed back to the orphanage. There would be no sale; somehow they would manage. Since that eventful day, bees have held an honored place in St. Catherine's story.

---

* The honorary title of "Mother" was given to Sisters Amanda Bednartz, Felicitas Weiss, Gonzaga Buehler, and Seraphina Maerz in 1903 and retained for life. The correct title is applied in the text according to the context. Sister Dolorosa was given the title officially in 1912. See Chapter 8, page 190 for the full explanation.

St. Catherine's Military Academy

By a combination of long hours and cautious economy, the sisters managed to make ends meet until 1916, when the Bureau of Catholic Charities introduced a policy of placing orphans in private homes rather than in institutions. To support the resultant declining enrollment, the sisters began to accept boarders and day students again and to engage men as teachers for the older boys. As a special attraction, physical education was highlighted in the daily program; and, by a sort of natural progression, it developed into a course of military training under the direction of a "pro," Captain D.M. Healy. After a two-year experiment, St. Catherine's School became, with the approval of Bishop John J. Cantwell of Los Angeles, St. Catherine's Military Academy (1925). A new and exciting chapter in the history of the school had begun.

Appointed prioress during these years (1924–1930) Mother Dolorosa Wallrath was pleased when, in December of her first year at the academy, St. Catherine's received a check from the Community Chest totaling $1,391.56. Devoted to St. Joseph, she remarked with satisfaction that the check arrived on a Wednesday, a day traditionally dedicated by the Congregation to prayer to the saint. Surely this was a good omen! Such optimism would shortly be tested however, for a conflict between the Los Angeles Chancery and the school administration threatened to jeopardize St. Catherine's chances of survival.

At the center of the controversy was Mother Dolorosa who, at the end of her first year, declined to readmit students whose conduct or school record had proved unsatisfactory. Father William Carr, former director of the Los Angeles Bureau of Catholic Charities, was in full support of her policy. "It was the only thing to do,"[14] he agreed. There were others, however, who were vocal in their criticism. For a brief time Mother Dolorosa dared to hope that the controversy was over:

> I learned today that Bishop Cantwell is taking steps to buy property for an industrial school. I am wondering if this means that St. Catherine's is to be no further [tormented]. God knows how much happier I would be if I could work for God's poor and afflicted. I would feel some human satisfaction. But [is] it just and right to place the delinquent

and semi-delinquent boy side by side with the normal innocent boy?[15]

But the trouble was far from over. On June 3, 1927, a letter from the Chancery Office struck like a bolt of lightning. "After reading [it], I made my offering to the Sacred Heart in [the] presence of the Blessed Sacrament exposed in the Boys' Chapel. Then I resolved to go to the Bishop.[16] "It was not a happy meeting. The words "orphan" and "delinquent" were bandied about, ending in the Bishop's charging Mother Dolorosa with not wanting orphans, that is, not wanting poor boys. "This is not true. God knows it,"[17] she wrote in her diary. Seeking Mother Seraphina's advice, she was told to remain silent and continue accepting poor children sent by The Bureau of Catholic Charities, but not so-called "delinquents." Despite the costs to her personally, Mother Dolorosa stood her ground and informed Monsignor Joachim Cawley, diocesan vicar general, that the school would accept orphans sent by the Bureau, but not "delinquents."

Unpleasant as the situation was, it seems to have ended there. In any case, St. Catherine's reputation does not appear to have suffered unduly from the trouble, for some time later, the annals record that the June Drill was attended by more than 2,000 guests, including 30 representatives of the various branches of the military. Colonel E.J. Moran, USA, conducted the customary inspection of the plant and declared St. Catherine's in a most satisfactory condition.

Over the years, the building program at St. Catherine's kept pace with the needs of enrollment and the upgrading of facilities, including the addition of a swimming pool, another dormitory, an infirmary and more classrooms. At times construction was dictated by natural disaster, as for example, March 10, 1933, which dawned like any other day but ended in misfortune. A severe earthquake struck throughout California, destroying the oldest building on St. Catherine's campus. The boys had just assembled for supper when the heaving of the earth began, continuing at 15-minute intervals throughout the night. Supper, which had begun as usual in the boys' dining room, ended around a bonfire on the parade ground. The younger boys spent the night in the one-story infirmary building, judged the safest place on campus.

Five years later, adversity struck again, this time in the guise of water. A flood that devastated Southern California did not spare Anaheim or St. Catherine's. Shortly after midnight on May 3, 1938, the Santa Ana River overflowed its banks. By four in the morning, most of the city was under two to five feet of water, and the streets had become raging torrents; cars, garages, even small houses were carried "downstream."

St. Catherine's annalist provided the details close to home:

> By 5:30 [a.m.] supplies had been taken from the dining rooms and an attempt to save the floors had begun. Buckets, dishpans, even milk bottles, were used by the sisters, staff, and older cadets to hand-bail the twenty inches of water from the lower floors and not until nine that night did they cease their toil, for then only were the boards in sight. The oil and silt had so damaged the wood that it was necessary to replace the entire lower floor of the main building...
>
> As the kitchen building was not damaged, the cadets were able to have all meals on schedule, even though some were eaten on classroom desks.
>
> So, though we went through hours of wondering just what would happen next, we went smiling to work, cleaned as rapidly as we could, repaired as soon as it was safe, and put our sand bags in mothballs ... [until] the next one.[18]

But, the damage served as a warning, and the same year saw the erection of a two-story reinforced concrete structure that housed five classrooms and two offices on the first floor and a gymnasium on the second.

On October 6, 1934, Lt. Charles A. Schmitt followed Captain Healy as commandant and began what would become an unprecedented 40 years of distinguished leadership at the school, interrupted only by a four-year stint during World War II when he was called to active duty. A man of deep Christian faith, genuine integrity and meticulous courtesy, Lt. (later Major) Schmitt brought to the position of commandant a stature and respect that translated into a role model for the boys trained under his supervision.

St. Catherine's celebrated its Golden Jubilee over a three-day period, May 13–15, 1939. Celebrant of the Solemn High Mass in St. Boniface Church on Saturday, May 13, was Father Henry Gross, pastor, with Fathers Jeremiah Lehane and John Quatannens as deacon and sub-deacon respectively. Father Louis A. Naselli, O.P., preached the homily. Monsignor Cawley was present in the sanctuary as the Archbishop's representative. Luncheon was served at noon to priest guests and visiting sisters, and in the afternoon St. Catherine's cadets presented a program for the enjoyment of all.

Major Charles Schmitt, Commandant at St. Catherine's Military Academy

A Field Mass was scheduled for Sunday, May 14, at 10:00 a.m. Because morning brought a heavy mist, the Mass was transferred to the gymnasium. Luncheon was served to 35 priests in the school library and about 400 guests in the boy's dining room. At 2:00 p.m., guests heard the Hon. Thomas L. McFadden of Anaheim speak on the founding of St. Catherine's and its subsequent growth. The Anaheim Conservatory of Music followed with a delightful program of instrumental and vocal selections. Benediction concluded the afternoon.

The three-day celebration closed on Monday, May 15, with a Solemn Requiem Mass sung by the sisters' choir in the school chapel. The Mass was offered for the deceased sisters, students, clergy, relatives, benefactors and friends of St. Catherine's.

On the "day of infamy," December 7, 1941, the streets of Anaheim rang with the voices of newsboys shouting excitedly, "Extra! Extra! Pearl Harbor bombed!" The following day the United States declared war on Japan, and the nation geared for a united war effort. The situation had a direct impact on St. Catherine's. In November

1942 Lt. Schmitt was called to active duty and replaced by Captain W.A. Murphy. During the war years, enrollment at St. Catherine's was at full capacity, averaging 190 resident boys annually, with applicants turned away for lack of accommodations.

With the restoration of peace after the war, Father William Maguire, a veteran of 30 years' experience as a naval chaplain and Chief Chaplain of the United States Pacific Fleet at Pearl Harbor on December 7, 1941, was assigned to St. Catherine's where he was warmly welcomed by sisters, staff and students (October 30, 1950). The assignment would prove Father Maguire's last "tour of duty," as his untimely death occurred while he was celebrating Mass in a London hotel room on September 13, 1953. St. Catherine's mourned his loss, and the flag flew at half-mast for eight days. Father Maguire was buried with full military honors in San Diego, all arrangements taken care of by the United States Navy. A number of sisters and older cadets attended the funeral.

Following the death of Archbishop Cantwell in 1947, Archbishop J. Francis A. McIntyre of New York was appointed to the western archdiocese. At his first visit to St. Catherine's in July 1948, the Archbishop expressed concern for the safety of the sisters, who lived on the third and fourth floors of an old frame building. His point was well taken, and the following July, ground breaking for a new convent took place. Archbishop McIntryre was pleased to dedicate the new building on Palm Sunday, April 2, 1950. Monsignor Bernard J. Dolan gave the principal address for the occasion. After a tour of the convent, guests were served refreshments, and the clergy had dinner in the sisters' new dining room.

January 12, 1953 proved an eventful day for the Archdiocese of Los Angeles. On that day word was received from Rome that:

> James Francis McIntyre [had] received the highest office the Catholic Church can bestow upon a man under the Papacy when he was created a Cardinal Priest under the title of St. Anastasia. In him, the entire Archdiocese of Los Angeles was recognized by Pope Pius XII. The new Cardinal was honored by the priests of the diocese upon his return from Rome with a banquet.[19]

In September 1953 the first day students were admitted in Grades One and Two. The following year, day students were enrolled in all eight grades. At the closing drill on June 12, 1954, attended by a large group of parents and friends, St. Catherine's Drum an Bugle Corps made their first public appearance. Composed of second and third graders, they "stole the show"[20] with their routine. Brigadier General Francis Day, Fort McArthur, was the Reviewing Officer, and the Reverend John Fitzgerald, C.S.P., procurator general of the Paulist Fathers, speaker. Following drill, the cadets were dismissed for summer vacation.

Chapel of St. Thomas Aquinas

As tribute to their beloved chaplain, St. Catherine's community, under the leadership of Sister Verona Wittenzellner, prioress (1952–1958), made plans to erect a chapel in Father Maguire's memory. A meeting was called to organize a fiesta to initiate the necessary fund-raising, and the committee's enthusiasm gave the sisters the boost they needed to proceed with the plans. A huge success, the 1955 fiesta drew a large crowd, Hollywood providing the main attractions: Dennis Day (whose sons were students at St. Catherine's), Maureen O'Hara and Red Skelton. The proceeds of the first and succeeding fiestas added substantially to the chapel fund; and Father John Slavik, appointed Father Maguire's replacement, invited Father Valerian Jasinski, professor of Dogma at St. Mary's College, Orchard Lake, Michigan, to meet Sister Verona and discuss plans for the memorial. The outcome of their meeting was the St. Thomas Aquinas Chapel—"the dream of a theologian, Father Valerina Jasinski; the pencil plan of a priest architect, Father Joseph Myrda; and the single-minded energy of Sister Verona Wittenzellner."[21]

In June 1956 things began moving forward rapidly. St. Catherine's annalist made note in a later entry:

> Mr. John DeRosen of the Iconography Committee of the National Shrine in Washington, D.C., paid his first visit [to St. Catherine's] to discuss the murals with Sister [Verona] for the new chapel. Excavation for the new south wing was begun in February 1957. The cornerstone ... was blessed on May 26, 1957. Mr. DeRosen actually began his work on the murals on July 8 and the sisters were first able to enter their new chapel on September 14, 1957. The first Mass was offered the next day.[22]

St. Thomas Chapel and the adjoining new convent wing were dedicated by His Eminence, Cardinal McIntyre, on April 26, 1958. The Very Reverend Joseph Fulton, O.P., provincial, was celebrant of the Solemn High Mass. He was assisted by Father Charles Carosella, O.P., as deacon and Father John Simones, O.P., as subdeacon. Monsignor Martin McNicholas gave the homily and Father Thomas McElhatton, O.P., served as the master of ceremonies. An augmented Sisters' Choir sang the Proper of the Votive Mass of St. Thomas. The Common, sung by a selected Cadet's Choir, was directed by Mr. George Arelano. Dr. Richard Derr Biggs, designer of St. Catherine's organ and supervisor of its construction, arranged the Common of the Mass and accompanied both choirs.

At ceremonies following the Mass, the memory of Father Maguire was duly honored when the cadets passed in review; Navy Chaplain, Comdr. Walter A. Mahler, CHC, USN, read a prayer commemorating the deceased; and taps were played as the flag was lowered to half mast. Dinner, served to visiting clergy and a number of other distinguished guests, concluded the ceremonies. His Eminence was so pleased with the day's program that he sent members of the clergy who were planning a dedication to Sister Verona for assistance in planning their day.

At the June drill preceding summer dismissal, Sister Verona was presented with a plaque in recognition of her "unselfish, courageous, and outstanding leadership"[23] in the chapel project. It was a recognition well merited. Dedicated to the Divine Truth under the patronage of St. Thomas Aquinas, the great Dominican theologian and saint, the chapel is an artistic expression of the saint's theology. The exterior north wall of the building portrays the "Ascent to Truth" by means of a larger-than-life mosaic, representing the great minds of the ancient pagan world (Hammurabi, Akhnaton, Cyrus the Great, Plato, Aristotle, Botehius) as well as the prophets and kings of the chosen People (Abraham, Moses, David, Isaiah).

The interior north wall contains John DeRosen's majestic 90-foot mural, the "Descent of Truth", which represents Christ the Teacher as the powerful central figure. Standing to the right of Christ are seven women—mystics and saints, outstanding in the story of the Church (including Sts. Elizabeth, Catherine of Siena, Teresa of Avila, Bl. Jane d'Aza); to the left of the Christ figure are 19 men—

apostles, fathers, doctors of the Church, and theologians, (among them are Sts. John, Peter, Paul, Augustine, Thomas Aquinas, Albert, and Ignatius; Dante Alighieri, Copernicus).

The south interior wall of the chapel is a symphony in stained class, depicting "The Burst of Creation," designed by Mr. DeRosen and executed by Max Ingrand of Paris, a magnificent window showing God the Father uttering his Fiat at the dawn of creation. It portrays in brilliant color the Hexaemeron described in the first chapter of Genesis—the work of the six days." Redemption, portrayed in stained glass through the Stations of the Cross, and Sanctification, represented by the Sacraments, complete the south wall and are the work of Max Ingrand.

Above the main entrance to the chapel (east wall) is another impressive stained glass window portraying Our Lady, "Seat of Wisdom", supported by seraphs' wings. Since its dedication, the Chapel of St. Thomas Aquinas has been visited by thousands who come to worship and to appreciate this artistic representation of Christian philosophy and theology.

The year 1955 brought excitement of a totally different kind for the cadets at St. Catherine's. Universal Studios requested permission to film on campus, *The Private War of Major Benson*, a full-length film starring Charlton Heston and Julie Adams. To the boys' delight, the studio invited the students to "stardom" as extras in several scenes! Some of the glamour began to fade, however, when the boys were marched wearily up and down the parade ground until their performance suited the casting director! On completion of the film, the sisters enjoyed a private viewing at Universal Studios. Selected to show the West Coast Premiere, the Anaheim Fox Theatre allocated the opening night's proceeds to the St. Catherine's Chapel Fund.

On May 2, 1959, St. Catherine's celebrated Major Schmitt's Twenty-fifth Anniversary as commandant. The day began with a Field Mass at which Bishop Alden Bell, auxiliary bishop of Los Angeles, presided and preached. Celebrant of the Mass was Father John Quatennens, pastor of St. Boniface, assisted by Father Donald Montrose, vice principal of Mater Dei High School, and Father John Fitzgerald, assistant pastor of St. Columban Church, Garden Grove.

Attending the ceremonies honoring Major Schmitt was a large representation of clergy and military personnel, as well as family, students, and friends of the esteemed honoree.

The decision to admit day students to the school bolstered the enrollment of St. Catherine's significantly. Over a five year period, 1955–1960, the student body increased from 160 to 292, of whom 120 were day students. Although parents enrolled their sons at St. Catherine's for a variety of reasons—as single parents wishing to provide residential care and a good education for their boys, as parents wishing to give their sons private school experience in a small student body with firm discipline, or as parents from foreign countries wishing their sons to gain a command of English[24]—expectations may be summarized in words taken from the school prospective:

> St. Catherine's is a school following the regular archdiocesan course of study... Through a well-balance religious, mental, physical, and social program, St. Catherine's Military Academy aims to train youth from its tenderest years in those habits and traits of character so necessary in later life for the responsibilities of good citizenship and active Catholicity.[25]

Recognition should be given also in any discussion of St. Catherine's to the Parents' Guild. Through the years, the parents provided generous assistance to the sisters in sponsoring the annual Military Ball, supervising the Carnival, publishing St. Catherine's Yearbook, and being on call whenever there was a need.

Sacred Heart Elementary School, Los Angeles

On March 7, 1890, an entry in Mother Pia's Diary reads simply: "Yesterday Sacred Heart School, Los Angeles, was accepted."[26] The parish of Sacred Heart, fourth oldest in the Diocese of Los Angeles, was situated in what came to be known as East Los Angeles, the city's first suburb "hardly out of its swaddling clothes."[27] Father Patrick Harnett, Sacred Heart's pioneer pastor, appealed to Mother Pia for sisters to teach the children of his far-ranging parish. Following consultation with her Council and earnest prayer, Mother Pia accepted the new foundation.

Sacred Heart Convent and School c. 1890

Acceptance was not without overtones of desperation. "Help, Jesus," she pleaded in the Diary. "We should build, but haven't a penny."[28] Father Harnett followed his initial request with a second: Would Mother Pia sign a contract for a school and convent building at an estimated cost of $5,659. "Do I intend to sign contract?" asked Mother Pia. "Lord, what shall I do? I have not a cent to build this house of Thine."[29] But the next day she sent her answer in a dispatch whose brevity gave no indication of her worries —"Yes." To the Diary she confided her fears: "O Sacred Heart! It is for Thee. Help us. The burden presses heavily on me. Help! Help!"[30] No help, she knew, would be forthcoming from the pastor, whose Sunday collection seldom exceeded $3.80.

Nine days later, on May 11, groundbreaking for the new building took place. That acceptance continued to weigh heavily on the already burdened superior is evident from the Diary entry of May 14: "O Lord! I am tired of the world and its commotion. How happy I would be to live alone in union with Thee. Give me strength and courage to carry on. Today I borrowed the first thousand dollars from the bank for the Sacred Heart Convent. I trust in Thee, Sacred Heart of Jesus, to pay Your debts."[31]

Presumably, the subtle shift of responsibility for the debt did not go unnoticed by the Sacred Heart.

Chapter 7 / SOUTHERN CALIFORNIA BECKONS 165

The unpretentious two-story frame building which was to serve as convent, school, and boarders' quarters was completed in little more than two months. On July 27, Sister Felicitas Weiss, prioress of St. Catherine's, Anaheim, arrived at Sacred Heart to see what was needed. With her were two sister volunteer helpers. "The large building," Sister Felicitas later recalled, "was devoid of every vestige of furniture, cooking utensils, and the like necessities. Not even a piece of board [to serve as a chair] ... was obtainable on the premises."[32] Fortunately, the pastor invited the sisters to the rectory for meals, as their kitchen boasted not a pot or pan, nor even more basically, a stove.

Following lunch on the first day, Sister Felicitas went shopping with the intent of purchasing furniture for the convent. But her Germanic background triumphed and she returned from her shopping tour with buckets, scrubbing brushes, and soap. Immediately the sisters set about cleaning the paint-spattered windows and floors. When the Mullers (Sister Walburga's family) arrived in the mid-afternoon with refreshments for the weary sisters, the versatile buckets were put to new use. Inverted, they could be utilized as stools. A week later, installation of the kitchen stove prompted Mother Felicitas to announce to the pastor that the Sisters would no longer trespass upon his hospitality for meals.

The next day was August 4, Saint Dominic's Day. "After Mass, in accordance with the pastor's expressed wish, a great number of parishioners visited the Sisters to extend a welcome and to assure them of their cooperation in the new work they were about to begin." [33] By the time the last well-meaning visitor had left, the sisters, who had had nothing to eat or drink that morning, sat down to dry bread and black tea, as the pantry shelves were bare. Towards evening Father Harnett was inspired to send over bacon and eggs for the next morning's breakfast, but the demands of the moment triumphed over the exigencies of the morrow, and the pastor's gift provided the sisters with their Saint Dominic's Day dinner! The convent annalist's comment on the occasion speaks for itself: "Thus passed slowly the first Saint Dominic's Day at the Sacred Heart."[34]

Sister Seraphina, appointed first superior and principal of the new mission, arrived a few days later with Sisters Augustina O'Connor and Agnes Mulligan as teaching staff and Sister Victoria Kine as convent cook and housekeeper. Wasting no time, the sisters began teaching catechism in the parish even before school opened. Forty-two children responded to the sisters' invitation.

School opened on September 1 with sixty pupils, aged four to nineteen, and three music students. Tuition was set at one dollar per month, with an increase of fifty cents for each additional child from the same family. Needy children were admitted tuition-free. For the more affluent, music lessons were offered at $5.00 per month for two one-hour sessions weekly. Despite financial challenges the school prospered, and by late October boasted an enrollment of 115, with an almost equal breakdown of 58 boys and 57 girls.

The curriculum was ambitious. In addition to religion and the basic subjects, classes included German, elocution, music, orchestra and art. Toward the end of the first month of school, the children sang hymns during Mass in Sacred Heart Church and on December 8 a *Missa cantata*, a liturgical feat of some accomplishment for children who had had no previous introduction to Gregorian Chant.

"Dedication of the school by His Lordship, Bishop Francis Mora, took place today [September 14]," recorded the annalist. "At 4 p.m. Vespers were sung, after which Reverend A. Meyer, C.M., [president of St. Vincent's College, Los Angeles] spoke of the necessity of parochial schools under the direction of religious."[35] Benediction of the Blessed Sacrament followed. Then, led by cross-bearer and acolytes, a long procession of children and sisters, parents and friends, members of the clergy and, last of all, Bishop Mora, filed from the church to the school for the blessing. Unwilling to let the opportunity slip by, Father Harnett ordered a collection taken up during Vespers for the benefit of the school. A total of $31.15 was realized.

In San Francisco, Mother Pia's thoughts turned southward many times that day: "Dedication of Sacred Heart School today," she wrote in the Diary "...Who could have thought nineteen years ago on the day when I was clothed in the holy habit, that on its anniversary my favorite convent should be dedicated."[36]

Two days later Sacred Heart's happy annalist wrote: "A most happy day!!! Our divine Lord deigned to enter the humble dwelling-place which we had prepared for Him in our little chapel. The first Mass in this house was said this morning at 6 a.m. by the Rev. P. Harnett. The Sisters received Holy Communion. Happy day! Happy Sisters!!!"[37]

The first year closed on July 1, 1891, with commencement exercises in the church basement. A number of parents, friends and clergy attended the program, which included the traditional exhibition and distribution of premiums (medals) by the Vicar General, Monsignor Joachim Adams. "Very successful,"[38] noted the annalist, summing up the afternoon with admirable brevity.

Father Harnett was more profuse. In a letter addressed to Mother Pia on July 4, he evaluated the year.

> The first year of our school's existence has passed. It is but right that I inform you that I am pleased with what has been accomplished. I examined the children myself and noticed a decided improvement since the Xmas examinations. The temporal remuneration of the poor Sisters—if estimated in gold coin—is little (if any); but I can assure you that they by their painstaking kindness have endeared themselves to the children and their parents and (needless to say so) to their unfortunate (fortunate rather because of the good Sisters that divine Providence sent him) pastor.
>
> ...I sincerely hope that you will find it possible and convenient to leave us our Sisters for the coming year. I do not believe that it will be for the interests of our school that changes be made. Our people in Los Angeles are peculiarly disposed, and as the children are not as yet well weaned from the public schools, it is necessary that they have attractions which strange Sisters cannot at this time easily supply.[39]

In the same letter Father Harnett predicted an enrollment of 150 to 175 children for the second year. "It is perhaps well," he concluded, "that you know this since such an increase would necessitate the occupancy of a third school room." Father's diplomatic appraisal alerting Mother Pia of the need for an additional teacher.[40]

By the end of the first year Sacred Heart's reputation had spread as far as northern California, for on July 22, 1891 *The Monitor* [San Francisco], reported:

> This institution [Sacred Heart] has just closed its first yearly term and has met with wonderful success, considering its youth. Commencing with just sixty pupils, it gradually grew in favor until now just twice that number are on the rolls.

> This school, besides being the parochial school for East Los Angeles, is also the nearest Catholic school to which parents can send their children from all points between Los Angeles and Pasadena. The... Sisters have succeeded in making special arrangement with the railroad companies by which scholars are conveyed from Glendale, Garvanza and other outside places for a very small charge.[41]

The publicity, unfortunately, did not fully reflect the true state of affairs. Although in 1892 a boarding school was added, the shortage of funds continued a constant threat. Six years later, the annalist was still describing the sisters walking the streets of East Los Angeles in extreme, record-breaking summer heat to interview parents regarding the enrollment of their children in the parish school. It was not an easy task, as Sacred Heart Parish covered an expanse that eventually became seven parishes! In addition, the sisters wore long woolen habits, serge mantles and stiffly starched veils. Streets were unpaved and dust prevailed. But these women were undaunted, and in the surrounding hills they found many who had abandoned their faith and were living in extreme poverty. Return visits were often required, but in the end the sisters' missionary endeavors paid off: and September brought an enrollment of 212 pupils and the return of several lapsed Catholics to the Church.

Now a new problem faced the sisters—parental grumbling and threats of withdrawal because of overcrowded classrooms. By way of solution, the sisters purchased at Christmas a cottage on Baldwin Street and outfitted it as a kindergarten; the addition, which opened on January 3, put an end to the criticism.

At the General Chapter of the Congregation held in the summer of 1900, Sacred Heart Convent was raised to a priory. Sister Patricia McSweeney was named first prioress, with Sister Dolorosa Wallrath as sub-prioress and Sister Clara Irwin as bursar.

In September of the following year, the sisters surrendered their community room to accommodate the influx of boarders. Enrollment, now at an all-time high of 241 pupils and 40 music pupils (26 piano and 14 violin and mandolin students), accounted for the move.

At the end of the school year, the sisters rented a cottage in Santa Monica for a month and went in shifts for a vacation at the beach. The "lucky seven" vacationers in the second week of July 1902 enjoyed a day also as guests of the Sisters of the Holy Names in their summer cottage in Santa Monica Canyon; the annalist records that the sisters "furnished a fine bus and provided a bountiful luncheon"[42] for their guests. Months' end, the last group of vacationers returned to Sacred Heart, tanned and rested. The only disagreeable feature, they agreed, were the sand fleas by day and by night!

Plans for a new building were submitted to Mr. Isidore Dockweiler, the community lawyer, who informed Sister Alberta Hocker she would be required to appear in court to declare that the $15,000 she wished to borrow would be used for building and improvements only. The legalities completed, work on the addition began on August 7, 1902. It was ready for occupancy on December 2, 1902. In December, also, the old school, built 12 years previously, was moved to its designated location behind the new building and attached to it.

Oral examinations, held at the close of the school year, were attended by the pastor, Father Michael McAuliffe, who pronounced himself well satisfied with the children's progress. And at the closing exercises held in the Y.M.I. Building, the hall was crowded, despite the fact that they were held at 10 a.m. to accommodate Bishop Montgomery's schedule.

Word from Rome (1903) brought news of the appointment of Bishop George Montgomery as the new Archbishop of San Francisco. Bishop-elect Thomas J. Conaty, who had just completed a six-year term as rector of the Catholic University of America, Washington, D.C., was his replacement. At Bishop Conaty's impressive installation ceremony on June 18, Sisters Alberta Hocker and Antonina Tschirner represented Sacred Heart. A week later, the school was privileged to welcome Bishop Conaty in person. Following a short program, the bishop spoke to the pupils and made the eagerly anticipated announcement of a school holiday! He then visited the sisters in the convent.

At the closing exercises held that year (June 23, 1903), Leo Dazé, brother of Sister Stanislaus (Bernadette) Dazé, enjoyed the distinction of being the first boy to graduate from Sacred Heart Elementary School. Pleased that a boy had finished the eighth grade, Father McAuliffe encouraged the sisters to keep the older boys until they had completed grammar school. Although it was not considered proper at the time for women to teach boys beyond the sixth grade, Father McAuliffe did not approve the custom of dismissing boys at so youthful an age for the purpose of seeking employment.

On July 3 Sacred Heart's boarders were placed under quarantine because of an outbreak of diphtheria. Despite the loving care of the sisters, little Sadie Matheson, one of the youngest children enrolled, died after a short illness. Sadie was baptized on her deathbed by Sister Bonaventura LaCroix. The following January the school was again obliged to suffer quarantine because of a recurrence of the disease; this time Sister Antonia Callahan was the victim. While the school was still closed, Sister Wilhelmina Maas, who had been suffering for some time from a lung ailment, died at Sacred Heart Convent. Because of the quarantine, services had to be held privately and only one carriage of mourners, containing four sisters, was permitted to follow the hearse to the cemetery. It was a sad cortege.

The following year (May 1, 1904) Sacred Heart's annalist wrote of the large First Communion ceremonies. Sixty-nine children received the Lord for the first time. After Mass the children were served a "bountiful breakfast" in the convent. First Communion pictures concluded the program.

Beginning in 1907, a ninth grade was added to the course of studies and four classrooms and a dining room were completed in time to provide for the enrollment increase to 370 pupils. The school day was shortened when dismissal was set at 3:00 p.m. instead of the customary 3:30 p.m.

In 1923, Monsignor Patrick Donohoe, pastor, erected a new school building and secured the services of the Christian Brothers to teach the boys from the sixth to the ninth grades. After three years the Brothers withdrew in order to open Cathedral, a college preparatory high school for boys on nearby Bishops Road. Sacred Heart upper-grade boys were again taught by the sisters.

Through the years eighth grade boys were frequent recipients of four-year scholarships to Loyola or Cathedral High Schools. The school proved a fertile source of vocations, and the number of boys who went to the seminary after elementary school made the church a favorite site for First Masses. Sacred Heart's Boys Choir, under the direction of Sister Mary Dominic Engelhard, was in popular demand to sing for the occasions, as well as for evening services. The boys were often heard also on the radio.

On January 2, 1934, the sisters rejoiced when "their boy," Father Robert Lucey, was named Bishop of Amarillo, Texas. A 1905 graduate of the elementary school, he had been a pupil of Mother Seraphina, and in May he offered Mass for her and his other teachers in the sisters' chapel.

Sacred Heart's first class, the Class of 1890, held its 45th reunion at the school on December 12, 1935. The Honorable Judge Thomas White, a member of the first group, was guest speaker. Present also were Mrs. Esther West and her brother, who were honored as the first pupils to register when Sacred Heart opened.

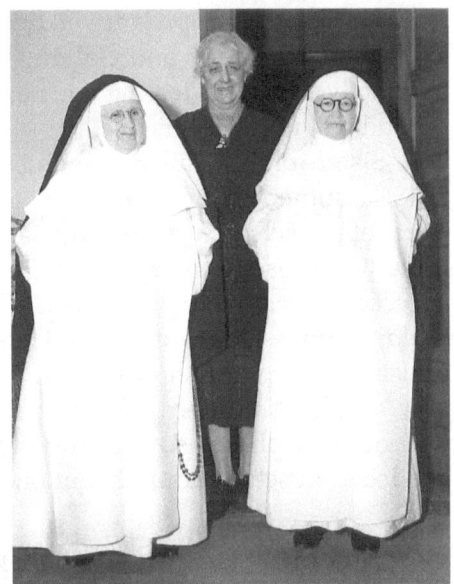

Mother Seraphina Maerz (left) and Sister Augustina O'Connor with first Sacred Heart student, Mrs. Lazier West, 1935

On February, 1938, the unwelcome sign warning of scarlet fever went up on the doors of the school. Responsible for the quarantine was the babies' dormitory. Following the confinement, the convent annalist observed that "Sister Dominica [Klein] would hardly mind prison after being confined to the dormitory with four of the little ones for ten days."[43]

On Thanksgiving Day, November, 21, 1940, Sacred Heart celebrated the Golden Jubilee of the sisters' arrival in Los Angeles. Celebrant of the Solemn High Mass was Monsignor George Donohoe, assisted by Father Patrick Donohoe, pastor of St. Ignatius Parish, and Father Henry Gross, assistant at Sacred Heart. Monsignor John McCarthy of Pasadena preached. The church was crowded to the doors with clergy, sisters and friends. A reception after the Mass was followed by a buffet luncheon for the visiting sisters. In the afternoon Archbishop Cantwell gave solemn Benediction, assisted by Fathers Hourihan and Galvin. The next day the annalist stated succinctly, but with feeling for her sisters: "November 22—Clean up and rest up for everyone."[44]

Sister John Dominic Samaha, appointed principal in August, 1948, assumed responsibility at a time when enrollment in the elementary school was usually around 535, but in the space of three years rose to its highest peak—671. Sister Mary Helen Bauer succeeded as principal in 1959. When civic officials declared the building unsafe for occupancy (1961), Father John Curran, pastor, appealed to his parishioners, and together they raised funds for a new school. A modern one-story brick building of 12 classrooms was built in phases so that the old classrooms could be used as needed, and school could begin on schedule in September, 1961.

Sacred Heart Academy/High School, Los Angeles

In 1907 Sacred Heart Academy opened as a boarding and day high school for girls, with Sister Alberta Hocker as principal. One of the first Catholic girls' secondary schools in the diocese, Sacred Heart Academy was the culmination of Father McAuliffe's ambitions for the girls of his parish. The first graduating class (1911) numbered a total of eight students. While the organ pealed jubilantly, the graduates marched with dignity up the church aisle, leaving wide spaces between them to make their moment of triumph last longer. Following graduation, four students entered the State Normal School and proved so well-prepared that the academy was given temporary accreditation the same year and official accreditation, the next. Four years later when the University of California was recognized as the official agency of accreditation for California, Sacred Heart's status was renewed on the record of fine academic work of its graduates.

But despite the recognition of academic proficiency, all was not well. That same year the Los Angeles Chief Inspector of Buildings notified the sisters that Sacred Heart School was not properly equipped in the event of fire. Sister Alberta took advantage of the warning to petition the Motherhouse for permission, not merely to purchase additional fire extinguishers and hoses, but also to build a new wing! Both permissions were granted and the school wing was completed in 1913.

When school opened in September 1916, the academy announced the addition of a business course consisting of shorthand and typing for juniors and seniors. The course supplemented the academic curriculum and was scheduled daily from 10:30 a.m. to 11:45 a.m.

Meanwhile, the academy had begun a series of trophy-garnering in the annual Los Angeles Fire Prevention Week activities. Three students were invited to read their essays over the radio, and the Fire Department sent a freshman's poster to New York for display at the National Fire Prevention Exhibition. There were other honors as well. In the annual Apologetic Oratorical Contest held at Immaculate Heart College, junior Lillian Nasef won the loving cup for her 10-minute talk on "Leadership of Catholic Youth in Preventing Juvenile Delinquency" and three-minute spontaneous talk on "Following Christ." An academy student also won Honorable Mention in the German contest sponsored by Stanford University. Unfortunately, competitive sports fared less gloriously. A volleyball game with Catholic Girls High resulted in the devastating score of 21 to 4, and although basketball fared better, Sacred Heart Comets were still on the losing side—St. Agnes, 14, and Sacred Heart, 4.

Left shepherdless since the death of Bishop Conaty in 1915, the Diocese of Monterey-Los Angeles received word from Rome of the new bishop's appointment, the Most Reverend John J. Cantwell. Bishop Cantwell's installation took place on December 12, 1916. Twenty years later, the announcement that Los Angeles was raised to an archdiocese caused ripples of excitement and general rejoicing among the Catholics of Southern California. Archbishop-elect Cantwell, the area's first archbishop was installed in the Cathedral on December 5, 1936. The day was declared a school holiday throughout the archdiocese.

World War II brought changes in the ordinary routine. On December 8, Sacred Heart experienced its first black-out and the fire department sent representatives to speak to the student body on incendiary bombs, demonstrate the use of gas masks, and give instructions on gas-tighting a room. Twenty-one sisters from Sacred Heart received certificates for completing a First Aid and Home Nursing

Course. Sacred Heart's porches took on a new look when they were outfitted with barrels of water, buckets of sand, and hoes in the event of incendiary bombs. Five Japanese seniors were sent to internment camps, three of whom were scheduled for Baptism on Holy Saturday. Classes dismissed for Christmas vacation on December 11 and resumed on December 28—an unwelcome novelty for students who went to class for the first time between Christmas and New Year's. The change in holiday schedule was intended to favor older students obtaining pre-Christmas jobs because of the work force shortage resulting from the war. Sister Jubilarians did not go to the Motherhouse in the summer to celebrate because of travel restrictions; local celebrations replaced the traditional congregational observance. Both high school and grade school held Defense Drives, buying War Bonds and Defense Stamps. The high school realized $2,697 and the grade school, $6,447.

The war barely over, Father Timothy Manning was consecrated Auxiliary Bishop of Los Angeles at St. Vibiana's Cathedral on October 15, 1946. The next day he presided at Benediction in the sisters' chapel. Members of his ordination class were present with him and renewed their vows privately before the Blessed Sacrament.

In 1945 Sacred Heart Academy, including the boarding department, was declared unsafe and ordered razed by city officials. Fundraising for a new girls' high school proved unsuccessful, and on June 4, 1947, Mother Bernardina wrote to Archbishop Cantwell apprising him of the situation.

> Most Reverend John J. Cantwell, D.D.
> Archbishop of Los Angeles
> 714 West Olympic Boulevard
> Los Angeles, California
>
> Your Excellency:
>
> For the past six years or more the problem of conducting the Sacred Heart High School has been increasing in difficulty due to the inadequacy of the facilities and the deterioration of the building. We have studied the problem of rebuilding from several angles, and the following facts have emerged:

Chapter 7 / SOUTHERN CALIFORNIA BECKONS

1. In order to make provision for the proper handling of the current enrollment it will be necessary to erect a new building and to make an addition to the convent that the replacement of the old building will necessitate. Mr. George Adams, the architect whom we consulted, is strongly opposed to the erection of any new permanent buildings on account of the changing nature of the district which is fast becoming industrialized. He advises that if the school is to remain on the present site, that some part of the existing building be salvaged and tied in with a new wing.

2. The only way that Sacred Heart High School could be maintained in the past was through the boarding school department. That has been reduced to a minimum—21 pupils—due to the encroachment of the high school upon the boarders' quarters and the prohibition by the authorities to use the attic for housing. The income from the salaries of the grammar school teachers, the high school tuition and the boarding fees is hardly sufficient to take care of the maintenance; hence, it is impossible to lay aside any amount toward a building fund. The district is an undesirable one for a girls' boarding school, but even if it were suitable, there is not enough ground for the erection of a boarding school unit.

3. The people whom Sacred Heart High School serves are not, so we have been told, in a position to subscribe the funds necessary for the erection of a building even of the nature suggested by Mr. Adams, and the religious community in charge of the school is not in a position to assume a debt, and guarantee the liquidation of such a debt within a reasonable time if at all.

4. If Sacred Heart High School is to continue to operate, something must be done soon. We are willing to continue, but we must have help to finance the undertaking. We have begun a campaign for raising a fund, but the returns are discouraging. Our alumnae and other friends advise against the erection of any building for the reasons that are urged by Mr. Adams. We humbly submit the above for the consideration of Your Excellency and await your advice.

With sincere expressions of profound respect, I am

Your Excellency's obedient servant,

Mother M. Bernardina, O.P.
Prioress General[45]

In the absence of Archbishop Cantwell who was in Ireland at the time, Auxiliary Bishop Joseph McGucken responded. He hoped to present a plan for Mother Bernardina's approval and that of the Archbishop when he returned. He acknowledged the importance of a solution "because of the large number of girls in the Sacred Heart district who need the benefits of the high school education which your Sisters are prepared to give them."[46] Bishop McGucken wrote also to Mr. George Adams, architect, asking for an estimate of the cost of bringing the existing building up to code for ongoing use.

A second letter from Bishop McGucken to Mother Bernardina raised a shocking alternative: Would the Congregation consider turning over the Sacred Heart property to the archdiocese for an archdiocesan girls' high school and under what terms? The option would update the project and relieve the congregation of an enormous debt. Initial consultation with the council revealed the members' reluctance to accept the proposal, but the fire department's prohibition had to be faced and eventually brought the Council to full support: The sisters would be willing to turn the property over by sale or lease after it had been appraised.

But George Adams was of a different mind. The City Building Department, he was sure, would not permit major alterations in the existing building because of its frame construction. Further, the Building Code permitted only one-story frame buildings; Sacred Heart was three!! Bishop McGucken, however, was still determined to keep Sacred Heart in the same district.

> While it may be true that there will be an increase in industrial establishments in the Sacred Heart area, I am inclined to think that it will be as it is at present, a district of congested population for many, many years. The present situation requires that we take care of the children in the area; the future prospects would seem to indicate that it would not be wise to undertake the enormous outlay of funds required for a new Class A school construction.

There is great apostolic work to be done in that area and the good work of the past needs to be increased rather than decreased. I agree with you that it would not be wise to think of the Community expending funds in that particular district for a boarding school. Other locations would be much better for that purpose. However, the need for a high school for girls to be continued at Sacred Heart is one that will exist, I am sure, as long as we are here to have anything to do with it.[47]

The unexpected death of Archbishop Cantwell on October 30, 1947, delayed further discussion until his successor, Archbishop J. Francis A. McIntyre of New York, was installed on March 19, 1948. In April, Mother Bernardina and Sister Louise Pfeffer, directress of schools, visited the new archbishop to discuss the future of the high school. Archbishop McIntyre was startlingly prompt in reaching a decision: the academy would become a parochial school; a new building would be erected on the same block; the convent would be relocated in the existing concrete building and enlarged; and the boarding school would close in June!

A planning meeting was scheduled at Sacred Heart. In addition to the Archbishop and the Auxiliary Bishop Timothy Manning, Monsignor Patrick Dignan, superintendent of Catholic Schools; Father Patrick Roche, assistant superintendent; Monsignor Martin McNicholas, archdiocesan consultor; Father John Curran, pastor; Mother Bernardina; Sister Louise; Sister Dolores Stopper, Sacred Heart Prioress; Sister Mary Thomas Lillis, academy principal; and Mr. George Adams were present. Definite plans were discussed, followed by a tour of the existing plant. On January 23, 1949, groundbreaking for a new high school took place, with Bishop McGucken officiating. In June the sisters living in the concrete structure moved into the old frame building in preparation for the remodeling and enlarging of the former.

At the Tenth General Chapter (July 28 to August 5, 1949), the Congregation was informed of Sacred Heart's change in status. "We announce that the property of the Sacred Heart Priory in Los Angeles has been sold to the Archdiocese of Los Angeles for a sum of $76,000. Because of the transfer of ownership, the Sacred Heart Convent has ceased to be a priory."[48]

The Chancery followed with a similar announcement: The

Sacred Heart High School and convent building (rear)

archdiocese would assume ownership of Sacred Heart High School; Father John Curran, Sacred Heart Pastor, was appointed financial manager of the school; Sister Mary Thomas Lillis, O.P., was to continue as principal. The new two-story brick building opened on schedule with a registration of 369 students and the sisters still quartered in the old frame building. Moving into the remodeled convent was scheduled to take place early in the new year, but on December 18, nature intervened. A violent winter storm flooded the lower floor of the old convent, and a new plan was implemented on the spot. A volunteer crew of sisters hauled dishes, pots and staples through the driving rain to the new kitchen. When all was transported without mishap, the exhausted haulers were rewarded with hot chocolate and cookies enjoyed on the floor in the absence of chairs—their first "meal" in the new dining room. It was a festive, though soggy, conclusion to the night's work.

The next morning breakfast was served in the new dining room, each sister arriving with a chair and making the best of missing items. Since moving had already begun the night before, the sisters spent the first day of the Christmas vacation transporting furniture to the remodeled convent. At 5 p.m. Father Curran brought the Blessed Sacrament to the chapel and celebrated Mass the next morning (December 20, 1949).

January 15, 1950, was Dedication Day. The student body assembled in Sacred Heart Church at 3 p.m., awaiting the arrival of Archbishop McIntyre. At the Archbishop's entrance, the students greeted him with "Ecce Sacerdos" and then preceded the clergy and religious to the school grounds where parents and friends awaited them. Father Vincent Molloy, Sacred Heart assistant pastor, introduced the program which began with the students' rendition of "Praise Ye the Father," directed by Sister Theophane (Marie) Lehner. Speakers for the occasion included Eleanor Grijalva, student body president; Arthur Will, County Superintendent of Charities; and Monsignor Patrick Dignan, Superintendent of Catholic Schools. After the blessing of the school and convent, Benediction was given. Tours of the school and refreshments, served to more than 1,200 guests by the Sacred Heart Elementary School Mothers' Club, concluded the afternoon.

February 17, 1950, was another memorable day for the students when Father Curran officiated at the laying of the cornerstone to the new convent addition. Enclosed were the street numbers from over the door of the old school—2108 (Sichel Street); a list of the 1949 graduates; and the names of the current year's faculty and senior class.

By 1954 enrollment had passed the 500 mark. The following year in September, Sister Mary Michael Phipps was appointed principal, and Sister Mary Martin Bush, superioress of the convent.

In 1957 Sacred Heart Parish raised funds for an auditorium, erected on the corner of Griffin Avenue and Baldwin Street. The new building, available for both elementary and high school use, permitted the latter to benefit from three additional classrooms constructed from the former social hall.

The same year and again in 1958, the sophomores held two-day bazaars to raise money for the erection of a roofed patio in the high school yard. Work on the project began in January 1958, the sophomore dads reporting for volunteer labor on Saturdays. Two chocolate drives later (1957 and 1958), the students had completely funded the enterprise, which was completed in November, 1958, and tastefully furnished with redwood tables, chairs, and benches.

In December 1961 the parish rejoiced to learn that Pope John XXIII had honored their pastor, Father Curran, by naming him a monsignor. He was invested with the title on February 11, 1962.

Monsignor Bernard Dolan read the Holy Father's letter announcing the honor. A clergy dinner, followed by a reception for the parishioners, was held in the evening.

Notes

[1] Backes 94.
[2] Backes 95.
[3] Backes 95.
[4] Backes 113.
[5] Backes 113.
[6] Anonymous, letter to Maerz, n.d.
[7] Annals of St. Catherine's Convent, 19 March 1889.
[8] *Anaheim Gazette*, 14 March 1889.
[9] *Anaheim Gazette*, 14 March 1889.
[10] Annals of St. Catherine's Convent, 4 August 1894.
[11] *The Tidings*, 26 August 1896.
[12] Annals of St. Catherine's Convent, 4 August 1894.
[13] Annals of St. Catherine's Convent, 19 September 1912.
[14] Father William E. Carr (St. Elizabeth Parish, Pasadena) quoted in Dolorosa Wallrath, O.P., diary entry for 4 May 1927.
[15] Wallrath, diary 24 May 1927.
[16] Wallrath, diary 3 June 1927.
[17] Wallrath, diary 3 June 1927.
[18] Annals of St. Catherine's Convent, 3 May 1938.
[19] Donald Montrose, et al, *The Story of a Parish: Its Priests and People* (Anaheim, CA: Saint Boniface Parish, 1961) 390.
[20] Annals of St. Catherine's Convent, 12 June 1954.

[21] Don May, *St. Catherine's Military School, 1889–1964: A Memorial Book Published on the Occasion of the Diamond Jubilee* (Anaheim, CA: St. Catherine's Parent's Guild, 1964.) 26.

[22] Annals of St. Catherine's Convent, 15 September 1957.

[23] Annals of St. Catherine's Convent, June 1958.

[24] Mary Catherine Antczak, O.P., "A History of the Schools Staffed by the Dominican Sisters of Mission San Jose, 1945–1982" (Thesis: Loyola Marymount University, 1985) 116.

[25] Mary Kevin Breen, O.P., "The Educational Work of the Sisters of Saint Dominic Queen of the Holy Rosary" (Thesis: Catholic University of America, 1946) 37.

[26] Backes 124.

[27] Backes 124.

[28] Backes 124.

[29] Backes 125.

[30] Backes 125.

[31] Backes 125.

[32] Weiss, "Memoirs," 27 July 1890.

[33] Weiss, "Memoirs," 4 August 1890.

[34] Annals of Sacred Heart Convent, 4 August 1890.

[35] Annals of Sacred Heart Convent, 14 September 1890.

[36] Backes 129.

[37] Annals of Sacred Heart Convent, 16 September 1890.

[38] Annals of Sacred Heart Convent, 1 July 1891.

[39] Patrick Harnett, letter to Backes, 4 July 1891.

[40] Harnett, letter to Backes, 4 July 1891.

[41] *The Monitor*, 22 July 1891.

[42] Annals of Sacred Heart Convent, February 1938.

[43] Annals of Sacred Heart Convent, 22 November 1940.

[44] Annals of Sacred Heart Convent, 22 November 1940.

45 Bernardina Michel, letter to Cantwell, 4 June 1947.
46 Joseph McGucken, letter to Michel, 6 June 1947.
47 McGucken, letter to Michel, 28 June 1947.
48 "Acts of the Tenth General Chapter," July 28—August 5, 1949.

CHAPTER EIGHT

AFFILIATION TO THE ORDER

Realist that she was, Mother Pia recognized with growing uneasiness the contradiction inherent in Dominican nuns of the Second Order compelled by circumstances to live as Third Order religious. Neither the rigorous fasts prescribed for the Order nor the rule of strict cloister could be observed by a community whose principal apostolate was education, and the inconsistency of interviewing parents through a grating when they called at the convent and meeting them face to face when they came to the classroom was awkward at best. In addition, the hapless grating had come under negative clerical and episcopal scrutiny. "Bishop Mora of Los Angeles came accompanied by his Vicar General, Father Adams, and another priest," wrote Mother Pia in the Diary. "... I was obliged to listen to another criticism on our grating in the parlor."[1]

Advice from Racine

From the Catholic Directory, she learned that the Dominican Sisters of Racine, Wisconsin, were affiliated to the Order as a Third Order congregation. Never one to hesitate in asking for information when she needed it, Mother Pia wrote to Mother Hyacintha Oberbrunner, Racine Prioress General, in November 1888, inquiring into the process of affiliation and its advantages, the need of the Ordinary's permission for the step, and the jurisdiction of the Archbishop in the event of affiliation occurring. A month later she wrote again, expressing gratitude for the information received and acknowledging that it had cleared up her difficulties.

The sequence of correspondence between Mother Hyacintha and Mother Pia regarding affiliation raises a question. Mission San Jose Archives contain no response from Mother Hyacintha to Mother Pia's first inquiry, although the latter thanks for the information received (December 3, 1888), and at the time of Mother Hyacintha's lengthy response, Mother Pia had already written to Rome (See Diary, October 30, 1889) requesting affiliation.

Regardless of the problem presented by dates, Mother Hyacintha's reply is a model of clarity and merits inclusion here:

> Racine, December 31, 1889
>
> Dear good Reverend Mother Pia:
>
> Read your letter of the twelfth of this month. Kindly excuse my delay in answering your letter. I was anxious to write details and was unable to find time before Christmas....
>
> Your inquiry regarding affiliation necessitates a long explanation. Our Convent became affiliated with the Dominican Order as early as 1877 as a convent of the Third Order and through J. Sanvito, at that time Master General. More than this cannot be claimed by the Sisters of our Order who are engaged in the schools, especially if they have charge of institutions and orphanages. The Second Order cannot dispense with the strict canonical enclosure. This enclosure forbids under penalty of excommunication travel under any pretext whatsoever. All visits, moreover, from externs are forbidden; and only a limited number of members may be received. Under these circumstances what would we be able to do and how could we obtain our livelihood? For a long time we were confused about the conditions and, like many other Dominican Communities in this country, considered ourselves Sisters of the Second Order. Our confessor, who for many years was professor of Canon Law, called our attention to this mistaken view of ours, and pointed out that we were not members of the Second Order and could not hope ever to be such, because we would never be able to observe strict enclosure. He told us, moreover, that if we desired to be members of the

Dominican Order, we would have to be affiliated with the Order; that is, that our Convent must be recognized as Dominican by the Master General. Dominican Fathers, as well as secular priests who are well informed in this matter, agreed with our Reverend Confessor.

We then applied to the Master General, who confirmed Father Birkhaeuser's statement. He wrote as follows: "Since you are unable to observe strict enclosure and other regulations of holy Mother Church which are incompatible with your life, you cannot possibly be affiliated as a community of the Second Order, but only as a Congregation of the Third Order of the Militia of Jesus Christ, and of the Order of Penance of St. Dominic, in which you will, however, have nearly all the graces, privileges, and indulgences which Rome has granted to members of the Second Order."

His answer clearly indicated that we could only become Dominicans by becoming affiliated with the Third Order and that bishops and priests did not have the power of admitting members into the Order unless they were especially or particularly empowered to do so. What were we to do? We had no choice, but to accept the advice of our confessor and the offer made by the Master General.

Since then we have the assurance of really belonging to the Order and of really being Dominicans. We have a quiet conscience and are happy. Don't hesitate to follow our example. Remember that the privilege and spiritual advantages of the Third Order are scarcely less than those of the Second. Besides, as members of the Third Order you have the privilege of following your good judgment in the circumstances that arise. Simple affiliation in the Third Order does not satisfy us, however. We strive after higher things. We want the approval of our Congregation by Rome, because if a congregation is not recognized by Rome, it is simply an episcopal association and depends in every respect upon the bishop of the diocese, who has full charge of the Sisters, and can act at will in their regard. It is, moreover, of greatest importance to have a Rule designed for our special circumstances and approved by the Holy

See. Our Father Confessor went to Rome last year in the interests of this matter. He called on the Master General and was minutely instructed by him. Among other things he was told that we must discontinue the large Breviary, and content ourselves with the recitation of the Marianum, that the Breviary was intended for the Sisters of strict enclosure only. The strict fast and abstinence of the Order was declared incompatible with the duties of Sisters engaged in teaching.

....The matter is so important for all of us. No doubt I have surprised you by the contents of this letter, but I hope that I will convince you of the necessity of affiliating with Rome, for we can get help from no one else—neither bishop nor priest. If we do our part, God will supply that which is missing.

If I can be of service to you in any other respect, I shall be happy to do all that I can for you. Let us hear from you again....

With heartfelt greetings,

Mother M. Hyacintha, O.S.D.[2]

Although by personality and formation the cloister was her predilection, Mother Pia faced the issue squarely. The time had come for her to seek Third Order affiliation, and sometime in October 1889 she wrote to the Master General, the Most Reverend Joseph Marie Larroca, O.P., in Rome, requesting affiliation as a Third Order congregation. Failing to receive a reply, she petitioned a second time on January 9, 1890, this time meeting with success. On February 14, the Document of Affiliation, dated January 28, 1890, arrived from the Generalate at Santa Sabina. The Foundress received it with mixed emotions, none of which was enthusiasm. She assuaged her feelings by envisioning the establishment of a Second Order branch sometime in the future. "On account of our activities here in America, we cannot belong to the Second Order," she wrote, "therefore, we have been affiliated to the Third Order. My ardent desire is, later, to combine a branch of the Second Order to the Third....I hope with God's help to accomplish this before I die."[3]

Though the desire for a Second Order branch continued to surface at intervals in Mother Pia's Diary and letters, such never became a reality within the Congregation. The principal obstacle was undoubtedly Archbishop Riordan's failure to approve the idea, but there were other contributing factors as well. The Foundress was too much taken at the time with founding mission houses, training novices, revising *Constitutions*, and resolving financial problems to give consistent attention to a Second Order project. There is in the Diary and letters a preoccupation with the need to establish the young community on a secure and thoroughly Dominican foundation before her death that is not without warrant in view of her chronic ill health.

Since the Minutes of General Council meetings begin only in 1900, no record of the Council's views on the subject of affiliation is available, but it seems reasonable to hazard an opinion that the majority of the members were in agreement regarding the change. What does appear odd is the fact that no record of consultation with the sisters at large regarding Third Order status is extant. It seems highly unlikely that all the members of the Congregation would be in accord with the decision, even though they were already living pretty much a Third Order lifestyle. The explanation may lie in the fact that early records are spotty at best. In any case, the changeover seems to have been remarkably calm.

Elections and General Chapters

In 1881, 1891, and 1894, at meetings called simply "elections," Mother Pia was elected "prioress of the Dominican Sisters of the Convent of the Immaculate Conception"[4] by all but one vote—her own, presumably. No mention is made of who served as electresses or how they were chosen. The 1891 election was witnessed by Father Eugene Puers, O.S.F., as representative of the Archbishop, with Sister Seraphina Maerz, O.S.D., and Sister Amanda Bednartz, O.S.D., as scrutineers, and confirmed by Archbishop P.W. Riordan. The 1894 election was witnessed by Father Leo Bruener, O.S.F., as the Archbishop's delegate and Sisters Seraphina and Amanda again acting as scrutineers. At the latter election the term of the prioress was recorded as six years, with no explanation for the three-year extension.

On July 20, 1896, the Diary noted that a General Chapter was convoked for the first time and important affairs were decided. Whatever happened to this Chapter remains a mystery, as there is no further mention made of it, nor is it reckoned among the General Chapters of the Congregation. Since it was only two years into Mother Pia's term as Prioress, it could hardly have been a Chapter of Elections.

At the election of 1900, affairs began to take a more formal turn. Sister Pia was elected first Prioress General of the Congregation, following a *tractatus* or period of reflection:

> San Francisco, Cal., August 2, 1900
>
> I, the undersigned, Father John Pius Murphy of the Order of St. Dominic, being appointed in absence of His Grace, the Mt. Rev. P. W. Riordan, Archbishop of San Francisco, California, by the Vicar General, Very Rev. Prendergast, to preside as Delegate, at the election of the first prioress General of the American Congregation of the Queen of the Holy Rosary, hereby certify, that after a previous *Tractatus* having been held, all the electresses assembled to the No. of (33). Sister Maria Pia Backes was elected (32) voices by secret suffrage, August 2, A.D. 1900, as the First Prioress General of the above mentioned Congregation for six (6) years.
>
> In witness whereof I have set my name and affixed the seal of the aforesaid Congregation, this second day of August A.D. 1900.
>
> Fr. John Pius Murphy, O.P.,
> Delegate of His Grace the Mt. Rev. P. W. Riordan
> Archbishop of San Francisco
>
> Approved
> P.W. Riordan
>
> Sr. Maria Amanda Bednartz
> Sr. Maria Felicitas Breitenbach [Weiss] } Scrutineers
> Sr. Maria Salesia Fichtner

Accepted, August 2, 1900 at 4:45 p.m.

Sr. M. Pia Backes
Sr. Marie Gonzaga Buehler   } Witnesses
Sr. Maria Bernardina Michel[5]

Except for the above document confirming the election of Mother Pia Backes as Prioress General (hitherto she had been designated prioress), the Congregational Archives contain little regarding this Chapter, nor does Mother Pia's Diary shed much additional light:

> Mass in honor of the Holy Ghost. Mother Gonzaga arranged everything for the election.

> Father Pius [Murphy], O.P. arrived shortly after 9 a.m. Voting passed off quietly. Announcement of the result was made in the chapter hall and again in the chapel. There were thirty-three vocals. In the afternoon the members of the General Chapter were photographed. In the evening an entertainment in honor of my silver jubilee of superiorship. Father Pius, O.P., presented a set of silverware, playing on spoons presented by Saint Dominic to his daughters.[6]

Insight into one piece of business effected by the Chapter is available, however, courtesy of St. Catherine's annalist. Written only a few days after the conclusion of the meeting, the annals announced: "This convent has now been raised to a Priory. Sister Raymunda [Wilson] is the Prioress, and Sister Ambrosia [Niedermeyer],[7] the Sub-prioress." St. Dominic's, Portland, and Sacred Heart, Los Angeles, were probably raised to the status of priories at this Chapter also, for from that time, annalists of the two convents use the term "prioress" when referring to their respective superiors.

The first and only Chapter of the Congregation designated "intermediate" (until the series of chapters updating the *Constitutions* in the 1960s) was held in Mission San Jose, July 23–25, 1903. Since there are no formal Acts extant, but only a series of "Regulations" covering such items as uniformity of clothing patterns, the quality of food served both sisters and children, restriction of newspapers to superiors who were permitted to read certain "useful" items to the sisters, and the non-use of surnames ("At our reception into the

Congregation, we voluntarily assumed a new name in order to forget the world and our families."),[8] one is led to wonder why such a Chapter was convoked, as such items could have been covered in a letter. But the *General Council Register* records that the initial business accomplished was the appointment of a General Council: Sisters Seraphina Maerz, Felicitas Weiss, Salesia Fichtner, and Sisters Raymunda Wilson, Bernardina Michel, and Sister Alberta Hocker, Bursar General. The register also referred to "various ordinances for the welfare of the Congregation [which] were framed and adopted after being voted for by the Chapter....[That were] placed in the hands of the Most Reverend Archbishop, August 3, 1903, [who] returned his approval and remarks in a communication of the same date."[9]

At the Third General Chapter of the Congregation (1912), the delegates decided that members of the General Council would be entitled "Mother" for the period of their incumbency. The succeeding Chapter (1918), however, must have experienced a change of heart. The title, "Mother," was reserved for the prioress general "in office" and the foundresses of the Congregation "for life." (Presumably, the delegates wished the title bestowed on the seven volunteers from New York.) An exception to the rule was Mother Dolorosa Wallrath, who was neither prioress general nor foundress, but who went to her grave as "Mother" at the designation of the sisters.

Papal Approval: The Journey Begins

Since their arrival in California, the sisters had been following the *Constitutions* brought with them from Brooklyn, that is, the *Constitutions* of the Second Order Dominicans as observed in Ratisbon. This Rule had been written by Blessed Humbert de Romans, fifth Master General of the Order (1254–1263), and updated in 1847 in conformity with current ecclesiastical legislation.

Separation from Brooklyn had given rise to a number of challenges for Mother Pia. Among them the writing of new *Constitutions* adapted to the Third Order and meeting conditions in the West was a priority. The task would consume a considerable portion of the young superior's time and energy and over the next several years would become a focus of her prayer.

In preparation for her task, Mother Pia devoted whatever time she could spare from her other duties to a study of the spirit and traditions of the Dominican Third Order and wrote to other Dominican communities of women, e.g., Racine, Wisconsin; Speyer, Germany; Benicia (San Rafael), California; and Stone, England, requesting copies of their *Constitutions* for study.

Mother Hyacintha's detailed and encouraging letter had provided the impetus for Mother Pia to seek papal approval for the Congregation. With papal approbation neither the bishop nor the general chapter could alter the *Constitutions* except under the provisions set forth in the document itself, and a new foundation needed only the consent of the Ordinary in whose diocese it was to be erected. Mother Pia had a tremendous love for the Church, and her loyalty to the Holy Father was beyond question. But on occasion she had problems with individual churchmen. A case in point was Archbishop Riordan's wish to interview applicants before approving their acceptance as postulants. Mother Pia was of a different mind, and Mother Cunigunda Schell's shocked reaction to the Archbishop's request, calling it "an unheard of arrogance,"[10] confirmed Mother Pia in her thinking. It was time, she decided, to seek papal approbation, even though it would be a far more complicated and drawn-out process.

Canon Law current at the time decreed three steps in the process of papal approval of a religious institute:
1. the Decree of Praise
2. the Approval of the Institute, and
3. the Approval of the *Constitutions*

Each step entailed the submission of specified documents to the Holy See. The first, "The Decree of Praise," required a petition to the Holy Father signed by the Superior General and her Council; testimonial letters from the bishops of the dioceses in which the Congregation had convents; a report from the Superior General and her Council giving the origin of the community, personnel statistics, economic status, account of the novitiate; and the examination of the *Constitutions* by the bishop/archbishop in whose diocese the Motherhouse was located.

After a specified length of time (seven to ten years), all conditions having been met and verified by the bishops in whose dioceses the Congregation was represented, the Congregation was eligible

192 SEED & GROWTH

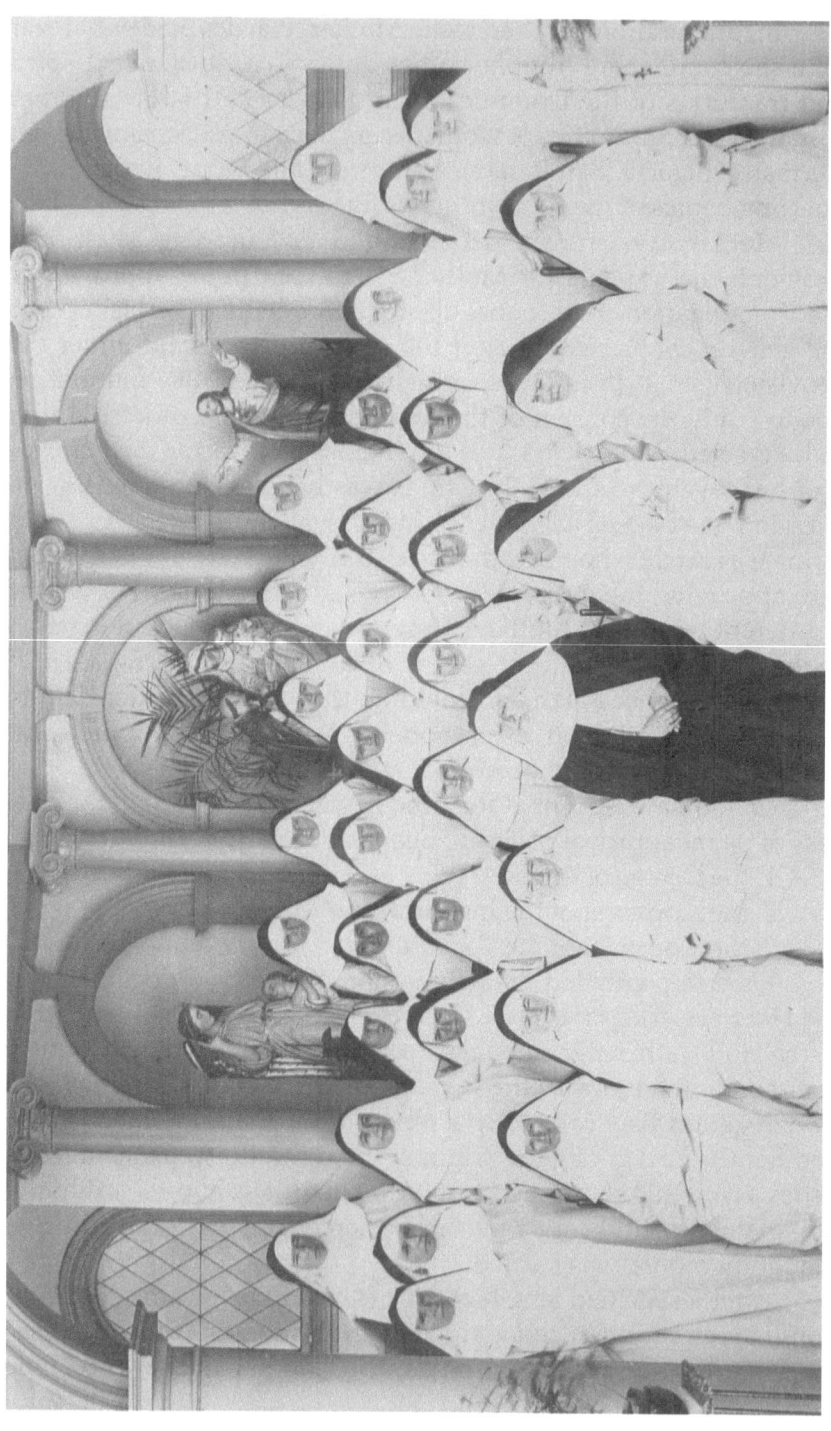

Members of the General Chapter 1900

(l to r) *front row*: Sisters Agnes Mulligan, Gonzaga Buehler, Amanda Bednartz, Maria Pia Backes, Salesia Fichtner, Felicitas Weiss, Columba Hagan;

second row: (standing) Alberta Hocker, Dominican Klein, Dolorosa Wallrath, (seated) Scholastica Kroutsch, Benedicta Kroutsch, Petrina Wiemand, Antonia Callahan, Hyacintha Holl, Innocentia Irving, (standing) Vincentia Powers, Thomasina Brueggen, Aegidia Borgemeister;

third row: Jordana Kneusel, Antonina Tschirner, Agatha Watts, Augustina O'Connor, Bernarda Hornung, Bernardina Michel, Regina Konigsberger, Imelda Meyer, and Evangelista Grisez;

back row: Bonaventura LaCroix, Ludovika Schumacher, Celestina Brandmeier, Clara Irwin, and Patricia McSweeney.

to receive "The Approval of the Institute." The conditions requiring verification included faithful observance of the *Constitutions,* proper discipline, zeal of members, and prudence of superiors.

For the final step, "Approval of the *Constitutions,*" a petition signed by the Superior General and her Council, testimonial letters from the Ordinaries of the dioceses in which the Congregation was represented, and a copy of the *Constitutions* sent again to the Congregation for Religious for approval were required.

Beginning in 1888, entries regarding work on the *Constitutions* run like a thread through the Diary, though with sometimes lengthy gaps at times between items. But finally, in mid-1894, Mother Pia was ready to write to Archbishop Riordan for the required permission to adapt the Second Order *Constitutions* to the Congregation's current needs.

> Most Reverend Archbishop,
>
> I have several points to put before Your Grace in reference to the *Constitutions* which we have until the present *tried* to observe. I said tried, for the work we have to perform as teachers is not at all in accordance with the *Constitutions* of the Second Order of Dominicans whose object is more the contemplative life. Besides, strict enclosure and almost constant fasting are required by it, the former of which, as Your Grace well knows, we cannot keep and the latter is just as impossible.
>
> Now, for a long time I have been desirous of having matters arranged in such a way that we will be able to keep our *Constitutions* strictly and not be under the necessity of making constant use of dispensation.
>
> In the year 1874, the Holy See approved a constitution which Rev. F. [Henri] Lacordaire, O.P., had adapted for the teaching Sisters of the Third Order of St. Dominic in France. Our Sisters in Germany and a Province in America have already adopted this *Constitution* and they have sent me copies of it and say that it is satisfactory in every way. I applied to the Rev. F. General of the Order about the matter and was advised by him to adopt this *Constitution* for our congregation.
>
> Several points must be changed in order to make it suit the

needs of a country like America. Later on we will put these changes before you for approval. I have placed this matter before the Council and they have *all* given their consent.

I therefore humbly beg Your Grace to give your approval to the proposed change and also to give us permission to translate the Rule and *Constitutions* into the English Language.

Humbly asking Your Grace's blessing for the Community, I am most respectfully

Your Grace's obedient spiritual child,

Sister M. Pia[11]

The following month (July 9, 1894) the first draft of the revised *Constitutions* was ready for typing. By November it was finished and prepared for submission to the Archbishop for approbation and permission to print. Although he assured Mother Pia verbally that the revision was good (December 9, 1894), his letter of approval did not arrive until May 6, 1895, the day he was leaving for Rome. Meantime, the document had been misplaced in the Chancery Office! Presumably this was the sole typed copy, for the community immediately began a frantic novena to Saint Anthony for its reappearance. Recovery brought rejoicing, and the *Constitutions* went to press!

A "notice" preceding the printed edition acknowledged that the first part of the document is a translation from the German of the *Constitutions:*

> ...used by the Sisters at Speyer and approved by the Holy See, August 14, 1874. The second part is chiefly taken from the *Constitutions* approved by the Holy See for the Sisters at Stone, England...With permission of Most Reverend Andrew Fruewirth, Master General of the Order of Preachers, and His Grace, the Most Rev. P. W. Riordan, Archbishop of San Francisco, we have made such changes and alterations as were found necessary to suit the existing conditions in America.

The body of *Constitutions* thus drawn up, having been accepted by the Chapter, was submitted to the Most Rev. Archbishop P.W. Riordan who approved them on the 1st day of May, 1895.

At the same time His Grace allowed that the *Constitutions* so approved should be printed and distributed among the Sisters, until such time as they should receive the approbation of the Holy See.[12]

It was the hope of the "Prologue," which followed,

...that the sisters who live under one Rule, and are bound by vow to one profession, should be uniform also in all observances of Religion in order that the outward uniformity of our practice may both represent and maintain the inward unity which should exist in our hearts.

Now this uniformity will doubtless be more easily and more perfectly observed if everything that ought to be done be committed to writing, that all may know by means of what is written, how they ought to live....

In order to provide the better for the unity and peace of the Sisters, we have written this book, which is called the *Constitutions*.[13]

On the feast of Saint Dominic, August 4, 1895, a grateful Mother Pia thanked God for the partial fulfillment of her dearest desire for the Congregation, the completion of the first step toward a papally approved *Constitutions*:

After seven years of prayer and desire, the day has arrived when we are handed the episcopally approved *Constitutions* of this Congregation. Reverend Father Leo [Breuner] O.F.M., gave an appropriate allocution and then handed each Sister a copy of the *Constitutions* adapted to our lifework. Thanks be to the Queen of the Most Holy Rosary, to our Holy Father, Saint Dominic, and to Blessed Jordan for this grace. Grant, O Lord, that we may be faithful in the observance of these *Constitutions* and that the seal of papal approbation may some day be imprinted on them. My dear Father, Saint Dominic, bless us and love us.[14]

Though she experienced a sense of accomplishment on gaining

the Archbishop's approval, Mother Pia would not rest easy until she had achieved her long-desired goal of papal approbation. This determination strongly influenced, no doubt, her giving serious thought to a trip to Europe as early as 1890. According to her custom, she recommended the intention to the Queen of the Holy Rosary and Saint Joseph. "If it be for the benefit of the Congregation," she wrote, "I am willing to undertake the tedious journey."[15] But despite her expressed willingness, she was troubled by misgivings about the entire project and finally abandoned it altogether when a "Miss Margaret," from whom she had borrowed $1,000, asked for its return. Funds for the trip were simply not available. Four years later, however, Europe was again on the agenda, this time for the dual purpose of procuring missionary-minded postulants and studying the rules and practices of the Order preparatory to drafting the *Constitutions* for Rome. Although her intent was to recruit postulants, she had no notion at the time of making a permanent foundation in Europe.

As the year 1895 drew to a close, Mother Pia sent the Master General, the Most Reverend Andrew Fruehwirth, a draft of the revised *Constitutions* to critique. She asked also for his recommendation of a few European women's convents where authentic Dominican life was flourishing in order to experience it herself. The answer came through Father Dominicus Scheer, assistant to the Master General and one who would remain her faithful friend and wise counselor until his death. The Master General approved the trip and recommended three convents as models of Dominican observance: Speyer, Germany; Nancy, France; and Stone, England. But in order to examine the *Constitutions*, he would need a copy of the text in German. Discouraged by the request, Mother Pia decided to postpone the trip for another year in order to allow time for translation.

The following November Father Dominicus wrote Mother Pia in his own name encouraging her to make the trip, which would be to her benefit, he thought, as well as that of the community. Archbishop Riordan also gave his blessing to the trip. Hence, she decided once more in favor of Europe, though the prospect still troubled her:

> The journey will be undertaken in accordance with the

Sisters' desire and the wish of the Master General, and as we hope, in conformity with God's Holy Will. The permanent security of the community requires this sacrifice. The *Constitutions* should have the approval of the Order and of the Holy See. The ceremonies and the customs of the Order are to be studied and adopted. May God and Saint Dominic bless, guide, and direct our endeavors in order that we may constitute a fervent and solid community. The entire community shall offer every Tuesday during the whole year all their prayers and good works for this intention.[16]

This time the trip would become a reality. On April 23, 1897, Mother Pia, accompanied by Sister Seraphina, took leave of the sisters in San Francisco to travel east the Santa Fe route. Arriving in Chicago, they changed trains for Racine, where they spent four rewarding days visiting the sisters there and discussing spiritual topics with Mother Hyacintha and Sister Cecilia, novice director. On their return to Chicago, they entrained for New York, and after a few days spent pleasantly with the Montrose Avenue community, boarded the steamer, *Kaiser Wilhelm*, for Naples. The "floating Mother," as Mother Pia described herself, began her first letter home somewhat emotionally: "Tears fill my eyes whenever I think of you...; my only desire is to be home....I had the feeling that I would have to jump off the boat. This leaving the homeland was a most painful moment."[17] In contrast, Sister Seraphina was in high spirits, greeting her first morning at sea in song until Mother Pia reminded her that they had not yet prayed Morning Prayer.

The days on board ship ran the gamut from calm and pleasant to rough and stormy. The first encounter with turbulence obliged the crew to secure the deck chairs by cable to prevent their sliding overboard. Ignoring the elements, the two sisters sat on deck from 8:00 a.m. to 8:00 p.m. as an alternative to their pitching cabin below. The towering waves were chronicled as "a grand spectacle."[18]

Mother Pia derived much pleasure from distributing fruit to the Italian passengers in steerage, who had little enough to comfort them. But she was shocked and saddened when a workman was buried at sea, the third to die during the trip. Employed as firemen whose duty was to keep the engine heated, they could endure the temperature in the boiler room for no longer than four-hour shifts and frequently collapsed from lack of oxygen. The thought of men working in such cramped and airless quarters diminished the joy Mother Pia was beginning to experience on board the *Kaiser Wilhelm*, the ocean now "as calm as San Francisco Bay."[19]

The crowning social event of the voyage was to be the Captain's Ball. Approached by an elderly major with an invitation to attend as his guest, Mother Pia thought fast and excused herself, explaining that she was just too old now for dancing. Her characteristic shyness, though, did not deter her from making friends with members of the ship's crew.

At last, on May 20, she was able to record in the Diary: "Naples. After five years of deliberation, we are finally seeing our plans materialize in this trip of four weeks over land and sea."[20] Aboard the train to Rome after a day's layover in Naples, she felt like shouting for joy when she first caught sight of St. Peter's in the distance, but restrained herself for fear of giving a bad example to her fellow passengers.

In Rome her first meeting with Father Dominicus Scheer impressed Mother Pia. He is a "lovable, friendly, vivacious man," she decided. "I think that we can settle our affairs successfully with him. Tomorrow Father Scheer will introduce us to the Master General, Father Fruehwirth. Then work begins." [21]

Bound the next morning for the Dominican Generalate at Santa Sabina, the travelers had scarcely seated themselves in the carriage when the unfortunate horse dropped dead, a turn of events that led to some delay. Despite the sisters' discomfiture at arriving late for their appointment, the introduction went well, and the second meeting even better:

> 9:45 a.m. To Most Reverend Father General Fruehwirth. With him from ten to twelve. He is a very amiable man—sane views, in keeping with the times. Said he: "I am in favor of modifying the *Constitutions* which were intended for the contemplative Second Order. Draw from the laws of the First, Second, and Third Orders, and add what may be fitting to your circumstances. Have recourse to me—write to me—do not be strangers toward me. We should be bound together in some way." He spoke fully two hours in the

most affable manner.²²

While the Master General ranged more widely in his comments on the *Constitutions* and the customs of the Order, Father Scheer was startlingly specific: Mother Pia should dispense the teaching sisters from the Advent fast and should introduce Plain Chant into the liturgy. The sisters should wear white stockings and short belts; should observe perpetual silence in the refectory; should not teach boys above 14 years of age or conduct boys' sodalities; and should alter their guimpes (which he thoroughly disliked—altogether too pretty!).

Reverend Dominicus Scheer, O.P., spiritual director of Mother Maria Pia Backes

The pressure of constitutional matters notwithstanding, the travelers still found time to be typical tourists, visiting churches and catacombs; attending Pope Leo XIII's Mass and the canonization ceremonies of Saint Zacharia Maria Antonius; praying in the rooms of Saints Dominic and Pius V in Santa Sabina; and calling on the Dominican nuns of San Sisto.

All too soon the time in Rome came to an end. The sisters' next destination was Munich, a trip that did nothing to cheer Mother Pia. The train was hot and dusty, they had to sit up all night, and drinking water was unavailable. "All beaten up"²³ was her summation on their arrival in Germany, and her spirits were not improved by the thought, however mistaken, that she would never see Rome again. She felt "like crying out in longing for what we [had] left behind us... O Rome—there is only one Rome—thou hast taken possession of my heart."²⁴

Sister Salesia's aunt met the weary travelers at the station in Munich and drove them to the hospital of the Servite Sisters. Two days later they boarded the train for Wettenhausen, where the Dominican Sisters received them kindly and impressed Mother Pia by their charity and piety, as well as by their beautiful singing in choir.

St. Mary Magdalen, Speyer, one of the three convents recommended by the Master General for religious observance, was the sisters' next stop. "Everywhere we are received with love, genuine sisterly love," noted Mother Pia. "O Lord, it is beyond my merit."[25]

But in spite of her interest in everything she saw and heard, her thoughts often turned homeward, and she made plans to return to California in August. Not so Father Dominicus, who wished her to remain in Europe until October and make a retreat under his direction in Venlo, Holland. Although she found the decision difficult, she accepted it, thanking God "for this boon of a spiritual director. All my life, I have been praying for one; now Thou dost give him to me in this true son of Saint Dominic."[26] In reality, it was concern for Mother Pia's health that prompted Father Dominicus to insist on her prolonging her stay and going at once to the Black Forest for a much needed rest. Accordingly, the sisters spent the following days in the beautiful wooded country along the upper Rhine, where they walked daily with Father Dominicus, discussing questions of constitutional import. It would be better, he agreed, to pray one nocturn of the Breviary than to abandon it entirely, and he recommended the *Constitutions* of the Dominican Sisters of Stone, England, as her model.

Meanwhile, Mother Pia eagerly anticipated the arrival of Father Albertus Trapp, German Dominican provincial, with whom she had been corresponding for some years. Soon she would meet him face-to-face! But "what a disappointment! So cordial in correspondence—yet displaying such brusque mannerisms upon personal contact. What a contrast between Father Dominicus and Father Albertus!"[27] Fortunately, the latter made a better impression in the evening, and the next day's conversation boosted his standing even higher. "A saintly, zealous priest,"[28] she decided, though she could not refrain from comparison: "Father Dominicus, love and tranquility; no hasty step; no rash word. Father Albertus, impetuous in his zeal; energetic in word and deed."[29] Nevertheless, the latter impressed her, for in spite of his many responsibilities, he still found time to pray daily, in addition to the Divine Office, the Little Office of the Blessed Virgin and three rosaries!

At the end of August, the sisters left the Black Forest for the

Dominican Convent of Marienthal in Venlo. They were followed shortly by Fathers Albertus and Dominicus who wished to anticipate Mother Pia's Silver Jubilee of Profession. Beginning with a *Missa cantata* celebrated by Father Albertus and sung by the Marienthal Sisters, the day progressed through congratulations, gift giving, and singing of Vespers, to an entertaining skit in the evening. The Master General sent congratulations from Ireland where he was visiting, but for Mother Pia the crowning joy of the festivity was the Apostolic Blessing of Leo XIII, obtained by Father Hyacinth Cormier, O.P., Procurator General. "The day was one, equal to which I have had but few," she summarized gratefully. "I thank Thee, O Lord."[30]

Bidding farewell to the Marienthal community on September 27, the travelers left early the next morning for Herzogenrath to meet Mother Hieronyma, O.C.D., to whom Mother Pia had been directed by Father Dominicus. "As vivacious a person as ever I met,"[31] wrote Mother Pia of the Carmelite nun who was to become her staunch and lifelong friend. During the ensuing days the two talked "soul affairs" frequently, their friendship steadily deepening.

In Dusseldorf, where the sisters arrived on October 1, they met Father Ceslaus Hansen, O.P., who would serve the Order as prior, provincial, and assistant to the Master General and would prove of invaluable assistance to Mother Pia in her quest for papal approval of the *Constitutions*.

But soon time was running out, and Mother Pia, for whom leave-takings were generally painful, found each goodbye an ordeal, notwithstanding her frequent spells of homesickness. Saying farewell to Father Dominicus was especially painful, but she offered the heartache to God before the altar.

Accompanied by six postulants who had applied for entrance during the sisters' visit in Germany, the travelers sailed from Bremerhaven on October 19 on the steamer *Saale*. With the exception of a cyclone that left the ship bobbing "like a nutshell on the water,"[32] the voyage was uneventful, the weather at times even delightful. After stopovers in Brooklyn and Racine, the sisters arrived home on November 26, the postulants having preceded them directly from New York. Their welcome was warm and enthusiastic.

Major Issues

Although Rome had cast its magic over Mother Pia and left her nostalgic for its sights and sounds, she soon found herself absorbed by concerns close to home. Sister Raymunda Wilson was critically ill in Anaheim; a new convent was under consideration in Portland; and the need for money was great, as always. But she resolutely continued to work on the *Constitutions*, incorporating all she had learned from the Dominican Fathers in Rome and Germany. The same concerns, however, continued to distress her: the Divine Office, the lay sisters, and the enclosure.

Third Order or not, Mother Pia was unwilling to let the Divine Office (or Liturgy of the Hours, as we know it today) be lost. But the Master General was of a mind that all Third Order Dominican Sisters should have *Constitutions* basically the same, and current practice in other women's congregations did not support Mother Pia's thinking. "Benziger wrote that Holy Cross Convent, Brooklyn, New York, and the Second Street Convent have given up the Breviary," she noted in the Diary. "They will recite the Little Office of the Blessed Virgin Mary. This is a matter that affects me deeply. I love the Divine Office."[33] On December 8 she was again troubled: "We are ridiculed because of our adherence to the Divine Office. It is being predicted that eventually we shall be obliged to discontinue it. Dear Father Saint Dominic, I do not want to be different from other good religious women. But, do help us retain the Breviary."[34]

She was opposed in her thinking also by several clerics, Father Raphael Fuhr, O.F.M., pastor of St. Joseph's, Los Angeles, and Father Francis Dubbel, pastor of St. Boniface, Anaheim, among them. The length of the Office, so ran the reasoning, was a deterrent to its adoption as the daily prayer of a community with school obligations. Representing the opposing line of thinking, Father Dominicus strongly supported the retention of the Office. He urged the sisters to "hold on to the prayers and devotions that are customary in the Order. Carry out well the choral recitation of the Divine Office, and that suffices."[35] Torn by conflicting opinions, Mother Pia seemed at an impasse when a practical solution presented itself: Pray the Office with one nocturn at Matins. This idea was proposed by Father Leo Bruener, O.F.M., who shared with Mother Pia that in

Munster, Westphalia, teaching priests were granted such a privilege. Did she dare propose such a resolution to the problem in Rome? Father Dominicus urged caution. He approved the suggestion, but thought it should not be inserted in the *Constitutions*. Further to confuse the issue, the Most Reverend Hyacinth Cormier, Master General of the Order, not only agreed with Mother Pia, but strongly recommended including the proposal in the *Constitutions*. He would defend the matter in the Propaganda and the Congregation of Rites. Needless to say, the diversity of opinions did not solve the problem for the beleaguered superior.

The lay sister question was a second sensitive area. Should a Third Order congregation continue to have two categories of sisters? The lay sisters, whose principal charge involved domestic duties within the convent, were not obliged to the recitation of the Office but to other prescribed prayers. Neither were they allowed to vote in convent elections or chapters; and their garb, black scapular and white veil, differed from that of the choir sisters. As early as 1890, Mother Pia had been startled to learn that the lay sisters were contemplating petitioning for the elimination of distinction in dress, an apparently thorny issue among themselves. Nothing seems to have come of it, however, and for the next few years affairs remained comparatively quiet, although worried references to the lay sisters surface at intervals in the Diary.

But, in 1898, a letter from an unidentified lay sister brought the clothing issue to a head. The letter stated Sister's preference for a convent where distinction in garb was not observed. Within the month Mother Pia summoned the General Council to a meeting in which the garb of the lay sisters constituted the main agenda. Lengthy discussion resulted in a decision to abolish difference in dress. The question appeared settled, but eight months passed and the lay sisters were still wearing their black scapulars and white veils. The explanation may be found in the more radical decision toward which Mother Pia was beginning to lean. Her latest thinking was summarized in a letter to Mother Hyacintha (1899) in which she observed that lay sisters "were not a matter of law." One class of sisters would solve the problem, but there was still Father Dominicus to be reckoned with, who continued to hold out in favor of retaining the lay sisters. Deciding to present the clothing option to the lay sisters themselves, Mother Pia was relieved when they voted unanimously to keep the black scapular and white veil.

But for all their apparent unanimity, the problem refused to go away. Four years later it surfaced anew; the lay sisters had suffered a change of heart and were petitioning for the white scapular. The issue of dress was once and for all put to rest at the Intermediate Chapter of 1903, when all differences in garb were abolished. It must have been a troublesome issue, not only for the lay sisters, but also for the Congregation, for in a letter to superiors announcing the change, Mother Pia stated emphatically that the subject was not to be discussed either with seculars or among themselves. It was her hope, she added, that the modification would bring more harmony and satisfaction to the lay sisters.

When all distinction between lay and choir sisters was finally eliminated is not easily determined. The Intermediate Chapter legislated only the matter of dress; nothing was said about prayer or voting power, though these would appear more significant issues than garb. The *Constitutions*, approved by Archbishop Riordan in 1895, carry legislation specifically for lay sisters, but the papally approved *Constitutions* of 1922 state definitely in Article 3: "The Congregation contains but one class of sisters."[36] This addition was the recommendation of Father Ceslaus Hansen, O.P., though the Congregation had evidently eliminated distinctions among sisters some time previously. In a letter to Mother Seraphina, dated November 12, 1921, Father Ceslaus wrote:

Reverend Ceslaus Hansen, O.P., Socius to the Master General

> The Consultor [presumably Father Louis Nolan, O.P.] asked me if there was only one class of sisters in the

Congregation. That he had read here and there about "house sisters" or of sisters who were appointed for housework... . It would be good to state that there is only one class of sisters in order to avoid misunderstanding... . I put at the end of the chapter dealing with the "Purpose" and "Name" of the Congregation a new Article: "The Congregation has only one class of sisters." This is correct, isn't it?[37]

The only conclusion that can be drawn with certainty is that the lay sister question had been finally laid to rest by the time the *Constitutions* were submitted to Rome for final approval.

Sister Sebastiana Schreiber, wearing the lay sisters' habit

Enclosure as a component of religious life was close to Mother Pia's heart. Enclosure, she wrote to the sisters in the language of the time, "is the custodian of silence, simplicity, and mutual love; it is the rampart for the spirit of prayer and for inner peace. It is enclosure that converts a convent into an enclosed garden in which the Spouses of Christ walk with the Heavenly Bridegroom."[38] For Mother Pia enclosure was the safeguard of contemplation and the groundwork of "holy preaching." In this she was supported by Father Dominicus, who advised her to retain the enclosure—with or without the grating. It comes as no surprise, then, that the *Constitutions* of 1895 contains specific directives in regard to the parlor. No sister was to go to the parlor with a visitor without a sister companion, unless with the permission of the prioress:

> This permission may be given in the case of persons well known to the Community, or such as require religious instruction, and other cases; but the Prioress must very rarely allow sisters to go unaccompanied to speak with men, whether priests or laymen; nor can this be done with doors closed, or after sunset....These wise restrictions give us a correct idea of the religious spirit which should guide the intercourse of Sisters with the world. The further they keep from exposing themselves to the public view, and from every worldly distraction and useless acquaintance, the truer they will be to their sublime vocation. The receiving of unnecessary visits should be avoided as much as possible, and they should not be prolonged over an hour because more or less they are great distraction in the way of perfection.[39]

Recognizing, however, that the sisters' ministry made some contact with the public unavoidable, the 1895 *Constitutions* further declared that the General Council should appoint:

> ...such sisters to speak to... strangers as are capable of receiving and conversing with them in an edifying way. Religious desirous to converse with the world soon lose the spirit of their vocation....Seculars coming from the company of a Sister should carry with them the conviction that Religious are the happiest and the holiest persons in the world, and that they are truly deserving of full confidence in the education of young girls.[40]

The tension between strict cloister and apostolic work was an ongoing challenge for Mother Pia, although her good judgment had led her to remove the parlor grating sometime around 1900. But the first *Constitutions* clearly favored enclosure and laid down detailed rules regarding the entry of externs into the convent. The sisters were allowed to leave the convent only to fulfill their responsibilities in church or school or to consult a physician. They were to be home before sunset unless there were an urgent reason. The cloister was still very much a part of Mother Pia's thinking.

For the next several years, the sisters lived out their religious commitment under the episcopally approved *Constitutions* of 1895, adapted in large part from those of Speyer and Stone. Meanwhile Mother Pia geared for the acid test yet to come—papal approval.

A long journey of miles and years, frequently interrupted, awaited her (see Chapters 11, 16, and 20).

Notes

[1] Backes 71.

[2] Hyacintha Oberbrunner, O.S.D., letter to Backes, 31 December 1889.

[3] Backes 124.

[4] Gerard Becher, O.S.F. and Eugene Puers, O.S.F., "Documents of Election, 1888, 1891, 1894."

[5] Pius Murphy, O.P., "Document of Election," 2 August 1900.

[6] Backes 242.

[7] Annals of St. Catherine's Convent, 8 August 1900.

[8] "Regulations," 25 July 1903.

[9] "General Chapter Minutes," 3 August 1903.

[10] Schell, letter to Backes, 17 September 1890.

[11] Backes, letter to Riordan, 28 June 1894.

[12] *The Rule of Saint Augustine and the Constitutions of the Third Order of Saint Dominic* (San Francisco: Congregation of the Queen of the Most Holy Rosary, 1895) 3–4.

[13] *Constitutions* (1895), 33–34.

[14] Backes 171–172.

[15] Backes 131.

[16] Backes 182.

[17] Backes, letter to Sisters, n.d. (probably May 1897).

[18] Backes 185.

[19] Backes 185.

[20] Backes 186.

[21] Backes 187.

[22] Backes 191–192.

[23] Backes 195.

[24] Backes 195.

[25] Backes 197.

[26] Backes 197–198.

[27] Backes 201.

[28] Backes 201.

[29] Backes 201.

[30] Backes 205–206.

[31] Backes 208.

[32] Backes 210.

[33] Backes 180.

[34] Backes 180.

[35] Backes 192.

[36] *The Rule of Saint Augustine and the Constitutions of the Third Order of Saint Dominic* (Mission San Jose, CA: Congregation of the Queen of the Holy Rosary, 1923) 55.

[37] Ceslaus Hansen, O.P., letter to Maerz, 12 November 1921.

[38] Backes, letter to Sisters, Feast of the Holy Rosary 1915.

[39] *Constitutions* (1895) 114–116.

[40] *Constitutions* (1895) 117.

CHAPTER NINE

MISSION SAN JOSE

La Misión del Gloriosísimo Patriarca Señor San José, fourteenth in the chain of 21 historic California missions and the "garden spot of Alameda County,"[1] was founded on June 11, 1797, by Father Fermin Francisco de Lasuen, O.S.F., on the site of the old Ohlone Indian village of Oroysam. The Franciscan missionary had arrived two days earlier, accompanied by an escort of Spanish soldiers from the Presidio in San Francisco and a small band of Christian Indians from the Mission in Santa Clara.

In a setting of uncommon beauty, Father Lasuen began the blessing ceremonies, dedicating the site to God under the patronage of St. Joseph. With becoming solemnity the raising of the cross and the hoisting of the flag of Spain followed the blessing. Six rifle volleys, fired by a detail of soldiers, accompanied the raising of the flag. At an outdoor altar, erected beneath an *enramada*, or bower of branches lavishly decorated with wild flowers, Father Lasuen offered the first Mass in Mission San Jose, the little choir of Christian Indians singing the responses. The Padres had come to preach the Gospel, administer the Sacraments and save souls; this would be their only pride and ambition. "For the next 35 years Mission San Jose was the economic, religious, and governmental center of the East Bay and areas to the east"[2] until it became a casualty of the secularization of the Missions in 1834 when the Mexican government awarded them as land grants to private owners. The small town that developed around the Mission was also called Mission San Jose.

Early in his episcopate (1855) Archbishop Alemany's concern

at the injustice of the mission take-over spurred him to apply to the California Land Commission for the return of the mission lands to the Church. His claim duly processed and validated, the Church received a patent for 28.33 acres, thereby regaining control of the surviving adobe buildings on the mission site.

In 1878, Father Peter Kaiser was named pastor of the Mission's debt-ridden St. Joseph parish. A priest of the Diocese of Limburg, Germany, he had been one of Archbishop Alemany's recruits while on a tour of Europe in 1867. He arrived in Mission San Jose to find the Mission's nearly 30 acres of old vineyards and olive groves abandoned and overgrown. A builder in his native Germany, he had brought with him to California his keen business insight. With an eye to reducing the parish debt, he set about rehabilitating both grape vines and olive trees and restoring the old processing equipment left to rust on the mission grounds. He would return Mission San Jose's natural assets to a condition to be rendered profitable—should the Archbishop so desire.

But Archbishop Alemany's mind was focused in another direction. The need for quality clergy for his Archdiocese had long weighed heavily on his heart. "He was convinced that the needs of the Church on the frontier demanded a native clergy receiving such formation as would provide worthy and zealous priests for the ministry."[3] Such a goal, he concluded after touring his diocese, required both standards and stability in his priests. Father Eugene O'Connell, who had come to California from Ireland to assist in the training of seminarians, agreed. He pleaded with his alma mater, All Hallows College in Dublin, for additional priests:

> Doctor Alemany hopes you will send him two talented young men if possible, but what he lays the principal stress upon is piety and zeal, and having these latter qualifications he will be content with *mediocris scientia* [average intelligence]. The Irish missioners that have hitherto figured here didn't reflect much credit on our country.[4]

The Archbishop, whose earlier attempts at establishing a seminary had failed, was determined to try again. Accordingly, he designated a section of land in Mission San Jose as a desirable location because of its quiet and pleasant climate. "A fine brick building"[5] accommodating 40 students was soon built. With high expecta-

St. Thomas Aquinas Seminary 1884

tions five young men arrived in Mission San Jose to begin classes on January 15, 1883. Their optimism was short-lived. After only two years of operation Saint Thomas Seminary closed. Shortage of students, strained finances and isolation of site accounted for the demise.

For five years the seminary building stood idle until Archbishop Patrick J. Riordan, successor to Archbishop Alemany, approached Mother Pia regarding the purchase of the building and surrounding property for a novitiate. The proposal, though startling, was not totally unacceptable to her; and on September 27, 1890, she set out to view the place for herself. This was not easily accomplished. It involved taking the ferry from San Francisco to Oakland, the Southern Pacific train from Oakland to Irvington and a carriage (if available) the last three miles to Mission San Jose. To avoid the eventuality of a walk at the end, Mother Pia contacted the Sunderer family, long time residents of the mission town. According to Mrs. Rose Whiteside, the former Rose Sunderer, born in Mission San Jose and a lifetime resident:

> In 1888 my sister Abbie went to San Francisco to the

Dominican School at Twenty-fourth and Guerrero Streets. The Superior of the Congregation, Mother Pia Backes, having become acquainted with our family wrote saying she would like to come to Mission San Jose to look over the Saint Thomas Aquinas building and property connected with it. My parents [Joseph and Rosa Sunderer] invited her to our home and my father engaged a hack and team of horses, and I had the pleasure of riding to Irvington with my father to meet the Sisters coming from San Francisco by train.

The Sisters spent the morning looking over the property and then came to our home for lunch. After lunch my father and I took Mother Pia and Sister Felicitas to see Father Governo, pastor of Holy Spirit in Centerville. Father enthusiastically encouraged the Sisters to take over the property vacated by the seminarians who had moved to Menlo Park.[6]

The town of Mission San Jose with St. Joseph Parish rectory and Church (left); the one remaining structure of the old Mission (right) (1909)

The little town of Mission San Jose that greeted Mother Pia on her first visit boasted a population of some 800 inhabitants. In addition to the surviving mission buildings and the Gothic-framed church dedicated to Saint Joseph, its one main street, Vallejo (now Mission Boulevard), held the usual shops catering to the inhabitants' basic needs—and six saloons!

Mother Pia's first impression of the site was mixed. "A beautiful place, but... not quite suitable for a novitiate. The Lord will inspire me what to do."[7] Two days of prayer and mulling over the proposal rendered her more positive in outlook; the mission site, she decided, would work well as an orphanage!

At this juncture Miss Katherine Drexel entered the picture. Daughter of a wealthy philanthropist, Katherine Drexel was active in support of missionary projects, reserving the bulk of her share of her father's estate to found schools for Native Americans and Blacks. From Sister Seraphina Maerz, ever alert where Indians were concerned, Mother Pia learned that Miss Drexel had offered Father William Dempflin, O.P., Western Dominican missionary to the Indians, $15,000 or $20,000 for a Native American school in Fresno. The government would support the project by contributing annually the sum of $12,000 on condition that the school serve at least 100 children and be staffed by a minimum of 10 sisters.

Sister Seraphina was ready to go! Her long-time desire to minister to the Indians would at last see fulfillment. Mother Pia, however, ruled out Fresno in favor of Mission San Jose as the location of choice. Archbishop Riordan approved the site, and Miss Drexel declared herself open to the change of place. All parties involved appeared well-disposed toward the project until politics intervened in the distribution of the Drexel moneys after Miss Drexel entered religious life. "God's Will be done!"[8] wrote Mother Pia, accepting the disappointment with good grace.

Despite the setback, Mother Pia was now more resolved than ever to take over the former seminary. "Even if Miss Drexel does not help, we shall accept the place for boarders," she determined. "The grape crop will probably pay the interest, and the olive crop, the capital. The board will support the house."[9] In her eagerness she recommended the purchase to the intercessory power of her late esteemed friend, Archbishop Alemany, who had, after all, been responsible for the building. But despite her brave words, misgivings continued to trouble her. Finally, on February 25, she made up her mind to set aside her fears and act. "Today I gave my consent," she wrote. "We shall make a contract with His Grace to purchase the building and twenty-nine acres of land for the sum of $30,000. Since we have not the money for cash payment, we shall pay annually the sum of $1,500 interest."[10]

The Josephinum

Sister Felicitas Weiss was named first superior of the new foundation. She was to be assisted by Sisters Josepha Sailer and Bartholomea Deckert. At the time of her appointment, the new superior was still assigned to St. Catherine's, Anaheim, a mission she had come to love. For some reason she failed to read the note appended to Mother Pia's letter until a few days after its arrival. "When you come north," the postscript read, "bring your trunk in case I need you here."[11] Sister Felicitas's heart sank, and she went north hoping that Mother Pia had forgotten what she had written. But the die was cast for Mission San Jose! As Sister Felicitas related several years later.

> I cried for a whole day. Mother let me cry it out; she kept me in her office, so that other hearts might not grow sad. In God's name I went forth. Sister Bartholomea went with me, also Mother Pia's sister, Mrs. Berge, with little Tommy Berge (seven years old) who carried "Watchie," our future watchdog, in a basket....
>
> The old seminary was in a most neglected state. Dead birds, especially woodpeckers, were strewn about the corridors and rooms; the place had been vacant for two [sic] years. With night came the bats!... and coyotes....
>
> The brick building was a most gloomy place. Sister Bartholomea and I went to sleep on the third floor. I chose the room at the southeastern corner so I could view and protect that end of the country. Sister Bartholomea chose the room at the northwest corner of the building and we begged Abbie Sunderer [daughter of Mission San Jose's unofficial mayor and local shoemaker] to come and sleep in one of the rooms...and we tried to rest in peace.[12]

Mrs. Berge and the youthful Tommy slept on the second floor near the stairway. In the event of intruders, it seems likely that they would be the first to have to deal with them, an unenviable distinction that only Tommy found exciting.

Corroborating Sister Felicitas's account, Mrs. Whiteside recalled in her letter, "Abbie went every evening to sleep at the convent in order to bolster the courage of the sisters in the large, empty building. Evidently the sisters had faith in her, though I assure you Abbie would never have won a medal for bravery."[13]

The sisters spent their first weeks of residency cleaning up after workmen engaged by Mother Pia had left the premises. These included, besides the seminary, a brick kitchen building and a barn. To the sisters' relief, Mother Pia hired a workman to assist with farm and maintenance tasks and purchased a cow and a horse in support of the sisters' first venture in farming. But it was soon evident that additional help was needed for the care of the orchards, which totaled 1,400 fruit-bearing trees.

The school, dedicated to Saint Joseph and known as the Josephinum, opened on January 4, 1892. Twenty-three pupils on opening day soon increased to 43 day pupils, 14 boarders, and 7 music pupils. According to Mrs. Whiteside:

> The Sisters were received kindly and many were the gifts of welcome showered by the farmers and orchardists.... My teachers were Sister Bernardina [Michel] and Sister Augustine [O'Connor]. Sister Teresa [Meyer] was my music teacher, as well as my sister's embroidery instructor. We had a shorthand course, too and Sister Felicitas gave me lessons in German.[14]

The following year Sister Felicitas initiated a Young Ladies Sodality group; about 30 girls responded. "We sat monthly at the convent," Mrs. Whiteside remembered, "and participated in civic affairs, too. During the summer months when the Sisters were without an organist either my sister or I played for them."[15]

For two years the Josephinum reflected the serenity of its rural setting, but gradually the need for a change had to be faced. Reluctantly Mother Pia admitted that distance from the surrounding towns was a serious deterrent to enrollment; consequently, in 1894 the day school was discontinued and, with Archbishop Riordan's approval, replaced by an orphanage. "There are now twenty children at Mission San Jose orphanage,"[16] noted Mother Pia on July 28. The boys—all of whom arrived afflicted with whooping cough!—were transfers from the Franciscan Fathers' orphanage in Watsonville, California, and were quartered above the old brick kitchen. The girls occupied the second floor of the seminary building.

Meanwhile, the sisters' payments on the Mission San Jose site were proving too slow for Archbishop Riordan, who suggested to Mother Pia that she mortgage the Motherhouse in San Francisco for $20,000 to be used toward payment of the debt. Her response was equal to his proposal: She would settle the entire debt for $15,000! It was a nice try, but the Archbishop was not persuaded, and the purchase price held. Following input from the Council, Mother Pia decided to continue the orphanage for at least another year on condition that State Aid would be obtained. The latter Sister Felicitas was pursuing doggedly. A trip to Sacramento proved futile, as the Legislature had recently called a moratorium on the licensing of more orphanages. She had, however, made the acquaintance of one Colonel O'Byrne, a San Francisco neighbor, who promised to use his influence to the sisters' advantage. Within three days Sister Felicitas had a check for $700 for orphan support and Mother Pia wrote happily in the Diary: "April 18 [1895]—Received State Aid from Sacramento for the orphans at Mission San Jose for the first time. Thanks be to God and Saint Joseph."[17] For the time being, the future of the orphanage was secure.

For whatever reason, Mother Pia had never fully shared Archbishop Riordan's thinking that the original seminary building would answer her need for a novitiate house. But something had to be done—and quickly! The increase in boarders at Immaculate Conception Motherhouse, San Francisco, made an immediate solution critical; moreover, a new turn of events caused the problem to escalate. An excess of candidates awaiting entrance to convents in Germany explained the willingness of the German cloisters, limited to a certain number of postulants each year, to share their vocations with America. In 1891 seven postulants arrived from Europe—three from the Dominican convent of Dusseldorf in the Rhineland and four from the Dominican convent of Wettenhausen, Swabia. The solu-

"Little Ones" at the Josephinum Orphanage c. 1900

tion was a stopgap one: On at least four occasions, 1892, 1895, 1898, and 1901, the novitiate seesawed from San Francisco to Mission San Jose and back again according to space needs in the City. The move was made permanent in April of 1901.

But the overflow simply transferred the problem to Mission San Jose. The Motherhouse chapel proved inadequate for the number of professed sisters, novices and postulants, and children. At Mother Pia's request, Mr. Celestine Grisez (Sister Evangelista's father) drew up plans for a larger chapel; and some weeks later, there was reference to construction in the Diary: "The erection of the chapel is proceeding slowly, but it will be beautiful."[18]

God's Acre

By 1900 three sisters had died in the community—Sister Hyacintha Schneider (on board ship from Oregon), Sister Brigitta McCarthy (Portland), and Sister Reginalda Kiesel (Los Angeles). Mother Pia decided that it was time to select a site for a sisters' cemetery on the Mission San Jose property. She chose a section to the northeast of The Josephinum, verging on the north property line.

A month after the selection was made, Sister Eugenia Becker died of tuberculosis. Her interment, however, was at Holy Cross,

Colma (San Francisco's Catholic cemetery). Mother Pia had meantime learned that neighbors, the Gallegos family in particular, were opposed to the cemetery location. Their resistance was not unwarranted; the proximity of the site to the neighbors' water supply was justifiable cause for objection. Two years elapsed before a new and acceptable site was determined. This time it was the land immediately behind the old Mission cemetery that would become the sisters' final resting place. A letter, signed simply "Dominican Sisters," was addressed to Archbishop Montgomery of San Francisco: "If agreeable," it read in part, "we would respectfully request Your Grace, in Mother Pia's name, to grant permission to our Community to have the plot in our grounds in Mission San Jose consecrated which we have selected as a cemetery for our sisters."[19] Following episcopal permission and blessing of the ground, the bodies of Sisters Hyacintha Schneider, Eugenia Becker and Victoria Kine (who had died on January 12, 1901), were exhumed and relocated from Holy Cross, Colma, to "God's Acre" in Mission San Jose. "Mother Felicitas and Mother Salesia accompanied the remains of our beloved deceased,"[20] was Mother Pia's entry in the Diary.

November 11, 1901, marked the Twenty-fifth Anniversary of the sisters' arrival in San Francisco. Mother Pia reminisced gratefully, "Three Sisters, forty children. At present: 95 Sisters, 2,000 pupils in our parish schools, 350 orphans. A thousand thanks to God for pain and suffering, cross and anxiety—also for Thy love and care, O my God. All for Thy honor!"[21]

Father Maximilian Neumann, O.S.F., ever a faithful friend of the Congregation, celebrated Solemn High Mass in St. Boniface Church, San Francisco, on November 28, in commemoration of the Silver Jubilee of the sisters' coming West. After Mass the ladies of the parish served luncheon to the sisters. Father Maximilian explained the celebration simply: "There is reason for thanksgiving."[22]

Motherhouse, Mission San Jose

In the early years of the Congregation, the financial condition of the struggling young community made a measure of self-support a necessity. In addition, candidates from Europe often came trained in the domestic arts such as sewing, weaving and embroidery, or had experience of life on a farm. Gradually, the land at Mission San Jose began to take on the characteristics of a medieval monastery as the Congregation engaged in a greater variety of supportive occupations. Sometime during the Mission's secular period, a number of racing stables had been built on the Mission property also; now, as the need arose, these were converted into workrooms.

First in order of immediacy was a sewing room. Before the separation from Brooklyn, the sisters had obtained their clothing from the New York Motherhouse. This source was no longer available to them; and so, when Sister Henrica Lehrenfeld made profession in 1894, Mother Pia appointed her seamstress for the Congregation. It was a wise choice, as Sister had been trained in dressmaking in Europe before her entrance into the community. When the Motherhouse was moved to Mission San Jose [in 1907], Sister Henrica and her machines were among the transfers. In one of the remodeled stables, she worked for the next 38 years, supplying the sisters' clothing, as well as items for the orphans. An appreciative annalist noted in 1909: "Today for the first time, Sister Henrica enjoyed the pleasure of running her sewing machines by electricity."[23]

Sister Henrica's successor, Sister Conrada Maier, had been taught to sew in Germany by her aunt, a professional seamstress. As soon as she arrived in Mission San Jose, she was assigned to the sewing room and placed under Sister Henrica's tutelage. When the latter retired, Sister Conrada was given full charge of the sewing department, a responsibility that she carried for the next 48 years, doubtless the longest assignment in the history of the Congregation. As the community increased in number, Sister Conrada wrote her own Guinness Book of Records in the thousands of yards of fabric cut and the number of habits sewn—always with pleasant smile and cheerful mien. During 1950, for example, the Motherhouse sewing room produced 264 habits, 415 guimpes, and 1,728 coifs—among a variety of other articles that the little work force was asked to make.

Habit material became an increasingly expensive item as the Congregation continued to grow in membership and the amount of yardage needed increased. Providence provided in Sisters Placida Struett and Pudentia Philipp, friends from girlhood in Germany who had learned the weaving trade together, entered the commu-

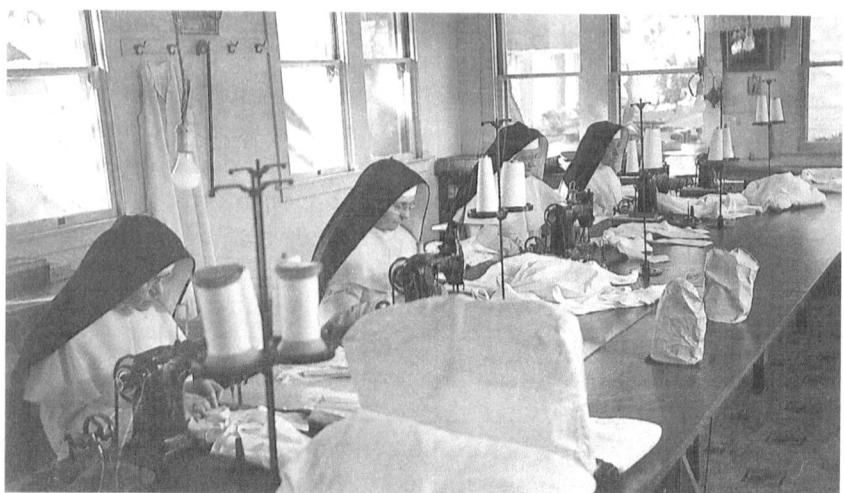
Sister Conrada Maier and her sewing room assistants

nity together, made profession together, and sailed for California together. When the Congregation purchased a loom in 1909, Sister Placida was a natural choice as community weaver, working at the outset under Mother Felicitas, whose practical bent of mind made her enthusiastic to try anything new. Sister Placida was soon turning out an average of 100 yards of wool, or material for about ten habits a month. Her quiet, patient ways fitted her admirably for the task, for preparing the loom was a tedious task. Threading the loom meant tying by hand (one at a time) 2,500 threads! For more than 30 years, Sister Placida provided material for the sisters' habits until World War II made the purchase of good thread unavailable; and the weaving department closed down.

But the sisters were not the only beneficiaries of the sisters' abilities. The Motherhouse annalist bears witness: "Sister Gertrude [Kuhn] has a new sewing machine. She is now sewing aprons for the children... she has finished 20 aprons and 15 dresses this week."[24] And Sister Rosita Suarez-Peredo, returning to her native Mexico after teaching sewing in the United States, set up sewing classes in the convent at San Miguel Allende. There, with the aid of volunteers, she made dresses for needy girls from the nearby ranches. Sister Rosita carried on her "trade" in a large room near the front entrance of the convent where racks of dresses according to size drew patrons to "Sister Rosita's Dress Shop."

When a knitting machine was acquired by the Motherhouse in 1908, Sister Pudentia Philipp was given full responsibility for the department. The annalist recorded with enthusiasm that Sister Pudentia knitted eight dozen pairs of stockings for the orphan boys at Ukiah, and later, "proudly exhibited 215 pairs of gray stockings"[25] knitted on her new machine. While the sisters were grateful for the sweaters, shawls, and other knitted goods produced by Sister Pudentia, the orphan boys, who often arrived at the convent barefoot, were the happy recipients of "Sister's socks."

The embroidery room became the territory of Sister Magdalena Thyke, a native American who as a girl had been trained in needlework by the Daughters of Charity. After her profession, Sister was assigned to the care of children; but, when the orphan girls moved from The Josephinum, Sister was free to work full time in the embroidery room. Vestments, stoles, altar linens and other items were produced with a respect for beauty of design and precision of workmanship. When newly professed sisters were assigned to the embroidery room as assistants, their apprenticeship unfailingly began with the floor. Only when they swept to Sister's satisfaction were they advanced to the needle. At the age of 96, Sister Magdalena suffered a fall that put an end to her work in the embroidery department, a work in which she had taken pride and delight.

Siena Studio succeeded the embroidery room. Through contact with Father John Meehan, artist and poet, Sister Clare Coon became interested in vestment making, her creative genius no doubt influenced by her early home environment. Testimonials to her father's artistic ability may still be seen in several public buildings in Grand Rapids, Michigan, where he was a stone cutter; her mother, a seamstress, was much in demand for the exclusive

S. Clare Coon, founder of Siena Studio

Liturgical art pieces on and behind the Motherhouse chapel altar, designed and sewn by Sister Clare Coon

women's fashions she created. Sister Clare taught sewing in the high schools of the Congregation until 1949, when she was called to the Motherhouse and, with the encouragement of Mother Pius Marbaise, Prioress General, opened Siena Studio, naming it after St. Catherine of Siena, whose father was a textile dyer and merchant. Experimenting with various materials, Sister Clare was delighted with the work of a company of Japanese weavers in Goten, Japan, and soon became a steady customer. It was her pride that only pure raw silk and pure gold thread were used in the work of Siena Studio. The application of original textile design with sensitivity to color and material made her work well known, and orders poured in from throughout the United States. Siena Studio made the Japanese weavers sought after in this country, and their beautiful material boosted Sister Clare's popularity as a vestment maker. Theirs was a happy association in the workplace.

Printing was introduced at the Motherhouse when Father Michael Wallrath, Mother Dolorosa's uncle, donated a printing press to the community. Sister Paula von Tessen was the community's first self-taught printer on the press, which was set up in the basement of The Josephinum; her assistant was Sister Berchmans Hudson. At the outset the chief items printed were lesson plans and courses of study, but as the sisters gained experience, book binding was added. Sister Euphrasine Dormann, who began as Sister Paula's helper, gradually advanced to "head printer" with Sister Polycarp Struffert as assistant. Sister Blandina Dumoulin, assigned to the printing department from 1913–1956, expanded the items printed, though production was still in-house, including the *Acts of the General Chapter*, the *Constitutions*, the *Catechism of Vows*, and the *Cantemus*, an organ accompaniment book. In 1952 the printing department went public when Beatrice "Cookie" Ballesteros, an alumna of Sacred Heart High School, Los Angeles, persuaded the sisters to purchase a Heidelberg press (vintage 1916!) and to name the department "Mater Dei Press." Employing community artists, Mater Dei was soon in business, producing greeting cards, stationery, and brochures and before long had patrons across the country. Sister Michael Marie (Giulii) Zobelein, assigned to the printing department in 1956, single-handedly managed the entire operation for almost three decades.

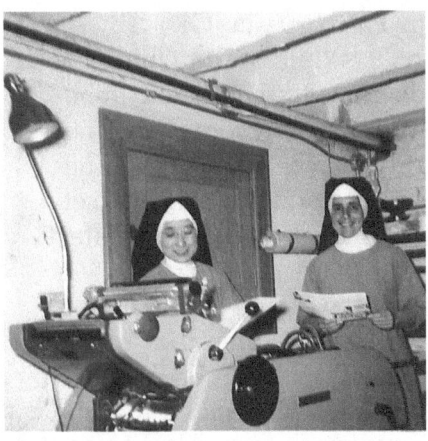

Sister Marie Seraphine Hatanaka assists Sister Michael Marie (Giulii) Zobelein with a special Mater Dei Press project

The Congregation's artistic achievements would continue under Sister Justina Niemierski's genius. A true contemplative is probably the most accurate description of Sister Justina by her contemporaries, who remember the familiar sight of Sister seated in chapel—Latin, Hebrew, or Greek Bible open on her knees—oblivious to all but the contemplation of the Word. A true daughter of Saint Dominic, she exemplified in her living the Dominican motto, *"contemplata aliis tradere."*

Anna Niemierski was born of Polish parentage in a small town in East Prussia, Germany, in 1879. While still a child, she displayed remarkable ability in art. On completing her studies, she moved with her parents and two sisters, settling near Berlin. Shortly after, one of Anna's sisters was asked to cater a dinner honoring several celebrities of the region. A crisis threatened when it was decided that the centerpiece for the head table was inferior for the occasion. Alerted to the trouble, the caterer suggested that they call in her sister to make something. The only material on hand was an immense lump of butter! Nothing daunted, Anna set to work and carved a lion, majestic and lifelike, to grace the center of the table. The admiring guests asked to meet the artist and were taken aback when the young girl was introduced. The result of Anna's afternoon's work was an invitation to attend the Berlin Academy of Fine Arts, where she studied under renowned sculptors.

Sister Justina Niemierski

At graduation she received first and second place awards for her original work, and both family and friends looked forward to a promising career for her. But to the surprise of all, she announced that she was entering the convent at Altenberg! On completion of the postulancy, she was clothed in the habit in 1910 and given the name "Justina;" she pronounced first vows in 1911. The following year Sister Justina bade farewell to Germany and sailed for California, where she devoted herself to the contemplation of Sacred Scripture and sacred art. The Motherhouse grounds bear witness to the fruits of her contemplation: the small Gothic Mater Dei chapel, constructed and decorated in commemoration of Mother Pia's Golden Jubilee of Profession; the Stations of the Cross, designed and executed in memory of Sister Evangelista Grisez's parents; the frescoes adorning the college building; and the statue

Sister Justina Niemierski's Stations of the Cross with Mater Dei Chapel in the background

of Our Lady, Queen of the Universe, standing high on its 25-foot pedestal on which Sister was working in 1960 at the time of her last illness. In the 1930s she was asked to design and execute an exterior frieze for the front wall of St. Anne's church in San Francisco. An impressive portrayal of Biblical history, it reveals "a wealth of Scriptural knowledge... and penetration into divine revelation contained in prophecies and types."[26]

An art studio at the Motherhouse was a later addition, built about 1932 for Sister Evangelista. A gifted wood carver, Sister fashioned the large wooden crucifixes and many of the picture frames that enhance the paintings in the Motherhouse. She also was responsible for the carved altar and ornate choir stalls in the chapel.

The Congregation's first baker of altar breads was Sister Ignatia Mullally, a native of Roscommon, Ireland. For her, the work was a labor of love and a signal honor. When engaged in baking or cutting the breads, Sister maintained strict silence out of respect for what the hosts would soon become. For the last 30 years of her life, Sister Ignatia supplied altar breads for most of the parishes around Mission San Jose, as well as for the Motherhouse and St. Mary of the Palms.

228 SEED & GROWTH

Frieze at St. Anne's Church, San Francisco, one of Sister Justina's major works

Production of honey was introduced by Sister Evangelista Grisez, who kept a few hives on the Motherhouse grounds. When Sister Balbina Schallwig replaced her as beekeeper, she increased the number of hives to 30, producing about 80 gallons annually. Although not a significant source of revenue, honey from the mission bees represented a saving as it replaced butter on the sisters' table at breakfast.

The grape crop failed to realize Mother Pia's plan to meet the interest payments on the Motherhouse when phyloxera struck the vines. The olives, however, could still be depended on. The 334 olive trees on the Mission San Jose site had early come under the scrutiny of Mother Felicitas Weiss, who was never one to let God's gifts go to waste. The industry was inaugurated without fuss. In a small adobe building near the parish church, Mother Felicitas worked an old hand press found on the property, turning the black olives into rich golden oil for a variety of uses. Later, a barn on the northeast corner of the sisters' property was remodeled to accommodate a new and larger electric press purchased in 1905. The following year, when the Motherhouse was moved to Mission San Jose and the industries were departmentalized, Mother Felicitas was placed in charge of the weaving; and Mother Salesia Fichtner, assisted by Sister Zita Kellerer, took over the producing of olive oil. Annual production netted about 400 gallons, though in 1911, a peak year, the trees produced such a bumper crop that the sisters had to enlist the help of the older orphans from St. Mary's in harvesting the olives for a yield of 750 gallons.

Sister Balbina with her bees

The oil became a modest source of income for the community. Used chiefly for sacramental purposes, it numbered among its patrons the bishops of the dioceses of Texas, Illinois, Hawaii, Wisconsin and California. During World War II the oil served a further purpose. Nearly 60 gallons were sent overseas for the use of chaplains in anointing the wounded. Mission San Jose's "genuine pure extra virgin olive oil"[27] was also popular for cooking purposes, and loyal customers came regularly to the convent door to purchase gallon cans for home use.

During the 21 years that she presided over the press, Mother Salesia grew quite fond of her work with the olives. When she became critically ill in 1924 and the Motherhouse chaplain was called to her bedside to administer the Anointing of the Sick, she brightened visibly and exclaimed, *"Das ist das Oel"*(That is the oil).[28] She was ready to go to God, the beloved oil scarcely dry on her forehead.

After Mother Salesia's death, manufacturing of olive oil continued under the direction of Sister Pudentia Philipp, who keeps reappearing in this chapter in a variety of guises. In 1948 a two-story "olive house" was erected on the northeastern corner of the Motherhouse property, the first floor housing the olive oil extracting equipment. When poor health finally forced Sister Pudentia to relinquish her responsibility, the oil presses at Mission San Jose shut down for a hiatus of 35 years.

But memories linger on, and many a former postulant and novice remembers the back-breaking task of collecting olives from the ground "for the souls in Purgatory" after Motherhouse employees had shaken the fruit from the trees. Perhaps the greatest blessing, though, was that by Archbishop Cantwell of Los Angeles. In a letter addressed to "Sister Superior," he wrote: "May Almighty God pour forth upon you and yours the oil of gladness. The Holy Oils will make you a sharer in all the good works of the diocese during the year."[29]

The Motherhouse sisters lived a simple life, getting along mainly on what they themselves produced or neighboring farmers shared. There was a communal effort to get things done. White habits and the orphans' clothing made the laundry a major item each week. In the early days, all—postulants, novices, and professed sisters—rose each Monday at the ghostly hour of 3:00 a.m. to hand-scrub the week's laundry before Morning Prayer; and on Tuesdays the sisters hurried home from school to deal with the ironing. When the first mangle was installed about 1906, the laundry became the joint responsibility of the long-time friends, Sisters Placida and Pudentia, assisted by the community. Only the quick and capable were allowed to "run the new contraption"[30] (mangle), which was viewed with suspicion by several of the veterans. Not until 1911 were electric hand irons introduced and the old flat irons abandoned.

Shoe repair, poultry raising, fruit and vegetable growing, and bread making comprised other efforts at self-support of the Motherhouse that have long since vanished from the premises. Only Mater Dei Press and the recently revived olive oil production remain as evidences of what were once thriving enterprises at Mission San Jose.

The town of Mission San Jose was incorporated into the City of Fremont in 1952. Contrary to the practice of Dominican Sisters' Congregations in the United States of identifying themselves by the town or city of their current motherhouse, the Dominican Sisters of Mission San Jose remain loyal to their historic identity.

Notes

[1] Holmes, Phillip. *Two Centuries at Mission San Jose: 1707–1997*, (Hayward, California: Folger Graphics, 1997) 130.

[2] Holmes 8.

[3] Harry B. Morrison, "Before the Sulpicians: Formation of Priests in Early Diocesan California, 1841–1885," *The Patrician*, Spring, 1992.

[4] Morrison (no page)

[5] Donald Pyne, "St. Thomas Aquinas Seminary," *The Patrician*, Spring, 1992, 21.

[6] Rose Whiteside, letter of reminiscences: Diamond Jubilee of St. Joseph's Convent [chart] 1966.

[7] Backes 129.

[8] Backes 133.

[9] Backes 134.

[10] Backes 137.

[11] Weiss, [sister's reminiscence] *Cor Unum*, "75th Anniversary edition," (1951) 55. *Cor Unum in Deo* was a quarterly newsletter initiated by M. Seraphina in 1927. It was discontinued in 1935 and resumed publication in 1943 with the shortened title *Cor Unum* until it was discontinued.

[12] Weiss 55.

[13] Whiteside, Diamond Jubilee of St. Joseph's Convent [chart] 1966.

[14] Whiteside.

[15] Whiteside.

[16] Backes 159.

[17] Backes 170.

[18] Backes 250.

[19] Dominican Sisters, letter to Montgomery, 6 September 1904.

[20] Backes 298.

[21] Backes 252.

[22] Backes 252.

[23] Motherhouse Annals, 7 April 1909.

[24] Motherhouse Annals, 30 January 1909.

[25] Motherhouse Annals, 30 October 1908.

[26] "Justina Niemierski, O.P." Necrology: 1955–1961, 32–33.

[27] Motherhouse Heritage Room [label].

[28] "Salesia Fichtner, O.P." Necrology I: 1889–1937, 50.

[29] John J. Cantwell, letter to Sister Superior, 16 April 1938.

[30] *Cor Unum*, "75th Anniversary," 1951, 37.

CHAPTER TEN

WORKING WITH THE FRIARS

Once again the sisters found themselves called to meet the religious and educational needs of the children of German-speaking Catholics when Father John Metzler, pastor of St. Joseph's church, Los Angeles, visited Sacred Heart convent in November 1892 in quest of sisters for his school. Begun in 1889 by the Reverend Florian Bartsch, pastor pro tem, the school consisted of 12 pupils taught by a lay woman. With Bishop Thomas Conaty's approval and Mother Pia's acceptance, St. Joseph's school came under the direction of the Dominican Sisters on December 1, 1892.

St. Joseph School, Los Angeles

In pelting rain Sister Seraphina, accompanied by a Native American girl, known to us only as "Nancy," made the long trip by horse car from Sacred Heart convent on Sichel and Baldwin streets to St. Joseph's on the far side of the city at Twelfth and Santee. Although 12 children met them that first day, the following morning the number had almost doubled, and by January it had increased to 39. "Classrooms" were the organ loft of the church and a small room adjoining. A second small room in the rear of the church was reserved as the sisters' lunchroom. The ever helpful Mrs. Bruttig (Sister Walburga Muller's aunt) was once again on hand to take care of the lunchroom and its few utensils.

A week after school opened, Clara Strauss, a postulant, joined Sister Seraphina as assistant teacher, commuting from Sacred Heart. The following April, Sister Emilia Moore replaced Sister Seraphina, whose principal role during the early years seems to have been that of "founding mother."

The school operated in the style of most parochial schools of the day. Whatever tuition collected was retained by the sisters because they received no salary or stipend from the parish. The parish provided the school space and benches, or in some cases, desks; the sisters provided such things as maps, charts and pictures funded from the tuition and an occasional raffle. The raffle of a sofa cushion at St. Joseph's for example, netted enough "to renovate the school and...buy maps and blackboards."[1] "Renovate" should probably be read to mean hire a worker to do the summer cleaning.

The future of St. Joseph's school seemed assured the following year when the Franciscan Fathers assumed responsibility for the parish. Convinced of the key role of the school in parochial life, Father Victor Aertker, O.S.F., pastor, and Father Cornelius Schoenwelder, O.S.F., assistant, promoted attendance with admirable zeal and vigor. As a result, the school year that had begun with a registration of 34 closed in June with 103! At the concluding exercises, Father Victor addressed the assembled parents and friends, praising the school and noting that at the Chicago World Exhibition he had examined the work done by the students of the Dominican Sisters in their San Francisco schools and had been very much satisfied.

To accommodate the increase in enrollment, the pastor ordered two classrooms built in time for the opening of the fall term. The sisters moved into a small five-room house located within the parish, bringing to a welcome conclusion the twice daily ride across the city. Constituting the pioneer community were Sister Gonzaga Buehler, superior-principal; Sister Bernarda Hornung, teacher; and Sister Mechtilde Kuhn, housekeeper.

Through the years the steadily growing enrollment necessitated a series of additions to the school. These included the raising of the building one story to allow the addition of classrooms, a library and a lunchroom, and the later remodeling of the old church to provide six additional rooms for the 300 children then enrolled.

As the sparsely populated district comprising St. Joseph's parish developed into a solidly established residential community, a more spacious building became a necessity. On May 7, 1905, amidst another "great downpour of rain," Bishop Conaty broke ground for a new school, returning in July of the following year to bless the completed building. "This was a beautiful day for St. Joseph's," the convent annalist recorded.[2]

> In the morning the Bishop presided at the conferring of Confirmation, and in the afternoon at the dedication of the new school. A grand procession, in which children, sodalities, and societies took part, accompanied the Bishop and priests through the school. After the blessing the Bishop gave a beautiful address, [commending the sisters] who had labored so indefatigably, energetically, and perseveringly in this parish for many years. Benediction in the Church closed the ceremonies for the day.[3]

Summer brought a welcome respite. With the sisters from Sacred Heart and St. Catherine's, the St. Joseph community boarded the streetcar for Santa Monica to enjoy a well-earned vacation at the beach. There, a daily 3:00 a.m. swim in the Pacific—to avoid the eyes of the curious, no doubt—was a chilling but apparently satisfying daily experience. Prayers and meals excepted, the vacationers spent their days on the sand, delighting in the salt air and invigorating sea breeze.

Returning refreshed, the sisters began school in the new building with an enrollment of 320 children divided into eight classes, each teacher responsible for a single grade—a definite improvement over past practice. The three-story building contained "ten large classrooms, real models of ventilation and light... with all modern equipment, [and a] spacious auditorium with stage."[4] It also provided meeting rooms, a kitchen and a dining room for the use of the parish.

But the sisters would not enjoy the amenities of their new accommodations for long. Changes in clergy personnel in 1904 had brought Father Raphael Fuhr, O.F.M., to St. Joseph's as pastor. Prior to this appointment, he had been pastor of St. Anthony's parish in San Francisco (Cf. below), where his penchant for interference in the sisters' affairs at times strained his relationship with Mother Pia. Their association did not improve a great deal at St. Joseph's and came to a head toward the end of the 1907 school year. Unbeknown to the sisters, Father Fuhr had invited Franciscan Sisters from Buffalo, New York, to take over the school in the fall—much to the chagrin of Mother Pia and the little community at St. Joseph's when they learned of the pastor's action. An official letter informing Mother Pia of the turn of events arrived at the Motherhouse on May 19, but she had had a few days' forewarning (May 14) from Sister Dominica Klein whom Bishop Conaty had alerted to Father Fuhr's move. "To our great consternation," wrote the annalist, "we learned today [May14] that Father Raphael had contracted with other sisters for the coming school year." [5]

Mother Pia wrote immediately in protest to Bishop Conaty. She sent a letter also to Archbishop Riordan of San Francisco, relating the particulars of the affair and assuring him that neither Bishop Conaty nor Father Fuhr had expressed dissatisfaction with the management or teaching in the school. The Archbishop, she hoped, would send a few words of favorable representation to Bishop Conaty, as she feared the pastor had misrepresented her sisters to him. Archbishop Riordan rose manfully to the sisters' defense, assuring her: "I will write at once to the Bishop," he assured Mother Pia, "and ask him to reconsider the case. He is evidently not acquainted with your side of the story and with the good work your Sisters have done in that Diocese and in this. It will give me great pleasure to be of any assistance to you that I can be."[6]

Thinking that he might not have been sufficiently directive, the Archbishop wrote a second time to Mother Pia:

> Now in reference to the difficulties in Los Angeles I say this. You are not to leave St. Joseph's School until you are formally dismissed by the Bishop himself in writing no matter what scandal may occur. You will therefore write to Father Raphael that you have orders from me that your Sisters are not to leave St. Joseph's School unless formally dismissed by Bishop Conaty and that you and your Sisters will remain. You will write to Bishop Conaty to that effect; I will also write to him. We cannot help scandals and we are not to be blamed for them without our doing. Father Raphael has no authority under Civil or Canon law to put you out of that building, therefore you may tell him very plainly that you will yield only to the Bishop's dismissal or to the physical violence of a constable. It is time to

make him understand that law must be obeyed....I write to Bishop Conaty this very day on this matter.[7]

When a third letter arrived from Archbishop Riordan, Mother Pia began to doubt the wisdom of her appeal to him. She had not counted on involving the Apostolic Delegate! Furthermore, talk was beginning in the parish; and withdrawal, she now felt, would be the more prudent course. But by this time the Archbishop was completely committed to the sisters' cause and meant to see justice done, come what may.

July 11, 1907

Mother Pia,
The Josephinum, Mission San Jose, Cal.

My dear Mother Pia:

I have a letter from Bishop Conaty to this effect: that Sister Serraphina [sic] and Sister Domenica [sic] are willing, and anxious even, to give up the school and that they are acting on your advice. Now I wish to say that Sisters Serraphina and Domenica have no authority to give up the school; the only one who could give it up is yourself and I do not wish you to do it. If your Sisters are to leave that school they must be put out formally by the Bishop or by force. You have appealed to me to see justice done and I will see justice done no matter what the consequences are. You must remain perfectly firm in this matter and if necessary carry your case to the Apostolic Delegate. I write this letter to you for your own guidance. You need not send a copy of it to Los Angeles except that you will warn the Sisters of Los Angeles not to interfere at all but refer the Bishop to you.

Sincerely yours,

P. J. Riordan[8]

Meanwhile, Bishop Conaty, wishing to avoid publicity—much less scandal—was opting for a more peaceful settlement. On July 26, 1907, he wrote to Mother Pia:

My dear Mother Pia:

After most careful consideration of the question of

> St. Joseph's school, giving consideration to all the circumstances, I have come to the conclusion that it is advisable for the best interests of all concerned that you should make the sacrifice of abandoning the school to another community. The usefulness of the Sisters seems endangered and therefore in view of all the circumstances I would kindly ask you to withdraw them.
>
> On the other hand, I will take care that whenever there is an opening in the city, I will offer it to you....I will also see that nothing will be said at St. Joseph's reflecting upon the Sisters or their competency.
>
> I regret to have to come to this conclusion but as the Sisters who are here know, this seems to be the best solution, and I trust it will be satisfactory to you as well as to all concerned.
>
> With my very best wishes to you and to the Sisters, I am,
>
> Yours very sincerely,
>
> Thomas J. Conaty
> Bishop of Monterey and Los Angeles[9]

Mother Pia's reply left little doubt about her view of the matter. She would comply with the Bishop's wishes by withdrawing the sisters and would "do so quietly in order to prevent further scandal, although we feel this ignominious expulsion to be an act of the grossest injustice on Fr. Raphael's part."[10] But she would do so on her own terms, which involved the settlement of the disputed ownership of a lot in Los Angeles:

> Allow me to add, however, that I cannot permit our Sisters' departure until we receive your assurance as Bishop of the Diocese, that the Reverend Franciscan Fathers of St. Joseph's Parish will re-deed to us, in due legal form, the lot in Los Angeles, (now held by them) donated to us by Mrs. [Emeline] Childs, or pay us its present value.
>
> If your Lordship is unable to give us this assurance, I fear that we shall be under the unpleasant necessity of appealing the case to the Most Rev. Apostolic Delegate.[11]

Archbishop Riordan's earlier counsel had evidently taken hold; Mother Pia was now ready, if necessary, to involve the Apostolic Delegate!

But when the time actually came to withdraw from the school, sadness prevailed over any other sentiment, and Mother Pia's letter to a sister whom we know only as "My dear Child" expresses her deepest feelings: "Our little Nazareth in Los Angeles—St. Joseph—is being abandoned today. May the dear Lord be served better by its...[new] occupants than He was by us."[12]

And the convent annalist closed her chronicle with admirable restraint: "August 9–10. On both these days we left St. Joseph's, as Fr. Raphael wishes to have Franciscans. It was heart-breaking, but the Lord has allowed it. His Holy Will be praised. *Finis.*"[13]

It was not quite *"finis,"* however. Despite the sisters' withdrawal, the problem of the lot was still not resolved, and the question of ownership, which had lain dormant for a number of years, had surfaced again. In 1894, when visiting the Franciscan Provincial at St. Boniface, San Francisco, Mother Pia had been "... astonished to hear from him that Mrs. Childs did not present the lot to us, but to the community teaching at Saint Joseph's, Los Angeles. We are to transfer the property to the parish. The parish will provide a home for the Sisters."[14]

Now, in response to Mother Pia's letter specifying the return of the property or an appropriate cash settlement, Bishop Conaty's reply was mild, but resolutely impartial. He, too, was determined to see justice done.

> August 3, 1907
>
> Mother Pia.
> The Josephinum,
> Mission San Jose, Cal.
>
> My dear Mother Pia:
>
> Your letter of July 31st is at hand. I am very glad to have this matter settled and I am grateful to you for your consideration of it in the way which in the circumstances seems the best.
>
> With regard to the assurance which you ask from the

Bishop relative to the lot spoken of I can assure you that so far as Father Raphael is concerned he is prepared to do anything recommended to him by the Bishop. Of course he has nothing to do with the lot and it has long since been sold and passed out of the possession of the Franciscans. If it can be shown that it was donated to the Sisters by Mrs. Childs for their own use, there will be no question in the matter. I feel perfectly satisfied that the question of money will not enter into the matter as a disturbing element. Whatever is right and just will be done and you can rest perfectly satisfied in the fulfillment of any obligation which will be shown to me as incumbent upon St. Joseph's Church and the Franciscan Fathers.

I think now the sooner the Sisters retire the better before matters become more generally discussed.

Begging God's blessing upon you and your work, I am,

Yours very sincerely in Christ,

Thomas J. Conaty[15]

It is evident from his letter that the Bishop wished the Dominican Sisters out of St. Joseph parish as quickly as possible—that is, before the exodus of the sisters and the affair of the controversial lot became matter for parochial debate.

About this time also, Mrs. Childs herself added to the general confusion. Following a conversation with Mother Pia, she wrote that while she could "not remember all the particulars of such transaction,"[16] she knew she had given the lot to the sisters for a parochial school. Appalled by this news, Mother Seraphina wrote at length in reply for Mother Pia:

Mrs. E. Childs
Los Angeles

My dear Mrs. Childs:

I know well that it is impossible for you to remember the details connected with the donation of the property on account of your manifold duties and cares, but you remember, dear Mrs. Childs, that I solicited it from you as a site for a house for our Sisters teaching at St. Joseph's School, who were then living in East Los Angeles, and you very kindly observed in bestowing it that a house in the Parish would obviate the inconvenience of their going daily back and forth, particularly during the rainy season. Father Victor himself admits this.[17]

Whether this letter, a pencil draft of which remains in the archives, was ever sent or whether Mrs. Childs ever answered the letter, if sent, cannot be determined. But supporting the sisters' understanding of the matter are the following entries of the Sacred Heart annalist, at whose convent the staff of St. Joseph's were then living:

May 23 — Mrs. Childs promised us a lot

May 30 — Ven. M. Seraphina went with Mrs. Childs to look at lots; one, 50 x 150, the other, 60 x 160.

June 28 — Mrs. Childs and Miss Tirnen came to settle matters about lot. Deed to be transferred to us.

June 29—Sent Mrs. Childs $1.00 to procure deed. Lot is located on Maple Ave. near 12th St

July 8 — Obtained deed from Mrs. Childs.[18]

In a letter dated August 15, 1907, Bishop Conaty guaranteed the sisters a check from Father Raphael for expense items totaling $618.95. But "as to the question of the lot that is a matter which will have to be investigated with some care in order that justice may be done to all the parties concerned."[19] Although both "parties concerned" were firm in their belief that their claims were just, it was Mother Pia who in the end had to surrender all claim to the lot or its equivalent value.

St. Elizabeth Elementary School, Oakland

The first intimation of a foundation in Oakland, California, is found in Mother Pia's Diary under date of August 21, 1893: "Visited Fruitvale, Saint Elizabeth's School. There seems to be a future there. I like the place."[20]

Permission for a German national parish in Oakland under the direction of the Franciscan Fathers was officially granted on July

17, 1892, when Archbishop Riordan met with the German-speaking Catholics of the area in St. Mary's parish hall in downtown Oakland. A decision regarding the location of the parish, however, was not reached without controversy, at times quite heated.

As a national church, St. Elizabeth's was intended to serve the spiritual needs of the German Catholics of Alameda County. But the Oakland clergy had their own ideas, and the Archbishop informed the newly appointed pastor, Father Seraphin Lampe, O.S.F., that the location of the church could not interfere with already existing parishes; it should, therefore, be located somewhere on the outskirts of the city. Fruitvale, a pleasant suburb of Oakland, was favored by the Chancery. Originally a part of the Rancho de San Antonio land grant made to Don Luis Peralta by the Spanish governor of California, Fruitvale was supported as choice because of its accessibility by train from Oakland and Alameda. But Father Seraphin thought it too far out for the German Catholics who would comprise his congregation; he was convinced he would not have sufficient support and opted, therefore, for a mixed parish, that is, one serving both German and English-speaking parishioners. This proposal the Archbishop refused to approve, as it would probably draw from already existing English-serving parishes in the area.

Matters were at a stalemate when the Franciscan Provincial ordered Father Seraphin to abandon the project. The plan worked! St. Mary's pastor, Father Michael King, for whom Father Seraphin had been functioning meantime as a quasi-assistant, appealed to the Archbishop for Father Seraphin's retention and was heard. After a series of consultations with Archbishop Riordan, the Franciscan Provincial relented on both scores, agreeing to a German national church in Fruitvale and to Father Seraphin's remaining as pastor.

Since a mixed parish was for the present out of the question, the astute Father Seraphin settled his problem by establishing a mixed school simultaneously with the foundation of the parish. The Franciscan tactic was not subtle: "If we have... the children we get the parents, and if we get the people we will certainly get a territory."[21] Accordingly, the parish blueprints included not only a church on the second floor, but also a school and a monastery on the first. To ensure the success of his plan Father Seraphin asked Mother Pia to provide sisters for the school.

On October 2, 1893, Sister Seraphina Maerz, superior, Sister Vincentia Powers and Sister Eugenia Becker left the Motherhouse in San Francisco, their destination Fruitvale. There, according to the annalist:

> ... in God's name [and] under the protection of the Guardian Angels they took possession of the new convent. The sisters were received most cordially by Rev. Fr. Seraphin Lampe and... several ladies. The convent was completely furnished. Office, rosary and night prayer were said in common in the chapel before a picture of the Holy Rosary.[22]

October 4, the Feast of the great Franciscan founder, St. Francis of Assisi, had been selected as date for the dedication of the convent and the "entry of the Great King of Heaven and Earth into the little chapel....With what joy we worked," attested the convent annalist, "and all tried to finish the chapel beautifully."[23] The next morning Father Seraphin blessed the building and solemnized the historic moment by celebrating the first Mass in the convent before an appreciative congregation composed of Mother Pia; Sisters Seraphina, Salesia, Felicitas, Vincentia, and Eugenia; and Rosa Ortner, an extern from the Poor Clare convent nearby. "All received Holy Communion. May the Most Holy Sacrament be adored and praised without ceasing in this house and may He never be dishonored here."[24]

Volunteering out of generosity if not necessarily expertise, Sisters Salesia and Felicitas, assisted by Sister Vincentia, set about preparing breakfast equal to the occasion. In her haste and excitement, the unidentified chef flipped the eggs so energetically that they flew out of the pan and had to be salvaged from the stovetop where they sizzled in happy abandon. Though all assured the flustered cook of their amusement at the blackened objects set before them, the annalist's comment seems more germane: "Too many cooks spoil the broth."[25]

On October 22, 1893, Archbishop Riordan solemnly dedicated the church amid ceremonies that included a parade originating at Fruitvale station and proceeding to the church, a distance of five blocks; the celebration of Mass; the singing of the *Te Deum;* and a festive dinner prepared by the women of the parish.

Two days later, October 24, 1893, St. Elizabeth's school opened with 20 children—9 boys and 11 girls—of varied ethnic backgrounds. Father Seraphin had his mixed school! Since the majority of the children had no knowledge of German, all classes were taught in English. At the outset Mother Pia permitted the sisters assigned to teach to waive their stipends.

To the delight of Father Seraphin and the parishioners, the school children celebrated the first Christmas by singing at the six and eight o'clock Masses. After the second Mass, the Fathers invited the choristers to breakfast at the monastery. The following afternoon the children participated in the dismantling of the Christmas tree, which, faithful to German custom, was decorated with cookies, candy, and nuts. "All went home satisfied,"[26] wrote the annalist by way of summation. And she concluded her first year chronicle with thanksgiving to God "for all joys, as well as for many deprivations, sorrows and troubles which have not been mentioned—yet will never be missing in a new foundation."[27] With wry humor she noted that the closing of the sisters' financial account was not difficult, as they had so little.

Overall, increase in enrollment was slow, despite the sisters' summer visits to parishioners encouraging attendance. The economy was a determinant. It was not uncommon at the time for children to withdraw from school in order to seek employment to assist their parents. Nor was the situation helped when several dropped out of school because of a Southern Pacific Railroad change in policy. Free rail passes were no longer available for pupils who had to travel a distance to and from school. At the close of the first decade the school could lay claim to a registration of only 105 pupils, but after 1903 enrollment began to improve, attaining a record 400 students by the middle of the second decade.

By the early 1900s, English-speaking Catholics outnumbered German in the parish. Though Father Seraphin was long since gone, St. Elizabeth's finally saw his dream come true. In 1910 the Archbishop declared the parish territorial or mixed.

The grade school was still confined to the first floor of the original church, but when the latter was replaced in 1921, Father Burchard Dietrich, O.F.M., pastor (1922–1924), began plans for a new elementary building. The appearance of a steam shovel on the premises incited the annalist to new heights of lyricism:

> A large, black, prowling, puffing monstrosity may be seen snorting and stamping about the site selected for the new school. It is termed "a steam shovel," but it resembles

St. Elizabeth Parish first convent (left); to the right, the church (top floor) and Elementary School (bottom floor), c. 1893

an antediluvian monster for all that—yes, a great dirt-eating monster of the Eozaic age as it scoops up incredible mouthfuls of soil and gravel into its ponderous iron jaws, then snorts and shrieks unmercifully as though it were filled with a vicious joy at its own rapacity. The air is thick with its heavy exhalations and the clean white habits of the grade teachers are almost turned black within a week's time.... The teachers have to emulate Demosthenes when he spoke above the roar of the waves, if they wish to be heard above the obstreperous din of that famous steam shovel![28]

Although Father Burchard saw the laying of the cornerstone in 1923, he did not live to see the school completed, dying unexpectedly during the construction. It was left to Father Ildephonse Moser, O.F.M., to bring Father Burchard's plan to completion. The new building was ready for occupancy on August 25, 1924. A two-story concrete structure, the entire first floor was reserved for the elementary school and the second, for the high school (Cf. below.)

First Holy Communion for 80 children from the elementary school and 27 from the public school took place on April 30, 1939. In the afternoon the First Communicants joined the parish organizations to take part in the May procession and crowning of Our Lady in St. Elizabeth's Church. The following morning the children received in a group and were enrolled in the scapular of Our Lady of Mt. Carmel. Breakfast was served them in the parish dining room.

Registration in the latter days of August, 1939, merited the annalist's comment as unusual: The boys, 303, exceeded the girls, 269! A faculty of 13 sisters taught eight single grades, a pre-primer class, with a supervising principal.

During the early years of St. Elizabeth's, a relationship developed between the school and the parish that could best be described as healthy and supportive. The St. Elizabeth's School Club (Mothers' Club) worked hard to contribute assistance to the school, and many of their functions became popular parochial social events. Plays, whist parties, bazaars for the support of the school served to unite the parish in a common purpose—the well-being of their children. Later, when the Fathers' Club was organized, it served a similar purpose, that of benefiting the school through its athletic program. For the children, too, the school was the hub of their social experience, often extending the school day beyond classroom hours. These were good years at St. Elizabeth's.

Two outstanding educators left their mark on the early St. Elizabeth's: Sister Claudia Kolezar, principal from 1923–1940, and Sister Eusebia Lins, principal from 1948–1955.

Born in San Francisco, Sister Claudia was a product of Dominican training, receiving her elementary schooling at St. Anthony's and her high school education at Immaculate Conception Academy. She entered the Order at Mission San Jose on August 3, 1912, received the habit the following year, and made profession on

Sister Claudia Kolezar, Principal, 1923–1940

February 12, 1914. Three years later, she was sent to St. Elizabeth's where she spent the next 25 years. Within six years of her assignment Sister was made principal and eighth grade teacher. In 1930 when enrollment reached 600, Sister Claudia was relieved of classroom teaching. Named to the San Francisco Archdiocesan School Board, she developed an Elementary Art Course that was adopted throughout the Archdiocese. In 1941 Sister suffered a massive heart attack and died a month later. She was buried amid the mourning of parishioners and students alike. According to one parishioner:

> Sr. Claudia helped pull the parish through the Depression. She made special provisions for families unable to pay the modest school tuition, and worked to provide clothing for families in need. As her obituary read, "There is scarcely a family in St. Elizabeth's that is not indebted to her zeal and love."[29]

Sister Eusebia Lins was an equally impressive figure. A no-nonsense administrator, she ran a tight ship, but the students recognized that she had their best interests at heart. Sister first became acquainted with St. Elizabeth's as a teacher in 1937 and was appointed to the principalship in 1948, a position she held for the next seven years. Her students recall fondly the old portable phonograph in the classroom window, blaring out John Philip Sousa's "Under the Double Eagle" march while Sister tapped the beat briskly with her hand bell, moving the children into their respective classrooms for another day of discovery and learning.

In October 1942, St. Elizabeth's Parish observed its Golden Jubilee with a three-day celebration, opening with a Mass of Thanksgiving on Sunday, October 9. Wishing the sisters present for the dinner that followed, Father Victor assured Mother Bernardina that their privacy would be respected. In his after-dinner remarks, Father expressed "regrets" that the "privacy committee" had failed in its duty. All present—including the sisters—enjoyed the humor, though there is some question regarding Mother Bernardina's response!

World War II had its usual impact on the school. School functions were restricted to day time; sisters found themselves responsible for gathering classroom contributions to the Bishops' War Relief Collection; and teachers became students in a 20-hour First

Aid Class at Holy Names College.

Registration closed early in 1946 for all grades except the double first. The long waiting list was in sharp contrast to the early days when the sisters spent their summer vacation visiting families in quest of students! Mounting enrollments (1947–608 pupils; 1948—649) continued to tax the facilities of St. Elizabeth's to such an extent that Father Dennis Mahoney, O.F.M., pastor (1955–1961), inaugurated a major building campaign for a new elementary school in January 1956. The drive elicited a good response, collecting a total of $220,000 in pledges. Meantime, in a quest of more solitude, the Poor Clare Sisters moved from their convent on Thirty-fourth Avenue to Capitola. The parish purchased the vacated convent to serve as club rooms. Now, to accommodate the new school building, the convent was razed.

Ground-breaking took place on May 16, 1958. In addition to classrooms, plans called for a gymnasium, parish library, hall, and cafeteria. The new school fronted on 33rd Avenue with the parish library and hall facing on 34th. July 21 and 22 were scheduled as moving days. Sister Annette Mackey, principal and "mover and shaker" of the change, was ready! Books and materials were stowed in cartons and carefully labeled. Employing a score of boys, available parishioners, and a pickup truck, Sister oversaw the move with drill-sergeant precision with the help from Sister Siena Lawrence at one end (the old building) and Sister Annette on the other (the new). "Thanks to Sister Annette's fine system," the annalist wrote with approval, "each classroom's material was easily placed in its designated room."[30] Ready for occupancy at the beginning of the 1959 school year, the school was dedicated by Bishop Merlin Guilfoyle, auxiliary bishop of San Francisco, on October 18, of the same year.

On Saturday/Sunday mornings the sisters from St. Elizabeth's taught catechism also at St. Mary Magdalene Parish, Berkeley; St. John the Baptist, San Lorenzo; and St. Elizabeth's. For the year 1936, the convent annalist noted that both Berkeley and San Lorenzo classes averaged 110 students each week, and St. Elizabeth, 45. In addition, the sisters taught vacation schools in the summer, the program climaxing with the reception of First Holy Communion. At the request of Father Francis Gliebe, O.F.M., summer teaching at Lakeport was added to the sisters' list, beginning in 1948, and in the school term, 1952–1953, Sister Mary Gregory Duignan and Sister Benilda Desmond of the elementary school staff taught speech classes to handicapped children on Saturdays at St. Jarlath's Elementary School.

In the early 1960s, Fruitvale began to shift from a predominantly Irish-German population to large numbers of Hispanics, African Americans, and Asian Americans, who gradually impacted the student body. St. Elizabeth's continued to meet the needs of its changing population and the challenge of new programs. As an inner city Catholic institution, St. Elizabeth's elementary school is one of several to which the Dominican Sisters have committed themselves in their option for the poor.

St. Elizabeth High School

St. Elizabeth High School was a need envisioned by Father Ildephonse Moser, O.F.M., pastor, who wished to provide additional Catholic education for the graduates of the elementary school, as well as for those of neighboring parishes. The high school opened in August 1921 when 24 freshmen were admitted as students. Classes were held in the rear of the old church. From the outset, the high school was parochial, that is, the pastor exercised the highest authority in the school and bore responsibility for its functioning; it was also co-educational after several conversations with the pastor persuaded Mother Pia to consent reluctantly to make an exception to her ironclad rule and allow the sisters to teach high school boys as well as girls! Consequently, the high school opened with Franciscan Fathers and Dominican Sisters composing the staff. Four sisters formed the original sister-faculty: Sisters Bernardina Michel, principal, Amanda Meyer, Alacoque Densmore, and Emily Spada. Franciscan Fathers conducted the religion classes, in which boys and girls were taught separately.

The second year a tenth grade was added, and for two years thereafter an additional grade each year. Sister Perpetua Juenemann, a dedicated school woman, assumed principalship of the high school in 1922, a responsibility she carried for 18 years. Early in her administration the program was expanded to include a two-year alternative course leading to a commercial diploma and adding typing, shorthand, business English and commercial law to the curriculum. To accommodate the additional classes, two rooms in the sisters' convent were renovated for school use.

In 1924 the erection of the new elementary school provided accommodations for the high school in the same building. The grade school occupied the first floor and the high school, the second. The auditorium was used by both schools and the parish.

Sister Perpetua Juenemann, Principal of St. Elizabeth High School, 1922–1940

The first high school graduation took place in St. Elizabeth's Church. Seven students—six girls and one boy—received academic diplomas before a large audi-

Reverend Ildephone Moser, O.F.M., Pastor of St. Elizabeth Parish, with one of the first graduating classes of St. Elizabeth High School 1925

ence of relatives and friends. In the fall of 1924, with the addition of the fourth year of the academic program, school authorities applied for accreditation to the University of California Agency for Accreditation of High Schools. After visitation by representatives of the University, St. Elizabeth's received notice that it had been placed on the A list of accredited California secondary schools.

Through the years, St. Elizabeth High School students figured prominently in competitive contests. Senior Joyce Nunes was awarded the first place trophy in a declamation contest sponsored by St. Mary's College, Moraga (May 24, 1947). Don Anderson, a senior, received first prize, a $250 U.S. Savings Bond, in the history examination sponsored by Hearst Newspapers. Sister Mary Edward Manning, sponsoring teacher, received a $100 bond and a set of history books for the school library. The following year Joan Elliot, St. Elizabeth senior, carried off the Hearst award. Sister Stanislaus (Bernadette) Dazé was the sponsoring teacher. In the Ladies Auxiliary, Veterans of Foreign Wars, Essay Contest, senior Georgina Williams and junior Margaret Halligan were awarded second and third prizes, respectively, for their essays on the topic, "Freedom's Open Door".

With the appointment of Father Victor Bucher, O.F.M., pastor (1937–1948) and a native son of St. Elizabeth's parish, the Franciscans gradually took a more prominent role in the high school. In addition to assigning Friars to teach religion, Father Victor appeared on the 1941 roster as president of the high school and Father Seraphin Muller, O.F.M., as dean of boys. In 1943, the Franciscan Fathers assumed responsibility for the school administration with Father Damien Lyons, O.F.M., as principal. Sister

Father Victor Bucher, O.F.M., Pastor of St. Elizabeth Parish, 1937–1948

Mary Kevin Breen, O.P., was named assistant principal and dean of girls. Completing the staff were two Franciscan Fathers, eleven Dominican Sisters, and a number of lay teachers. Father Everett Chandler, O.F.M., the last Franciscan to hold the principalship, took over in 1961. Following the Friars, the Diocese of Oakland assumed responsibility for the high school. After a series of lay administrators, responsibility was once more returned to the Dominican Sisters.

With the erection of the new elementary school in 1959, the former school building was renovated for the sole use of the high school. It was high time. Enrollment soon stabilized at 900!

St. Anthony School, San Francisco

With the influx of immigrants from Europe into San Francisco, Archbishop Riordan judged it time to establish a second German national church in the City. His thinking favored the Mission district, south of Market Street. A beginning was made when a temporary place of worship was set up in a vacant store building on Mission Street near Twenty-sixth and the administration entrusted to the Franciscan Fathers. There Mass was offered initially on July 23, 1893, by Father Cletus Gierschewski, O.S.F., of St. Boniface, who had been placed in charge of the preliminary organization of the new parish. Within the year, a suitable location was found on the block bounded by Army, Folsom, Precita and Shotwell streets, and purchased for $22,500. Construction began shortly on a combination church and school building.

The new parish was placed under the patronage of the venerated Franciscan saint, Anthony of Padua. The following July 15, 1894, Father Leo Breuner, O.S.F., pastor, celebrated the first Mass in the new church-school and dedicated the building. For the occasion the sisters from Immaculate Conception priory sang the *Missa de Angelis*. On the same day Mother Pia wrote in her Diary: "Saint Anthony's combined church and school in San Francisco was dedicated today. At the end of the month the new school will open under the direction of our Sisters."[31]

Thinking to strike while the iron was hot, Mother Pia prayed to St. Anthony for help in solving her problems that had arisen in Oregon and in finding $1,000 she needed to cover her indebtedness.

First Class at St. Anthony School in 1894, Tom Berge (standing, third from left), nephew of Mother Maria Pia Backes

In return, she promised the saint that she would give his name to one of the new novices. A benevolent St. Anthony complied; and on Edocia Callahan from Freestone, California, fell the honor at the next reception ceremony. The unsuspecting novice would henceforth be known as Sister Antonia of the Queen of the Holy Rosary.

When the school opened its doors on August 12, 1894, fifty-two children found three Dominican Sisters waiting to receive them. Sister Bernardina Michel was the pioneer principal, assisted by Sisters Dominica Klein and Emilia Moore, teachers. Twice each day until 1918, the sisters walked the half-mile from Immaculate Conception to St. Anthony's and home again at the end of the school day.

At the rate children were applying for entry, it soon became evident that the entire church-school building would be needed for school use. Accordingly, plans for a separate church were formulated; and on August 12, 1894, Father Peter C. Yorke, representing Archbishop Riordan, presided at the laying of the cornerstone. On March 10, 1895, the Archbishop dedicated the new church, and the school took over the original building. With the addition of a grade each year, St. Anthony's boasted a full complement of eight grades by August 1899. Three years later the school building was moved from its Folsom Street frontage to a new location on Precita Avenue. In the moving it was raised and enlarged.

Following a pastorate of five years, the beloved Father Breuner was replaced by Father Raphael Fuhr, O.S.F. The relationship between the new pastor and Mother Pia would prove an uneasy alliance. Father Fuhr's tendency to interfere in the lives of the sisters at times disturbed Mother Pia. He opposed the sisters' praying the Divine Office on the supposition that they did not understand Latin. He declared that he had no obligation to follow the Dominican Ordo when saying Mass in the sisters' chapel. Mother Pia also found him difficult to please in regard to the sisters assigned to teach in the parish. "Only novices," he said. Strictly speaking, the sisters appointed had completed the novitiate and were already, though recently, professed.

The quarter century of commuting from Immaculate Conception to St. Anthony's came to an end for the sisters on November 22, 1919, when they moved into a rented house adjacent to the school site. With mixed emotions the little community of eight bade goodbye to Immaculate Conception Priory, their home for nearly 25 years. "The departure from all the good sisters was not so easy; we shed a few tears....All we could do on that day was to put up our beds and straighten up a little bit, so that we would not fall over the boxes."[32]

But a potentially worse fortune awaited them! On their first Sunday of occupancy a pre-dawn cry for help awakened the sisters who hurried from their rooms to find Sister Ildephonsa Gerber and Sister Ludgera Rolland dragging a fainting Sister Alma Holzman and an unconscious Sister Jacobina Rentfle into the hall. "Gas," was the terse explanation. The doctor, summoned immediately, soon pronounced the victims out of danger because of the quick action of the rescuers. Leaking gas was the responsibility of a workman who had installed a stove the previous day and had accidentally left a meter open in one of the bedrooms. By afternoon the sisters were sufficiently recovered to attend the dedication of the new church organ built for the parish by Louis Schoenstein, father of Sister Mary Mark, O.P.

For the first week, Sister Ildephonsa, superior, slept with a hatchet under her bed! The hatchet was a safeguard against the number of Italians who lived in the neighborhood; Sister feared that the war would not find them well-disposed toward the "German Dominicans." After a week of peaceful co-existence, however, Sister Ildephonsa returned the hatchet to the basement.

On the first Thanksgiving Day in their new home, November 28, 1919, Father Aegidius Herkenrath, O.S.F., pastor, blessed the convent. From then on, cloister was imposed and the steady stream of visitors eager to see the sisters' house came to an end. On New Year's Day, when the Fathers dutifully observed the social custom of formally calling on the sisters, the latter were happy to have chairs to offer them. Christmas had brought a gift of six from a gracious parishioner!

The year 1924 brought exciting word of a new convent. Bazaars for the sisters' benefit proved so successful that workmen were able to begin excavating in late July 1925. In a little less than six months (January 7, 1926) the community moved into their new home facing on Folsom Street. Archbishop Hanna offered Mass and blessed the convent on March 26. He remained for breakfast and visited with the sisters in the community room. A "day of grace and joy," reported the annalist.[33]

At the beginning of the school year 1925–1926, the seventh and eighth grades were introduced to the wearing of school uniforms, a practice that was gradually adopted by the entire student body. The following year, the school participated in Music Week, held annually in the Civic Auditorium, when a chorus of 80 girls sang in a special program.

"Such excitement,"[34] noted the annalist, commenting on the teachers' reaction to the archdiocesan tests administered by the school. January 16, 1940, marked the introduction of the diocesan practice of measuring the progress of students annually.

St. Anthony's observed its Golden Jubilee as a parish with a three-day celebration, beginning on November 28, 1943. His Excellency, Bishop James M. Sweeney, Bishop of Honolulu, represented

Archbishop Mitty at the Mass. Celebrant was Father Lousi Schoen, O.F.M., assisted by Father Lawrence Mutter, O.F.M., deacon, and Father Donald Gander, O.F.M., sub-deacon. The school was proud to note that the three priests were former St. Anthony students. The church was crowded for the occasion, as well as for the dinner which the ladies of the parish served in the sisters' community room. On the third day of the festivities, the school children sang a *Missa cantata*.

St. Anthony's Golden Jubilee booklet of 1943 concludes a brief history of the parish with the following:

> It is hoped that in the not too distant future a new school may be built to replace the historic structure that this year is rounding out its fiftieth year of service for the glory of God and the edification and up-building of God's kingdom on earth.[35]

Not long after, the hope was realized. Groundbreaking for the new school saw Father Adrian Erlenheim, O.F.M., pastor, turning over the first spadeful, followed by Sister Alberta Oehlke, vicaress; Mrs. Clarke, Mothers' Club president; and two eighth grade students. The following month work began. The 1951 graduates held the distinction of being the last class to graduate from the old school, and the next day the transfer of the books and supplies began. On September 4, the new school was opened with 400 students under the new pastor, Father Brice Moran, O.F.M. (1951–1953), and the school administration of Sister Mary Patrick English, O.P. (1949–1952). The following October, Archbishop Mitty dedicated the building. Constructed of reinforced concrete with stucco exterior, the building was substantial and spacious. The first floor housed three classrooms, library, health room, faculty room, principal's office and lobby. The second floor contained five classrooms and two music rooms. A multi-purpose room—a combined cafeteria and social hall—and kitchen comprised the lower floor.

On May 28, 1953, St. Anthony's held registration for the first grade. Before the day was over, registration had closed and disappointed parents and children were put on a waiting list. St. Anthony's had become "big time!"

At the open house held in November 1955, over 600 guests were present for the evening program and tour of the classrooms.

Invited for the afternoon was the faculty from Le Conte Public School nearby. Over the years a friendly association had developed between their Le Conte neighbors and the sisters of St. Anthony's, the schools exchanging invitations to their respective open house and programs.

Following World War II, a wave of immigrants, the majority Hispanic, began settling in the Mission District, many worshipping at St. Anthony's Church. Father Michael Egan, O.F.M., pastor (1941–1949), deemed it time to appeal to Archbishop John J. Mitty to establish St. Anthony's as a territorial, rather than national church. The Archbishop acquiesced, signing the document specifying the change on July 30, 1947.

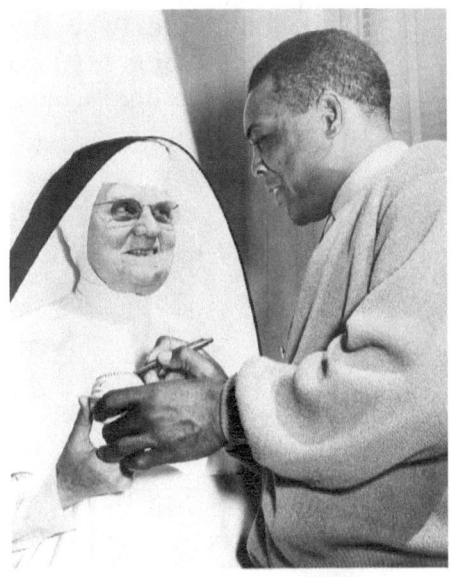

Sister Eusebia Lins, Principal 1955–1967, with her favorite Giant, Willie Mays.

St. Anthony's friars, sisters, and students rejoiced when Bishop-elect Hugh Donohoe, former student from the first to the seventh grades, was elevated to the episcopate as first Bishop of Stockton, California. They could not claim the new bishop as their graduate, as St. Paul's School opened in his home parish in time to graduate the future prelate.

Writing the history of the schools owned or staffed by the Dominican Sisters of Mission San Jose for her Master's thesis, Sister Mary Catherine Antczak concluded her account of St. Anthony Elementary School with the following:

> In the same spirit that Saint Anthony's was begun by German immigrants in 1894, it continues....Although the generation that founded the school has long since moved from the area, the sense of devotion to the parish and its

school continues to be 'alive and well' among a new multi-ethnic population of Hispanics, Filipinos, Blacks and other groups who compose the school community at this time."³⁶

It was a concise and accurate summation.

Notes

[1] Annals of St. Joseph's Convent, Los Angeles 15 July 1906.

[2] Annals of St. Joseph's Convent, Los Angeles 15 July 1906.

[3] Annals of St. Joseph's Convent, Los Angeles 15 July 1906.

[4] Annals of St. Joseph's Convent, Los Angeles 14 May 1907.

[5] Annals of St. Joseph's Convent, Los Angeles 14 May 1907.

[6] Riordan, letter to Backes, 18 May 1907.

[7] Riordan, letter to Backes, 5 July 1907.

[8] Riordan, letter to Backes, 11 July 1907.

[9] Thomas J. Conaty, letter to Backes, 26 July 1907.

[10] Backes, letter to Conaty, 31 July 1907.

[11] Backes, letter to Conaty, 31 July 1907.

[12] Backes, letter to Unidentified Sister, 9 August 1907.

[13] Annals of St. Joseph's Convent, Los Angeles 9–10 August 1907.

[14] Backes 152.

[15] Conaty, letter to Backes 3 August 1907.

[16] Emeline Childs, letter to Backes, 8 August 1907.

[17] Maerz, letter to Childs, 31 August 1907.

[18] Annals of Sacred Heart Convent, May – July 1907.

[19] Conaty, letter to Backes, 15 August 1907.

[20] Backes 147.

[21] Seraphim Lampe, O.F.M. quoted in Oliver Schutz, "Of German Roots:

St. Elizabeth's Parish, 1892–1914," in *St. Elizabeth Parish, Oakland, California: A Centennial History* (Unpublished collection of essays, 1992) 6.

[22] Annals of St. Elizabeth's Convent, 2 October 1893.

[23] Annals of St. Elizabeth's Convent, 3 October 1893.

[24] Annals of St. Elizabeth's Convent, 4 October 1893.

[25] Annals of St. Elizabeth's Convent, 4 October 1893.

[26] Annals of St. Elizabeth's Convent, 26 December 1893.

[27] Annals of St. Elizabeth's Convent, 31 December 1893.

[28] Annals of St. Elizabeth's Convent, 19 November 1923.

[29] Jeffrey Burns, "100 Years of Educational Excellence: the History of St. Elizabeth Elementary School, 1893–1993," (Unpublished essay, 1993) 16.

[30] Annals of St. Elizabeth's Convent, 21–22 July 1958.

[31] Backes 159.

[32] Annals of St. Anthony's Convent, 22 November 1919.

[33] Annals of St. Anthony's Convent, 26 March 1926.

[34] Annals of St. Anthony's Convent, 16 January 1940.

[35] Saint Anthony's Parish, "The Golden Jubilee Program," 1943.

[36] Antczak 47–48.

CHAPTER ELEVEN

THE FOX CATCHER

Once again Sister Seraphina Maerz found herself bound for Europe. This time her mission was well-defined: to set up a house abroad for the purpose of recruiting vocations to the Congregation. The responsibility did not entail establishing a permanent foundation, but rather selecting a suitable house and location for a limited time—two or three years—just long enough to make the California Congregation known abroad. It would not prove as simple as it sounded.

On August 7, 1899, Sister Seraphina and Sister Margaretha Griffin left San Francisco by train for New York. Ten days later they boarded the *Bremen,* their destination Southampton, England. Sister Margaretha, a gifted violinist, was born and baptized Eva Rosa Griffin in Bogota, Colombia. She entered the Congregation at the San Francisco Motherhouse on June 16, 1892, three days before her twentieth birthday. She was professed on July 21, 1894, and was still in temporary vows at the time of the mission to Europe. Sister Margaretha was chosen as Sister Seraphina's companion in order to avail herself of the opportunity to study church music and organ under European masters. Sister Seraphina was to devote whatever time she could spare from vocation recruiting and the study of regular observance and liturgical ceremonies to the pursuit of art.

After brief visits with the Dominicans of Stone, England; Dusseldorf, Germany; and the Carmelites in Herzogenrath, the sisters set up temporary quarters with the Dominican Sisters in Cologne, who conducted a home for retired women. Once settled, they began their studies under highly qualified teachers. For Sister

Sister Seraphina's sketch of the Bremen deck before and after a storm warning August 1899

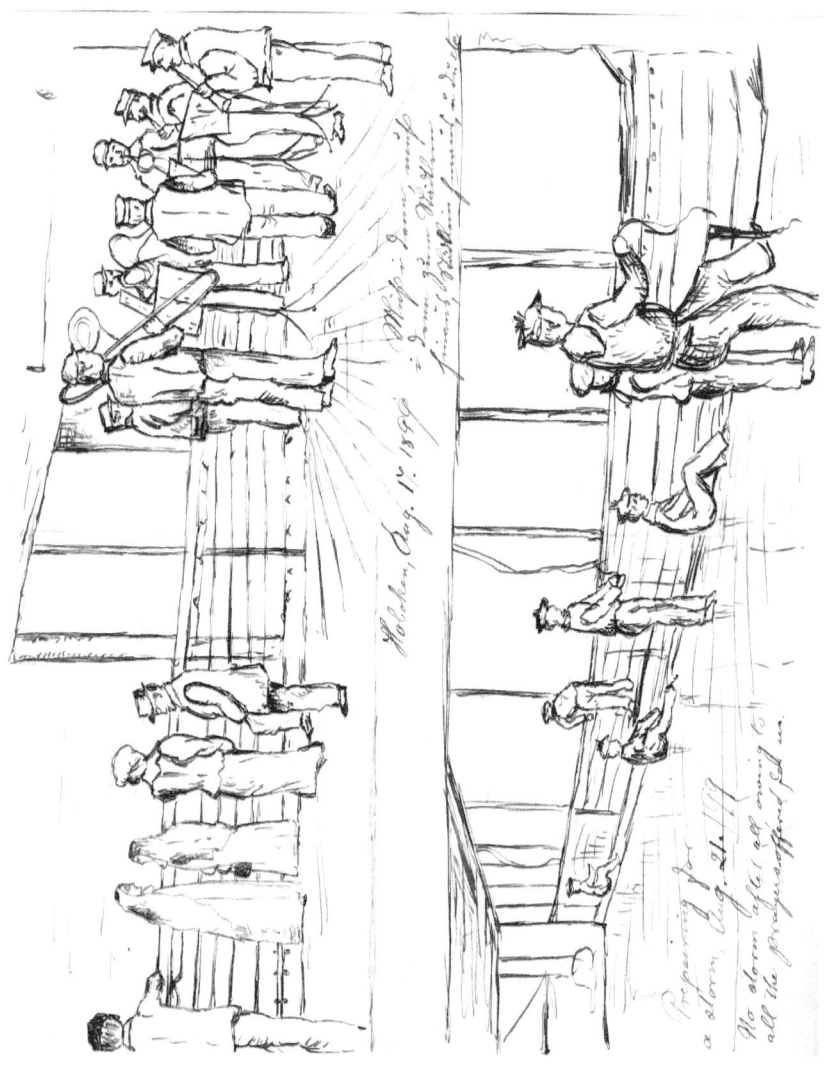

Margaretha music was a full-time occupation; for Sister Seraphina art was a satisfying but secondary pursuit.

Assessing the situation shortly after their arrival in Cologne, Sister Seraphina decided that her first move would be to cultivate the acquaintance of the local clergy, who were in the best position to direct young women inquirers to the California mission. Her second would be to visit the bishops in dioceses where the establishment of a house appeared to have the possibility of success. She would also have to be attentive to Father Albertus Trapp, Dominican provincial of Germany, and Father Dominicus Scheer, O.P., both of whom regarded themselves as "delegates" of Mother Pia and the travelers as their personal responsibility.

Sister Seraphina's personality served her well in her new circumstances. She had a simplicity about her that was disarming, coupled with an astuteness that was often underestimated. Dubbed by the German clergy "the fox-catcher from California," she soon had their friendship and interest. Bishop Anton Fischer of Cologne was also taken with her charm, endorsing her project and urging her to visit him often. And the Wettenhausen cloistered Dominicans, blessed with a surplus of vocations, offered to send girls with missionary aspirations to apply for acceptance in California.

With the entry of two postulants on January 6, 1900, conditions in Cologne became almost intolerable. Sister Seraphina's room, fourteen by sixteen feet in dimension, served as oratory, refectory, study, music room, sewing room, art studio, community room, postulancy, parlor, and bedroom. Sister Margaretha and the two postulants shared a second room designed for a single occupant. As part payment for their room and board, the postulants helped with the housework, which entailed by agreement cleaning the rooms of the residents, but gradually by extension included serving the residents' other real or fancied needs. Although Sister Seraphina's limited funds made caution a virtue, she canceled the arrangement when the two had to work from morning to night "almost like slaves;"[2] time to further their religious formation was more important to her. At the same time the need for a larger house became every day more apparent.

Over the next few months, a number of possibilities emerged: Venlo, Holland, seemed especially promising. The Marienthaler sisters offered a small house or the option of building on their property, and Father Ceslaus Hansen, O.P., Venlo prior, urged buying property near the Dominican Fathers and building there. From Diekirch, Luxemburg, came an offer of a house that the owner was willing to rent. But the bishops of the respective dioceses, though gracious, turned skittish when it came to granting the requisite permission. Anticipating the expulsion of religious orders from France any day, they feared that large numbers of religious would soon be crowding into their dioceses and they were uneasy lest the influx presented problems of housing and financial support with which they were not prepared to cope. Hence, the Bishop of Roermond refused permission to settle in his diocese on the grounds that his Diocesan Council had recently passed legislation forbidding the establishment of new convents; he suggested Marienthal, which involved only a simple addition to an already existing convent or, better yet, Nijmegen, which was in another diocese! The Bishop of Luxemburg refused with regrets. Luxemburg, a country of 200,000 inhabitants, already had 102 religious communities and, furthermore, was "a nest of liberals." [3]

The High Royal Government of Prussia presented an even more formidable barrier. Describing a visit to a government official in Cologne, Sister Seraphina wrote of being received courteously enough, but denied her request. The sisters could not teach girls (postulants) as that would be private instruction and would require permission of the City School Deputation. "Did you ever hear anything like that in your life?" she wrote in exasperation to Mother Pia. "To teach the children "cat", "rat", "fat", we would have to apply to the 'Kingly Government' through the City School Deputation. Our English 'lessons' consist usually in English conversation during recreation, and this nobody can forbid us."[4] They might, however, have boarders, but would have to register them with the local police.

The choices had narrowed almost to a point of nonexistence and Sister Seraphina was beginning to turn her thoughts toward Rome when an invitation arrived out of the blue from a Dr. Enteneuer in Rhoendorf-on-Rhine, a beautifully situated spot between Cologne and Koblenz. Following injury in a train accident, Dr. Enteneuer had been compelled to abandon the management of his Kneipp Sanitarium and consequently had a house available for the sisters' use. Sister Seraphina explained to Mother Pia that the doctor was "of the opinion that the government cannot have anything against our taking some treatments here. This is a government business; everything here is 'government, government.'"[5] Weighing the balance in favor of the Rhoendorf location was the frequent presence of the Dominican Fathers, who were often the doctor's guests, availing themselves of the baths at the sanitarium. A confessor would often, therefore, be on hand.

Sister Seraphina went to inspect. The house was old, built in 1571, but in good condition. It was large; 10 rooms on the upper floor, completely furnished, would serve nicely as a convent. The lower floor comprised storage, with one room assigned to the gardener as living quarters. His presence, Sister Seraphina took pains to assure Mother Pia, would guarantee protection. Needed, of course, was the Bishop's permission, as well as the approval of Father Dominicus Scheer in Rome and Father Albertus Trapp in Dusseldorf, who "wants to do everything himself."[6]

In comparison with Cologne, Rhoendorf appeared almost palatial. Sister Seraphina was jubilant when Father Trapp secured the Bishop's permission, attributing his success to the intercession of St. Catherine of Siena, her beloved patron. On February 6, the little community of four left Cologne for Rhoendorf, where Dr. Enteneuer met them with open arms. "One would think we had fallen from heaven,"[7] wrote Sister Seraphina happily. She seemed to relish the idea that their circumstances would be somewhat suspect. "Like the Jesuits," she noted in a letter to Mother Pia, "we are here under cover and have to be careful. The government thinks we are here for the baths."[8]

Although candidates continued to apply, most came without funds for the trip to America. Sister Seraphina stormed heaven for a few postulants of means who could underwrite passage for themselves and for their less well-endowed companions. By this time her experiences in Europe were causing significant shifts in her thinking. She was now persuaded that candidates should receive the habit and make profession in Germany before leaving for the States; parents wished their daughters settled, i.e., professed, before going so far from home. She had come to the further realization, with which the German clergy concurred, that to accomplish her mission a longer time—eight to ten years—was a more realistic expectation than the two or three originally intended. She began to envision a European house of studies where postulants would pursue music, pedagogy, art, and embroidery. So many decisions had still to be made!

Inhibiting Sister Seraphina at times was the seriousness with which the Dominican Fathers took their responsibility. She could not make a move without permission from Father Trapp, who steadfastly maintained that Mother Pia had entrusted the sisters to his charge. From Rome Father Dominicus felt obliged to exercise a similar responsibility, and Father Bartolomeus Bremer, O.P., Sister Seraphina's newly selected spiritual director, was turning out to be a strict, no-nonsense guide. Such diligent supervision was offset from time to time by a certain deviousness on the part of Sister Seraphina. The better wisdom, she decided, was not to tell everything, and she explained to Mother Pia, "You should have Father Provincial as your superior; you would contract yellow jaundice.... Still, he means well,"[9] she concluded charitably.

She acknowledged gratefully the Fathers' help in directing to her girls seeking vocational guidance. Occasionally, however, their would-be candidates proved a source of embarrassment. Among the young women Father Dominicus sent to Sister Seraphina was a former penitent, who came highly recommended also by her pastor and the proprietor of the dry goods shop where she was employed. Deferring entrance day, scheduled for April 20, when the storekeeper asked that the girl remain in his employ until after Pentecost, this was his busiest season, Sister Seraphina agreed obligingly. No one was prepared for what followed. On April 21 the police arrived at the store to take into custody the trusted employee and two accomplices. A search of the girl's room, where she lived with her employer's family, revealed suitcases crammed with goods removed from the store secretly over a period of time. Two carriages, traced to a relative's home, were found loaded with contraband, bringing the value of the pilfered merchandise to about 6,000 German marks. "In truth," wrote a grateful Sister Seraphina to Mother Pia, "God was good to us."[10]

Weary of Prussian bureaucracy and the petty annoyance of frequent inspections and summonses to the offices of local officials, Sister Seraphina wrote home to her superior:

> Their official manners anger me....As long as one has a red

stripe on his cap and jacket, he thinks he is important. And with the clergy here, little can be done; they haven't the courage....Even Father Provincial ordered that...groceries, meat, etc. should be bought in the postulants' names so that no one will find out we have our own kitchen and the police investigate.[11]

At last, her patience worn thin, Sister Seraphina decided it was time to take matters into her own hands and go straight to the top, bypassing all men with "stripes." A letter to the Emperor, Wilhelm II, "can't do any harm," she rationalized. "Shall I keep going from Pontius to Pilate? In the end, each one makes his role so important that no one gets to the point."[12] She would at least see what she could do! And so, on May 15, 1900, Sister Seraphina sent off a letter to Emperor Wilhelm II, asking permission to be allowed

> ...to live in Germany and establish a House of Study where workers in our German-American Schools will be trained. It is of great importance to us that German methods of pedagogy are studied thoroughly and can be used in California, so that our German Schools will be counted among the best.[13]

Meanwhile, a notice from the Mayor of Rhoendorf informed Sister Seraphina that the *Landrat* (Prefect) wished to receive from Mother Pia and the San Francisco Chancery Office a declaration of permission for the sisters' presence in Germany. The notice did nothing to buoy Sister Seraphina's spirits. "More red tape,"[14] she said with disgust. Father Trapp wrote out a form for Mother Pia to copy and sign:

> I hereby declare that Sisters M. Seraphina Maerz and Margaretha Griffin were sent by me from the Motherhouse in San Francisco to Germany for the purpose of accepting new candidates for our German schools and sending them to California to test their vocation for a period of time, since because of a lack of sufficient help we cannot supply the requests of German families. The period of the Sisters' stay here should last only a few years.
>
> Sister Maria Pia Backes
> Superior General of the Dominican
> Sisters in California and Oregon
>
> SEAL[15]

No answer from the Emperor was forthcoming—at least directly. But despite Sister Seraphina's talent for making friends and representing the sisters so favorably, she was becoming daily more aware that conditions in Prussia were tightening. Her thinking was confirmed when a mandate from the government (February 8, 1901) ordered the immediate dismissal of all postulants and forbade further acceptance.

The situation became even more discouraging when the Archbishop of Cologne refused to approve the sisters' establishing a house in Rhoendorf. Politics figured prominently in the refusal. The Archbishop and the Prussian Minister of Public Worship were long-time friends, and the prelate would do nothing to jeopardize the relationship. If the American sisters did not enjoy the patronage of the government, the Archbishop would by no means support their presence. Father Provincial's comment on the situation piqued Sister Seraphina. Instead of sympathy, he merely marveled that the sisters had been allowed "to walk around so undisturbed for a whole year."[16] Writing to Mother Pia, she asked, "Did you ever in your life hear language like that?...He knew that all my work with Bishop Anzer, Bachem [Cologne newspaper editor], etc., would be of no use. I told him that he could have said something, but not one of our Fathers said, 'Do this or that.' I did my best and that consoles and quiets me."[17]

Father Dominicus was no better. His remarks Sister Seraphina considered heartless. He always knew, he said, that her stratagems would accomplish little, as nothing could be achieved with the Prussians! But he partially redeemed himself by mentioning, "a place that belongs to no government. It was forgotten at the time the division was made in 1815. It is a neutral district, but what it is called I do not know. It must be between Aix-la-Chapelle and Verviers."[18]

Altenberg, Moresnet Neutre

From her friend, Bishop Fischer, Sister Seraphina learned that the region was called Moresnet Neutre or Neutral Moresnet. She decided to investigate. The little village of Altenberg in Moresnet Neutre, sandwiched between the German and Belgian borders and a part of the Diocese of Luttich, would put the sisters right "under the nose of the Prussians,"[19] but independent of them, a fact which suited Sister Seraphina just fine! Moreover, the bishop of the diocese, Most Reverend Victor Joseph Doutreloux, was amenable. The sisters moved to Altenberg in time for Easter 1901, establishing themselves in a small rented house, which they immediately christened "Little Nazareth."

Removed from Prussian bureaucracy, Sister Seraphina was now free to pursue vocations with singleness of purpose. But though things were turning out satisfactorily and vocations were increasing, other concerns began to occupy her, particularly anxiety about Mother Pia's health. Already the previous year she had written:

> If only I were at home with you! I would help you to the best of my strength....How I implore the dear Lord to give you the needed strength, health, and all you need for your difficult office....I have also had hours when I thought that perhaps it was a mistake that I was sent here. [But] Father Bartholomeus said, 'You are here because God wanted it and not because human beings wanted it.' In other words, it is God's Will that I am here.[20]

Nevertheless, concern for Mother Pia nagged at her and she continued to feel a strong pull toward home.

By November, 1901, Mother Pia had come to a similar way of thinking and sent word that she would like to recall Sister Seraphina and Sister Margaretha to the Motherhouse. Their replacements would be Sister Thomasina Brueggen and Sister Josephina Schreiber. Sister Thomasina, a native-born German, had taught for 10 years in Germany before entering the community. Her final profession took place on July 28, 1900. Sister Josephina born also in Germany, had at some time migrated to the United States, where she entered the community in June 1894. At the time of her assignment to Altenberg she had been professed for five years. In Altenberg she would be known among the sick poor as their "good Samaritan."

Shortly after the 1901–1902 school term ended, Sisters Thomasina and Josephina bade farewell to their California colleagues and set sail for Europe. Arriving in Altenberg, they were welcomed heartily by the sisters, the little house resounding with excitement. Sister Thomasina's first impression of the Altenberg convent was of "a poor 'little Nazareth' [where] peace and God-loving joy reigned."[21] The house was quickly explored. On the ground floor were two small rooms, the one doubling as refectory and study; the other, as community room and parlor. For desks the postulants had wooden boxes covered with white oilcloth. The ground floor also contained the tiny chapel, a Rosary group and a few other statues constituting the principal furnishings. A narrow staircase led to the first floor where two small rooms served as postulants' bedrooms.[22] To the right of the stairs was Sister Margaretha's music studio. On the second floor were located rooms for the novices quarters. Sister Seraphina and Sister Margaretha had their rooms on the third floor. Kitchen and laundry were located in the yard, the walls covered with oilcloth, as wall paper could not withstand the dampness.

Hardly had the two sisters settled in Altenberg when Father Albertus Trapp arrived to inspect the new location and to preach a retreat, which ended with the first profession of Sister Victoria Borgemeister and Sister Lamberta Menne. As the first sisters of the Congregation to complete their training and make profession in Germany before setting out for America, Sisters Victoria and Lamberta have earned honored place in the annals as pioneers of a long line that generously supported the early missions of the Congregation.

A few days later Father Dominicus Scheer also made his appearance to welcome the newcomers. The following month five postulants entered. Although there was a steady stream of candidates making application to enter, only a small number could be accepted. Poor health or lack of vocation were the usual deciding factors.

After a transition period of three months, Sister Seraphina, Sister Margaretha, recently professed Sister Victoria, and the five postulants bade tearful goodbyes to the sisters in "Little Nazareth" and left for Antwerp (probably October 1902), where they boarded a steamer for the United States. With Sister Seraphina's departure, Sister Thomasina assumed the office of superior; and the first phase of the European experiment came to an end.

Four new candidates soon filled the places of the California-bound postulants. Their entry was occasion for the Altenberg annalist to take a somewhat biased view of the youthfulness of one, "a young child of fifteen years."[23] Her opinion was reinforced a few weeks later when fire broke out in the girl's room. The terrified postulant ran to alert the community, who seized buckets, bowls, or anything else handy and fled outside for water from the rain barrel. Solid ice awaited the would-be fire fighters, who had to resort to the kitchen sink and wait their turn at a single faucet. With an eye for the dramatic, the annalist reported "a running and a rushing, a coughing and a gasping, a shock and a mix-up. Only a few more minutes and the whole place would have gone up in flames as two close-by...attic rooms had eight beds with feather quilts."[24] Fortunately for the "miscreant," damage was limited to a single wall and a window-frame.

Father Albertus Trapp's term as provincial of Germany expired on May 5, 1903. On his frequent visits to the Altenberg community he often expressed a desire to spend his last years in solitude. But now, to the sisters' amazement, on May 10, 1903, he appeared at the door, meager possessions in hand, and announced he had come to be their chaplain! Relieved of responsibility as provincial, *"Vaterchen,"* (Little Father) as the sisters affectionately called him, spent his last years in prayerful and contented retirement among the sisters he had grown to love, serving the "Little Nazareth" community faithfully until his death on November 7, 1908. The convent annalist summarized the sisters' feelings toward him when she wrote: "Never will we forget the beautiful example of humility, child-like simplicity and piety of the dear, venerable old priest; he showed himself in all things as the caring Father of the sisters."[25]

Reports of severe weather, excessive dampness, and critically limited space elicited a welcome directive from the Motherhouse in California bidding the sisters look for property on which to build. Obeying happily, they found a lot conveniently near the parish church and purchased it for 5,300 D.M. On the recommendation of the Moresnet Neutre pastor, Sister Thomasina engaged an out-of-town architect. His appointment met with instant opposition from the townspeople, who regarded the employment of an outsider as an injustice committed against the entire town. But it was the pastor, not the sisters, who became the focus of their outrage, which led finally to a petition to the Bishop for the priest's removal. The Bishop refused, and gradually calm was restored in the little village.

Cost of the proposed building was estimated at $7,000, which Mother Pia agreed to underwrite. Actual construction began on July 2, 1903. Despite delays caused by severe weather and the architect's partiality for more important projects, the building was eventually completed, and the community of the Nazareth Novitiate House moved in during Holy Week of the following year. Father Albertus blessed the house on Good Friday, April 1, 1904, and celebrated the first Mass in the new chapel on Easter Sunday. The community, expanded now to 19 by the addition of 11 postulants, was jubilant.

The excitement of moving into the new convent was surpassed only by the announcement of Mother Pia's impending arrival. The days preceding the Foundress's visit were spent in cleaning, polishing, and arranging and re-arranging the furniture. Finally, on May 17, the long-awaited day dawned. Accompanied by Sister Clara Irwin, Mother Pia arrived in Altenberg after an 11-day voyage, marked by towering seas, heavy rains and high winds. "The joy was so great, so unbelievable in its anticipation," exulted the Altenberg annalist, "that even with effort the Sisters could not work themselves into holy indifference....Yes, this was the happiest day to be noted in the Annals."[26] Mother Pia had come for a number of reasons: to see the new house, to visit the Dominican convents recommended by the Master General and to seek advice from Rome regarding the *Constitutions*. In the days following her arrival she announced the new convent appointments: Sister Clara Irwin, superior; Sister Josephina Schreiber, treasurer; and Sister Thomasina Brueggen, novice mistress. Out of consideration for the latter's failing health, Mother Pia relieved her of the additional responsibility of superior.

Papal Approval: The Journey Continues

In July Mother Pia traveled to Marienthal in Venlo, Holland, to meet Father Dominicus Scheer. Although she had been looking forward to seeing him again, she admitted disappointment: "Approached Father Dominicus concerning the *Constitutions*. Not much satisfaction on account of his poor hearing. Father has become very serious—has lost his former congeniality. He is ailing."[27] Time proved her right. A month after her return from Venlo, Mother Pia received a note from Mother Augustina, Marienthal prioress, informing her that Father Dominicus' health was declining at an alarming rate. Deeply affected, she wrote immediately for permission to visit him again. Receiving a favorable reply, she left at once for Venlo, where she found the patient much improved. In fact, the next day he wished to work on the *Constitutions,* but was exhausted after three-quarters of an hour.

On September 12, Mother Pia and Sister Clara left Aachen for London, taking the boat at Ostende, Belgium. Their destination was the Dominican Motherhouse in Stone, England, one of the convents recommended for observance by the Master General. The community made an excellent impression on Mother Pia:

> A very good spirit reigns in this community. Very quiet measured demeanor, but not cold; rather plain, mild, friendly. The Mothers understand different languages; are prudent and sensible. Very monastic; very sisterly. Towards superiors, the Sisters are not shy...[or] timid; filial submissiveness.[28]

In Mother Philomena Dormer, provincial, Mother Pia found a kindred spirit with whom she could speak freely: "She agrees with me regarding Breviary, Domestic Sisters, Enclosure. I feel greatly relieved that others think as I do. I do not want to insist on my opinion, for I trust little in myself. But I thank God for the relief afforded me by this interview."[29]

Mother Philomena encouraged her to seek papal approbation for the Congregation. Mother Pia left England greatly reassured. "I profited by this trip to England. There I found truly genuine religious, uncontaminated by the Zeitgeist [spirit of the age]. Educated but simple. Nothing of the butterfly spirit."[30]

From Father Albertus Trapp, Mother Pia learned that in Rome Father Thomas Esser, O.P., was willing to assist her with the *Constitutions.* Father Esser, a well-known professor of Thomistic philosophy and a member of the Congregation for Religious, was a tempting contact. Mother Pia pondered the matter at length. The thought that Father Dominicus might possibly be offended concerned her, but his health was so precarious that she hesitated to burden him further. It took her two days to compose a letter that satisfied her. "The letter to Father Dominicus...cost me an untold struggle to do what I thought impossible....How will it affect the poor old offended man? My Jesus, preserve him from sorrow. Let him not be disappointed in Pia." [31] To her relief Father Dominicus was not at all disappointed and remained a steadfast friend.

In October, the new Provincial of Germany, Father Ceslaus Hansen, O.P., and Father Gregor Banten, O.P., prior of Santa Sabina Convent in Rome, visited Altenberg. They remained five days, an indication of the interest Father Ceslaus was taking in the Congregation. Concerned for Mother Pia's health, he insisted on Mother Seraphina's return to Germany to accompany her to Rome and on the longer trip home. Accordingly, Mother Pia sent a dispatch to her friend inviting her to come. Not surprisingly, the next morning she received a favorable reply.

Daily it was becoming more evident to Mother Pia that Sister Thomasina would not survive another German winter and needed the milder climate of California. At the beginning of the new year, therefore, (January 5, 1905) Mother Pia wrote to Mother Seraphina recommending Sister Dolorosa Wallrath as novice director for Altenberg. The General Council concurred; Sister Dolorosa was a wise choice.

A "pillar" of the Congregation, Maria Wallrath was born in Haupstadt, Indiana, on August 20, 1870. Maria's father, Peter Wallrath, was a school teacher and from him she acquired a lifelong appreciation of learning and a passion for reading. When she was 21, she bade farewell to her family and boarded the train, her destination San Francisco. Despite the restrained language of her diary, the trip must have been a terrifying experience for the young woman. On February 17, she wrote: "Mr. Meyer, a traveling salesman from New York, and the Pullman conductor were shot and killed in my presence near Bald Knob, Kansas, at about 12:30 p.m."[32] No further details of the shocking experience are recorded in her diary.

In San Francisco Maria lived with an aunt, and there she met the Dominican Sisters who taught at St. Boniface School. The association led to her entrance into the Congregation on July 8, 1893. She received the habit and her religious name and title, Sister Dolorosa of the Holy Cross, on July 19, 1894, and made profession on July 20, 1895. Five years later Sister Dolorosa made her final profession. She always remembered July 28, 1900, as one of the happiest days of her life. For the occasion Sister's uncle, Father Michael Wallrath, was celebrant of the Mass.

Her first assignment was to Portland, Oregon, where she taught at St. Joseph's School and later served as prioress of St. Dominic's convent, Albina (1903–1905). From there she received her call to Germany, (March 14, 1905) traveling in the company of Mother Seraphina and Miss Parsha Clark, a lay teacher in our schools.[33] For the next seven years Sister Dolorosa would serve the Congregation in "Little Nazareth."

Sisters Dolorosa Wallrath, Josephina Schreiber and Clara Irwin in Altenberg

Two weeks after Sister Dolorosa's arrival in Altenberg, Sister Thomasina, accompanied by recently professed Sister Pulcheria Reichert, Sister Amalia Weber and two postulants, left their beloved Germany for California.

Notes

[1] Maerz, letter to Backes, 2 November 1899.

[2] Maerz, letter to Backes, 17 January 1900.

[3] Maerz, letter to Backes, 31 December 1899.

[4] Maerz, letter to Backes, 18 October 1900.

[5] Maerz, letter to Backes, 4 January 1900.

[6] Maerz, letter to Backes, 11 January 1900.

[7] Maerz, letter to Backes, 4 January 1900.

[8] Maerz, letter to Backes, 17 January 1900.

[9] Maerz, letter to Backes, 26 April 1900.

[10] Maerz, letter to Backes, 2 May 1900.

[11] Maerz, letter to Backes, 6 April 1900.

[12] Maerz, letter to Backes, 14 May 1900.

[13] Maerz to Wilhelm II, 15 May 1900.

[14] Maerz, letter to Backes, 3 February 1901.

[15] Maerz, letter to Backes, 3 February 1901 (with copy of form for *Landrath*).

[16] Maerz, letter to Backes, 21 February 1901.

[17] Maerz, letter to Backes, 21 February 1901.

[18] Maerz, letter to Backes, 7 March 1901.

[19] Maerz, letter to Backes, 7 March 1901.

[20] Maerz, letter to Backes, 4 July 1900.

[21] Thomasina Brueggen, O.S.D., letter to unidentified Dominican Sister, 15 July 1902.

[22] In Europe it is customary to designate the first floor the ground floor, and the next floor the first.

[23] Annals of Altenberg, Moresnet Neutre, 3 November 1902.

[24] Annals of Altenberg, Moresnet Neutre, 3 November 1902.

[25] Annals of Altenberg, Moresnet Neutre, 10 May 1903.

[26] Annals of Altenberg, Moresnet Neutre, 15 May 1904.

[27] Backes 281.

[28] Backes 283.

[29] Backes 284.

[30] Backes 284.

[31] Backes 285.

[32] Wallrath, diary, 17 February 1891.

[33] Miss Parsha Clark was a lay teacher in our schools. No explanation is given for her traveling with the sisters during the school year.

CHAPTER TWELVE

CRISIS IN COMMUNITY

On January 1, 1902, Mother Pia wrote in her Diary: "With Jesus at the helm, I shall sail safely. Whatever may come during this new epoch of my life, I shall bear for the love of Him. I shall nurture only one desire of my heart, to love Jesus, and to do His Holy Will. I fear the future, yet I place all my worry and all my incapacity in the hands of God. He is our Father."

Little did she suspect what her words foreshadowed. But by the end of April she had reason to be concerned. "My heart is sore on account of a partisan spirit which is beginning to show itself among some of our Sisters,"[2] she confided to the Diary.

Trouble was brewing. The struggle between Irish and German first-wave immigrant Catholics that continued into the next generation originated primarily in differences that cut deep into the respective nationality's concept of church. In her study, *Immigrants and Their Church*, Sister Dolores Liptak, R.S.M., writes: "More than perhaps any other immigrant group, the Irish realized the value of integrating with American society"[3] and were ready to situate themselves within, not apart from, the American environment. In striving for acceptance they had the advantage of sameness of language, and post-bellum United States following the Civil War saw them improving their economic and social status and beginning to experience a new sense of self-importance. Further, their sons and daughters chose to serve the Church in such numbers that by 1900, they held almost all the positions of ecclesiastical power in the country.

Several major consequences resulted from the pervasive

presence of Irish Americans in church affairs. One was their effect upon the institutional development of the church. From the time of their initial involvement, Irish-Americans manifested a paternalistic, even controlling, attitude toward the development of the local church. Their first concern for Catholics was simple enough: members of gathered Catholic communities should be provided with a pastor and a place of worship. Almost as soon as a Catholic congregation...could be defined, negotiations for these were commenced. Under an authorized priest, church property was purchased and a church erected.... Only if the church could be established firmly within a community did the Irish-American leadership encourage other institutions, such as schools, orphanages, or other social or health agencies.[4]

Meanwhile, the escalating number of German immigrants to the United States soon made them the largest non-English speaking Catholic population in the nation. It was not long, therefore, before they too made their presence felt in the Church. They took issue with the Irish who, in their opinion, were entirely too tolerant in adapting to American ways. Friction between the two groups was inevitable, especially in regard to the school. German-Americans wanted schools for their children in which the faith would be protected and their own language and culture taught (their motto was "Language Saves the Faith").[5] For them it was essential that their children develop a spirituality that included their traditional and cherished values. In their thinking the school possessed the key to the future.

For Irish-Americans, the concern for schools was predicated on the degree to which public schools had been overly influenced by Protestant or secular values. Moreover, it was only when Catholic education could not be obtained within the family setting (preferably at the mother's knee) that the concept of schools was strongly advanced....Once assured that their children would, in some way, receive sufficient religious education, the Irish seemed more easily able to divert their concern for schools toward other social issues than the German-Americans or other ethnic minorities, who remained totally committed to the establishment of parochial schools.⁶

Convinced of the need to protect their faith by preserving it in their own language and culture, German-Americans supported the national church as an alternative to the territorial parish. Further, they began to demand German representation in the predominantly Irish episcopate to safeguard their rights as bona fide members of the American Catholic Church.

It should not surprise, then, that a "reverse-friction" would eventually find its way into the convent. Sisters from Ireland or of Irish descent, plainly outnumbered, found themselves immersed in German language and culture. Discomfort on the part of the minority gradually led to resentment and discontent. Disturbed by the unrest she sensed, Mother Pia felt that she was "living between a volcano that threatens to explode at any time and an iceberg that causes the marrow of my bones to freeze."⁷

Compounding her worries was a letter from Rome in which the writer quoted an unknown source:

> What a surprise came in the mail this afternoon...."M.P. [Mother Pia] boasts of her power in Rome. P.D. [Pater Dominicus] writes every month. He meddles with diocesan affairs. M.P. is at variance with the confessor; she will lose her mind yet." Remain tranquil, Pia"⁸

Although the contents cost her a restless night, the morning found her tranquillity restored:

> The darkest hour comes just before the dawn....Tomorrow is the beautiful feast of the Immaculate Mother [December 8]. I place the entire matter calmly in God's hands and am silent. I forgive Sister N. and Father X. Jesus, help me to control my tongue in this trouble.⁹

Still, the discontent was taking its toll, and a week later she recorded in the *Diary*:

> How dark, void, and destitute of love is my inner life at present. Outwardly, misery and the cross; inwardly, disconsolate and dry. Jesus, guide me. Jesus, help me in placing this misunderstanding before the Archbishop. Direct him according to Thy Holy Will. Father X's affair?

> Jesus, be Thou my advocate. I forgive all and accept this trial as penance for my sins.[10]

On Christmas Day Mother Pia received word to be at the Archbishop's residence the following afternoon. His reason for summoning her, she learned, was to announce that he would conduct a visitation—his first with reference to the community—at Immaculate Conception Convent. The news pleased her until she learned from a sister (who had heard it from another!) that the Archbishop's recent sojourn in Los Angeles had been occasioned, in part at least, by the trouble within the community. "Can the cause of the canonical visitation here be connected with this visit in the South?" she questioned. "I am indignant at the duplicity of Sister P. [Patricia McSweeney]. I am filled with sorrow, pain and worry."[11]

Father Raphael Fuhr, O.F.M., who keeps resurfacing in Mother Pia's life like a recurring dream, was in the thick of things, espousing Sister Patricia's cause with a vengeance. On December 29 Mother Pia wrote sorrowfully:

> Archbishop Riordan was here with Father Raphael Fuhr. All our present trouble comes from Father R. and his connection with Sister P.'s 'case' as she calls it.
>
> Shall we be obliged to give up the Divine Office? Soliciting alms must be given up. Why, even the poor dog we had in the convent has been drawn into this conflict! Jesus, Jesus, my heart is almost breaking. Is this pride, dear Lord? I put my confidence in Thee. Thou wilt help me in the right time.[12]

The last day of the year saw Mother Pia kneeling in prayer before the Blessed Sacrament, thanking God for all the graces and blessings, the crosses and trials that He had sent. "Please, dispel this bitter misunderstanding that is threatening to disturb the harmony of hearts in our dear Congregation. Regulate this affair according to Thy own sweet Will. O Jesus, I desire only to love Thee and to serve Thee."[13]

New Year's, 1903, must have been a depressing day in the community. Mother Pia observed that the spirit of joy was missing among the sisters; little wonder that the day was dismal—she had prescribed silence in the convent as an act of reparation!

It was time, she thought, to inform the Archbishop. In a

lengthy letter she related the entire sorry tale to him, concluding with a petition:

> My nerves are...a total wreck. I, therefore, humbly beg Your Grace to appoint Mother Seraphina in my place and to let me go to Oregon until spring and then to Europe to find the needed rest in our little mission house at Moresnet. Although my time of office expires only in 1906, you can let the sisters elect a new Prioress General at the next chapter. I hope you will see the necessity of this change and accede to my wishes.[14]

Reverend Raphael Fuhr, O.F.M.

A brief note in Mother Pia's handwriting, appended to a rough draft of the above letter, states that Archbishop Riordan gave her permission to rest in Moresnet as requested, but refused to accept her resignation.

Adding to the Foundress's pain was the discovery that Father Pius Murphy, O.P., whom Mother Pia had long regarded as a trusted friend of long-standing, had become involved in the affair as champion of the dissidents. On January 14 Mother Pia wrote him a letter that reflected her distress:

> The poorest criminal has a chance to defend himself before sentence is passed upon him. The Community and I were denied this act of justice by our own Brother, Friend and Father. Why I cannot fathom....It is only since December 28, that we are aware of having bitter enemies to combat...one outside the community, and the other, one of its members....

> Taking your advice [they] did...[their] best to promulgate this evil spirit of dissension and nationality among the sisters. They visited you secretly, received your encouragement—even money from you to enable them to work against us.
>
> Then our outside enemy said triumphantly, 'Even Father Pius Murphy, your own brother, is your greatest enemy.' All this is like a nightmare. No doubt God permits it, and we must humbly submit, although our hearts almost break. The crisis in our Congregation has come. God will send the necessary grace and strength to tide [us] over the evil time. This is our consolation—our hope. The community has nothing to be ashamed of and, thanks to the good spirit among the sisters, only five among thirty-five are...guilty. I forgive all and pray that God may forgive them because they do not know what they are doing...[15]

As shattering as the experience was for Mother Pia, her steadfast faith upheld her. "How bitter and disconsolate is this chalice," she wrote in mid-January, 1903. "Some of my own children rise up against me. Lord, should the destruction of the Congregation be decided, then Thy most holy and adorable Will be done! Only, permit not my sins to be the cause."[16]

Two days later she wrote again: "How dull and dreary from the human viewpoint everything looks in these days of anxiety. Today it seems to me again that the Congregation will be destroyed. I am undergoing untold spiritual anguish. I live only when I pray."[17]

Since she had not heard from Archbishop Riordan, Mother Pia sent Mothers Seraphina and Gonzaga to the Chancery to tell him a second time of her willingness to resign. The Archbishop's response was definite: "The visitation is settled. Mother should continue her work as heretofore."[18] Relieved, she told the community that the visitation was over. Presumably, the sisters also relaxed at the news, for they, too, had been affected by the strained situation in the house. Still, for Mother Pia the pain continued; the resistance of some of her sisters, even though so few in number, was for her a crushing blow. But on March 4, 1903, came a letter of retraction from the leader of the little group. And on March 10, the Archbishop summoned the recalcitrant to his office to talk to her. To Mother Pia he said: "From the beginning I saw that all was treachery and therefore I kept calm and kept away."[19] At his words Mother Pia admitted in her Diary: "I did feel some satisfaction. O Lord, forgive me this weakness."[20]

The unfortunate offender came to Mother Pia in tears and said: "I have no rest until I come to you and tell you that I'm the fault of all this. I'm the instigator of this plot against you and the community. Oh, can I ever be forgiven?"[21] All was forgiven, and those responsible were restored to the good graces of the community. A painful episode in the history of the community was past. But a lesson had also been learned. The community needed to become more sensitive to national and cultural differences.

Once again Archbishop Riordan called Mother Pia to his office and said: "So, the storm is over. The day of visitation, I saw through the whole affair. Never mind, Mother, that was something for heaven." Mother Pia replied, "I took it all as penance for my sins." But the Archbishop had the last word: "No, it was something good for heaven." [22]

Notes

[1] Backes 253.

[2] Backes 256.

[3] Dolores Liptak, R.S.M., *Immigrants and Their Church* (New York: Macmillan, 1989) 61.

[4] Liptak 82–83.

[5] Liptak 94.

[6] Liptak 84–85.

[7] Backes 257.

[8] Anonymous letter quoted in Backes 263.

[9] Backes 263–4.

[10] Backes 264.

[11] Backes 265.

[12] Backes 265.
[13] Backes 265.
[14] Backes, Unpublished diary, January 1903.
[15] Backes 265–6.
[16] Backes 266.
[17] Backes 266.
[18] Backes 266.
[19] Backes 267.
[20] Backes 267.
[21] Backes 267.
[22] Backes 267.

CHAPTER THIRTEEN

MISSION TO UKIAH

Expansion of the Congregation's apostolic efforts eventually took the sisters northeast to Ukiah, California—the gateway to the Redwood Empire, approximately 120 miles northeast of San Francisco. The first white men to lay eyes on the Ukiah Valley were probably trappers, but with the discovery of gold in 1848, the area came under control of the United States, and the town of Ukiah awakened to new life when in 1859 it was named county seat and dignified with a courthouse. On Sundays the courthouse doubled as church for the Catholics of the region, priests from Mendocino celebrating Mass. In 1887, Ukiah ceased to be a mission and was raised to parish status under the patronage of St. Mary (a title expanded in 1924 to St. Mary of the Angels). To help fund a church for Ukiah Father Luciano Osuna, Mendocino pastor, sold his team of horses (reputedly handsome) along with his buggy, and thereby doubled the church building fund. With the goal in sight, construction got underway; and when the church was completed, the parish received its first resident pastor, Father Victor Aertker, O.S.F.

Sacred Heart Elementary School had been educating the children of Ukiah since 1883 under the direction of the Sisters of Mercy. But a combination of financial problems and dwindling enrollment obliged the sisters to announce their withdrawal after a ministry of 20 years. Archbishop Riordan prevailed on Mother Pia to send sisters to serve as staff. Accompanied by Sister Seraphina Maerz, four sisters arrived in Ukiah on the feast of the Transfiguration, August 6, 1903. Comprising the first Dominican community were Sister Agatha Watts, superior; Sister Benedicta Kroutsch; Sister Cecilia

Linneweber; and Sister Hieronyma Borgemeister. For Sister Agatha it was a homecoming of a sort.

A Native American from Mariposa, California, near Yosemite, Sister Agatha had been introduced to the Dominican Sisters rather curiously. Shortly after Sister Seraphina's arrival in California, she expressed keen disappointment to Mother Pia on not finding Indians to evangelize in San Francisco. Not long after, Father William Dempflin, O.P., the Indians' beloved "Padre Blanco," happened to visit Mother Pia, who told him of Sister Seraphina's frustration. On his next visit Father arrived at the convent with two little Indian girls in tow. To the sisters' surprise, he announced that he had brought the little ones to stay! Equal to the turn of events, the sisters welcomed the girls as boarders and outfitted them for school. After some years, one left to seek employment and the other asked to enter the community. Now, professed with final vows, she was sent to Ukiah to serve Indians of the Pomo tribe. In the years ahead, Sister Agatha would figure prominently in the sisters' work among the natives of the surrounding missions.

Affairs did not get off to a smooth start. The Sisters of Mercy had been greatly revered by the resident Catholics of the town, who resented the newcomers and made no effort to conceal their ill will. The sisters' one consolation was the Protestant and Jewish population, who made every effort to show the newcomers marks of respect and civility. Discouraged if not demoralized by the low school enrollment—15 students, Grades One to Eight—and the negative attitude of the resident Catholics, pastor included, the sisters would willingly have withdrawn even before the first month was over had it not been for Mother Pia, who was convinced that there was work for God to be accomplished in Ukiah.

The dark and lonely days of the beginning were eased by the occasional presence of Father Marianus Fiege, O.F.M.Cap., who traveled by springboard some 80 or 90 miles over rough and mountainous roads every six or eight weeks to reach Ukiah. Father's arrival was greeted with great rejoicing by sisters and boys alike, his visits generally lasting three days while he heard the confessions of boys and sisters and bolstered the spirits of the latter by including a conference. On the day of his departure the sisters would rise at 1:00 a.m. to assist at his Mass and receive Communion. Following a pre-dawn breakfast, Father Marianus would bid the community goodbye and leave on his long drive home. Unfortunately, on one such trip he met with an accident on a narrow mountain pass that left him incapacitated for further priestly ministry. The sisters were bereft.

Although they stood firm in their opinion that a day school would never flourish in Ukiah, the sisters admitted somewhat cautiously that it might be a good location for an orphanage; Mother Pia listened and agreed. Negotiations with the Archbishop and the State were accordingly introduced little more than a month after the sisters' arrival. Archbishop Riordan's reply was affirmative, and Secretary W.S. Melick of the State Board of Examiners wrote in confirmation of the Board:

> I think that your proposed arrangement will be an admirable one. They [the orphans] have needed a home in that vicinity. There will be no need of any formal authorization from the state, so that your claims will come in from the new Home the same as from the old one."[1]

The way was wide open for a change!

The Albertinium

On January 4, 1904, five months after the sisters' arrival, Mother Salesia Fichtner and Sister Wendelina Faltermeier escorted a group of 30 boys, aged three to twelve, from The Josephinum in Mission San Jose to their new home in Ukiah. The presence of the orphans bolstered the school enrollment to almost 40, a slight but nevertheless definite improvement over past figures. With the arrival of the boys the name of the school was changed from Sacred Heart to The Albertinum after the illustrious thirteenth century Dominican teacher, Blessed Albert the Great.

But though permissions were forthcoming, funds were not. A letter from Archbishop Riordan's secretary, Father P. E. Mulligan, informed the sisters:

> If with the money you receive from the State for orphans maintained at your Convent in Ukiah, the House can be comfortably supported, it is not fair to ask the Archbishop to make a monthly contribution, even though this would be on account of the Indian schools....His Grace sends the enclosed check of $50 to pay preliminary expenses for the opening of the Indian Schools.[2]

The discussion regarding finances, however, was not at an

end. September brought an answer from Mother Seraphina to Father Mulligan:

>Dominican Convent,
>Guerrero and 24th Sts.,
>San Francisco, Sept. 12, 1904.
>
>Reverend and dear Father Mulligan:
>
>We acknowledge with thanks the receipt of the Most Reverend Archbishop's check for $50. Through the sisters in Ukiah, we have also received your letter of August 23, in which you say that in view of the State Aid we receive for the support of the orphans, etc., it is not fair to ask the Archbishop to make a monthly contribution even though this would be on account of the Indians. Well, Reverend dear Father, we shall try to do the best in Ukiah in order to render the little charity we can to the Indians.
>
>When our Community took charge of Ukiah, we had no thought of opening an orphanage, but endeavored to obtain a few boarders; this plan failing, we applied to the Most Reverend Archbishop to transfer the small boys from our orphanage in Mission San Jose to Ukiah. The accommodation there is sufficient for only forty children, and up to the present the sisters have had but thirty-eight. On going to Ukiah the sisters had to purchase a surrey, horse, harness, etc., to drive to the Indian Schools and were also obliged to build a stable and hayloft which entailed considerable expense.
>
>You may not be aware that the income from the day school is almost nothing. From September to January it amounted to only $32.30. You will see by this, that the $50 we counted on receiving from the Archbishop would be little more than sufficient to pay the expenses of the horse and stable. The sisters also have to contribute $20 per month to the support of the Pastor, as his income is very small.
>
>I sent you a statement of the money expended for the Ukiah Convent since its opening in August, 1903, to January 1, 1904. The entire expense was borne by our various houses,

and the money they lent ought, of course, be repaid.

The first State Aid from January to June 30 has just been received and it amounts to $1,395. Please judge for yourself, Reverend dear Father, if that sum is sufficient for the comfortable support of six sisters, 38 orphans, and the monthly allowance to the priest, repairs, stable expenses, and debts.

It may be that when the sisters have paid their debts and matters are in running order, the income from State Aid will be sufficient for the maintenance of the House.

Although the number of Indians in both schools is only some 23, the work of the sisters does not consist merely in spending the day with these, but they visit the families, particularly the sick. The sisters also assemble the Indians at the schools on Sundays, adults and children, for instruction and the recitation of the Rosary. The attendance on these occasions is sometimes over 40.

Although I have not corresponded with Mother Pia on this subject, I think she would readily endorse what I have written. Begging your prayers, I remain with best wishes.

Yours gratefully in Christ Jesus,

Sister M. Seraphina[3]

While restrained in character, the letter was nevertheless clear on the points Mother Seraphina wished to make. A gracious, mild-mannered lady, she could on occasion speak her mind. In this instance she was probably ruffled by Father Mulligan's use of the words "not fair." In any case, she was not yet finished, for October brought another letter to the Archbishop in which she feared that she must appeal to His Grace again in regard to the situation in Ukiah. She wished to know what the Archbishop expected of the community in regard to current expenses, such as insurance, taxes, repairs, etc. The oldest building, she explained, was in such wretched condition "that extensive repairs will soon again have to be undertaken, [and] we trust that we are not asking too much if we request Your Grace to furnish us with a written agreement in regard to the matter."[4]

Meantime, the sisters were becoming wise in the ways of the world. Following the General Chapter of 1912, Sister Bernardina Michel, Chapter secretary, wrote to Archbishop Riordan concerning "our community interests in...Ukiah."[5] She called the Archbishop's attention:

> ...to a few particulars in regard to our management of affairs in the Ukiah institution since Your Grace placed it under our charge. The expenses incurred in behalf of the Indian schools, principally for care of horse and buggy, amount to $1,047.44. The sisters' services have been given gratis. The amount expended for repairs to the old building is $3,099.03. The amount paid for taxes to date is $761.55 and for insurance, $297.15. These respective amounts, as Your Grace will see, total the sum of $5,205.17.
>
> As the value of the Ukiah property hardly exceeds five thousand dollars ($5,000), and as we have already expended more than that amount in cash, exclusive of the labor of the sisters, we trust it may not be amiss to petition Your Grace to consider the aforesaid expenditure as payment in full for the property, and transfer the title to us.
>
> Should Your Grace consider our wishes favorably, which we humbly hope may be the case, both deeds are to be made over to the Corporation known as the "Female Religious of the Order of St. Dominic."[6]

The Archbishop was gracious in his response dated September 4, 1912:

> As regards the property at Ukiah, the Archbishop is pleased to consider most favorably the proposal you make, namely, that the five thousand and some odd dollars that you have spent on that property should be regarded as a purchase price for the same. His Grace has instructed that a deed be drawn up transferring the Ukiah property to your corporation.[7]

The deed of transfer was subsequently received at the Motherhouse.

Gradually, circumstances began to change for the better and both orphanage and school to thrive. Within a 10-year period, the number of resident children more than tripled, increasing to 130 orphan boys cared for by 16 sisters, with 10 day students from Ukiah attending the school. On July 23, 1912, the General Council voted unanimously to raise the convent to priory status under the name of Blessed Albert Priory, the conditions for doing so having been met. Sister Raymunda Wilson was appointed first prioress and three sisters were named "outdoor sisters,"[8] that is, those responsible for conducting the business affairs of the community. Remnants of cloistered days were slow in disappearing!

Relations between the public schools of the area and The Albertinum (as the school was now known) were becoming quite cordial also, for the annalist recorded in May of the same year: "The Public School Teachers' Institute of Mendocino County was held in Ukiah. Our boys sang the opening chorus and gave a program of several numbers. We also sent our school work to the Exhibit."[9]

Formalities were few in those early days, and the sisters met each new situation with equanimity. Returning by ferry from San Francisco to Ukiah one day, Sister Aegidia Borgermeister met an elderly lady with her three grandchildren. The grandmother shared her story tearfully. She was searching for a Catholic home for her little ones whom social workers wished to place in a Protestant residence with, she was sure, consequent loss of faith. Her story struck a sympathetic chord in the heart of Sister Aegidia, who then and there took the children under her wing and arrived that evening at The Albertinum with no admission papers but three more orphans.

Nor were children the sole recipients of the sisters' largess. Friend and benefactor of the orphanage, David Frazier had moved to Ukiah the previous year and was accustomed to drop in on the sisters for an occasional visit. One afternoon he arrived at the convent door and announced that he was ill and had come to stay! The sisters received the announcement calmly and placed the elderly gentleman in a small cottage on the premises. During the ensuing six weeks he confided to the sisters caring for him that he loved Jesus deeply, but had never been really baptized. Over the years he had asked for baptism in a variety of faiths, but since he did not believe in any of them, he was always refused. He solved his problem, therefore, by baptizing himself! Now, during his illness, he began to question the sisters about Catholicism. Liking the answers and avowing belief in what he heard, he once again asked for Baptism, this time as a Catholic. The chaplain complied, and the edified annalist recorded that Mr. Frazier made "his First Holy Communion with great fervor...and died a most peaceful and holy death."[10]

A final item from the convent annals merits inclusion here, as it reflects the contrasting attitudes of the citizenry of Ukiah toward the sisters at the time of their first arrival and their later acceptance by the townsfolk:

> June 16, 1914 — Outing to Redwood Valley. The people of Ukiah defrayed all the expenses of this most enjoyable outing. They had all the children conveyed to the grounds in automobiles, and it was a joyous sight to see the happy crowd flying off on their first auto ride, the autos decorated with flags. Tables were prepared and luncheon served, and many little lads felt that they had had 'the day of their lives.'[11]

Over the years The Albertinum was forced to extend its facilities in order to keep pace with the increasing enrollment. A "Babies Cottage" was opened, and 30 little boys moved happily into their new home on May 30, 1916. Some years later, 1922 or 1923, The Albertinum took a significant step forward when the sisters' desire to keep children of the same family together led them to open their facilities to girls as well as boys. In consequence, brothers and sisters, suffering a ruptured home life following the death or departure of a parent, could at least be kept together. The arrangement made The Albertinum unique in the State, resulting in increased enrollment and inaugurating a building program to provide accommodations for girls. El Rosario, a two-story stucco structure housing the girls, was erected in 1929.

In the same year a new school building, designed to accommodate the increasing number of day students (120), was added. By 1949, the number had escalated to more than 200 and necessitated the building of a second wing, which provided two additional classrooms, as well as a craft and hobby shop. Reflecting on the increase in enrollment, Sister Henrietta Friese, prioress, predicted: "The number of pupils has increased considerably, and we anticipate an even greater number of Catholic day scholars in September, due to the increased population of Ukiah, including many Catholic families."[12]

The Albertinum Boarding School Campus 1961

Integrated into the year-round program of The Albertinum was Camp St. Albert in the heart of the redwoods, which the sisters purchased as a summer camp for their children in 1939. Located between the towns of Willits and Fort Bragg on 17 acres of natural beauty along the Noyo River, the camp was reached from Ukiah by the train known affectionately as "the *Skunk*." Regularly through the summer months "the *Skunk*" brought new groups of children to enjoy swimming, hiking, fishing, and campfire entertainments. Nellie, the children's mascot, enjoyed the privilege of only-dog-allowed-a-seat-on-"the *Skunk*" as she rode back and forth with returning and arriving campers.

The camp also provided a popular summer activity for the seminarians of St. Patrick's, Menlo Park, who served as counselors. One of their favorite capers was taking the younger boys "snipe-hunting." Armed with paper bags and long poles, the boys would go out after dark to beat the bushes, hoping to catch a "snipe." Despite their fruitless quests, they never caught on, but returned to camp ready for a good night's sleep. Following the boys' sessions, the girls had their turn, guaranteeing all the children of The Albertinum fun time at camp.

In the 1940s, new residences for senior and junior boys were constructed. Since plans involved the razing of the old building, the sisters faced a full-scale challenge. They met it by moving 35 boys, 4 sisters, and a chaplain to the summer camp for the duration. Two classrooms were set up and school went on as usual, though the occupants found the camp less fun during the cold and wet winter months. On May 4, 1941, Archbishop John J. Mitty of San Francisco arrived in Ukiah for the dedication of the completed buildings. A gala affair, it was attended by more than 750 guests. Luncheon was served in El Rosario by the girls of The Albertinum.

In May 1953, The Albertinum observed its Golden Jubilee. Bishop Merlin Guilfoyle, auxiliary bishop of San Francisco, presided at the Solemn Mass in The Albertinum chapel. The sisters were proud to have two alumni take part in the celebration: Father Vincent Cavalli, O.P., celebrant of the Mass, and Father Raymond Smith, O.F.M., homilist.

Up to this point, The Albertinum had struggled to maintain itself largely from state and county welfare funds and the mod-

Dormitory building at Camp Saint Albert

est fees charged parents if financially able. Encouraged now by Monsignor William Flanagan, director of Catholic Social Services for the Archdiocese of San Francisco, Sister Henrietta invited business and professional men to membership on a lay advisory board. In March 1953, the board assembled for the first time: 21 men representing San Francisco, San Mateo, Marin, Sonoma, and Mendocino counties. The group's first major project was the erection of a gymnasium. Located on the corner of Hope and Stephenson streets, the property was the gift of Mr. and Mrs. John Isnard, residents of Ukiah. So successful were the Board's fund-raising activities that work on the gymnasium began in the summer of 1955.

Encouraged by success, the Board next undertook the triple responsibility of building an administration wing and broke ground for a new convent and a chapel in 1959. Bishop Hugh Donohoe, auxiliary bishop of San Francisco, dedicated the completed buildings on October 29, 1960. The Albertinum had grown from a single frame building accommodating 30 boys and 4 sisters into a series of units covering more than 5 city blocks and housing 23 sisters, 10 lay workers, and over 150 students.

In her Master's thesis, Sister Mary Catherine Antczak summarized the sisters' work in Ukiah:

Sister Henrietta (Loretta Marie) Friese, welcoming a brother and sister to The Albertinum as boarders.

The ministry of the Dominican Sisters of Mission San Jose at The Albertinum was from the very beginning characterized by a spirit of response to the needs of the people in the Ukiah area. Initially, the Dominicans came to Ukiah to maintain a grammar school from which the Sisters of Mercy had withdrawn. Then, realizing that a day school would not succeed, the Dominicans opened an orphanage, which together with a school became the main ministry of the sisters. Change came about twenty years after the orphanage for boys began with the admission of girls as well. Growth accompanied these various changes and it was acknowledged by Archbishop John J. Mitty on the occasion of the Golden Jubilee of the Albertinum when he wrote:

"The burdens of the Archdiocese of San Francisco in caring for dependent children are many and are constantly on the increase. The great success of this work is due in no small way to the patience and Christ-like efforts of the Sisters of the Albertinum. For their share in building up this corner of the Lord's Vineyard, God will certainly bless them abundantly with His graces."[13]

Saint Mary of the Angels School

The Mission San Jose Dominicans had been at The Albertinum 50 years (1903–1953) when Father Celestine Quinlan, O.F.M. Cap., pastor of Ukiah's St. Mary of the Angels parish (1949–1956), initiated a capital funds campaign to build a parochial school. "A man of vision and energy with the skills of a diplomat,"[14] Father Quinlan had on appointment as pastor recognized the growth potential of his parish and had felt obligated to provide a Catholic education for the children who were being brought to him in increasing numbers for baptism. Looking around for property suitable for a parochial school, he found what he wanted in nine acres of vineyards and walnut trees owned by John Freitas of Ukiah and located about four blocks from the parish church. Employing his diplomatic skills, he persuaded Mr. Freitas to make a donation of the land. On May 4, 1953, a drive for funds was launched with Alex Thomas of Ukiah as chairman. The parish rallied to the cause, and the necessary funds were raised. Plans called for a four-classroom school (with four more added in the second phase of the drive) and an auditorium seating 300. Actually, the auditorium was designed to serve a triple purpose: hall, gymnasium, and cafeteria.

Scheduled to open in September 1953, St. Mary of the Angels school met its goal—in The Albertinum! Prior to the erection of St. Mary's, The Albertinum had opened its doors to the children of the parish who wished to attend a Catholic school. Now again the orphanage came to the aid of the parish. The annals of The Albertinum record the procedures involved in housing two schools harmoniously under one roof:

> The Albertinum prepared for the first day of school with about 320 children, six teachers, two principals—two schools in one; a unique event in the history of The Albertinum.
>
> The children attending The Albertinum proper moved over

to make room for the children awaiting completion of Saint Mary of the Angels Parochial School.

The group of day scholars will make up four separate classes under the principalship of Sister Jeanette [Wilhelm]. She will have the aid of Sister Frances Marie [Henriques]...Sister Jeanette will teach the third and fourth grades and Sister Frances Marie...the first and second.

With the completion of the parochial school building, the children of these four grades will move into their new building which will be located on South Dora Street about 8 to 10 blocks south of The Albertinum.[15]

St. Mary of the Angels school opened with six grades rather than four, (to meet the needs of the enrollees), and 96 children. The following year the new building was ready for partial occupancy.

Bishop Merlin J. Guilfoyle, auxiliary bishop of San Francisco, dedicated the school on October 15, 1955. At the time of dedication 215 students were enrolled in 7 grades. The first graduation was held in 1957, when 25 graduates received their diplomas from Father Isidore Kennedy, O.F.M. Cap., St. Mary of the Angels pastor.

Ukiah Home Missions

Closely associated with The Albertinum was the sisters' long and fruitful missionary work among the Indians of Mendocino County. The Indian schools referred to in Father Mulligan's letter to Mother Seraphina were small, even by one-room schoolhouse standards. The first—St. Mary's, Guidiville, presided over by Sister Benedicta Kroutsch—had 10 children enrolled. The second—St. Patrick's, Yokayo, located some seven miles south of Ukiah—claimed a higher enrollment: 11, ten boys and one girl. Sister Agatha was in charge of St. Patrick's. The two schools would enjoy only a limited existence, however. When government aid was obtained for Native Americans, the children were introduced to the public school system; school buildings were erected to meet their needs and public school teachers were employed. The sisters now became full-time missionaries to the Pomo tribe, traveling by horse and buggy each day to one of the seven *rancherias* in the area to instruct in the faith and visit the sick. Besides St. Patrick's and St. Mary's, they added to their responsibilities St. Dominic's, Pinoleville; St Francis, Hopland; Redwood Valley; Calpella; and Potter Valley. Obstacles not withstanding, they persevered in their purpose, which was ridiculed by some and termed hopeless by others. But persistence won the day, and Sister Benedicta became the Indians' beloved "Bossy Lady," a title she carried for 35 years.

With remarkable patience and untiring zeal Sister Benedicta cared for the spiritual and temporal well-being of her Indians. She had marriages validated, brought lapsed Catholics back to the Sacraments, and spent hours praying at the bedside of the dying. On Sundays the pattern for each mission was the same. The sisters drove to the *rancheria* scheduled for Mass that day, rang the church bell, and assembled the congregation. During the winter months of rain and snow, Sister Benedicta would start out an hour before Mass in order to heat the church for the people who came fasting, often from great distances. After Mass the congregation would gather around their "Bossy Lady" to receive food provided by Mother Pia, share problems and receive advice, or ask Sister to visit someone ill at a *rancheria*.

During the week a room in The Albertinum, popularly known as the "Indian parlor," became a favorite stopping-off place for the natives when they rode into town; there they knew they were guaranteed a warm meal, would find a sympathetic ear to listen to their problems, or receive clothing for themselves or their children. They knew that they could come at any time—morning, noon, or night—for Sister Benedicta always made time for them. Because of her influence, the Indians gradually omitted their ceremonial dances at the gravesites—or at least waited until Sister had left the cemetery!

When the missionaries' work increased and distances lengthened, horse and buggy were no longer adequate and the Archdiocese provided a car for Sister. In wintertime, mud, washouts, snow, and ice often made the roads impassable. The mission car was subjected to rough treatment and on occasion balked. For Sister Benedicta the alternative was to walk the rest of the way! On one occasion, after a particularly frustrating episode, Sister appealed to Archbishop Riordan for a new car. The Vicar General, to whom the request was referred, asked Sister if she drove. "Of course, Sister Benedicta drives," interjected the Archbishop, "she has just driven the Archbishop to buy her a new car."[16]

Sister Huberta Golz holds the distinction of being the first Mission San Jose Dominican permitted to drive a car—a distinction bestowed in order to permit ministry to the Indians to continue. Sister served as Sister Benedicta's faithful assistant and daily driver from 1929 to 1938.

When advanced age and failing eyesight forced Sister Benedicta to retire in 1938, Sister Rufina (Mary) Doran replaced her, with Sister Elizabeth Kuppers as assistant. Catechetical instruction now assumed a more formal aspect, reflecting Sister Rufina's years of classroom teaching. Monthly tests were given in catechism, Bible history, liturgy, and church history, and each quarter the children received a report card. Sister Rufina also organized the Sodality of Mary for the girls and the Holy Name Society for the boys. When the number of children enrolled in the classes increased to 250, Sister Rufina asked the Archdiocese for a bus. The "Catholic Mission Bus" became a familiar sight picking up children around the *rancherias* for class.

Sisters Aloysa Carroll and Robertina Pidgeon were the last Mission San Jose Dominicans to serve full-time in the *rancherias* around Ukiah. The sisters followed in the footsteps of their predecessors, instructing children and adults in the faith and serving their physical needs. San Francisco merchants, as well as those in Ukiah, became accustomed to visits from the pair seeking donations for their proteges.

Catechetical Outreach

From early times catechetical instruction played an important role in the teaching mission of the Dominican Sisters. From the Motherhouse in Mission San Jose, sisters fanned out in every direction each Friday afternoon and Sunday morning to teach catechism in the surround-

Sisters Aloysa Carroll and Robertina Pidgeon

ing parishes where no Catholic schools existed. Early Motherhouse annals credit Mother Amanda Bednartz with initiating classes for public school children in the towns of Niles, Centerville, Irvington, and Warm Springs as early as 1909, though quite possibly instruction began earlier before the recording of annals on a regular basis. She also introduced the Rosary Confraternity for girls, conducting meetings in the shadow of the old Mission, the choir loft of the parish church, or under the convent olive trees.

Following Mother Amanda, Mother Gonzaga Buehler took charge of the classes and supervised the young professed sisters and postulants who taught in the nearby towns. Conditions were anything but ideal, and "classrooms" had a tendency to be mobile from week to week—under a walnut tree one week and in a neighbor's backyard the next.

Sister Rosalia Monaghan's "Journal," covering the years 1933–1936, is a valuable source of first-hand information on conditions prevailing in some of the towns around the Motherhouse, which by that time included also Decoto, Alviso, and Mission San Jose. With Sister Blandina Dumoulin as companion, Sister Rosalia taught in the old mission hall in Mission San Jose, where she had to contend with bats, pigeons, and omnipresent dirt. "But there are little souls to save," she explained. "Jesus help us!"[17] In 1933 Sister Rosalia's First Communion class numbered 27, including 9 from Mission San Jose; 12 from Irvington; 3 from Warm Springs; and 3 from Sunol. (Sunol and Pleasanton were the latest additions to the sisters' list of nearby towns where catechism classes were taught.)

Of concern to Sister Rosalia were the children from the First Communion class of Irvington, many of whom, she felt certain, would not see the inside of a church again until Confirmation. She determined, therefore, to organize a religious vacation school in Irvington. Mission San Jose's pastor, who was responsible for Irvington also, had no objection, but neither did he offer any assistance. Sister had to fend for herself consequently and beg supplies—pencils, crayons, needles, thread, etc.—from local merchants. On June 16, the opening day, Sister Rosalia, Sister Blandina (boys' handicrafts), and Sister Fidelis Espinosa (girls' sewing) were ready bright and early to set out in a neighbor's "castaway" car. To their dismay it refused to budge! With driver, three sisters, a college student aide, and a month's supply of school materials, the old "Starr" succumbed to overload. It required pushing by all available hands to get the car started and narrowly avoid a no-show. Although the vacation school was declared a great success by parents and children alike, it was forced to close a week early. It could not compete with the apricots, which were ready for summer harvesting in late July.

As the summer drew to a close, Sister Rosalia requested the pastor of St. Joseph's, Mission San Jose, to announce the beginning of fall catechism classes at the Sunday Masses. The announcement was not what she had anticipated:

> You may do as you please about sending your children to Catechism. It would be a good thing to send them, but I don't believe in compulsion of any kind; this is a free country. If you think your children need it (instruction) send them to Catechism; if you don't, don't send them. Do as you please in this matter. It is your business, not mine. I don't believe in going into your homes and dragging your children to Catechism. I won't do it! I don't want it done![18]

On September 1, Sister Rosalia and three young professed—Sisters Mary Helen Bauer, Geraldine Kelly, and Raphael McCarthy—set out for Irvington to begin classes in a hall offered for their use by the owner. But when they arrived, they found it had been rented out as a skating rink. The manager refused to allow the children entry; he did not want "those kids coming in here with...dirty feet."[19] Following prolonged discussion, Sister Rosalia and the manager arrived at a reluctant compromise: The children could occupy the space behind the counter. This meant 58 children crowded into a 40-foot space, 3 children to a bench, with the "leftovers" (20) standing. To make the situation even less appealing, the manager turned his radio up full volume. Obviously this state of affairs could not continue, and Sister Rosalia went looking for another site. She thought the problem was solved when another gentleman offered his store. But the following Friday the "store" proved to be a storage room stacked with boxes of potatoes, dried peas, and sacks of flour. The real challenge of the situation, however, was the absence of windows. Seventy-four children, jammed between stacks of produce without benefit of air on a warm Friday afternoon would probably daunt the most zealous missioner!

The following week conditions were no better. "Seventy-seven children and no hall! We crowd smaller children into storage room. I take the big boys with me and start for the side of the highway.... The boys squat or kneel among the weeds and stickers. Lesson proceeds."[20] And the next week, 96 show up for class!

But despite the ever-present challenges, Sister Rosalia succeeded in establishing the Rosarian Sodality and the Christian Doctrine Guild for graduates of the catechism classes. Boys and girls met separately once a month at the Motherhouse to discuss topics of current Catholic interest. Sister was instrumental also in bringing the Boy Scouts into the area under the auspices of the C.Y.O. (Catholic Youth Organization).

A message from the principal of Warm Springs public school informed Sister Rosalia that 150 children of pea pickers, camped temporarily on the slopes of Mission Peak, attended his school in the afternoons, but received no religious instruction. Would Sister Rosalia want him to distribute a form for the parents announcing a First Communion class as well as regular catechism classes for older children? She would indeed, and on Easter Tuesday, April 21, 1935, Sister Rosalia and Spanish-speaking Sister Beatrice Díaz stood waiting in Warm Springs to see if anyone would arrive. Seventy-five children appeared, aged six to twelve. "What poverty!" lamented Sister Rosalia, "...their bodies were barely covered, their feet without shoes."[21] The next day Sister resolved to visit the adults in the camp the next day, but could not find a driver. "Our only alternative was to walk. We made up our minds to say nothing to those at home, hoping that 'a walk' might bring a blessing on the new work."[22] Thumbing a ride part way and walking the rest, the sisters eventually made it up the hills to the camp. "Tents—hundreds of them. What a picture of poverty and wretchedness greeted us!"[23]

The following day the missionaries set out again for camp, reinforced by the addition of two more Spanish-speaking sisters, Sister Adelaida Domínquez and Sister Catalina Gutiérrez. After teaching the children, the sisters went from tent to tent taking note of the older people who had not made their Easter duty. Some adults, they discovered, had not received the sacraments for six or seven years, and older brothers and sisters who worked during the day had never made their First Communion. Sister Rosalia had her work cut out for her. The workers were invited to come to the

Motherhouse in the evening for instruction. Anticipating three or four at least, Sister was delighted when 24 made their appearance!

In spite of difficulties with St. Joseph's pastor and lack of facilities in which to teach, Sister Rosalia never lost heart, but overcame any and every obstacle in order to instruct the children and the adults in the faith. She was the champion of the poor and counted no sacrifice too great that involved their interests. Sister Rosalia was gifted with a true missionary's heart.

Among the Congregation's later missionaries to the migrant people were Sister Vincentia Rusting and Sister Isabel Espinosa. For 10 years the two sisters gave their summers generously to work in the migrant camps near Patterson, California, and in Woodburn and McMinnville, Oregon. Besides preparing children and adults for the reception of the Sacraments, the two sisters were responsible for the enthronement of the Sacred Heart in over 100 homes of workers. The account of their ministry is contained in the book *Missionaries in Migrant Camps* by Sister Bernadine.

In addition to sisters in full-time catechetical work, sisters engaged in classroom teaching ministered to public school children by catechetical instruction and sacramental preparation in almost every parish in which they taught. Classes were usually held once a week after school and on Saturday or Sunday mornings. Many teachers also volunteered a good part of their summers to teach in parochial vacation schools. In several instances, e.g., Sacred Heart and St. Ignatius, Los Angeles; St. Mary Magdalene's, Berkeley; and St. Mary's, Fullerton, catechetical instruction preceded the opening of the parochial school.

Notes

[1] W.S. Melick, 25 August 1903, Chancery Office, Archdiocese of San Francisco.

[2] P.E. Mulligan, 23 August 1904, Chancery Office, Archdiocese of San Francisco.

[3] Maerz, letter to Mulligan, 12 September 1904.

[4] Maerz, letter to Riordan, 5 October 1904.

[5] Michel, letter to Riordan, 7 August 1912.

[6] Michel, letter to Riordan, 7 August 1912.

[7] John J. Cantwell, 4 September 1912.

[8] Conditions for priory status: At least six sisters must be assigned to the house; the property must belong to the Congregation; and the ministry must be compatible with the goals of the Order.

[9] Annals of The Albertinum, 20 May 1913.

[10] Annals of The Albertinum, 10 April 1914.

[11] Annals of The Albertinum, 16 June 1914.

[12] Henrietta Friese O.P., 21 December 1955.

[13] Antczak 198–199.

[14] St. Mary of the Angels Church Centenary Book, (1887–1987) 16.

[15] Annals of The Albertinum, 10 September 1953.

[16] "Benedicta Kroutsch, O.P." Necrology, Vol. III, August 1943–1949.

[17] Rosalia Monaghan, O.P. "Journal," (1933–1986) 1.

[18] Monaghan 12–13.

[19] Monaghan 16–17.

[20] Monaghan 26.

[21] Monaghan, "Memories—Mission to the Pea-Pickers," 1935.

[22] Monaghan, "Memories," 1935.

[23] Monaghan, "Memories," 1935.

CHAPTER FOURTEEN

MOTHER ANTONINA FISCHER

The first mention of Mother Antonina Fischer in the Mission San Jose story appears in Mother Pia's Diary under date of November 22, 1900: "What a surprise! Who are the three Dominicans who have announced their visit? I should be pleased to welcome our own sisters! My expectation has been fulfilled—they are Mother Antonina Fischer, Prioress; Sister Placida Bednartz; and Sister Seraphina Eppig, from Brooklyn, Holy Cross."[1]

Visitors from New York! Mother Pia was delighted, and Sister Amanda, overjoyed. Since the trip to New York seven years earlier, Sister Amanda had not seen Sister Placida Bednartz, her blood sister; it was a happy reunion and an evidence of Mother Antonina's kindness in selecting Sister Placida as traveling companion. The purpose of the visit, however, or the reason for including Sister Seraphina Eppig is not clear. During the ensuing days the visitors were taken to Mission San Jose; Golden Gate Park; San Jose; St. Elizabeth's convent, Oakland; and St. Anthony's convent, San Francisco.

Shortly after the visitors' arrival Mother Pia learned the disturbing news that Mother Antonina wished to take SisterAmanda back with her to New York! That the information caused pain is evident from the Diary: "My Jesus, remain with me, for the night is approaching. I feel abandoned."[2] Nevertheless, she gave her friend and coworker permission to visit New York for six months, and her hospitality and graciousness toward the visitors remained unchanged.

The New York "visit" was to extend well beyond six months,

however. After a lapse of nearly three years Mother Pia was still mourning the absence of her companion: "A letter from Mother Catherina, Holy Cross, Brooklyn, and a picture from Sister Amanda. Oh, how I yearn for her. Wrote her to come home. She was the friend and collaborator of my youth."[3] The absentee was slow in responding, and another year would elapse before Mother Pia could write that she had received word from New York that Sister Amanda was coming home. But her happiness was premature, for yet another year would slip by before Mother Amanda's return. Finally, on July 6, 1905, when Mother Pia stopped at Holy Cross Convent, New York, en route to Mission San Jose from Europe, she rejoiced to learn that Mother Amanda had arranged to return with her. This time the homecoming would occur.

Mother Antonina Fischer, O.S.D.

In the years following her San Francisco visit, Mother Antonina Fischer, Mother Pia's companion of novitiate days, would be closely associated with the Mission San Jose community. Born in Bavaria on November 22, 1848, Anna Fischer had, at the age of three, traveled with her parents to the United States. The family settled in Williamsburg, New York, where Anna attended St. Alphonsus School, staffed by the Dominican Sisters of Holy Cross. Drawn by the example of the sisters, she entered the Holy Cross Congregation on February 2, 1863, and after the postulancy and novitiate made final vows at age 17. Appointed local superior at 19, she held the position for the next 30 years in numerous Holy Cross convents until elected Prioress of the Congregation. The years that followed were challenging ones. According to her biographer, Sister Irene Hartman, O.P., "Mother Antonina was destined to lead Holy Cross Convent through the turbulence occasioned by the change from Second to Third Order status."[4]

As might be expected, not all the community supported the change. Hence, "it was the lot of Mother Antonina to bear the brunt of the inevitable criticism occasioned by the uprooting of cherished traditions."[5] Consequently, when her first term as Prioress ended, she was not re-elected, losing the election by a narrow margin of seven votes. She was, instead, elected Subprioress, i.e., second in command. But "the call to be a missionary was stronger than the call to serve as Subprioress on Long Island,"[6] and her thoughts began to turn westward to Kansas, where earlier the dry climate had led Mother Seraphina Staimer to consider establishing a house there for her invalid sisters, especially those suffering from tuberculosis. Mother Seraphina's unexpected death, however, had prevented the realization of the plan. It was Mother Antonina's turn now to think, not simply of a new house, but of a new Dominican congregation based in the mid-Western state.

The requisite permissions having been obtained, Kansas was destined to be the site of Mother Antonina's missionary labors for the next several years. Accompanied by six sisters and two candidates from New York, she arrived in Great Bend on April 23, 1902. Intent on instructing poor children in the faith and spreading the Dominican Order, Mother Antonina opened St. Mary's Academy the following September. But the citizenry of Great Bend were of the opinion that they needed a hospital even more than a school and convinced the Foundress to open St. Rose hospital in an old college dormitory across the street from the convent.

The new community's early years were marked by financial anxiety and related troubles. Sister Irene Hartman summarizes the situation as follows: "Internal dissent had been growing for some time. Overwork and poor nourishment took their toll. Some of the sisters gave reports to the bishop and/or local clergy, and asked them to intervene in the internal governing of the Congregation."[7] Gradually prayer and reflection led Mother Antonina to the conviction that her withdrawal from the community would be the best course to pursue. Accordingly, she wrote to the Bishop of Wichita, Kansas, the Most Reverend John J. Hennessy, asking permission to serve in another diocese. Thereupon, Bishop Hennessy appointed Sister Seraphine Weisenberg, a sister in temporary vows, as Prioress of the Kansas community. Two days later, Sister Seraphine went to the Wichita Chancery Office to make final profession in the hands of Monsignor J. H. Tihen, chancellor of the diocese!

From May to December, 1910, Mother Antonina petitioned a series of bishops for admission to their respective dioceses, but, as Bishop Hennessy refused to write the prescribed recommendation, the requests could not be granted.[8] On December 8, 1910, Mother Antonina and five companions—Sisters Catherina Dentlinger, Ursuline Suger, Petrina Tannheimer, Florentina Lindner (novice), and Katie Meier, (postulant)—left Great Bend for the last time. One month later Mother Pia welcomed her old friend and traveling companions to Mission San Jose.

Their arrival seemed providential. The preceding summer the Mission San Jose sisters had responded to the pleading of Father Michael Wallrath, (Sister Dolorosa Wallrath's uncle), to staff his parish school in Colusa, California, a small community northeast of San Francisco in the Diocese of Sacramento. As early as 1891, Father Wallrath had initially petitioned Mother Pia for sisters. Regretfully, she had refused him on the grounds of a shortage of personnel. But in 1910, when Father Wallrath, a model of tenacity, again approached Mother Pia, she brought the matter to the General Council for a second time. The Council agreed to help him temporarily by staffing his school for one year while he searched for another community of teaching sisters.

On August 2, 1910, Mother Felicitas Weiss and Sisters Columba Hagan, Augustina O'Connor, Philomena Fister, and Flavia Althaus opened St. Aloysius School in Colusa. From the beginning, the undertaking was a disappointment; the sisters found themselves in a spacious building, with a mere 30 children to fill the seven classrooms awaiting them.

Within a month after arriving in California, Mother Antonina and Sister Petrina went to Colusa to support the sisters there, and not long after were joined by Sisters Catherina and Ursulina. Their stay was brief, however, for when school closed in June, Mother

Antonina and one of the sisters (name not given) returned to Mission San Jose, to be followed in October by the remaining two.

Sometime in May of 1911, Mother Antonina and Sisters Ursulina, Catherina, and Petrina signed a petition asking admission into the Mission San Jose community. Uncertain regarding the procedure to be followed, Mother Pia consulted Monsignor Diomede Falconio, Apostolic Delegate in Washington, D. C. His reply set forth clearly the procedure to be pursued:

> [...] your first proper step...would be to inquire of the Bishop of Wichita concerning the sisters whom it is proposed to admit to your community; since if any of them have been dispensed from their vow[s] or have been dismissed from their former community, they cannot be received into yours without the permission of the Holy See.
>
> Should the information thus obtained prove to be satisfactory, and should your community decide to receive the sisters in question, it would be necessary to observe all the provisions of your *Constitutions* in reference to these matters, and also to draw up a formal petition asking for permission to receive these sisters, which petition should be sent directly by you to His Eminence, Cardinal Vives y Tuto, Prefect of the S. Congregation of Religious...and you should await his response, and act in accordance with it. The petition should set forth all the principal features of the matters affecting these sisters.[9]

Unfortunately, Bishop Hennessy again disclaimed any jurisdiction over the sisters and refused to sign the required release. Meanwhile, Katharina Meier, the postulant from Great Bend, had gone through the postulancy and novitiate at Mission San Jose and, as Sister Corona, made first vows in the Congregation on July 19, 1912.

As the enrollment at St. Aloysius School continued low and the promised year of service had been fulfilled, Mother Pia and the Council decided the time had come to withdraw the sisters from Colusa. "We are unable to sacrifice six or eight Sisters," she explained in a letter to Bishop Thomas Grace of Sacramento, "for the sake of teaching fewer than thirty children. This number of Sisters is necessary to keep that large house in order."[10] The Bishop's reply was gracious.

> January 11, 1912
>
> Dear Mother Pia,
>
> I am extremely sorry that you find it necessary to withdraw your Community from Colusa. If there were anything in the world I could do to prevent it, I would most gladly do it, and if there is any cause but the one you allege I might be able to remedy it. I know the departure of the sisters will have a bad effect on religion in Colusa as the people there were proud of your Sisters. However, if it cannot be helped, we must take it as God's will.
>
> Thanking you for all the good you have done, I am
> Yours sincerely in our Lord
> + Thomas Grace[11]

In reply Mother Pia offered an alternative proposal involving Mother Antonina and her sisters "who intended to open a house in North Dakota in the near future. They are willing, however, to drop this plan in order to take the school in Colusa, if Your Lordship will accept the offer. These Sisters would form a separate Community."[12]

Bishop Grace readily agreed, but two days later retracted his acceptance. He had not reckoned with Father Wallrath, who still maintained a proprietary interest in the Colusa school, even though he had been transferred to Woodland, California, and replaced in Colusa by Father McGrath. The Bishop wrote in explanation:

> Dear Mother Pia,
>
> Father Wallrath has written to me opposing the going to Colusa of the new colony, and as Fr. McGrath in Colusa would not be likely to encourage them, I think it best in the name of God to avoid scandal that we give up the plan altogether and let the Sisters go where they first intended to go. Hence, while thanking you for your interest in the matter and regretting greatly the departure of your own Sisters, I return the papers of Mother Antonina.
>
> Sincerely yours in our Lord,
> + Thomas Grace[13]

Meanwhile, the Bishop of Fargo, North Dakota, must have looked the other way as far as Bishop Hennessey was concerned, for he did indeed welcome the sisters to his diocese. With Mother Antonina went Sisters Petrina, Catherina, Ursulina and Florentina. But the sisters did not remain long in Fairmount, a little town in the southeast corner of the state, for in 1916, they again asked admission to Mission San Jose. Mother Antonina's "poor health, the poverty of the mission, and the small enrollment of the school"[14] were the reasons given for leaving North Dakota. On Rosary Sunday, Mother Antonina, Sister Catherina and Sister Petrina arrived at the Motherhouse. Of Sisters Ursulina and Florentina all that is known for certain is that they did not return to Mission San Jose. On November 1, 1916, Sisters Catherina and Petrina made vows in the California community, where Sister Catherina served for many years as cook until her death in 1955. Sister Petrina, a practical nurse, took care of her beloved Mother Antonina for the few remaining years of the latter's life. Mother Antonina's status was apparently that of guest of the sisters at Mission San Jose until her death on January 15, 1920.

Mother Pia, who was absent from the Motherhouse at the time of Mother Antonina's death, received the following account from Sister Petrina, the deceased's faithful nurse:

> Her dissolution was welcomed because her illness had developed so during these last days that we could not look upon her suffering any longer....I wish to thank you above all for the care dear Mother found here, especially for the great consideration and devotion shown her in her last illness. All her Sister nurses send you greeting and heartfelt thanks for all the time so kindly allotted them to take care of Mother. We do not doubt that Mother Antonina will obtain a great recompense from God for this community for she was fully appreciative of all that was done for her. Her attachment to Reverend Mother and all the good Sisters here was boundless. During her illness she often expressed herself in admiration at their love and generosity. We all shall surely have a great intercessor in heaven....Her death was a blessed one; her last moments consoling....All were disposed to feel consoled. Poor and humbled during life,

but rich in grace and merit, at the hour of death she died with courage and a feeling of happiness. A thousand times I pitied poor Mother in life....She was always following the example of her dear Saviour—she was silent, she never justified herself nor sought to win back her good name, but merely knelt weeping and praying before the Tabernacle and sought strength and consolation there. And now I thank God that Divine Providence permitted all this. Honor and glory would have disappeared, merit and humiliation went with her to the grave.[15]

Mother Antonina was laid to rest in the sisters' cemetery at Mission San Jose behind the old Mission. Some three decades later, on the occasion of their congregational Golden Jubilee of Foundation, the Dominican Sisters of Great Bend requested that the remains of their Foundress be returned to them for interment. Accordingly, Mother Antonina's remains were exhumed by the sisters' mortician and sent to Kansas in May 1952.

As a final note to the story of this talented and remarkable woman whose love for religious discipline cost her so much, her devoted nurse, Sister Petrina, requested to be buried in Mother Antonina's grave and religious habit at Mission San Jose. Her request was honored when she died on January 2, 1963.

On receiving notification of Sister Petrina's death, the Sisters of Great Bend immediately sent the following telegram from Mother Mary Francesca (Schinstock): "Sincere sympathy to you and community. We pray for Sister Petrina. She and Mother Antonina will repay their debt in kindness to you." [16]

Sometime between January and August (probably March of 1912) Mother Pia and her Council must have experienced a change of heart regarding withdrawal from St. Aloysius school, because the Third General Chapter of the Congregation (August 2 to 6, 1912) announced "that owing to the repeated requests made by his Lordship, the Right Reverend Thomas Grace of the Diocese of Sacramento, it was decided by the General Council to retain the school at Colusa."[17] On receiving the happy news, Bishop Grace wrote to Father Wallrath:

> Dear Father Wallrath,
>
> I assure you *ex corde* that I have not heard news for a long time so pleasing to me as the determination of Mother Pia to leave her Sisters in Colusa. It lifts a load from me and I feel like doing anything possible to help the Sisters to make their stay pleasant. Let her know that at least two railroads are under way to enter Colusa and that there is every likelihood of the place becoming important....[18]

In May the sisters directed a retreat for 41 *confirmandi*. The Colusa annalist noted that in his questioning, Bishop Grace gave the most difficult questions to the children from St. Aloysius School, examining them on the "civil and ecclesiastical laws regarding the marriage contract, the difference between perfect and imperfect contrition, sanctifying and actual grace, and such like questions. They were all promptly answered, and His Lordship praised them for answering so promptly."[19]

Despite the students' excellent showing, enrollment did not improve significantly, even though First Communion records attest to the large number of children (112 in April, 1914) in the area. But it was the critical shortage of sisters that influenced Mother Pia to write one last time (1915) to Bishop Grace, informing him regretfully that she was compelled to withdraw her sisters. This time the Bishop was more sympathetic, noting in his reply that "the people were not enthusastic and...the pastor took little interest in the convent."[20] Not so Father Wallrath, the former pastor and a staunch supporter of Catholic education. In an impassioned letter to Mother Pia, he criticized harshly her decision to withdraw:

> On my return yesterday from a visit to Humboldt and Del Norte Counties, I learned your actual withdrawal of the sisters from St. Aloysius Convent. Alas, your grave mistake!!! Some time you will recognize it and weep over it. I hold the move as a crying injustice in the apostolic labors to bring Sacramento Valley to bow its knee to the Bl. Sacrament, when a priest and his people labored so extraordinary [sic] hard to build, furnish and support the beautiful school for the propagation of our Holy Faith in this worldly heathen land.[21]

Accusing Mother Pia of doing "immeasurable damage...to the Catholic education of the whole diocese for generations," he begged her to reconsider, and he concluded his denunciation with "Love in Christ."[22]

Notes

[1] Backes, 245.

[2] Backes, 246.

[3] Backes, 268.

[4] Irene Hartman, O.P., *The Dominican Women of the Sunflower State* (Great Bend, Kansas: Golden Belt Printing, 1997) 7.

[5] Crawford, 1938, 155.

[6] Irene Hartman, O.P., *Mother Antonina Fischer, O.S.D.*, (Great Bend, Kansas: Dominican Sisters, 1977) 8.

[7] Hartman, *Mother Antonina Fischer, O.S.D.*, 21.

[8] The permission of the bishop from whose diocese the sisters were withdrawing had to be received in writing before another bishop could admit them to his diocese.

[9] Diomede Falconio, letter to Backes, 9 June 1911.

[10] Backes, letter to Thomas Grace, 8 January 1912.

[11] Thomas Grace, letter to Backes, 11 January 1912.

[12] Backes, letter to Grace, January 1912 [draft].

[13] Grace, letter to Backes, 16 January 1912.

[14] Hartman, *The Dominican Women of the Sunflower State*, 28.

[15] Petrina Tannheimer to Backes, Account, January 1920, in Hartman, *Mother Antonina Fischer, O.S.D.*, 95.

[16] Account of the Last Illness and Death of our Dear Sister M. Petrina Tannheimer, O.P., January 2, 1963. Mission San Jose: Dominican Sisters Archives.

[17] Acts of the Third General Chapter, 2–6 August 1912, 23.

[18] Grace, letter to Michael Wallrath, 25 March 1912 [copy].
[19] Annals of St. Aloysius Convent, 17 May 1913.
[20] Grace, letter to Backes, 2 August 1915.
[21] Michael Wallrath, letter to Backes, 20 August 1915.
[22] Wallrath, letter to Backes, 20 August 1915.

CHAPTER FIFTEEN

CATASTROPHE!

Catastrophe struck early on the morning of April 18, 1906, when at 5:18 a.m. San Francisco was rocked to its foundations by an earthquake of devastating proportions. Two shocks, registering 8.25 on the seismograph, followed within 10 seconds of each other, the first lasting 40 seconds and the second, 25. The treacherous San Andreas Fault, paralleling the central California coastline for approximately 600 miles, was the culprit, and its shifting caused damage for a distance of some 30 miles on either side of the fault.

With a penchant toward purple prose, an anonymous writer at Immaculate Conception Convent described the event:

> As the first rays of the morning sun tipped the Golden Gate hills, we were startled by an unusual sound—a low rumble, chilling in its ominous tone, that seemed to come from the bowels of the earth. Instantly following, the ground rose and fell, swayed and shivered with awful motion, and hell was loosened. The shrieks of women and children and the imprecations of men were drowned in the roar and crash of falling buildings, the grinding thunder of the upheaving earth, and the groaning, cracking, and splitting of timbers as homes and business places of the peerless city were being wrenched to pieces. With a last vicious tremble, as of a terrier shaking a rat, the terrible subterranean power ceased with a groaning sigh and quiveringly the earth settled to quiet, a cloud of dust arising from the shattered city. As that mantle of destruction was being borne toward

the calm bay on the morning sea breeze, there was an instant of silence as the people gasped in the dumb realization of the cataclysm.

But the horror had but begun. From every direction red spears of fire shot from among the ruins, and as men rushed to the work of preservation, the blood in their veins was frozen when the pumps brought forth only air. The wracking of the earth had torn the water pipes from the ground, and with a greedy roar the flames mounted higher and leaped upon their prey with little hindrance.

The details of the ghastly conflagration, the heroic fight of the people to save the city, the suffering and privations of the tens of thousands of homeless ones, and the unexampled rush to the rescue by the American nation have been told by a thousand pens.[1]

Although shattered glass, broken crockery, and cracked plaster were the order of the day, far greater havoc was wrought by the fire that raged throughout the city as the day wore on—overturned stoves, leaking gas pipes, and damaged electrical wires sparking the blaze. The city firemen[2] fought valiantly to bring the flames under control, but lost the battle when water mains gave way under pressure from recurring temblors. Without water the men were helpless.

Father Victor Aertker, O.S.F., St. Anthony pastor, arrived at the Motherhouse to check on the sisters, offer Mass, and impart General Absolution. It was a solemn moment when Father asked, "Sisters, are you sorry for your sins?" and all...answered with a ringing: 'Yes!'"[3]

At 9 a.m. word arrived at the convent that casualties were being taken to the downtown Mechanics' Pavilion, set up as a temporary hospital. Mother Pia immediately sent three sisters to help care for the injured and comfort the dying. Armed with holy water and indulgenced crucifixes, the sisters picked their way through the still falling debris, forced to cover on foot the long route from Immaculate Conception Convent on Twenty-fourth and Guerrero Streets to the Pavilion across from the City Hall on Larkin and Market, as no streetcars were running in the city. Later in the day when fire threatened to engulf the overcrowded Pavilion, patients and caretakers were loaded into wagons and transported to the Presidio, which was out of line of the flames. Despite the efforts of San Francisco police to persuade Sister Bartholomea Deckert to leave the Pavilion for her own safety, she adamantly refused until all the patients assigned to her care had been evacuated. In the afternoon four more sisters from Immaculate Conception made their way to Buena Vista Park and to Bernal Heights to assist.

All through the long and terrifying day the scene outside the Motherhouse was one of endless lines of people tramping heavily past the convent in a death-like silence. Dragging what belongings they could manage, they made their way toward Bernal Heights, the hills their only refuge. "I could not watch this sad spectacle any longer,"[4] wrote Mother Pia in her account. "...The sight of so many people walking silently by was too much. At 3:00 p.m. the Blessed Sacrament was removed from the convent chapel; their Support gone, the community felt bereft. *"Dies magna et amara valde!"* (A terrible and exceedingly bitter day!)[5] was Mother Pia's description of the catastrophe.

Following a sleepless night (under community room tables for those who elected to try to rest), the sisters were notified that the fire would reach the convent sometime after 11 p.m. Little hope was held out for its preservation. As the day wore on, there was even less reason for optimism. Increasingly the sisters felt the heat of the encroaching flames and breathed with difficulty the smoke-filled air. By evening, ashes covered the streets and rooftops. Concerned for the boarders, the sisters took them to St. Paul's and St. Anthony's churches, which were judged out of the path of fire. For the next few days the children's "home" would be the church basements.

To save what they could, the community carried among other things the altar, altar picture and chapel stalls from the convent out to the sidewalk. From there they were carted by horse and wagon to outlying areas. Sister Pulcheria Reichert and an unidentified companion rode in a dray, holding erect the large altar picture of the Immaculate Conception. As the wagon moved slowly down Guerrero Street toward St. Anthony's, people knelt in the street invoking the Virgin's protection in their affliction. Meantime, the sisters at home buried smaller articles, such as Office books, candlesticks and statues, in the convent garden, the safest place the sisters could think of on short notice.

Just before nightfall, the word they had been fearing arrived. Although water flowed in the streets from broken water mains, not a drop was available to put out the fires. Dynamite was the only alternative! St. James Church on Twenty-third and Guerrero, one block north of the convent, was scheduled for destruction at midnight and the Motherhouse at 2:00 a.m. By then the fire was already at Twentieth Street. The sisters sat outside on the convent steps, watching tongues of flame begin to appear over the crest of the hill and listening to the sound of explosions as the dynamiting drew closer. "No sister wept or complained," wrote Mother Pia. "...I went with good Mother Seraphina into the middle of the street to see better the terrible spectacle, and it was in truth a frightening beauty—the...stately, beautiful tower of St. James Church against the red sky."[6]

But the sisters were not to see their convent destroyed! Two factors were decisive in saving both St. James Church and Immaculate Conception Convent: a sudden shift in the wind and the discovery of an unbroken water main in the neighborhood. "God preserved us!" rejoiced Mother Pia. "How can we thank Him?"[7] Recalling her feelings as she reentered the convent for a little rest late that night, she wrote:

> Am unable to describe my feelings of gratitude to God, as I once more ascended the steps and entered the room from which I had taken leave with a saddened heart....At six o'clock I got up and sang: "Jesus lives, Jesus lives, Alleluia, Jesus lives!" This was my expression of joy and, if possible, I would have shouted it to the whole world.[8]

But though the convent was spared, life was far from normal. Mother Pia wrote in the Diary:

> ...people received some food for the first time. No Holy Mass. Everything belonging to the Chapel is in the country. The Divine Office [is] said privately. With great trouble we were able to get something to eat. Nobody may make fire or have light at night. NO WATER! ... Under "Martial Law!" What that means you know, but have no idea of it. After 8 o'clock no one allowed outside the house. No one is allowed to strike a match. Rosaries are recited during the whole night... Today there is fire from North Beach to the Bay.

> [That same day] the altar was the first thing to be brought back and replaced for the celebration of the Holy Sacrifice. What exultation! Father Lynch of Saint James considerately inquired if we were in need of food. Martial law was enforced throughout the city. Transportation from the overcrowded city to other parts of the country was free as were also mail deliveries.[9]

The following day was not much better:

> Holy Mass and Holy Communion; but Father had to wait at the Offertory for a long time until we had hosts. We did not know how...[or] where to get them, for no fire can be made. We can cook only in the street. The Divine Office is recited again, but all of it during the daytime, for at night we may not have any lights.[10]

The after-shocks continued. "My God, will You annihilate us?" questioned Mother Pia after one particularly severe temblor. "Have mercy."[11] Eight days after the earthquake people were still cooking in the streets. Several weeks passed before life regained any semblance of normalcy. At night the sisters' "wakeful rest," as an anonymous survivor described it, was snatched under the long tables in the community room; no one was courageous enough to ascend to the dormitories, as the after-shakes were frequent reminders that danger was still lurking. Further, with each new temblor the sisters feared that the convent chimneys would come crashing through the roof!

> We take in everyone that is sent to us, namely, refugees. The Most Reverend Archbishop came to see how we were. The priests send us wagonloads of provisions and so we do not have to stand in the breadline.
>
> St. Anthony's is a hospital, and our sisters take care of it. The sisters also go to the hills to help the people and take care of the sick. For weeks this work [will] continue. For all this suffering and privation we thank the Lord, and a thousand thanks for our safety.
>
> Fifteen Catholic Churches and more than eighteen convents and schools are destroyed. Why was that sacrifice not asked of us? Are we still too weak in the spiritual life to bring

such a sacrifice? To the Lord be honor, praise, and gratitude for all. AMEN! [12]

In the meantime, letters of sympathy poured in. From the sisters in New York came the following:

Jamaica, April 22, 1906

Dear, good Sisters,

> Please let us know immediately if you too were struck by the disaster. We are so sorry and all we can speak about at recreation is our dear Sisters in California. It is very sad, but we must console ourselves with the thought that God permitted it and that we do not know what may happen to us here.
>
> We are praying for you. In all love and sympathy, I am
> Your loving Mother Catharina [Herbert], O.S.D
> Prioress[13]

Throughout the month the sisters continued to visit the sick and bring food, clothing and comfort to the destitute living in the hills. When doctors asked that the Noe Valley School be converted into an emergency hospital, the sisters were quick to volunteer, unscrewing and removing desks and arranging beds in the improvised "wards." Accommodations still being inadequate for the number of sick and injured, the sisters converted the boarders' house on Guerrero Street into another temporary hospital. At St. Anthony's School, they cared day and night for over 100 refugees. They not only nursed the sick, but also prepared their meals and provided clothing for them.

Martial law almost brought tragedy to the convent. Sitting up one night with a dying man, a sister nurse was confronted by an angry soldier, who threatened to shoot her because of a candle burning in the room by doctor's orders. The physician's note finally convinced the zealous enforcer of the law that the candle was a necessity.

Again Mother Pia met Archbishop Riordan's request that the sisters take charge of children left without home or parents. Somehow or other, 500 girls were cared for at Immaculate Conception over a six-week period following the quake. The first children brought to the sisters were daughters of a man who had lost his home and family possessions; he begged Mother Pia to take his girls and offered her all he had—five dollars. Mother took the children, but not the offering.

At Mission San Jose, The Josephinum had not been spared. The large brick building which housed the orphans, novices and sisters was declared structurally sound with only minor damage. Worse was the fate of the dining rooms and kitchen building with great gaps in its brick walls. For six months all meals had to be cooked on an outdoor stove and served under the trees as the kitchen and dining rooms were declared beyond repair. Fortunately, the spring and summer months provided a cooperative climate, permitting something of a picnic atmosphere to be maintained. This delighted the children—at least, at the outset; but for the sisters it meant additional work and inconvenience. Nevertheless, the sisters continued to accept all children brought to them, refusing no one in need. "Father Mulligan and an official called and asked us to take poor children. Hearts and rooms are open to them," wrote Mother Pia on April 25.[14]

A letter from C. S. Leavey, assistant secretary of the office of the State Board of Examiners, asked for help also:

Sacramento, Cal., 4/27/06

To the President and Secretary:

As a result of the fearful disaster to San Francisco and vicinity there is urgent need that accommodations be provided for many homeless children. In this hour of necessity the State is looking to the child institutions outside of the injured district, insofar as their capacity will allow. ...Will you kindly determine immediately how many and what kinds of children you can accommodate and write at once. Send your reply directly to Secretary A.J. Pillsbury, 675–32nd Street, Oakland.

Very truly yours,
State Board of Examiners
C.S. Leavey
Assistant Secretary[15]

St. Boniface Church, San Francisco, leveled by the April 18, 1906 earthquake

In San Francisco the recently built St. Boniface Church (1902) and School (1898) were in total ruins. On May 14, Sisters Bernarda Hornung and Remigia Gatschen reopened the school in the basement of St. Joseph's Hospital. Since no streetcars were running, the move necessitated the sisters walking each day from Twenty-fourth and Guerrero Streets all the way to Buena Vista Park Avenue at the summit of one of San Francisco's hills. In contrast to Immaculate Conception Academy, which was doubling in enrollment weekly, the relocated St. Boniface had only 40 children registered, a harking back to the early days of 1876, when the original enrollment was 40. Although the Franciscan Fathers in time rebuilt both church and school, enrollment never again reached the 400 mark, which it had enjoyed at the time of the earthquake.

The sisters' ability to feed and clothe so many was in large part due to the generosity of the people. California Governor George Pardee sent a personal donation of $500, in addition to a carload of provisions and clothing. The San Francisco Relief Committee made a gift of $1,000 towards the maintenance of the orphanage in Mission San Jose, sending a second check later for $2,000 in appreciation of the services rendered by the sisters during the harrowing aftermath of the quake. The gifts were a blessing, as the carpenter's estimate for replacing the kitchen and dining room at Mission San Jose came to $3,000! Mother Pia had written to Archbishop Riordan earlier asking permission to send two sisters to New York to seek funds from relatives and friends. Although the Archbishop readily gave permission, no further mention is made of the proposed trip—neither the names of the two sisters nor the results of the money-raising project. Presumably the checks sent in relief eliminated the need for the trip. In any event, a "temporary" kitchen/dining room was erected which served the community for the next 74 years until replaced by a new facility.

Despite the devastation everywhere, the citizenry of San Francisco showed an unquenchable spirit that refused to succumb to adversity. With 450 dead and an estimated $350,000,000 in property damage, the City began clearing and rebuilding even before the ashes had cooled. The quarter of a million homeless were housed in tents set up in Golden Gate Park and any other open space throughout the City. Everyone, rich and poor alike, cooked in the street and stood in line for rations. For the time being at least, the earthquake and fire had abolished privil**ege!**

St. Boniface School, San Francisco

The earthquake brought its own far-reaching consequences to St. Boniface School in San Francisco. Less than five months after the catastrophe, a new school building was blessed by Archbishop Montgomery, a tribute to the undaunted spirit and courage of the parishioners. Up to that time, the school enrollment remained consistently healthy, but with the rebuilding of the City after the earthquake, the parish found itself in the heart of the business district, an undesirable location for an elementary school.

For a time enrollment soared, largely through the efforts of Father Alfred Boedekker, O.F.M., St. Boniface pastor, who opened the additional classrooms in the new building and hired lay teachers to supplement the staff. Hitherto all double grades, the school could now accommodate children from parishes that were without schools.

But by 1946, when Sister Verona Wittenzellner took over the administration of the school, the handwriting was on the wall. Though by the end of Sister's term (1949) the enrollment had begun to show faint stirrings of new life, it could not be termed vigorous, as it had increased a mere 28 students to a total of 142. Sister Mary Jane Dennis was named principal in September 1949 and was followed by Sister Eucharia Heidt in 1953. The following year the enrollment received a shot in the arm and rose to 340. The reason for the significant increase was the plan, mentioned earlier, that Father Alfred put into action involving the opening of additional classrooms. The parish that responded most enthusiastically was St. Paul of the Shipwreck, while the parishes in the avenues from which Father Alfred had expected to draw were poorly represented. In consequence, the encouraging increase soon began to slip, so that by 1957 during the principalship of Sister Marcellina Gatschene (1955–1957) enrollment was down to 283. Sister Evangela Balde followed as principal. Aware that because of its location the school could not continue to attract a sufficient number of students to make its operation feasible, Father Alfred initiated a program of phase-back during Sister Evangela's principalship beginning with the first grade. In the fall of 1959 Father accepted only 98 students in Grades Two to Eight. By the spring of 1961, closure was inevitable as St. Paul of the Shipwreck opened its own school. Sister Marguerite Mendoza, principal, had the unenviable task of closing St. Boniface. Prior to closure, the sisters secured the placement in Catholic schools of all students whose parents desired a Catholic education for their children.

Cor Unum, the Congregation's newsletter, expressed the feeling of the community:

> St. Boniface, the cradle of the Congregation's endeavors, closed its door for the last time on February 3 after an existence of eighty-five years.
>
> Our revered Mother Pia, Mother Amanda, and Mother Salesia opened the school doors for the first time in 1876 with a student enrollment of 40 pupils. Sister Marguerite,

principal, closed them in 1961 with an even smaller enrollment of 20 pupils. Over the span of years, 84 sisters taught at Saint Boniface.[16]

St. Thomas School for Boys

The earthquake had other ramifications as well, one affecting the boys of St. James Parish. As early as 1900, concern for the education of the boys of St. James had prompted Mother Pia and her Council to inquire into the possibility of buying the house on the southwest corner of Twenty-fourth and Guerrero Streets, which was owned by the Foundress's sister and brother-in-law. Mother Pia's powers of persuasion accomplished the desired result, and she purchased the house for $8,250. Short as always of cash she resolved her problem by becoming something of an entrepreneur—she decided to raise chickens at Mission San Jose for the market as a means of boosting the Congregation's income! The enterprise was apparently successful, as it continued until 1955.

The boys' elementary school had opened in the newly acquired house on August 7, 1900, under the patronage of Saint Thomas. The initial enrollment of 65 had by month's end increased to 80, divided into two groups. One sister was assigned to teach the four lower grades and one, the four upper. The marvel is how 65—much less 80—boys could be accommodated in a house whose rooms could by no stretch of the imagination be described as large.

In the mind of Father Lynch, pastor, St. Thomas School for Boys was a temporary arrangement only. Strongly of the opinion that older boys should be taught by men, he wrote to the Provincial of the Brothers of Mary in Dayton, Ohio, requesting teachers (1905). The Provincial agreed, but could send men only in 1907. Circumstances, however, brought a swift change of plan. Among its victims, the earthquake had severely damaged St. Joseph's School, San Francisco where the Brothers were already teaching. Learning of the Brothers' plight, Mother Pia offered the boys' school to Father Lynch for the Brothers, who readily accepted. The Brothers opened school on July 23, 1906, with 157 boys from St. Joseph and St. Thomas Schools, grades four through eight. The sisters were to continue to teach the primary grades. Meantime, Father Lynch was busy; and in November, the laying of the cornerstone for a new

(l to r) Immaculate Conception Academy 1888–1928, Immaculate Conception Priory, completed in 1883 and Saint Thomas School for Boys (right)

boys' parochial school on the corner of Twenty-third and Fair Oaks Streets, took place. Ready for occupancy in April 1907, the new school was blessed and christened St. James Boys School.

With the passage of years, appeals for a four-year boys' high school in the area began to come from all sides. Again, the Provincial of the Brothers agreed to staff the school and by 1920, a complete secondary program was in operation in the building. The Brothers of Mary continued to staff both elementary and high schools until 1950, when, on condition that they be relieved of responsibility for the two existing schools, St. James Elementary and St. James High School, they would provide staff for the newly completed Archdiocesan Riordan High School for Boys.

Expansion at Immaculate Conception Academy[17]

Immaculate Conception Academy had gained additional classroom space when the Motherhouse moved to Mission San Jose in 1907; this allowed the Academy to begin operating as a full four-year high school. Its curriculum offered both academic and business programs. The initial enrollment was 17: 4 in the academic program and 13 in the business tract.

Enrollment would increase steadily in the next decade with the curriculum expanded to include four years of both religion and English, three years of history, three years each of mathematics, science and a foreign language and one year of American government. By the 1930s the program was expanded to include Algebra II, world history, physical science and several business courses.

In 1915 the academy was accredited by the University of California. The need for additional classrooms to accommodate the increasing enrollment and expanded academic program was felt as early as 1918. Partial relief was provided in 1924 when Father Patrick Lynch, pastor of St. James parish, erected St. James Parochial School for Girls independent of Immaculate Conception Academy. The three-story concrete structure was built on Fair Oaks Street adjoining the Academy and staffed by the Dominican Sisters. Sister Bernarda Hornung served as the first principal. The transfer of grades one through eight of the Academy to the parish school, including the first three grades of the boys of St. James, provided room for expansion. From this date the Academy building was de-

Immaculate Conception Academy after 1928

voted solely to the high school classes. Excavation for a new building, however, did not begin until 1927; the building was complete by August 1928. No one was more dedicated to the project than Sister Dominica Klein, whose energy may have been consumed by the project; she died on February 21, 1929 within months of the opening of the building. The first graduates received their diplomas on May 31, 1929.

As the years progressed, the students of Immaculate Conception Academy would maintain their academic successes, host visitors, celebrate the 700th anniversary of St. Dominic and join in the golden jubilees of Mother Seraphina , Sister Amanda, and Mother Felicitas. They also celebrated the sesquicentennial of the death of Father Junipero Serra and petitioned President Franklin D. Roosevelt to abstain from supporting the government of Mexico in its religious persecutions.

As St. Mary of the Palms had done earlier, the administration of Immaculate Conception Academy sought to comply with the 1935 California law that mandated year-round resident schools provide summer camps for their children. In 1936 the sisters found

Chapter 15/ CATASTROPHE!   335

Sister Agnella Hauner caring for a camper

an ideal spot on the Russian River, a vacation area popular among northern Californians. "Sully's Resort," a three-acre site complete with hotel and cottages, became Camp Imelda, a Catholic camp under the ownership and direction of the Dominican Sisters. Here girls ages 8–13 were given the opportunity for healthful and wholesome summer days among the beautiful redwoods of the Russian River area.

The camp operated four two-week sessions from late June to mid-August. Full staff consisted of Dominican Sisters as directors, the popular duo of Alfred and Julia Bohny as cook and caretaker respectively, head counselors and assistants and resident chaplain. Later the camp ran a session for children sent by the Guardsmen, a charitable organization that provided vacations for children who would not otherwise enjoy one. With the close of the boarding department at ICA, the camp had served its primary purpose. Camp Imelda posted a "closed for good" sign at the entrance, and the sisters eventually sold the site.

Summer session at Camp Imelda on the Russian River

Based on reports from the Department of Public Health, City and County of San Francisco, the Chancery Office advised the closing of Immaculate Conception Academy's boarding department in June 1959. After 75 years of uninterrupted service the old frame building was declared a fire hazard and ordered razed. For the old-timers, demolition of the original Motherhouse was an emotional experience, enveloped as it was in early memories of the youthful Congregation. Construction of a new two-story convent, erected on the same site, began one month after the leveling of the old building. Sister Rita Marie Brown, prioress, planned and supervised the construction, which involved the further responsibility of tactical planning for housing the faculties of Immaculate Conception Academy, St. James, and St. Boniface Elementary School staffs in the flats vacated by the resident students.

After a year of "camping out," the sisters moved happily into the newly completed convent on August 3, 1960, following the blessing of the building by Father John Walsh, St. James pastor. On the following day, the Feast of St. Dominic, Father Christopher

Byrne, O.F.M., with Father Walsh present in the sanctuary, celebrated the first Mass offered in the new chapel. Dedication of the convent was reserved for Sunday, October 30. Most Reverend Hugh Donohoe, auxiliary bishop of San Francisco, presided. Open House concluded the ceremony.

Solemn consecration of the altar took place on Saturday, December 10, at nine o'clock. Bishop Merlin Guilfoyle, auxiliary bishop of San Francisco, was assisted by the Reverend Thomas Bowe and the Reverend Chester Thompson as deacon and subdeacon respectively. Reverend Patrick O'Shea acted as master of ceremonies. Immediately following the consecration, a Dominican Solemn High Mass was celebrated. Very Reverend Joseph Agius, O.P., newly appointed provincial, was celebrant; with Very Reverend Joseph Fulton, O.P., former provincial, deacon; and a visiting Spanish Dominican, sub-deacon in place of the Very Reverend Paul Zammit, O.P., who was detained. Clergy guests included Father John Walsh; Father Matthew Poetzl, O.F.M., St. Anthony pastor; and Father Raymond Daly, St. James assistant pastor. Father Walsh hosted the clergy for luncheon in the rectory after the ceremony.

Notes

[1] Annals of Immaculate Conception Priory, 18 April 1906. "Earthquake File," Dominican Sisters Archives.

[2] *The Independent*, "Fire Hydrant Honors Firefighters, City" 18 April 2001. The "miracle" is commemorated by a gold-painted fire hydrant at the corner of Twentieth and Church Streets, although some maintain that it is not the correct site. Annually on April 18, a group of stalwarts gather at the hydrant at 5:18 a.m. to commemorate the saving of the Mission District.

[3] Annals of Immaculate Conception Priory, 18 April 1906. "Earthquake File," Dominican Sisters Archives.

[4] Annals of Immaculate Conception Priory, 18 April 1906. "Earthquake File," Dominican Sisters Archives.

[5] Backes 301.

[6] Eye Witness Account, Anonymous. "Earthquake File," Dominican Sisters Archives.

[7] Backes 302.

[8] Eye Witness Account, Anonymous. "Earthquake File," Dominican Sisters Archives.

[9] Backes 302.

[10] Eye Witness Account, Anonymous. "Earthquake File," Dominican Sisters Archives.

[11] Backes 303.

[12] Eye Witness Account, Anonymous. "Earthquake File," Dominican Sisters Archives.

[13] Catharina Herbert, O.S.D., letter to Sisters, 22 April 1906.

[14] Backes 303.

[15] C. S. Leavey, letter to Backes, 27 April 1906.

[16] *Cor Unum*, 3 February 1961.

[17] Rita Marie Brown, O.P. "The History of Immaculate Conception Academy, San Francisco, California." Thesis. University of San Francisco, 1953.

CHAPTER SIXTEEN

FOUNDATIONAL WORK

In an attempt to get back to normal after the catastrophic events of April, Mother Pia began preparations for the Second General Chapter of the Congregation, as six years had elapsed since the first. Held in the Motherhouse in San Francisco from August 2 to 5, 1906, it was attended by 15 delegates or "vocals"—the retiring Prioress General, the General Council, the five conventual prioresses, the three vicaresses (all members of the Chapter by right of office), and the associates of the five prioresses, elected by their respective communities. The number of delegates marked a significant departure from the Chapter of 1900, which had a total of 33. No record is available of how the 33 were determined.

Under the presidency of Bishop George Montgomery, Auxiliary Bishop of San Francisco, Mother Pia was again "unanimously" re-elected, with Mothers Seraphina Maerz, Felicitas Weiss, Salesia Fichtner and Sister Thomasina Brueggen as councilors, also chosen "unanimously." The use of the word is debatable, since the respective sisters may be presumed not to have voted for themselves. Sister Raymunda Wilson was elected General Procuratrix or Treasurer. All, with the exception of the Prioress General, were elected "for an indefinite period of time!"[1]

Two pieces of legislation enacted by the Chapter had their impact on the Congregation's future: authorization of the Prioress General to send the *Constitutions* to Rome for papal approbation and the transfer of the Motherhouse from San Francisco to Mission San Jose. The latter move has been attributed by some to the recent earthquake, but was motivated more probably by a desire for a more rural and open location, as the Mission District of San Francisco was fast becoming too citified and populated for Mother Pia's liking:

> We authorize our Venerable Mother Prioress General to propose to the Most Reverend Archbishop the necessity of transferring our Motherhouse from San Francisco to Mission San Jose and to purchase there more property for the purpose of erecting when means allow, a spacious convent, in true conventual style, where our young Sisters may be trained according to the spirit of our holy Founder, and our aged and weak Sisters prepare for their last summons in the quiet of a truly religious atmosphere. Let all the sisters pray for the speedy realization of this wish.[2]

A third commission authorized the Prioress General "to send able Postulants from Altenberg [Moresnet Neutre] to England to study English Literature."[3] The Acts of the Chapter dealt also with a number of other items. A series of admonitions urged the sisters to be mindful of the law of enclosure and the observance of silence and poverty. The sisters were forbidden to have their pictures taken without permission of the Prioress General or to spend their vacations in public bathing places.

Included for the first time in the published Acts of the General Chapter was the necrology of the seven sisters who had died since the last Chapter: Sisters Eugenia Becker, Victoria Kine, Constantia Cunningham, Cecilia Linneweber, Clothilda Stolz (novice), Petrina Wiemand and Bertranda de Flou. Five of the seven were under the age of thirty-five, at least three—and possibly five—dying of lung ailments.

With some trepidation Mother Pia submitted the Chapter decisions to the Archbishop for approval on August 14, 1906. She was especially apprehensive regarding the *Constitutions,* as papal approval would significantly reduce the Archbishop's control of congregational affairs. On the following day, the Feast of the Assumption, she prayed to Our Lady, "O Mary, assist us with regard to our *Constitutions*. If they correspond to the Will of God, then help; if they are not at one with His Will, then let me be satisfied with their rejection. Only God's Will is my aim."[4] However, she need not have been so concerned, because she had already laid the groundwork.

Papal Approval: Dominican Support in Rome

Mother Pia had spent eight months in Altenberg consulting her Dominican advisors, visiting observant convents, and drafting a new *Constitutions* (see Chapter 11). Leaving nothing to chance, she then sought support and encouragement from the highest Dominican authority in Rome. With Mother Seraphina as companion, Mother Pia set out by train from Moresnet Neutre for Rome on April 10, 1905. They arrived in the Eternal City the next day and went directly to *Casa di Salute on Via dell' Olmata* conducted by the Sisters of Saint Elizabeth, popularly known as the Gray Sisters.

The visiting Mothers soon found themselves impressed by the consideration of Father Ceslaus, recently appointed assistant to the new Master General, Father Hyacinth Cormier, who had organized things most conveniently for them. On their return from Mass the day after their arrival, Brother Christopher, O.P. was waiting to see to their needs. The Master General was most cordial also, offering to arrange an audience with the Holy Father, Pope Pius X. Although encouraged by the Fathers gracious reception in Rome, Mother Pia awaited uneasily her appointment with Father Esser, fearing the outcome. But summoning her courage, she outlined the request for the sisters to pray the Divine Office with one nocturn at Matins. Father Esser advised insert-

Very Reverend Hyacinth Cormier, O.P., **Master of the Order, 1904–1916**

ing the article into the *Constitutions* by way of testing the waters to see what the Congregation of Religious would allow. The Master General, however, was more encouraging, viewing the petition in a more favorable light than his predecessor; the sisters were reassured to hear that he would "defend the matter in the Propaganda and the Congregation of Rites. He hopes there will be no difficulty."

True to his word, Father Cormier made arrangements for the visitors' audience with the Holy Father:

> Today...[we] saw the Holy Father, Pius X. Christ's Vicar on earth. 3:30 — Arrived at the Vatican. Swiss guards in their gorgeous uniforms: red, yellow and black. The audience took place in the hall of Clement VII....The Holy Father passed from one to the other giving his hand to be kissed. I clasped the hand of His Holiness in mine. What a grace![6]

As before, Rome offered the Mothers many consolations: attendance at Mass in St. Dominic's room in Santa Sabina and in St. Pius chapel on Mother Pia's patronal feast, and an opportunity to assist at the Holy Father's Mass, which Mother Pia described as an honor and a grace.

On May 9 the travelers bade a reluctant farewell to Rome. They did not return directly to Moresnet Neutre, however, but boarded the train for Florence. Bologna and Venice followed, with Ratisbon (Regensburg), "the cradle of our Congregation,"[7] the high point of their trip home. By May 18 they were back in Moresnet. Shortly after her return Mother Pia wrote to Father Zeno, O.P., prior of Santa Sabina in Rome. The ice had been broken, and she felt comfortable enough with her Dominican brothers in Rome to seek help on matters that still troubled her. Not two weeks after the sisters' return, Father Ceslaus Hansen was again at Moresnet, where Mother Pia discussed with him several items about which she was still doubtful. In the meantime, wishing to utilize their time well, Mother Seraphina and Sister Clara went to Aachen to learn leather craft and weaving.

At last the day for departure from Moresnet dawned, June 23, 1905. At the Cathedral in Cologne, faithful Father Ceslaus awaited them to impart the travelers' blessing. Then taking the train for Bremerhaven, they boarded the steamer, *Barbarossa*. The only break in the monotony of the trip, other than a few stormy days, was "a splendid iceberg in the midst of a boundless ocean. A grander sight than this white mass glittering in the sun can hardly be imagined. It resembles a church with steeples pointed heavenward."[8] On arrival in New York, they went by horse-driven hack to Holy Cross Convent at Montrose and Graham Avenues, where Mother Pia found Sister Amanda awaiting them, ready to return to California. After a stopover in Racine, where the sisters received them graciously, they left for San Francisco; there on July 31, 1905, the sisters welcomed them home with great rejoicing.

Although the Roman visit seemed to have accomplished little, in reality the contacts made served Mother Pia well. She had gained the understanding of many Dominican Fathers, who pledged their support of her desires regarding the Divine Office, a risk she was willing to take even if it meant chancing all. While she awaited word from Rome, she would bide her time, imploring heaven for a favorable outcome.

When Archbishop Riordan's reply arrived on August 17, 1906, she did not have the courage to open it, but decided to wait until Mother Seraphina arrived on the following day. Disappointed when Mother failed to appear, Mother Pia slit the envelope at the foot of the statue of the Queen of the Holy Rosary. Steeling herself to accept God's Will whatever the outcome, she was overjoyed to receive full episcopal approval of the Chapter action, including sending the *Constitutions* to Rome for approval.

The episcopal hurdle crossed, Mother Pia forwarded the *Constitutions* to Father Hansen, O.P. He soon assured her that Father Cormier was himself examining the *Constitutions*. She was worried about the acceptance of the article regarding the Divine Office which permitted the praying of only one nocturn at Matins in place of the customary three. Complying with the Master General's request, she sent letters to the various bishops in whose dioceses the sisters were ministering, requesting testimonial letters for Rome. "After twenty years of anxiety concerning our *Constitutions*," she wrote in the Diary on November 21, 1906, "our work is now accomplished. All now depends on Rome and the Bishops."[9]

Mother Pia also sent a petition to the Holy Father, which read:

> Most Holy Father:
>
> Since the foundation of our Institute it has been the intention of the Foundresses, as well as of the vocals assembled in General Chapter, to adhere in all points to the instructions and usages of the Holy Apostolic See in arranging our *Constitutions*.
>
> *The Constitutions* according to which we now live, are those which were approved by the Holy See on April 18, 1877, for the Sisters in Stone, England—and for us, by our Archbishop, the Most Reverend P.W. Riordan, on May 1, 1895.
>
> The present *Constitutions*, made in conformity with the decree of His Holiness, Pope Leo XIII, *Conditae a Christo*, (Dec. 8, 1900) and with the new laws of the holy Congregation of Bishops and Regulars (June 28, 1901) differ so essentially from the former *Constitutions* that our General Chapter has unanimously decided to humbly petition Your Holiness to approve our Congregation and the aforesaid *Constitutions* for a time only, so that when put into practice, any change, addition or modification deemed necessary may be made which may then be submitted to the Holy See before they are definitely approved by Apostolic authority.
>
> At the same time we humbly beg Your Holiness to sanction the vows the Sisters have already made and those yet to be made.[10]

Although the copy of the petition contained in the Mission San Jose Archives is unsigned, the original signed petition must have found its way to Rome, for shortly thereafter came an answer. "*Laudate Dominum!*" she exulted in the Diary on May 1, 1907. "Rejoice in the Lord, dear Sisters. On the 25th of April, God graciously granted our Congregation the privilege of obtaining from the Congregation of Religious the Decree of Praise for our *Constitutions*. We are now approved by the Holy See. *Deo gratias.*"[11]

One month later, Archbishop Riordan informed Mother Pia that he had received the Decree of Praise from Rome as a first step in the process of papal approval. The *Constitutions* had survived the first scrutiny.

Normal School, Mission San Jose

Mother Pia now turned her attention to another cause dear to her heart—the education of her sisters. She did not favor the practice common at the time of sending postulants out to teach, but wished her sisters proficient in their ministry as teachers. Consequently, on November 3, 1908, she established a normal school at Mission San Jose. Sister Paula von Tessen, who held a doctoral equivalency from the Dominican School at the University of Fribourg in Switzerland, was appointed first director. She was assisted by Sisters Bernardina Michel and Pius Marbaise.

The school enjoyed a modest debut. Summoning the nine sisters who were to constitute the first student body, Sisters Clotilda Hoffmann, Petrina Becker, Bertranda Piernikarczyk, Berchmans Hudson, Loretto Schafer, Vincent de Paul Breslin, Guadalupe Torres, Juana Brun and Rosario Healy, Mother Pia led the little group into the Motherhouse chapel where together they prayed the *Veni Creator*. She then addressed the sisters, exhorting them to be exemplary religious and to seek knowledge in order to teach children to live Christian lives.

Classrooms were the spacious room at the southern end of the seminary building and the postulancy. Sometime later, Aquinas Hall, its half-walls open to the beauties of nature around it, was erected on the hillside behind the Motherhouse for class and study

Normal School outdoor classroom 1908

purposes. The normal school continued to function until it was succeeded by Queen of the Holy Rosary College in 1931.

The founding director, Sister Paula von Tessen-Wesierski, was the daughter of Count Joseph von Tessen-Wesierski and Francesca Sawicka. She was born on June 11, 1872, in Schleswig, at that time a part of Prussia. Baptized Antonia, she was always known as Helena before her entrance to the convent. She received her early education in Berlin and in 1898 entered the University of Fribourg in Switzerland, where she studied under Albert Weiss, O.P., dean of the Department of Religious Studies.

On June 4, 1905, she entered the Dominican Sisters in Altenberg. She received the habit on January 6, 1906, and made profession a year later. Five days after profession, she sailed for America with three companions. When the normal school opened shortly after her arrival in California, Sister Paula was named directress and in 1908 General Directress. In 1909 Mother Pia sent her East "to visit the best Catholic and public schools for the benefit of our schools."[12]

The benefit appeared in a course of study developed for our teachers in 1910. "The purpose of the Graded Course of Study and Manual is to establish and to introduce gradually a well-organized definite system of education and instruction in the day schools, boarding schools, and orphanages of our Congregation in order to secure uniformity of matter and method in our various institutions."[13] The course was presented to the Congregation accompanied by a letter from Mother Pia, who called it "a book of duty and obligation, a treasure."[14]

Sister Paula taught at San Rafael and acted as educational consultant to other Dominican Congregations. Gifted in many fields, Sister also taught violin and art and trained the young sisters at the Motherhouse in liturgy. After 1926 she engaged in research. Her last work was a comparative translation of a Cambodian Monastery manuscript and an ancient document from the library of the University of San Francisco. This multi-talented religious died on February 11, 1959.

Notes

[1] Acts of the Second General Chapter, 2–5 August 1906.
[2] Acts of the Second General Chapter, 2–5 August 1906.
[3] Acts of the Second General Chapter, 2–5 August 1906.
[4] Backes 306.
[5] Backes 291.
[6] Backes 290.
[7] Backes 293.
[8] Backes 295.
[9] Backes 308.
[10] Backes, letter to Pope Pius X, n.d.
[11] Backes 309.
[12] Backes, letter to the Congregation, 16 April 1909.
[13] Paula von Tessen, *Course of Study and Manual for the Sisters of the Third Order of St. Dominic.* (Mission San Jose, CA: Dominican Sisters, 1910).
[14] Backes, letter to the Congregation, 16 April 1909.

CHAPTER SEVENTEEN

LA PALMERA

When the Motherhouse of the Congregation was transferred to Mission San Jose in the wake of the 1906 earthquake, the orphanage was still housed at the Mission. Overcrowded conditions, however, were beginning to present a serious problem. A solution was imperative. Consequently, an offer from Father Patrick Blake, pastor of St. Helena church, St. Helena, California, seemed a direct gift from heaven.

> May 15, 1908
>
> Dear Reverend Mother,
>
> I wish that the beautiful La Palmera, site of 17 and more acres would not be too inconvenient for your community for asylum or convent. The grounds are so beautiful. I would donate the lovely tract to the Community provided that [a] building consecrated to the good work in which you are engaged be erected on it. With kindest wishes in
>
> Corde Jesu
> Yours truly
> Fr. Blake[1]

Mother Pia's reaction was immediate, as evidenced in the Diary: "One of our Banner Days: 24 of our little orphans approached for the first time the Banquet Table of the Lord. Reverend Father Patrick Blake, too, gave us a happy surprise *Deo gratias*. Father had intended to put up a T.B. Sanatorium on the property but his plans fell through."[2]

La Palmera was situated on a slope south of the Irvington-Mission Road in Mission San Jose about a half mile west of the Motherhouse. Although the idea of a sanatorium for tubercular patients had met with strong opposition from neighboring landowners, the location seemed acceptable for an orphanage.

Mother Seraphina wrote a note of reply expressing deep gratitude. It is extant only in a rough, undated draft without salutation:

> Your kind letter, dated May 17 [sic], was received and simply took my breath [away]. Should God have really heard our supplications and sent us help at a time when we were in the greatest need! Our poor children are so crowded, which is surely not conducive to their health and which troubled us very much. I know God will bless you for this great charity towards His poor little ones.
>
> I do not know how to express my feelings. I am so overwhelmed with surprise that I do not know what to say. I fell on my knees before the Tabernacle and thanked God and asked Him to bless you.
>
> Dear Rev. Father, would it not be good if we could speak to each other before seeing His Grace? Could you not come here, or would you rather have me come to St. Helena? Please pardon this suggestion.
>
> I beg to remain, dear Rev. Father,
> Your grateful
> Sister Seraphina[3]

A delighted Father Blake answered immediately:

> May 16, 1908
>
> Thanks for your note....I hope His Grace may bless and encourage the good work of providing a home for the orphans. I mentioned to His Grace in my note thanking him, on behalf of the Sisters of San Antonio,[4] that I had given the property at Mission San Jose to you, so that it will not be news to him. You may look for his blessing and encouragement.[5]

The priest wrote again on May 19, promising even more benefits, a presage of the voluminous correspondence (50 notes and letters) to follow:

Dear Rev. Mother,

I am in receipt of your note and am delighted to know that you can use the beautiful site. Now if you will get His Grace's permission to go ahead with the good work, I think I can do so much for you that the site is but the smallest part of the gift which our Blessed Lord offers you by my hand. You will rejoice and all your dear ones with you when you see what will be done for you. You know when we are dead, we can work no more and that is why our Blessed Lord tells us to hurry up while it is day. "When the night cometh, no man can work." Just get His Grace's permission to go ahead; tell him you will not make any debt.

You will pardon me for the freedom with which I write, but you know how things go if we [don't] take advantage of opportunities. Sometimes they pass from us. I hope you will agree with me that there is no need in this land of earthquakes, to build brick or stone or mortar. For the foundations yes, but for all above that a good strong framework of wood, with pressed steel sidings and ceilings. This kind of building is most sanitary. It is fire and earthquake proof. If you approve of this kind of building, then with God's blessing before the winter sets in, your dear Sisters and their charges shall be comfortably located in their new house. Just see how things will go on....Oh, how truly happy shall we not be on the day of dedication. To take such interest in your work shall be for me the most acceptable of all vocations.

In speaking with His Grace you may or may not mention my name, as you see fit. But should you do so, I beg you to not mention what I hope to do for you, if pleasing to you.

Your prayers and the prayers of your dear daughters in Christ and your children shall be for me a most coveted reward for what is offered you with a full heart. In Corde Jesu, I beg to remain,

Yours truly,
P. Blake [6]

The following day he was even more explicit. In a letter addressed to "Rev. Mother" (whether intended for Mother Pia or Mother Seraphina is difficult to determine), Father Blake specified:

> I beg to tell you that the benefactor of your dear orphans wishes not to be known. If you will kindly remember this well when speaking with His Grace, it will be better. Just a friend of the orphans, no more. I can promise you besides, if you go to work soon and get all the necessary approval from His Grace you will soon with God's blessing have the happiness of seeing your dear children in their new house. How happy you will be on the day of dedication, I am sure that your dear daughters in Christ and your children will pray for your unknown benefactor.[7]

Father Blake's enthusiasm for the project continued, as a steady stream of letters made their way to Mission San Jose, urging the sisters to obtain the Archbishop's permission without delay so that the orphans would soon enjoy their new home. The Archbishop, however, was away on business; the best that Mother Pia could do was to schedule an appointment on his return. The priest's stipulation that he did not wish to be known is something of a puzzle though, as he himself had already informed Archbishop Riordan of his intentions, at least of donating the property to the sisters. But, in any case, he must have had second thoughts, for he followed with a letter that began: "I hope your good judgment will see that, in wishing you to withhold my name, I seemed to require too much. There should be no such condition, nor was it meant as a condition, simply a preference and wish to remain the unknown friend of your dear orphans."[8]

As the letters multiplied, Mother Pia began to experience uneasiness. A draft of a letter unsigned but probably in Mother Seraphina's handwriting at Mother Pia's request, expresses gratitude for Father Blake's release from his request for anonymity and asks for a clear description of his offer so that the sisters will have the correct information to present to Archbishop Riordan. She asks for a clear understanding of his intentions: is he donating the property; will the orphanage be debt free; if he means to help the sisters build, can he give her an idea of the amount he is proposing to donate? The letter is embarrassingly blunt, but Mother Seraphina may be forgiven, for the sisters' obligations in the building of the orphanage were becoming increasingly obscure.

Father Blake replied the next day.

St. Helena

May 28, 2008

Dear Rev. Mother,

Your note of yesterday just received. In reply I beg to say that 1st I donate for an orphanage the tract of 17 1/4 acres near your convent. The deed of gift will be made out when the corporate title is sent to me or to the French American Bank. 2nd, I think that a very comfortable home—plain and roomy and light—same can be put up for 6 or 7 thousand dollars. A frame building about 120 x 60, two clear stories and one dormer story, after the plan of your convent. The side walls, inside and outside and roof of pressed steel with concrete foundation. Such a building is both fire and earthquake proof....If such a building meet your approval, I think I can manage without calling on you. Should you wish a building say about $10,000 then I would expect you through your funds to give say $3,000. I am of opinion that you would be pleased with the building which I suggest....I would be so glad to see the work begin, for you have a good neighbor in Mr. Lachman and you may have from his generosity a gift *in perpetuam* of the water and this is a gift that would be as valuable as the building. He is my friend and he likes the sisters and their work....

Yours truly,

P. Blake

[P.S.] It is understood that no debt be contracted in putting up the building. Every dollar shall be paid when due. The building will owe no man a dollar on the day of Dedication.[9]

Reassuring as the letter was, it offered small comfort to Mother Pia. With increasing frequency the priest mentioned the hospital for consumptives that he was still determined to build:

> ...Dear Mother, I have not given up the hospital for the dear ones stricken with the white plague. I am praying and I have many praying that His Grace may give me permission to begin. I have two sites in view, but I cannot think of doing anything till I know if I can get the good sisters....I have a community down in Texas that would be willing to take up the work....Of course, dear Rev. Mother, for the hospital I can only give encouragement and get all the friends I can for them. They will get besides from dear St. Joseph $10,000 to start. They ought to be able to get along. You know how much better it is not to take away all energy from willing workers. It should never be done whether for a church or institution of charity. Let the good and willing ones get in their part. I assure you I would build your orphanage, but you know how I have dear friends in India and Africa and China and many other points to whom a little help is most acceptable.[10]

Following an appointment with Archbishop Riordan, Mother Seraphina wrote to Father Blake to tell him of the Archbishop's wishes:

> Dear Reverend Father Blake,
>
> Today I called upon the Archbishop and he told me that he was perfectly satisfied with your proposal to give us an absolute deed without conditions. His Grace told me that he would write to you today concerning the matter, and he directed me to request you kindly to have such a deed, absolute and without conditions, drawn up and to send it to us. I presume you are still in favor of calling the institution "Nazareth" after the home of our blessed Lord, to which we do not object. You may remember that the name of our Corporation is "Female Religious of the Order of St. Dominic."
>
> Your kindness in bestowing this property is indeed great. Be assured of our sincere estimation of your goodness. We

can only say: "May God repay you a hundred-fold and bless all your undertakings." May God grant also that this Home become a nursery of virtue and good training for young girls. We shall do all in our power, with God's grace, to make it such. It seems at last the prayers of our little orphans are heard, and they shall soon have the pleasure of living in the new Home, which for so many months has been the object of their desires.

Asking your priestly blessing, I remain with best wishes,

Yours most gratefully in C.J.,[11]

But on November 4 came a letter from Father Blake that strained the former cordiality almost to the breaking point. Wishing to be up-front and sincere, the priest informed Mother Pia of the interpretation put on his actions by members of the clergy:

Dear Rev. Mother,

I have received the deed for making corrections in title. Before proceeding to make the corrections I think it is proper to be candid and sincere with you and your community in regard [to the] way in which my action is viewed and spoken of by clergy, both secular and religious.

They ask me, 'What does your gift require to be done *in perpetuam* by the Community?' What return is to be made for all the money invested? The interest on the money invested would be about $125.00 per month, at least. How many children are the Sisters prepared to guarantee that they shall keep even if they receive nothing from the State? Then again, these Sisters are well off. They own any amount of real estate in San Francisco and elsewhere. They are all the time receiving help. No wonder that they should increase.

Everybody is giving to them and they are always asking for more. You are, they say to me, a fool to hand over all that beautiful property asking nothing in return. Then again, to finish the business they say that when once the property is turned over, you will be hardly welcome at the place; in fact, you will be an unwelcome guest—if you consent to be a guest. Such, dear Rev. Mother, is the manner in which I have been spoken to, and I give you my word not by secular but religious priests. They are those who I hope are saints or are striving to be. I have thought it wise to be candid with you before proceeding further. You know how I have no wish to pose as one doing things. I prefer that my name [be] unknown as it should be. If the good is done for love of God and humanity, it is all I wish.

Now before proceeding to make the deed, I would beg you to let me know your pleasure in the matter. It is good to know what people say. It guides us many times and gives an opportunity of acting more cautiously. I have thought that should you prefer to have an absolute deed to the property for a nominal price, it might be as well. Then I had no more to say. I would, of course, always be the friend of the orphans, but you and your community and those who would come after you would be free to do as you wish with your own property. In this case I would make your Community a gift of $12,000. The property up to the present has cost nearly $25,000. You might not be able to pay the $12,000 at one time, but you need not do so. Then I would be not obliged to answer so many questions. The property simply passed into your hands, and I had nothing further to do with it, than to be a friend of the children and the good work.

Should you not wish to do this, then I would beg you to give me, in writing, what the Community agrees to do for all time, and which may be incorporated in the deed as your part of the bargain, so that I may be able to point out to those who say "fool" what you are doing and what those who are to come after you will do and be obliged to do. In this latter case, I shall attend to the perfecting of the deed and the same shall be handed to you as head of the Community on the day of dedication.

In Domino I beg to remain

Yours truly
P. Blake[12]

The troubled priest could not have derived much consolation from the typewritten unsigned copy of a letter in the archives, probably written by Mother Pia:

> Nov. 10, 1908.
>
> Reverend P. Blake, Pastor,
> St. Helena, Calif.
>
> Reverend Father, —
>
> Your letter dated Nov. 4, is at hand. After prayer and due consideration kindly allow me to say the following:
>
> You know, Reverend Father, that we did not ask you for the gift of that property. Of your own free will, you offered it to us for the orphans. I feel very sorry that your act of charity is ridiculed by the Clergy, and to spare you this humiliation we herewith release you of the promise to donate that property to us for the orphans. My advice would be to use it for your desired Sanitarium.
>
> I will refrain from commenting on the other points in your letter. I hope you are well and believe me to be
>
> Yours in Christ,[13]

The exchange of letters that follows increases the confusion. Father Blake sends Mother Pia the deed for the property on November 10, the same day that she releases him from his gift. He wishes her to draw a line through any conditions not agreeable to her and return the deed to him. She must have done so, for his next note informs her that he is sending the deed to the Archbishop that very day (November 20). Three days later, however, he still has the deed and asks to omit her corrections that mention "donor" and a $10 consideration for the document. Mother Pia is willing to accept his recommendations, but first wishes to know the debt on the building for which she will undoubtedly be responsible.

In the meantime, Mother Pia must have written to the Chancery, for a letter from Father Charles A. Ramm, secretary to the Archbishop, advised her:

Dec. 2, 1908
Mother Pia,
Mission San Jose, Cal.

My dear Mother Pia:

In reply to your letter of Dec. 1st enclosing another from Father Blake, the Archbishop directs me to say that he thinks Father Blake should trust your Community to carry out conscientiously the purpose for which the Orphan Home has been built and that therefore it should be handed over to you without any annoying conditions or restrictions. Unless the Home is thus freely entrusted to you he does not think it wise to accept it at all.

Very truly yours,
Charles A. Ramm
Secretary[14]

On December 4, Father Blake countered with a new proposal. Since Mother Pia had not answered him immediately, as she was waiting for the Archbishop's reply, the anxious priest concluded that the conditions of the deed were not to her liking. He then offered her $10,000 toward the cost of "the entire amount expended up to the present, your Community to take over the property and run the orphanage without any outside interference. The deed will be made to you as if you had paid for the property in full."[15] Although $10,000 was no small gift, it was well below the original offer. Mother Pia and the Council found themselves unable to meet the cost of the building as Father Blake now proposed. A note from her stated simply that the sisters were sorry that they could not afford to purchase the building, even if Father donated the land. Father Blake responded by saying that if the sisters did not accept the property, he would complete the building as a home for children of unhappy parents who were worse off than his poor consumptives, but did not qualify as orphans.

Eight days later, he wrote again.

St. Helena
Dec. 12, 1908

Dear Rev. Mother,

> In reply to your note I beg to say that the site of the Home, together with my time and labor go to the orphans. You would have a deed without condition or restriction. You can have it, and you can call the Home by any name you please and manage it without interference or suggestion. The improvements—material and labor—your Community will pay for [about $15,000]. You shall have all the time you ask or require from the French American Bank of San Francisco. The interest shall be the lowest. In giving you the site and my labor and trouble I feel satisfied that I have done my part. You will get other friends to help you, for there are many kind people in and out of California. *In Domino,*
>
> Yours truly,
> P. Blake
>
> P.S. Kindly look upon what is stated here as final.[16]

Final or not, the letters continued. In January, Father Blake informed Mother Pia that he had sent the deed to the Archbishop and would accept whatever His Grace decided in regard to the property. "Even if it were disposed of for a small sum, this would be of benefit to sisters and priests working on the foreign mission....No matter how things go, I am sure Our Dearest Lord will judge me, according to the motives and intentions I had while working for His sake, outside my own field."[17] Father Blake also mentioned a church he hoped to build near Saint Helena in the spring.

On May 1 Mother Seraphina explained in a letter that Mother Pia had been obliged to go to Europe on business, but that in her name she would accept Father Blake's latest "kind offer of an absolute deed, to use the property for the purpose which seems best to promote the honor of God and the salvation of souls."[18] Father Blake responded promptly, promising the new deed within the week. Mother Seraphina's reply (May 17) was friendly, even warm. Cordiality seemed restored, but Father Blake's answer told a different story:

> It will be better not to bring up the matter of the property to the Rev. Mother again. Evidently she does not wish to possess it. Since she would not be willing to allow me even the privilege of naming it after the house of our Blessed

> Lord, the only house He ever had on earth....I may tell you that I shall offer the place to the Sisters of Charity for a summer house for their orphans, and should His Grace not approve of this, I shall find a way of disposing of the property. The proceeds shall all be sent to good and holy Sisters working out among the savages of China and India and Africa. No one will doubt but these are all saints. They give everything, body and soul, to Christ.[19]

The letter revealed also that Father Blake was under the impression that the sisters had "turned adrift" from their orphanage at Mission San Jose:

> ...a poor child worse [off] than any orphan...Mother and child to go where they pleased. What you received for her during her short stay came out of my pocket. I suppose the child is now in a Protestant orphanage or home and the mother will never enter a Catholic Church again.[20]

The accusation struck a sensitive chord in Mother Seraphina's heart and elicited a lengthy response from her:

> May 18, 1909
>
> Dear Rev. Father:
>
> You are undoubtedly mistaken, dear Father, in regard to Rev. Mother not wishing us to possess the property. As we were under the impression that there was no hope of our getting the new home for our orphans, and we have already about 20 children above the number that we can readily accommodate, we were in the act of getting ready to build an addition to our orphanage here.
>
> In order to have a *final* understanding, we beg leave to make the following *final* proposition.
>
> I. The new home may as you desire be named after the home of our Dear Lord: "Nazareth."
>
> II. We will finish the building of the home [at] our own expense (with His Grace's permission) providing we [will] not be obliged to pay the debts which perhaps may rest on the building.

III. As you are already aware we cannot accept any deed imposing cumbersome conditions.

It is impossible for us to do better in this matter. Should you not feel inclined to let us have the property under the above mentioned conditions, kindly let us know that we may begin to build here; as our orphanage is overcrowded, we cannot wait much longer. If the property should pass into the hands of the Srs. of Charity, these good Sisters will have our best wishes [on] their acquirement. Neither would we grudge the Sisters laboring in China, India and Africa the alms they might receive from you, as they are really worthy of your charity.

Now, in regard to the little child you mentioned, I beg leave to state that the mother took the child of her own accord, saying that she left the place where she was working as the people were too mean and that she was able to have the child with her. She seemed to have been pleased with the good care the child had received and thanked the Sister in charge repeatedly.

While the child was with us, we received ten dollars ($10.00) sent by the Jesuit Father in San Jose. The...ten dollars ($10.00) which were sent by you, dear Father, we returned to you directly. After that we did not receive any money...[from] anyone for the child. We did all we could for the little one in spite of not having had the proper accommodations for such small children, and did it for the *Love of God,* not for cash. One thing is consoling that God judges one according to one's motives.

Asking a memento in your prayers at the altar and wishing that only God's Holy Will may be accomplished in this matter,

Yours most sincerely in Christ Jesus,

Sister M. Seraphina[21]

An equally long letter from Father Blake crossed Mother Seraphina's in the mail. The deeply wounded priest repeated all the comments previously made about the "wealthy" sisters, told how offended he was when the name, "Nazareth House," was rejected, and hoped the sisters were not shocked when he announced that the property would be sold. It was for him:

> ...a sad blow to see that name blotted out. I mentioned the matter to the Rev. Mother of the Dominicans who came to visit here some time ago. She said she could not understand. To me, Rev. Mother, it should make no difference after I did my part....You will see by my note that I promised to try and get the home without asking Mother to use her checkbook if I could help it. All the correspondence will show my sincerity in the matter....You will see how I am justified in having the business brought to a finish of some kind, and since your Community does not seem to want the property and since the Sisters of Charity would not, I suppose, accept it for a summer house for their children, nothing remains for me to do but call a real estate house and place the property for sale at whatever price it will bring. The sum realized shall be sent to Sisters working on the foreign missions....
>
> It would have been the joy of my life if the Sisters had taken over the property as it was handed to them. Should they use the premises for any other purpose they would never have heard from me a word of complaint, because they would in such case have given something as good to the orphans. I would be proud to see the place utilized, whereas I feel bad to see it as it is, and am therefore fully determined to bring the business to a close. I need not tell you, Rev. Mother, that I shall never visit the Mission unless the premises built for the orphans is occupied by Sisters and orphans.
>
> It would have been the joy of my life to visit the children in their new home and to take always an interest in their welfare. It would be to me as a sacred duty to enlarge and embellish the house according as my means would permit. Now I say *fiat voluntas tu*....I ask a thousand pardons for any fault on my part and beg to remain
>
> Yours respectfully
> P. Blake [22]

Mother Seraphina's reply was brief. She simply acknowledged receipt of Father Blake's letter and expressed regret that the affair was the cause of such pain. It was her hope that God would turn everything to good purpose.

June brought another letter from Father Blake. He informed Mother Seraphina that the decision regarding the property now rested in the Archbishop's hands and he had no objection to the Archbishop's making the property over to the Dominican Sisters without conditions. He further stated that if the sisters took possession of the property and moved the children in, he would again take an interest in their work. At this juncture Mother Seraphina remained silent, doubtless awaiting the next development. In August he wrote again, chiding Mother Seraphina gently for what he deemed a lack of trust.

> Had you taken your children and you into the new premises, you surely would have, by this time, your beautiful chapel and many more things. It pays to put unbounded trust in our Blessed Savior. He will see to it that those who work in His service and trust in Him and leave to His kind Providence the future will always be more than provided for. I beg you to never think of what I did as done for any other motive than for His honor and glory. What I did, I did, and there it remains. Whether used or unused, my Lord will give me as much credit for what I did as if the place was occupied the next day after I left. Even should the place be never occupied, my reward will be the same, for my wish and intention in giving so much time and money had no other motive than the honor and glory of our Lord and the love of those who are dear to Him. Should the place even be destroyed, the news would not disturb me. My part was done and more than done when I left the Mission and got back to my work.[23]

In her reply Mother Seraphina prayed that God's Will would be done and included kind regards from the sisters and children. Father Blake wrote the same day saying he had sent the deed to the Archbishop to do whatever he thought best. The sisters might have an absolute deed, as requested; he advises the sisters to go to the Archbishop because a society is negotiating with him for the purchase or rental of the property to be used as a hospital.

At this juncture, the story of La Palmera took a surprising twist. Father Blake wrote of the need for a "first class sanitarium where patients threatened with tuberculosis will always have the right of way"[24] and informed Mother Seraphina that the previous year Mother Pia had promised him

> ...six or eight sisters to take up the work...in case I could get no sisters... If you are ready to make good that promise and if you are willing to help and encourage the good work, then, I have hope that the new house will belong to your orphans. But if you cannot find sisters to go at this good work of caring for consumptives, then I must only do the best I can, and soon the society [for the care of tubercular patients] which is trying to acquire the property at the Mission will begin. Any reply you give please give it to His Grace *Yes* or *No*.[25]

A second letter from Father Blake, written the same forenoon, explained his dilemma:

> But should the society not be able to acquire the property there, I must start in again....Now if I give your order the property for the orphans, in case these people cannot buy it, I wish you to let me know what your community proposes in return, that I may have my hospital, or rather your hospital, for, should you be prepared to give six or eight sisters and your good will to them to begin the good work, the property to be acquired, like the home for the orphans, would be yours. If I should send you a deed of gift to the property at the Mission without your promising me any aid for my hospital then I would be out in the cold and could never hope to go any further.[26]

Mother Seraphina's reply (September 19, 1909) left no room for doubt.

> Rev. and dear Father:
>
> In response to your two letters of yesterday I can only state that it is not in our power to comply with your wish that we should take care of poor consumptives, for the simple reason that we have not a sufficient number of Sisters to take up the work, although there is no lack of good will

nor of readiness on the part of the Sisters to engage in that good work....Since it is therefore utterly impossible for us to assist you as you desire, Rev. Father, we must abandon the hope of obtaining the house. As the work to which we are devoting our lives is as dear to our hearts as is that of caring for unfortunate consumptives is to yours, our first and only thought is the welfare of our poor friendless little charges.

We are at present in great straits owing to the fact that we did not build the much needed addition to our house as we had expected to have your home. With the certainty that we were soon to occupy your house, we took more children than we can really accommodate in our limited quarters, and now as the place is overcrowded, we are in constant fear of some sickness breaking out....Besides, we are obliged almost daily to refuse applicants for admission. Last week we were asked to receive six poor orphans, and as we could not we are much worried, as they have doubtless been placed in a Protestant asylum. Another application, the refusal of which caused us much pain was that of a poor widow with nine children. Can you not, Rev. Father, imagine what a source of sorrow it is to be thus obliged to turn from our door poor helpless, homeless little ones?

Now, Rev. Father, once again I must state that we cannot accept the home on the conditions you have proposed, and this being our *final decision* we will as soon as possible take steps to build an addition to our orphanage. Mother Pia has not yet returned from Europe; however, I presume we are acting in accordance with her wish.

Thanking you, Rev. Father, for the kindly interest that prompted you to offer us the home, and asking a little memento in your prayers for our community and for our children, also presenting our sincerest wishes for the success of your good work for the poor consumptives,

I am yours respectfully in the Sacred Heart,

Copy unsigned
[Sister Seraphina][27]

Mother Seraphina followed with another letter that was a model of good will. She informed Father Blake that the Brothers of Mary wished to establish a novitiate in California, described their good work there, and proposed that Father offer the Brothers the building as gift or purchase. Father Blake's reply made no mention of "gift," but stated that the property and building had cost $24,000 to date and that, if the Brothers bought the property, they would be pleased with the help he would give them. Nothing further was heard of the proposal.

The following month (October) Father Blake wrote "Rev. Mother" a lengthy letter that began:

> I hope you will not look upon me as regretting what I undertook for the sake of your orphan children. For love of God and these helpless ones I did what I did, with the hope too of being able to help the poor consumptives later. Far from giving up the hope of having a house for consumptives, [I] looked upon the act as being one that would help me to my end and aim of starting the work upon which I set my heart. If I fail, God will reward the good intention. Had you taken over the premises a year ago when my part was done, you would have seen a happy home of Nazareth, and I would be bound to stand by you to the end of my life...
>
> In the name of the Father, Son and Holy Ghost, take over the property as it was offered, and begin your work. I say that till Judgment Day if your community should last till then no one will question that you are rightful owners of the property for the benefit of orphan children in your charge. Should you ask at any time to turn the place into a novitiate, leaving your present home for the use of the orphans, I would not only say by all means do so, but feel happy. In doing our Master's work we ought to trust in Him for all time. He has protected and will protect us to the end. With kindest wishes to each and to all I beg to remain,
>
> Yours truly,
> P. Blake[28]

Another letter from Father Blake, dated "All Souls' Day," welcomed Mother Pia home from Europe, offered to come down for the opening of the orphanage, and promised:

> ...with God's blessing if I see it prosper, you may expect not only a new chapel but also a duplicate of the large building on the East side of the kitchen and also a house or cottage for the chaplain. I may tell you that if your sisters take my hospital, you will be obliged to get some of your wealthy friends to help me. [29]

Later in the same month, Father Blake sent three beautiful statues for the sisters' chapel in the new building and offered Mother Pia any doors or windows left from the building project which seems to be at a standstill. As disturbing as the course of events had been, affairs must have calmed down and an acceptable settlement been reached.

St. Mary of the Palms

For whatever transpired in the meantime, on February 27, 1910, the General Council voted to expend $3,000 for the completion of the building; and, on July 25 of the same year, sisters and children took formal possession of St. Mary of the Palms, as it would henceforth be known. Father Blake accepted Mother Pia's invitation to be present for the dedication of the building and to celebrate the opening Mass and address the sisters and children. Until his death in 1921, he wrote occasionally to the orphans and remembered them at Christmas with gifts of candy.

The last communication received from Father Blake is a long letter addressed to "My very dear Children of St. Mary's" under date of March 26, 1920.[30] Father thanks for their feastday remembrance for the feast of St. Patrick. He writes at length on the necessity of avoiding bad companions and closes hoping they keep faithful and receive the Sacraments of Penance and the Eucharist regularly. Father Patrick Blake died one year later on March 25, 1921. He went to his Lord peacefully, confident that he would be judged on his intentions, not his achievements. He never realized his heart's dream—his home for "poor consumptives."

The story of the beginning of St. Mary of the Palms leaves a number of questions unanswered. Why was the revised, often-promised deed not returned? What provoked the fuss over the name of the orphanage that so offended Father Blake? Did the sisters actually refuse to accept the name change? True, in a rough draft of a letter, Mother Seraphina wrote: "We find that we cannot possibly change the name of the orphanage."[31] The sentence was crossed out, however, and presumably, was not sent. Why was Archbishop Riordan apparently uninvolved in the transaction, or was it his decision to give the property to the Dominican Sisters? (He did have the property incorporated under the title, "St Mary's Orphanage".) Despite the extensive correspondence at hand, some answers are not forthcoming.

The principals in the story were certainly well meaning. Father Blake seemed driven by a desire to help the less fortunate, particularly orphans and "poor consumptives." Nevertheless, his frequent changes of mind had an unsettling effect on those negotiating with him. Mother Pia and Mother Seraphina were challenged by the barrage of letters that the anxious priest seemed compelled to write and disappointed when the anticipated windfall did not appear. In the end, it was the orphans who benefited!

With the transfer of the orphans to St. Mary's, the postulants and novices moved into the former children's quarters at the Motherhouse, and the priory was transferred to St. Mary's, with Mother Gonzaga Buehler as first prioress. The new arrangement at the Motherhouse gave everyone more breathing space.

This was not the case at St. Mary's, however. Orphans placed by state and county agencies increased the number of children at St. Mary's so dramatically that in 1914 a second building containing dining room, kitchen and sewing room was constructed. A few years later, an auditorium, purchased by the sisters from a resident of Mission San Jose, was moved to the St. Mary of the Palms grounds. Taking advantage of their purchase, the sisters added a second story to the auditorium for additional dormitory space. A steady program of development in the following years brought new music and recreation rooms, additional classrooms and dormitories, and a laundry.

In 1935 a ninth grade was added, the students transferring to other high schools for their remaining years until a directive from the San Francisco Archdiocesan Superintendent of Catholic Schools

Main building of St. Mary of the Palms

(1943) ordered the termination of all similar ninth grade programs in favor of four-year high schools.

By 1946 the sisters were educating not only dependent girls, but elementary school day students from the area as well. According to St. Mary's annalist, "The people of the neighboring villages are clamoring for an eight-classroom elementary school building where they can send their children, boys and girls, to a Catholic school." [32] In response to the demands, plans were initiated for a one-story frame building, containing four classrooms, an office, and a bookroom. Father James N. Brown, San Francisco archdiocesan superintendent of schools, presided at the groundbreaking on December 19, 1948. By the following September, the school was ready for occupancy under the principalship of Sister Ildephonsa Gerber, O.P. Through the first half of the 50s, enrollment increased steadily, verging on 200 (86 resident and 112 day students) by 1956.

Meanwhile a gradual change was occurring in the character of the child-care institution. Sister Mary Dominic Engelhard, O.P., community director of schools, alerted the sisters in a statement to the community:

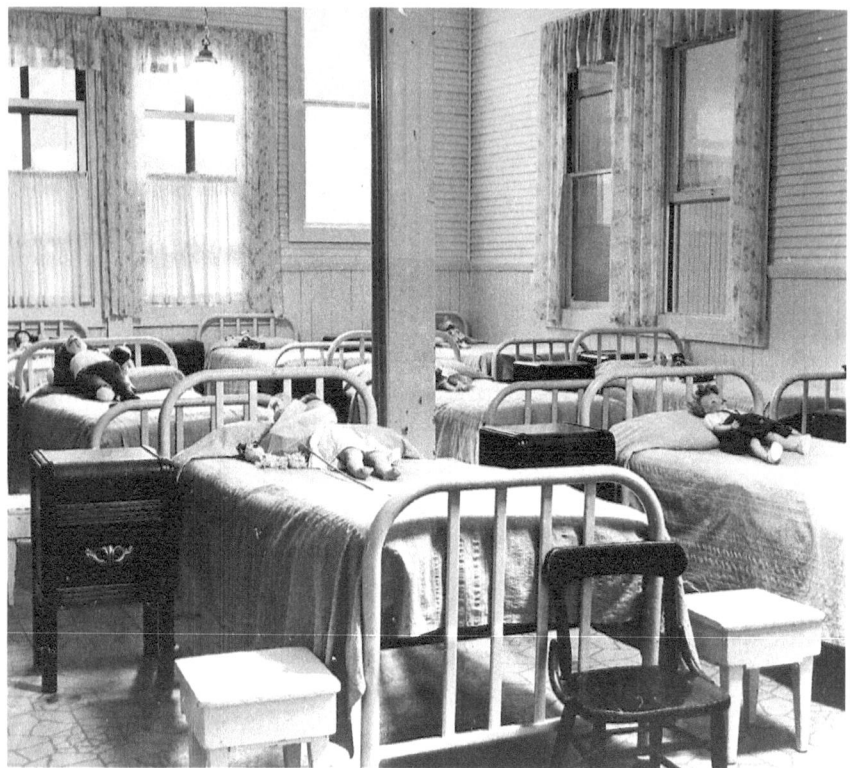

Dormitory for older girls

> From the custodial type care traditionally offered to the homeless orphan, the institution...[has been moving] into the more highly specialized care extended to the child needing out-of-home placement. The consequent need for new kinds of services and increased trained professional staff has come to be recognized as imperative for the institution that hopes to meet adequately its responsibilities in a changing contemporary society.[33]

About the same time, a report compiled by a member of the State Department of Social Welfare provided an accurate description of St. Mary of the Palms in 1957. It profiled the institution as:

> An independent corporation whose board of directors are all members of the religious community; subsequently, it

does not include any community members; financially, it relies almost completely on fees paid by child-care,... only through the personal sacrifices of the religious staff has the institution been able to maintain itself and pay off a remarkably large portion of the debt incurred....No support is received from the Community Chest, the United Crusade, archdiocesan or local church organizations.[34]

Although the financial condition of the institution could certainly not be described as strong, the review stated that the school was adequately staffed and met a real community need, but its weakness was in casework services since the institution did not have professionally trained social workers. In addition, the diversified population of St. Mary's—girls from broken homes, children requiring remedial education, children from the local community attending day school, and relatively undisturbed children in boarding school—led the State Department representative to conclude:

> ...because the resources of Saint Mary's of the Palms are not unlimited (both financial and available personnel are in short supply), it seems important to clarify objectives selecting a major emphasis and developing programs according to what is necessary for the major purpose.[35]

In summary, the report named three problem areas: finance, absence of a representative board, and need for professionally trained staff.

Following study of the report, Mother Pius Marbaise wrote to Archbishop Mitty of San Francisco asking permission to draw up a plan that would address the following:

> Over the years, Saint Mary's has operated as a sort of hybrid boarding school-home for dependent children, with the result that its status has never been clarified to the satisfaction of the welfare groups that would normally be interested in its program. The institution has not, in consequence, received assistance from these agencies to the extent to which it would seem entitled if it were to fulfill exclusively its original purpose as contracted with the Archdiocese in 1910.
>
> In order to function in its proper character, Saint Mary's needs to re-study its program, gradually expanding its

facilities and offerings until it is in a position to meet adequately the needs of the particular type child it was originally intended to serve.[36]

In collaboration with the sisters, Rt. Reverend James M. Murray, archdiocesan director of Catholic Charities, initiated the selection of an executive committee that would develop a proposal for the restructuring of Saint Mary of the Palms. The general intake policy of the institution was re-defined to provide for girls needing:

> ...a constructive group living experience in a therapeutically oriented group environment. Girls may be dependent, orphaned, homeless, abandoned, or emotionally troubled. These girls, of whom there is a growing number, need the benefits of care outside homes but cannot now adjust to foster home care.
>
> The services of the center will be available to girls between the ages of 11 and 16 years (grades 5–10) without regard to race, religious beliefs, or residence [. . .]. Excluding factors will include infectious diseases, mental deficiency (80 IQ or below), serious physical abnormality, hostile or aggressive delinquency (adjudicated), addiction to liquor or drugs, confirmed or overt sexuality.[37]

The plan included construction of six residential cottages with a total capacity of 120 girls. Grades Five to Eight would be taught on campus; older students would attend "outside" schools.

In its Golden Jubilee year, St. Mary of the Palms was off to a fresh start. It displayed a new name, "Serra Center," and looked forward to group residence living. Sister Linda (Rosalinda) Henriques, the first director of the modified institution, undertook the implementation of the plan with her customary enthusiasm. The annalist described the Golden Jubilee observance, November 20, 1960:

> Today, fifty years ago, St. Mary of the Palms opened its door to nineteen boarders, who were transferred from the Josephinum, their first home...The highlight of [to]day was a Board of Directors meeting at which outstanding personalities of the diocese assisted.
>
> Mr. Gerike, attorney and chairman, welcomed the guests.... The program included an open board meeting, Benediction

of the Blessed Sacrament by His Excellency, the Most Reverend Merlin J. Guilfoyle, [auxiliary bishop of San Francisco] followed by a tour of the premises concluding with tea.[38]

Glenwood Summer Camp

St. Mary of the Palms was founded as a home for dependent children needing custodial year-round care. The sisters cared for them during the summer months, as well as the school year. Between 1920 and 1966, resident and day camps in the United States grew in number from 2,000 to more than 11,000. The phenomenal growth was the result of a 1935 California State Law requiring year-round resident schools to provide summer camps for their children. In compliance with the law, St. Mary of the Palms looked south to the Glenwood area in the Santa Cruz Mountains for a campsite. There they found an ideal location on property owned by Charles Martin.

Charles C. Martin, born in Nova Scotia but raised in Maine, did what most Maine boys did in his day—went to sea at an early age. When his ship anchored in San Francisco Bay, Charlie jumped ship, deciding he had had enough of the ocean. Eventually he made his way south to Santa Cruz County and began taking up land in the beautiful area later known as Glenwood.

By 1876 the first passenger train, a narrow gauge *South Pacific Coast,* joined the town of Santa Cruz with that of Alameda by way of San Jose and Los Gatos. Alert to the future possibilities, Martin built the Glenwood Hotel on the most beautiful section of his property. The hotel consisted of a large frame building, enhanced by guest cottages, camping sites for those who preferred a more rugged experience, and a small outdoor "swimming tank," a novelty in its day. An outdoor dance floor, built in the center of a ring of redwood trees, harbored a saloon below, out of sight so as not to offend the female guests' sensibilities. A California Historical Marker, located across the road from the former railroad depot, recognizes Charles Martin's contribution to the district:

GLENWOOD

Historic town founded by Charles C. Martin, who came around the Horn 1847, and his wife, Hannah Carver Martin, who crossed the Isthmus. First homesteaded the area in 1851 and operated tollgate and station for stagecoaches crossing mountains. Later Martin developed lumber mill, winery, store and Glenwood Resort Hotel. [State Registered Landmark No. 499. Tablet planned by California Centennial Commission. Base provided by Santa Cruz Parlor, No. 26, Native Daughters, Santa Cruz Parlor No. 20 Native sons, and descendants Martin family. Dedicated June 22, 1950][39]

With the advent of auto travel and Highway 17, the railroad began to lose money and eventually ceased to run. The hotel followed as a casualty around 1924, and lay abandoned for the next 12 years. Comprising 138 acres, Charles Martin's property lay midway between Los Gatos and Santa Cruz, and the sisters from St. Mary's saw it as the answer to their needs. Sisters Bertranda Pierikarczyk and Nemesia Schwarzenback pioneered Glenwood, a camp for girls aged six to eighteen.

Glenwood proved a popular summer attraction until 1944 when war-time conditions made transportation so difficult that it was decided to hold "camp" at St. Mary of the Palms. An onsite swimming pool built in 1940, the gift of San Francisco benefactors, was a compensating attraction for the girls obliged to spend their summer "at home."

Notes

[1] Patrick Blake, letter to Backes, 15 May 1908.

[2] Backes 314.

[3] Maerz, letter to Blake, n.d. (probably 15 May 1908).

[4] Father Blake was evidently negotiating with a community of sisters in San Antonio, Texas to staff the sanitarium he hoped to build at Mission San Jose.

[5] Blake, letter to Maerz, 16 May 1908.

[6] Blake, letter to Maerz, 19 May 1908.

[7] Blake, letter to Backes, 20 May 1908.

8 Blake, letter to Backes, n.d.
9 Blake, letter to Maerz, 28 May 1908.
10 Blake, letter to Backes, 25 October 1908.
11 Maerz, letter to Blake, n.d.
12 Blake, letter to Backes, 4 November 1908.
13 Backes, letter to Blake, 10 November 1908.
14 Charles Ramm, letter to Backes, 2 December 1908.
15 Blake, letter to Backes, 4 December 1908.
16 Blake, letter to Backes, 12 December 1908.
17 Blake, letter to Backes, 21 January 1909.
18 Maerz, letter to Blake, 1 May 1909.
19 Blake, letter to Maerz, 17 May 1909.
20 Blake, letter to Maerz, 17 May 1909.
21 Maerz, letter to Blake, 18 May 1909.
22 Blake, letter to Maerz, 18 May 1909.
23 Blake, letter to Maerz, 28 August 1909.
24 Blake, letter to Maerz, 18 September 1909.
25 Blake, letter to Maerz, 18 September 1909.
26 Blake, letter to Maerz, 18 September 1909.
27 Maerz, letter to Blake, 19 September 1909.
28 Blake, letter to Maerz, 28 October 1909.
29 Blake, letter to Backes, 2 November 1909.
30 Blake, letter to orphans, 26 March 1920.
31 Maerz, letter to Blake, n.d.
32 Annals of St. Mary of the Palms, 1946.
33 Mary Dominic Engelhard, O.P., "Community Statement," 1955.
34 State Department of Social Welfare Report, 1957.
35 State Department of Social Welfare Report, 1957.
36 Mary Pius Marbaise, O.P., letter to Mitty, 1957.

[37] "Executive Committee Report," n.d.
[38] Annals of St. Mary of the Palms, 20 November 1960.
[39] California Centennial Commission (marker), 22 June 1950.

CHAPTER EIGHTEEN

MISSION TO MEXICO

The poor were never far from Mother Pia's heart. For some time she had been experiencing a growing desire to serve God's children south of the border in the land favored by Our Lady, but the San Francisco earthquake had diverted her attention until a fresh incentive was provided from an unexpected source. The three Torres sisters from Mexico were enrolled by their father as resident students in Immaculate Conception Academy, San Francisco. One day Raquel, the oldest, observed to Mother Seraphina, "It's a shame that no school exists in Mexico staffed by the Dominican Sisters. There are many cloistered Dominican Congregations, but no teaching Dominicans."[1] That was enough for the missionary-minded Mother Seraphina, who immediately relayed the observation to Mother Pia. The latter regarded the message as a nudge from on High and forthwith called a meeting of the General Council to discuss the feasibility of a Mexican foundation.

As outcome, Mother Seraphina, accompanied by the delighted Raquel, was en route to Mexico City on September 28, 1906. Señor Angel Sebastian Torres, Raquel's father, welcomed the travelers at the depot and escorted them to the Dominican Fathers, where they met the Vicar Provincial, Father José Bayon, O.P., and his assistant, Father Joaquín Rodríguez, O.P. During the lively interchange that followed, the Fathers assured Mother Seraphina of their keen interest in a school taught by Dominican Sisters. A visit to the Most Reverend Prospero María Alarcon, Archbishop of Mexico City, also promised the sisters a warm welcome in the Archdiocese.

From Father Joaquín Mother Seraphina learned that for some

time he and Father Elías Fierro, O.P., had been recruiting young women for active Dominican life and, as a preliminary step, had received several into the Order as Tertiaries. The priests pledged their assistance with vocations. As evidence of good will, Father Joaquin introduced Mother Seraphina to Sister Rosa de la Torre, a novice in the cloistered Dominican community of Santa Catalina de Siena in Mexico City. Delicate of health, she had entered the cloister in order to receive spiritual formation, but her real desire was to establish schools in Mexico staffed by Dominican Sisters of the Third Order.

On returning to the United States, Mother Seraphina gave a glowing account of the visit to a receptive Mother Pia and Council. "Mother Seraphina returns from Mexico," Mother Pia recorded in her Diary. "The Archbishop, priests, and lay people ask for a foundation there. God grant it be realized."[2] Though the Council gave unqualified approval, three years would elapse before a foundation would actually be made. The Dominican Fathers had informed Mother Seraphina of two possibilities: The sisters could accept property and build a convent and school in a wealthy American colony, or they could have a small house belonging to Señor de la Torre, Sister Rosa's father, in Atzcapotzalco, a poor suburb of Mexico City. Advice was plentiful on all sides, almost all of it favoring the American colony, but for Mother Pia the decision was easily made; it was to the poor that she would send her sisters.

In April 1907 Mother Seraphina, with Sister Teresa Meyer as companion and interpreter, returned to Mexico, staying with the cloistered sisters of Santa Catalina de Siena in Mexico City. On their return they brought with them Sister Rosa de la Torre to enter the formation program at the Motherhouse. The following November Raquel Torres entered the postulancy in San Francisco and was soon joined by Mercedes Veloz, Guadalupe Brun, Soledad Gutiérrez and Elizabeth Healy from Mexico. True to their word, the Dominican Fathers had sent four candidates. Their arrival was welcomed by Mother Pia, who was convinced that the best way to insert the Congregation into a foreign country was by forming native vocations.

Wishing to see for herself, Mother Pia left for Mexico City on March 16, 1908, with Sister Teresa Meyer again as companion. They arrived in the capital on March 20, where they were welcomed by Father Joaquín Rodríguez, O.P., now Vicar Provincial, the faithful

Señor Torres and the Olaguibel family, whose two daughters had been students at Immaculate Conception Academy. The sisters' 10-day visit was marked by discussions with the Dominican Fathers and visits to the Dominican Church in Mexico City. But another year passed before the Dominican Vicar Provincial wrote Mother Pia from Mexico that he would be ready for the sisters to make a foundation in time for the opening of school in 1910:

> He thinks it will be well to have a few Sisters in Mexico for six months preparatory to the opening of the school, so that they may accomplish the necessary preliminary work. Father Provincial is building a Day School in Atzcapotzalco, a suburb of Mexico City, for the poor children. We are to go daily from our convent to this school. At the convent we should have a pay school.[3]

Mother Pia's concerns were realistic: "How many sisters...[will] the Provincial require of us for his poor school? Will his school be ready at the time of our foundation?"[4]

Satisfactory answers must have been forthcoming, for in November Mother Seraphina and the recently professed Sisters Rosa de la Torre, Guadalupe Torre, and Josefina Veloz left for Atzcapotzalco to establish the foundation. Two weeks later, December 16, 1909, Sisters Loretto Schafer, Rosario [Elizabeth] Healy, Catalina [Soledad] Gutiérrez and Juana [Guadalupe] Brun arrived in Mexico to complete the community.

The first few days saw the sisters separated, forced to stay with relatives and friends in Mexico City until the arrival of beds for the convent. By December 21 all was in order, and the community joyfully took possession of the little house. Its furnishings were minimal: eight beds and mattresses, two small tables, one desk, a crucifix and 12 chairs. Dishes and silverware were borrowed from relatives, contributing to a diverse and colorful table. From the neighborhood strays, the sisters adopted an aging yellow cat, who soon became a community regular. Shortly before Christmas the sisters acquired a sewing machine on loan in order to make muslin curtains to replace the unsightly sheets and white aprons with which they had covered the windows.

At midnight on Christmas Eve, they knelt in shadowy candlelight around their improvised crib—a borrowed table covered with branches and green hay. Gently Mother Seraphina laid the Infant in the manger, the setting not much removed from the poverty of Bethlehem. On Christmas morning they made their way on foot to a little chapel outside the town where the Indians worshipped. Sitting on the floor with them, the sisters "were happy to be with the poor of Mexico."[5]

Academia Santa Rosa, Atzcapotzalco

As the school was not yet finished, Santa Rosa Academy opened on January 10, 1910, in the convent. The statistics were not impressive: eight sisters, eight children and 12 chairs. The significance of the chairs should not be minimized. They moved with the community through the day: from chapel to refectory to parlor to schoolroom to community room and back again to chapel to begin the circuit anew. The chairs served school purposes adequately for the first three days until a thirteenth child was registered. Then the children took turns sharing chairs until the new desks arrived a few days later, thereby avoiding a developing seating crisis, as by January 17, the school reported an attendance of 24.

In February the sisters began catechism classes in the parish church for the servants of neighboring families and in a nearby chapel for the Indian children. Sisters Juana and Rosario scouted the surrounding villages gathering the Indians to be taught. They began classes also at the San Lucas Catechism Center with 23 children in attendance. For lack of chairs the children sat on *petates* or straw sleeping mats.

Ever mindful of the sisters' needs, Mr. Torres donated a small organ for the convent oratory. The first hymn sung to accompaniment was *"Wir preisen dich"* ("We praise You"), rendered heartily in good German flavored with a Spanish accent.

The Feast of Our Lady of Lourdes, February 11, celebrated throughout the world for the first time that year, was scheduled for the blessing of the convent. Father Joaquín Rodríguez, O.P., led a procession, composed of Dominican Fathers and a Brother, the sisters, 40 girls in white dresses and veils, and a number of guests carrying lighted candles, through the house, blessing each room in turn. Following the blessing, Father Macario López, O.P., celebrated the Eucharist in the sisters' chapel. At the reception after, the sisters served wine and cookies, Father Joaquin having thoughtfully dispensed all present from the Lenten fast. The guests sat on chairs borrowed for the occasion from the neighbors. "The Blessed Sacrament is with us forever,"[6] exulted the annalist, little dreaming of what lay ahead.

On April 4 the school moved from the convent to the newly finished classrooms below the church, signaling an increase in registration. In the same month, a dormitory for resident girls was declared ready. The month of May brought the introduction of the Rosary Confraternity, and June, the addition of two more classrooms. Then came the sobering word of Mother Pia's grave illness and the necessity of Mother Seraphina's return to the Motherhouse. Replacing her as superior was Mother Amanda Bednartz, who arrived with Sister Armella Schlickenrieder, a native of Bavaria, destined to serve the sisters in Mexico as cook until her death seven years later.

In June, 25 Indian children and family servants, prepared by the sisters, received their First Holy Communion. On August 15 the first postulant from Pueblo, Amalia Suárez-Peredo (Sister Rosita) entered the convent in consequence of Mother Seraphina's visit to Pueblo in quest of native vocations. December brought a visit from the government inspector, who rated the school satisfactory, and the same month the Indian children enrolled in catechism classes increased to 94. In the happy community's opinion things were shaping up beautifully. "A year ago," the annalist wrote on December 31, "we had practically nothing but an empty house; now we have the Blessed Sacrament with us, Holy Mass daily, and more or less, all we need."[7] But an ominous note made its way into the entry, even though the annalist, a little naively, gave small importance to it: "All speak about revolution; yet, we neither see nor suffer anything indicating this. We enjoy perfect peace in our happy little house, ignoring all rumors."[8]

Actually at the time of the sisters' arrival in Mexico, the country was ripe for revolution. With the exception of one four-year period, Porfirio Díaz had been in power for 34 years, transforming what had been a constitutional government into a personal dictatorship. By 1910 there was general unrest and sporadic opposition throughout the country, but no leadership to counteract Díaz's control. Mexico's military and political figures were loathe to risk their lives in conflict with the dictator.

The man who finally succeeded in overthrowing Díaz was the unlikely Francisco Madero. A little man, five feet two inches tall, with a high-pitched voice and a nervous tic, a vegetarian and a teetotaler, Madero belonged to a wealthy creole family in Coahuila. He had been educated in Europe and the United States, where he had picked up a number of humanitarian ideas. Entrusted by his family with the management of a cotton plantation, he spent the profits on housing, schools and medical services for the workers and regularly fed 50 to 100 of their children in his home. Porfirio Díaz did not regard Madero as a serious threat.

About the same time Emiliano Zapata, a Morelian peasant leader, began stirring things up by recruiting Indians from the sugar plantations to wage war on the *hacendados*. Soon uprisings were occurring throughout the whole of Mexico. The Díaz dictatorship, which heretofore had appeared invincible, was on its way out. Zapata's forces, called Zapatistas, were greatly feared for their brutality; wherever they went, they burned the haciendas, murdering the administrators and dividing the lands among the peons. Such was the situation at the time of the sisters' arrival in Mexico.

On Ascension Thursday, May 25, 1911, the people of Mexico City revolted, leaving many dead and wounded, and the following day President Díaz resigned and fled to Europe. Francisco Madero, who took over in Díaz's place, was greeted by the people as a savior. In Atzcapotzalco there was a great ringing of bells and honking of horns as the train bearing Madero to Mexico City rumbled by. As a measure of prudence, Mother Amanda added to the general din by ringing the convent bell vigorously. Fearing that a second outbreak in Mexico City might reach the suburbs, the sisters held no classes during the week.

Sometime in 1912 Sister Teresa Meyer replaced Mother Amanda as superior of Santa Rosa. Scarcely had she arrived when Doña Concepción García-Conde, a widow of means, approached her regarding the staffing of an orphanage and school for poor children in Tlalpam, another of Mexico City's many suburbs. The offer seemed providential, as Sister Rosa de la Torre had recently left the community in order to found a new Dominican congregation in Atzcapotzalco. Fearing that Sister Rosa would lay claim to her father's house any day, Sister Teresa regarded Doña García-Conde's offer as a blessing from heaven.

[Her] beautiful and spacious building which had been in the course of erection for six years was now completed.... After many exchanges of mail [with Mother Pia, or in her absence, Mother Seraphina, and the Council as Mother Pia was in Europe], conditions agreeable to all parties concerned were at last about to be accepted and signed, when war broke out in Mexico City on February 14, 1913. [9]

A ten-day bombardment ended with the capture and death of President Madero and Vice President Piño Suárez.

For the time being, communication with the Motherhouse was temporarily suspended and negotiations came to a halt. Finally, sometime in February 1913, a telegram arrived from California granting permission to accept the Tlalpam school and orphanage, but making no mention of Atzcapotzalco. In the general turmoil a letter from the Motherhouse containing further instructions never reached its destination.

Meantime, Doña García-Conde was growing desperate, as she had her heart set on opening the school and orphanage in March, the month of St. Joseph. A second Motherhouse telegram received in late March advised consultation with the Archbishop of Mexico City, the Most Rev. José Mora del Rio. After hearing the sisters' dilemma, the Archbishop declared that God had permitted the loss of the letter and wished the sisters to have two houses. Solomon-like, he decreed that the community be split, half going to Tlalpam, half remaining in Atzcapotzalco. Consequently, on March 31, Sisters Teresa Meyer, Armella Schlickenrieder, Josefina Veloz, Catalina Gutiérrez, and two postulants, Francisca Narváez

Sister Teresa Meyer

Sisters in courtyard at *Academia de Sta. Rosa, Primaria,* Atzcapotzalco, Mexico, D.F., c. 1910

(Sister Susanna) and Trinidad Alonso (Sister María de Chantal) bade farewell to the community at Atzcapotzalco and left for Tlalpam. Remaining at Santa Rosa were Sisters Laurentia Sharkey, Guadalupe Torres, Teresita Coghlan, Rosita Suárez-Peredo, and a postulant, Guadalupe Alvarez (Sister Mercedes).

Colegio Inmaculada Concepción, Tlalpam

Shedding tears of gratitude to God for this answer to her prayers, Doña Garcia-Conde welcomed the sisters to their new home, *Colegio Inmaculada Concepción*. The house was devoid of furniture and that first night they prayed the Office in the dormitory, kneeling around a trunk on which a solitary candle provided the only light. For a week the order of the day was housecleaning, and the sisters quickly made the acquaintance of women from the area who came with their servants to assist the sisters in scraping lime and mortar from windows and floors.

On Sunday, April 4, 1913, Father Luis Cea, pastor, celebrated the first Mass in the convent for the sisters and their friends. With the presence of the Blessed Sacrament the convent was now complete. By mid-April the backyard had become home to chickens, ducks and rabbits, which the sisters hoped would provide food in the future for the children. On April 30, the first orphan arrived, to be followed the next day by 10 more. Since mattresses and bedding had not yet been delivered, the sisters gave up theirs for the benefit of the children. The latter had arrived in a condition most accurately described as unwashed, and the sisters were looking forward to bathing them. Their enthusiasm turned to frustration when boilers leaked, bathtubs clogged, and plumbers either failed to respond or worked so casually that the hot water shortage seemed a way of life. These were hurdles they had not anticipated.

The Feast of Corpus Christi, May 22, marked the first High Mass celebrated in the convent chapel. Sisters Teresa and Josefina constituted the Mass choir, with the rest of the community and the children singing at Benediction which followed. Conchita and her many friends "were edified by the piety and good behavior of the children, who when first admitted to the institution, were untrained and wild as young savages."[10]

By June, enrollment had increased to 50, the youngest four or five years old. Visitors to the school were delighted, all expressing admiration at the work of the sisters and the children. Dominican Fathers Domingo Fernández and Ramon Carrión were among the callers. Father Domingo summed up the general feeling: "It is superb! And you cannot ask for more. This place is really a blessing from God....When God wants something, it is bound to succeed."[11]

On the last day of June, however, the serenity was shattered. Conchita arrived breathless with the news that Zapatista forces were expected in Tlalpam that night and troops from the Capital were on their way to confront them. "The children," she said, "must sleep with their clothes on, so that if the Zapatistas do come, you can all begin to run."[12] To this news the sisters responded with a show of outward calm, though they were not sure what they could actually do to protect the children if war broke out in the town. Preparing for the worst, Sister Armella buried the tabernacle key and what money the sisters had in the chicken yard. The long and frightening night dragged on, but although the government troops arrived, the Zapatistas did not, and peace was maintained. It would not be for long.

In October Sisters Magdalena Serranía, Inés Perochena, María Cueto and Dominica Ochoa arrived from the Motherhouse to bolster the staffs of the two schools, and the following month Sister Laurentia Sharkey returned to the United States with six postulants in tow.

Just before Christmas Sister Teresa announced a decision that brought pain to all involved. The question of closing the house at Atzcapotzalco in order to have all the sisters in one place (Tlalpam) had been settled only after lengthy discussion. Sister Teresa explained the move sadly:

> The country being so unsettled and times so hard on account of the continual war, the Academy and house of St. Rose, Atzcapotzalco, had to be suppressed and all the Sisters transferred to Tlalpam. The Sisters were heartbroken at having to leave a place where they had labored so hard and with so much fruit. For in the four years that they had taught there, they had done much good for all the parish children. The people were inconsolable.[13]

The sisters left the school to the direction of Sister Rosa de la Torre, whose father owned the property.

In April a news report confirmed that American troops were expected to arrive any day in Veracruz. Sister Teresa Meyer and Sister Teresita Coghlan, Tlalpam superior, who had gone to Mexico City to stock up on provisions, encountered angry mobs burning the American flag and attacking American shops. They were advised by the American Consul General to close their school and seek refuge in the capital. Community friends urged an even more extreme measure—the sisters' immediate return to California for their own safety. Sister Teresita Coghlan, Tlalpam superior, was in a quandary. During a sleepless night, she suddenly remembered Mother Pia's words to her sometime earlier: "One must leave all to God. He is able to help and assist us. And, if necessary, you must go from door to door to beg daily bread for your poor little ones."[14] Her mind was made up! The sisters would stay! Their only concession would involve the safety of the children.

On June 30, 1914, the sisters began to dismiss the children. "Poor children," Sister Teresa wrote, "you should have seen how touching it was to see them all crying and begging for a blessing."[15] Soon only six –those who had no families to receive them—remained. After much soul searching, Sister Teresa decided that the sisters, too, should disband and return to their families or friends; only she and Sister Armella would remain, staying in the convent by day and in the local hospital by night. "Even though we may lose the crown of martyrdom by leaving Tlalpam," wrote Sister Teresa to Mother Pia, "we had better take advice by putting ourselves out of danger. These Zapatistas are incarnate demons who respect no one."[16] Yet she worried about the sisters' safety in Mexico City:

> "I hope that I am doing the right thing. I have not acted without advice....People say that when the rebels arrive, Mexico [City] will be like the Day of Judgment. But better to have our young sisters blown up in Mexico City than to be carried away by those terrible Zapatistas."[17]

As a precautionary measure, the sisters buried the monstrances and chalices from the convent and parish church in a large pot under the back porch. Each day one of the priests consecrated just enough hosts for the morning Mass, leaving only one large host in the convent. "In case of danger," Sister Teresa wrote Mother Pia, "I can take It out and run with It."[18]

Then just as the sisters were about to leave for their homes in

Mexico City, word arrived that danger was over. Peace had been approved by the United States, and all was calm again. Relieved, the sisters determined to stay and invite the children to return. But the decision presented a new problem for Sister Teresa. "If the situation lasts much longer," she wrote, "we will have to starve; instead of being martyrs....We have been living on our chickens, geese, ducks, rabbits and pigs."[18] Her concern was real enough. By this time the refugees, children and sisters living in the convent totaled 105, and daily demands were far exceeding the supply of food on hand. Nevertheless, she scheduled profession for August 4, the feast of Saint Dominic, shortening the customary eight-day retreat to three "on account of the dangerous situation and the nervous state we are in from shots and shells and cannon balls." She explained to Mother Pia, "...we escaped unhurt, except for the terror we experienced, which took away my little hips and [I] now find that my clothes are falling off."[20]

But by the end of August it was the same old story. "It is nearly a week now," Sister Teresa had written earlier to Mother Pia, "since our nerves have been strung to the highest pitch, jumping at every little noise."[21] It was not surprising, for the Carrancista forces of General Venustiano Carranza, the constitutional chieftain, made an unwelcome appearance at the convent, threatening to break down the door if it was not opened immediately. On learning that the house was a school for poor children, the soldiers became friendlier, but returned the next morning to announce that they were setting up their cannon on the convent roof. Hastily the sisters gathered children, bedding and a few provisions and set out for the homes of Doña Concha and the Canalizo family. After a quiet night they returned to the school the next morning in time for Mass.

But Sister Teresa's worries were multiplying. Linked with wealth and privilege in the minds of the revolutionaries, the Church had become part of the Revolution. Catholic schools and colleges were closed, and the majority of sisters and clergy had gone abroad. Those remaining were holed up in private homes and went out only in disguise. But word was out now that teaching communities would be spared. Gradually, in order not to attract attention, Sister Teresa began to bring the sisters back to Tlalpam, and she went personally to the Minister of Brazil seeking assurance of the children's safety before she would take them back. To Mother

Pia she wrote that she now appeared in public as an "independent American lady. Where I got the courage, I do not know, except that Our Lord has pity on a poor little coward like me and makes me a lioness in this land of wild bulls." [22]

On September 1, 1914, school reopened. Only 30 children were present, the others prevented by fear—not without reason, for shooting in the surrounding hills had become the daily fare.

In November the Zapatistas made their entry into Tlalpam, creating an uproar that succeeded in its objective of intimidating the people. Shouts, shooting, blowing of horns, setting off of fire crackers and sky rockets, and roaring of cannons left the citizenry terrorized. Houses were broken into and stores looted and trashed. Conchita and her household, accompanied by a mob of townsfolk, came running to the sisters, begging shelter from the invaders.

> [The next morning] the *Colegio* was visited by two bands of Zapatistas; the first band nearly broke the front door by beating it with the butts of their rifles; the second, threatened to blow up the back door with bullets. But as soon as the doors were opened and they saw the religious in their white habits, they stared and changed their attitude immediately. They told them not to fear, that they did not come to hurt them, but to protect and deliver them from the enemy.
>
> So while every other house in Tlalpam was broken into and robbed, God protected the *Colegio García-Conde*. Nothing was touched; on the contrary, on the following day, corn, beans and rice were sent to the Colegio from the Zapatista authorities.[23]

Although news of rioting in Mexico City and sporadic cannon fire in the hills surrounding Tlalpam kept the people tense and fearful, life for the sisters and children was beginning to return to normal. Then came a telegram from the Motherhouse, which stunned the community: "Danger. Come home all of you. Pia."[24] Sister Teresa went to the American Legation for advice. "It would be madness to leave," she was told, "as nearly all traffic...[is] suspended and the only train running north...[is] in great danger of attack."[25] For the time being, obedience was out of the question.

On February 5, 1915, the moment, long dreaded, finally arrived. Carrancista forces clashed with Zapatistas in Tlalpam. Entering the convent, the Carrancistas hauled their machine guns to the roof from where they began firing. The children screamed and wailed in fright as bullets penetrated the convent walls. Sister Inés Perochena became a near casualty when a bullet missed her by inches, embedding itself in a dormitory floor. In mid-afternoon the Carrancistas, claiming victory, withdrew from the convent, only to be followed by the defeated and infuriated Zapatistas, who smashed the convent doors with their rifles, cursing and calling the sisters names for permitting the Carrancistas on their roof. In revenge they carried away blankets, sheep, chickens and all the bread in the house.

Despite the alarming conditions, the sisters managed to have Mass almost daily and Benediction of the Blessed Sacrament on high feasts of the Church, even though the long-suffering chaplain, a Spaniard, had to be hidden in the house whenever the soldiers reappeared, as orders had been issued to kill all foreign priests. His presence sometimes produced a creative spark. On one occasion when the soldiers appeared at the convent without warning, the sisters ran the chaplain, clad in his Dominican habit, into the kitchen where they hastily put a veil on his head, stuck a spoon on his hand, and bade him stir the pot on the stove! Thinking he was the sister cook, the soldiers left him to his task!

Community prayer was often accompanied by gunfire, but through it all the convent stood as an island of peace. As a guard at the crossing line into Tlalpam told a mother who came frantically seeking her child: "Well...madam, return in peace, for your child is safe. That *Colegio* is surrounded by angels and no harm will come to her."[26]

Sister Teresa Meyer put it a different way for Mother Pia, "We have heard all the shooting and the Carrancista detachments here are dashing about in all directions on horseback. But God saved us before and he will save us again. If only they [would] shoot us and be done with it."[27]

By late August the food situation at the convent had become so critical that the sisters had to dismiss 45 children. Learning of the remaining children's need, General del Viliar of the *Constitucionalistas*, sent fresh buns to the convent, the first bread the delighted children had tasted in weeks.

Surprisingly, in the midst of the turmoil and general unrest, vocations continued to come. In 1915 three postulants received the habit: María Pascal became Sister Concepción; Josefina Gazano, Sister Amada; and Guadalupe Domínguez, Sister Adalaida. Between January and April 1916 another group — Irene Bustamante (Sister Juana), Mercedes Dávalos (Sister Columba), Rebecca Uriarte-Healy (Sister Auxilia), and Sara Vásquez-Dávila (Sister Soledad) — were accepted into the community. A fifth, Angelita Aguerrebere (Sister Rosario), hitched a ride in an old hay wagon from Mexico City part way to Tlalpam, as no trains were running at the time. Walking the remaining miles in the hot sun, she arrived at the convent a blistered but eager candidate.

But at length, conditions finally improved. Slowly, during the years of Venustiano Carranza's presidency, the activities of peace began to reappear. So much so, that when Alvaro Obregón assumed the reins of government in November 1920, "Mexico was at peace, and more nearly united than at any time in its history."[28] Sister Teresa's troubles were over for the time being, and the sisters could live in tranquility, but there was more, much more to follow!

Notes

[1] Raquel Torres in Maria Victoria Hernandez, O.P.; *Ministry Under Fire: 1906–1946* (Mission San Jose, CA: Dominican Sisters, 1998) 2.

[2] Backes 307.

[3] Backes 315.

[4] Atzcapotzalco Annals, 25 December 1909 in Hernandez 21.

[5] Atzcapotzalco Annals, 11 February 1910 in Hernandez 26.

[6] Atzcapotzalco Annals, 31 December 1910 in Hernandez 33.

[7] Atzcapotzalco Annals, 31 December 1910 in Hernandez 33.

[8] Teresa Meyer, O.P., "Introduction," in Hernandez 45–46.

[9] Tlalpam Annals, 22 May 1913 in Hernandez 50.

[10] Tlalpam Annals, 18 May 1913 in Hernandez 50.

[11] Tlalpam Annals, 30 June 1913 in Hernandez 52.
[12] Tlalpam Annals, 23 December 1913 in Hernandez 56.
[13] Tlalpam Annals, 23 April 1914 in Hernandez 59.
[14] Meyer, letter to Backes, 30 June 1914.
[15] Meyer, letter to Backes, 28 June 1914.
[16] Meyer, letter to Backes, 30 June 1914.
[17] Meyer, letter to Backes, 3 July 3 1914.
[18] Meyer, letter to Backes, 28 July 1914.
[19] Meyer, letter to Backes, 28 July 1914.
[20] Meyer, letter to Backes, 3 July 1914.
[21] Meyer, letter to Backes, 25 August 1914.
[22] Tlalpam Annals, 17 November 1914 in Hernandez 65.
[23] Tlalpam Annals, 25 January 1915 in Hernandez 66.
[24] Tlalpam Annals, 25 January 1915 in Hernandez 66.
[25] Patrick Mary Kearney, O.P., Personal Interview, 28 September 2003.
[26] Armella Schlickenrieder, O.S.D., letter to Backes (translated from the German), 10 April 1915.
[27] Meyer, letter to Backes, 28 July 1914 in Hernandez 93.
[28] Henry Bamford Parkes, *A History of Mexico, Sentry Editions 61* (Boston: Houghton, 1970) 367.

CHAPTER NINETEEN

LOOKING SOUTH AGAIN

St. Michael Elementary School is distinct in the annals of the Congregation in that, although a parochial school, it antedated the parish, the sisters arriving before the clergy. Credit for the foundation, however, should be given to the Catholic parents of the area, whose earnest desire to have a Catholic elementary school in Manchester Heights, as the outlying district of Los Angeles was then known, was the real motivating force behind the grassroots initiative. Children of the area—if they attended Catholic school at all—traveled by horse and buggy the considerable distance to St. Joseph's parish in Los Angeles. But by the turn of the century Manchester parents were becoming restive and talking about a school closer to home. On January 16, 1903, they decided to act, and their appeal to Bishop Thomas Conaty of Los Angeles met with a positive response and permission to take action.

St. Michael Elementary School

With an eye to enrolling his numerous progeny, John Wagner (father of Margaret, one of St. Michael's first pupils and our future Sister Vibiana) donated property on the corner of Manchester and Vermont Streets for the school. The project became a family enterprise. The brothers-in-law, Messrs. Wagner, Merten and Thill, took it upon themselves to build the school, which they named St. Michael's in honor of Michael Wagner, John's father. Father Victor Aertker, O.S.F., St. Joseph's pastor, blessed the building, which consisted of two classrooms and a tiny lunchroom for the sisters. Small though it was, it stood as a triumph; the parents had their Catholic school!

St. Michael's opened on September 8, 1903, with 33 children spread over six grades and taught by Sisters Hedwig Infanger and Marcolina Schriever. The sisters lived at St. Joseph's and each day made the long trip by interurban car out to St. Michael's. For four years the daily excursion continued until the sisters' dismissal from St. Joseph's (Cf. Chapter Ten) worked to the benefit of St. Michael's. Rendered homeless by their termination at Saint Joseph's, the sisters rented a small house some eight blocks from St. Michael's to accommodate the community that had grown to four: Sisters Rosaria Huber, superior; Barbara Huber; Diana Biro; and Pulcheria Reichert. Monthly rental payments ($13.00) proved a challenge, as so few children paid tuition—the Wagner, Merten and Thill offspring providing the main financial support.

Sister Diana taught Grades One to Four and Sister Rosaria, Five to Eight, in addition to holding the dual responsibilities of principal and superior. Monday through Friday Sister Pulcheria commuted to Sacred Heart where she taught music, and Sister Barbara served the little community as cook. To Sister Diana, youngest member of the group, fell the custodial task of sweeping the two classrooms daily, as well as the bulk of convent duties—cleaning house, mending clothes and helping with the laundry and ironing.

Early accounts of life at St. Michael's spark the imagination. The snugness of the little house demanded a degree of agility on the part of the occupants. "Bedrooms" were upstairs under the eaves. Lodged between the staircase and the exterior walls of the house were two beds, one to the right of the stairway and one to the left. To retire was a dual enterprise: one member had to climb on the bed and hold aloft a chair so that the other could squeeze her way between the banister and the wall. The alternative was to stand on the chair at the foot of the bed and jump! The "closet" was a rope tied around the brick chimney that ran through the center of the attic floor to the roof. Over the rope the sisters had draped sheets to protect their white habits from the brick dust. To reach the "closet" one had to crawl through a small opening, making sure that a wayward foot did not go through the ceiling below.

In the absence of a chapel, the sisters turned the tiny parlor into an oratory, its one window adorned with a lace curtain, which

St. Michael's convent built and gifted to the sisters by Mr. and Mrs. Peter Thill

did not prohibit passersby from bunching on the sidewalk to watch the sisters at prayer.

The community attended daily Mass at St. Vincent's, the nearest church, rising early to catch the first electric car of the day from Redondo Beach. The pre-dawn exodus was perforce a necessity, as the smell of the freshly caught fish carried by a later San Pedro car was too much of a challenge for empty stomachs. Arrived at St. Vincent's, the sisters made their contemplation until Mass time. On returning home, they breakfasted on black coffee and dry bread; then, rain or shine, they set out through tall grass and hay fields to walk the distance to school. On Sundays they worshipped with St. Michael's Catholic community, as Mass was celebrated in a nearby home by a priest from the Cathedral.

Fortunately, living in the little house did not endure for long. Once more the Wagner contingent came to the sisters' relief when Peter Thill offered to build a more comfortable home on his Manchester Avenue property, a short distance from the school. The new house was a spatial, as well as financial relief. Not only was it larger, but it came rent-free! Although the strain was somewhat alleviated, the sisters' monetary problems did not disappear. When Mother Pia came to visit, she reproved a sister for having only soup for dinner at noon. Under the table the cook nudged the corrected one and whispered, "Nothing else in the house; wait until after school"[1] when teachers would be recruited to visit the neighboring farmhouses to beg bread and potatoes. Distressed when she discovered how poorly the sisters were living, Mother Pia made arrangements with Sacred Heart convent to assist the sisters at St. Michael's with donations of food. From then on, they fared better, but not always. On one occasion when potato salad was on the menu, the cook mistakenly substituted machine oil for olive oil. The long-suffering community attributed the unpalatable dish to an absence of vinegar, a not unusual circumstance, given their limited funds. "A sorry looking lot"[2] was Sister Diana's description of the community that evening.

St. Michael's first closing exercises were held in John Wagner's granary amid bins of grain, piles of gunnysacks and a variety of farm implements. The unique character of the setting did nothing to inhibit the enthusiasm of the audience, who applauded each song and recitation vigorously.

In 1907 Bishop Conaty erected St. Michael's into a parish. Work on the church began on the Feast of the Epiphany, January 6, 1908, and the first Mass was celebrated in the nearly completed structure on the feast of St, Joseph, March 19. Ten years later, an ironic twist as far as the sisters were concerned was the appointment of Father Raphael Fuhr as pastor of St. Michael's. Now a diocesan priest, Father Fuhr found himself once again working with the Dominican Sisters he had had removed from St. Joseph's!

To accommodate the steadily growing student body, a new elementary school was built in 1913 and replaced by a brick structure in 1926. The latter is still giving service, though after its first 20 years, Father Michael Lee, pastor, undertook

Sister Raphael McCarthy with her First Communion class

the renovation of the building. The convent annalist approved:

> This evening the Reverend Pastor, Father Lee, paid us a visit. He is very anxious to have each sister give suggestions as to where the necessary improvements in the school building should be made. He plans on having Mr. Ross Montgomery, outstanding architect and contractor, come Monday and consult with the sisters....[A] complete renovation of the school cafeteria will be undertaken immediately.[3]

When enrollment climbed beyond 500, Father Lee authorized the addition of four classrooms, which were ready for occupancy in March 1953. The same year marked the school's fiftieth year of service for the children of South Central Los Angeles, (the name by which the district was eventually known). Enrollment figures spoke for themselves: from 42 pupils in 1903, St. Michael's lay claim to a registration of 610 in 1953.

Mission San Gabriel Elementary School

San Gabriel was a drowsy little village east of Los Angeles when the Dominican Sisters arrived in 1912 to open an elementary school. Adobe and wooden shacks lined its dirt walks and narrow lanes, and "the only great disturber of...[the] little town's quiet atmosphere was the electric trolley car which came clanging down the unpaved street every half hour, bringing tourists to see the venerable Mission situated in the midst of San Gabriel."[4]

Founded on September 8, 1771, by Fathers Benito Cambon, O.S.F., and Angel de la Somera, O.S.F., *Mission San Gabriel Arcangel*, located approximately nine miles east of Los Angeles, was the fourth oldest of the Franciscan missions in California. The "Queen of the Missions" lay claim to its royal title because it "gathered into its fold thousands of neophytes, its flocks and herds were thick in the deep fertile valley, and its granaries were never empty."[5] Following the secularization of the missions in 1834, Mission San Gabriel was entrusted to the diocesan clergy for three-quarters of a century, but in 1908 Bishop Conaty invited the Missionary Sons of the Immaculate Heart of Mary, popularly known as Claretians after their Founder, Saint Anthony Mary Claret, to take charge of the Mission parish.

The Reverend Andrew Resa, C.M.F., the Mission's second

Mission San Gabriel

Claretian pastor, dreamed of a school for his parish, poor as it was, and made plans accordingly. His successor, the Reverend Miguel Onate, brought the dream to reality. Appealing to the Mission San Jose Dominicans who were already established in Sacred Heart parish, Los Angeles, he received from Mother Pia a promise of sisters. The annals of Sacred Heart convent make reference to the new foundation somewhat matter-of-factly: "Two sisters went to San Gabriel to consult on the foundation of a school there, proposed by the Claretian Fathers."[6] Plans evidently progressed without difficulty, for the Acts of the Third General Chapter, August 2 to 6, 1912, state that "in the month of January of the current year there was accepted a new mission school at Mission San Gabriel in the Diocese of Monterey and Los Angeles."[7]

In the same month Father Onate wrote to Sister Angela Harnett, prioress of Sacred Heart convent:

San Gabriel, Cal., Jan. 29th, 1912

R. Sister Angela, O.S.D.

Rev. dear Sister:

As I told you, I was awaiting the letter of my V.R. Fr.

> Provincial. He says that the terms of our contract are all right and gives me the permission to sign it.
>
> The Bishop read attentively the same contract, without asking for any correspondence else, and on handing me it, said: "I think it will be all right." He wishes the architect or anybody else to call on you and settle every particular in regard to the building, and then to notice [sic] him. I have said everything to the Committee of the Mission Society.
>
> Now I will go and sign the contract when you please. Let the I [mmaculate] Heart of Mary and St. Dominic bless this work!
>
> Yours very sincerely in Jesus Christ,
> Michael Onate, C.M.F.[8]

The following September a member of the San Gabriel Mission society drove four sisters from Sacred Heart convent to enroll the children of the parish and to view their future home. What the sisters saw was "a neat little convent and school...being now built there by the members of the Mission Society directed by the zealous pastor, Rev. Father Onati [sic] C.M.F."[9] Two classrooms occupied the first floor, with the sisters' living quarters on the second.

> ...At four o'clock the sisters went over to the pavilion, a large hall which had served for a fair. Here a large number of children, many with their parents, awaited them. All crowded about the sisters as the Indians had crowded about the Padres on the memorable day when the joyous singing of the hymns and sound of bells announced the opening of the Mission San Gabriel. Many of the grown people and also of the children spoke no English, but they contented themselves with shaking hands with the sisters... Fortunately Ven. Sr. Teresa, who has been appointed superioress of the new foundation, speaks Spanish.[10]

At the outset the situation was a challenge for teachers and students alike. The annalist describes the first day of school, September 23, 1912:

> Today two sisters, Ven. Sisters Teresa and Loretto, came

from the Sacred Heart Convent to San Gabriel to open the new school. As the schoolrooms were not yet finished, school had to be opened in the pavilion. It was not thought prudent to wait with the opening of school until the rooms were finished for fear the children would start at the public school and then there would be difficulty in getting them to leave and come to our school.

The situation was a difficult one. One hundred thirty-five children [six to sixteen years old], two teachers, no books, no blackboards. Absolutely nothing. However we had to make the best of it...Some tables...were brought to the pavilion and used as desks for the larger children. The lower grades were taken to the back room where they had nothing but benches without backs on which to sit.[11]

The second day was no great improvement over the first, except that most children came equipped with a notebook and pencil. To write, the younger pupils knelt on the wooden floor and used the benches as desks, a situation inviting the breakdown of discipline, but contradicted by the testimony of the faithful San Gabriel annalist: "They were all very docile and diligent."[12] Toward the end of the month the classrooms were enhanced by a gift of three portable blackboards and a few pieces of chalk. Shortly after, to the teachers' relief, the first textbooks arrived. Until then, they had managed with "a few classics, [something entitled] *Washington* and *Red Riding Hood* to serve as reading matter."[13]

Dedication of the convent-school took place on October 6, 1912, Bishop Conaty officiating. Father Onate, C.M.F., chartered an electric car so that the 60 boarders at Sacred Heart could attend the ceremony. Confirmation of some 30 children and several adults followed. The ceremony closed with Benediction of the Blessed Sacrament at which the girls from Sacred Heart sang. A brief entertainment given by the children preceded a banquet prepared by the ladies of the Altar Society.

Ten days later the pioneer community, composed of Sister Teresa Meyer, superior, Sister Callista Stopper, Sister Loretto Schafer and Sister Cesla Ziesche, left Sacred Heart convent for their new home. Up to this point, they had traveled by electric trolley from Los Angeles to San Gabriel daily.

On January 6, 1913, the annalist made note of the increased

enrollment in the school: 185 children. By the following month the number of children had so increased that the First Grade had to be moved into the pavilion. "This building lacks all accommodations necessary for school, the light being admitted by two doors and by wooden shutters. Room, however, is the only advantage and attraction (over the previously used passageway)."[14]

Blessed with a practical bent of mind, Sister Teresa had the northeast corner of the sisters' garden fenced off with barbed wire to serve as a chicken yard. Its first occupants were "two handsome fowls, namely, a set of Plymouth Rock,"[15] donated by a Mr. and Mrs. Rios. The idea caught on and soon several Rhode Island Reds arrived as gifts. Under Sister Cesla's diligent supervision, the chickens prospered and the number rose to an astonishing 125!

To provide the sisters with privacy a 10-foot wooden fence was erected along the west side of the sisters' garden. But it proved no barrier to the children who climbed it daily to beguile Sister Cesla into giving them something to eat. No matter how busy, she could not resist the children's stories of their hunger, genuine or embellished.

First Communion Day, May 18, 1913, drew praise from the parishioners. "All was very solemn, the children (68 little ones) were very devout, and all the people were greatly edified....Many of them were moved to tears, for never before had so many children received First Holy Communion at one time or in so solemn a manner."[16]

The first Mission school graduation exercise occurred on June 22, 1913, its solemnity unmarred by the fact of only one graduate. Solemn High Mass, sung by the boys of the upper grades, preceded the ceremony. The solitary honoree, Dolores García, received, in addition to her diploma, a gold medal for general excellence, not surprising since there was no competition. According to the annalist, Dolores "carried a bouquet of flowers and wore a wreath. During Mass she knelt on a priedieu which was placed in front in the middle aisle."[17] The children's work was also on display—freehand drawings, maps, needlework and compositions. According to the annalist: "All [the people] were much pleased and said that their fondest hopes had been far surpassed."[18]

With Father Eustace Flemenco, C.M.F., Father Onate's successor, the school became totally free—tuition, books, even lunch. The latter was Sister Cesla's responsibility, which she discharged with loving care for the children who, regardless of weather, came to school barefoot and thinly clad. Each noon the children lined up for a large tin cup of nourishing soup. For many, perhaps most, "Sister's soup" was a daily treat, as they came to school without lunch.

The Claretians' fatherly interest in the school children sometimes took an unusual turn. One hot afternoon Father John Maiztegui, C.M.F. (later Bishop of Panama), visited a classroom and remarked to Sister that the children looked hot and grimy from the dust. The next morning he returned with soap and towel. Taking the children to a basin in the yard, he washed the grime from their little faces. Obviously pleased with the results, he returned to the rectory, satisfied with his morning's labor.

As enrollment increased, additional classrooms were added. But in 1918, influenza, reaching epidemic proportions, accounted for a critical fall-off in attendance. By order of civil authority, churches and schools were closed in October, and on November 3, Bishop John J. Cantwell of Los Angeles prescribed Exposition of the Blessed Sacrament in all private chapels from sunrise to sunset for the cessation of the epidemic. One month later, the scourge had abated enough to warrant the reopening of the schools, and enrollment at Mission San Gabriel slowly climbed back to normal, necessitating the addition of a bungalow to accommodate two classrooms.

The new school year brought the welcome news that the San Gabriel Mission society had opted to increase the sisters' stipends from $25 to $30 per month. The members had also voted to underwrite the convent utility bills—gas, electricity and telephone. This unexpected bolstering of the community finances was

Mission San Gabriel Convent

welcomed by the convent treasurer.

World War II brought in its wake an influx of new families into the San Gabriel Valley, with the result that the school enrollment increased sharply. In September 1946 Mission San Gabriel School opened with 638 children enrolled in eight classrooms. The state of affairs was reflected in the minutes of the first faculty meeting: "How to stem the influx of 'too many' pupils was discussed with little hope of betterment since the children belong to the parish."[19]

The following semester the situation was no better, enrollment increasing to 675. The minutes again expressed concern:

> Next term enrollment may positively not exceed the required number. That, of course, will not be easy since the present enrollment is too large in some grades, and if the pupils are parishioners, it is almost impossible to turn them away. However, the neighboring parishes are erecting their own schools, which of necessity will diminish the number of our pupils. Let us hope for the best.[20]

Construction of additional classrooms, a logical alternative to overcrowded conditions, would not begin for seven years, even though enrollment would continue to range between 576 and 635. Improvisation became a common theme, and the parish library, hall, cafeteria and rectory were utilized in turn for school purposes. A new cafeteria, built in 1947, relieved the pressure to a degree.

Finally, under Father Peter Caballer, C.M.F., pastor, and Sister Dolores Stopper, O.P., principal, an addition to the school was begun in 1953. The convent annalist commented:

> This week the grammar school yard has begun to bear a close resemblance to a bomb-gutted countryside. Huge holes lie open where workmen have removed the old pepper trees; branches and leaves are scattered round. The crumbled old first grade foundations look for all the world like war rubble. With all this tearing down, something must be going up soon.[21]

The following year, September 1954, something did go up: a new addition, comprising five classrooms, opened to relieve the pressure in the primary grades.

With the phenomenal growth of the parish, the Mission

Sister Juliana Weber with her 95 first graders at Mission San Gabriel Elementary School

church was proving entirely too small to accommodate the congregation, and Father Michael Montoya, C.M.F., pastor, began making plans for a church that would seat over 800. On January 4, 1959, the Chapel of the Annunciation was dedicated by His Eminence, James Frances Cardinal McIntyre, Archbishop of Los Angeles. The same year construction began on a new school building under the direction of Father Montoya and Sister Verona Wittenzellner, principal. The original school building and convent were demolished so that the new school could be erected on the same site. It consisted of six classrooms, a health room and administrative offices. Of attractive mission style, it was ready for occupancy by October 1959. Mission elementary school was now a double school with 16 rooms and 735 students.

St. Ignatius School, Los Angeles

St. Ignatius of Loyola parish had its origin in 1911 under the aegis of the Society of Jesus when Bishop Conaty of Los Angeles invited the Jesuit Fathers to establish a church and school in the Highland Park—Garvanza district of the city. Not surprisingly, the new parish was dedicated to St. Ignatius honoring the founder of the Jesuits. On his appointment as first pastor, Father Richard Gleason, S.J., at once set about purchasing property at Avenue 52 and Monte Vista Street where he erected a frame building to serve as a temporary school. There, in lieu of a church, Mass was offered in a classroom each Sunday and holydays.

Prior to the arrival of the Jesuits, the Catholics in the area had had the good fortune to attend Sunday Mass in the private chapel of the home of Father Hartnety. The ailing priest had come to California from Stuebenville, Ohio, in 1904, in the hope of regaining his health. His presence proved a blessing for the Catholics of Highland Park, who would otherwise have had to travel by horse and buggy all the way to the Cathedral in downtown Los Angeles.

The Jesuit influence in the area was brief; however, for after a stay of only three years, they moved to Blessed Sacrament Church, Hollywood, and the orphaned parish of St. Ignatius came under the direction of the diocesan clergy. Father Thomas O'Regan, successor to Father Gleason, is generally considered, therefore, the true founder of St. Ignatius parish. The consideration may be warranted since, with the future development of parochial facilities in mind, the new pastor purchased the present site at Avenue 61 and Monte Vista Street and built a church and a rectory. In March 1916 the first Solemn High Mass was celebrated in the new church, which was then dedicated.

Three years later Father Jeremiah Burke succeeded Father O'Regan as pastor. Delicate in health, he devoted all his energy to the task of building a parochial school and obtaining the services of the Dominican Sisters. St. Ignatius Elementary school opened on September 5, 1922, with 127 students—64 boys and 63 girls—arranged in double grades. Sister Frances Dunne, O.P., was the first principal. Monday through Friday four sisters comprising the original faculty commuted by car from Sacred Heart convent. They were no newcomers to the parish, as they had been teaching catechism classes on Saturdays and Sundays for the previous four years. They continued to commute until a convent was built in 1929, during the pastorate of Father Patrick J. O'Donaghue. "After eight long years of patient waiting," noted the convent annalist, "St. Ignatius Parish [is] at last to have a convent for its teaching sisters. It now stands a silent but effective witness of the zeal and generosity of the faithful parishioners, guided and encouraged by their most zealous pastor, Rev. Fr. Patrick Joseph O'Donaghue."[22]

Typically, the departure of the workmen heralded the arrival of the sisters. Armed with a variety of implements, they set about eliminating traces of the work crew and cleaning the house with vigor to ready it for Open House on the following Sunday.

According to the annalist, the event was a financial, as well as social success. After the Sunday Masses, the sisters escorted parishioners through the convent, explaining and dispelling "many an erroneous notion concerning convent life. All were loud in their praise of the new convent, and not a few offered their share to the convent fund."[23] At four o'clock the blessing ceremony began in the church with the recitation of the rosary, followed by a homily given by Monsignor John McCarthy in which he told his listeners that "the erection of a convent in their midst is one of the greatest blessings God can bestow on a parish."[24] Benediction of the Blessed Sacrament and the dedication of the convent followed. The final event of the afternoon was a supper served parishioners in the parish hall, the proceeds benefiting the convent.

The next day the sisters began their exodus from Sacred Heart convent. A tiny caravan consisting of a trailer carrying the sisters' simple possessions and Sacred Heart's venerable Buick conveying the sisters made its way to St. Ignatius. At 8:30 a.m., the entire student body managed to squeeze into the tiny chapel, convent patio and adjoining parlor for the first Mass offered in the new building. Father O'Donaghue was celebrant and Father Noel Dillon, Los Angeles superintendent of Catholic schools, homilist. The annals credit the speaker with an inspiring talk in which he referred to the chapel as "the workshop of the sisters, where they receive the necessary light and strength to carry on their arduous tasks in the classrooms."[25]

Comprising the initial community were Sisters Dolores Stopper, superior and principal; Clare Coon, Carmel Doran, Rosina Hageman, Peregrina Henglberger, Gemma Kozell, Benedict McNeil, Elisa Sandoval, and Agnes Mary Tiffany. On May 1, the sisters organized a May procession through the convent halls, singing hymns in honor of Our Lady, Queen of May. Arriving at the chapel, they recited the rosary and the Litany of Loretto, concluding their

May Day observance with Benediction of the Blessed Sacrament offered by Father O'Donaghue.

Graduation took place on Sunday, June 23. So taken was the annalist with the ceremony that she neglected to record the number of graduates, but described at length the 24 girls who, "dressed in white, with a dainty bow of pink, marched down the main aisle supporting flower-decked arches, thus making an adorned archway through which the graduates were to pass. The measured step and the perfect order with which all was carried out added beauty to the scene and credit to the school."[26]

School opened for the new year on September 10, 1929, with an enrollment of 310 pupils. Twenty-nine children made their First Holy Communion on December 8, and 150 children and 50 adults received the Sacrament of Confirmation on December 10.

St. Patrick's Day, a celebration of gala proportions in parishes with Irish pastors, becomes even more jubilant when it coincides with a beloved pastor's personal feastday. At St. Ignatius, Father

St. Ignatius School pupils

Pat's feastday celebration customarily began with a Solemn High Mass attended by the entire school. Following Mass, the children assembled in the schoolyard for a short program, presentation of gifts, and an annual "surprise," the pastor's privilege of giving the rest of the day free. The year 1932 was an especially memorable one at St. Ignatius. A few days before the feast, the children had presented a program in the parish hall for the entertainment of a standing-room-only audience. The pastor's feastday gift was the proceeds—$100 in gold! It took all of the recipient's Irish eloquence to express his gratitude for so munificent a gift.

At the end of the scholastic year, the boys gave an entertainment at which parents and friends expressed themselves pleasantly surprised by the excellence of the program. Two weeks later the girls presented their version of a closing entertainment. The separate programs continued for two years when they were succeeded by combined presentations.

At the beginning of the 1936 school year, the annalist reported the highest enrollment in the history of St. Ignatius school—377 pupils, only to be eclipsed the following year by a registration of 414. Average class size was 50, though on occasion additional desks had to be moved into a classroom to allow "extra" students to be received.

By 1952 plans for a new and larger church were underway; it was completed and dedicated on October 24, 1954. Within five years the parish was again raising money, this time for a new elementary school. The rationale for the second drive in such close proximity to the first was the failure of the school building to meet the standards of an earthquake-proof structure. Although the old building was not scheduled for demolition until August, Archbishop McIntyre asked that classes in the new term continue without interruption for the students' benefit. The sisters met his request by scheduling half-day sessions in four classrooms created by partitioning off the four corners of the auditorium.

Despite the inconveniences, both workmen and students proved good neighbors, and the building was completed on schedule. The new school contained 11 classrooms and satisfied all the safety requirements. On September 10, 1960, classes began in the new building, and on March 5, 1961, Auxiliary Bishop Timothy Manning of Los Angeles blessed the school before a large assembly of clergy, parents, students, and friends.

In its first 39 years of serving the needs of the elementary school children of Highland Park (1922–1961), St. Ignatius proved worthy of the trust parents placed in it. In the years to follow, it would prove a steady source of moral and educational integrity in the community.

St. Mary's Elementary School, Fullerton

Since February 2, 1912, two sisters from St. Catherine's orphanage, Anaheim, had been traveling to the nearby town of Fullerton each Saturday and Sunday to teach Christian Doctrine to the children of St. Mary's parish. "Twenty-five eager little children formed the first class,"[27] recorded St. Catherine's annalist, a statistic that in two weeks' time had almost doubled. For 10 years itinerant teaching prevailed until Bishop Conaty visited St. Mary's in 1922 and gave permission for the erection of an elementary school. Father John J. Prendiville, appointed pastor the following year, lost no time in implementing the Bishop's authorization. Already familiar figures in the parish, Mission San Jose Dominicans were a logical choice to staff the school. Mother Pia agreed to provide sisters; and, on September 5, 1923, St. Mary's school opened with an enrollment of 29 pupils which soon increased to 47: 29 girls and 18 boys spread through the first to the fifth grades with three enrollees in something called "the baby class."

The pioneer staff consisted of three sisters: Sister Frances Dunne, principal and teacher of the third, fourth, and fifth grades; Sister Sybillina Lingelser, teacher of the first and second grades; and Sister Lioba Doehman, music. The following year the sixth and seventh grades and a third classroom teacher were added, enrollment increasing to 85. In 1925, the school was complete with four teachers, an eighth grade, 112 students, and Sister Annunciata Henke as principal.

The original contract between the Dominican Sisters "acting by and through the Prioress General, Mother M. Pia, party of the first part, and the parish of St. Mary's School acting by and through its authorized representative, the Reverend J. J. Prendiville, Rector of the said parish, party of the second part,"[28] specified that the Congregation would provide sisters with competency to teach and follow the diocesan program. The Congregation also agreed to:

> ...teach the boys of the parish with the permission of the diocesan Bishop; [to] accompany their pupils to the church and there watch over them any time during the day, but not in the evening, except on some exceptional occasions when the children are required to take part in a procession; [and], if required, [to] teach their pupils Plain Chant and suitable hymns to be sung during the children's Mass. Outside of this, the sisters cannot take charge of the organ. Neither shall they take charge of the sacristy."[29]

Further, they cannot be required to "take charge of sweeping and cleaning the classrooms." The contract also stipulated that the sisters would "consider it a pleasure to meet with the wishes of the Pastor and co-operate with him in all educational matters."[30] For her services each teaching sister would receive an annual stipend of $300, to be paid monthly or quarterly. Previous experience had taught the sisters the wisdom of specifying what they would or could not be required to do in the line of duty, though "the pleasure of the Pastor" seems to neutralize the negatives in the contract.

In Father Prendiville's plans for the parish, the rectory would eventually become the sisters' convent, an arrangement happily anticipated by the sisters. A change of pastors at the end of the first year, however, altered circumstances, and although a 1930 version of the contract specified a monthly stipend of $40.00 for each sister teaching in the school until the parish supplied a convent, the latter was not provided during the sisters' presence in the parish. When a convent would be provided, so the contract read, the sisters' stipend would be reduced to $35.00 monthly.

Dominican presence in the parish ceased when the opening of Flintridge Sacred Heart Academy, Pasadena (Cf. Ch. 26), had repercussions on St. Mary's school. With regret the sisters withdrew after a teaching commitment of nine years. The school continued to operate, however, under the capable direction of the Sisters of St. Joseph of Orange.

In its Centennial Edition (May 7, 1987), the *Fullerton News Tribune* wrote of St. Mary's school early years:

> St. Mary's continued to be a comparatively small school,

but it was a very fine one. It was with regret that the sisters relinquished it to the care of the Sisters of St. Joseph of Orange in 1932 when the need of the sisters at Flintridge Sacred Heart Academy, opened the year previously, necessitated the withdrawal of the Dominicans from Fullerton.

...St. Mary's school was always a well-equipped school equal in every respect to the public schools of Fullerton, which were exceptionally fine. The people of Fullerton are of a very fine class, but not predominantly Catholic. In fact, the majority were quite prejudiced against the sisters at first. Public school trustees carefully scrutinized the school and compared it with their schools, finding to their surprise that the pupils from St. Mary's were usually considerably more advanced than those in the public schools. In 1927 an examiner from the Fullerton High School examined the eighth grade class for the purpose of accreditation and St. Mary's came out at the head of the list of schools examined.[31]

Notes

[1] Annals of St. Michael's Convent, n.d.

[2] Annals of St. Michael's Convent, n.d.

[3] Annals of St. Michael's Convent, n.d.

[4] Smeaton Chase, *California Coast Trails* (Boston: Houghton, 1913) 6.

[5] John McGroarty, *California, Its History and Romance* (Los Angeles: Grafton, 1911) 78.

[6] Annals of Sacred Heart Convent, January 1912.

[7] Acts of the Third General Chapter (2–6 August 1912) 23.

[8] Michael Onate, C.M.F to Angela Harnett, O.S.D., 29 January 1912. [Early business transactions regarding the Mission San Gabriel foundation were negotiated with the Prioress of Sacred Heart Convent].

[9] Annals of San Gabriel Convent, 8 September 1912.
[10] Annals of San Gabriel Convent, 8 September 1912.
[11] Annals of San Gabriel Convent, 23 September 1912.
[12] Annals of San Gabriel Convent, 24 September 1912.
[13] Annals of San Gabriel Convent, 26 September 1912.
[14] Annals of San Gabriel Convent, 13 February 1913.
[15] Annals of San Gabriel Convent, 14 January 1913.
[16] Annals of San Gabriel Convent, 18 May 1913.
[17] Annals of San Gabriel Convent, 22 June 1913.
[18] Annals of San Gabriel Convent, 22 June 1913.
[19] Minutes, Mission San Gabriel Elementary School Faculty Meeting, 10 September 1946.
[20] Minutes, Mission San Gabriel Elementary School Faculty Meeting, February 1947.
[21] Annals of San Gabriel Convent, 1953.
[22] Annals of St. Ignatius Convent, 28 April 1929—8 December 1932.
[23] Annals of St. Ignatius Convent, 28 April 1929.
[24] Annals of St. Ignatius Convent, 28 April 1929.
[25] Annals of St. Ignatius Convent, 30 April 1929.
[26] Annals of St. Ignatius Convent, 23 June 1929.
[27] Annals of St. Catherine's Convent, 2 February 1912.
[28] Contract, St. Mary's School, Fullerton.
[29] Contract, St. Mary's School, Fullerton.
[30] Contract, St. Mary's School, Fullerton.
[31] *Fullerton News Tribune,* 7 May 1987.

CHAPTER TWENTY

ALTENBERG AND ROME REVISITED

As early as March 1909, Father Kept, Altenberg pastor, approached the sisters, asking them to open a school for boys. Just one classroom would be enough, he assured them. The sisters' response was positive, and Sister Dolorosa wrote at once to Mother Pia for the requisite permission. On June 14, 1909, a one-room school under the patronage of St. Joseph opened in the convent with 45 boys, aged 6 to 13, in attendance. Sister Alexandra Heim, recently professed and a teacher before she entered, assumed charge as principal. Sister Leo Greb constituted the faculty of *St. Josef Schule*.

Father Kept to the contrary, the following year (October 1910), boys had to be turned away, the single classroom unable to contain them. So pleased were the townsfolk with this turn of events that they decided to build a schoolhouse for the sisters. By May 1911, when the building was completed and blessed, 100 boys were enrolled and Sister Thoma Possberg, professed only one week, was promptly recruited for classroom service. Within the next year or two, the steadily increasing enrollment necessitated the hiring of a lay teacher.

At the Third General Chapter, held at the Motherhouse from August 2 to 6, 1912, Sister Dolorosa Wallrath was elected a member of the General Council and Secretary General. The election *"in absentia"* necessitated Sister Dolorosa's rather hasty return to California. On September 20 she bade a sad farewell to the little convent she had learned to love. The following month on October 30, Mother Pia arrived in Altenberg, and the next day Sisters Anna Thoren and

Bonifacia Stabel, having spent a day visiting Sister Anna's elderly mother, appeared. On November 2 Mother Pia installed Sister Anna as superior of Altenberg and Sister Bonifacia as novice director. Since both sisters were originally from Germany, language presented no problem. After assuring herself of the sisters' adjustment to their new responsibilities, Mother Pia, with Sister Coletta Breidinger as companion, sailed for the United States in October 1913.

The first rumors of war reached Altenberg in late July 1914, followed shortly by an announcement from the mayor that no one would be allowed to leave town without permission from the police. Rumor quickly merged with reality when the school building was taken over by the German army and converted into a hospital for the wounded. Sixty-four cots replaced desks, and teachers and boys were ordered to vacate the premises. The hospital, however, proved no more than a makeshift measure; for, by the end of August, the wounded had either recovered or been moved to nearby Aachen. In a semblance of normalcy, sisters and boys moved back into the abandoned school building.

To the accompaniment of cannon rumbling in the distance (about six miles away), the sisters went on "crisis alert." Hastily they made black habits for themselves and packed suitcases in the event that they would be required to make a quick exit. With Christmas in the offing, they engaged also in knitting socks, wristlets and caps for the soldiers as protection against the cold of the

Reverend Thomas Kept, Pastor of Altenberg—message on back of card: "…Please, Rev. Mother Pia, take me along to your country that I may be near you so that I will have a greater part in your prayers. Have a good journey and God take care of you." Moresnet Neutre the 22nd of June, 1905. *Signed:* T. Kept, Pastor

Chapter 20 / ALTENBERG AND ROME REVISITED

Altenberg Parish Church (left) and Nazareth Novitiate (right)

German winter. The pupils did their part by contributing postage for the packages sent to the front.

At the reception ceremony held at the convent on December 8, the sisters' families were not able to be present. Travel was considered much too dangerous.

With the onset of World War I, the Congregation faced a series of new and potentially divisive challenges. Family members of the sisters from Germany were involved in the armies on both European fronts, and in the United States the arrival of black-bordered letters was anticipated with dread. When America entered the war in April 1917, tensions inevitably mounted, though the sisters made heroic efforts to be sensitive to one another.

As the war continued, conditions in Europe became ever more desperate and the community in Altenberg was not exempted. Hunger became a frequent companion. Food was not only scarce, but, even when available, beyond the thin purse of the convent treasurer. In consequence, the sisters decided to send the postulants home for the duration. An exception was made for Magdalena Eberl (Sister Germana), who had entered from Lobsing, Bavaria, and whose family home was at such a distance (17 hours by train in normal times) that prudence dictated she remain in Altenberg.

The work site for the lone postulant became the convent garden, where she and Sister Josephina Schreiber were commissioned to raise vegetables for the community's generally sparse table. The success of their efforts seems to have been confined to potatoes and lettuce, especially the latter of which they shared with the Franciscan Sisters in Aachen. From the beginning the sisters had raised chickens, which now had to be eaten or destroyed because of the shortage of feed; and the sisters' one little pig, purchased with the ambition of starting a farm, had to be sold reluctantly when he grew pitifully thin. Since the bread ration for the town was extremely limited, the sisters bought a crushing mill in order to be able to provide their own flour. When all else failed, they might at least have bread.

On February 1, 1915, the German army once more preempted *St. Josef Schule*, this time for the quartering of soldiers. Sisters Leo and Thoma were allowed to continue teaching in the building, but the lay teacher fared less fortunately, being ordered to move elsewhere. The new school year heralded the arrival of more children, which necessitated the hiring of a second lay teacher. Once more the convent parlor became a classroom. By the following year, the original one-room school, as envisioned by Father Kept, had escalated to six rooms. Sister Theodora Stute taught first grade in the convent parlor; Sister Arsenia Lins, second grade in a little house set in the midst of a meadow across from the convent; and Sisters Leo, Thoma, and the two lay teachers taught the remaining boys—the sisters in the school building and the lay teachers elsewhere. Regrettably, the Altenberg annals give no clue as to the location of "elsewhere."

With the signing of the Armistice on November 11, 1918, relief seemed imminent; but the fallout brought fresh problems. By the terms of the peace treaty on June 28, 1919, Moresnet Neutre lost its neutrality and was annexed to Belgium. Henceforth, persons of German origin were no longer welcome, and the sisters' situation in Altenberg became precarious. They continued to teach, however, until 1921, when the Minister of Education and Culture suddenly became aware of them and ordered their dismissal before the end of summer, contrary to the appeal of the Parish Council, whose members spoke out in the sisters' defense, and the requests of the citizenry who made interventions on their behalf. On the advice of the Motherhouse, the sisters tendered their resignations in the spring and on April 30 left their classrooms saddened in a last farewell. It was time for the sisters to think about moving again.

Papal Approval: A Dream Fulfilled

On October 19, 1919, Mother Seraphina set out for Europe for a third time. Her mission was twofold: to hand deliver the *Constitutions* for final approval by Rome and to look for a new location for the Altenberg community. The General Council Minutes for November 4, 1916, confirmed that "This...was the fiftieth and final meeting of a series...held for the purpose of revising our *Constitutions* before placing them for a second approval before the Holy See."[1] The war years had brought to an abrupt halt the Sacred Congregation's work on sisters' *Constitutions*. It was time now to get things moving again, and in the Council's opinion the best way to spark action was by personal appearance. To Mother Seraphina, Mother Pia and the Council delegated the sensitive task of moving the approval of the *Constitutions* forward while not making a nuisance of herself.

Sister Liberata Monotti, a native of Cavigliano, Canton Ticino, in the Italian sector of Switzerland, was selected as Mother Seraphina's traveling companion. As a young woman, Liberata Monotti had become acquainted with the community through pursuit of the commercial course offered by Immaculate Conception Academy, San Francisco. The course completed, she entered the Congregation on August 4, 1913, at the age of 19 and had been professed four years at the time of the trip. Alfred Monotti, Sister Liberata's uncle and a man of some means, agreed to defray the sisters' traveling expenses. Choice of Mother Seraphina's companion, one suspects, was related to the anticipated financial assistance and Sister Liberata's fluency in Italian.

By early January 1920, Mother Seraphina and Sister Liberata were in Rome. There Father Ceslaus Hansen, O.P., assistant to the Dominican Master General, Father Ludwig Theissling, found a place for them to stay. *Il Cenecolo* was "a very nice boarding house for ladies of the better class," Mother Seraphina assured Mother Pia. "It means about two dollars [per day] for both of us. Everything: food, clothing, etc., is very expensive here."[2]

In Father Ceslaus, Mother Seraphina found her strongest support. On the sisters' arrival, he invited them to visit him frequently and advised Mother Seraphina to entrust the *Constitutions* to Bishop Thomas Esser, his fellow Dominican who was, conveniently, a consultor to the Congregation of Religious. Heartened by Father Ceslaus's positive attitude, Mother Seraphina informed Mother Pia that Father Ceslaus was optimistic regarding the outcome of the *Constitutions* "because they contain everything that belongs to the Order."[3]

The following day the sisters met Bishop Esser, to whom they restated their desire to retain the Divine Office. More cautious in his responses than Father Ceslaus, Bishop Esser said that it would depend on the Master General, who favored identical *Constitutions* for all Third Order congregations. Rather than daunt Mother Seraphina, however, this news made her more determined than ever. She resolved to go to the Master General herself and ask for his endorsement, since she had Father Ceslaus's assurance that the *Constitutions* were in accord with the spirit of the Dominican Order. Bishop Esser, she wrote to Mother Pia, asked "if I thought that we had done well and that there was nothing to correct. I answered that that must now be found out; this amused him very much."[4]

Through the good agency of His Eminence, Cardinal Andrew Fruewirth, O.P., who would also prove a devoted supporter, the sisters were scheduled to have a private audience with His Holiness, Benedict XV, on January 26. This was an opportunity too good to miss! Mother Seraphina determined to place the important question of the Office before the Pope. But as she waited in the papal chambers on the fateful day, the possibility of refusal loomed ever larger, and she found her courage waning in direct proportion to the length of the wait. At last, accompanied by Cardinal Fruewirth, the sisters entered the papal chambers and knelt to kiss the Holy Father's ring. The Cardinal guided the conversation skillfully; they spoke of California, the Congregation, the novitiate at Moresnet and the schools staffed by the community.:

Then came the critical moment. Cardinal Fruewirth informed the Pope that the sisters had a special petition to place before him. They were in Rome, he said, to have their *Constitutions* approved, and they sought permission to continue praying the Divine Office, even though Third Order sisters. At the first mention of the Office, the sisters fell on their knees in supplication of the requisite permission. Nodding his approval, the Holy Father replied: "You wish to continue to say the Divine Office? From all my heart I say that is something very, very good."[5]

Scarcely able to contain her joy, Mother Seraphina presented the Pope with the gift of a zuchetta or papal skull cap. By then, Sister Liberata's courage was building also, and to the Holy Father's question, "Something else?" she replied in Italian, "If possible, Holy Father, may we have an exchange?"[6] Smiling, he removed his cap and gave it to Sister, putting the new one on his head. The sisters were delighted with their trade.

Andrew Cardinal Fruewirth, O.P., Cardinal Protector of our Congregation; Master of the Order 1891–1904; Cardinal 1915–1933

Writing to Mother Pia, Mother Seraphina said: "It was not easy," –a modest enough description of the audience in which the Office hung in the balance. She continued:

> As we descended the steps and walked through the halls, the Cardinal said, "The most important...point you have accomplished; the rest I will take care of for you." I tell you, dear Mother, we have a Cardinal! I am sure you will approve that we asked for...him as our Cardinal Protector. He will surely protect, advise and help us. You have no idea how dear our Congregation is to him. He will do his best that the approbation of our *Constitutions* will take place soon. If only our Master General will do the same![7]

It was a sincerely meant wish for, although a challenge had been met, the sisters were not yet in the clear. If the Master General imposed identical *Constitutions* on all Third Order Dominican Congregations, the Mission San Jose sisters would be obliged to accept them. The Office would then be lost to the Congregation. Further, Mother Seraphina was convinced that not all congregations could follow the same *Constitutions*. On this latter point, Bishop Esser just as firmly disagreed with her. She replied rather tartly that, if he had lived for 40 years in a community of women, he would certainly think differently! Mother Seraphina found Cardinal Fruewirth easier to deal with.

On March 11 Mother Seraphina noted that on the morrow they would pay their eighth visit to Cardinal Fruewirth and had already consulted Bishop Esser 15 times, almost every visit by invitation. But despite the prelates' willingness to help, the approval of the *Constitutions* dragged on. A backlog of Church related work, stacked high during the war years, demanded the officials' immediate attention. "You can see," wrote Mother Seraphina, "that this is the *Eternal* City; everything takes an *Eternity*."[8]

But the truth, she admitted to herself, was that the approval appeared at a deadlock. Favoring the same *Constitutions* for all Third Order Dominican Sisters' congregations were two powerful supporters: the Master General and Bishop Esser. Aligned with Mother Seraphina's conviction that each congregation should be permitted to design its own document were Cardinal Fruewirth; Father Ceslaus; Father Aldridge, American assistant to the Master General; and Father Gabriel Horn, Santa Sabina prior. Father Aldridge expressed the thinking of the latter group when he said that the sisters know what they are capable of doing, e.g., praying the Breviary, and should be allowed to write their own *Constitutions*. With the outcome in the balance, Mother Seraphina felt obliged to remain in Rome and see the *Constitutions* through to the end. Father Ceslaus, she wrote to Mother Pia "is very much worried about us," "and regrets the delay in the *Constitutions*. He is dissatisfied with Bishop Esser and advised me to beg the Cardinal again that since our *Constitutions* are written according to the spirit of the Order, to have them put in order."[9]

Mother Seraphina's experiences were persuading her that, if someone had not come personally to Rome to represent the *Constitutions*, the question of the praying of the Office would have been ignored and a uniform document would have been imposed on all congregations.

Meanwhile at home at the Motherhouse, Mother Pia fretted as the reports from Mother Seraphina told of little accomplished.

Although pessimism was not a characteristic of Mother Seraphina, she admitted dismay with the Roman way of doing things. After receiving another discouraging report regarding the fate of the Breviary, Mother Pia wrote to her friend in exasperation:

> What will we be when the last of the monastic spirit is taken away? Just try to visualize Christmas, Holy Week, Easter, etc., without the Breviary. The news gave me a terrible shock which I am not yet over. These men of God do not know *everything*, and they take no time to think about the harm they are doing. They are not infallible. My days are numbered, and I shall not have to see the havoc all this will do to the Congregation. In Eternity, I shall praise the Lord by chanting the psalms for all time. But to this, dear good Mother, I am completely resigned. I surrender everything, everything to His Divine Providence.[10]

The "men of God" were not infallible, and although Mother Pia expressed herself as "completely resigned," her words were not particularly submissive.

In the meantime, Mother Seraphina and Sister Liberata kept up a barrage of prayer for their intentions. Their persistence stood them in good stead. Influenced by his conversations with Father Ceslaus, the Master General gradually changed his thinking regarding a uniform constitution for all. The documents must, however, satisfy two conditions: they must be arranged according to the new 1918 Code of Canon Law and comply with the Norms he himself had written for Sisters of the Third Order. Having met his requirements, each congregation would then be free to incorporate its own practices according to its circumstances. "We really have to thank good...[Father Ceslaus] for most of this," Mother Seraphina wrote home, "first by the good counsel he gave me and secondly because he fought for our *Constitutions* and expressed his opinions freely [to the Master General]."[11] The critical barrier crossed, Father Ceslaus took heart and informed Mother Seraphina that he had thought the matter over and would take the *Constitutions* into his own hands and arrange them according to the most recent norms. With evident relief Mother Seraphina wrote to Mother Pia:

> He knows...your wishes exactly. He advised me to go to the Cardinal and tell him I've thought the matter over and have spoken about it to experienced Fathers. I believe the

> *Constitutions* can be arranged a little more logically, and, at the same time, coincide with the Norms of the Master General. Naturally, I will have to go to Bishop Esser and ask for the *Constitutions*....[12]

Confident that the *Constitutions* could not be left in better hands, Mother Seraphina made ready to leave Rome. On April 23, 1920, after farewell visits to their Dominican brothers, the sisters returned to Altenberg.

With the *Constitutions* evidently home free, Mother Pia wrote her friend on November 17, 1920: "I would really be glad if you were here again. There is so much to be organized and done that my strength is scarcely sufficient any longer....This immense weakness often makes me think that I shall not see you again. Take care, therefore, that *your* work is finished soon and particularly that the *Constitutions* are completed."[13]

To Mother Pia's disappointment, Mother Seraphina wrote the following February that she could not possibly return before the summer, if then. "Well, I shall say nothing more," Mother Pia replied. "I'll just keep working *alone* as long as our dear God gives me the strength; then I shall stop. You could often be less slow, but you just aren't too fast. With love...."[14]

Added to Mother Pia's other physical problems at the time was a painful neuralgic condition of the right hand which made writing extremely arduous for her. She found such difficulty approving the corrections made by Father Ceslaus that she authorized Mother Seraphina to finalize all changes with him. But she managed, nevertheless, to make her opinion known when something not to her liking was inserted. A case in point was an article on "nursing care." She ordered it removed immediately. She had changed her mind about hospitals.

Father Ceslaus meanwhile continued his painstaking work, article by article, making sure that each was in harmony with the revised Code of Canon Law and the norms of the Order; it was a long and tedious process. But at last there arrived a letter for Mother Pia from Father Louis Nolan, O.P., consultor for the Congregation of Religious in Rome:

Chapter 20 / ALTENBERG AND ROME REVISITED

July 6, 1922

Very Rev. and dear Mother General:

Today, before the Commission of Consultors of the Sacred Congregation of Religious, the Final Approval of your *Constitutions* was discussed. The decision has been not only favorable, but laudatory in the highest degree to yourself and your Institute. The *Constitutions* have been pronounced the most satisfactory of all that have passed through our hands this year.

Owing to the recent death of the Cardinal Prefect of the Sacred Congregation of Religious, the Plenary Commission of the Cardinals, which is presided over by the Cardinal Prefect, and which was to be held at the beginning of July, has had to be postponed until the end of July, with the result that the Plenary Commission which was to take place early in August, and before which your *Constitutions* were to pass before going on to the Holy Father for the ultimate seal of approval, will now have to be postponed until after the summer vacation, that is, until November. Your *Constitutions*, therefore, will have to wait until November for the Pontifical Decree of Final Approval, but this need not disturb you, for once they have got the approval of the commission of consultors, which was given today, they are already regarded as approved, and what follows is only a formality, though a necessary formality.

There have been only a few alterations necessary in the *Constitutions* as presented by you in French, and such are merely minor matters required by the Code, and not in any way derogatory....

I cannot express to you, Very Rev. and dear Mother General, how happy and proud I am that your *Constitutions* have passed, and passed with such a high encomium. I congratulate you and all the Sisters of your Institute on this, and feel that it is a happy augury, in this Jubilee year, of still greater strides in the way of perfection and in your work for souls. May God ever bless you and all the members of your dear Congregation, and may the spirit of our Holy Father St. Dominic ever inspire all his children of the Congregation of the Holy Rosary of [Mission] San Jose to faithfully correspond with their grand vocation for the salvation of souls.

I am offering a Mass of thanksgiving on behalf of your Congregation for the favors received by all its members in the final approbation of the *Constitutions* worthy of the highest traditions of the Order.

Recommending myself and my work to your holy prayers and asking our dear Lord to bless you all with His choicest graces and blessings, I remain,

Very Rev. and dear Mother General,

Yours very sincerely and fraternally in S. D.

Fr. Louis Nolan, O.P.
Consultor of the Sacred Congregation of Religious[15]

Father Nolan's letter arrived during the July retreat at the Motherhouse. Father Stanislaus Olsen, O.P., retreat master, read the letter to the community assembled in the chapel. He congratulated the sisters warmly and especially Mother Pia "for her years of endeavoring to have the Congregation approved by the Holy See and to leave her children laws that are approved by the Church and are according to the spirit of the Order."[16] He then intoned the *Te Deum*, which a grateful community continued with enthusiasm.

As Father Nolan had foretold, the document of Final Approbation of the *Constitutions*, signed by His Holiness, Pope Pius XI, was received at the Motherhouse on November 25, 1922. Mother Pia was so happy that she entered the dining room and, despite the rule of silence she so ardently supported, announced to the community at dinner: "Sisters, our *Constitutions* are finally approved!" She then added, by way of the most special treat she could think of, "This day should be celebrated from now on by serving ice cream!"[17]

Some time later Mother Pia sent an "Instruction" to the sisters regarding the Final Decree of Approbation. After summarizing the three steps involved in the process, she reminded them that they had received special favor from Rome in that only two steps had been required and went on to say:

> We have been informed by several of the Consultors of the Sacred Congregation of Religious that our *Constitutions* were praised by the Sacred Congregation and also by the Cardinals as among the very best proposed for approbation. No wonder, for no less than four theologians in Rome worked at them in order to arrange and revise them according to the new Codex of Canon Law.
>
> You, dear Sisters, have no idea of the care and work bestowed on our *Constitutions* in Rome (apart from our own years of worry and sleepless nights) even after the *Constitutions* had been arranged and ready for approval....
>
> Therefore, let us thank our good God from the bottom of our hearts, and ask Him to give us the grace to reproduce in our daily lives a faithful copy of these, our sacred laws....
>
> We have received many congratulations from prelates and priests all over, who read the account of the final approbation of our *Constitutions* in the *Vatican Edition*, the *Ecclesiastical Review*, the *Analecta*, which is the official paper of our Holy Order printed in Rome, and other periodicals. We were informed from Rome that our finally approved *Constitutions* will in future serve as a model and basis for other *Constitutions* of the Sisters of the Third Order of St. Dominic, which are to be sent to Rome for approbation. Of course, each Congregation must arrange theirs according to their work and conditions, for instance, hospital work, etc.....
>
> Again I say, let us thank God each and every day for this great blessing and ask Him for the grace of perseverance.[18]

Papal approval of the *Constitutions* had loomed in the forefront of Mother Pia's mind for years as a Goliath to be conquered at all costs. Its attainment had cost her years of anxiety. She now felt that the Congregation was on a secure foundation and could respond to her friend, Bishop Francis Aguirre, O.P., vicar apostolic of Foo-Chow, China, who had written to congratulate her on the approval: "The definite approval of the *Constitutions* of my Congregation is an event for which I have long worked and prayed. It is the crowning of my life's work and I can therefore with a joyful and grateful heart sing my *Nunc dimittis*." [19]

Notes

[1] General Council Minutes, 4 November 1916, General Council Register 260.

[2] Maerz, letter to Backes, n.d.

[3] Maerz, letter to Backes, n.d.

[4] Maerz, letter to Backes, 10 January 1920.

[5] Maerz, letter to Backes, 26 January 1920.

[6] Maerz, letter to Backes, 26 January 1920.

[7] Maerz, letter to Backes, 14 March 1920.

[8] Maerz, letter to Backes, 4 April 1920.

[9] Maerz, letter to Backes, n.d.

[10] Backes, letter to Maerz, n.d.

[11] Maerz, letter to Backes, 7 April 1920.

[12] Maerz, letter to Backes, 7 April 1920.

[13] Backes, letter to Maerz, 17 November 1920.

[14] Backes, letter to Maerz, n.d.

[15] Louis Nolan, O.P., letter to Backes, 6 July 1922.

[16] Stanislaus Olsen, O.P. July 1922 (as recalled by retreatants).

[17] Winifred Gallagher, O.P., "Personal Reminiscences."

[18] Backes, "Instruction on the 'Final Decree of Approbation,' of our Beloved *Constitutions*," October 1923.

[19] Backes, letter to Francis Aguirre, O.P., 8 June 1923.

CHAPTER TWENTY-ONE

ALTENHOHENAU

In July 1920 Mother Pia and the General Council authorized Mother Seraphina in Europe to negotiate the sale of the Altenberg property if the sisters would no longer be allowed to teach or "receive postulants from any country, for thus the primary end in founding Altenberg is frustrated." Mother Seraphina was further empowered to seek permission from the Holy See for the transfer of the novitiate house to a site in Switzerland. The proposed move to Switzerland was undoubtedly dictated by Mother Seraphina's experiences in Germany and by the situation in Europe following World War I. Hyperinflation had resulted in the German Mark sinking to a thousand-billionth of its prewar value against the dollar. The aftermath of inflation subsequently weakened the German economy and made the country especially vulnerable in the Great Depression.

Cavigliano, Switzerland

In response to the Council's directive, Mother Seraphina again went house-hunting, this time in the vicinity of Cavigliano in the Italian sector of Switzerland. With little effort she succeeded in finding a house, which she described as admirably suited for their purpose. Beautifully situated in the Italian Alps, *La Providenza* belonged to a Mrs. Edwina Peri, who had built the villa, but had later moved to the United States and settled in Oakland, California. At the time of the sisters' visit the house was functioning as a small health resort. Inquiry revealed that Mrs. Peri was willing to lease the property for five years at 6,000 francs ($1,000) per year. Sister Liberata's uncle, Alfred Monotti, encouraged the project by agreeing to contribute $20 monthly toward the lease payment. Further, both pastor and people were eager for the presence of the sisters, who would provide religious instruction for their children.

Heartened by the evidences of goodwill, Mother Seraphina wrote to the Apostolic Administrator of Lugano for permission to open a house in Cavigliano. Clearance came quickly in a letter from the Vicar General of the diocese.

> Lugano, September 9, 1920
>
> To Reverend Sr. M. Seraphina
>
> Vic. Gen. for the Rev. Sisters of the Third Order of St. Dominic in Cavigliano
>
> After having seen the recommendation of the Most Eminent Cardinal Boggiani, Archbishop of Genoa, we grant that you and your Sisters may take up residence in Cavigliano according to the aims of your Congregation. But we desire that you should come to Lugano, in Curia, in order to have more detailed information and also to understand one another better.
>
> There remains intact all the existing general ecclesiastical prescriptions for Religious.
>
> Noseda
>
> Vic. Gen.[2]

Mother Seraphina's enthusiasm for Cavigliano was not shared to the same extent by Mother Pia. The best she could do was profess herself not against the move if: a) Rome would approve the establishment of a second novitiate; b) the mortgage [first mention!] would be left standing; c) the health resort would be continued only until the debt was paid; and d) the sisters could live separately from the lay guests. October brought an upsurge of optimism, however, which was reflected in a letter from Mother Pia to her representative in Europe:

> Only this morning...while meditating on dear Mother Teresa, my instructor, I found these words, 'Learn from my experience never to listen to the fears of nature and never

to treat God's loving kindness with distrust, even if He tries you. If His honor is our only intention in achievement, never doubt the results, because this great God is almighty.'

Therefore, my dear Friend, I will follow and see how she will help us. Cavigliano has been accepted. God must be served, loved, and praised there, His honor promoted, His holy Will done. I firmly believe that He will bless this difficult project. This new house must produce saints; if not, the foundation should not materialize....

Now I must talk about Moresnet. I have much concern.... The more I think about it, the clearer it becomes to me that, if it is possible, we should sell the whole place with house and yard....[3]

But despite her resolve to abide by Mother Teresa's counsel, Mother Pia could not discount the weaknesses in the proposed plan for the use of the villa, and her next letter to Mother Seraphina spoke of her anxieties. Her heart was just not in the project: "I am not heart and soul in this foundation because it is outside our sphere of work....If there would be any hope of having a school, I would be more at ease because that is our work, but I will be quiet and give everything into the hands of God."[4]

Mother Pia's distaste for the project was increased, no doubt, by problems at home, where her worries were compounded by difficulties within and without the community. At home, she was being criticized by members of the clergy for accepting foreign, non-English speaking postulants. "And what will happen if perhaps some Italians come?" she wrote to Mother Seraphina. "We do not dare even mention a single word about the foundation in Cavigliano."[5]

Within the community also, individuals were not shy in voicing their disapproval of non-English speaking candidates. "I did not tell anyone further because I dread the criticism," Mother Pia continued. "As soon as the approved *Constitutions* are in our hands and you are home, we will invite the superioresses of all the houses to the Mission, and then it will be given out."[6] For the time being, Cavigliano would remain the Congregation's best-kept secret, only Mother Pia and her Council aware of the intended move.

On December 6, 1920, five sisters formed an interim community at

Cavigliano for the purpose of preparing the house for occupancy: Mother Seraphina Maerz, Sisters Liberata Monotti, Anna Thoren and Thoma Possberg.

Mother Pia's little relish for the project became even more apparent in the following weeks. Things were not working out to satisfy her, and in January 1921, she wrote to Mother Seraphina at Altenberg:

> My dear Mother Seraphina,
>
> ...I do not like to hurt you, dear Mother, but I cannot be enthusiastic about the place in Cavigliano. Whole half-nights I lie here and think it over; what I especially dislike is that the Sisters must live in the same house with outsiders, use the same stairs, the same halls and the same chapel. It is not to my taste or my comprehension of a religious house....
>
> I have no objection to girl boarders for education, but to... have a sanitarium, I do not like. Educational purposes, all right, but a sanitarium, no! It would not go with our observance and the recitation of the Divine Office....
>
> Think it over, and do not accept sick people or those who wish to come for a rest. The Sisters could visit the sick as the Sisters in Altenberg did, or they could instruct poor children as they do in Niles, Centerville, etc. If Italian postulants enter, they must receive instruction in English and learn convent life; how can they do this if they are employed all day in working and waiting on sick people and boarders?[7]

It is regrettable that the Archives at Mission San Jose do not contain Mother Seraphina's answers to Mother Pia's objections. Whatever the exchange, in February, the first community assigned to Cavigliano arrived from Altenberg in February: Sisters Anna Thoren, Theodora Stute, Germana Eberl, Fabiana Panhaus, and Leonarda Meuer. From the first, the sisters struggled to make ends meet. Sister Theodora opened a kindergarten and at noon served soup to the children whose families were too poor to provide them with lunch. Often there was not enough for both children and sisters, and the sisters gave preference to the children. At the end of the year the kindergarten closed, to be followed by day care, but it was the same story all over again. Although Sister Germana planted a vegetable garden and worked diligently at it, a six-month drought thwarted her efforts. According to Sister Fabiana, all the sisters had for dinner sometimes was boiled grass! Sister Leonarda, a dentist by profession, offered her services to the townspeople, but as the town was small (about 200) and the majority of them were poor, the income from Sister's dentistry helped little. As a last resort, a few elderly women were taken in and cared for by Sister Fabiana, but it was a losing battle.

In a letter to Mother Pia, written on May 20, 1922, Sister Anna Thoren summarized her thinking in regard to the future of *La Providenza:* the house was built as a family home and was unfit as an institute; the city of Locarno had several excellent institutes, and none was needed in Cavigliano; the villa might serve as a *pensione*, but it was too far removed from Locarno; and it would have to depend on the Swiss for residents, but the rate of monetary exchange was so high that people could not afford to come.

In October, the General Council admitted defeat and voted "to give up Cavigliano, as conditions there are such that the Sisters are unable to make a living."[8] But, for some unexplained reason, another year went by with no action taken. Finally, sometime in the spring of 1924, Mother Pia wrote to Bishop Aurelio of the Canton of Ticino in which Cavigliano was located, announcing the withdrawal of the sisters. A rough draft of her letter with neither heading nor date or signature, but in Mother Pia's handwriting, is preserved in the Motherhouse Archives at Mission San Jose:

> It is with deep regret that I am obliged to communicate to Your Lordship the decision, which after mature deliberation, I have been constrained to take, namely, to have to recall my Sisters from Cavigliano. The Institute in Cavigliano presents a variety of problems from the material side. Of this I am sure that Your Lordship is well aware.
>
> To have to pay the entire rent and, moreover...send a monthly allowance for the current expenses is an impossibility for the Motherhouse. I have done the little that was in my power for the house in Cavigliano, and I regret my inability to do more. The Sisters will leave Cavigliano some time in autumn.

> I take this occasion to express my sentiments of profound gratitude for the kindness and the paternal interest which Your Lordship has always had for my Sisters. May God recompense so much charity with His richest and choicest blessings.
>
> It pains me to know that the health of Your Lordship leaves much to be desired. I hope and pray that before my letter arrives, Your Lordship's health will be completely restored.
>
> (The ordinary closing, asking his blessing, etc.)[9]

The Bishop's reply came from Zurich, where he was hospitalized following surgery. He referred to the withdrawal of the sisters as "sad news" and continued:

> I have tried, but without success, to obtain a reduction in the rent. I have also tried to find for them another place in the diocese, but in this also I have not succeeded. Perhaps if my long sickness would not have forbidden it, I could have done more. In September, when I shall be again in Lugano, I will still try something, so much does it pain me to see your sisters leave this, my poor diocese....[10]

The Mission San Jose archives contain a letter also from Mr. Albert Pedrozzini, who identifies himself as "a member of the commission before the government for the work which was taken up by the members of the Reverend Dominican Sisters."[11] He acknowledges that conditions do not correspond to the sisters' desires "to develop their activity, the ardor of the holy mission which they feel in their heart,"[12] and he urges Mother Pia to obtain a house in Locarno. "I feel almost certain that here we would find that support in order to facilitate the continuation of the pious work...[whereby the sisters] could dedicate themselves to the care of abandoned poor children or the many reliefs of the afflicted of humanity."[13]

Mother Pia's reply was gracious but firm. "The crisis which is the sad outcome of the great world war is making itself felt strongly also in Switzerland...this is a situation which could not be foreseen two years ago."[14] She explained that Father Ceslaus Hansen, O.P., was in Cavigliano at the time and would clarify for the pastor, Father Pompeo Corti, how matters stood. It was impossible, she said, for the sisters to purchase a house in Locarno as Mr. Pedrozzini was suggesting, and she concluded by apologizing for typing her response, justifying it as an American practice.

Another letter, presumably from Father Corti and addressed to Sister Liberata, states that he is sending a few words that he has much at heart.

> I have very tangible proofs of the great good that the Sisters are doing in our parish, and of the still greater good which they would not fail to do for the good of the entire Canton if the opportunity would be given them to carry out their activity which at present is forced to such a small sphere. You cannot imagine how day by day my thoughts and pre-occupations are concentrated more and more on the Institute, on the future of which are, or rest, my most beautiful hopes. I wish that I could do the impossible in order to open to the good Sisters a vast field of labor; for this I wish to interest His Lordship and other influential persons, but before I do this I would like to know what your intentions are....[15]

But the sisters' "intentions" had already been determined, and on April 30, 1924, they left Cavigliano for the last time. In the end, the war and its aftermath had proved too much for them. Not surprisingly, Mrs. Peri was not pleased, especially since the sisters had failed to inform her of their departure. She wrote at once to Mother Pia.

> Reverend Mother Superior
> Mission San Jose
>
> Dear Rev. Mother,
>
> I have been informed that the Nuns have left Cavigliano, for which I am very sorry.
>
> Would you kindly let me know at your earliest convenience what arrangements you have made of [sic] the place? Has some one been left in charge of it, or will it be closed? I shall feel quite uneasy should it be the latter, as there is an element in Cavigliano that would not hesitate to cause

damage to the premises knowing it was <u>not</u> occupied, and of course should anything of the kind happen the lessee is responsible....

Sincerely yours,
Edwina A. Peri[16]

Although the sisters left Cavigliano before the expiration of the lease, they paid the full term rent on departing. It was money lost, but preferable to starvation!

As serving the sisters' primary purpose in establishing a house in Europe—the quest for vocations, Cavigliano might have worked out in time. But as providing a ministry compatible with the apostolate of the Congregation or one that would be self-supporting, it was a failure. A happier chapter was to follow.

Sts. Peter And Paul Convent, Altenhohenau, Bavaria

In an undated circular letter written to the Congregation sometime in 1922, Mother Pia shared with the sisters amazing news—the restoration of the ancient Dominican Convent of Sts. Peter and Paul in Altenhohenau, Upper Bavaria. The circumstances, she explained, were startlingly providential.

From a Father Friederick Haselbeck, C.Ss.R., novice master at the Redemptorist monastery in Gars, Bavaria, Mother Pia described receiving a letter in which the priest explained:

> A communication from the Convent of the Holy Cross at Ratisbon...has reached me today, inquiring whether the former Convent of Dominican Sisters at Altenhohenau were not an appropriate place for the training of missionary Sisters for America and Mexico. Special efforts for the restoration of Altenhohenau are being made by a Dominican [Father Bonifatius Vordermayer], who has also published a booklet treating on the Venerable Mother Columba Weigl of Altenhohenau.[17]

Father Haselbeck then shared his hope that Mother Pia and her sisters would undertake the work of the restoration:

> It would be too good, if your Reverence were to be the cause of restoring Altenhohenau as a Dominican Convent.

> I cherish great devotion to the Venerable Maria Columba Weigl. May she intercede at the throne of God, that her Convent, now in private possession, be resuscitated as a Temple of God....
>
> The tomb of Venerable Columba is in a miserable condition; it may be, however, gloriously restored with the church. Her probable beatification is also a cause of consolation.[18]

After quoting from Father Haselbeck's letter, Mother Pia continued:

> Immediately upon the reception of this unexpected proposal, I cabled to Mother Seraphina, who was still in Europe, to go to Altenhohenau for the purpose of inspecting the buildings there. She could not give adequate expression to the beauty and antiquity of the place. And as to myself? For two weeks I lived in a world of rapture admiring God's goodness in selecting us, His poorest creatures, to restore this ancient and venerable Dominican sanctuary....I consider it the keystone of our foundations, yes, as the crown of my 50 years of labor in the garden of our Holy Father, St. Dominic. Indeed, a heavenly Jubilee Gift![19]

The "heavenly Jubilee Gift" was indeed an "ancient and venerable Dominican sanctuary." Founded as a cloister for Second Order Dominican Sisters in 1235, by Konrad, Duke of Wasserburg, the convent was beautifully situated in the little village of Altenhohenau, Bavaria, on the banks of the Inn River. At the height of its vigor the convent encompassed 200 acres and provided employment for over 400 villagers. It reached its greatest renown in the late eighteenth century during the lifetime of two Dominican mystics, Mother Columba Weigl (1713–1783) and Sister Paula Grasl, lay sister (1718–1793).[20] As a convent of the Second Order, the venerable structure had seen over 500 years of cloistered Dominican life when, in 1803, it was secularized and came under private ownership. By government order visitors were forbidden to enter the church, the nuns' gravestones were removed, and Mother Columba's tomb, which had been a popular place of pilgrimage, was abandoned and well nigh forgotten. The tomb lay to the right of the main altar in what was formerly the sacristy, later known as St. Anne's Chapel.

Over the centuries the church had undergone extensive changes. In 1308 and again in 1379, it was severely damaged by fire. In the eighteenth century it was enlarged as well as beautified by frescoes done by the master hand of Matheus Guenther (1705–1788). The new main altar and statues were the work of his brother, the celebrated rococo sculptor, Ignaz Guenther (1725–1775). A side altar in the church held the tiny, carved figure of the widely venerated "Altenhohenau Christchild" who, following the secularization, fell into oblivion, and was replaced in the people's affection by the *"Columba Jesulein,"* Mother Columba's "Little Jesus," to whom miraculous powers were attributed.

Mother Columba Weigl's *Jesulein* statue

Early in the twentieth century Father Haselbeck had become interested in the convent after reading Father Bonifatius Vordermayer's booklet, *Strahlenkranz um das Eucharistische Herz Jesu (Wreath of Glory Around the Heart of Jesus)*, extolling the virtues of Mother Columba. Father Haselbeck determined to reestablish the convent as a religious house and to this end made a vow at the mystic's tomb that he would not cease his efforts until he had found a Dominican community that would once again occupy the convent. God favored his desire, and the chain of events bridging two continents began.

Sister Ignatia Reichert of Holy Cross Convent, Ratisbon, the sister of Sister Pulcheria Reichert, a Mission San Jose Dominican stationed in San Francisco, knew from her sister that the California community was looking for a site in Germany suitable for recruitment of candidates. She shared the information with her Ratisbon sisters and one, Sister Hyazintha Igl, originally from Gars, relayed the news to Father Haselbeck. He wrote immediately to Mother Pia, who in turn cabled Mother Seraphina in Altenberg to visit Father Haselbeck as soon as possible at Gars.

Accompanied by Sister Bonifacia Stabel, Altenberg novice director, Mother Seraphina set out for Gars on October 31, 1921. Father Haselbeck received the sisters enthusiastically and introduced them to several young women whom he had been grooming for entry into religious life once the convent at Altenhohenau was restored. From Gars the sisters traveled to Altenhohenau where it was love at first sight. Idle as a place of worship for over 100 years, the church bore sad evidence of its use as a granary, but to Mother Seraphina's artistic eye it was a place begging for restoration. After five months of searching for a suitable novitiate location, here it was—dropped by Providence into her lap!

The sisters' next move was to call on the owner of the property, Frau Katarina Soyer, who expressed willingness to return the church and a part of the land to Dominican ownership, but balked at parting with the old convent, which she had meantime converted into a guest house and restaurant. Despite the prospect of an eager buyer, negotiations were not finalized without frustration. For five months Frau Soyer temporized on one pretext after another. Finally, on March 5, 1922, she came to terms, and the sale was notarized in the nearby city of Wasserburg.

Determined to cover all bases as quickly as possible, Mother Seraphina and Sister Bonifacia went at once to Holy Cross Convent, Ratisbon, to obtain from the prioress a letter of introduction to His Eminence, Michael Cardinal von Faulhaber of Munich. The cardinal was welcoming and gracious, and the requisite permissions to open a house in Alterhohenau and initiate a charitable work were readily granted. Mother Seraphina thereupon procured the services of an architect in Munich, whom she commissioned to draw up plans for a convent and children's home. Motherhouse approval of the plans was the next step; once obtained, Mother Seraphina was free to return to the United States. With her in late September 1921, went Sister Liberata and three recently professed: Sisters Gertrudis Schonborn, Lambertina Schrickler, and Aquina Hauer. On Sister Bonifacia Stabel, novice director, now fell the responsibility of overseeing the restoration progress. In this she received valuable assistance from the Very Reverend Dean, Father Joseph Kratz, pastor of Cologne-Ehrenfeld and brother of Sister Gregoria Kratz, O.P.

The principal obstacle was, as usual, funding. Although construction of the new convent and renovation of the church had begun on schedule, the effects of the war soon told. The scarcity of building materials and their consequent high cost, as well as the continual devaluation of the dollar, imposed a heavy financial burden on the Motherhouse. At a meeting on July 20, 1922, the General Council addressed the situation and voted unanimously in favor of using Sister Bernardina Michel's inheritance from her parents ($30,000), which she had recently renounced, to underwrite the Altenhohenau purchase and building costs. The following year (July 11–12, 1923) Altenhohenau was again on the General Council agenda. Discussion of the purchase of an additional 20 acres adjacent to the convent resulted in a favorable vote. (Purchase price: $300.)

Meanwhile, Frau Soyer was proving a difficult neighbor. Ordering the grass in the sisters' meadow cut and hauled to her barn! This in Sister Bonifacia's opinion, "was an unscrupulous action! On Sundays the place is filled with people who come to see... [our] new building and then spend their money...[at] Soyers on food. For that, she could be much nicer to us."[21]

With the convent at Altenhohenau nearly completed, Sister Bonifacia bade farewell to Altenberg on September 25, 1923. She was accompanied by three newly professed—Sister Mauritia Bleiker, who as a postulant had been "smuggled" into Belgium from Germany on a false passport (the Congregation's first and only "illegal alien"), Sister Raphaela Dorr, Sister Marka Grips—and a postulant, Cecilia Kassel (Sister Isnarda) who would constitute the pioneer community.

In her memoirs Sister Mauritia tells of the sisters' leave-taking:

> ...Although our train left [Altenberg] early on that memorable morning, many people had assembled to bid farewell to their Sisters, who for many years had been the devoted teachers of their children, who had cared for their sick, and had given comfort and advice in hours of trial and sorrow. A kind businessman presented the sisters with seventy white woolen blankets. These [would be] especially useful when the first home for children was

opened in Altenhohenau.

> Our first stop was Frankfurt. A woman came aboard...with her two daughters. Her face brightened on seeing the Sisters [and] she entrusted the girls to their care to Duesseldorf. "What! Duesseldorf!" exclaimed Sister Bonifacia. "We are going to Munich!" Unaware that the cars had been separated, we grabbed our belongings and rushed out. I was the last to leave, for I had been entrusted with the precious altar stone. Holding on to my umbrella and satchel I hurried to join the Sisters, but to my consternation they were nowhere to be seen. The train [had] started when I spied Sister Raphaela at a window. What was I to do?
>
> ...Without a penny in my purse, I knew only one thing: I must reach the Sisters. I ran after the train, paying no heed to the conductor, who tried to stop me. I reached the last car and jumped in. In desperation the conductor threw the satchel and umbrella after me. Exhausted, I sank into a plush seat. It was a first class compartment![22]

In Munich the sisters were met by Father Kratz, who advised them not to continue their journey that evening. But youth and enthusiasm prevailed and the little band, baggage in tow, boarded the train for Rott-am-Inn, walking the last hour to Griesstaett, the village nearest Altenhohenau. Arrived in Griesstaett, Sister Mauritia continued her narrative:

> The venerable...[pastor] welcomed us kindly. He was courtesy personified, and invited us to supper, which we gratefully accepted. He regaled us with stories until our eyes drooped. 'You can't go to the convent this evening,' he announced. 'You may all stay here.' He showed us to our quarters...[The sisters} were pleased with theirs. I, poor sinner, perhaps on account of my height, was assigned to the attic. There, in the corner stood a huge bed...I didn't mind the hole in the mattress, but there was another problem. The Reverend Father pointed to a [cloth-covered] figure, 'Don't be afraid,' [he said, removing the cloth and pointing to a skeleton.] 'This is Blessed Claudius. In times past vandals stole the jewels from his eyes; otherwise, he is intact. Good night.'[23]

With blessed skeleton for roommate, Sister Mauritia slept soundly.

After Mass and breakfast the next morning, the sisters set out down the path bordering the river for the first glimpse of their new home. Spying the tower in the distance, Sister Bonifacia joyfully intoned the *Magnificat* in which the little band joined heartily. Singing from full hearts, they entered the church, their emotions soaring. "Like wildfire the news spread: 'The Sisters are here.' When we came from Holy Mass the following morning, we were surprised to find a large basket filled with apples, tomatoes, butter, bread, and sandwiches awaiting us."[24] It was a warm and welcoming gesture from an anonymous neighbor!

Although the Columba chapel was cluttered with paint brushes and buckets, the sisters managed to clear enough floor space to hold the first *Salve Regina* procession in over 100 years. With lighted candles they walked from the body of the church to the little chapel, singing the beloved anthem that closes a Dominican's day. Replicas of crutches and canes as well as votive plaques mounted on the chapel walls attested to the faith and gratitude of Mother Columba's many clients in years past. Once again, her patrons would be welcome to express their devotion at her tomb.

For the time being, the sisters had their work cut out for them. Days were filled with scraping paint from windows and floors, sweeping up debris left by workmen, and scrubbing more than a century of dirt and dust from church pews and altar. For the first week they availed themselves of the pastor's hospitality in Griesstaett, as the convent was not yet finished. But when the chaplain's quarters were completed, they moved into them above the church. According to Sister Mauritia:

> We still had to get water from the neighbors, because our well was not yet functioning...[The pastor] thought perhaps we might take care of the altar linen. We could only say: "Lord, Thy will be done!" The scarcity of water urged us to melt snow, and we had marvelous results. We brought the immaculate work to the parish church....Mr. Schmitmeir of Griesstaett lent us a cow so we could have milk. We baptized her Olga....
>
> We were still waiting for our furniture. Money was scarce. Sister Bonifacia's purse was often empty. With St. Philip she

might say, 'Wherewith shall we buy bread?' It happened more than once that we asked a kind farmer for bread.... Holy poverty was still the main chef in the kitchen."[25]

Since the grave of Mother Columba had been badly damaged, the sisters received permission to open it. They beheld only bones and the buckle of a belt. Reverently, Sister Bonifacia removed the skull and carried it to the roof, imploring Mother Columba to bless the new convent.

In October, two of Father Haselbeck's postulants, Teresa Eisenberger and Ursula Geidobler (Sisters Kiliana and Fredericka), entered. The next day a neighbor wishing to give the sisters a treat prepared a chicken dinner for them with all the trimmings. They were about to sit down when the doorbell rang. There stood three more of Father Haselbeck's candidates—Julia Hengelberger (Sister Peregrina), Maria Linner (Sister Ruperta), and Katharina Stellner (who returned home as a postulant). As the sisters watched, they saw their anticipated banquet enjoyed by the newcomers!

Although there was still much work to do, the little community—now increased to 10—moved into the convent proper on November 16. Three days later seven novices from Altenberg joined the group: Sisters Ceslava Eigenmann, Columbina Precht, Delphina Schmitt, Gaudentia Kunz, Angelina Gassner, Gerarda Sturz, and Alphonsina Kronseder. On the same day the newly appointed chaplain arrived—to the sisters' delight, Father Bonifatius Vordermayer, O.P.

Gradually Altenhohenau began to take on the features of a hundred years before. From Griesstaett came the wood-carved figures of Sts. Anne, Joseph, and Florian, which the pastor had removed years before to preserve from desecration or theft. "A hay wagon, splendidly decorated and drawn by stately horses, brought...them down the valley to the church."[26] Others arrived later. At the time of the secularization the Altenhohenau sacristan had removed two ancient life-sized statues of the Lord in agony and the Sorrowful Mother and had stored them in his home. When fire destroyed his house—all but the room in which the statues were stored—he vowed that he would return the figures to the sisters, should they ever return. Now, the promise was faithfully fulfilled by relatives of the deceased.

A large wooden crucifix, the corpus hollow and the wound in

the side open, had through the years, been left hanging unharmed on the church wall. In times past, so the story went, it had floated up the Inn River to the convent, its origin unknown. For the surrounding villagers the crucifix had become a treasured possession. Into the open wound in Christ's side both prince and pauper placed their petitions. Now they would be free once again to resume their cherished practice.

In their explorations the sisters discovered that a large stone slab in the church floor could be removed. Curious, they withdrew the stone and descended a narrow staircase, discovering that it led to the burial place of former Altenhohenau chaplains. Arms crossed, the bodies lay undisturbed in a vault of brick. After her first descent, a sister observed that one didn't need a book to meditate down there. But the tomb was not destined to become a place of pilgrimage; in the interests of sanitation, the slab was hermetically sealed before the year was out.

One item remained to be recovered: Mother Columba's miraculous statue of the Infant Jesus, missing from the cloister for 122 years. At the time of suppression Mother Claudia Weigl, Altenhohenau's last prioress, entrusted the Infant to her relatives for safekeeping. Before her last relative died, he gave the Infant to the Capuchin Fathers in Munich. When the sisters went to retrieve him, they were told by the Brother at the door, "That Baby stays here."[27] But on August 22, 1925, Mother Columba's "Little Jesus" came home in an ornately decorated horse-drawn wagon, amid the joyous pealing of church bells and the enthusiastic welcome of sisters, children and neighbors. "An unforgettable day," recorded the Altenhohenau historian, "which included the answer to many prayers and continued efforts for His return."[28] The infant's homecoming had required the intervention of the Capuchin provincial; the Master General's assistant; and the mediation of two Cardinals, their Eminences Andrew Cardinal Fruewirth, O.P., and Michael Cardinal Faulhaber!

January 1, 1924, was the last New Year's Day the sisters would spend in Altenberg. On April 10, their beloved "Little Nazareth" was purchased by the parish; hence there was nothing to hinder the remaining sisters from moving to Altenhohenau, especially when two wagons arrived to remove with whatever was left of the sisters' effects. Sisters Arsenia Lins, Maria Muller, Febronia Hauer, and Victorina Bertram left Altenberg for Aachen, where they spent the night at the convent of the Franciscan Sisters. Sisters Leo Grebs and Nazaria Busch remained in Altenberg, working through the night to leave the house in perfect order for its new owners. The next morning all six boarded the train for Rott-am-Inn, the nearest station to Altenhohenau.

Two weeks later (April 30, 1924) the sisters from Cavigliano—Sisters Anna Thoren, Thoma Possberg, Brigitta Gantner, Theodora Stute, Germana Eberl, and Leonarda Meuer—arrived under rather dramatic circumstances. The trip had gone smoothly enough until they reached Wasserburg when the heavens opened and a drenching storm—accompanied by thunder, lightning, and hail—greeted the travelers. The last seven miles were memorable. In an open horse-drawn wagon they were pelted with hail and soaked to the skin within a matter of minutes. Suddenly the storm grew so violent that at a particularly explosive clap of thunder the horses reared wildly and started to bolt. Pitched from side to side, the sisters struggled to hold on in the lurching wagon while the driver fought desperately to bring the frightened animals under control. Bruised and saturated, the sextet arrived in record time at Altenhohenau, grateful to set foot on solid ground again and be reunited with the community.

"For the rededication of the church the flag must wave on high,"[29] decreed the pastor of Griesstatt with an eye for diplomacy. To Sisters Mauritia Bleiker and Barnaba Friesinger fell the task of climbing the convent bell tower to fulfill the pastor's pronouncement. Their duty accomplished, the two decided to remove the century of dust covering the bells and, as long as they were up there to test their tone quality. To the astonishment of the country folk the noonday stillness was broken when the strains of the Angelus rang out across the fields after a century of silence.

The new convent was given priory status by Mother Pia and her Council, and rededicated to the apostles, Sts. Peter and Paul. Sister Bonifacia Stabel was appointed prioress; Sister Anna Thoren, subprioress; Sister Arsenia Lins, novice director; Sister Leo Grebs, trea-

Sts. Peter and Paul Priory, Altenhohenau, the River Inn in the foreground and the Bavarian Alps in the background

surer; and Sister Thoma Possberg, school directress. Appropriately, on June 29, the Feast of Saints Peter and Paul, the convent patrons, the bells once again summoned neighbors to Mass. Life was back to normal in Altenhohenau!

According to Sister Leonarda Meuer the sisters recently professed at the time worked diligently preparing the convent for the arrival of 55 girls from the Ruhr, aged 8 to 13. The girls were war casualties in need of rest and fresh air; and for the time being, the new building would function as a children's convalescent home.

In preparation for the girls' arrival, Sister Leonarda was charged with making dresses for the statue of the Blessed Mother above the main altar in the sisters' church. "How many times I climbed up behind the altar to try on her...[new wardrobe],"[30] Sister remembered. But, when the girls arrived, she had no reason for regret; they sang the praises of the statue, lovely in her beautiful new dress.

Sister Leonarda's talent for dressmaking would soon be put to a variety of uses. One of Altenhohenau's first vocations to be mis-

Maria Maeusl (second from right, back row) studies home economics at Sts. Peter and Paul Priory—our future Sister Thecla Maeusl

sioned to the United States, she was assigned the task of outfitting her eight fellow travelers and herself with black habits for the long trip.

> On February 2, [1925] we received a special blessing...and a mission cross. We left the next day by car, but the car got stuck in the deep snow. A farmer came to our rescue and used his two horses and wagon to bring us to the Rott train station. In Munich we were met by the Reverend Kratz. He ordered for us a good Bavarian soup and dumplings. They were delicious. After that we continued our trip to Bremen and then by ship to America....[31]

Altenhohenau had begun its selfless mission of sending Dominican women from Europe to evangelize the Church in the United States. Until World War II, Germany would continue to be a strong and steady source of vocations to the Congregation and account significantly for its growth. The sisters from Germany have left their stamp on the community, imparting to it a solid, faith-filled, dedicated-to-duty character. Their contribution should be neither overlooked nor undervalued.

Beginning in 1929, Sts. Peter and Paul Convent responded to a variety of needs. It served as a retreat house for women, a home for refugees, and a facility for teaching home economics and sewing classes to adults. Meanwhile a concordat, signed between the Holy See and Germany, specified that religious superiors had to be German citizens. Sister Gregoria Kratz, the prioress of Altenhohenau, had been born in Germany, but had acquired American citizenship after her assignment to the United States. Word received from a nervous Chancery Office in Munich advised Mother Pia appoint Sister Thoma Possberg, a German citizen, as prioress. The General Council concurred, but created a new title of unspecified canonical status for Sister Gregoria, "Mother Seraphina's representative in Germany."

World War II

During World War II, Altenhohenau became a home for refugees from the south Tyrol, the number at times reaching as high as

St. Peter and Paul School students

90. Despite the increase in care, four sisters were drafted for Attl, a nearby monastery of the Brothers of Charity, converted into a wartime military hospital. The sisters were ordered to take over the kitchen for the Brothers, who were called to military service. Sister Stilla Sinseder was one of the draftees. From Attl she could see in the distance the spire of Altenhohenau. Miserably homesick, she shed so many tears over the kettles as she stirred the midday soup, that the German officer in charge finally told her to go back to Altenhohenau and stay there! Never was an order more cheerfully received!

Other sisters, however, were not so fortunate. Sisters Ludovica Sewald, Mechtildis Okos, and Ermelinda Deisohl had been at Altenhohenau only two years when World War II broke out. Shortly after making profession, they were called for service. Sister Paulina Getz, prioress, petitioned without success for their release. While awaiting a decision, the three missed the prescribed physical examination, which preceded military duty. From the young women drafted at the same time, the sisters learned how fortunate they had been. The girls were bunched in a large room and told to remove their clothing. Left to wait in line, they were forced to submit to offensive remarks. But the sisters who arrived late were told to obtain medical certificates from their own physician in Wasserburg.

Sister Mechtildis, who has left an account of the experience, was sent for her tour of duty to Esdrenbach, Oberpfalz; Sister Ermelinda was scheduled for duty in Amerz; and Sister Ludovika was assigned to the Bavarian Woods. The weather was bitterly cold and the sisters wore bulky, shapeless coats, but "We couldn't have looked too bad," writes Sister Mechtildis, "for the soldiers greeted us at the train station as 'Munchener Kindl' (Munich children).[32] From Munich they left for their various destinations; the separation was painful, and the sisters parted in tears.

Sister Mechtildis arrived in Esdrenbach late at night and had difficulty finding someone who could direct her to the camp. Last to arrive, she managed to find an empty bed in the barracks, but soon discovered it was covered with ice. In the middle of the barracks stood an iron stove, which warmed the dormitory—when there was firewood! But the girls soon discovered that removing straw from their mattresses was a comforting substitute.

The day after arrival they were issued identical blue dresses and rough linen aprons. Their "morning prayer" consisted of assembling around the flag in the freezing courtyard, with right arm upraised, singing a German song with arms upraised. For services assigned them the girls received 20 cents per day. Meals were often indescribable, as three girls would be appointed cooks for the day whether they knew anything about cooking or not. The best part of the experience was the occasional assignment to a family, (usually four to six weeks) to help in the fields or in the housework. The families were always kind, but promptly at 6:00 p.m. the girls were obliged to return to the reality of the camp where they were assigned chores in the kitchen or laundry. They also had to take turns at all-night guard duty. This was not too bad once they learned to make the rounds of the camp and then sneak into the leaders' barracks, which were comfortably furnished and warm. One night when Sister Mechtildis was on night duty, soldiers broke into the leader's quarters and threatened to report the culprits to the officer in charge. "Although the threat was not carried out, the fright we experienced, I cannot tell,"[33] said Sister Mechtildis, shivering at the memory.

The spiritual life of the sisters was of little concern to the camp officials. Of private prayer they could not deprive them, but they were allowed to attend Sunday Mass only with special permission. They were not permitted to wear their uniforms to church and had to look for other clothing wherever they could find it. Some "civvies," when finally assembled were little short of appalling, but because it was wartime, fashions were not of uppermost importance!

When her period of service ended, Sister Mechtildis was given a three week visit with her parents. Vacation over, she returned to the convent and renewed her vows. "It was not quite so easy to feel at home in the convent," she admitted, "but God helped me,"[34] There was triple work in Altenhohenau at the time, as the Tyrolean refugees had arrived while the sisters were away.

As the war dragged on, the situation in Altenhohenau became critical. A section of the American army was encamped across the Inn River from Altenhohenau, and the German troops began an attack perilously near the convent, which was in the direct line of fire. After five harrowing days, the German army withdrew—to the sisters' relief. But scarcity of food, particularly after the refugees' arrival, was a constant threat. Many a day the soup on the table was watery thin.

Postwar Challenges

Meantime, the sisters in the United States had heard nothing from their sisters in Germany. Taking advantage of New York Archbishop Francis J. Spellman's elevation to the cardinalate, Mother Bernardina, prioress general, included in her congratulatory note to the new cardinal a request for assistance. Explaining her concern for the sisters in Altenhohenau for four years, Mother asked him to deliver a letter to Cardinal Faulhaber of Munich at the forthcoming consistory. Cardinal Spellman graciously complied and following the consistory, Cardinal Faulhabler wrote to Mother Bernardina:

> Having received your anxious letter, I went personally... to Altenhohenau in order to ease your mind by giving you definite information. The convent at Altenhohenau... remains unharmed by bombs, and likewise the convent church was not damaged. Indeed bombs fell quite close,

some dropping into the River Inn, yet without doing injury to the convent and church....The sisters in Altenhohenau are devoted to the Motherhouse in California with filial loyalty, and the solicitude of the Motherhouse for them has strengthened the bond of union. [35]

On hearing this reassuring news from Cardinal Faulhaber, the sisters at the Motherhouse rejoiced. Actually, the sisters in Germany were faring better than most groups at the hands of both armies. The American soldiers identified them as members of an American congregation, and the German army recognized them as German citizens. Still, there were challenges. One day someone reported hearing moaning in the cornfield beyond the convent. The sisters went out to investigate and found a wounded German soldier who had gone AWOL. His presence presented the sisters with a serious dilemma; they were unwilling to report him to either army. Bringing blankets and pillows as soon as darkness fell, and bandaging his wounds, they made him as comfortable as possible under the circumstances. Each night they visited him, caring for his wounds and bringing him food for the following day. But at last there came a night when they crept out as usual, only to find the blankets empty. Had he felt well enough to escape, or had he been captured? The sisters hoped it was the former.

By Nazi command the bells in the sisters' church tower were ordered removed and hauled away. But, when men came to fulfill the charge, they removed the two large bells only, leaving a small third one in place. The story of the retrieval of the bells is told in an account sent to the sisters by Herr Hans Schoeffler, brother of a long-time lay resident of the convent in Altenhohenau:

> After my return from captivity at the end of 1945, I received a letter from my sister Lenchen, who was then and still is in the Convent of Altenhohenau [now deceased]. Among other things she told me, that all in Altenhohenau had heard that there was in Hamburg a "Camp" of Church Bells. She gave me the inscription on the bells and asked me to do something about it. At the Police Office I learned that in the Hamburg Free Harbor several bells were supposed to be there.

Now, first of all, I got myself a bicycle, because there was no other facility for travel as yet, and went to the Free Harbor. After several mistaken trips in the Harbor, I found the place where hundreds of bells were lying, partly in the open field and partly in public dumping grounds. I also found a responsible caretaker. After I made myself known... he could tell me only to search the place, and if I should find what I was looking for to let him know.

In the afternoon...I had to leave the camp without any result....The next morning...I made my appearance again. At last, I found one bell and my hope increased to find the other one. Shortly before closing time, I had the [good] fortune to find the second bell.

With white chalk I marked both foundlings with the name of the owner. After that I came to an agreement with an official, who promised to take care of all the rest. A few cigars, which I, thanks be to God, still had, did all the rest.

I learned later from my sister that the two 'runaways' were again in their old place performing their duty. This was a joy for me, because now I know that all my trouble was not in vain. Let us all hope that the 'runaways' will never leave again.[36]

The last refugees from southern Tyrol left Altenhohenau in 1950, and were replaced by children sent by Catholic Charities. Because several of the children were crippled, the sisters asked and obtained permission from the German government to establish a school on the premises. In January 1953, a special class (*Foerderschule*) was introduced to meet the government requirement that children entering Germany from a foreign country must have special instruction in the German language for one year.

In 1958 Father Karl Wildenauer, C.Ss.R., was appointed chaplain to the sisters at Altenhohenau. During his years as chaplain he did much to publicize Mother Columba's sanctity by his writings and lectures. From Father Haselbeck, his novice master, he had early learned to venerate the saintly Dominican. Gradually, through Father Wildenauer's influence, interest in Mother Columba

Sister Tharcisia Ertl, assigned to Sts. Peter and Paul as Prioress, 1953–1960; Superior 1960–1962 at Wallgau; Prioress Sts. Peter and Paul 1962-1969

Sister Mary Thomas muses by the River Inn while visiting Altenhohenau.

returned, and once again, her tomb became a place of pilgrimage.

When German-born Sister Tharcisia Ertl was called from the United States to be prioress of Saints Peter and Paul Convent in 1953 she faced a series of post-war challenges. One of the first was the building of a larger school and residence for the children applying for entrance. The new school provided classrooms from the third to the sixth grade levels, the *Foerderschule*, and special instruction in religion, English, and needlework.

Between the years 1925 and 1956, Sts. Peter and Paul Priory sent 57 sisters to the United States in support of the Congregation's mission for the Church. Their contribution continues to be a blessing to the Congregation.

NOTES

[1] General Council Minutes, 5 July 1920.

[2] Noseda (Vicar General for Cardinal Boggiani), letter to Maerz, 9 September 1920.

[3] Backes, letter to Maerz, 13 October 1920.

[4] Backes, letter to Maerz, 23 & 25 October 1920.

[5] Backes, letter to Maerz, 17 November 1920.

[6] Backes, letter to Maerz, 23 & 25 October 1920.

[7] Backes, letter to Maerz, 20 January 1921.

[8] General Council Minutes, 22 October 1922.

[9] Backes, letter to Bishop Aurelio, (probably 1924).

[10] Bishop Aurelio, letter to Backes, (probably 1924).

[11] Albert Pedrozzini, letter to Backes, (probably 1924).

[12] Albert Pedrozzini, letter to Backes, (probably 1924).

[13] Albert Pedrozzini, letter to Backes, (probably 1924).

[14] Backes, letter to Pedrozzini, (probably 1924).

[15] Pompeo Corti, letter to Liberata Monotti, O.P. (probably 1924).

[16] Edwina A. Peri, letter to Backes, n.d.

[17] Friedrich Haselbeck, C.Ss.R., letter to Backes, n.d. in Backes, circular letter (1922).

[18] Haselbeck (1922).

[19] Backes, circular letter (1922).

[20] Columba Weigl, O.S.D. was born on 8 March 1713. She entered the Dominican cloister of Saints Peter and Paul, Altenhohenau, on 16 April 1730, at the age of seventeen. She was chosen prioress in 1774 and died on 31 August 1783. She was buried in the former sacristy, now the Saint Anne's Chapel. Ten years later, a lay sister, Sister Paula Grasl, who died in the odor of sanctity, was buried beside Mother Columba.

[21] Bonifacia Stabel, O.P., letter to Backes, n.d.

[22] Mauritia Bleiker, O.P., "We Take Leave of Little Nazareth," (1924) 1–2.

[23] Bleiker 2.

[24] Bleiker 3–4.

[25] Bleiker 3–4.

[26] Bleiker 3.

[27] Leonarda Meuer, O.P., "Transfer of Novitiate from Moresnet-Neutre to Sts. Peter and Paul, Altenhohenhau," (personal report translated from German, 1924) 2.

[28] Annals of Sts. Peter and Paul Convent, 22 August 1925.

[29] Annals of Sts. Peter and Paul Convent, 22 August 1925.

[30] Meuer 2.

[31] Meuer 3.

[32] Mechtildis Okos, O.P., (Sister's remembrance), 1924.

[33] Okos, 1924.

[34] Okos, 1924.

[35] Michael Cardinal von Faulhaber, letter to Michel and Sisters, 26 April 1946.

[36] Hans Schoeffler, letter to Altenhohenau Sisters in "History of Altenhohenau," 10.

CHAPTER TWENTY-TWO

MISSION TO MARIN

Timoteo Murphy, the "Irish Giant" from County Wexford, Ireland, was a man to be reckoned with. Towering over six feet and weighing 300 pounds of solid muscle, he arrived in California to set up a beef-packing plant in Monterey. Though the enterprise failed, Don Timoteo did not. He emerged from his failure everybody's friend.

In 1828, California was still under the control of Mexico, and Murphy soon made friends with both Mexican soldiers and government agents. Sometime during these years also he became a naturalized Mexican citizen. When the decree secularizing the missions was issued in 1834, it was only a matter of time until the despoiling began, and Mission San Rafael de Arcangel, lying north of San Francisco, was not excepted. Soon the Indians of the region were in desperate straits. Trappers and hunters were depriving them of much of the game on which they depended for food and, with the departure of the missionaries, the fields which had provided them with grain lay untilled. To deal with the situation Governor Alvarado appointed Don Timoteo administrator of the Mission and Indian agent. His was a fortuitous choice. He immediately petitioned for a land grant (57,000 acres) for the 1,400 Indians in his custody, and as long as he was their agent, they lived peacefully and well provided for off the land.

The Don, meanwhile, thought it time to look after his own interests. Seeking a land grant for himself, he was awarded some 22,000 acres around San Rafael by the Mexican government. But, when Mexico was forced to cede California to the United States in the Treaty of Guadalupe Hidalgo (1848), the Indians lost their rights to the land, which was sold to speculators. Don Timoteo's grant, however, was approved by the United States Land Commission. It had come at an opportune time. The American occupation, coinciding with the gold rush, served the Don well in acquiring wealth, and his San Rafael hacienda became famous up and down the coast as a popular gathering place.

Taken suddenly ill on the night of January 10, 1853, Don Timoteo bethought himself to make a will. He tended to the Church first, deeding some 317 acres to Archbishop Alemany of San Francisco with the "express condition that the grantee...within two years from the date hereof, cause a school or seminary of learning to be established and maintained upon said land."[1] The deed was duly recorded on January 13, 1853, at 8 a.m. and, in a matter of hours, Don Timoteo lapsed into unconsciousness and died.

St. Vincent Orphanage: Early Years

The gift was a challenge. Situated some 25 miles across the bay from San Francisco, the land could be reached by sail or row boat as far as San Rafael, and from San Rafael by carriage or horseback over five miles of dirt road that turned to thick mud in winter; the alternative was by boat across the bay and up a creek that ran through the deeded property—a hazardous enough trip in good weather and outright perilous in bad. Ranches were few at the north end of the bay at the time; hence, the number of children did not warrant building a "seminary or institution of learning" in the area. And, to crown matters, Archbishop Alemany lacked the money to build anything! (He himself was living in a single room behind St. Francis church in San Francisco.) But time was rapidly moving on in terms of the conditions stipulated in Don Timoteo's will. If he could not build, he figured perhaps someone else could. The Daughters of Charity had an orphanage and school in San Francisco and might have use for the property.

Accordingly, he offered the land to Sister Frances McEnnis, D.C., superior, on condition that she build and staff a school there. The sisters' superiors in Emmitsburg, Maryland, accepted the offer, and Sister Frances undertook the erection of the school, including housing for the sisters and a few boarders—the latter required to make the operation financially sound. Placed under the patronage of the great St. Vincent de Paul, founder of the Daughters of Charity, the building was completed and Sister Corsina McKay, D.C., was sent across the bay to take charge just 10 days before Don Timoteo's deadline.

The Emmitsburg superiors were not pleased when they learned of the boarding school and wished the children replaced by orphans—a ministry to which they were dedicated. Ten little orphan girls were soon housed in the boarders' quarters and attending school at St. Vincent's. But the inaccessibility of the site and the absence of a priest, even for Sunday Mass, led the superiors in Emmitsburg to intervene again, this time instructing Sister Frances to go back to San Francisco and return the property to Archbishop Alemany. Sister Frances was not disappointed. "I...feel more satisfaction in giving up Mr. Murphy's property than I have in taking it," she wrote. "The Sisters will be home in two days. I have spent $5000 on the property, and of course it must be lost....It's no use grieving over it."[2]

For the sisters the problem was solved, but for the Archbishop it was trouble revisited. Sister Frances, however, did not abandon him. With her help he reached a solution; the sisters would move the boys from their San Francisco orphanage to St. Vincent's, and the Archbishop would provide a priest director for them. With Father Robert A. R. Maurice as designated director, 14 boys crossed the bay in January, 1855, to take up residence in the new school. By the end of the year St. Vincent's housed 28 orphans and provided a tuition-free school attended by 40 pupils.

As the only priest in Marin County, Father Maurice soon found his responsibilities extending to all Catholics in the vicinity and including the care of Mission San Rafael approximately five miles to the south. The mission was in a deplorable condition, and Father Maurice added the building of a new church to his other duties. Transferred to Stockton, California in August of the following year, Father Maurice has gone down in history, short as his time was, as the first pastor of San Rafael and the first priest director of St. Vincent's.

The priests who followed him seemed cut from the same cloth—zealous, fathers to the boys, and remarkable for the amount of territory they covered in their care of the Catholics of San Rafael, Sonoma, Novato, Santa Rosa, and Petaluma. By the end of 1861, under the direction of Father Louis Lootens (1859–1868), third priest director and a native of Belgium, St. Vincent's numbered 133 orphans, who received eight years of education at a time when most pupils received six. With the rapid increase in student population the director faced the challenge of expansion; a building program was essential. The result was the erection of Most Holy Rosary chapel and a new building providing dormitories on the second floor and classrooms on the first.

Under Father Lootens' successor, Father Peter Birmingham (1868–1875), a change took place. When the priest director was absent tending to parochial duties, the hired staff often grew careless, doing only the bare minimum. Father Birmingham sought to remedy the situation by petitioning Archbishop Alemany for sisters to care for the boys. The Archbishop appealed to the Dominican Sisters of Benicia (San Rafael), who agreed to send two sisters for three months as a stopgap measure, since the Archbishop hoped to procure the services of sisters from Canada within that time. The sisters were to supervise the boys' dormitories and take care of their clothing. Whatever happened to the sisters from Canada, the three months stretched to twenty-six years, and the two Dominican sisters expanded to thirteen as the number of boys increased. "By 1884, a staggering 554 boys called St. Vincent's home. A student body that was once predominantly orphans now consisted of mostly 'half-orphans' and abandoned or neglected children. St. Vincent's found itself at the forefront of the fledgling field of social work."[3]

For some time Archbishop Riordan, believing that the school would benefit by having both teaching and administration under the same religious community, had been appealing to the Christian Brothers to take over St. Vincent's in its entirety. The Brothers admitted interest, but asked for time to prepare.

Finally, on August 15, 1894, after the Dominican Sisters of San Rafael withdrew from the school, the Christian Brothers arrived at St. Vincent's. Brother Michael Dorgan, former director of St. Mary's College, Oakland, replaced the priest director and the Brothers took over the classrooms and supervised the dormitories, playgrounds, and dining room. St. Vincent's had become an all-male institution. For 27 years the Brothers carried on, adding instruction in Greek and Latin to the curriculum, as well as the trade-oriented disciplines of agriculture, tailoring, and shoemaking. But on August 2, 1921, Archbishop Edward J. Hanna of San Francisco received word from Brother Joseph, the Brother Visitor of the District, requesting permission to withdraw the Brothers from St. Vincent's. His letter explained his petition:

> ...[Before World War I] thirty to forty boys made up our normal first year high school class, sufficiency for a teacher, surely. Today in one of our schools, we have registered well nigh 200 applicants for this same class. Others of our institutions are almost similarly situated. All of which means that from three to five Brothers are now needed to teach in the lower high school classes to do the task of one of past years, while a relatively like condition must arise in the upper classes as promotions are successively made. Hence our desire to transfer the personnel of St. Vincent's to other of our schools as a measure of immediate relief to overworked Brothers and congested classes....[4]

The Brother Visitor's letter evidently did not come as a complete surprise, as Archbishop Hanna's reply indicated that he had been negotiating on his own: "After consultation with the Sisters of St. Dominic at Mission San Jose, I am able to inform you that they will take over most of the Asylum at San Rafael in August, 1922."[5] He then expressed his regret that the Brothers' need for teachers compelled them "to leave the work to which...[they had] consecrated such fine ability."[6]

Meantime, Mother Pia had written to the Vicar General of the Archdiocese:

> The Councillors have decided that we should do the utmost, even at the cost of sacrifice, for the sake of helping the Most Rev. Archbishop in his project with the Boys' Home. Considering that the boys will attend the public school to be erected for them, we are willing to furnish ten Sisters (although twenty would be necessary for the undertaking) to take charge of the Home after August 4, 1922, stipulating however for a trial of five years.[7]

Although the Archbishop was assured of sisters for St. Vincent's, he still needed teachers, as Mother Pia had agreed to supply the domestic staff only. The solution nearly brought closure to the school. Archbishop Hanna petitioned Superintendent of Marin County Public Schools James B. Davidson for teachers, and Mr.

Davidson agreed to help. St. Vincent's was situated in the Dixie School district, which consisted of one small rural school and fewer than 10 pupils. Suddenly to explode into a district with a student population of nearly 400 was asking for trouble. Classes would have to be held at St. Vincent's, since the Dixie district had no building large enough to accommodate the sudden escalation. This circumstance fretted the State Superintendent of Public Instruction, Mr. Will Wood, who criticized the withholding of school funds "because people cannot readily understand that a non-sectarian school can be conducted in a sectarian orphanage. If the buildings were separate, the distinction could be readily understood."[8] Finally it was settled that the state would rent a classroom wing and the school would be exclusively under the control of the public school authorities, the course of study would be the one used by the public schools of Marin County, and denominational doctrines would not be taught in the school.

Teachers constituted another problem. The Dixie School district had no funds to maintain the school for the rest of the year (It was only October!). In addition, the Superintendent believed that the type of boy at St. Vincent's called for strong teachers. He did not think proper teachers could be employed "without liberal supplementing of State and County funds."[9] In a nice mixture of Church and State, Archbishop Hanna resolved the problem by volunteering to underwrite the teachers' salaries for the remaining months of the school year, an expenditure of $9,600! But generous as the offer was, the situation raised too many questions in Superintendent Wood's mind. Uneasily he addressed a letter to Mr. Davidson:

> Since leaving you yesterday I have given thought to possible complications growing out of the plan for St. Vincent's. The thing that brought it most strikingly home to me was the plan to take people out of teaching positions and put them in the proposed school. I think this should be done if we are to secure good teachers, but I should feel quite blamable if after these teachers had resigned and accepted a place at St. Vincent's, a legal point were raised and an adverse opinion on the legal status of the plan were rendered. Moreover, I should feel culpable if the Archbishop, assuming that the matter could be fully settled by us, were induced to expend a considerable sum for the school, only to find that

legal difficulties prevented carrying out the plan of public support.

In consequence, I have decided to submit the entire matter to the Attorney General for opinion....I am sure that all of us will feel much more easy in mind if the legal points are cleared up now rather than later.[10]

On December 21, 1921, the California Attorney General handed down the opinion that he saw no legal difficulty in establishing the school as proposed. Mr. Wood could now be at ease.

Msgr. McElroy and the Sisters from Mission San Jose

Monsignor Francis P. McElroy, Director

To the Brothers' credit, they made provision before leaving for all replacements except the director. In replacing the latter, Archbishop Hanna made a happy choice—Father Francis P. McElroy, a man eminently fitted for the responsibility that lay ahead. He had already provided for boys who had no home to return to after work by buying a house for them near Sacred Heart church, San Francisco. The home became known as the San Francisco Working Boys' club, with Father McElroy as director. Now, on January 13, 1922, he received his appointment as director of St. Vincent's.

Shortly before sending sisters to make up the domestic staff, Mother Pia paid her first visit to St. Vincent's. It was only then that she realized what a public school on the premises actually meant, and the reality shocked her. The classrooms were completely devoid of religious symbol—crucifix, holy water font, or religious picture. It was too much for her, and she announced that by August she would provide sisters for the classrooms also—somehow!

August 7, 1922, marked the arrival of the Mission San Jose Dominicans at St. Vincent's. Mother Seraphina was the first to appear with Sister Anastasia Maas and Sister Sebastiana Schreiber. The next day the staff was boosted by seven additional sisters: Sisters Emygdia Joras, Hyacintha Holl, Wilhelmina Preun, Osanna Weber, Felicia Westmark, Cornelia Leitner, and Petronilla Buchmann. Two days later, the last two, Sister Innocentia Irving and Sister Petrina Becker, arrived—11 in all, one more than originally promised.

As school would begin soon, Mother Seraphina considered it her duty to have the classrooms ready. On August 16, she organized the boys into a procession, one boy from each class carrying a crucifix. The procession filed through the school, entering each classroom where a crucifix was hung and prayers were recited. With satisfaction she noted that St. Vincent's was once again a Catholic school. Three sisters would join the teaching staff: Sister Anastasia, eighth grade; Sister Cornelia, second; and Sister Osanna, first. Five lay women would constitute the remaining staff, and 298 boys, the student body.

The sisters soon discovered what had occurred since the Brothers' departure eight months before. All the boys arrived for Sunday Mass in overalls! Horrified, the sisters determined to remedy the situation at once and set to work sewing day and night. On Sunday, October 1, the Feast of the Holy Rosary, their efforts paid off. They had the satisfaction of seeing every boy arrive at Mass neatly outfitted in a new "Sunday best" wardrobe.

On December 1, Father Peter Weber joined the staff as assistant to Father McElroy, bringing a new stimulus to the school. A farmer by birth and background, Father Weber managed the farm at St. Vincent's for the next 18 years. A better choice could not have been made:

> Under his care, St. Vincent's became almost self-supporting as far as food was concerned...he produced all the beef, the pork, the bacon and the chickens needed for food. He bred and raised his own calves. He increased the cows to

sufficient numbers that there was ample milk on the table twice a day for three hundred boys. He turned the reclaimed lands into hay and alfalfa fields sufficient to feed his stock. The orchards bore enough fruit that with the hard work of the Sisters during canning season there was abundant fruit of every description for dessert throughout the long winter months. Eggs and cream and butter abounded.[11]

Father McElroy, meanwhile, concentrated his efforts on the boys' housing. The buildings were old and in poor condition. His dreams, however, required funds. From Archbishop Hanna he obtained permission to preach in the parishes. Sunday after Sunday he stood in the pulpits of the Archdiocese and told the story of St. Vincent's. He shared his ambitions for the boys. He hoped to replace the old institutional type buildings with a cottage system—with one difference: He would not separate the units. The boys would live in groups of 30. He envisioned a living room in each unit with a fireplace, and upstairs a dormitory containing 30 beds and a private room at one end for the housemother. He pictured an auditorium for the boys with stage and projection room. His enthusiasm caught on, and the money poured in—so generously that ground-breaking for the first building consisting of three units took place on December 8, 1923, and construction began in January.

On December 15, 1924, Father McElroy blessed the first completed cottage and the same afternoon Sister Sebastiana and her boys moved into their new home. Two evenings later, an excited student body initiated the auditorium by viewing their first film in the new theater.

The previous June, 13 boys had received their elementary school diplomas. It was time to "farm them out," but Father McElroy was averse to turning boys out at so young an age and decided to keep them another year. He therefore added a ninth grade. The staff would now consist of four sisters, two lay women, and one layman responsible for teaching a combined eighth and ninth grade.

School closed that year with 394 boys, 13 of whom were graduates ready to enroll in the ninth grade. What to do with the boys ready for the tenth grade? The solution, obviously, was to add another grade. The director decided to make the ninth and tenth grades into a commercial high school in which business English, typing, shorthand, bookkeeping, math, and religion constituted the curriculum. Five sisters and three laymen made up the faculty, the laymen teaching the older boys.

The erection of the next building presented a real financial hurdle. Priests, sisters, and boys began a novena to the recently canonized St. Therese of Lisieux, more widely known as the "Little Flower." Within a week $57,000 in contributions came in! Encouraged by the amazing results, Father McElroy decided to hold a novena to the Little Flower once each month, beginning on the First Friday. So strong was his faith that he ordered the tearing down of another dormitory immediately in preparation for the erection of a third cottage. With every building Father McElroy's philosophy became more clear. He was convinced that his boys would respond to their surroundings. Consequently, the new structures were done in attractive mission style architecture, departing from the usual institutional type building. He engaged his brother, a skilled landscape architect, to design formal gardens for the grounds. The older boys poured concrete blocks for the walks surrounding the gardens and leading to a large, ornamental fountain in the center.

Construction continued through 1929, when the crowning achievement of the new St. Vincent's was completed with the generous help of an anonymous donor—the Italian Renaissance-mission style chapel, built to seat 400. Dedication was postponed, however, until June 29, 1930, when St. Vincent's celebrated its Diamond Jubilee. On the Jubilee day, attended by thousands, Archbishop Hanna preached at the Mass, Bishop John J. Cantwell of Los Angeles gave the Benediction, the 90-voice St. Vincent's Boys' choir sang, and the St. Vincent's band presented a concert before and after the ceremonies. Choir boys and band were dressed in smart, new uniforms—another evidence of the priest director's philosophy. To the gratification of all present, Father McElroy's work for the boys was recognized by the Holy Father, Pope Pius XI, when Archbishop Hanna invested him in the robes of a monsignor.

In addition to the construction program, Monsignor McElroy was responsible also for other important changes at St. Vincent's. Perhaps the most significant was the decision made in 1935 to introduce a two-year academic high school program to replace the commercial curriculum. The number of college graduates who re-

Chapter 22 / MISSION TO MARIN

The new dorm buildings and gardens at St. Vincent School for Boys

St. Vincent Chapel

ceived their early secondary preparation at St. Vincent's attests to the solid foundation, as well as to the incentive given them to aspire to higher education. Monsignor McElroy next changed the name of the institution. Dropping the use of such labels as *orphanage* and *asylum*, he renamed the home St. Vincent's School for Boys. He had justification for the change. Recently introduced social practice sanctioned the placing of orphans in foster homes rather than orphanages. With scarcely any full orphans left on the roster, St. Vincent's was now becoming identified as a home for boys forced by circumstances to be placed outside their families for reasons of parental illness, divorce, or other like causes.

Other changes followed in rapid succession. Placed in charge of the Catholic Youth Organization (C.Y.O.) when it was introduced into the Archdiocese, Monsignor McElroy enthusiastically endorsed the program at St. Vincent's. Teams were organized, and soon green and white basketball and baseball uniforms dotted the grounds. When a St. Vincent's team went out to play, the band accompanied it, resplendent in green and white. Not only the band but a newly organized drum corps, also in uniform, were soon marching on the streets of San Francisco. Swimming was added next. An outdoor pool, the gift of a generous donor, was constructed in the boys' yard, and St. Vincent's became the scene of annual swimming meets.

Another outlet for the boys that the director introduced was the annual Christmas play. To the sisters was assigned costume-making, which usually began around Thanksgiving. The success of the productions guaranteed their continuance until interrupted by World War II, but once peace was declared, the house lights glowed again.

In August, 1942, a sixth sister was added to the teaching staff, bringing the Dominican community to twenty. The number did not hold for long, however. On December 1st, St. Vincent's beloved infirmarian, Sister Coletta Breidinger, who had served the boys faithfully for 13 years, died of a heart attack.

Five months later, tragedy struck again. Monsignor McElroy had suffered a heart attack in January, but was well enough by Easter to sing the *Missa cantata* for the boys and staff. Later in the day, he enjoyed dinner with his sister and brother in San Francisco, returning to St. Vincent early in the evening. At 10 p.m., he suffered a massive heart attack and died within minutes. Shocked and saddened, the boys sang a Requiem Mass for Monsignor on Tuesday morning in his beloved St. Vincent's Chapel. His body was taken to San Francisco, where the funeral took place in St. Mary's Cathedral on the following day. Father Leo Powelson, Working Boys' Club director, summarized Monsignor McElroy's work for the boys at St. Vincent's:

> From an orphanage he converted an institution into a home in which he was the father, the Dominican Sisters the mothers. From an orphanage, he pioneered the cottage system wherein he was the elder brother of the family. From an orphanage he established a school, the graduates of which he always spoke proudly, followed their careers closely, shared their joys gladly, shouldered their sorrows intimately.[12]

St. Vincent's had lost a true father and friend, who instilled in the boys self-respect and wholesome pride. It was good to be a "St. Vincent's boy".

Father William Burke, who had served as Monsignor McElroy's associate director for seven years, was appointed director in Monsignor's place. Named associate director and principal of the school was Father John T. Dwyer, recently ordained priest of the Archdiocese of San Francisco. Father Burke's experience as associate director was excellent preparation for his new role. Under him the St. Vincent policy of having every boy off the premises at Thanksgiving, Christmas, Easter, and at least two weeks during the summer, was initiated.

During his administration also he replaced the heating system, installed hot water, renewed the mattresses in all dormitories, and had the buildings painted. Maintenance was Father Burke's forte, but not his only concern. During Monsignor McElroy's administration, library books had been collected, but not catalogued. An appeal was made to the sisters for help, and from the Motherhouse in Mission San Jose came Sister Carmelita Keogh, with a degree in library science, to spend four months cataloging the library for the boys use.

Monsignor Clement McKenna, Director, poses with the cast of Sister Mary Edward Manning's play, "Under Mary's Mantle," directed by Sister Isabel Espinosa 1951

Msgr. McKenna: A New School and New Growth

In January, 1951, Father Clement McKenna succeeded the recently honored Monsignor Burke as Director of St. Vincent's, and Father Aloysius Sullivan followed Father John Dwyer as principal. During Father McKenna's administration a gradual but significant increase in staff took place. A new position, that of assistant administrator, was created and filled by Mr. Raymond Hebel, M.S.W. Teachers were relieved of prefect work and replaced in the role by additional staff members. The sisters' community remained constant at 20: Sister Rosalia Monaghan, superior; Sisters Wunibalda Schmidbauer, Guala Wimmer, Mauritia Bleiker, Simplicia Heim, Thecla Maeusl, and Gerarda Sturz, house mothers, Grades One to Six; and Sisters Rosalia Monaghan, Josephine Koehl, Bertrand Salas, Antonia Leber, Mary Jordan Martin, and Consolata Espinosa, teachers, Grades One to Six. Sister Marka Grips and Sister Walburgis Schmidbauer presided over the kitchen and were responsible for over 1,000 meals a day, while Sister Gertrudis Schonborn had charge of the boys' dining room. Sister Loyola Farnham, who spent 32 of her 34 years at St. Vincent's as sacristan, also served as teacher, assistant superior, and receptionist. Completing the sister staff in the sewing, laundry, and housekeeping departments were Sisters Gertrudis Schonborn, Angelina Pérez, Manessa Spagl, and Florentina Steinberger.

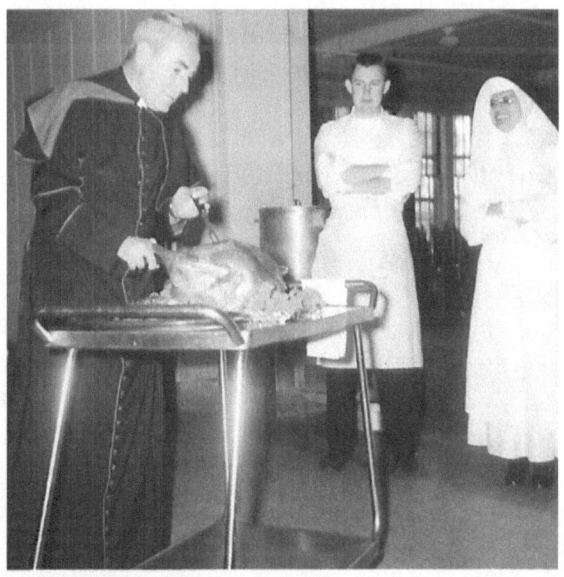

Monsignor Clement McKenna carving the Thanksgiving Day turkey

In 1954, during Father McKenna's administration, construction was begun on a new elementary school, containing six classrooms and a seventh reserved for remedial work. The students moved in on October 21, 1954. Before the year ended (December 6), Father McKenna was honored with the title of Monsignor by Pope Pius XII in recognition of his work with the boys. St. Vincent's rejoiced at the honor bestowed on the school and its director. With the dawning of the New Year, preparations began in earnest for the celebration of St. Vincent's centenary.

The celebration was observed in gala fashion on the weekend of May 21–22, 1955. Ceremonies began with an open house for religious communities in the Bay Area. The day included a pageant portraying St. Vincent's history performed by the boys and the blessing of the shrine of Our Lady of Fatima in memory of Mr. and Mrs. Vincent de Laveaga, donors. The next day, Sunday, was the public observance, which opened with a Solemn High Mass celebrated by Father John Dwyer and followed by open house, barbecue, second presentation of the pageant by the boys, and blessing of the new school by Archbishop John J. Mitty of San Francisco. Mr. Thomas J. Mellon, president of the San Francisco Chamber of Commerce and member of the California State Board of Education, was principal speaker for the occasion.

On October 19, 1958, St. Vincent's was declared a California historical landmark, the Native Sons and Daughters of the Golden West making the presentation. A bronze plaque affixed to a large boulder situated on the grounds relates the founding of St. Vincent's School for Boys.

In his *One Hundred Years an Orphan,* Father John T. Dwyer concluded his account of St. Vincent's with a tribute expressed in terms of its hundredth year:

> Under the care of Monsignor McKenna, Father Sullivan and the Dominican Sisters, nearly 300 boys are presently finding a home, an education, and character training as well as emotional stability at St. Vincent's through the excellent program maintained there. As the institution commences the second century of its existence...it has found its place as a leader among child-care homes.[13]

NOTES

[1] John T. Dwyer, *One Hundred Years an Orphan* (Fresno: Academy Library Guild, 1955) 10.

[2] Dwyer 20.

[3] Peter Rudy, *A Mission that Endures: A History of St. Vincent's School for Boys* (San Rafael: St.Vincent's School for Boys, 2001) 6.

[4] Dwyer 104.

[5] Dwyer 105.

[6] Dwyer 106

[7] Backes, letter to Vicar General, 21 September 1921.

[8] Dwyer 107.

[9] Dwyer 107

[10] Dwyer 108.

[11] Dwyer 117.

[12] Dwyer 140.

[13] Dwyer 154.

CHAPTER TWENTY-THREE

GOD ALONE

In the early morning hours of Septuagesima Sunday, February 8, 1925, Mother Maria Pia Backes, revered foundress of the Dominican Sisters of Mission San Jose, Congregation of the Queen of the Holy Rosary, answered the summons of the One Whom she had loved and served for more than 50 years of consecrated life. With a slight twitch of the lips, she died peacefully in the Lord just as the strains of the *Salve Regina,* sung by the sorrowing sisters gathered at her bedside, faded from the room.

For 20 years diabetes had complicated the pulmonary problems that had afflicted Mother Pia almost since her arrival in California. A letter to the sisters from Sister Coletta Breidinger, Mother Pia's nurse for the last 14 years of her life, described the Foundress's final days. Recurring weak spells, accompanied by loss of appetite, signaled her deteriorating condition. Nonetheless, she insisted on her daily custom of rising before the morning bell to pray the Litany of the Saints for the sisters and to be present at Mass, celebrated at 6:20 a.m. With the arrival of the day's mail she would begin her work, which generally lasted all morning. Attendance at Vespers and Compline was part of each afternoon. But as Sister Coletta reported:

> All my representations that she should not exert herself so much and should rest at least here and there in the week (what the doctor wished also) were without result. She answered, "Who knows how long I can still attend Holy Mass and receive the Lord?" [1]

It seemed as if she was in a race with death and had pressing things to do before the end. So it went until Thursday, February 5, when a definite change took place and Mother Pia's strength seemed to fade. On Friday she said to Sister Coletta:

'Oh, we must pray when we are well, for when we are ill we cannot do so anymore. Today I was not able to pray.' Dear Mother suffered so patiently and was so deeply satisfied with everything; and as often as I gave her something, she accepted it with a 'Vergelt's Gott' (May God reward you).... Since she never wanted to give any trouble for her sake, she told me to go to bed. I obeyed, but lay down fully dressed and listened sharply to every sound. [2]

On Saturday morning, according to her wish, Mother Pia received the Anointing of the Sick, praying the *Confiteor* with the chaplain and making the Sign of the Cross devoutly during the Absolution. Prior to this, she had received the Sacrament of Reconciliation and Viaticum, making her thanksgiving with profound recollection. From Saturday afternoon on Mother Pia spoke no more and asked for nothing. About ten minutes before the end, her appearance changed. Her features appeared peaceful and beautiful, becoming "more and more spiritualized....It was exactly 12:55 [a.m.] when we knelt weeping around her bed,...[that] a twitching of her lips"[3] indicated all was over.

A sorrowing Mother Seraphina set aside her own grief to share by letter with the grieving sisters the events surrounding the Foundress's death. On Monday, February 9, a Requiem Mass for the repose of Mother Pia's soul was sung in St Joseph's church, Mission San Jose, by Father John A. Leal, pastor. Word of Mother's death had spread quickly, and the Mass was attended by numerous friends, the children of St. Mary's Orphanage, and the children from the Mission San Jose public school.

Preceding the burial on the following day, Masses for Mother were celebrated in the Motherhouse chapel by Father Rodergas, Motherhouse chaplain, and three Dominican Fathers from the Western Province—Fathers Damian O'Brien, William McClory and Aquinas McDonnell. At 9:30 a.m., Mother's body was brought from the chapter room to the chapel where the Office for the Dead was prayed by the priests and sisters present. Solemn Requiem Mass followed. Very Reverend Lawrence McMahon, O.P., provincial, was celebrant; Father Gregory Rourke, O.P., deacon; and Father William McClory, O.P., sub-deacon. Father Aquinas McDonnell, O.P., served as master of ceremonies. The Right Reverend Monsignor P. J. Ryan, vicar general of the Archdiocese of San Francisco, represented Archbishop Hanna, who was out of town at the time. Members of the clergy, Mother Pia's family, sisters from other communities, our own sisters from Bay Area convents, and numerous friends joined the Motherhouse community in forming what one newspaper described as a "vast concourse"[4] of mourners who crowded into the chapel to pay their last respects to the one who had been their Mother and friend.

In his eulogy Father McMahon commented:

> If we were to regard the wishes of her whose remains are in our midst, no mention would be made of her except that which is made...in the Liturgy, but His Grace, the Most Reverend Archbishop, who would have been here this morning except for an engagement he had outside the City, feels that something should be said by way of expressing the regard the loss he feels in the passing of one who had so much to do in great part in the work of the diocese.[5]

The Provincial then spoke of Mother Pia's accomplishments for the Church, her admirable blend of a missionary and contemplative spirit, her work on the *Constitutions*—"so that after years passed and every Mother General passed, there would be something that would endure, something of promise, something of stability, something that would always guide the Sisters toward the same end, the Salvation of Souls."[6]

Mother Seraphina concluded her letter by describing for the sisters the familiar procession to the convent cemetery, where Mother had escorted so many before her:

> Then the Very Reverend Father Provincial spoke the final absolution over the body after which the sorrowful procession of Sisters, clergy, and relatives wended its way from the draped chapel to accompany the mortal remains of our beloved Mother to their last resting place at the foot of the cross in the center of our cemetery....[There] we laid to rest our dearly beloved Mother, knowing that she will be refreshed eternally by the abundance of gladsome light which in the body man cannot enjoy. Our Mother is gone

but her spirit endures. As her devoted children, let us strive to imitate her virtues; let us endeavor to remain faithful to her admonitions; let us strive to preserve her spirit in the Congregation.[7]

Mother Pia's last participation in community occurred shortly before her death when, on February 2, she took part in the observance of the Golden Jubilee of Profession of her lifetime companions and collaborators, Mother Seraphina Maerz, Mother Amanda Bednartz, and Mother Felicitas Weiss. She entered into the celebration wholeheartedly, taxing her ebbing strength to the limit and honoring the Jubilarians with a last address. With affection and gratitude she spoke:

> Let us open this sisterly gathering to honor our dearly beloved Jubilarians in the name of the Blessed Trinity—the Father, the Son, and the Holy Ghost. Amen.
>
> Although all our Houses sent their good wishes to the dear Mothers' feast...I desire to extend my heart's feelings personally. Therefore, my honorable and dearly beloved Companions, including the two dear souls who have left us for their heavenly home [Mother Gonzaga and Mother Salesia], accept the deep and sincere felicitation which I place in the Heart of the Divine Master, begging Him to pour out upon you Divine Grace and sanctifying benedictions in abundance, similar to the millions of dewdrops that cover God's earth in the early morning.
>
> I wish also to make use of this occasion to thank you for your cooperation, your prayers and sacrifices, your loyalty, good will and helping hand in the foundation and up-building of this, our Holy Father's family—our dear Congregation. The Lord be praised and thanked forever and ever!
>
> Our community is now—after much suffering, many trials and dark hours, contradictions and criticisms—on a solid footing, bearing on its brow the approval, sanction and blessing of our Holy Father the Pope and Holy Mother Church. Never can we sufficiently understand, appreciate

and give thanks for this, God's gift, which makes us true daughters of our saintly Founder and his holy Order. Considering all this, you and I might think we have finished our course, have completed our lifework and can therefore sing our *Nunc Dimittis,* but let us give this sighing for heaven into the Master's hands.

And now again, may our holy Father St. Dominic love and bless you, my venerable Jubilarians, and if God wills Ad Multos Annos. [8]

One week later Mother Pia was dead. The death of the Foundress is an event of unique significance in the lives of a religious community. For the first time the members walk without the presence of the one who formed them in the spirit and tradition of the lifestyle they have embraced. For 48 years Mother Pia had borne the responsibility of leadership, nurturing the young community in a context at once strongly contemplative in its crafting and at the same time broadly apostolic in its ambition.

In her youth Sister Pia had been captivated by Dominic's vision, had embraced it with a passion and tenacity characteristic of her, and had yearned to share it with the entire world. In Brooklyn the young Pia had no way of knowing what would be the trajectory of her life. In all likelihood, she thought to live out her span of years in the familiar surroundings and friendly security of the Eastern seaboard. And when she stepped off the train at Benicia on November 11, 1876, founding a religious congregation was probably the farthest thing from her mind. But God's designs have their own way of unfolding and would lead her, not merely to an unfamiliar land, but to a responsibility of which she had never dreamed. The challenge accepted and her fears offset by her deep faith and trust in God, she led the young Congregation through its greening years of struggle and uncertainty—at what cost to herself only God knows. Success was never a guarantee, and the bitter taste of failure and disappointment was a familiar one, but she forged ahead steadily, impelled by the vision entwined round her heart.

By nature Mother Pia was surprisingly shy, a quality that often forced her to do violence to herself in maintaining the numerous contacts with people imposed by her responsibilities. Only those who knew her well were aware of what lay concealed behind that calm and dignified mien. Father Dominicus Scheer warned her that her shyness might prove an obstacle in her work and cautioned her regarding appearances:

> Let your features portray those kind qualities of your heart; then you shall be the best of mothers. Discipline must be maintained with firmness, but with love. Before acting, ask yourself: 'How would Jesus act?' When people come to visit in the parlor, think: "God has sent them." [9]

This advice Mother Pia did not always find easy to follow. A strain of melancholy in her personality seemed aggravated by her frequent spells of illness, causing her to over-react at times and she worried on occasion about the impression the Congregation was making, tending to take the responsibility to herself. "It seems that people here begin to realize that we are doing something for the Church," she wrote. "I do not wish to glitter—only to be counted among the laborers. We have not been making enough show—a certain dash is necessary." [10]

A woman of heart and intensity of purpose, Mother Pia had an unshaken loyalty to the Church and the Order that shaped the totality of her dedication. She never deviated from her first loves and gave to them without measure. Offsetting her physical frailty was an indomitable will. "God alone" was the motto by which she lived and died.

Through the years Mother Pia strove to penetrate the Dominican charism; and to attain a better grasp of it she went to the sources—the Dominican Fathers in Europe, even though doing so brought criticism upon her. It was simply her way—to seek advice from experts—wherever they could be found.

Central to an understanding of Mother was the love of God which engendered in her a love of neighbor, especially the less fortunate. Her hand was always out to the poor and vulnerable, and no orphaned or abandoned child was ever denied her motherly affection and support.

A gifted teacher, Mother Pia missed the children when Archbishop Alemany forbade her continuing in the classroom, and she welcomed excuses to maintain contact with them by substituting for a teacher whenever an occasion presented itself. Regularly she examined the plan books and personally conducted the end-of-term examinations to assure herself of the children's progress. If time permitted, she would drop into a classroom for a friendly visit with the children. Sister Bernadine Rusting recalled her first meeting with Mother Pia:

> It was my very good fortune to start my early education with the Dominican Sisters of Mission San Jose. I had attended St. Elizabeth's School [Oakland] only a few days when our first grade teacher, Sister Callista [Stopper], told us to be back in our places on time after lunch because an important person was coming to visit us. Sure enough, Mother Pia came....She carried a rather large package which she placed on the teacher's desk, asking, 'Sister Callista, do you have a good class this year?' 'Oh, yes indeed, Mother,' Sister answered and continued to sing our praises. Evidently pleased, Mother Pia took the bag and went down the rows, placing something on each pupil's desk. I couldn't imagine what it was until I saw my share....What a pleasant surprise!...All colors of delicious jelly beans! In return for her gracious kindness and beautiful smile, we all stood up and thanked her heartily. [11]

Sister Winifred Gallagher, a centenarian who entered the convent under Mother Pia, remembers her concern for the young teachers. In an era when the bishops did not readily excuse teachers from the Lenten fast, Mother would ask the Archbishop for a dispensation for her teachers and tell them: "Eat your breakfast, Sisters, and not your children." [12]

Affirming Mother PIa's interest in her sisters, an elderly sister who knew Mother Pia personally left her impression of the Foundress:

> One was always aware of her keen interest in the individual sister. One could always approach her, assured of a kind and motherly reception. If on occasion she found it necessary to administer a reproof, she was straightforward and could be quite emphatic....However, one was always aware...that Mother sought only the best interests of the sisters and of the Congregation in general. An act of kind, motherly concern towards one admonished or corrected invariably followed such an experience. Nothing that she said or did aroused bitterness. Her success in the classroom resided in

her ability to combine firmness with understanding and her sympathetic heart easily won children to her.[13]

Mother Pia's fondness for the young extended to the novices of the Congregation. Three times a week—Monday, Wednesday, and Friday—she went to the novitiate for evening recreation if she was free. She wished to get to know the newest members of the community, and she encouraged superiors to be attentive to the young. Frequently she gave instructions to the novices on some aspect of religious life, taking special interest in their formation.

Mother Pia's love for the sisters found expression in a variety of ways. To a convert sister whose family would have nothing to do with her after her entrance, Mother suggested that she have her picture taken for them, a rarely given permission in early times. Sister made an appointment with a photographer, and Mother ordered 12 copies of the most complimentary photo, one for each member of Sister's family. The "plot" worked, for the opposition dissolved with the reception of the pictures.

Of another sister Mother Pia observed: "Sister N. wrote to me. I must have hurt her feelings. Shall go South to make up. Could procure no tickets for Los Angeles earlier than the fifth—sorry."[14] But on the fifth she boarded the 4:00 p.m. train that arrived in the South at 1:30 p.m. the following day. It is safe to presume that a reconciliation was effected.

Sister Innocentia Buss was 25 years old and professed six years when she felt called to leave the convent to persuade her brother to return to the Church. Mother Pia was desolate. She invited the sisters to keep a night vigil before the Blessed Sacrament on sister's behalf and took the midnight watch herself. But despite her efforts, Sister Innocentia persisted in her intention and left the Congregation on New Year's Day, 1895. "A sad beginning," wrote Mother Pia in the Diary. "Sister Innocentia Buss left the Order at one o'clock from Los Angeles....A heavy blow."[15]

In her superiors Mother Pia encouraged charity above all. When a superior was told that she was too good to her sisters and that no one wanted to be transferred to another community, she asked what she should do, and Mother's answer was to continue just as she had been doing![16]

"Patience and kindness at home and in school, and also with Father Victor [pastor]," Mother Pia wrote to Mother Gonzaga

Buehler, superior of St. Joseph's Convent, Los Angeles. "To practice virtue is better than to do good business." And two days later she added a note:

> Just let Father Victor grumble! When Father Provincial comes, have a quiet talk with him and tell him that we are not able to fulfill all the wishes of Father Victor until we live there. He is too inconsiderate in his wishes. As to the leaving of the children, tell Father Victor without excitement to let you know when he takes children free; otherwise, this could happen again! Only no getting excited on your part.[17]

It must have been balm to Sister Gonzaga to know that Mother Pia recognized Father Victor's lack of consideration and that whatever the trouble, it was not entirely her fault. But in another letter Mother Pia admonished:

> What you told me about Sister Raymunda and Sister Hieronyma was no act of charity. Sister Raymunda told me how very good you were when you gave her...twenty-five dollars. This act of charity was not entirely pure, or you would not have reported it to me...the way you did. Well, Rome was not built in one day, and my Gonzaga cannot... be without faults all at once.[18]

The "little over-excited sister in the South,"[19] [Sister Gonzaga] was the frequent recipient of letters from Mother Pia, as she attempted to form her into a model superior. Their correspondence is a fascinating combination of spiritual reflections and homey, practical details, not to mention admonitions. But, Sister Gonzaga's devotion proved too much even for Mother Pia, who was incensed when she learned that her superior had had Mother Pia's picture enlarged at a cost of $5.00! Sister Gonzaga must, in fact, have been something of a spender in Mother Pia's eyes, for she chided her on more than one occasion for her expenditures. "You are seven sisters in the house," wrote Mother Pia, "and your milk bill is $8.85. In Oregon there are eight sisters and their milk bill is $2.25. Your vegetable bill is $2.25. Theirs is 25 cents....In November...your butcher bill was $26.79—butter $7.20—this is really grand style!"[20]

In her relations with the sisters Mother Pia proved a wise and compassionate guide. From childhood she had been a leader among her peers; as an adult she learned to temper control with understanding. It was the latter that so endeared her to the sisters.

But the sisters were not her only concern. She derived joy also from instructing adults for the reception of the Sacraments and was delighted to assist lapsed members in returning to the Church.

Mother Pia's last words to the sisters were penned some time before her death and found among her papers after her demise:

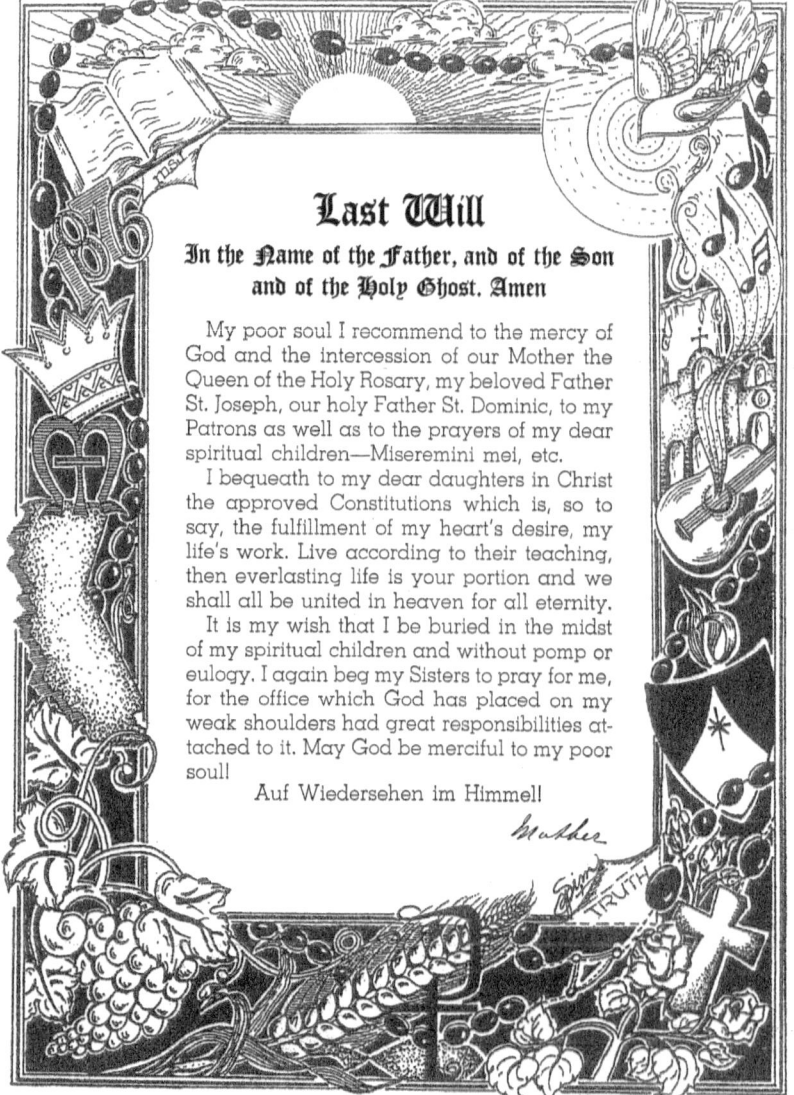

Last Will

In the Name of the Father, and of the Son and of the Holy Ghost. Amen

My poor soul I recommend to the mercy of God and the intercession of our Mother the Queen of the Holy Rosary, my beloved Father St. Joseph, our holy Father St. Dominic, to my Patrons as well as to the prayers of my dear spiritual children—Miseremini mei, etc.

I bequeath to my dear daughters in Christ the approved Constitutions which is, so to say, the fulfillment of my heart's desire, my life's work. Live according to their teaching, then everlasting life is your portion and we shall all be united in heaven for all eternity.

It is my wish that I be buried in the midst of my spiritual children and without pomp or eulogy. I again beg my Sisters to pray for me, for the office which God has placed on my weak shoulders had great responsibilities attached to it. May God be merciful to my poor soul!

Auf Wiedersehen im Himmel!

Artwork by S. Irene Mary Diones

Mother Pia's Legacy

Faithful to her call and vision, Mother Pia moved resolutely forward during her years of congregational leadership despite obstacles and opposition. Her breadth of vision is evident in the goals she set for the Congregation: the adoption of the Church's prayer as the communal form of daily worship, the providing of professional preparation for the sisters engaged in the ministry of education, and the procuring of papal approbation of the *Constitutions*. In the goals she established, she resonated to the vision of Dominic, who urged his brothers to prayer, walking up and down the choir encouraging them; *"Fortiter, fortiter,"* who sent the brothers to the great universities of Europe to study theology in preparation for preaching and teaching, and who sought approval for the *Constitutions* for the brothers before his death.

The Divine Office / The Liturgy of the Hours

At a time when the Divine Office was the entitlement of clergy and cloistered religious, Mother Pia dared to think differently. She had learned to love the Breviary in Holy Cross Convent, Brooklyn, and wished her sisters—whether Second or Third Order—to benefit from praying with the Church.

The decision to retain the Office became an increasingly painful one, but so convinced was she of liturgical prayer as a constitutive element of Dominican life that she sought it unremittingly for the Congregation. "Love the Divine Office, the *Opus Dei*, God's Work," she urged the sisters, "The Divine Office is the prayer of our Holy Mother Church;...let us appear with her before the Throne of the Most Holy Trinity. Recite it with all the solemnity possible...."[22] The praying of the Church's Prayer was Mother Pia's treasured bequest to her sisters.

From the beginning, music played a significant part in the community prayer of the Congregation and in the training of the sisters. More than a decade before Pope Pius X's *motu proprio* on Church Music (1903), Mother Pia had made up her mind to provide a firm liturgical foundation for the sisters' prayer. She determined to have them trained in Gregorian Chant, the approved chant of the Church, and entrusted the Motherhouse Chantress the responsibility for training the formation groups. As members of the Motherhouse choir, the sisters were taught to sing a *Missa cantata* on Sundays and the principal feasts of the liturgical year, as well as to render the daily Office in both its simple and solemn forms, with beauty. From Pope Pius X's *motu proprio* Mother Pia drew strong support. The Pope ordered the restoration of the Gregorian Chant, which, he said, possessed the qualities proper to the liturgy, namely, sanctity and goodness of form (#2).

Motherhouse choir practices were part of the weekly program, and the sisters became quite proficient in sight-reading. To the present day, the liturgy has retained a central place in congregational celebrations.

When Teresa Kratz made application to enter, Mother Pia felt she had the one she wanted. Born in Essen, Ruhr, Germany, on December 28, 1879, she entered the Congregation at Altenberg on May 4, 1907, received the habit and religious name, Sister Gregoria, on October 3 of the same year, and made profession on October 7, 1908. The early years of her professed religious life were spent in Altenberg teaching music until she was sent to study liturgical music with the monks of the renowned St. Gregory Academy of Church Music in Beuron. The ancient German cloister had been restored as a Benedictine abbey in 1868 under the leadership of its first abbot, Dom Maurus Wolder, who promoted vigorously the study of the liturgy and the Chant. Modeling his efforts on the work of Dom Prosper Gueranger of the monastery of Solesmes in France, he set in motion the modern liturgical revival in Germany and for two years. Sister Gregoria eagerly absorbed the monk's teaching.

After completing her studies, Sister was missioned to the United States to direct the Motherhouse choir and teach organ and liturgical singing to the novices. Sister was also asked to give courses in the Chant at Conaty High School and Mt. St. Mary's College, Los Angeles. As Motherhouse chantress, Sister Gregoria exercised a profound influence on the sisters' rendering of the Divine Office and the celebration of daily Mass.

To assist the sisters of the local communities in keeping current in liturgical practice, Sister Gregoria introduced *Opus Dei*, a quarterly publication of the Congregation. It was her aim to improve and establish more firmly the recitation of the Divine Office and the celebration of the Holy Mass as a worthy unified prayer-worship. She compiled also a *Ceremonial,* translated and adapted from that of the Dominican Fathers and other approved sources. It was corrected and approved by Father Bruno Hespers, O.P., cantor at Santa Sabina in Rome.

In 1929, Sister Gregoria published *Cantemus,* a compilation of English hymns and liturgical chants. Originally intended for limited use, the demand for the hymnal called for wider distribution than she had anticipated. Sister Gregoria, who identified herself in the preface simply as "The Author," explained that the hymnal

> ...meets the needs of the pupils in our Catholic schools from the kindergarten to and throughout college and is adapted to the use of every Church service. The melodies, partly ancient, partly modern, and partly original compositions, are elevating and melodious in form, possess emotional life, and supplement the texts in their very essence....A new feature which is lacking in most of our hymn books is presented in the prelude for each English hymn, thus making prelude books unnecessary.[23]

Among several commendations Sister Gregoria received for the hymnal, Father Edgar Boyle, director of music for the Archdiocese of San Francisco, called the *Cantemus* "one of the notable liturgical offerings made in commemoration of the twenty-fifth anniversary of the promulgation of the *motu proprio* of our late Pontiff, Pope Pius X." Declaring the hymns "in strict conformity with the *motu proprio*" and the preludes "a decided improvement in hymnody," Father Boyle heartily recommended "the book as being particularly suited to the liturgical needs of convents and parochial schools."[24]

In much the same vein, the choir master of St. Joseph's College, Mountain View, California, B.F. Marcetteau, lauded Sister Gregoria's work:

> The calm, graceful, and devotional style of the melodies, the sweet and easy flow of the harmony, reveal the inspiration of an able musician deeply imbued with the spirit of Gregorian Chant, which Pius X gives as 'the supreme model of all sacred music,' and well acquainted with the classic polyphony of the Palestrinian School which the same Holy Pontiff praises so highly in his *motu proprio* on Church Music.

The present work is therefore worthy of commendation for its musical value and liturgical character.[25]

A revered tradition in the Congregation is the annual choral rendering of Felix Knubben's three-voice composition, *Jubilate Deo*, at the solemn entry of the Sister Jubilarians in the Motherhouse chapel on the morning of Jubilee Day. The beautiful anthem was composed by the maestro for the annual celebration at the request of Sister Gregoria.

Sister Mary Bertha Rehers

A few months before her death, Sister Gregoria suffered a severe heart attack, from which she never fully recovered. In May, while walking in the garden of St. Mary's Priory, she suffered another attack, which proved fatal. Sister's burial took place at the Motherhouse, where the girls from St. Mary's formed a guard of honor leading to "God's Acre."

Because of its close linkage with the prayer life of the sisters, the position of Motherhouse chantress or choir director has always been held in high esteem in the Congregation. Among the sisters responsible for directing the choir following Sister Gregoria were Sister Mary Catherine Schmidt, Sister

Sister Concepta Maciel

Mary Bertha Rehers, Sister Concepta Maciel, and Sister Mariella Savant.

Classical, as well as sacred music, also figured prominently in the story of the Mission San Jose Dominicans. As early as Mother Seraphina Maerz's arrival on the West Coast (1878), music was added to the curriculum. A little later, Mother Pia could write to her friend, Mother Hyacinthe of Racine: "Yes, every mission has a music teacher. Music is in much demand here."[26]

Sisters Aloysia McSweeney, Callista Stopper, Cyrilla Poschmann, and Lioba Doehman built up a strong music department at Immaculata Academy in Portland. Sister Lioba, an accomplished violinist in Belgium, taught violin, piano, and organ at Immaculata and Sacred Heart, Los Angeles, for a total of 64 years. Sister Pulcheria Reichert and Sister Stella Zimmerman established a music department at Immaculate Conception Academy, San Francisco, that earned an excellent reputation throughout the City.

The sisters in Mexico also introduced fine arts into their program of offerings. Sister Teresa Meyer taught piano and voice, and Sister María Cecilia Díaz, who made her novitiate in the United States, returned to Mexico to assist in teaching piano. Sister Josefina Veloz, gifted with a beautiful voice, attended music conservatory in Mexico City and gave voice lessons until the persecution forced her recall to California.

In the late 1940s, Sister Clementina Lafevre and Sister Paula von Tessen established Rosary Studio at the Motherhouse, Mission San Jose, with the intention of teaching a few students in the area. But in 1948, Sister Alberta Oehlke, vicaress, informed Sister Mary Bertha of a request she had received from a neighbor for violin and clarinet lessons. Would Sister take care of it? Sister would! After a year at Immaculate Heart College, Los Angeles, where she earned an advanced degree in piano performance, Sister Mary Bertha returned to the Motherhouse and began a program of music instruction, affiliated to the College as Queen of the Holy Rosary School of Music, with Sister as chairperson. Soon over 200 students were enrolled, ranging from four to seventy years of age, and although the teaching staff expanded, there was an annual waiting list!

By the 1960s the College was graduating a number of music majors each year, who were eager to begin teaching under the direction of the School of Music. Among them were Sisters Marie

Yvonne Armstrong, Imelda Pellettieri, Clare Haltermann, Andre Marie Fujier, and Miriam Joseph Afflerbaugh. Students came from Fremont, Newark, and other parts of Alameda County. With a highly respected reputation, Queen of the Holy Rosary School of Music was recognized as a valuable resource in the fine arts offerings of Fremont. Mother Pia was proved right. "Music...[was] much in demand here."[27]

Study and the Ministry of Education

Describing the purpose of the Order, Saint Thomas Aquinas does so in a formula familiar to every Dominican, *"Contemplari contemplata aliis tradere"* (Contemplate in order to give to others the fruits of contemplation). Taking her cue from Saint Thomas, Mother Pia understood study as integral to the Dominican way of life.

> For a Dominican teacher...study is not something accessory, nor something more or less necessary; it is an essential element. It is an absolute duty.
>
> The study of theology, as an essential part of our Dominican formation, has a contemplative as well as an intellectual dimension. It is not divorced from, but rather grows out of our apostolic commitment. Indispensable for our work of preaching, it does not draw us away from pastoral concerns, but allows us to respond more effectively to the needs and sufferings of people.[28]

Though without personal ambition, Mother Pia wished her teachers as professionally prepared for their work as their public school colleagues; hence, her desire to have the postulants complete high school, if they had not before entrance done so already, and proceed at once to normal school. As early as 1887, she was already thinking: "A letter from Mother Superior, telling me that the Sisters in Brooklyn are preparing for the Regents' examination for teachers....The thought struck me today to have Sister Alberta [Hocker], Sister Dominica [Klein], and Miss Maggie O'Connor [postulant] obtain public school diplomas."[29]

In a communication addressed to the superiors of the Congregation the Foundress summarized a General Council meeting (January 3, 1916) that dealt with teacher preparation. Among the decisions reached was one permitting the sisters to attend the summer sessions of the University of California in Berkeley in order to pursue courses other than those dealing with religious or moral issues. Another announced that selected sisters would be allowed to attend summer school at Creighton University in Omaha. The letter was to be shared with the sisters.

In 1917, Mother Pia proposed to the General Council that the Congregation open a House of Studies in Washington, D.C., for the purpose of sending sisters to study at the Catholic University of America. The Council endorsed the plan enthusiastically and designated Mother Seraphina Maerz and Sister Dolorosa Wallrath to represent them in investigating sites. The two left by train for Washington on Sunday, September 23, on a mission that included, in addition to searching for an appropriate site, enjoying the fringe benefits of a visit with Mother Seraphina's relatives in New York, Sister Dolorosa's family in Illinois, and the Motherhouse of the Dominican Sisters in Brooklyn. They arrived in Washington, D.C., on Saturday, September 29, where they were met by Sister Bernardina Michel, who was studying at the Catholic University. The days in Washington were occupied in making themselves known. Strategic contacts were made with the Apostolic Delegate, Msgr. Bonzana; Bishop Shahan; and the Dominican Fathers. They also inspected a number of sites but did not come to a definite decision.

Leaving Washington for New York on October 12, they were welcomed heartily at the Motherhouse on Montrose Avenue. The sisters took them to Amityville, which Sister Dolorosa described in her diary as "a beautiful place [with a] wonderful chapel and a real convent....The sisters were all very lovely to us and I wept when we left the convent."[30] Visits to Mother Seraphina's relatives; to Mother Aveline in Caldwell, New Jersey; to Sister Dolorosa's family in Evansville, Illinois followed in rapid succession. Five days later, on October 29, Sister Dolorosa wrote in the diary:

> Left all my dear ones early this morning and I shall never see my dear parents again this side of the grave....My dear father followed us to the station just to see me once more. God bless him![31]

The sisters' next stop was the Motherhouse of the Dominican Sisters of Racine, Wisconsin (October 31). Sister Dolorosa, with her sharp eye open for detail, pronounced the Motherhouse, "a very nice convent."[32] In the company of Mother Romana, Racine prioress, the travelers left for Chicago to call on Archbishop Mundelein and then set out for Peoria, Illinois to visit Mrs. Theresa Hagemann, Sister Rosina's mother. Returning to Chicago, they spent the afternoon with Sister Mary Catherine Schmidt's mother, brother Herbert, and sister Edith and children, as well as Sister Leopolda Brzeska's aunt. The relatives were overjoyed to receive first-hand reports of their dear ones so far away from home.

At length the weary travelers arrived in Oakland (November 8, 1917) after an absence of some six weeks, and reported to Archbishop Hanna the next day. To their surprise the Archbishop, who had heartily endorsed the idea of a Washington House of Studies earlier, now advised delaying pursuit of the project until the war was over. On the strength of his advice, Mother Pia decided to postpone implementing the plan. Though in the ensuing years sisters were sent to Catholic University to study, the house in Washington, D.C., never materialized.

First mention of a School Board for the Congregation is found in the General Council Minutes for August 1, 1918. The early members were: Sisters Innocentia Irving, General School Directress; Dominica Klein; Bernardina Michel; Rosaria Huber; and Pius Marbaise. The Board was policy-making for the schools owned or staffed by the Congregation and functioned in a consultative capacity to the Prioress General and her Council.

Perhaps the best expression of Mother Pia's views on the training of the sisters is found in Chapter XXII of the 1923 *Constitutions*, where she addresses preparation of the sisters for their work: "Our Congregation is devoted to the education of...young children, with special love for the poorer class, without excluding, however, children of more advanced age or of higher social rank....This vocation imposes the duty of careful and zealous preparation."[33] A recurring theme follows:

> We must consider it a point of honor that our institutions be nowise inferior to the State or to other private or public associations. As far as circumstances permit, we shall, therefore, endeavor to obtain the same diplomas and college degrees as are required in public institutions of learning.
>
> The Prioress General must...take care to afford the

> young sisters, according to their aptitude, the academic and professional training...[that] will qualify them for the creditable discharge of their duties in our various departments of education....
>
> A thorough course of studies terminated by a successful examination must not, by any means, be considered an adequate preparation for so difficult a task as teaching. It is necessary that study be continued in order to avail ourselves of every possible means for rendering our instructions more fruitful and efficacious for our pupils.[34]

Concluding the section is a caveat reminding the sisters that they "guard themselves against the passionate pursuit of knowledge."[35]

A sister who recalled Mother Pia's concern for the sisters' preparation for teaching writes of the difficulties she encountered, particularly from pastors:

> Great were the difficulties she encountered when she established the so-called "Professed Novitiate," now the Juniorate. In her attempt to carry out...[the idea] designed for the two-fold purpose of continued systematic spiritual formation and professional training, she met with opposition both from within and without, but particularly from pastors who, almost without exception, were loathe to engage lay teachers, maintaining that one year of canonical novitiate was sufficient to insure acceptance and success in the classroom.[36]

Section Two of the same chapter, entitled "Education and Instruction of Pupils," begins::

> The term "education" comprises all the means enabling us to implant, cultivate, and render fruitful the Christian spirit in souls, so as to lead them to an open and sincere profession of the Catholic Faith....The teaching sisters shall consider themselves as co-operators of Jesus Christ....The sisters shall endeavor to form the characters of the children conformably to the principles of the Gospel.[37]

Mother Pia then writes at length of the importance of religious instruction, but she does so without minimizing preparation in other subjects:

> The importance attached to religious instruction shall, by no means, be detrimental to the secular branches. Our Congregation must bestow the utmost care upon the proper management of the schools and upon the improvement of the methods employed, fully aware that by these means the blessing of a Christian education shall be extended to a greater number of children. For this reason, it is the duty of every sister engaged in teaching that she strive to attain the highest proficiency in the branches she teaches and that she apply her modest talent to best advantage. She does not thereby fail against humility, for her aim is not vain display, but with trust in God for success, she seeks only to accomplish the duty imposed by obedience.[38]

From Europe Mother Pia wrote home to the sisters encouraging them at the beginning of a school year:

> Your schoolwork will soon begin again. Try to do your very best in the classroom—educate first—then teach. To be able to do this, as God wishes done, you must sanctify yourself first of all. Then prepare every lesson scrupulously and lastly teach with heart and soul, not minding the voice of self-love. You may rely on my poor prayers and blessing.[39]

Today, the Dominican Sisters of Mission San Jose still rely on Mother Pia's "prayers and blessing" in their ministry of preaching and teaching.

The *Constitutions*

The Constitutions of 1923 was for Mother Pia her most important contribution to the Congregation. In compiling them, she sought the advice of her Dominican brothers, and they did not fail her. Father Ceslaus Hansen, assistant to the Master General in Rome; Andrew Cardinal Fruewirth, Dominican Master General; Bishop Thomas Esser, consultor to the Congregation for Religious; Father Dominicus Scheer, assistant to the Master General; and Father Louis Nolan, consultor to the Congregation for Religious, gave generously of time and advice in preparing a constitution acceptable to Rome. Father Ceslaus went over the *Constitutions* line by line, word by word, and admitted in a letter to Mother Seraphina that "it...

[was] a work ten times more difficult than I had imagined."[40] The modifications required by the Congregation he found "both good and desirable. All those points which you have at heart have remained unchanged."[41]

It would be indeed difficult to over-estimate the importance of Father Ceslaus's work. His letters testify to the painstaking quality of his labor. Any article he modified he submitted to Mother Pia through Mother Seraphina, stating his reasons for the change, which he often discussed initially with Father Nolan. Article 264, for example, dispensed the sisters from abstinence if the feast of a saint of the Order or St. Augustine fell on a Wednesday—customarily a day of abstinence in the Congregation. Father Ceslaus wrote to Mother Seraphina:

> Father Consultor [Nolan] advises to add: feasts of Our Lord, Christmas, Epiphany, all feasts of the Blessed Mother, Saints Joseph, Peter and Paul, and All Saints. I agree with this because they are great ecclesiastical feasts. I hope dear Mother you also agree.[42]

And when about to wind up his work on October 26, 1921, he wrote to Mother Seraphina: "I will let the whole business go once more through my head."[43] The contribution of this "always devoted brother" (as he signed his letters) in obtaining papal approbation of the *Constitutions* merits the prayerful gratitude of the Mission San Jose Dominicans.*

When the *Constitutions* were papally approved in 1922, Mother Pia recognized the achievement as the culmination of her life's work. She could now die in peace. But the words of her "Report of Forty-eight Years Incumbency, 1876–1924," addressed to the delegates of the Fifth General Chapter the year before her death, convey little of the worry and effort expended. "Sincere thanks to God," she concluded her report, "and also to the Most Reverend Prelates in Rome who gave their assistance towards the accomplishment of this difficult task."[44]

But the truest summation of Mother Pia's life's work is contained in her simple words: "We came to the most distant point of

---

* Father Hansen spent his remaining years as chaplain of Sts. Peter and Paul Priory, Altenhohenau. He died July 6, 1928, and is buried among his "devoted sisters."

the United States to work in the vineyard of the Lord and to spread the work of our holy father, Saint Dominic."[45]

NOTES

[1] Coletta Breidinger, O.S.D. (nurse to Mother Pia) "An Account of Mother Pia's Last Days," (16 February 1925) 1.

[2] Breidinger 3.

[3] Breidinger 4–5.

[4] "Valiant Woman, Worn With Years and Labors, Goes to Her Reward," *The Leader*, (San Francisco) 14 February 1925.

[5] Lawrence A. McMahon, O.P., 10 February 1925.

[6] McMahon.

[7] Maerz, letter to Sisters, 16 February 1925.

[8] Backes, letter to Jubilarians, 2 February 1925.

[9] Backes 202.

[10] Backes 220.

[11] Bernadine Rusting, O.P., "Memoirs of Mother Pia," Interview 1976.

[12] Winifred Gallagher, O.P., Interview 2002.

[13] Anonymous Account, Dominican Sisters Archives, n.d.

[14] Backes 169.

[15] Backes 166.

[16] Backes, letter to Buehler, 27 November 1893.

[17] Backes, letter to Buehler, 29 November 1893.

[18] Backes, letter to Buehler, 1 October 1896.

[19] Backes, letter to Buehler, 18 June 1895.

[20] Backes, letter to Buehler, 8 February 1899.

[21] Backes, "Last Will of Mother Pia," n.d.

[22] Backes, "Retreat Book" n.d. (possibly 1911).

23. Gregoria Kratz, O.P., *Cantemus*, Preface, 1929.
24. Edgar Boyle, *Cantemus*, "Recommendations," 1929.
25. B. F. Marcetteau, *Cantemus*, "Recommendations," 1929.
26. Backes, letter to Oberbrunner, n.d.
27. Backes, letter to Oberbrunner, n.d.
28. *Constitutions* (1923) 160.
29. Backes 83.
30. Wallrath, diary, 17 October 1917.
31. Wallrath, diary, 29 October 1917.
32. Wallrath, diary, 1 November 1917.
33. *Constitutions* (1923) 160.
34. *Constitutions* (1923) 160–161.
35. *Constitutions* (1923) 161.
36. Anonymous n.d.
37. *Constitutions* (1923) 161.
38. *Constitutions* (1923) 162–163.
39. Backes to Sisters on retreat, n.d.
40. Backes, letter to Sisters, n.d.
41. Hansen, letter to Maerz, 20 January 1921.
42. Hansen, letter to Maerz, 22 December 1922.
43. Hansen, letter to Maerz, 26 October 1921.
44. Backes, "Report of Forty-Eight Years Incumbency: 1876–1924."
45. Anonymous, "Sketch of Mother Pia's Life," 8 February 1962.

CHAPTER TWENTY-FOUR

MINISTRY UNDER FIRE

Conditions were worsening in Mexico. The focus of persecution was now the Church and its properties, the clergy and the religious. The *Constitution* of 1917 was specific. Article 3 stated that all teaching in government and private schools was to be done by lay teachers, and Article 130 ordered the confiscation of any school teaching religion. Private schools were subject to governmental supervision, churches were national property and could be used for other purposes, and priests and religious institutions were no longer recognized as legal entities. All hope for the Church seemed lost when the self-styled "iron man" of Mexico, Plutarco Elías Calles, was elected president in September 1924. "The die is cast,"[1] wrote Sister Pius Marbaise, novice director in Mexico, to Mother Seraphina at the Motherhouse in California. Cast or not cast, the die in no way deterred the sisters from continuing their missionary endeavors, if not in one place, then in another.

Prior to the election of Calles, the sisters had managed, though with growing uneasiness. Sister Teresa Meyer remained at *Colegio García-Conde*, Tlalpam, until 1919, when the sisters responded to a request to open a day and boarding school in a second suburb of Mexico City, San Rafael. Within the first month of its opening the school increased in enrollment from an initial 75 to 119, and by 1921, to a high of 375. *Colegio San Rafael* continued to flourish until Calles's Penal Code forced its closure in 1926. Other than the above enrollment figures and the years of origin and termination, little is

Community of Inmaculada Concepción in Tlalpam 1919: Front Row (l to r) Sisters Rosita Suárez-Peredo, Catalina Gutiérrez, Teresa Meyer, Superior, Josefina Veloz and Teresita Coghlan; Back row Sisters Amada Gazano, Concepción Pascal, Inés Perochena, Adelaida Domínguez, Christina Gomez, Verónica Landaverde, and Rosario Aguerrebere

known of the school since neither chronicles nor correspondence remains. The same is true of a foundation of even shorter duration (1923–1926) at Chimalistac, San Angel, D.F., the *Colegio de Nuestra Señora de Loreto*. An elementary day and boarding school for girls, it opened in a home owned by Señor Luciano Tagle, a friend of the sisters. Fearful of having their benefactor's property confiscated when religious persecution broke out in earnest, the sisters withdrew and returned the house to the Señor.

On January 2, 1923, four sisters—Sisters Carolina Canalizo, superior-principal; Rosario Aguerrebere; Joaquina Nuñez; and Columba Dávalos—left San Rafael by train to open *Colegio Santa Rosa de Lima* in the town of San Felipe in the northern part of the State of Guanajuato. On their arrival they were met by pastor, parishioners, and children who "came out to greet us with respect and tokens of affection. It seemed like the triumphal entry of Our Lord to Jerusalem. As...[we] entered the illuminated little chapel,... the organ thundered loud peals of joy to announce the arrival of the new teaching sisters." [2]

Awaiting the sisters was a spacious classroom, large enough to accommodate 80 students. Word of the newcomers' arrival spread rapidly, and within two days the sisters noted with satisfaction the growing enrollment that would allow them "opportunities to practice charity by accepting poor children without tuition." [3]

For two years all was quiet at Santa Rosa and the school made rapid progress, but in January, 1925, the sisters received a warning to be on the alert. Someone, the caller advised, had informed the civil authorities that religion was being taught in the school. This was in direct opposition to the *Constitutions!* Failure to conform would result in their immediate arrest.

Concerned on the sisters' behalf, the townspeople urged the sisters to exchange their religious habits for secular garb, and a procession of friends bearing black suits and dresses appeared at the convent door throughout the day. Admirable as such generosity was, it created a challenge within the convent, seamstresses working far into the night adjusting hems and taking in or letting out seams depending on the height and/or girth of the recipient. Presently all were outfitted reasonably, if not fashionably, for the arrival of the inspectors. But change of garb proved no help. On February 12, a saddened annalist recorded: "The dreaded day has

Students of *Colegio Santa Rosa de Lima* at San Felipe 1923

arrived. Since the last visit by the civil authorities, all that we knew would happen has come to be realized—that our school would be closed, that we must leave or else be apprehended."[4] And the tension mounted when a friend arrived breathless with the announcement: "I bring you very alarming news. Tomorrow at 9:00 a.m., the commandant will be here to apprehend all of you."[5]

Hastily the sisters prepared to leave. In the event that the official might decide to arrive early and take them by surprise, the sisters spent the night on the roof where Father Juan Pérez, pastor, had ordered a ladder placed for their escape to the house of a neighbor. Nothing out of the ordinary occurred, however, and in the early morning hours the sisters prayed their Office quietly and received Holy Communion. Then, ghostlike, they filed silently from the convent and entered the cars provided by friends. Their destination—San Luis Potosí. They would not return to their convent in San Felipe again. *Colegio Santa Rosa de Lima* bears the unenviable distinction of being the first house of the Congregation confiscated by the Mexican government.

Not to be underestimated, however, was the courage of the "fugitives." Refusing to abandon the children of San Felipe to godless education, the sisters returned one by one to the town in "disguise," that is, in lay clothes, and took up residence with various families, who risked imprisonment and confiscation of property in order to harbor them. In the quasi security of private homes the sisters taught small groups of children, never more than nine in a house, as ten, by government decree, constituted a "school."

Meanwhile, Sister Teresita Coghlan, superior of the abandoned convent in San Felipe, had become critically ill, and Sister Pius Marbaise assumed responsibility for the sisters in Mexico. In the harrowing months that followed, she would make her mark!

El Rosario Novitiate

Sister Pius had had her first glimpse of Mexico in 1922. On arriving at El Rosario, the recently purchased novitiate house next door to *Colegio García-Conde*, she first met the eight novices who awaited her and was pleased to note that their Dominican vocations were being nurtured by frequent visits from Fathers Domingo Fernández, O.P., and Elías Fierro, O. P. Even minimal contact with the priests from Spain convinced her that the Fathers were true sons of St. Dominic, and she thanked God that they took such an interest in the novices. In preparation for her arrival, the sisters had put the house in excellent order, and the poverty she witnessed around her she found enchanting. As for the beauty, she was enthralled. "In the valley of Mexico," she wrote, "one feels the nearness of God and the full meaning of the *Sursum Corda!* The whole of nature invites you to praise His omnipotence, mercy, and wisdom! What would Mexico be, if it could enjoy a lasting peace? It would certainly be a true earthly paradise, but as it is, this poor country is never at rest."[6]

The poverty was real enough. In the novitiate boxes covered with oilcloth or muslin were utilized as chairs, bookcases, desks, etc. In the kitchen Sister Rosa María Zimbrón, assisted by Sister Benita Medrano ("Mama" to the novices), was ingenious in making the sisters' simple diet palatable. "We never see butter; fruit but rarely, only when visitors bring a bagful," wrote Sister Pius to her aunt. "The washing is done...around the fountain—in cold water, of course. Those who never laundered anything in their life are as willing as those who look back on an experience of years."[7]

Meantime, next door at *Colegio García-Conde*, life was not proving tranquil. Ill health and the nerve-racking revolutionary years had left Conchita irritable and demanding, a condition that her niece María's entry into the community had considerably aggravated. The latter's entrance had dealt a severe blow to the Señora, as María had managed her fortune, taken care of her correspondence and accompanied her wherever she chose to go. The Señora's love for the sisters "turned almost to gall," [8] and she began to treat them as slaves. To add to their problems the government sent an accountant to check the school's financial records and to announce that he would return shortly to take inventory. In a letter to Mother Seraphina, Sister Pius wrote: "[Conchita's] advisors will have to answer to God if this beautiful place will finally pass into the clutches of this godless government....Our sisters must put into safety their furniture and books, and we must be ready for whatever may happen in the near future and accept it now already as His Will."[9]

Sister Teresa went looking for another location for the novitiate and found a potential, but run-down property at Calle de la Moneda 2, not far from the *Colegio García-Conde*. The house had a picturesque history. Originally a gambling den for the fashionable world of the capital, it had served also as a meeting place where politicians hatched their devious plots. An elderly Spanish gentleman recalled vividly for Sister Pius the "front salons where he had seen the gold stacked a foot high. You have no idea, [he added] how many have lost their lives in this place and have been buried most probably in one of the caves under your garden."[10] But despite such tales, the sisters rented the house. Its possibilities were excellent, agreed Sister Pius. The garden was large and could accommodate their needs, which, as perceived by Sister Pius, would be two cows (since they could not afford to buy milk), chickens, geese, rabbits, sheep, and possibly a few pigs. They would also have to plant vegetables and cultivate the 400 fruit trees on the property. For this, she informed Mother Seraphina, they would need "a good German sister with common sense who will try to learn how things must be done here. She must not stubbornly want to adhere to California or German methods. The soil, the seasons are different here."[11] Meanwhile, acutely aware of her own limitations, she ordered a book on gardening!

Sister Polycarp Struffert was the German sister of Mother Pia's choice. She was well suited for the tasks assigned her. In an undated letter sometime after 1923, Sister Pius wrote to Mother Pia in glowing terms:

El Rosario Community, the second foundation in Talpalm, 1929, in the midst of the persecution: seated (l to r) Sisters Leo Greb, María de Chantal Alonso, Pius Marbaise, Teresita Coghlan and Polycarp Struffert; standing, center row, Adelaida Domínguez, Benita Medrano, Paz Madrid, María Lourdes Pons, Concepción Pascal, María Victoria Reyes and Angelica González; back row María del Pilar González, Vincenta Regalado, Carlotta Serranía and Carmelita Aureocochea

> [Sister Polycarp] is really doing wonders in the immense garden with only three Mexican boys. You should see her marvelously large cabbages, the big heads of lettuce of several kinds, the sweetest peas and beans you ever tasted, etc., the promising young plantation of quite a number of fruit trees. Next year we can invite you to sample the avocados, quinces, that were here already, and the first crop of immense golden persimmons, *toronjas* or grapefruit, the red and green plums, etc. Besides, you should see her hens that lay big eggs, and we have a litter of little pigs, and what not![12]

Despite the rave review of the garden, the threatening reports reaching the Motherhouse via refugees persuaded the General Council to form an Advisory Board for Mexico and to appoint Sisters Teresa Meyer, Pius Marbaise, Josefina Veloz, Annunciata Henke, and Margarita Lira as members. They were to consult on all important matters.

The Perils of Persecution

After a brief interlude of relative calm, President Calles showed his true colors by setting up a Mexican Catholic Church independent of Rome. Armed men entered the venerable Church of La Soledad in Mexico City and drove out the worshippers (February 1925). They were followed a few minutes later by Father Joaquin Pérez, who had been confined for some time to a mental institution, but who now appeared declaring himself the Patriarch of the Mexican Catholic Church!

That the situation was becoming more perilous the sisters soon experienced personally. One day Sisters Pius and Rosario Aguerrebere ventured into Mexico City for a doctor's appointment. Suspected of being religious, they were apprehended by the police and taken to the *Comandancia,* where they were accused of begging in the city streets, an offense strictly against the law. Elegant in her borrowed furs and jewelry, Sister Pius was an unlikely beggar, and the police were hard put to make the accusation stick. Not easily cowed, she proved a match for her accusers. Thrust in the company of drunkards, pickpockets, and prostitutes, Sister Pius asserted her American citizenship and demanded a telephone to inform the American Embassy of the outrage. The *Comisario* experienced a sudden change of heart and released the two immediately. But it had been a warning!

Advised that trouble was about to break out with renewed fury, the sisters decided to follow the advice of their German-American neighbor, Adam Weimar, and camouflage the novitiate as a residence for convalescent women, a ruse that would allow a few sisters at least to remain and take care of the house. The novices and postulants were invited to take temporary refuge in the Weimars' spacious home, and the remaining sisters would go to the homes of relatives and friends. But first things first, and six novices, Sisters Fidelis Espinosa, Isabel Espinosa, Paz Madrid, María de Lourdes Pons, Carlotta Serranía, and Carmelita Aureocochea, were ready to make profession. At 9:00 p.m. that night, while Tlalpam lay shrouded in darkness and the tension of fear, the six novices quietly entered the little chapel, the few candles bracketed on the wall providing the only light. Accompanying them were Sister Teresita Coghlan, superior, and Sister Margarita Lira, novice director, softly singing a psalm without benefit of organ. Father Francisco Franco, a young Dominican priest recently arrived from Spain, was so overcome by the similarity of the scene to the early catacombs that he could not begin the ceremony until he had conquered his tears. Following the prescribed prayers, one by one, the novices pronounced their vows, the light from the candles casting long shadows on the chapel walls. The ceremony over, all retired; there would be no fiesta that night!

The next morning the sisters, 13 in all, went quietly to their neighbor's house where Mass was offered in the reception hall, the grand piano serving as altar. A daily routine was soon established. Each evening at 8:30 p.m. the sisters pushed back the furniture in the reception hall and rolled up in sheets and blankets on the carpeted floor. Each morning at 4:15 a.m. they arose, hid their bedding in Mr. Weimer's workshop, moved the furniture into place, and began another day. Classes, prayers, meals, and recreation all took place in the reception hall. It could be described as close living!

Meanwhile, the persecution, wrote Sister Pius to Mother Seraphina on March 28, 1926, was spreading like wildfire from state to state, but the faith of the people was strong and would not be quelled without resistance. When soldiers arrived at the Church of the Sagrada Familia to arrest the foreign-born Jesuits in charge, they faced a cordon of some 3,000 parishioners, mostly women with their servants, surrounding the church. Failing to disperse the protesters at pistol shot, the soldiers called for firemen who directed their hoses into the crowd, targeting women and men indiscriminately. Making little impression on the people, they called for police backup. The officers rode into the resisters, beating them into submission with clubs. But a second cordon of women was soon formed and once again whipped brutally. Sometime later, 5,000 women advanced on the Governor's Palace demanding an audience, which was refused. Again the violence was repeated, the Police Inspector General himself galloping full speed into the crowd and striking the women viciously in their faces.

Pressure continued to mount. Orphanages, homes for the elderly poor and schools were closed without warning—desks, statues, crucifixes burned. Religious, orphans, and elderly were thrown ruthlessly into the street without provision of food or shelter. In some cases, children were offered to anyone who happened to be passing. But despite the barbarities, Sister Pius opted to stay and wrote to Mother Seraphina: "I understand your anguish, Mother dear, but we must not lose courage! If all foreign communities of teaching Sisters leave the Republic, the various Protestant sects will take over the abandoned schools; and what then?" [13]

From a trustworthy friend the sisters received word that mail sent to foreign countries was now subject to governmental inspection. From that time on, Sister Pius's letters to Mother Seraphina were coded and addressed to Mrs. Seraphina Maerz de Guzman, President. The Archbishop was henceforth referred to as "Mr. Bishop"; the Dominican Fathers as "uncles"; and Sister Leo Greb as "husband Leo."

In June the full intent of Calles' plan was revealed when his Penal Code was published. Its 23 articles forbade the teaching of religion in primary schools, demanded the immediate dissolution of all monasteries and convents, suppressed the liberty of the religious press, and declared churches, bishops' residences and private colleges property of the state. The Federal Government would decide which churches would be allowed to continue functioning. The Code went into effect on July 31, 1926. Daily Mass was no longer possible in the convent, as so many priests had been exiled or slain. Spies were everywhere, and the convent portress had to be constantly alert. Daily the list of martyrs grew longer, and when Father Miguel Pro and his companions were executed, the tension came to a head. In the face of all this, God's work continued, as priests—disguised as charcoal or kindling vendors—brought Holy Communion to private homes, heard confessions and encouraged the oppressed.

Once more the sisters moved, this time to the Espinosa country home at the rear of the novitiate garden, since Mr. Weimar had decided to sell his home and return to the United States. Moving took place as inconspicuously as possible. Dr. Manuel Infante and his family, friends of the sisters, moved into the vacated novitiate building to prevent its falling into government hands. Sister Teresita Coghlan assumed the role of housekeeper for the Infantes; Sister María Diez, receptionist; Sister Carmen, cook; and Sister Petrina, laundress. The sisters, Sister Pius assured Mother Seraphina, are "dressed in accordance with the role they are playing, and they are good actresses."[14]

Emboldened by the fact that government agents were so busy spying on priests that private schools were for the time being left in peace, the sisters reopened their school in Tlalpam on February 15, 1927. Although enrollment had doubled, it was a challenge to make ends meet, as several paid reduced tuition or no tuition at all, for the sisters refused no child in order to shield him or her from the godless teaching of the Mexican public schools. They had, in consequence, to resort to the sale of flowers from their garden, particularly magnolias which were in popular demand, as the petals, prepared in a tea, were considered a highly effective remedy for heart disease. In addition, fruit, vegetables, eggs and poultry, and rabbits were also in demand. Sisters María del Pilar González and María Luisa Flores baked a variety of homemade breads for sale and Sister María Diez provided tamales and cakes. The items proved so popular that families from Mexico City sent their servants by car to the sisters' "market" and paid well. By such means the sisters managed to make ends meet, as well as help feed the families of their poorer pupils.

About this time, Catholics calling themselves *Cristeros* (for their battle cry, "*Viva Cristo Rey!*" "Long Live, Christ the King") were proving a threat to the Mexican government. In response to the Holy Father's demands, Portes Gil, interim president of Mexico, offered amnesty to any *Cristero* who would surrender. Within a month, 500 *Cristeros* who had surrendered in good faith were shot or murdered in their homes and their property confiscated.

Since private schools were now ordered to use government textbooks, the sisters decided to follow the scriptural injunction and "Be cunning as serpents, but wise as doves" (Mt. 10:16). They would display the government texts on the teachers' desks, but teach from their own carefully prepared notes. More and more frequently government agents posing as electricians were appearing without warning to examine in detail "the lights" in every room of the school and convent, making nuisances of themselves! One stormy evening a so-called "electrician" appeared at the convent door and after the usual house inspection chose to wait out the storm in the parlor where he could observe everyone entering or leaving the building. As the hour grew late Sister María Diez, in her role as portress, had had enough of him and said: "Sir, you had better leave now as my husband will be home in a moment, and I should not like to witness the rumpus that he will make finding you here."[15] Taking the advice to heart, the agent left immediately.

Next came the census takers. To avoid questioning Sister Pius went to a friend's home disguised as a French chambermaid. Clad in a black dress, white apron and maid's cap, she was busily wielding a feather duster in the reception room when the agent appeared. Barely able to speak Spanish (although she was fluent), she escaped interrogation. From Sister Pius's letters one is led to suspect that though she describes her courage at times as "sinking below zero,"[16] it is more likely that her early attraction for the stage found an outlet in the various roles in which she enjoyed outwitting the government agents. "I think," she wrote to Mother Seraphina, "that these few examples serve to illustrate the present situation, where from morning till night you have to be prepared! Absolute trust in God and a good sense of humor are our only weapons."[17]

On March 4, 1930, Emilio Portes Gil stepped down as interim president, and on November 28, the "inept and despised"[18] Pascual Ortíz Rubio was elected in his place. Following the inaugural ceremony, the new President was seriously wounded when a would-be assassin fired several shots at him. The attack left Rubio a frightened man, suspicious and incapacitated. But standing in the wings, primed and ready, was the "iron man," Calles, who once more assumed the reins of government.

The year 1931 brought new and annoying restrictions on private schools. Sister Pius wrote that they were ordered to keep the entrance gate open from morning until late afternoon; government agents had the right to inspect all rooms, even private apartments, as well as books, music, presses, even beds!

Finally, on September 6, 1934, the blow so long anticipated fell. A notice from the Secretariate of Education stated curtly: "Your school is closed by the government." [19] The sisters were not unprepared. Commercial high schools were not affected by the order and since the girls of the fifth and sixth grades were unusually tall for their age, the sisters regrouped them as "Comercio A" and the regular commercial students as "Comercio B" and carried on as usual. The children of the other grades had to be taught in private homes in groups of no more than nine.

On December 1, a new law was promulgated, stating that any house harboring a priest, religious school or community would be confiscated and become national property. Sister Pius realized that the handwriting was on the wall. Once the children were called for by their parents, the only course available to the sisters would be to disband and return to their families. The departure began with the tearful exodus of all but four children—three Russian youngsters who awaited their grandmother's arrival from New York and one little boy whose absent father was expected back any day. Government inspectors, including *la Loba*, the "she-wolf" whose reputation was worse than any man's, continued to search the convent until satisfied that school was not in session. The house now became the temporary "home" of the wife of General Ortíz. Six "señoritas" (sisters) had their roles to play as the staff of Señora Ortíz.

In the meantime, a possible solution presented itself as an alternative to disbanding. Father José María Preciado, C.M.F., former pastor of Mission San Gabriel, had been consecrated Bishop of Colon, Panama, and he applied to Mother Seraphina for sisters to staff his Cathedral School. Mother Seraphina decided that Sister Pius should be the one to investigate Colon since she was already half way there. In preparation for her first trip by air, Sister Pius visited the airport in Mexico City, where she sought permission to view the interior of a plane. Pleasantly surprised to find it air-conditioned and comfortable, she took Step Two in her preparation: a visit to the doctor to have her heart checked for high altitude flying. All was A-OK! So off she flew to Panama and thoroughly enjoyed the ride!

Her report of the visit for Mother Seraphina began with a detailed description of the flight and a brief history of the country; she then got down to the business for which she had come. Two schools would be needed, she informed Mother Seraphina, one for black children and one for white. Since almost everyone spoke English, each school would need at the very least one English-speaking sister. A music teacher would be required for each school also. And because of the intense heat, the sisters would need habits made of a lighter material in place of wool. During her stay in Panama, Sister Pius visited several schools and was impressed by the order and discipline, as well as the furnishings and equipment. After discussing the Sister's report, the General Council voted (October 7, 1935) not to accept the mission, as the required number of English-speaking sisters could not be spared.

In January, the sisters in Mexico thought their end had come for sure when some 30 to 35 government agents invaded the house and began a thorough search of the premises. Two sisters, Sister Polycarp Stuffert and Sister María Diez, managed to escape by climbing a back wall into a neighbor's yard. Those detained in the convent were herded into the corner of an upstairs room and forbidden to speak. The four children remaining were subjected to frequent questioning though without result, and Mrs. Ortíz had to submit to a three-hour grueling, again without result.

According to Sister Imelda Espinosa's eyewitness account:

> The agents devoured everything they found in the bakery and the kitchen, and ran from one room to the other the whole night, cursing and blaspheming. Finally the sisters arranged four mattresses on the floor of one of the now empty rooms for the poor, hungry and exhausted children. Even now, they all were left without food or water. The sisters, of course, passed the night without closing an eye....In the meanwhile, these ruffians had taken whatever they found suitable for their homes. The leader had immediately ordered our beautiful chapel carpet and the Aztec furnishings of our parlor to be taken to his home. Most of the others followed his illustrious example.[20]

The next morning Mrs. Ortíz reminded the agents that the children and "señoritas" had not eaten since the previous noon. She was answered with abuse and told that all should leave the house at once and would not be allowed to return. The property now belonged to the government! To the sisters' relief, the absentee parent arrived at this juncture for his son and was given permission to take the three Russian children also.

Ousted from the convent, Sister Pius, accompanied by Mrs. Ortíz, found a suitable house in Mexico City that would accommodate six. The owner, a Catholic, was willing to rent to them. With the other sisters placed in individual homes, the sisters were soon functioning almost normally, teaching 130 children, the younger classes in groups of eight or nine—one group in the morning, another in the afternoon. The fifth and sixth grades attended class all day, but circumvented one law at least by observing the small group restriction.

Mexico, meantime, had a new president, Lazaro Cardenas, who issued an alternative directed toward private schools: Teach Socialist doctrine or be closed. A brutal attack on the Church of El Espíritu Santo in Tacubaya while services were being held resulted in 10 dead and 50 wounded. It was clear that under the new president the situation would not improve.

The next episode Sister Pius branded "ridiculous." A friend came secretly to warn her that at the sisters' former house in Tlalpam, government agents had found the skeleton of a 10-year-old Yaqui boy buried beneath the floor. Sister Pius, her friend warned her, was wanted for murder and the Mexican government had put a price on her head! That the boy had died sometime between 1910 and 1913 when the Yaquis had used the house as headquarters and Sister Pius was still in the United States seemed to have little bearing on the case. Imploring her to go into hiding, the friend left. After giving this new threat consideration, Sister Pius opted in favor of an alias; henceforth, she would be Angela Braschi, borrowing her Italian great-grandmother's name. Posing as Señora Braschi, she managed to escape arrest!

The Exodus

Finally, however, the unhappy day could no longer be postponed. A letter to Mother Seraphina announced the inevitable:

> Mother dear, you know my great love for Mexico, this mysterious land of Mary, so beautiful, so worthy of a better lot, and yet so utterly wretched on account of the inhuman cruelty of its presidents and their minions. You also realize, I am certain, that all of us, with only a few exceptions, have

strained every nerve to save as many souls as possible in our schools, and in finding ways and means to train our pupils to become apostles in their own families. Our foundation here, we know, is the apple of your eye. But now, I am forced to come to the conclusion that we must not continue, so to say *usque ad infinitum,* to stem this tide of unbelief and immorality rampant here....We can, with God's help, hold out until the end of the school year....The giving up of this foundation after all the sacrifices it cost is a sorrow to all, but I must repeat, I cannot and must not take the responsibility on my conscience for more than the end of the scholastic year.[21]

Gearing for the exodus, Sister Pius wrote again:

So far, the sisters are resigned, and their families also. Let us pray that they may be happy in their new surroundings, assuming their new duties for the love of God. You, of course, as well as I, realize that it is a tremendous sacrifice for them to leave their beloved country, their language and customs, and the never-relinquished hope to help in the building of a new Mexico in which God will have the supreme place, and human rights will be protected.[22]

Despite the dangers, it was indeed a "tremendous sacrifice" for the Mexican sisters to leave their country, but between January and April 1936, nine sisters left for the United States: Sisters Mercedes Alvarez, Albertina Ortega, and Rosita Suárez-Peredo via El Paso; Sisters Auxilia Uriarte-Healy, María del Pilar González, and Paz Madrid via Laredo; and Sisters Agustina Cerezo, María Diez, and Pius Marbaise via Nogales. The last group left by night train on April 25. Four had already gone to the Motherhouse before Christmas; the three remaining members of the Congregation in Mexico were at the Dominican Convent in San Miguel Allende, State of Guanajuato.

Convent of Santo Domingo, San Miguel De Allende

The Convent of *Santo Domingo,* located in the picturesque colonial town of San Miguel in the mountains of Guanajuato, had been founded in 1735 as a *Beaterio,* that is, a religious house in which holy women (*Beatas*) devoted their time to prayer and penance. From its foundation *Santo Domingo* had conducted a flourishing school for girls until the revolution under Juarez when soldiers took over the convent and expelled the *Beatas*—with one exception! A determined Sister María Luisa Hernández obtained from the mayor of San Miguel the keys to a small room in the convent where she established herself behind locked doors and did her best to safeguard the building. From time to time she suffered verbal abuse from the soldiers and their women, who also occupied the convent.

Following the revolution, the sisters returned to the convent and elected Sister María Luisa prioress, an office which she held until her death in 1895 at an advanced age. According to Mexican custom of the time, her body was exhumed after five years and found to be incorrupt. The sisters kept her body in a room in the *Beaterio* for three months until a vault was built for her beneath the sisters' choir. During this time the convent became a place of pilgrimage for the people of San Miguel, who venerated Sister María Luisa as a saint.

In 1880, almost a century and a half after the foundation of *Santo Domingo*, the parents of María Soledad Almaguer Soto ("Julia" to her family) entered her as a boarder in the *Beaterio*. At the time five *Beatas* were living in the convent. When Julia was 15, after two years' experience of convent life from a boarder's perspective, she asked admission to the *Beaterio* and was accepted. The prescribed postulancy completed, she received the Dominican habit and her religious name, Sister María. She was admitted to temporary vows in May 1910, and made perpetual profession in 1915.

Sister María Almaguer

The *Beatas'* lifestyle at the time of Julia's entrance might be described most accurately as that of "neighboring tenants in apartment houses."[23] Although Mass was celebrated daily and the Office of the Blessed Mother and rosary were prayed in common, each *Beata* had her own apartment and managed her own finances. Each had a personal servant who cooked the meals the *Beata* ordered and served them in her room. But in 1922, a major change occurred. Father Juan Menéndez, O.P., visited the community and, hearing their story, realized that they were neither properly affiliated to the Order and nor living a lifestyle that could, by any stretch of the imagination, be characterized as Dominican. Father Menéndez urged the sisters to communicate with the Dominican Vicar Provincial of Mexico who recommended that they affiliate with an existing Dominican congregation. He further advised them to seek admission with the Dominican Sisters of the California Congregation of the Queen of the Holy Rosary who had sisters in Mexico.

The *Beatas* began a series of canonical proceedings involving, first of all securing permission from the Bishop of León, Guanajuato, in whose diocese the convent of San Miguel is located to make the move:

July 27, 1923

San Miguel de Allende, Gto.

To: His Lordship

Msgr. Emeterio Téllez Valverde

León, Gto.

Illustrious and Right Reverend Monsignor:

The community of Religious of the Third Order of St. Dominic of San Miguel de Allende in your diocese, presided over by its prioress, Sister María Almaguer, respectfully wish to place before Your Excellency the following:

We desire to serve God by entering the Third Order of Regulars of our Holy Father, St. Dominic de Guzman in order to perfect and save ourselves and not having in this Institute the facility to attain this and for want of direction and...having had until now but little communication with the religious of the same Order. Having now learned their

Rule and their practice of it by having lived with them in their community as well as in our own and knowing the advantages of the religious life, and the great difference that we observed in our mode of living; feeling at the same time the great charity which each and all of its members have towards us, especially the Reverend Mother [Seraphina Maerz], Vicaress General of the Motherhouse and the Reverend Sister Teresa Meyer, superioress of the houses in Mexico...we do not hesitate for one moment to entreat Your Excellency to deign to take the step for our incorporation in this for us so kind and dear Institute. In it we know that under the direction of its charitable superiors, we shall be able to attain with more assurance our much desired perfection.

For now, by stating our considerations in order to attain our purpose, we wish to place as the most important necessity we have to be true religious by the practice of the three vows: poverty, chastity and obedience. We do not make such vows, because those that we make at present are made only in a private manner.

Secondly, this incorporation will help us participate in the graces, the favors and the privileges of the said Institute of which we are in need.

If Your Lordship will be interested in our favor our petition you will increase the glory of God, honor in a special manner our Holy Father St. Dominic, and you will bless us with special grace.

May God preserve Your Lordship for many years to come.

(Signed) Sister María Almaguer
Sister Margarita Lopéz
Sister Francisca Olvera
Sister Magdalena Rivera
Sister Bernarda Almanza
Sister Dominga Sánchez [24]

The Bishop's approval was not slow in coming. On July 31, 1923, he wrote to Sister Teresa Meyer in Mexico.

León, July 31 1923

M.R.M Teresa de Jesus Meyer
Superior of the Third Order Dominicans in Mexico

Reverend Mother:

There exists in the city of San Miguel de Allende in this Diocese a religious Community which bears the name of: Blessed St. Dominic," founded in the year 1750 with the permission of the Right Reverend Bishop of Michoacán and with the necessary warrants sent by two Reverend Father Provincials of the Dominican Order in Mexico.

As you will see by the letter sent me by the members that now form the present said Community, the original of which I am enclosing, they desire to join the Institute of the Third Order of St. Dominic which has various houses in Mexico, because they believe that in this way they will be able to regulate their religious life and participate in the grace which the said Institute enjoys.

By this virtue, I beg you, Reverend Mother, to place these desires before those who have the faculty in your Institute to incorporate the Community to which I refer, in such a way that for the future that Community will be considered regarding the government and the direction as one of the Institute, neither more nor less than one of the houses which it has already established.

Moreover, I wish to state that as Prelate of this Diocese, I give consent for this incorporation for which the said Community has solicited my authorization.

If you desire other information for the expressed purpose, I am disposed to give it.

(Signed) Emeterio, Bishop of León[25]

Sister María was now free to approach Mother Pia with the sisters' request for affiliation. This she did in a letter signed by the members of the community:

Santo Domingo Convent
San Miguel de Allende, Gto.

October 15, 1923

Feast of St. Teresa

Ven. Mother M. Pia, O. P., Prioress General

Very dear and esteemed Mother,

According to the wish and consent of the Most Reverend Emeterio Valverde, Bishop of León, I from my very heart and in the name of my community make a humble petition hoping that your maternal heart will deign to attend.

For about eight years we have been praying God to permit us to find a Congregation of the Third Order of St. Dominic who will admit us. Our Lord and God has done us the favor to direct us to your Congregation through the medium of our present pastor, Reverend Father Refugio Solís, delegated by the Most Reverend Bishop, already mentioned.

We are well informed of the Rule and _Constitutions_ of the Congregation of the Queen of the Holy Rosary under your maternal direction.

We are very unworthy; we know nothing, and can do nothing, yet we hope that your maternal heart will not reject us. We all have a very good will and we propose to obey in all that you command us, to go where you send us, to learn all that we shall be taught, and, in fine, we will be submissive in all [things]. So, very dear Mother, we beg you to receive us as your children in the name of our Lord. We sign ourselves your obedient daughters.

Signed: Sr. María Almaguer, Prioress
Sr. M. Francisca Olvera, Mistress of Novices
Sr. Magdalena Rivera, Procuratrix
Sr. Margarita Lopéz, Sacristan
Sr. Luisa de la Soledad Flores
Sr. Ma. de los Angeles Pérez
Sr. Bernarda Almanza [26]

Supporting the sisters' petition, Sister Teresa added a note of reassurance for Mother Pia:

> Following St. Teresa's day [October 15, 1923], Sister María Almaguer assembled her community and in our presence, read the petition to them after which Mother Seraphina and I interrogated the sisters each in turn privately to see if they were well-informed of the contents of the petition and if all were in earnest and really desired affiliation. Having been satisfied of that point, we had each one sign her name as you see.[27]

With an eye to the practical, Mother Seraphina reported to Mother Pia on the physical aspects of the convent in San Miguel:

> Revolution and poverty have caused damage to the buildings. Three years ago the Most Reverend Bishop allowed the sisters a collection throughout the entire diocese for the restoration of the convent. Up to now they have been very successful....A large refectory and a new kitchen have evolved out of the ruins. The sisters' choir, as well as several large rooms, is completely finished, too.... The convent has been built on a steep hill...[and has] seven to eight cells with numerous small rooms (called "holes") added to them at a later time that served as hiding places during the revolution.
>
> ...Their income comes from: sale of hosts, quince jelly, chocolate, candles; doing the laundry for several of the churches in neighboring communities; sewing. One girl is boarding there. Jelly, chocolate and candles are made by the sisters. They have about 15 chickens and a pig.
>
> Behind the building uphill there is a large garden. Many different fruit trees, especially quince; a great reservoir, much water. Could start a good vegetable garden! A wonderful place for relaxation and suited for retreats.
>
> This piece of land is owned by a gentleman who is willing to deed it over in the name of anyone of the sisters of the community at any time. Unfortunately this gentleman lives in Mexico City. Therefore, we are unable to see him [at the present time].[28]

As a preliminary step in the merging process Mother Pia asked two sisters from each community to live for four months in one another's convents in order to experience their respective lifestyles. Sister Catalina Gutiérrez and Sister Dominica Ochoa moved into the *Beateria* for four months, and Sister Francisca Olvera and Sister Bernarda Almanza, into San Rafael. At the end of the trial period, the respective sisters expressed satisfaction.

The canonical requirements having been duly fulfilled and the necessary permissions obtained, Mother Pia appointed Sister María Almaguer superior of the new group; she remained in that capacity for 22 years (1924–1946) with the exception of a three-year period during which Sister Natalia García de la Cadena held the office. Sister Dominga Sanchez, Sister Francisca's mother, was not accepted into the Congregation because of her age (64) and lay sister status. (The Congregation had no lay sisters at this time.) She was allowed to remain, however, as a lay Dominican and extern sister.

A ripple effect from the merging of the *Beatas* with the Congregation was the founding of *Colegio Santo Tomás de Aquino*. When Mother Seraphina and Sister Teresa paid their initial visit to the pastor of San Miguel, Father J. Refugio Solís, he took advantage of the situation to ask the sisters to open an elementary school for boys in his parish. They promised to do so the following year. In fulfillment of their promise *Colegio Santo Tomás de Aquino*, located near the parish church of San Miguel, opened in July 1923.

When religious persecution broke out in Mexico under President Calles in 1926, the convent in San Miguel once again fell victim to confiscation. The annalist says simply, "On November 22, 1926—a date never to be forgotten—our house was confiscated."[29] The sisters had been warned to expect government agents, but in not so melodramatic a fashion. They arrived through the classroom windows! The school would not be closed, they announced, but as of that precise moment it was government property!

Later the same day (about 5 p.m.) the agents made a second appearance, announcing their presence this time by a fearful pounding on the convent gate. The sisters, Sister María Almaguer excepted, seized their little bundles prepared for just such an emergency and headed out the back door for the hills behind the convent. Responding somewhat leisurely to the pounding at the entry in order to give the sisters a little advantage, Sister María opened the gate where she was confronted by five agents, accompanied by 10 soldiers. Angry at being kept waiting, the men shoved their way in rudely, declaring the convent government property driving home the fact by sealing rooms and cabinets with the government seal. In vain Sister María explained that the house belonged to Señor Javier Alvarez, that she was the landlady, and that the other residents were boarders. She was answered with insults. At 7:30 p.m. the intruders finally left, having nothing more to seal. Their parting warning to the crowd gathered outside in the street was that harboring nuns would mean imprisonment and confiscation of property.

Meantime, as darkness fell, the sisters began making their way cautiously down the hillside. They found the street still filled with people, and police guarding the convent. At sight of the sisters, a great wailing went up, some of the bystanders offering the sisters hospitality in spite of the agents' earlier threats. Keeping a low profile, the sisters quietly made their way to various neighbors' homes for the night and gradually the crowd dispersed.

As the night wore on, Sister Natalia, from her hideaway in a neighbor's house, began to worry about articles left behind—sacred vessels locked in a convent press and books containing the registry of Apostolic League members, which in desperation she had thrust into the oven when the agents arrived. These must be recovered at all costs. Sister María de la Cruz Vásquez-Dávila, her companion in hiding, was the obvious choice to accompany her. In the dead of night the two slipped out of the neighbor's house and circled the hills heading for the convent. Entering by a back gate that had fortunately been left unlocked, they crept silently through the pitch dark convent, freezing at every sound. Slowly they felt their way to the press, which was sealed. With her penknife Sister Natalia managed to open the seal without breaking it. After recovering the sacred vessels and resealing the press, they groped their way to the books in the oven. During the entire time they kept hearing strange noises in the convent; their hearts pounding, they were sure the soldiers were in the house with them. On their way out, at last, they were pleased to find two black shawls thrown over the clothes line in the yard; these they fashioned into makeshift bags in which to carry their "loot."

Meantime, unknown to the trespassers, Sister María Almaguer

and Sister Bernarda Almanza had also made their way in secret to the convent for the purpose of collecting the holy oils. Their plan of entry involved climbing to the roof. Once on the roof Sister María tied a rope around Sister Bernarda's waist and let her down through an open window to the floor below. With sheets brought from their host's home, Sister Bernarda made bundles of the sacred oils, sending them up to Sister María by the multi-purpose rope. After three such loads, she tied the rope once more around herself and signaled Sister María to haul her up. Climbing down from the roof, they were horrorstruck to find the shawls they had thrown over the clothesline missing! Panicked at the thought that others, most probably soldiers, must also be in the house, they beat a hasty retreat from the convent and spent the rest of the night sitting on a bed of boards in the neighbor's attic, sure that at any moment soldiers would arrive to arrest them.

The next morning word passed through the neighborhood that houses in the area would be searched for articles removed from the convent. Not wishing to jeopardize their neighbors' safety, the sisters left San Miguel secretly and went to their family homes for the duration of the persecution. According to one story, however, that persists to this day, the convent was not abandoned. Sister María Luisa Hernandez, the indomitable former prioress who had died in 1895, was seen in the convent garden on several occasions by soldiers guarding the house. They not only saw her, but heard her strongly admonish them to return the convent to its rightful owner. This was reported to the Mexican authorities who began to show an uneasy interest in returning the property to Señor Javier Alvarez in whose name it was held. With unprecedented dispatch the convent and school were returned to the Señor who immediately surrendered the keys to the pastor. The latter went to great lengths to locate Sister María Almaguer. He at last found her discouraged and reluctant to undertake the reopening of the convent.

At his insistence, however, she finally yielded, and the call went out early in January 1936 for the sisters to return after a 10-year absence. It was an emotional reunion, and joy mingled with shock as they observed the condition of the premises. The convent was beyond recognition. Horses had been stabled in the refectory; pigs had been allowed the free run of the cloister. The sisters went to work scrubbing and replacing what the horses and pigs had ruined. Their diligence prevailed; and when all was in order, they began the challenging task of reorienting themselves.

The following year (1938) the school reopened under the title of *Colegio Santo Domingo* with a registration of 60 children and five boarders. In 1949, it was incorporated under the title *Colegio Fray Bartolomé de las Casas*. Later a *secundaria* was added, and in 1962, a normal school with the name shortened to *Instituto Las Casas*. With the addition of a junior college (*preparatoria*) affiliated to the University of Guanajuato, the institute was complete.

La Sta. Escuela de María

One additional foundation needs to be mentioned here to complete the early chapters on Mexico. In 1949, Monsignor José Mercadillo Miranda, pastor of the parish church in San Miguel Allende, turned for help to Sister Fidelis Espinosa, at that time superior of Santo Domingo Convent. Stricken earlier with a grave illness, Monsignor Mercadillo had vowed to found a religious community in gratitude to God should he be cured. Now in fulfillment of his vow, he was requesting the services of a sister for three years to assist him in the spiritual formation of the candidates of his new group. Sister Fidelis appealed to Mother Bernardina Michel, Prioress General, for the requisite permission, which was granted. Both Sisters Mercedes Alvarez and Margarita Lira declined the responsibility when asked; hence, on Sister María fell the obligation of forming the members of *La Sta. Escuela de María* (The Holy School of Mary) as their novice director and superior. Nine candidates awaited her when she arrived in Atotonilco, Guanajuato, on September 8, 1949.

Her three years terminated, Sister María found herself reluctant to leave the sisters in the midst of their training. Mother Pius Marbaise, elected Prioress General in August 1949, recalled her, and although Sister María obeyed, it was evident that her heart was with the little group at Atotonilco. Mother Pius appealed to the local Bishop for direction, and together they referred the case to the Holy See. The latter extended Sister María's stay for two years. A third time Rome ruled in favor of an additional two years, but no more. At the end of the seventh year Sister María was faced with the same soul-wrenching choice. Sister María's distress evident in her words: "I am between the sword and the wall; there is no other way out. I shall ask God to show me His Divine Will and then do whatever He requests." ³⁰

After a reasonable lapse of time Mother Pius wrote Sister María, stating in clear terms that she must return to the Congregation or request a dispensation from her vows; she further specified the date by which she was to answer. This letter, according to Sister María, she never received. Meantime, Sister María shared her dilemma with the Vicar for Religious in the Diocese of León, who brought the matter swiftly to termination by dispensing her from her vows as a Mission San Jose Dominican and receiving her as a member of La Sta. Escuelo de María.

Oddly enough, Monsignor Mercadillo, who had initiated the idea of the new community in fulfillment of his vow, disassociated himself from the little group and left them to fend for themselves. But, by the time of Sister María's death (1982) she had the happiness of seeing the young Congregation firmly established as a Dominican foundation, making a valuable contribution to the work of the Church in Mexico.

NOTES

[1] Marbaise, letter to Maerz, 11 October 1924 in "Kaleidoscopic View of Mexico: 1922–1936" (Series of Letters) 117.

[2] Annals of Santa Rosa de Lima Convent, 2 January 1923 in Hernandez, *Ministry Under Fire: the First Foundations in Mexico (1906–1946)* (Mission San Jose: Dominican Sisters, 1998) 142.

[3] Annals of Santa Rosa de Lima Convent, 4 January 1923 in Hernandez 142.

[4] Annals of Santa Rosa de Lima Convent, 12 February 1925 in Hernandez 166.

[5] Annals of Santa Rosa de Lima Convent, 13 February 1925 in Hernandez 166.

[6] Marbaise 35.

[7] Marbaise 38.

[8] Marbaise 40.
[9] Marbaise 55.
[10] Marbaise 66.
[11] Marbaise 59.
[12] Marbaise 92.
[13] Marbaise 146–147.
[14] Marbaise 159.
[15] Marbaise 202.
[16] Marbaise 158.
[17] Marbaise 203.
[18] Marbaise 206.
[19] Marbaise 261.
[20] Imelda Espinosa, O.P., quoted in Marbaise 272.
[21] Marbaise 303.
[22] Marbaise 305–306.
[23] Hernandez B-39.
[24] María Almaguer, O.P., et al., letter to Emeterio Téllez, Bishop of León in Hernandez A-9.
[25] Valverde letter to Teresa Meyer, O.P., 31 July 1923.
[26] Almaguer, et al., letter to Backes, 15 October 1923 in Hernandez A-12.
[27] Meyer, report to Backes, 18 October 1923.
[28] Maerz, letter to Backes in "Report," 18 October 1923.
[29] Annals of *Santo Domingo* Convent, 22 November 1926 in Hernandez 367.
[30] Almagauer, letter dated 11 September 1956 in Hernandez B 43–44.

CHAPTER TWENTY-FIVE

THE LEGACY CONTINUES

Following the death of Mother Pia on February 8, 1925, a special General Chapter (the Sixth) was called by Mother Seraphina, Vicaress General, on August 3 of the same year for the purpose of electing Mother Pia's successor. To the surprise of no one, her co-worker and confidante, Mother Seraphina Maerz, was elected the second Prioress General of the Congregation. To fill the vacancy on the Council by Mother Seraphina's election, the chapter elected Sister Bernardina Michel as Vicaress and Sister Innocentia Irving as Councilor. No other business was transacted, as the Sixth General Chapter followed the Fifth by an interval of only six months.

Mother Seraphina would lead the Congregation for two terms (1925–1931; 1931–1937). Although she had, as it were, "grown up" in the shadow of Mother Pia, she was not without experience of her own. Over the years she had opened schools, founded convents in Europe, Mexico and the United States and negotiated the approval of the *Constitutions* in Rome. Because her understanding and appreciation of Dominican life was similar to Mother Pia's, there would be no radical departure from the direction in which the Congregation was heading. She was as devoted to the liturgy as Mother Pia, and her clear, sweet soprano was a welcome addition to the Motherhouse choir whenever she was at home.

Self-effacing by temperament, she never allowed this trait to interfere with duty, meeting her publics with a courage that was at one and the same time disarmingly gracious and surprisingly resolute. During her two terms of office, Mother Seraphina opened 11 schools and established Queen of the Holy Rosary College in Mission San Jose.

Besides filling the offices of vicaress general and local prioress for several terms, Mother Seraphina assisted Mother Pia by founding Sacred Heart Convent, Los Angeles; St. Elizabeth Convent, Oakland; and Sts. Peter and Paul Convent, Altenhohenau, Bavaria. Although she experienced close ties with all her foundations, perhaps those dearest to her heart were the houses in Mexico: Santa Rosa Convent, Atzcapotzalco; San Rafael; and San Felipe. The children of Mexico were her special love, and they fully reciprocated. An excerpt from a letter written by an unidentified sister in Mexico witnesses to Mother's place in the hearts of the Mexican people:

Mother Seraphina Maerz, Prioress General, 1925–1937

> Mexico owes dear Mother Seraphina a debt of gratitude because in her great zeal for the salvation of souls she offered herself to come to Mexico to plant the first seeds of our dear Congregation...in the land of our Lady of Guadalupe. During her sojourn in this country she learned to love the people, and by her holy and amiable and winning ways, she endeared herself to all who came in contact with her. We all loved her and venerated her as a saint, and we can never forget her.[1]

Mother Seraphina had a heart for the poor and disadvantaged wherever she met them. She was a frequent visitor at San Quentin and came to know many of the prisoners on Death Row. One young man, a native of Germany, was sentenced to be hanged for murder. A lapsed Catholic, he refused to speak to her or anyone else representing religion. His language was so vile and abusive that no one wanted to go near him. But Mother Seraphina's quiet, gentle manner and words in his native tongue gradually wore him down and he opened his heart to her. "A few more of dear Mother's visits, and a truly repentant sinner went to the gallows...fortified by the worthy reception of the Last Sacraments."[2] Before he died, he told her that his aged mother still lived in Germany; and Mother promised to visit her on her next trip to Europe. True to her word, Mother Seraphina called on the grieving mother and left her greatly comforted after assuring her of her son's repentance and return to the Church.

Those who knew her in her retirement years recalled seeing "our little Mother emerging from her room...clad in an apron, palette and paint brush in hand, going through the Motherhouse parlors and corridors painting out her name on the oils bearing her signature."[3] No recognition for her, if she could prevent it!

After a fall in 1947, Mother Seraphina went into a slow decline until death appeared imminent. It seemed significant to the sisters that she who had done so much to establish the Congregation in Mexico should be visited in her last hours by the Dominican Vicar Provincial of Mexico, Father Claudio, and his companion, Father Juan Zavala, O.P., who happened to be in the Bay Area at the time. Mother Bernardina Michel, Prioress General, who as president of the Dominican Mothers General Conference was at Flintridge Sacred Heart Academy for the biennial meeting, left immediately on adjournment to return to Mother Seraphina's bedside. The next morning, April 25, 1949, while the sisters were singing the last strains of the *Salve Regina* and Mother Bernardina was praying quietly at Mother's bedside, she died as she had lived—gently and peacefully.

During her long lifespan of almost 94 years, Mother Seraphina had endeared herself to many by her simplicity and kindness, her humility and gentle humor—traits that made her easy to approach. Her remarkable confidence in Divine Providence prompted the prayer—together with the rosary—heard most frequently on her lips: "Providence can provide; Providence did provide; Providence will provide. O holy and provident God, have mercy on us."

Present for Mother's funeral were Mother Anselm and Mother Hedwig of Amityville, Mother Cleopha and Sister Gerald of Racine, and Mother Margaret and Sister Mercedes of San Rafael, all of whom had been attending the Dominican Mothers General Conference at Flintridge. After the funeral Mother Anselm remarked, "How providential it is that a member of the Amityville convent should be present at the funeral of the last link of the California province with its Motherhouse in New York." [4]

Among the letters and telegrams of sympathy that poured in at the time of Mother Seraphina's death was a note from Alice Irwin Shone for whom Mother Seraphina had been appointed legal guardian by the Court:

> The world seems bleaker today because of her passing. She was so tiny in physical stature but so big in spiritual stature, and what an abundant life of work she gave to God! Mother was such a kind guardian to me during my childhood and girlhood at the Mission and Guerrero Street...her inspiring conversations in the beautiful gardens of the Mission! I feel strongly my inadequacy in front of her great contribution to me. [5]

During the twelve years of Mother Seraphina's governance, the Congregation continued to expand its missions, including those that, though of short duration as far as the Congregation was involved, introduced inner city children to the benefits of Catholic education.

St. Therese School, Alhambra, California

St. Therese parish, lying east of Los Angeles in the suburban town of Alhambra, was established in 1924 by the Most Reverend John J. Cantwell, Bishop of Los Angeles. To the Discalced Carmelite Fathers, recently arrived in the diocese, Bishop Cantwell assigned responsibility for organizing and staffing the new parish, which was placed under the patronage of the Little Flower.

The first unit planned was a combination church and school which, according to *The Tidings*, the diocesan weekly newspaper, was "modern in every respect. Adequate provision is made for the immediate scholastic needs of the parish by the well-equipped classrooms. On the second floor a temporary church has been fitted up in what will one day be the auditorium of the school."⁶

Since Mission San Jose Dominicans from Sacred Heart Convent, Los Angeles, had been teaching catechism in the parish from the beginning, it was no surprise that Father Malachy Cranfield, O.C.D., pastor, sought the sisters' services for his school. Mother Seraphina complied with the request, even though the parish had no convent for the sisters. It was understood that they would travel the distance from Sacred Heart to St. Therese daily until a residence would be built for them.

On September 8, 1926, St. Therese School opened with forty-four pupils and three teachers assigned respectively to grades one to two, three to five, and six to eight. Sister Beata Gloria served as school principal, with Sister Stanislaus (Bernadette) Dazé and Sister Rosemary Kaffer completing the staff. Within two years enrollment had practically doubled, 42 boys and 44 girls comprising the student body. Although the school was off to a good start, the Dominican Sisters' association with it was brief. Accounting for the sisters' withdrawal in 1930 was the opening of St. Boniface School in Anaheim, for which sisters had been pledged several years earlier. Reluctantly the sisters left St. Therese, which, fortunately, was taken over by the Sisters of Providence.

Immaculate Heart of Mary School, San Antonio, Texas

Coinciding with the opening of St. Therese School in Alhambra, the Congregation moved further afield to the Diocese of San Antonio, Texas. Immaculate Heart of Mary Parish, entrusted to the care of the Claretian Missionary Fathers, had as pastor Father José María Preciado. Prior to his pastorate in San Antonio, Father Preciado had been pastor at San Gabriel Mission where the Congregation staffed the school and Sister Annunciata Henke presided as principal. Impressed by the latter's efficiency, Father Preciado petitioned Mother Seraphina for sisters to staff his school in Texas and in particular for Sister Annunciata to be appointed principal.

Located in a poor section of San Antonio and destined to serve the needs of the children of Mexican immigrants, the school held an appeal for Mother Seraphina, but she declined regretfully, lacking sisters to serve as staff. Undaunted, Father Preciado and his parishioners began a novena to St. Joseph. The power of prayer was manifest when on March 19, the patronal feast of the beloved saint, Mother Seraphina experienced an unaccountable change of heart and sent a telegram of acceptance to Father Preciado. One circumstance probably influencing the reversal was the strategic location of San Antonio; the convent could serve as sanctuary for sisters forced to flee Mexico in the likely event that conditions there became desperate.

On September 16, 1926, three Dominican Sisters arrived in San Antonio where Father Preciado awaited them at the train station. He was delighted to welcome Sister Annunciata Henke as principal and Sister Benedict McNeil and Sister Soledad Vásquez-Dávila as teachers. After dinner in the rectory, he toured the sisters through the spacious building that would be home to school and convent and was gratified at their appreciative comments. Since the convent was totally bare of furniture—not so much as a single bed or chair, the sisters spent their first night in Texas at the Motherhouse of the Sisters of Divine Providence. Bright and early the next morning Father Preciado appeared at the Motherhouse door to take the sisters shopping for the missing items. Never was furniture held in higher regard, as each sister carried her chair from room to room according to need. Meals were another challenge. A gas stove had been delivered, but not connected. For three weeks the sisters managed on a two-burner electric plate, its limited capacity necessitating their serving in "courses." But gradually

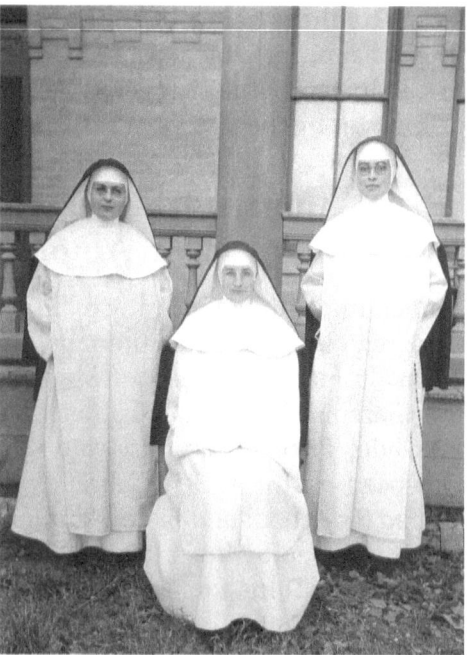

Immaculate Heart of Mary Community: (l to r) Sisters Benedict McNeil, Annunciata Henke and Soledad Vásquez-Dávila

things fell into place. October 13 was a welcome day in the convent when workmen arrived to install two laundry tubs! Up to that point, the sisters had been compelled to wash their white woolen habits in the bathtub or kitchen sink!

Sister Benedict's recollection of her pioneer experiences supplies a fair idea of the life of the sisters in the early days of the Texas mission:

> Being [convent] treasurer, I was concerned about our rapidly diminishing funds. We had only $160, and from this we had to pay for our berths on the train, for transportation of our trunks, and for food. This money had to last us until we received our first salary at the end of October. Sister Annunciata agreed to my going to a wholesale grocery store where I identified our school...and asked if I might purchase some staple foods on credit. The manager decided I was honest and we got our groceries: flour, sugar, beans, rice, cereals, dried fruits, and a few more items. Thus one of our worries was dissolved.
>
> It was in San Antonio that we saw dire poverty—and, to a certain degree, practiced it. Our salary was only $25 a month for each teacher, and although in 1926, the dollar had more purchasing power, we had fewer luxuries....
>
> To save a few precious cents I'd walk into the city. If my companion and I took the street car, we'd have to pay 40¢. I also went once a week to the central market where the farmers brought their produce. I carried a gunny sack into which I put my purchases and my donations. Sometimes the good farmers would give me...free vegetables and fruit. And I was indeed grateful!
>
> Though we were poor, we were happy. We loved our children, all of whom were Mexican with the exception of one Anglo-American family and two or three Italian families. They were a simple, loving, joyous people. [7]

The day before school opened (September 26), the Most Reverend Arthur J. Drossaerts, Archbishop-elect of San Antonio, celebrated Mass and dedicated the new building. For the occasion the church was crowded with clergy, sisters from other communities, and parishioners. Following the dedication, the archbishop and clergy were served dinner by the young ladies of the parish. Archbishop Drossaerts used the occasion to welcome the sisters to his archdiocese.

On September 27, opening day, 162 pupils presented themselves for class. As no textbooks had arrived, catechism and Bible history classes were taught in the forenoon only, for the first week. To the relief of both sisters and parents, school began in earnest the second week when the textbooks arrived. Though English was the language used in the classroom, it was obviously the children's second language. This fact made teaching more of a challenge, but the children's eagerness to learn helped compensate, and their efforts were apparent at graduation when annually one or more students received scholarships to a Catholic high school in the city.

Prior to the opening of school, the Diocese of San Antonio had been honored by being elevated to an archdiocese (August 1926). The following February the investiture of Archbishop-elect Drossaerts took place. A Pontifical High Mass, celebrated in the civic auditorium, was crowded to the doors with members of the clergy, religious, and well-wishers. Seven thousand children from the Catholic schools of San Antonio sang the Mass. "A great and beautiful day for the Catholic people of San Antonio,"[8] summarized the convent annalist, pleased that their new school was represented in the choir.

Archbishop Drossaerts proved a faithful friend of Immaculate Heart of Mary School. Annually he presided at graduation and attended all programs given by the pupils. He was also a generous contributor, on one occasion presenting the school with a check for $1,000 to underwrite the cost of additional desks and materials.

Immaculate Heart began its second year with 200 children in attendance. Four sisters were added to the faculty: Sisters María de la Cruz Vásquez-Dávila, Tomasina Aranda, Columba Dávalos, and Dominica Ochoa. The new faculty members were assigned to the primary grades and the kindergarten to help the children with English as a second language.

On Pentecost Sunday, May 27, 1928, Immaculate Heart's first graduates received their diplomas from Archbishop Drossaerts. Sixteen students—13 girls and 3 boys—were congratulated by the

Archbishop, who commented favorably on the way the students conducted themselves.

The following September, school reopened with 458 students in attendance at the Mass of the Holy Spirit. A newly added commercial class, consisting of eight girls, was introduced.

On December 23, 1928, the children of the school presented a Christmas play for clergy, parents and friends. Among those present were the Archbishop, five refugee bishops from Mexico and several priests—Dominican, Claretian, and diocesan. "Everyone was surprised and delighted with the wonderful results which have been obtained with these poor children,"[9] wrote the annalist in approval. Expressing his personal appreciation to the sisters later, the Archbishop said, "We cannot thank God enough for having sent you here."[10]

As Mother Seraphina had anticipated, Immaculate Heart Convent quickly became a temporary asylum for the sisters exiled from Mexico. They tended to arrive at odd hours of the night "in disguise." The common guise was lay garb, but some arrived as "widows," that is, attired in black. "Widows they might well be," observed the annalist wryly, "mourning for their beloved Church persecuted in their native land."[11] Others, such as Sisters Carolina Canalizo and María de la Cruz Vásquez-Dávila, traveled by preference "as young ladies in modern, though modest fashion."[12] Gradually the San Antonio community became accustomed also to welcoming episcopal refugees from Mexico, the exiled prelates arriving at times in groups, as many as five at a time.

By its third year Immaculate Heart of Mary School boasted an enrollment of 450 pupils and a staff of 8 teachers. But when San Fernando school in nearby Cathedral parish opened (1930), enrollment at Immaculate Heart of Mary dropped to 230, as students from Cathedral parish withdrew to register in their new school. There was no need, however, for alarm. By mid-September, Immaculate Heart attendance had stabilized at 330—with the return of the older children from the cotton fields.

Poverty continued to be a daily reality that the sisters and staff tried to alleviate in any way they could. "Through the kindness of our school nurse," the annalist noted appreciatively, "we are now receiving ten gallons of creamy milk [daily] for the benefit of our most needy children."[13]

But in spite of the poverty, Immaculate Heart of Mary School was a happy place, where teachers and pupils worked together in harmony and mutual respect.

Our Lady of Sorrows School, San Antonio, Texas

Exiled from Mexico during the religious persecution, the Spanish Dominican Fathers were assigned to take charge of Our Lady of Sorrows Parish. In 1929 the Fathers approached our sisters with a request for teachers to staff their recently completed elementary school. A poor parish, Our Lady of Sorrows tugged at Mother Seraphina's heart, and she felt she could not refuse. Forming the first community in 1929 were Sisters Josephine Koehl, superior; Ancilla de la Maza; Imelda Espinosa; and Soledad Vásquez-Dávila, the last three fluent in Spanish, their native tongue. Classes were arranged in three groups low first grade, high first to third grades, and fourth to seventh grades. There was no graduating class the first year. "All beginnings are hard," observed the annalist in retrospect, "and this school has been no exception. However, work done in the shadow of the Cross will not fail to reap its reward in God's good time."[14] Whatever prompted the foregoing reflection was not elaborated, unless the statement that "The school building, which was built of homemade bricks...proved unsatisfactory,"[15] is a clue.

But despite the fact that conditions improved steadily at Our Lady of Sorrows, Mother Seraphina announced regretfully at the close of the 1932 school year that the Congregation could no longer supply sisters for the Texas schools. A shortage of sisters, coupled with the distance from the Motherhouse and the effects of the intense heat on the health of the sisters, weighted the decision in favor of withdrawal from the Texas missions. The news was received with deep regret, not only by clergy, parents, and children, but by the sisters themselves. "We, too, feel it, leaving these poor people who have always been so good to us," mourned the Immaculate Heart annalist, expressing the sadness of the sisters of both convents. "However, we are perfectly convinced that the dear Lord knows what is best for us."[16] And her final entry expressed the sisters' gratitude and regret, "A thousand thanks to our dearest Jesus for all the countless benefits which He has bestowed upon us during our stay in the beautiful city of San Antonio....The last set of sisters today leaves our beloved school....*Fiat voluntas tua!*"[17]

Responsibility for Immaculate Heart of Mary and Our Lady of Sorrows schools was assumed by the Benedictine Sisters, and the sisters left with less heavy hearts knowing that the children would still be taught and cared for by sisters.

St. Boniface School, Anaheim

The lack of Catholic parochial schools in the area surrounding St. Boniface Parish, Anaheim, and the number of Catholic families desiring a Catholic education for their children led Father Patrick Browne, pastor, to build an elementary school for his parish. For him this would become the most significant accomplishment of his years as pastor.

The natural choice of sisters to staff the school was the Dominican Sisters of Mission San Jose, who were already teaching on the same property at St. Catherine's Military School. Under the leadership of Sister Stanislaus (Bernadette) Dazé, O.P., the school opened on September 15, 1930. The five-classroom school boasted an enrollment of 179 students.[18]:

Sister Stanislaus had fond memories of the opening years. She found the students especially eager to learn and admired the dedication of their parents who struggled to bear the cost of Catholic education during the Depression. She later had the privilege of meeting many of the former students in their adult years.

Hallmarks of St. Boniface were its excellent curricular and co-curricular programs. The students competed among themselves in spelling and mathematics and entered reading contests at the Anaheim City Library. In the 1930s the school had its own soccer

St. Boniface Church (left), parish hall (center) and school (right) c. 1930

field and an accompanying landscaped area with trees and benches. Sister Mary Bertha Rehers, O.P. established an orchestra for the students.

During the 1950s significant improvements were made in the school's physical plant under the leadership of Sister Mary Peter Traviss, O.P. Enrollment grew steadily over the years necessitating the construction of additional classrooms. The annex with 12 new classrooms was filled in 1962 with an enrollment of 777.

St. Boniface School was one of the parish's wonderful success stories when the parish celebrated its centenary in 1960.

America's Most Scenic Hotel

Situated high in the San Rafael hills above the cities of Pasadena, Altadena, and La Canada, Flintridge Sacred Heart Academy is unique among the schools staffed by the Dominican Sisters of Mission San Jose in its evolution from a luxury hotel to an academy. "America's Most Scenic Hotel" was built in 1927 by United States Senator Frank Flint and completed just prior to the stock market crash of 1929 that launched the Great Depression and left the country economically paralyzed. Despite its having received the "Honor Award of Exceptional Merit for Design and Execution" in 1930, the hotel was an early victim of the debacle and went into the hands of the receiver, Security First National Bank of Los Angeles, who offered it to Bishop John J. Cantwell of Los Angeles for "church" purposes.

On July 3, 1931, the Bishop sent his Vicar General, Right Reverend Monsignor John Cawley, to Sacred Heart Convent, Los Angeles, to propose to the astonished sisters that they purchase the bankrupt hotel! True, at an earlier canonical visitation conducted by Monsignor Cawley, the sisters had alluded to a need to move Sacred Heart's boarding department to a new locale, preferably in the Glendale area, because of the Los Angeles Fire Department's recent condemnation of their old frame building, but a luxury hotel was beyond their wildest imagining! The Monsignor, however, was a persuasive delegate and, their interest piqued, Mother Dolorosa Wallrath and Sister Thomasina Rehers, prioress and treasurer of Sacred Heart Convent, decided it would do no harm to view the site.

Chapter 25 / THE LEGACY CONTINUES

Flintridge Hotel nestled in the San Rafael Mountain Range near Pasadena 1929

Losing no time, a representative of Security First National arrived at the convent that same afternoon to escort the sisters up the hill to Flintridge. "So charmed were the two sisters by all they saw that they left [by train] for the Motherhouse, Mission San Jose, that very same evening,"[19] reported the Flintridge annalist, basing her first entries on notes made by Mother Dolorosa. Mother Seraphina listened calmly to their enthusiastic recital and terminated the interview with a flat refusal: "No. We could never raise $150,000."[20]

Her unequivocal closure to the discussion drew strong support from the Council, who advanced substantial reasons for their negative stance: lack of personnel, existing conditions (the Depression) and subsequent shortage of funds. Deflated, the two returned to Los Angeles where the Sacred Heart community urged them not to give up hope; the sisters were convinced that, if Mother Seraphina were to see the site, she would surely change her mind.

Yielding at length to the pressure of the community superioresses in the South, who had taken occasion to see for themselves and been captivated, Mother Seraphina boarded the train to Los Angeles for only a look. Just as the sisters had figured, she was delighted with the beauty and possibilities of the site. Nevertheless, she steadfastly refused to succumb to the temptation of a Spanish hacienda with red tiled roof and white stuccoed walls that followed the contour of the hills or the attraction of matching cottages that nestled snugly against the adjoining hillside. In addition, the 40 acres that went with the hotel accommodated an Olympic-sized swimming pool, tennis courts, bridal paths and a dance pavilion. Further, the hotel came "as is," that is, enhanced by $185,000 worth of specially designed furniture, draperies, bedding, linens, china and silver. The answer was still an unqualified "No." Bishop Cantwell was not happy when he was told of Mother Seraphina's decision; in his thinking this was a once-in-a-lifetime opportunity, and the Congregation was making a grave mistake in letting it pass.

Urged by clergy friends and sisters to give it another try, Sisters Dolorosa and Thomasina set out somewhat hesitantly for the Motherhouse a second time. There they met little encouragement and returned home downcast and a little cowed. In the meantime a novena of Masses offered for Mother Pia went heavenward from the still hopeful community at Sacred Heart. Mother Seraphina made a second trip to Los Angeles, "took the matter into consideration, prayed much, and finally on the day that the novena of Masses for dear Mother Pia...[ended, decided to accept] Flintridge."[21] Somehow she would find the funds. Evidently Mother Pia was still looking out for her community!

The Congregation now had the unprecedented challenge of converting a $1,250,000 hotel into a school for girls in less than a month. The founding sisters had little time for amenities. On a hot summer afternoon (August 15, 1931) Mother Dolorosa and Sisters Thomasina and Frances Dunne—superior, treasurer and principal respectively—made their way up the hill to begin an exhilarating, if at times terrifying, mission. Under her arm Mother Dolorosa carried a statue of the Blessed Mother and in her pocket a five-dollar bill, sole capital for the new undertaking!

That same evening Bishop Cantwell arrived with Monsignor John McCarthy; Father Joseph McGucken, the Bishop's secretary; and the Bishop's sister, Nellie Cantwell. The next morning a new chapter of hotel history began when Bishop Cantwell offered the first Mass on the hill at approximately eight o'clock, the precise time dependent on the arrival of Mothers Seraphina and Amanda who came by night train from Mission San Jose for the occasion. Joining the little congregation for the historic occasion were members of the Flint family and a few friends. After Mass the sisters served breakfast to all present, initiating the hospitality characteristic of Mother Dolorosa and Flintridge from the beginning. On October 11, Bishop Cantwell would return again for the formal blessing of the school and convent.

At the request of the Flint family the name "Flintridge" was retained; the school would henceforth be known as Flintridge Sacred Heart Academy. Open House, well publicized by Security First National Bank's representative, brought an estimated 2,000 persons to visit the hotel *qua* school. Interested parents took advantage of the occasion to register their daughters; as a result, 200 students of "all ages [Grades One to Eleven] and all sizes were present when classes...[began] on Tuesday, September 2."[22] The grade school was housed in the former servants' quarters below the hill, a spacious building that adapted itself well to its former use. The academy moved into its place of preeminence in the hotel proper. Board, room and tuition were priced at an astonishingly low $40 per month. The sisters also established a nursery for children as young as three years of age.

The first weeks were challenging. Rooms were overcrowded, grade school classrooms not completed, teachers new. In the opinion of the annalist, "Patience and forbearance were the order of the day."[23] In addition to her responsibility as academy principal, Sister Frances served as mistress of boarders and high school teacher. To complete the original staff, Mother Seraphina sent Sisters Odilia Engelm, Cortona Wittemann and Miriam Jackson as housekeepers and housemothers for the resident students. To Sister Natalia Garcia was entrusted the nursery. Lay teachers formed the grade school staff, and Sister Frances, assisted by two lay teachers, constituted the high school faculty. In December Sisters Beata Gloria and Johanna Stein were sent as reinforcements; and in March of the following year, Sister Charitas Delahoyde arrived to teach in the high school.

Miss Lillian Fitch, drama coach, quickly became identified with Flintridge's best loved traditions. Under her direction the students staged Monsignor Hugh Benson's Christmas miracle play, which became an annual holiday offering of the Academy. In June the entire student body participated in Shakespeare's "A Midsummer Night's Dream," an evening production on the front lawn. The dramatization of a Shakespearean play became an annual spring presentation, impressively produced and beautifully enhanced by charming choreography. In those early years also, Flintridge established its own rituals that included alumnae teas and weekly banquets for which students were expected to "dress," May crownings and Corpus Christi processions, and evenings at cultural events—concerts, stage plays and operas. From the beginning Flintridge emphasized fine arts in the curriculum. Instruction in instrumental music, primarily piano and violin, was provided, and choral, dance and drama were prominent in the program. Mr. Roger Wagner, internationally famous as a choral director, was hired as choral teacher in the 1940s and taught on campus for several years.

The first graduation of students took place in 1933 on the front lawn, establishing another tradition when the junior class in white uniforms formed a pathway outlined by a chain of red roses down which the graduates walked. Bishop Cantwell conferred diplomas on the honorees, who were presented by Monsignor

First Graduates of Flintridge Sacred Heart Academy 1933 with John J. Cantwell, Bishop of Los Angeles 1917–1936, Archbishop of Los Angeles 1936–1947: Top row (l to r) María Carmen Terroba, Elizabeth "Liz" Sterkel, Mary Inez Schall, Eleanor "Bunny" Harrington, Margot Milburn; bottom row (l to r) Mary Frances Zerwekh (Sr. Mercia Zerwekh's sister), Betty McCray, Leonora Lombardi and Alice Blacker

John McCarthy. With its first graduating class of nine seniors, Flintridge was granted full accreditation by the University of California. The recognition followed annual qualifying visits from University representatives.

At the Eighth General Chapter of the Congregation in August 1937, Flintridge Sacred Heart Convent was raised to the status of priory, with Mother Dolorosa Wallrath as prioress. Meantime, withdrawal from the schools in San Antonio, Texas, and St. Mary's, Fullerton, worked to advantage for Flintridge, bolstering the high school and grade school staffs, the former by three teachers and the latter by one. Also added were a music teacher and two sisters in support of household management.

Over the years, Flintridge became a showplace of the Archdiocese. Archbishop Cantwell, accompanied by his sister Nellie, was a frequent visitor, often bringing or sending visiting bishops and clergy to view the site. Among the visitors were the Most Reverend Emmanuel Suarez, O.P., Master General; Monsignor Fulton J. Sheen; Alfred Noyes and his wife from England; the Irish Consul to San Francisco, Mr. Murphy, with his wife and son; Father Louis Nolan, O.P., delegate of the Dominican Master General in Rome; Una O'Connor, Hollywood actress (who came for a rest); and Monsignor James Campbell, Catholic University of America Summer Session Director, an annual visitor following the summer program at Dominican College, San Rafael.

On October 18, 1940, at the urging of Archbishop Cantwell, Miss Trixie Friganza of Hollywood and vaudeville fame came to reside as a permanent guest at Flintridge. Her presence added a certain color or flair to the sedate dignity of the Academy. On special occasions Trixie could not resist contributing a little entertainment for the benefit of guests, by drawing upon "her unlimited repertoire to help entertain them."[24] Her spontaneous appearances were at times a source of discomfiture to Mother Dolorosa, as Trixie's choices now and then bordered on the risqué! Trixie lived out the last 15 years of her life at Flintridge in contented independence, dying on February 27, 1955, after a short sojourn in the hospital. She was buried from Blessed Sacrament Church, Hollywood, on March 2, at a Solemn Requiem Mass attended by a number of Hollywood celebrities. The sisters from Flintridge were among the mourners also.

December 7, 1941, brought the shocking news of Pearl Harbor and war. Although the sisters tried to carry on normally, the war loomed in the background of most decisions for the next few years. Blackouts interrupted the routine of days and nights, and the annual Shakespearean play had to be moved indoors for the duration. On occasion, the sisters provided hospitality, including Mass and breakfast, for as many as 70 soldiers at one time.

By the early 1940s enrollment averaged 179 boarders. Up to that point Flintridge had maintained itself by tuition and board. Operating expenses were kept down, as teachers and boarding department supervisors were largely sisters. During the war years when help was hard to find, many of the students lent a hand with chores usually assigned to the employees, especially serving in the dining room. Dish washing and like tasks were often shared by sisters and students. Meantime, enrollment was soaring! Over 100 students had to be refused because of a lack of accommodations. One positive effect: between 1944 and 1945, the remaining indebtedness on the school, $100,000, was completely liquidated.

Annual Day, inaugurated on June 10, 1946, marked the distribution of the first yearbook published by the Academy. Immediately popular, the *Veritas* became a yearly publication to which the students looked forward with eagerness and pride.

November 3, 1949, was a day long remembered by the residents of Flintridge. Around 11:00 a.m. fire broke out on Linda Vista Boulevard below the Academy. Soon out of control, it raced up the hill, the shortage of hydrants accelerating its progress. Fire trucks from surrounding cities and as far away as Los Angeles came to assist, but the fire raged from 11:00 a.m. to 3:00 p.m., destroying more than 800 acres. Shortly after noon police and firemen arrived on the hill to order the evacuation of the students. Flintridge Preparatory School for Boys and Lyon Van and Storage Company sent buses and trucks to transport the girls to St. Francis High School in La Canada, where the Capuchin Fathers had graciously offered the students hospitality. Hardly had the girls arrived when the flames jumped Foothill Boulevard and headed toward St. Francis. Frantic, parents who were within driving distance called to pick up their daughters; the remaining students, mainly from out of state, were directed back into the buses. This time they were taken to La Canada Elementary School, where members of the Red Cross registered the girls and served them and their accompanying teachers supper.

Back on the hill, Mother Dolorosa and Mother Bernardina Michel, who happened to be visiting at the time, watched the flames advancing toward the Academy. As they topped the last hillside, Mother Dolorosa made a promise of 200 Masses for the Poor Souls if Flintridge were spared. Hardly had she spoken when the wind shifted dramatically, turning north along the lower ridgesite where it came within 20 feet of the grade school, but left it unscorched. Flintridge was spared! From the annalist's perspective, it was as if someone "drew the line of demarcation [near Our Lady's statue]— 'thus far and no farther'."[25]

At 7:00 p.m. the girls from out of state—about a bus load—

returned to the Academy, the school being declared out of danger, though without the convenience of light or water. As a safeguard firemen remained on the hills looking for hot spots through the night and the following day. Although the sisters were convinced that a miracle had occurred, possibly a greater miracle involved the students who, when informed of the need to evacuate, marched quietly across the lawn to the waiting trucks and buses, praying the rosary and showing no sign of panic.

The following day a woman passing by asked one of the firemen watching on the hill how they had succeeded in stopping the fire. His answer: "Lady, we didn't stop anything. A Higher Power did."[26] Fortunately, as there were few homes on the hillside in the 1940s, little property damage was sustained.

By 1951 the high school had outgrown itself to such an extent that a larger building was judged imperative. Moreover, residents of La Canada were asking to enroll their daughters as day students, now that roads leading up the hill were much improved. The site chosen for the new building was on land already owned by the sisters, with the exception of a single lot that, fortunately, they were able to purchase. Blessing of the site is probably best chronicled as "unrehearsed." Father Gerald Bolger, C.Ss.R., a frequent visitor at Flintridge had just finished saying Mass one morning when Mother Dolorosa told Sister Mary Benigna Krug, principal, and Sister Rosemary Kaffer, faculty member, to escort Father to the hilltop and to bring with them stole, holy water and ritual. She would await them there, as she had scheduled a meeting onsite with the architect and contractor. On the sisters' arrival the blessing of the land took place without fuss—attended only by the little group.

Approval of the site by Archbishop J. Francis A. McIntyre, Archbishop Cantwell's successor, and a low bid of $200,000 from J. J. McNeil, contractors, signaled the arrival of bulldozers to begin the site work for the new academy.

September 17, 1951, was an exciting day on the hill. Students arriving for the first day of the fall term were escorted to the Spanish style structure of reinforced concrete and tile roof that harmonized with the hotel and cottages already on campus. They roamed the halls of their new school, exploring classrooms, study hall, science labs, typing room, library and offices with evident approval. On October 14, Archbishop McIntyre dedicated the building before a large gathering of clergy, sisters, lay faculty, parents, friends and students. Monsignor Patrick Dignan, Los Angeles Superintendent of Catholic Schools, was principal speaker, and the high school students under the direction of Roger Wagner sang. Flintridge was now in a position to open its doors to day, as well as resident students.

With the high school moved into the new building, Father Paul Early, pastor of St. Bede's, La Canada, seized the opportunity to ask permission to move his elementary school into the vacated rooms. Under construction, St. Bede's School had been housed in Holy Redeemer, which was no longer able to accommodate the additional children. For the first and only time, Flintridge opened its doors to boys as well as girls. With Flintridge's 21 elementary school boarders, the total number of grade school students was brought to 164 in eight grades. Sister Mary Hilary Miller, principal of Flintridge grade school, organized the temporary merger. Sister Theodora Stute and three lay teachers, assigned to double grades, constituted the elementary school staff. By December 18 of the following year St. Bede's had its own staff of six Sisters of St. Louis and one lay teacher and was ready to move into its new building. Flintridge had responded to the emergency and had served its neighbor well.

At the request of the Pasadena Rose Bowl committee the Ohio State football team, coaches, physicians, and chaplains—in Pasadena for the "big game"—were guests of Flintridge during the 1954 Christmas recess. In 1956, an auditorium seating 300 was added to the complex. On December 8, Father William Lulloff, O.F.M. Cap., blessed the building in the presence of the sisters, lay faculty, and students. A *Missa cantata* and luncheon followed. The same year the grade school was discontinued.

The following year the community purchased two houses at Lake Arrowhead, California, as a vacation spot for sisters and resident students. The blessing took place on August 10, 1957. Mother Dolorosa, Sister Thomasina Rehers, and Sister Louise Pfeffer attended. Father Clavin, pastor of Our Lady of Fatima Parish, Lake Arrowhead, blessed the houses. Both sisters and students continue to enjoy holidays in the snow or sunshine in the spring at the three mountain cabins.

Committed to a program of academic excellence and moral

integrity since its foundation in 1931, Flintridge Sacred Heart Academy continues to support an environment that respects cultural diversity and scholastic achievement.

Queen of the Holy Rosary College

Chartered under the laws of the State of California in December, 1930, Queen of the Holy Rosary College opened the following January. "Dedicated to the religious, humanistic and professional education of Dominican Sisters engaged in a life-time pursuit of truth and in various forms of education,"[27] the college was founded as a four-year liberal arts institution. The first members comprising the Board of Trustees were Mother Seraphina Maerz, Mother Amanda Bednartz, Sister Bernardina Michel, Sister Augustina O'Connor, Sister Laurentia Sharkey, Sister Rosaria Huber, Sister Louise Pfeffer, Sister Innocentia Irving, and Sister Dolorosa Wallrath.

Located in a newly erected three-story concrete building on the Motherhouse campus, the college was practically debt-free at the time of its completion. Its healthy financial condition was largely the result of Mother Amanda Bednartz's enthusiastic and untiring efforts. She spearheaded the campaign for funds, assisted by a committee composed of many of her former pupils and faithful friends. In the archives is a letter from Mr. Louis Schoenstein, father of Sister Mary Mark and chairman of St. Anthony's Parish Division of the fund-raising campaign, explaining the purpose of the drive. The occasion was the celebration of the fiftieth anniversary of the sisters' arrival in San Francisco. As a token of gratitude and as a deserving jubilee offering, the *Staats Verband,* with the "cordial support and approval of the Reverend Clergy, has inaugurated a drive for needed funds to enlarge the Motherhouse at Mission San Jose... The drive is to take place during the month of January."[28] The recipient of the letter—"Dear Friend"—was invited to a sectional meeting at St. Anthony's on January 3, 1927, at eight o'clock.

Organized by parishes and societies, the drive was a success and the erection of the college building began. The college housed lecture rooms, library, auditorium, administration offices, reception and dining areas on the first and second floors and faculty residences on the third floor. On Sunday, May 3, 1931, the building was dedicated by the Most Reverend Archbishop Edward J. Hanna. St. Vincent's School for Boys sent its choir of 90 resplendent in red

Chapter 25 / THE LEGACY CONTINUES   547

Queen of the Holy Rosary College Building c. 1932

cassocks and white surplices; and Father Kennedy brought his band from St. Paul's Church, San Francisco. During the luncheon, which followed the blessing, many prominent guests were called on to speak. The afternoon was pronounced a huge success. As described by the Motherhouse annalist, "The celebration was a success in every respect: the ceremonies were beautiful, the program appropriate, the weather unsurpassable, the visitors numerous and enthusiastic."[29]

The first college session began on June 29 and was attended by 55 sisters. Course offerings included "New Trends in Elementary Education" taught by Miss Bertha Roberts, Deputy Superintendent and Supervisor of Practice Teaching, State Teachers' College, San Francisco; "Citizenship" taught by Mr. A. Cloud, Chief Deputy Superintendent of San Francisco Elementary Schools; "Wesco Methods of Handwriting," taught by Mr. E. Ludovici, co-author of the Wesco System of Handwriting and faculty member, Behnke-Walker Business College, Portland, Oregon. Sister Louise Pfeffer taught English and Sister Redempta Prose, chemistry.

The presidency of the College has traditionally been held by the Prioress General of the Congregation. The first president, therefore, was Mother Seraphina Maertz (1931–1937). Appointed by the Council to assist her in carrying out the immediate direction of college affairs was Sister Bernardina Michel as dean. Serving as deans during Mother Seraphina's presidency were in addition to Sister Bernardina, Sister Louise, and Sister Pauline Lang.

The Board of Trustees, appointed by Mother Seraphina, had the following officers: Sister Bernardina Michel, vice president; Sister Rosaria Huber, secretary; Sister Laurentia Sharkey, treasurer; and Mr. Charles Sullivan, assistant secretary.

At the first meeting of the board (January 2, 1931), Sister Rosaria, secretary, attested that the Articles of Incorporation had been "duly filed in the office of the Secretary of State and that the Certificate of Incorporation...[had been] issued by the Secretary

Diploma of Sister Edmunda Klinkenberg, first graduate of Queen of the Holy Rosary College 1934

of State and she then and there presented the same."³⁰ A certified copy of the Articles had been filed also in the office of the Alameda County Clerk. A Code of By-laws was also presented and unanimously approved for adoption.

Among the faculty members during the early years of the college were: Mrs. Lucy Lockwood Hazard, Ph.D., associate instructor in English, Mills College; Reverend John Greenan, Ph.D., Logic; Mr. Edwin Beilharz, Ph.D., University of Santa Clara; Reverend Acquinas O'Donnell, O.P., philosophy; Reverend Joseph King, S.J., religion and Reverend Joachim Walsh, O.P., church history.

Sister Edmunda Klinkenberg

Sister Edmunda Klinkenberger holds the distinction of being the first graduate of Queen of the Holy Rosary College, followed by Sisters Mary Benigna Krug, Alacoque Dinsmore and Geraldine Kelly. Through the years the line of graduates stretches out, bearing witness to Mother Pia's goal of having her sisters well-prepared for their teaching mission.

During the presidency of Mother Bernardina Michel (1937–1949), the College was affiliated with Catholic University of America through the Sister Formation College Program. Acting as deans during this period were Sister Antoinette Forgeng, Sister Redempta Prose and Sister Mary Kevin Breen. Mother Pius Marbaise followed as president of the college (1949–1961) with Sister Mary Dominic Engelhard as dean.

NOTES

[1] "Seraphina Maerz, O.P." Necrology, August, 1943—August, 1949.

[2] "Seraphina Maerz, O.P." Necrology, August, 1943—August, 1949.

[3] Oral History, Dominican Sisters Archives, n.d.

[4] "Seraphina Maerz, O.P." Necrology, August, 1943—August, 1949.

[5] Alice Irwin Shone, letter to Michel, 27 April 1949.

[6] Mary Kevin Breen, O.P., "The Educational Work of the Sisters of Saint Dominic of the Congregation of the Queen of the Holy Rosary" (Thesis: Catholic University of America, 1946) 100.

[7] Benedict McNeil, O.P., "Our Convents in Texas," n.d., 5–6.

[8] Annals of Immaculate Heart of Mary Convent, 17 February 1927.

[9] Annals of Immaculate Heart of Mary Convent, 23 December 1928.

[10] Annals of Immaculate Heart of Mary Convent, 31 December 1928.

[11] Annals of Immaculate Heart of Mary Convent, January 1927.

[12] Annals of Immaculate Heart of Mary Convent, 24 July 1929.

[13] Annals of Immaculate Heart of Mary Convent, 12 April 1931.

[14] Annals of Immaculate Heart of Mary Convent, 10 September 1930.

[15] Annals of Immaculate Heart of Mary Convent, 18 June 1932.

[16] Annals of Immaculate Heart of Mary Convent, 22 June 1932.

[17] Annals of Immaculate Heart of Mary Convent, 30 June 1932.

[18] Montrose, Donald, et al., *The Story of a Parish: Its Priests and People.* (Anaheim: St. Boniface Parish, 1961).

[19] Annals of Flintridge Sacred Heart Convent, "Introduction," 1930–1945.

[20] Annals of Flintridge Sacred Heart Convent, "Introduction," 1930–1945.

[21] Annals of Flintridge Sacred Heart Convent, "Introduction," 1930–1945.

[22] Annals of Flintridge Sacred Heart Convent, "Introduction," 1930–1945.

[23] Annals of Flintridge Sacred Heart Convent, "Introduction," 1930–1945.

[24] Annals of Flintridge Sacred Heart Convent, "Introduction," 1930–1945.

[25] Annals of Flintridge Sacred Heart Convent, "Introduction," 1930–1945.

[26] Anonymous report, Dominican Sisters Archives, n.d.

[27] Self-Study Report to Accrediting Commission for Community and Junior Colleges. October 25–26, 1988, 7.

[28] Louis Schoenstein, letter to the sisters, 1931.

[29] Annals of the Motherhouse, 3 May 1931.

[30] Minutes of the Board of Trustees, 2 January 1931, 12.

CHAPTER TWENTY-SIX

DOMINICAN COLLABORATION

An older and wiser Mother Pia wrote on October 27, 1895: "It is a pity that we who come from the same Motherhouse are separated. We could constitute a Congregation more than a thousand in number. If we worked in unity, how much we could do for souls and God's honor. The Superioresses do not seem to understand this advantage."[1]

The California superioress [with Sister Felicitas Weiss as companion] was on her way to Brooklyn intent on a threefold mission:
1. To borrow money at a low rate of interest in order to pay off the debt owed Archbishop Riordan for the Mission San Jose property.
2. To obtain sisters to help staff the school being considered for Sacramento.
3. To discuss amalgamation with the superioresses of Brooklyn, New York; Racine, Wisconsin; and Caldwell, New Jersey.[2]

On all three scores, the trip was unsuccessful, but the notion of amalgamation remained alive in Mother Pia's thinking. The following March she discussed the "amalgamation problem"[3] with Father Clementine, O.S.F. It may have some significance that she now referred to the topic as "problem" and recognized the hurdle that would have to be crossed regarding the authority of the respective Prioresses General. Father Clementine, she noted in her Diary, was of a mind that "an independent province would be a more workable arrangement."[4]

On her first trip to Europe in 1897, Mother Pia again pondered the idea of amalgamation, this time with a slightly different twist:

the union of the Dominican congregations in the United States under a central Motherhouse in Rome. The more she considered the idea the more enthusiastic she became. Father Dominicus Scheer agreed and thought that Rome would approve on a probationary basis, but cautioned her not to move too fast. She seemed to have taken his caution to heart, for the next mention of amalgamation is a Diary entry dated January 24, 1902, when her admiration for the Stone community led her to consider some kind of union with the sisters in England.

Sometime later, Mother Pia must have shared with Father Scheer her concern regarding information she had received about congregations being "forced" by Rome to unite. Father Scheer's reply denied such a possibility and assured her that no one in Rome thought of such a thing. But, he continued,

> ...something else was done by the *Congregatio Episcoporum et Regularium*; it has also the norm for all sisters with simple vows. According to that norm in the future all *Constitutions* must be in writing, if the approbation from Rome is asked for. With that it is left to each Order and every single Congregation of an Order to formulate and arrange the *Constitutions* according to the requirements and spirit of their Order. The newest book, *Analecta Ord. Praed.*, (now in print) contains complete instructions about the Third Order Congregations of our Order from which it can be seen how lenient the Roman Congregation had been in some cases and how it must be done in the future if a new Congregation asks for the approbation of its Institute and *Constitutions*.
>
> Therefore, do not worry about a union with other Congregations; you will not live to see such a happening.[5]

By 1905, however, Mother Pia was having second thoughts of her own. As she worked on the *Constitutions*, she saw with ever greater clarity the problems that dogged the topic of amalgamation. Nevertheless, discussion must have gone on with the Dominican Sisters of Tacoma, Washington, for the Acts of the Fourth General Chapter, August 2–5, 1918, contain the following under "Announcements:"

> 68—We announce that upon the request of Reverend Mother Thomasina, Prioress General of the Tacoma Province of Dominican Sisters, it has been decided to affiliate that Province to ours. The unification is to be put on trial for three years. The Sisters of the Tacoma Province wish to adopt our approved *Constitutions* and our *Customary* and to submit their Houses to the visitation of our Dear Reverend Mother. In all other respects, the Provinces are to be separate and distinct.[6]

The use of the term "province" raises a number of questions. It was not accurate when applied to Mission San Jose, an independent Congregation, and probably not to Tacoma as well. Further, it is difficult to understand the chapter announcement. Given Mother Pia's failing health at the time and Mother Seraphina's absence in Europe from 1919 into the first half of 1921, it is unlikely that Mother Pia ever visited the Tacoma community in an official capacity. This assumption must remain an assumption, however, as Mother Pia's Diary concludes in 1909, and the annals of both the Congregation and the Motherhouse are missing for this period.

A letter from Father Clement M. Thuente, O.P., of the Eastern Dominican Province, to Mother Pia bears witness to the fact that the idea of amalgamation was not dormant as late as 1915. Father's letter reads in part:

> I was in New York at Christmas and learned from our Provincial, Father Meagher that the old question of bringing together the various Dominican teaching communities is brought up again. It seems that the Papal Delegate in Washington is insisting much on it....
>
> As a first step in this movement the Provincial [is] consider[ing] inviting all the superiors with a few companions to one house to make a retreat together. It seems that this was done some years ago by Father Cormier in France with good results. I suggested Chicago for the place and in Chicago an academy belonging to the Milwaukee [Notre] Dame Sisters. I believe it would be good to have such a meeting to meet one another and exchange ideas. What do you think of the plan? I know it is an old desire

of yours. You have thought the matter over for a long time. Your ideas will be much appreciated.[7]

By this time, however, Mother Pia's thinking had come full circle; her reply certainly cannot be described as encouraging:

> Your letter of Jan. 17th has been received with thanks. Yes, I have, as you say, considered well the plan of uniting. The plan in itself is excellent, for much could be done for the glory and honor of God and our holy Order by this union. However, it seems to me that the arrangement of the temporal affairs would be an easier matter than that of forming a Congregation of good observant religious of the Order of St. Dominic....
>
> You know, Rev. Father, that some years ago I cherished the wish of seeing those Communities united that are off-shoots of the Brooklyn or Regensberg Convent. On my return from Europe, I visited the Convents of Brooklyn, New York City, Racine and New Jersey and proposed this union. The project was not welcomed. I returned to California disappointed, and with the help of the V. Rev. Dom. Scheer, O.P., I set to work to shape the little Community which God had given me into a religious body according to the spirit of our Holy Founder. With grace from above and the cooperation of my dear old companions, I believe to have attained some success in my attempts to combine the contemplative with the active life.
>
> You understand, dear Rev. Father that I would not like to sacrifice our ideals, for instance, the Divine Office and other observances peculiar to our Congregation for the sake of uniting.
>
> A meeting of the superiors of the various Congregations may also be productive of much good. Many of them are in a position to accept the invitation with ease, both with regard to distance and expense.
>
> The condition of my health makes it hard for me to do the necessary amount of traveling required by my office, and therefore I can scarcely venture to undertake this trip to Chicago...[8]

Although discussion of some form of unification appears to have been taking place about this time in several communities, no group seems to have had the desire to take the topic beyond the talking stage. In 1934, however, Father Louis Nolan, O.P., representative of the Master General in Rome, visited the motherhouses of the congregations of Third Order Dominican Sisters in the United States; and in a follow-up letter to the Prioresses General he summarized his reactions and outlined a proposal for the future:

> I have been most favorably impressed by all that I have observed and learned everywhere. However, I do feel convinced that as members of the same religious family, the various Congregations of Dominican Sisters have not all that unanimity of spirit and action that is desirable, and that would, no doubt, make for greater strength and efficiency.
>
> To remedy this defect, and to secure greater unity of spirit, I have decided to invite the Mother General and one of her Councillors of each Congregation to a Conference at which we could all together discuss the following points, as well as others that in the course of our meeting may seem necessary or advisable:
>
> 1. Uniformity of *Constitutions* and Ceremonial, as far as possible;
>
> 2. Uniformity of our religious Habit, especially with regard to material and form of guimp and head-dress;
>
> 3. The recitation of the Divine Office, in at least the Novitiate Houses;
>
> 4. Measures for the training of the young Sisters to meet the educational requirements of the day, conformably to the spirit and mind of the Church;
>
> 5. A great convent or hostel in Rome where the Sisters may receive at the centre of Christendom and of the Order the training and the knowledge that only Rome can give. [9]

The Conference was calendared for Dominican College, San Rafael, California, from January 1 to 4, 1935. Twelve of the twenty-eight Dominican Congregations in the United States accepted the invitation. Commissions based on Father Nolan's five points were formed, meeting daily during the Conference to discuss their area of interest. Although uniformity was judged generally desirable, practical aspects of the topics made those present realize that during their days together a mere seed had been planted.

As temporary president of the Conference, Father Nolan reminded the participants that the meeting was consultative, not deliberative. Mother Samuel Coughlin of the Sinsinawa Dominican Sisters, elected first president of the Conference, was at pains to reassure the congregations that were not present at the first meeting:

> Some of us were apprehensive of a movement towards an amalgamation of all Dominican Sisters in the United States. Let me assure you that that subject was never mentioned, and we have every reason to believe, was not intended to be considered at all....The matters proposed must be referred to the respective General Councils of the Congregations, then to General Chapters or to a vote of the members of each Congregation, to secure a Dominican, democratic procedure.[10]

Quite possibly, there was reason for the uneasiness felt in several congregations. On her first trip to Rome, Mother Pia had encountered a strong desire on the part of the Master General to have all Third Order Sisters' *Constitutions* uniform. A single constitution was true for the men of the Order, but the women were heir to a different history. Collaboration was for them a far less threatening word. In any case, Mother Samuel's letter undoubtedly allayed the anxieties of many superiors.

The following year Mother Samuel invited the Most Reverend John T. McNicholas, O.P., Archbishop of Cincinnati, to preach a retreat for the conference members preceding the meeting. The Archbishop not only agreed, but invited the sisters to be his guests at the Cincinnati archdiocesan seminary, Mount Saint Mary's of the West, in Norwood, Ohio. The meeting took the form of round table discussions yielding a number of specific resolutions that respected the difficulties the commissions were encountering in achieving uniformity. It was agreed at this meeting that the conference would henceforth meet biennially at a location and time determined by the Executive Board. Partial reason for the change was financial, and successive conferences included a note to the effect that confer-

Conference of Dominican Mothers General at Flintridge, Pasadena, April 21–24, 1949; Mother Bernardina Michel, President, standing to the left of Joseph T. McGucken, Auxiliary Bishop of Los Angeles

ence funds would be allocated in part to congregations that wished to attend, but could not afford transportation.

Some disquiet must have lingered, however, for in the Acts of the Ninth General Chapter (1943), Chapter One concludes with a statement on the binding force of the *Constitutions, followed by a brief referral to the Mothers General Conferences:*

> We declare that no authoritative power has been conferred by ecclesiastical authority on the Mothers General Conferences. Apropos of this matter Archbishop McNicholas, O.P., made the following statement in 1925 when he presided at the conference: 'The purpose of the biennial meetings of the Mothers General is that of elevating Dominican ideals and propagating the Dominican spirit and virtue. The conclusions arrived at there have no binding force; they amount only to opinions.' [11]

The Eighth Mothers General Conference took place at Flintridge Sacred Heart Academy in Pasadena during the presidency of Mother Bernardina Michel. It is worth noting that Father Nolan's five points offered for consideration at the first conference were still under discussion at the Eighth!

Over the years the Dominican Leadership Conference, as it was later known, broadened its understanding of its mission. From uniformity in certain areas, it came to an understanding of preaching as the heart of the Dominican vocation and committed itself to the struggle for justice that the claim implies. As a corporate body, the conference works to achieve a just world order; collaboration has become the order of the day. The sisters of the various congregations stand together in fidelity and witness to the Dominican charism.

Notes

[1] Backes 172.

[2] Backes 172.

[3] Backes 175.

[4] Backes 175.

[5] Dominicus Scheer, O.P., letter to Backes, 25 February 1902.

[6] Acts of the Fourth General Chapter (2–5 August 1918) 23.

[7] Clement M. Thuente, O.P., letter to Backes, 17 January 1915.

[8] Backes, letter to Thuente, O.P. 1 February 1915.

[9] Louis Nolan, O.P., letter to Prioresses General, 2 December 1934.

[10] Mother Samuel Coughlin, O.P., letter to Prioresses General, 29 January 1935.

[11] Acts of the Ninth General Chapter (28 July-3 August 1943) 8.

CHAPTER TWENTY-SEVEN

NATIVE DAUGHTER

The Eighth General Chapter of the Congregation (July 28 to August 5, 1937) would mark a departure from the past. For the first time in 60 years, the delegates would be convened to elect a prioress general who had not received her early religious training at the Motherhouse in Brooklyn. (Mother Amanda Bednartz and Sister Bartolomea Deckert, the only living survivors from the early days in New York, were both advanced in years and in poor health at the time). Nevertheless, the delegates favored a candidate in the same tradition; hence, their choice fell on Sister M. Bernardina Michel to serve as third Prioress General of the Mission San Jose Dominican Congregation.

Born in San Francisco on December 16, 1871, Louise Michel was the younger of two daughters of John and Margaret Gahr Michel, a prominent and well-to-do San Francisco couple. Baptized Elizabeth in St. Boniface Church, she was always called Louise. At the age of five, she was enrolled in St. Boniface School where she was taught by the Dominican Sisters. She entered the Dominican Sisters at fourteen at Immaculate Conception Priory, then the Motherhouse of the Congregation. She received the habit and her name in religion on July 2, 1888, and made vows on January 6, 1890. On the Feast of St. Dominic, August 4, 1899, she made her final profession.

Sister Bernardina began a successful teaching career at St. Catherine's in Anaheim and taught also at St. Boniface and St. Anthony Schools in San Francisco. From 1900 to 1908, she was director of novices and subsequently did graduate study at Catholic

University in Washington, D.C. Later appointments included directress of the schools of the Congregation and prioress of the Motherhouse. She served the Congregation as a member of the General Council, dean of Queen of the Holy Rosary College, and Vicaress General. Elected Prioress General, she served the maximum two terms (1937–1943). In 1953 she translated Mother Pia's Diary from the German. *Her Days Unfolded* is still today an invaluable source of congregational history and pertinent material on our Foundress's life.

Elizabeth Louise Michel

Mother Bernardina had great respect for scholarly research and its accuracy. She was ready to help the student sisters acquire the precise facts needed. In the archives of the Motherhouse is a six-page, hand-written letter that she sent to a student who had approached her for information on the Indian missions. Mother not only took the trouble to write sister, but was at pains to schedule an interview with Sister Blandina DuMoulin, one of the earliest members of the home missionary band. For five years Sister Blandina had driven the horse and buggy for Sister Benedicta, the Indian's beloved "bossy lady' (cf. Ch. 13). Mother verified names and dates with Sister Blandina.

Mother Bernardina's outstanding virtue was honesty, a trait that sometimes got her into difficulty, though it made her completely trustworthy. Until bedridden toward the end, she exercised her civic right to vote, a right she regarded as a sacred duty. Intensely loyal, she never swerved from her love of the Congregation and her country.

In an interview with Sister Louise Pfeffer, who served as a member of the General Council during Mother Bernardina's terms

Mother Bernardina Michel, Prioress General, 1937 —1949

of office, Sister shared that Mother inspired respect rather than love because she was of a reserved, though kindly nature. She had a gift for judging character, and was excellent at repartee, retaining her sense of humor to the end.

Mother Bernardina spent the last years of her life in the *Salus Infirmorum* the home for the Dominican Sisters needing care. There she died peacefully on December 31, 1968, at the advanced age of ninety-seven, just one week short of her 79th year of religious profession. On Friday morning, January 3, the Most Reverend Floyd L. Begin, Bishop of Oakland, celebrated the Requiem Mass for Mother Bernardina in the Motherhouse chapel. Concelebrating with Bishop Begin were the Very Reverend Paul Scanlon, O.P., prior of St. Albert's; the Reverend Martial Luebke, O.F.M. provincial secretary; the Reverend Cornelius Snyder, O.F.M.; and the Reverend John Williams, pastor of St. Joseph Church, Mission San Jose. The Very Reverend Paul Zammit, O.P., preached, and Dominican students from St. Albert's College assisted in the sanctuary. Among the many present for the obsequies were Father Seraphin Muller, O.F.M. and his 90 year old uncle, who had been Mother Bernardina's childhood friend. Mother was laid to rest in God's Acre beside her beloved companion of so many years, Mother Seraphina Maerz.

St. John Seminary, Camarillo

The Congregation's embarking on a new mission in 1939 was triggered by a letter to Mother Seraphina from Archbishop John

Cantwell of Los Angeles. The letter had reference to the new St. John Seminary in Camarillo, California, to be built for the students studying for the priesthood in the Archdiocese of Los Angeles. A land grant, received by the archdiocese from Don Juan Camarillo for the property located near the town that bears his name, specified its use for the sole purpose of the construction of a seminary. The gift coincided with the elevation of the diocese into a second metropolitan district of California, the Archdiocese of Los Angeles. The Archbishop's letter to Mother Seraphina concerned the seminary staffing:

> June Sixteenth, 1937
>
> Very Reverend Mother Seraphin, O.P., [sic]
> DOMINICAN CONVENT,
> Mission San Jose,
> Alameda County, California.
>
> My dear Mother Seraphin:
>
> I would be extremely grateful if at my expense you could arrange for your Community, with the help of a chef, to take general supervision of the new Seminary that I hope will open within two years. In the plans I am including a convent.
>
> I know the great difficulty that my request will propose at first reading. Your Community has done so well and is prospering with so much distinction in Southern California that I feel you would like to help me in my problem. It will be absolutely necessary to get a Community of Nuns to superintend the domestic arrangements of the Seminary. Every other system that has been tried in this country has failed.
>
> I want you to give this matter serious consideration in union with your Council.
>
> Very devotedly yours,
> John J. Cantwell
> ARCHBISHOP of Los Angeles[1]

One week later Mother Seraphina sent her considered reply:

June 23, 1937

Most Reverend John J. Cantwell, D.D.,
Archbishop of Los Angeles,
Los Angeles, California.

Most Reverend and dear Archbishop Cantwell:

I have seriously considered Your Excellency's proposal and have spoken the matter over with my councilors. Much as we would like to do you the favor, we see no possible way of complying with your request.

The scarcity of vocations, along with the growth of schools, renders it a difficult task to supply the necessary aid for the upkeep of existing institutions. Several of the larger Houses of the Congregation have already taken recourse to outside help in the kitchen for the reason that the Sisters were lacking in number.

Then, also, the work of the supervision of seminaries and the like institutions is outside the scope of work undertaken by the Congregation....

We thank you for your kind words of appreciation, and we wish to assure you of our earnest endeavor to be of service whenever possible.

Your Excellency's humble servant,
Sister M. Seraphina, O.P.
Prioress General[2]

The Acts of the Eighth General Chapter at which Mother Bernardina was elected Prioress General included the following announcement:

> We announce that in response to the urgent and repeated requests of the Most Reverend John J. Cantwell, D.D., Archbishop of Los Angeles, our Congregation will undertake the supervision of the domestic arrangements of the archdiocesan seminary to be erected in that archdiocese in about two years.[3]

The "repeated requests" cannot be verified, as only one additional letter from Archbishop Cantwell (February 6, 1939) relating to seminary staffing is found in the archives of the Congregation. It is an answer to a letter from Mother Bernardina relating to the duties of the seminary staff. The principal work of the sisters assigned to seminary duty anticipated, would be the "running of the kitchen and the care of the dining room."[4] A chef would be responsible for the cooking and students will wait on table. For heavier work, men would be hired. In addition, the sisters will be expected to supervise the laundry. "I am sure," the Archbishop added:

> ...that it will be a pleasure and a privilege for the Sisters to care for the main Chapel and the Priests' Oratory, and to care for the Altar Linens also. There will be no direct contact of the Sisters with the students, and their relations to the faculty will generally be arranged through the President or *Econome*. "Corridors and halls could be attended to" while the students were at prayer! "Any other services will be incidental....I am sure of the cooperation of the Sisters in

Dominican Staff at St. John Seminary, Camarillo: (l to r) Sisters Roberta Diaz-Martinez, Erharda Ensinger, Josephine Koehl, Marka Grips and Nemesia Schwarzenback c. 1942

anything that will contribute to the more perfect formation of the life of the Priest.[5]

The outline did not leave the sisters much free time or even prayer time apart from the early morning hours, and may have prompted Mother Bernardina's exhortation at the close of her first Visitation:

> ...Your hard labor, undertaken in the spirit of self-denial, is one of the means for the advancement of the good cause of educating young men to the priesthood of Christ. You are serving those who are, or are destined to be other Christs unto the salvation of souls. You are providing for their material needs in order that their bodies may have the endurance required for the hard study, which is necessary to prepare them for their future priestly ministrations.[6]

The words were addressed to the sisters comprising the first community two months after their arrival: Sisters Hedwig Infanger, superior; Marka Grips, Salome Esser, Canisia Getz and Roberta Diaz-Martinez. They were a sturdy lot, but it is evidence of her concern for them that Mother Bernardina held Visitation so soon after their arrival.

On its tenth anniversary *The Evangelist*, student publication of the seminarians, recognized the work of the sisters in fulsome tribute:

> Like their sisters in religion in the Archdiocese, they fulfill their Dominican vocation by their humble tasks in the Seminary, by their prayers and recitation of the Divine Office, and by praising, blessing, and silently preaching the Lord by their example and good deeds. We can only add our meager words of gratitude and appreciation on behalf of our alumni and the students of the Seminary because we have learned from the grand example of their consecrated leaven who have spurned the life of the world.[7]

Pax Erholungsheim, Bavaria

The success of the seminary work at St. John's encouraged the Congregation in 1940 to undertake service at the *Pax Erholungsheim*, in Wallgau, Bavaria, a vacation place for priests and children. A

Sisters at Wallgau: (l to r) Sisters Ludwig Maria Voggenauer, Paulina Getz, Mechtildis Okos and Geralda Steer

jewel of a setting at the foot of the Bavarian Alps, the Wallgau site provided an ideal rest and vacation spot and proved an unforeseen blessing during World War II, as it qualified as a place of service required by the government. Some sisters could be sent there to serve rather than be conscripted for service in military hospitals. With the restoration of peace, the *Pax Heim,* as it was familiarly known, returned to its role as a priests' vacation residence. Mountain climbing enthusiasts among the sisters enjoyed the facility on occasion, also.

In time the popularity of the place became its downfall. These were pre-Vatican II times and individually celebrated Masses meant that the sisters were often washing and ironing altar linens into the night. In addition, ailing priests required special attention. The sisters bade a regretful goodbye to the *Pax Heim* when the work became too much for the few that could be spared.

One reason for the sisters' personnel shortage was that, as the war dragged on, monasteries were frequently taken over as military hospitals and sisters were recruited for service. Such was the destiny of the Benedictine monastery of Attl high on the bluff above the Inn River near Altenhohenau. Sisters from Altenhohenau were not surprised when they were called to service. To her great disappointment, Sister Stilla Sinseder was among the chosen and assigned to domestic duty in the big kitchen. From a window on the bluff, she could see the spire of Altenhohenau in the distance and the sight was too much for her. Day after day she wept her way through her duties until the officer in charge finally sent her home and told her to stay there! Never did a recruit comply so happily; the reunion was a joyous one.

School of the Madeleine, Berkeley

The University of California established its first permanent campus in the city of Berkeley lying to the northeast across the Bay from San Francisco. Its growing reputation soon earned for the city the title of the "Athens of the West." St. Mary Magdalen Parish was founded almost within the shadow of the University Campanile and entrusted to the Dominican Fathers of the Western Province. Although established on February 1, 1923, the parish did not receive a pastor, Father Francis Pius Driscoll, O.P., until the following July. The five-month interim did not prove much of a grace period, however, as Father Driscoll found neither church nor rectory awaiting him when he arrived. For nearly a year Sunday Mass was offered in the auditorium of Thousand Oaks public school on Milvia Street between Eunice and Berryman. Another four months were spent in locating a site, which was finally found and purchased from the Southern Pacific Railroad in north Berkeley. Despite the delay in getting started, both church and rectory were completed in a little less than five months. Dedication took place on August 18, 1924.

After an interval of four years, the pastor, Father Daniel O'Brien, O.P., invited the Mission San Jose sisters to teach catechism in the parish. Dutifully each Saturday afternoon and Sunday morning, two sisters from St. Elizabeth's Convent, Oakland, made their way to Milvia Street in Berkeley to instruct the children of St. Mary Magdalen, about one hundred attending regularly.

In May, 1931, Father Christopher Lamb, O.P., pastor, wrote to Mother Seraphina, Prioress General, informing her that the Archbishop had granted permission for a parochial school to be completed by September 1, 1932. The letter shared his hopes:

> We expect to begin with about sixty children in the first five or six grades, and year by year, work up to the full eight grades. Of course, we expect you to take over the school. Two Sisters could teach the four grades of the primary school, and if the fifth and sixth are started, a third Sister will be needed. Please let me know as soon as possible what you will graciously do.
>
> Hoping to receive a favorable answer, and wishing you and all the Sisters God's choicest blessings,
>
> Yours very truly in St. Dominic
>
> C.V. Lamb, O.P.[8]

The Seventh General Chapter, meeting (from August 1 to 4, 1931) at the Motherhouse, had announced the acceptance of the School of the Madeleine to open in September 1932. Such would not be the case, however, as another letter from Father Lamb notified Mother Seraphina:

> The bids were opened at 11 a.m. and were satisfactory; but our finances were not. Just lately the Archbishop's Council made a rule that no new school could be built unless at least half of the necessary money was at hand.
>
> Therefore, it was decided _not_ to build our school at present.
>
> The Archbishop's Building Committee will take up the matter again after the first of next year. Our only hope of building immediately is by raising $15,000. But I am almost certain that cannot be done. The sisters you kindly promised us will be free to teach elsewhere for another year. By that time we hope to have the school ready without the present uncertainty. We must be satisfied with the sisters for an hour a week on Saturdays and Sundays until we have our school built. The sisters have done much good among the children and people. May God continue to bless them and their work.[9]

Father Lamb would not see the school built during his pastorate. It would take five years of vigorous fund raising—bazaars, raffles, card parties, variety shows, etc., –to bring the school to reality. But on May 16, 1937, the cornerstone of the school was finally laid, and on August 22, Archbishop John J. Mitty, archbishop of San Francisco, blessed the building before an assembly composed of Father Humbert H. Kelly, O.P., pastor, his fellow Dominicans, parishioners, friends, and sisters.

School opened the following month with 137 students and four teaching sisters, and in the short space of four days rose to 156. Each teacher had a combination class of two grades. Sister Amanda Meyers was superior and principal; Sister Rosalinda (Linda) Henriques taught the first and second grades; Sister Mary Helen Bauer, the third and fourth; Sister Clarita Center, the fifth and sixth; and Sister Amanda, the seventh and eighth. Adding to the community were Sister Valeria Cummings who taught music, and Sister Marka Grips who was responsible for domestic duties. Ten days previously the sisters had moved into their "temporary" convent, the Murphy residence at 1321 Milvia Street. Here they were destined to live for the next twelve years!

John J. Mitty, Archbishop of San Francisco, 1935–1961

By 1947 the school had increased in population from 156 to 287. Classes were still combined, and a waiting list grew longer and longer, not only from St. Mary Magdalen, but from neighboring parishes as well. Two years later, the school plant was extended by the addition of classrooms and a library, and a convent was built for the sisters. The addition allowed the school to open with eight single grades for the first time. Father William T. Lewis. O.P., pastor, was responsible for the single grade arrangement. During the pastorate of Father William A. Norton, O.P., (1952–1959) a kindergarten was added and the playground greatly enlarged. At about the same time, the school parents were instrumental in setting up a school cafeteria. The school that Father Lamb had envisioned more than two decades earlier was at last complete.

The School of the Madeleine celebrated its Twenty-Fifth Anniversary on September 23, 1962, with a High Mass, offered by the pastor Father W. G. Martin, O.P., followed by an open house. The occasion was one of general rejoicing and commendations were extended to the dedicated priests, sisters and lay teachers who had worked together since the beginning to promote a strong Christian spirit among the youth they served and to maintain a tradition of excellence in curriculum and scholarship.

St. Mary Magdalen Convent chapel altar

Before closing the account of the early years in Berkeley, the sisters' chapel deserves special mention. The altar, designed by Sister Justina Niemierski, Dominican artist and hand carved for the chapel by the Mayer Studio, Oberammergau, Germany, was erected onsite in 1952, the gift of Sister Benedict McNeil's family. According to Sister Benedict, "Both Sister Justina and Sister Gregoria [Kratz] gave much time and devoted their respective talents to [the] chapel."[10] The result of the cooperation between artists and studio is the beautiful wood-carved altar in the sisters' chapel today.

Restoration of the Congregation in Mexico

Soon after Mother Bernardina took office in 1937 there were clear signs of growing political stability in Mexico. She lost no time returning Sisters Natalia Garcia and Dominica Ochoa from California to their homeland in 1938. They were welcomed by Sister María Almaguer and the few sisters who had not left Mexico during the late revolution. In 1936 they were able to reoccupy *Santo Domingo* convent in San Miguel de Allende and open *Colegio Santo Domingo* in 1937. Sister Natalia was appointed Superior of Mexico in 1938.

In 1942 word was received that former properties which had been confiscated could be recovered. Sister Natalia then opened *Colegio San Rafael* in Colonia San Rafael in a rented house while working to recover the property in Tlalpalm. The rent payments were so high and the sisters so poor that Mother Bernardina assessed the priories in California for funds to help maintain *San Rafael*. After extended legal and financial negotiations Sister's efforts to regain Tlalpalm were achieved in 1943. With funds realized from the sale of that property, a home in the Tacubaya district of Mexico City was purchased. *Colegio San Rafael* with its rapidly growing enrollment was moved there and incorporated under a new title, *Instituto Lacordaire*.

Mother Bernardina, meanwhile, was taking further action to lay the groundwork for a novitiate in Mexico. Having given Sister

Chapel of Santo Domingo Novitiate, San Miguel de Allende

Natalia authority to receive postulants in San Rafael, she appealed to the proper authorities in Rome and Mexico for permission to open a novitiate in San Miguel. Permission was granted on August 7, 1943. Sister Margarita Lira, who had come to the United States at the time of the persecution and was teaching science at Queen of the Holy Rosary College, was appointed novice mistress. Despite restrictions on travel during World War II, Mother Bernardina, accompanied by Sister Teresa Meyer as translator, made a formal visitation in Mexico the following January. On February 2, 1944 she presided at the entry into the Congregation of our first two San Miguel novices: Sisters Rosa María (Francisca) Peralta and María Inés (Adda) Guerrero. They were followed by a steady stream of two or three novices each year.

Following the war additional sisters returned from California to help Mexico in its recovery, notably Sister Fidelis Espinosa in 1946, Sister Juana Bustamante in 1947 and Sister Paz Madrid in 1951.

At the urgent request of the parents in Delicias, Chihuahua, the Congregation assumed responsibility for a school in northern Mexico, *Colegio La Paz*, in September 1951. In existence for a number of years when the sisters took over, the school had been under the direction of lay teachers. In addition, two parochial schools, designated "poor schools," were opened in Delicias.

A new era began for the Congregation in Mexico when the 58 professed sisters were established as a Region, with Sister María Concepta Maciel as the first Regional Superior. It was a well-deserved recognition. The Congregation had weathered the hazardous and unsettling days of the persecution because of the faith and courage of the sisters. Now our sisters in Mexico were free to turn their energy and resolve into broadening their evangelization of the people to include catechetics for the poor, preparing children and adults for the reception of the Sacraments, visiting shut-ins in hospitals and homes, directing youth and Bible groups, teaching alphabetization, hygiene, and domestic arts to the poor in outlying districts, and serving on mission teams among the indigenous people. Theirs continues to be a proud chapter in the history of the Congregation

Notes

[1] Cantwell, letter to Maerz, 16 June 1937.

[2] Maerz, letter to Cantwell, 23 June 1937.

[3] Acts of the Eighth General Chapter (28 July-5 August 1937) 18.

[4] Cantwell, letter to Michel, 6 February 1939.

[5] Cantwell, letter to Michel, 6 February 1939.

[6] Michel, "Visitation Book," (1939).

[7] *"The Evangelist,"* Winter Anniversary Issue, 1949, 42.

[8] Christopher V. Lamb, O.P., letter to Maerz, 28 May 1931.

[9] Christopher V. Lamb, O.P., letter to Maerz, 7 July 1931.

[10] Sister Benedict McNeil, O.P., letter, n.d

CHAPTER TWENTY-EIGHT

GOOD MEASURE

At the Tenth General Chapter, July 28 to August 5, 1949, Sister Mary Pius Marbaise was elected fourth Prioress General of the Congregation. Born in Hoboken, New Jersey, on May 6, 1883, the elder of two daughters of Henry Otto Marbaise and Eugenie Marie Louise Deveaux, she was two years old when her parents returned to Europe, settling in Cologne. With the death of her beloved mother in 1897, Eugenie was sent to live with her paternal grandfather and maiden aunts, and her sister was enrolled in an elite boarding school. In her grandfather's home, Eugenie was reared in a cultural environment that quickly introduced her to the world of ballet, concert and stage, which captivated her. Her formal education included St. Leonard's Higher School in Aachen and Teachers' Training College, where she earned a diploma qualifying her to teach in any school in the Empire. Languages, music and art became her special interests, which she continued to cultivate throughout her life. But sometime in her seventeenth year, she underwent a conversion from her worldly way of life and attraction for the stage to a desire to dedicate herself to God.

Drawn to the Dominican Order and our Congregation in particular by its strong liturgical orientation, she entered the postulancy at Altenberg, Moresnet Neutre, in 1903 and was sent almost immediately to California. As a postulant she taught in San Francisco at St. Anthony and St. Boniface schools. In June 1904 she received the habit, asking for the name of Pius because of kinship on her mother's side to Pope Pius VI (1775–1799). Profession followed in 1905. The next years she spent in teaching in the parochial schools of San Francisco and the normal school at Mission San Jose. In 1912, the year after her final profession, Sister Pius was appointed novice director and began at once to organize a program of novitiate studies that included liturgy, Dominican and church history, and spirituality. Her facility in languages stood her in good stead, as she was able to conduct the novitiate classes in English, German, or Spanish as needed. She was indeed a woman of many talents. Despite her delicate health, she regularly marched the novices up the hill to the vineyards of Mission Peak to pick grapes for the community table.

Mother Pius Marbaise, Prioress General, 1949–1961

These were the formative years of the Congregation when Mother Pia was at work on the *Constitutions*. Sister Pius was of valuable assistance to her in translating the documents into Latin and French for presentation in Rome. Though without official title, she regularly acted as Mother Pia's "foreign correspondent" and assumed responsibility for communication with the Congregation for Religious, as well as with the Dominican Fathers at the Generalate in Santa Sabina, Rome. Many became her personal friends and faithful correspondents for life.

March 6, 1922 was a memorable day for Sister Pius. In the morning she was summoned to Mother Pia's office and told that Rome had granted the Congregation permission to open a novitiate in Tlalpam, D.F., Mexico, and that the Council had appointed her novice director. Immediately and characteristically, she set about using whatever spare time she had to study Mexican history, beginning with the early Mayan and Aztec civilizations, their mythology and religious beliefs. "Having to live in that mysterious country who knows for how long, I find it necessary to become informed as much as possible,"[1] she wrote to a relative.

On September 22 Sister Pius, accompanied by Mother Seraphina, left the Motherhouse en route to her new mission field. After a stopover in Los Angeles, their next destination was El Paso, Texas, where they crossed the Mexican border into Ciudad Juarez. There they boarded the one Pullman car available for the long trip to Mexico City. The Pullman was hot; the taco and tamale vendors were annoying in their insistence. Sleep was out of the question. The train groaned "like a poor asthmatic patient"[2] as it climbed to an altitude of more than 7,000 feet. When they reached the desert, the dust was so thick that the porter went through the cars four times a day, wiping the windows with a damp cloth, which turned the dust to mud. Finally on the evening of September 29, during a torrential downpour, the weary pair arrived in Mexico City. There they were welcomed by a former student and her husband who drove them to *Colegio San Rafael*, where, more dead than alive, they were greeted warmly by Sister Teresa Meyer and the eager community.

For the next 14 years, Sister Pius would play a cat and mouse game with officials of the Mexican government, managing to stay one step ahead of them despite her calm and deliberate manner. She was bred to the challenge, having come—she maintained— from Norman stock dating back to Charlemagne. Her forebears ravaged France and Germany with such fury that for a time the Church inserted into the Litany of the Saints the invocation, "From the fury of the Normans, deliver us, O Lord." She delighted in the shock value of her "pirate" ancestry, but was equally proud to claim as relative a contemporary of St. Thomas Aquinas, who, like the saint, was famous as theologian, philosopher, and Greek scholar and who translated the works of Aristotle from Greek into Latin, meanwhile purging the translation of error. In Mexico her forebears would serve her in good stead as she assumed increasing responsibility for the sisters there. Her steadfast courage under pressure served to bolster the self-assurance of the more timid members of the community. At no time, she often said later, did she feel God's presence and provident love more tangibly than during those harrowing years of persecution and pursuit. And despite the menacing conditions in which she was forced to live, she carried in her heart for the rest of her life a deep love for Mexico and its people.

After Mexico came six years as prioress of St. Catherine's, Anaheim; six as prioress of Immaculate Conception, San Francisco; and one as prioress of the Motherhouse, Mission San Jose. While prioress of St. Catherine's, she was summoned to the parlor one day to meet a visitor. There to her astonishment stood the former President of Mexico, the "iron man," Plutarco Calles, who had brought his two sons to be enrolled in the school. He explained that he had promised his deceased wife, a Catholic, that the boys would make their First Communion; he was here to fulfill that promise now. Enjoying the irony of the situation, Sister Pius accepted the boys with her usual calm demeanor. Whether Calles recognized his old adversary is not known.

Mother Pius leaves for Mexico, her first visit as Prioress General 1950

Warmly human, with a wealth of experience behind her, she radiated a kind of tranquility that had a quieting effect on the communities she served. Her way of handling most situations was simple. In time of difficulty, her counsel was usually, "Never mind, Sister. It will all work out. Nothing happens that the Lord does not know. We will pray about it."[3] Then out would come her rosary, one of the great loves of her life. And if things got really out of hand, she would take to the organ. Those who lived with her knew that something had genuinely upset Sister Prioress when she was at the organ again.

Sister Pius's term as Motherhouse prioress was ceased abruptly after one year when she was elected Prioress General at the Tenth General Chapter of 1949, a responsibility she would carry for the next 12 years. It was a time of rapid expansion and multiple vocations, a time in which the early years of struggle and uncertainty on the part of the Congregation matured into a seasoned acceptance of itself. As encapsulated scripturally by the eloquent Father Noel Moholy, O.F.M., in his homily at the Congregation's Diamond Jubilee Mass of Thanksgiving in St. Mary's Cathedral, San Francisco on November 4, 1951:

> We are assembled this morning to thank God for the blessings that have been lavished during seventy-five years upon the Dominican Congregation of the Queen of the Holy Rosary. This archdiocese has grown up with these sisters and they in turn have flourished and multiplied in and with this metropolitan See...We are amazed and they are astounded at the largess with which Christ has fulfilled His infallible guarantee: 'Give, and it shall be given to you: good measure, pressed down, shaken together, running over shall they pour into your lap. For with what measure you measure, it shall be measured unto you in return' (Lk 6:38).[4]

The Gospel passage from St. Luke would prove an apt description of Mother Pius's 12 years as Prioress General. The largesse of the good measure would be lavished on California, Oregon and Bavaria, coming full circle to the Motherhouse.

Four months after Archbishop Cantwell's death, Archbishop J. Francis A. McIntyre arrived in Los Angeles from New York to succeed to the vacant See. He lost no time in making his pres-

James Francis McIntyre, Archbishop of Los Angeles, 1947–1952, Cardinal of Los Angeles, 1952–1970

ence felt. Within a year of his arrival, he had launched a $9,000,000 campaign for the building of Catholic elementary and secondary schools in the Archdiocese. Well planned and orchestrated, the campaign was a success, and poor parishes received a shot in the arm when funds were made available to them for Catholic schools.

Santa Teresita School, Los Angeles

One parish to benefit from the Archbishop's campaign was Santa Teresita, which served the Mexican-American community in East Los Angeles. A letter addressed to Mother Pius from the Chancellor of the Archdiocese, Auxiliary Bishop Timothy Manning, alerted her to the part Mission San Jose Dominicans were expected to play in consequence of the drive.

January 30, 1950

Mother Pius, O.P.
Dominican Sisters
San Jose, California

Dear Mother Pius:

At the request of his Excellency, the Most Reverend Archbishop, I am writing this letter to you. As you know, here in the Archdiocese we have entered into an extensive program of providing schools for our children. This has entailed great sacrifices on behalf of our people. In an effort to provide Sisters for these schools, we have, in the past, requested communities that have already substantial schools in the diocese to make an extra effort to take over one of the schools in the less privileged areas.

At this time, I am writing particularly about the parish of Santa Teresita in the vicinity of the General Hospital. A new school and convent are being completed there at the moment, and we would very much like if the Dominican Sisters could arrange to provide a few Sisters to inaugurate the school.

I am sure that, while it would mean sacrificing personnel in some of the other schools, it would bring a great blessing on the community.

Thanking you for your attention to this request, I am

Very sincerely yours,

Timothy Manning
Auxiliary Bishop of Los Angeles
Chancellor[5]

The appeal did not fall on deaf ears. Mother Pius accepted the school, but stated clearly the number of teachers that would be available at the outset. Within the week came a second letter from Bishop Manning expressing his gratitude to Mother Pius for being "able to supply even two Sisters for the new school at Santa Teresita."[6] He noted the proximity of the school to Sacred Heart and informed her that he had already advised Father Antonio Boquet, pastor, who would communicate with her further.

On September 7, 1950, four sisters arrived in Los Angeles to form the first Dominican community of Santa Teresita Parish. Constituting the original community were Sister Amalia Weber, superior; Sister Marguerite Mendoza, principal; Sister Ignatia May, teacher and Sister Armella Flores, cook. At 10:45 a.m. the same day, Sister Dolores Stopper, superior of nearby Sacred Heart Convent, presided at a simple ceremony of installation of Santa Teresita's su-

Santa Teresita Elementary School, Los Angeles

perior. Then followed a tour of the sisters' new home, which proved to be a composite—two neighborhood bungalows joined. The next morning the chapel was blessed by Father Boquet, and succeeded immediately by a *Missa cantata*. Sisters from Sacred Heart, St. Michael's and Flintridge formed the choir. Father Charles Dignam, parochial assistant, was also present and welcomed the sisters.

Three days later, September 11, school got underway with 140 students assigned as follows: Grade One—55; Grade Two—35; Grade Three—25; Grade Four—25. In school little more than a week, both teachers and students were mildly surprised to receive a formal visit from the archdiocesan school supervisors, all three descending on the same day!

The sisters lost no time in getting established. By mid-November they had organized a Mothers' Club, and in December presented the students in their first Christmas play. On the following February 24, over 200 children received the Sacrament of Confirmation; and on May 27 nineteen students made their First Holy Communion. Dedication of the school, however, did not occur until February 4, 1952, Bishop Joseph T. McGucken, auxiliary bishop of Los Angeles, presiding.

At the end of the second school year, the sisters were stunned and saddened when Father Boquet suffered a severe stroke and died ten days later on August 10, 1952. His funeral, held from Santa Teresita Church on August 13, was crowded with clergy, sisters and parishioners. Appointed as administrator in Father Boquet's place was Father Charles Dignam.

School opened for the third year on September 15 with six grades and a student registration of 264. Comprising the staff were the following: Sister Emilia Techtman (Grade One); Sister Marguerite Mendoza (Grade Two and Principal); Sister Columba Dávalos (Grade Three); Sister Rosina Hageman (Grade Four) and Sister Geraldine Kelly (Grades Five and Six). Sister Marguerite was appointed superior of the convent also, as Sister Amalia's failing health did not permit her to continue. Sister Mathia Zircus completed the community as housekeeper.

With the addition of a seventh grade the following year, enrollment jumped to 345 and to 401 in 1954, when the eighth grade brought the school to capacity. Because the number of First Communicants was so large, Father Dignam judged it advisable to separate the boys from the girls. Ninety-five girls made their First Communion on May 23, succeeded the following Sunday by 125 boys. In the afternoon all First Communicants, to the number of 300 (including those from St. Lucy's Mission) took part in a procession in honor of Mary, Queen of May. Since the church could not hold all the people, the procession moved out to the school grounds. The year closed with the school's first graduation on June 16, 1955. Thirty students received their diplomas from Father Dignam at an evening ceremony in a packed church.

For the first time in 1954, summer vacation school was held at Santa Teresita. Almost 200 public school children attended the classes conducted by Sisters Marguerite Mendoza, Clarissa Marie Kozcielski and Mary de Sales Sondergeld. Summer vacation school climaxed with many children receiving their First Communion.

Santa Teresita Elementary School stands as a solid witness to Archbishop McIntyre's intention of providing Catholic education for inner city children and to the Mission San Jose Dominican Sisters' commitment to inner city children. The union was a happy one.

St. James Boys' School, San Francisco

Following the withdrawal of the Brothers of Mary from St. James Boys' School and St. James High School, San Francisco, in order to staff the new archdiocesan Riordan High School, Mother Pius agreed to take over St. James Boys' School, Grades Three to Eight, beginning in September, 1950. She would provide two sisters for the first year. But when Monsignor Patrick J. Quinn, St. James pastor, offered to hire an additional lay teacher for the Girls' School if she would assign three sisters for the Boys' School, she consented to the change. The sisters staffing the Boys' School moved into the Brothers' former residence, and on August 29 Monsignor Quinn celebrated the first Mass in the refurbished convent. Later the same day, Mother Pius installed Sister Angela Marie Boedigheimer as superior, adding to her responsibilities as principal and eighth grade teacher. Comprising the other sisters on the faculty were Sister Matthew (Mary Alice) O'Shea and Sister Mary Luke (Theresa) Braun. Sister Amanda Meyer, assistant, and Sister Valentina Droesch, cook, made up the St. James community roster. Sharing the convent with them were the sisters of St. Boniface School in downtown San Francisco: Sister Mary Jane Dennis, principal; Sister Consolata Espinosa, Sister Eucharia Heidt, and Sister Mary Peter Traviss.

The arrangement did not endure for long. One month into the third school year, Mother Pius announced that the St. Boniface sisters would return to Immaculate Conception Academy to live. By arrangement with the Franciscan Fathers, a taxi cab called for the sisters of St. Boniface each morning, returning them to the convent in the late afternoon. The drawback in this arrangement was that a change in schedule obliged the sisters to receive Holy Communion each morning before Mass and leave before the end of Mass. The sisters were given little time to ponder the change of residence, as the next day, October 12, was a school holiday and the day chosen for moving!

For 20 years St. James Parish maintained the Girls' School and the Boys' School as separate units, but the financial implications of operating two elementary schools within the same parochial boundaries influenced the decision to merge. It was further decided that the new entity, St. James Parochial School, Grades K through Eight, would be housed in the Girls' School building on Fair Oaks Street. The merger was effected under the efficient leadership of Sister Rosalinda (Linda) Henriques, principal.

St. Frances Cabrini School, Los Angeles

In recognition of the needs of a rapidly growing section of southwest Los Angeles, the new parish of St. Frances Xavier Cabrini was established by Archbishop Cantwell in October 1946. The site selected for the new church was on Imperial Highway, a few miles east of the Los Angeles International Airport. Father Paul Konoske, a staunch friend of the community since his early days of priesthood in Sacred Heart Parish, was assigned as first pastor. It was he who, a mere three months after the canonization of Saint Frances Xavier Cabrini, the United States' first citizen saint, proposed to Archbishop Cantwell that the new parish be named after the recently canonized saint.

Mission San Jose Dominicans staffed the school in the adjoining parish of St. Michael, and Father Konoske appealed to his old friends when he was ready to assume responsibility for a school. Once again Mother Pius responded favorably; and on September 17, 1951, St. Frances Cabrini School opened in the parish hall, each class utilizing a corner of the auditorium. Two sisters and a lay teacher composed the original staff: Sister Siena Lawrence, first grade; Mrs. M. Kosek, second; and Sister Florita (Margaret Therese) Seidle, principal and third and fourth grades. The 139 students who were on hand for the opening day initially attended classes in the mornings only. Within the month, however, the school was completed on October 1, and classes began full-time in the new building.

The Tidings, Los Angeles archdiocesan weekly, began its dedication story on the school with a tribute to the parishioners:

> A monument in concrete and steel to the sacrifices of 1000 working-class families to provide Christ-centered education for their children will be dedicated this Sunday in Southwest Los Angeles.
>
> The monument is the new eight-classroom St. Frances Cabrini School at 1400 W. Imperial Hwy., a modern educational plant which, without a cent of cost to taxpayers, will serve the people of California for generations to come.[7]

Auxiliary Bishop Joseph T. McGucken blessed the building on Sunday, October 26, 1952, in an afternoon ceremony beginning at three o'clock. Monsignor Patrick J. Dignan, archdiocesan superintendent of schools, was the principal speaker. More than 60 priests, 90 sisters and a large number of parishioners were present for the occasion.

For two years the sisters lived at St. Michael's Convent and commuted to the neighboring parish, but in the spring of '53 ground-breaking for the sisters' residence took place. The convent was ready for occupancy in time for the school term beginning the following September.

Sister Cabrini (Patricia Marie) Walsh followed Sister Florita as principal in September 1956. During Sister's administration a new wing was added, necessitated by the growing enrollment which, by 1958, had increased more than fivefold to 738 students. Inspection by the fire department in January 1959, resulted in a strong recommendation that a maximum of 50 students to a classroom be immediately implemented. Father Konoski called a special faculty meeting to discuss the situation. The solution, proposed by the faculty and accepted by the pastor, called for the hiring of three additional lay teachers to relieve the congestion. But despite the hiring, the school could not keep pace. Enrollment continued to escalate until in September 1961 it reached 791, and St. Frances Cabrini became a 16 room school.

St. Nicholas / St. William School, Los Altos

On Holy Thursday morning, March 25, 1942, Frank Marini of Los Altos, California, a town lying some 40 miles south of San Francisco, turned the first spadeful of dirt at a ground-breaking ceremony for a new Catholic church. On land donated by the Marini family, Archbishop John J. Mitty of San Francisco had established a new parish church in October 1937. For ten years it operated as a mission of St. Joseph's, Mountain View, with Mass offered on Sundays and holydays in the local Los Altos American Legion hall.

Frank Marini was given the privilege of naming the new church; and he called it St. Nicholas after his father, Peter Nicola Marini, whose patron was St. Nicola of Bari, Italy. St. Nicholas was upgraded to a parish proper on December 2, 1947, when Archbishop Mitty appointed as first pastor Father Stanley J. Reilly, who had just completed a 15-year stint as a United States military chaplain that found him in a Japanese prison camp at the end of World War II.

At the outset, a parish census showed a total of 250 families that two years later tallied 600, the phenomenal growth explained by the supplanting of orchards by housing developments. Of tremendous support in the early days of the parish were the Sulpician Fathers of St. Joseph's College, Mountain View, particularly Father Robert Guigere, S.S. professor of philosophy, who regularly assisted Father Reilly with the six Sunday Masses his burgeoning parish demanded. Father Andrew Forster S.S. college director of Church Music, rendered assistance by forming a men's parish choir and training its members in Gregorian chant.

As younger families with children moved into the area, support for a school mushroomed; and Archbishop Mitty authorized

Father Reilly to begin a drive for funds. A 5.72 acre site, purchased in 1950, provided the necessary land; and plans for a one-story, eight-classroom building and a convent accommodating eight sisters were approved. Construction began at once. Originally scheduled to open with three grades, St. Nicholas added a fourth at the request of enthusiastic parents who approached Father Reilly and offered to underwrite the salary of a lay teacher if he would add another grade. Father agreed; and, when school opened on September 14, 1953, three Dominican Sisters and one lay colleague were on hand to welcome the 187 students registered. Sister Mary Helen Bauer, principal and superior, taught the fourth grade; Miss Laverne Tocher, the third; Sister Clarissa Marie Koscielski, the second; and Sister Siena Lawrence, the first. The three sisters set up temporary living quarters in the two faculty rooms, as the convent was still under construction.

From the outset the parish took the school to heart. Father Reilly announced a Mass for school children and their parents on September 20 in the parish auditorium. Over 500 attended. Henceforth, the nine o'clock Sunday Mass would be designated the "Children's Mass."

Proud of his school, the pastor frequently brought visitors to tour the building. He was delighted when a superintendent of public schools visited St. Nicholas and declared the school more beautiful and better appointed than any he had seen in the area.

Father Forster lent his assistance also in training the children to sing. Six weeks into the first school year, the convent annalist recorded proudly: "Our children turned out 100% at the 8:30 Mass closing the Forty Hours Devotion. We were happy to have them play an active part in the Holy Sacrifice by singing *Et cum Spiritu tuo* under Father Forster's direction."[8] Modest though their contribution was, the children sang with gusto, relishing the opportunity to respond to the celebrant.

Dedication of the school building was scheduled for All Saints Day, 1953. On November 1 all was in readiness when promptly at 2:30 p.m. Archbishop Mitty and attending clergy left the library in procession for the entrance to the school where children and guests were assembled. After blessing the exterior of the building, the Archbishop and clergy moved to the foyer for the blessing of classrooms and crucifixes. Passing between the Knights of Columbus

Color Guard, the procession entered the auditorium where the flag was blessed. A detail of U. S. Marines from Moffett Field raised the flag, while the school children gave the Flag Salute and led those present in the national anthem. Speakers followed, beginning with the star of the day, Richard Fleming, a fourth grade student. According to the convent annalist, "More than one priest present was heard to remark, 'How happy I was not to have to speak after that lad had finished!'"[9] The Reverend T. Mulligan, president of St. Patrick's Major Seminary, gave the principal address, and Father John Foudy, archdiocesan assistant superintendent of Catholic schools, narrated the ceremonies for the benefit of the guests present.

December proved an eventful month at St. Nicholas. In the first week, a meeting of school mothers spurred the organization of a Mothers' Club, which lost no time in planning a Christmas Party for the children. A second major December event was the sisters' move from the faculty rooms to the convent. The sisters, Father Reilly and Father Kavanagh, a parish visitor formed a procession, the pastor carrying the Blessed Sacrament from the auditorium to the convent chapel. A third event of significance occurred the next morning when Father Reilly offered the first Mass celebrated in the chapel. Finally on December 23, the little community had the happiness of welcoming Sisters Seraphica Behm and Valentina Droesch, who brought the community to full membership, the former serving as assistant superior and the latter as cook.

Spring saw 50 children, prepared by Sister Clarissa Marie, receive their Lord for the first time in a solemn ceremony that impressed the parents. Some weeks later, Open House featured a display of student work which was praised by the delighted parents. Refreshments were served by the hospitable, recently formed Mothers' Club. June 10, the last day of the scholastic year, brought St. Nicholas's first year to a successful close.

In July a meeting of pastor, faculty and parent representatives led to a decision to add, not only a scheduled fifth grade for the school year 1954–1955, but also a sixth. Parents again agreed to pay the additional salary of a second lay teacher for their rapidly growing school. They were agreeably surprised, however, when Mother Pius managed to send two sisters for the new year, Sisters Sophia Kettlewell and Damian Wilson, so that the hiring of a second lay teacher was not necessary. At the time Sister Alan (Allyne) Ayres replaced Sister Siena Lawrence in the first grade. St. Nicholas School was set for its second year with five teaching sisters, one lay teacher and a student body of 304.

Meanwhile, the parish continued its phenomenal growth; and on June 30, 1959, Father Reilly announced a momentous change: Archbishop Mitty wished the parish formally divided into two! St. Nicholas Parish would suffer a name change and henceforth would be known as St. William's. Father Glenn Kelly would be pastor and newly ordained Father John Petroni, assistant. The school auditorium would serve as parish church, and the priests would move into the former Rodgers' home behind the convent.

Archbishop Mitty appointed Father Richard Meade as pastor of the new parish with the old name, St. Nicholas. He would have no assistant. As the new parish had St. Nicholas Church within its boundaries but no school building, school would begin in September with a first grade only, using St. William's School library as classroom. Miss Patricia Delgarde would form a staff of one to teach the 38 first graders. Sister Mary Hilary Miller, who replaced Sister Mary Helen as superior and principal of St. William's, would assist St. Nicholas School in getting underway. As principal of both schools, Sister Mary Hilary found herself in the delicate position of being accountable to two pastors at the same time. But the situation was only temporary. The following year the new St. Nicholas School opened on its own campus under the direction of the Irish Sisters of Mercy.

Mission San Gabriel High School

In the mid-1940s Father J. Nuevo, C.M.F., Mission San Gabriel pastor, wrote a letter to the parishioners sharing his vision for the future:

> For several years people in this community have felt the urgent need of establishing a Catholic High School to complete the moral training and religious education so ably imparted in our grammar school...For this reason ever since I was appointed Pastor of the Old Mission, my most cherished ambition has been to provide a first-class, up-to-

date High School for our boys and girls, to start them out in life with a well-balanced mind and a highly trained will.[10]

By the time of his transfer in 1948, Father Nuevo had raised a sizable $245,000 toward the realization of the project. His successor, Father Eugene Herran, C.M.F., enjoyed a pastorate of only 11 months, as his success in dealing with the complexities of the high school building project resulted in his election as General Treasurer of the Claretian Fathers.

The high school plan called for a co-institutional school; the boys would occupy one wing and the girls the other. The Claretian Fathers would provide the teaching staff for the boys, and the Mission San Jose Dominican Sisters, the staff for the girls. By design the plan would allow satisfactory social contacts between the boys and girls, but would avoid the possible distractions of a completely co-educational system.

On Sunday, January 16, 1949, groundbreaking ceremonies took place. Bishop Timothy Manning, auxiliary bishop of Los Angeles, officiated; and Monsignor Patrick J. Dignan, superintendent of Catholic schools, addressed the large crowd gathered to witness the ceremony.

Of an architectural style in harmony with the Mission, the high school was erected on the historic old Mission Quadrangle. The new school opened in September 1949 with a freshman class of 119 girls and boys, quartered temporarily in All Souls grammar school in nearby Alhambra. Six months later (February 1950) the freshmen moved into their new building. Father John Schneider, C.M.F., and Sister Redempta Prose, O.P., were the respective principals, with staffs that numbered three priests—Fathers Schneider, C.M.F., Leo Mattecheck, C.M.F., and Joseph Anglim, C.M.F.; three sisters—Sisters Redempta, O.P., Columba Dávalos, O.P., and Mary Raymond Carmody, O.P.; and two lay teachers—Mr. John Hanrahan and Mrs. Leo Ryder. In October Sister Maureen Murphy, O.P., joined the sisters' community as an additional staff member.

On Sunday, January 14, 1951, Archbishop J. Francis A. McIntyre dedicated the high school. The ceremony proved one of the highlights resulting from the Archbishop's Educational Fund campaign.

Sister Rita Marie Brown followed Sister Redempta as principal of the girls' high school in 1952. During the five years of her administration, the first graduation took place (June 1953). At an impressive ceremony, 110 graduates received diplomas and several awards. The following year the school was accredited by the University of California. Sister Alberta Oehlke served as principal of the girls' wing from 1957–1958, Sister John Dominic Samaha assuming responsibility for the girls' division the following September. During the latter's principalship space again became a problem, as the high school now drew students from 33 feeder schools, built during Archbishop McIntyre's drive for schools.

Missions in the Northwest continued to expand also. Between 1955 and 1958, the Congregation undertook the staffing of three new elementary schools in the developing district of Northeast Portland and relocating Immaculata Academy under a new name, Marycrest High School, in the same area.

St. Joseph the Worker School, Portland

St. Joseph Church, known also as the Kronenberg Church, was built in 1886 and is thought to be Oregon's second oldest Catholic Church on the east side of the Willamette River. In the fall of 1954, Archbishop Edward D. Howard, Archbishop of Portland in Oregon, appointed Father Jerome Schmitz pastor of St. Joseph Parish, encompassing 18 square miles and covering a good portion of East Multnomah County. A census taken at the time showed 700 Catholic families residing in the parish, a number which in five years would double.

On November 9, 1954, after a survey of the situation, Father Schmitz called a general meeting of parishioners at which those attending were unanimous in declaring that three parishes were needed to serve the area adequately. Further discussion yielded not only the name of the new parishes—the Kronenberg St. Joseph, to be known henceforth as St. Joseph the Worker; St. Therese of the Child Jesus; and St. Anne; but also in each case the parishioners demand for an elementary school. For the time being, Father Schmitz would remain pastor of the three parishes, subject to the approval of the Archbishop. The appeals met with a positive response from Archbishop Howard and from Mother Pius, who regarded the proposed elementary schools as feeders for the sisters' high school to be relocated shortly in the same general area.

Early the following year, Father Schmitz purchased a 10-acre tract on 148th and Division streets, a site judged central enough for the new St. Joseph the Worker Parish. A fund-raising campaign was immediately mounted and two classrooms, a sanctuary and a breezeway were ready and dedicated by the Archbishop in time for the opening of school in September 1955. Sister Rosalinda (Linda) Henriques was named principal and Sister Emilia Techtman appointed teacher. The school opened with three grades and 51 students. Sister Rosalinda taught 23 first graders and Sister Emilia, 16 second and 12 third graders.

According to Sister Emilia, the children were well-behaved and "a joy to teach,"[11] but the physical plant proved inconvenient. Each Friday afternoon the children packed their books in large bags and stockpiled them in the rear of the classroom, opened a curtain extending across the front of the room to reveal a simple altar and sanctuary, and readied the classroom for Sunday Mass. Each Sunday following Mass the process was reversed. As the sisters had no convent, they lived in a house on the newly purchased Marycrest property, approximately three miles distant. In the second year, the sisters' residence was moved to St. Dominic's Convent in Albina, a long commute of 8.6 miles, dangerous in the ice and snow.

Sister Paul Marie Batiloro replaced Sister Rosalinda as principal in September 1956, and taught the first and second grades, Sister Emilia moving to the third and newly added fourth grade. The following year an auditorium-church, kitchen and two classrooms were added to the original building.

While a satisfaction to the parishioners, the kitchen was not an unmixed blessing as far as the school was concerned. One day a mother brought her little son to be registered, but admitted that she could not pay tuition. "No problem," said Sister Emilia, "we'll take him."[12] Charity brought its own reward. A few weeks later the little boy came to Sister insisting that he smelled smoke. Sister checked the classroom, found nothing, but decided to look in the adjoining kitchen. To her horror smoke billowed into the classroom when she opened the door. Alerting the fire department and Father Schmitz, Father assured her that he would take care of the emergency. Within a matter of minutes, Sister was astounded to behold Father Schmitz running toward the school, holy water bucket and sprinkler in hand. Meantime, the fire department roared into the school parking lot. More effective than Father Schmitz with his bucket, the fire fighters quickly brought the fire under control. Cause of the fire was soon determined. Someone had forgotten to turn off the burner under the coffee pot, and paper goods stored by parishioners in the oven had ignited! Happily, severe damage was limited to a single wall; the little boy's insistence had saved the day. Embarrassed by the incident when they learned the cause, the sisters agreed to keep it a secret between them when they returned to the convent that evening. True to their promise, they said not a word; but unfortunately, the story made the morning newspaper!

In the summer of 1958, the parish purchased a house for the sisters in the proximity of the school. Dedication by Archbishop Howard took place on February 15, 1959; the sisters moved in two days later, delighted to be "next-door neighbors" to the school.

Through the years St. Joseph's advanced one grade annually until the eight grades were complete, the first class graduating in June 1961. The following September Sister Florence Cumbelich assumed the principalship of the school. Under Father Donald Denman, pastor, and Sister Mary Ignatius (Patricia) Layman, Sister Florence's successor, six additional classrooms were built to meet the rapidly growing enrollment.

St. Therese School, Portland

St. Therese of the Child Jesus Parish was canonically established by Archbishop Howard on January 1, 1955. For a time parishioners worshiped in an interim "Little Flower Chapel," located in a business building at N.E.122nd and Stark streets. Meantime, Father Schmitz purchased a nine-acre parcel at the corner of N.E. 132nd and Halsey streets; parishioners went to work to raise money for a church-school building, utilizing the identical floor plan of St. Joseph the Worker. Completed in the summer, the building was dedicated by Archbishop Howard on August 28, 1955, in good time for the opening of school on September 19.

Forty-five children made up the first three grades. Sister Rosalinda (Linda) Henriques' responsibilities were increased, as she now served as principal of two schools, St. Joseph the Worker and St. Therese. Sister Julia Perez was assigned to teach the first grade, and Mrs. Marian Edwards was responsible for the combination second and third grades. Under circumstances similar to St. Joseph's, the school was obliged to undergo a transformation every Friday afternoon in preparation for Sunday Mass. The multi-purpose use of the building entailed storing various school supplies and children's books and reversing the process after Sunday worship.

For the first year the sisters teaching at St. Therese lived with the sisters of St. Joseph in the house on the site of the future high school, but in the second year, a section of freshmen from Immaculata took over the house for classroom use. In consequence, the St. Therese community had to move to St. Dominic's Convent several miles west.

Unknown to Father Schmitz, a section of the new St. Therese Parish property had once been a gravel pit. Following the 1948 flood, that wiped out the trailer city of Vanport on the Columbia River near Portland, the debris—such as refrigerators, stoves, and sofas—were transported to the gravel pit and used as fill. Unaware of the prior use, Father Schmitz located the church-school partially over the filled area. The first winter, heavy rains caused the fill to settle and the building to collapse! Nothing daunted, Father Schmitz had the church-school rebuilt at once on another section of the property. Despite the setback, four classrooms and a parish hall were added in the years that followed (1957–1960). Eventually a three-bedroom house west of the school was purchased and enlarged to include a small chapel and two additional bedrooms. Sister Florita (Margaret Therese) Seidle, superior and principal, and Sisters Ignatia May, Paul Marie Batiloro, and Mary Ruth Buehrle, faculty, moved into the convent in March 1962.

The first graduating class consisting of 15 students—11 boys and 4 girls—received their diplomas from Father Schmitz on May 31, 1961. Since its foundation St. Therese has continued to serve the needs of the growing district of Northeast Portland.

St. Anne School, Gresham

In 1957 Father Schmitz made a pilgrimage to the shrine of St. Anne Beaupré in Canada to ask God's blessing on his third foundation, St. Anne Parish located predominantly within the boundaries of Gresham, a small town east of Portland and partially in Portland.

On his return he had the old Kronenberg St. Joseph Church moved from 166th and Powell Boulevard to 182nd Avenue in Portland to serve as the first St. Anne's Church. Later with a school in mind, he purchased a Methodist-Episcopal Church on Stark Street and had it moved adjacent to the St. Joseph Kronenberg Church. Combined, the two buildings constituted the parish church and school, the Methodist-Episcopal Church housing the first and second grades, and the St. Joseph Kronenberg Church basement, the third and fourth grades until the new classrooms were ready.

While occupied with the moving and remodeling, Father Schmitz found time for a third appeal to Sister Redempta Prose, prioress of St. Dominic's and principal of Immaculata Academy, for assistance in obtaining Dominican Sisters to staff St. Anne's. Accordingly, Sister Redempta wrote to Mother Pius at the Motherhouse in support of Father's request. In her letter Sister emphasized the advantage involved in staffing three parochial schools—St. Joseph, St. Therese and St. Anne—in the vicinity of the sisters' future high school. She assured Mother Pius that, despite the rapid housing development in Northeast Portland, parochial school plans were progressing at a more conservative rate. Hence, she need have no fear of a demand for a great number of sisters at any one time.

The reasons were evidently convincing enough to persuade Mother Pius and her Council to grant the requisite permission. St. Anne Elementary School opened in the fall of 1958. Sister Marcellina Gatschene was appointed founding principal and third and fourth grade teacher; Sister Agnes Mary Dembowski was assigned the first and second grades. The sisters commuted from St. Dominic's Convent on Stanton Street until February 1959 when they joined the St. Joseph School sisters in the house purchased for the latter. Father Daniel Kelly, who succeeded Father Schmitz as pastor of St. Anne's, later bought a house in Gresham for the sisters not far from the school.

In its second year, St. Anne's received a new principal and a fifth grade teacher, Sister Eileen (Angela) Molahan; the students moved into a new three-classroom building, which Archbishop Howard dedicated on February 14, 1960. For the school years 1960-1962, Sister Gonzaga Loftus served as principal of St. Anne's.

Immaculata Academy / Marycrest High School, Portland

Immaculata Academy had its humble beginning in 1911 in the parlors of St. Dominic's Convent in Immaculate Heart Parish, Portland (Cf. Ch. Six). For 18 years the former parish church, to which a wing had been added, served as the high school; but in 1929 a new one-story brick building was erected on Morris Street directly behind the old church.

Expanding enrollment (348 students in a building designed for 150), as well as a rapidly deteriorating neighborhood, made the search for a new location imperative; and in 1954 Sister Redempta Prose began looking for a new site. She found what she wanted in an 8.5 acre property in northeast Portland at 132nd Avenue and the Banfield Expressway within the boundaries of the new St. Therese Parish. The site had on it a house that could accommodate ten comfortably and would be available for temporary school use. Upon inquiring the sisters learned that the owners were asking $25,000 for the property. Terms were a down payment of $4,000 and $100 a month.

With the Motherhouse granting the requisite permission and the Apostolic Delegate approving the contracting of a loan, the purchase was soon completed. The sisters' agent must have been persuasive, for the actual price of the property was settled at $19,500. The new campus was christened "Marycrest." On December 8 the sisters ritually claimed the property when they formed a procession on campus and carried a statue of Our Lady into the house enthroning it on the mantle in the living room. Sister Redempta blessed the rooms as the sisters sang the *Salve Regina* asking Our Lady's blessing on the future Marycrest enterprise. In June groundbreaking for the high school took place, Father Schmitz presiding at the ceremony. According to approved plan, the school would consist of 10 units, two to be constructed beginning in March 1957. The estimated cost of the entire project was $1,496,810 and the capacity was set at 500 students.

Affairs moved forward rapidly, both City and County Planning Commissions approving the project in the spring of 1956. Fundraising events were scheduled to take place throughout the year, and negotiations for a succession of loans from the Knights of Columbus allowed construction to get underway.

The transfer of the Immaculata student body to the new campus was initiated in 1956 when half (50) freshman class moved to the Marycrest house for classes; the other half remained on the old Immaculata site. The following September, the entire freshman and sophomore classes were transferred to Marycrest, the juniors and seniors still attending Immaculata. In the same month, Archbishop Howard dedicated the new campus.

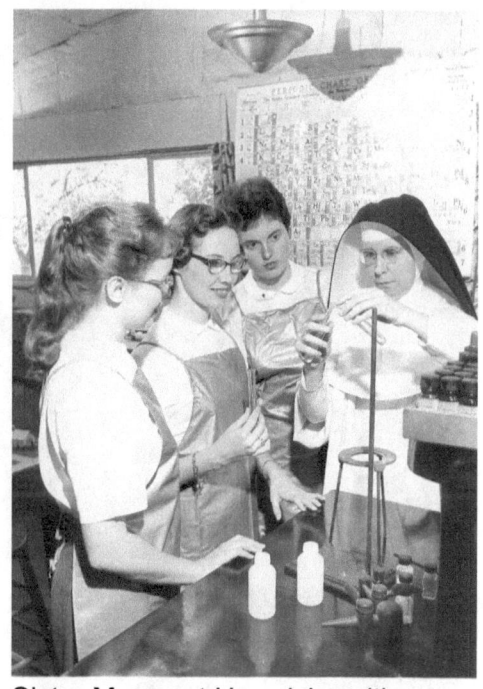

Sister Margaret Hewelcke with a science class

In 1958 the last senior class graduated from Immaculata, and the following term saw the entire student body attending classes on the new campus. As construction of the convent was delayed in getting started, St. Dominic's in Albina continued to be the residence of members of the Marycrest faculty until 1961. St. Joseph's and St. Anne's staffs moved from Albina in 1959. St. Therese and Immaculate Heart staffs moved in 1962.

The last building to be constructed on the site was the sisters' residence, which was planned to house the faculties of Marycrest and Immaculate Heart Elementary School. The early years with only the one house on a 21 acre campus were lonely, and quite possibly dangerous, a concerned parent gave Sister Redempta a dog and a rifle for protection. As far as is known, Sister had to take the gun after intruders only once. Whether or not it was loaded is unverifiable!

Illness necessitated the removal of Sister Redempta as principal and prioress in 1960; and Sister Mary Edmund Curtin, vice principal, replaced her in the former capacity. A memorable event

Senator John F. Kennedy at Marycrest

of the year was the on-campus visit of Senator John F. Kennedy, just six months before his election as president. A flagpole erected on campus commemorated the event.

In September 1961 Sister Mary Benigna Krug was appointed prioress and principal. A city-wide fund-raising drive proved disappointing in its results; and although the enrollment was satisfactory (428) and the Knights of Columbus were generous in the terms of their loans, the financial burdens confronting the school continued to increase and the inevitable occurred. After 62 years of dedicated service to the high school students of East Portland, Immaculata Marycrest was forced to close in 1973.

Immaculate Conception Elementary School, San Francisco

Immaculate Conception Church, serving primarily the Catholics of Italian ancestry in San Francisco, is located within the parochial boundaries of St. Anthony's Parish in the Mission District of the City. Since its founding in 1912, the church had been under the direction of the Franciscan Fathers of the Italian province. In 1955, Father Victor Bazzanella, O.F.M., pastor, began a series of discussions with the Franciscan provincial regarding the addition of an elementary school. He also began writing letters to Mother Pius requesting sisters to staff the school as soon as Archbishop Mitty granted permission to build. Her refusals were regretful, but firm.

Finally he requested an appointment, which she granted. Once again, Mother declined Father's request for sisters on the grounds of critical shortage with regrets; she declared that she could not give him half a sister! Father Victor, a man with the face of a medieval saint from a stained glass window and the tenacity of a bulldog, pleaded in vain. Finally he left the parlor, but not the grounds. About an hour later, the portress came to Mother Pius to inform her that there was a priest sitting on the front steps of the Motherhouse praying the rosary. "Mother, he refuses to move until you give him sisters for his school."[13] Mother's response was a deep sigh. Some time later she sent Sister to see if Father was still there. He was. At that, Mother Pius lost the battle and, going to the door herself, capitulated, "Father, go home. You will get one sister to open your school."[14] With that, Father Victor pocketed his rosary and left.

The site selected for the new school was on Treat Avenue on property behind the Italian Church. Ground-breaking, at which Monsignor James N. Brown, archdiocesan superintendent of Catholic schools, presided, took place on April 3, 1954. Completion of the building was celebrated by an Open House on January 27, 1957. The building was substantial—of reinforced concrete, with two stories and 13 rooms: eight classrooms, library, offices, storeroom, auditorium and kitchen.

On September 5, 1957, Immaculate Conception Elementary School opened with an enrollment of 119 children in the first and second grades. The boys outnumbered the girls better than two to one: 83–36. True to her word, Mother Pius assigned one sister to the school. Sister Frances Marie Henriques, principal and second grade teacher was assisted by Miss Diane Resch who taught the first grade. Dedication of the building on November 2, 1961, by Auxiliary Bishop Hugh Donohoe of San Francisco, was followed by a reception and open house. Each year one grade was added until all eight classrooms were filled.

Until 1961 the sisters resided at St. Anthony's Convent a short distance away. Ground-breaking for the convent took place on March 18; eight months later the sisters moved into their new home. Father Victor's dream had at last come true!

St. Joseph School, Mission San Jose

In the spring of 1959, Father James O'Neill, pastor of St. Joseph Parish, Mission San Jose, presented a twofold petition to Mother Pius. The first request concerned the purchase of three acres of Motherhouse property fronting on Mission Boulevard for the purpose of erecting a parochial school. The second was an appeal for sisters to staff the school, which Father hoped would be ready to open in September 1960. Responding favorably to both requests, Mother Pius and her Council promised two sisters for the first year.

With site and teachers assured, Father O'Neill approached Harry Downie, eminent authority on the California missions and restorer of the mission at Carmel, with the request that he design an elementary school authentically correct in terms of mission architecture and meeting the requirements of the State Code. The result was an eight-classroom building with low tiled roofs, adobe-like walls, and arches and porticoes typical of an original California mission.

Despite the dispatch with which the building was begun, it was not quite ready for the opening of school in September. The sisters met the emergency by providing classroom space on the grounds of St. Mary of the Palms a half mile away. The founding faculty consisted of Sister Alan (Allyne) Ayres, principal and second grade teacher, and Sister Emmanuel Jiménez, first grade teacher. One hundred students presented themselves on opening day, September 6, 1960. Classes continued at St. Mary's until mid-October when sisters and students used the holiday, October 12, to move into their new building and began class the next day.

According to Sister James Mary (Rose Marie) Hennessy, who followed Sister Alan as principal, the majority of parents were middle class, upwardly mobile and new to the area. They regarded the location of the school as an asset. Situated near the sisters' Motherhouse, no provision had to be made for a sisters' residence.

In addition, parents who wished could avail themselves of music lessons for their children at the Dominican School of Music located on the Motherhouse grounds. For the sisters, too, there were advantages. Experienced retired teachers could enjoy the contact with children that tutoring provided. All would benefit!

St. Michael High School, Los Angeles

One of Monsignor Michael Lee's unfulfilled ambitions was to provide a Catholic high school for the girls of his parish. With Archbishop McIntyre's encouragement and the parishioners' support, he launched a drive for funds which proved successful. Once again, the Wagner family came to his aid. Mrs. Anna Wagner Thill donating property on Manchester Avenue for the high school. Monsignor's next appeal was to Mother Pius for sisters. With her assent and the Archdiocesan Building Committee's approval of the plans, construction was underway.

St. Michael High School opened in September 1955 with an enrollment of 135 freshmen. Sister Cecile Marie Reams, O.P., was appointed founding principal, assisted by Sister Miriam Jackson, Sister Patricia Rielly and Sister Mary Martin. Delays in construction forced the high school to operate for a two-month period in the elementary school building, but eventually all was in readiness. On November 23, 1955, the move into the new building took place. The students found themselves in a handsome brick and concrete building that included, in addition to spacious classrooms, biology and chemistry labs; home economics, sewing, and art rooms; library; study hall; and suite of offices.

By the fourth year St. Michael's had an enrollment of 451 students, applicants coming from more than 20 parishes. Constituting the first graduating class, 91 seniors received diplomas on June 13, 1959. Two years later, the school was awarded full accreditation through the University of California Accrediting Agency.

The high school was one of Monsignor's last achievements in the parish. His death on October 28, 1960, was shocking and a deep sorrow to the parish and the student body. As his close friend, Monsignor William E. North, said in his eulogy at the Requiem Mass on November 3: "We have lost an eloquent witness to the undiminished splendor of the priesthood, and we are all

First faculty at St. Michael's High School: (l to r) Sisters Miriam Jackson, Cecile Marie Reams, Reverend Thomas Kiefer, Sisters Patricia Rielly, and Mara Martin

prelates, priests and people, poorer and sadder with this death."[15] St. Michael's students had in addition lost a faithful supporter and an understanding friend.

St. Frances Cabrini School, San Jose

Father Robert Essig, a longtime friend of the community since his junior high school days at St. Elizabeth's, Oakland, and his early assignment as a priest in St. James Parish, San Francisco, was named pastor of the newly established St. Frances Cabrini Parish in Cambrian Park, a San Jose suburb. A firm supporter of Catholic education, Father Essig wrote to Mother Pius within a month of his appointment, alerting her to his need for sisters to staff a school in possibly five years. Mother's reply was cautious: "There may be a possibility for us to take your school...after five or six more years."[16]

Father Essig's first glimpse of his parish must have been a disappointment. A dilapidated shed on the 10-acre site was proposed as interim church. Over 2,000 hours of donated labor on the part of parishioners transformed the shed, or "red barn" as it was affectionately known, into a respectable place of worship for the 475 families who in 1956 claimed St. Frances Cabrini as their parish. Four years later (January 1960) ground-breaking ceremonies for a school and convent took place, and Father Essig was knocking at the Motherhouse door seeking sisters. It was time for Mother Pius to make good her somewhat limp promise of staff.

Both buildings, school and convent, were completed in August of the same year; and in the first week of September, two members of the pioneer community, Sister Gabriel McCarthy, superior, principal, and second grade teacher, and Sister Karen Nelson, first grade teacher, moved into the convent. Sister Adelinda Delbrugge, cook, and Sister Casimira Weiss, housekeeper, arrived the next day.

School began on September 6, 1960, both class rooms filled to capacity (50). Dedication of the school and blessing of the convent took place on March 4, 1961, with Bishop Merlin Guilfoyle, San Francisco auxiliary bishop, presiding. In the second year the maximum enrollment of 50 to a classroom continued, and Sister Cecile Marie Reams arrived to teach the third grade. The usual custom of adding a grade a year was introduced until the increased enrollment warranted the addition of a grade and a half annually and St. Frances Cabrini became a 14–room school.

On the occasion of the school's 25th Anniversary, Sister Carmel Marie Silva, principal, paid tribute to the pastor: "This joint effort [of Father Essig and the Dominican Sisters] has proved to be a very warm, generous and fulfilling partnership....There is no pastor in the whole Archdiocese that could be commended more for his dedication to Catholic Education than our own beloved Rev. Robert G. Essig."[17] It was a tribute well merited!

St. Alphons Seminar, Ingolstadt, Bavaria

The expansion of the Congregational ministries during the administration of Mother Pius was not confined solely to the United States. In the city of Ingolstadt, Bavaria, the Redemptorist Fathers operated St. Alphons Seminar, a residence for boys from Grades Five to Twelve. Founded in 1956, it was not a seminary in the strict sense, but was designed in the hope of encouraging vocations to the priesthood. The boys lived at the seminary, attended schools in the vicinity, and supplemented their academic studies with programs of religious devotions, sports and art supervised by the Redemptorist Fathers.

The Fathers sought the assistance of our sisters at Sts. Peter and Paul Convent, Altenhohenau, Bavaria in managing the domestic department of *St. Alphons.* Permission obtained, five sisters were assigned: Sister Stilla Sinseder, superior; Sister Marietta Wittmann, Sister Delfina Schmidt, Sister Carola Dietl and Sister Ancilla Trippe. After a short time Sister Stilla was given complete charge of the priests' and boys' dining rooms, acting as hostess for the priests on all occasions. Sister Marietta's ability in the kitchen was soon recognized also and she was entrusted with the responsibility of menu preparation.

Sacred Heart School, Patterson, California

The town of Patterson lies on the west side of the San Joaquin River, a little more than 80 miles southeast of San Francisco. Founded in 1909 by T.W. Patterson, the town is central to some of the best orchard and crop land in California.

The Catholic Church in Patterson began as a mission of the parish in Newman and was serviced by the Claretian Fathers, who said Mass in the neighboring towns of Crow's Landing and Gustine. In Patterson, Mass was offered on Sundays and holy days in an open-air theater behind the town drug store. But it did not take the Catholics of the area long to raise funds for a small church of their own. The church was dedicated on May 17, 1917, by Father John Cantwell, vicar general of the Archdiocese of San Francisco.

Patterson did not become a parish, however, until 1925, when Archbishop Hanna gave it parochial status under the patronage of the Sacred Heart. Almost a quarter of a century later (1949), a new and larger church was built to meet the growing needs of the parish. It was dedicated by Bishop James T. O'Dowd, auxiliary bishop of San Francisco.

In 1955 the Vincentian Fathers entered the picture when they were invited by Archbishop Mitty to assume responsibility for the parish. Father James V. Connors, C.M., became the first Vincentian to serve as pastor of Sacred Heart. He began at once a Confraternity of Christian Doctrine Teacher Training class taught by the Sisters of the Holy Family and organized a School Building Committee to raise funds for a parochial school.

In 1961 the committee was ready to build, and Father Connors' successor, Father Harold Buetler, C.M., contacted the Mission San Jose Dominicans for sisters. Mother Pius agreed to provide a staff of two sisters—all that she could provide at the outset.

Sister Bonaventure Fritz and Sister James Mary (Rose Marie) Hennessy constituted the original staff with Sister Dominic Marie Tojo "on loan" to help the sisters get settled. They were joyously welcomed by Father Buetler and the people of the parish when they arrived on August 20, 1962, to move into the new convent and school that awaited them. A week later Sisters Fidelis Winschuh and Ancilla Althaus arrived to join the community. The fifth member, Sister Celestine Stiebritz, completed the community a few days later.

School opened on September 4 with 94 students reporting for class in Grades One through Four. The convent annalist remarked the support provided by parents:

Sister Bonaventure Fritz, Superior and Principal, Sacred Heart School, Patterson 1962

All the children are in Sacred Heart Parish which includes Crow's Landing, six miles southeast; Westley, six miles northwest; and Vernalis, fourteen miles northwest. In the earnest interests of Catholic education, several parents from Westley formed a corporation, purchased a bus and... provided transportation for the children of that area.[18]

Support for the fledgling school was also expressed by Bishop Hugh A. Donohoe, Bishop of Stockton, who welcomed the sisters in a letter to Sister Bonaventure, superior-principal: "I hope and pray that you and the Sisters will find much happiness in your new work. As pioneers in a new territory I am sure that you understand how many people and how many things depend upon your good judgment, your zeal for the work, and your love of souls."[19] Bishop Donohoe could not know how accurately he was describing the sisters' ministry in Patterson.

Motherhouse Chapel and Infirmary

Meanwhile, Mother Pius's attention was focused also on congregational needs. During her time in office, the need for a larger Motherhouse chapel and an infirmary for the ailing members of the Congregation had become ever more critical. A decision to build was finally made. To make room for the new buildings the little "white house" which had served as the Congregation's infirmary was razed. Succumbing to the same fate were the laundry, weaving and sewing rooms and on May 3, 1954, Father John Leal, St. Joseph, Mission San Jose pastor, broke ground for the new construction. Mother Pius assisted by ceremoniously turning a shovel of dirt.

The Spanish-Colonial or Mediterranean style chapel was designed to seat 228 in the nave and accommodate some 20 sisters from the infirmary in a side chapel on the first floor, another 10 on the second, and an estimated 50 visitors in the gallery to the rear. Plans called for access to the chapel from the infirmary on both floors so that sisters who were able could, despite diminishment in health, participate in the prayer of the community. The infirmary also had its own dining room and kitchen.

Below the chapel, plans called for a social hall seating approximately 350. A small kitchenette, serviceable despite its restriction in size, was an added convenience.

Motherhouse Chapel and Infirmary building 1955

The two-story, 34-bed infirmary, harmonizing in exterior architectural design with the chapel, was erected simultaneously and was ready for occupancy at the time of the blessing of the buildings. The generosity of our sisters from Bay Area convents allowed the deadline to be met; they came to the Motherhouse in large numbers on the Saturdays of May, armed with buckets and cleaning fluid, and polished and sparkled their way through the care center rooms.

Trinity Sunday, May 27, 1956, was the day chosen for the blessing. In the parking lot of the Motherhouse a canopied platform accommodated an outdoor altar for His Excellency, Auxiliary Bishop Hugh Donohoe of San Francisco, presiding before a huge crowd of clergy and guests. Promptly at three o'clock, the long line of clergy, headed by Dominican seminarians who served as cross bearer and acolytes, proceeded to the chapel for the blessing. Father William Norton, O.P., pastor of St. Mary Magdalen, Berkeley, acted as narrator of the ceremonies and assisted the guests in following the prayers of the Bishop. From the chapel the procession made its way into the infirmary for the rite of blessing there. The singing of the *Te Deum* by a sisters' choir under the direction of Sister Mary Bertha Rehers followed the blessing. Bishop Donohoe then addressed the more than thousand guests and imparted the blessing and good wishes of the Holy Father to Mother Pius, the members of the community and all present. Benediction of the Blessed Sacrament, given by Bishop Donohoe, assisted by Father James O'Connor of St. James Parish, San Francisco, and Father Stanley Reilly of St. William's, Los Altos, concluded the religious ceremony. Tours of the new buildings and a reception followed.

The chapel was dedicated to the Queen of the Holy Rosary, patroness of the Congregation; and the infirmary was given the title *Salus Infirmorum* (Health of the Sick) as it was known for several years. Later the name was changed to St. Martin's Residence.

The Dominican Guild

The Bay Area Dominican Guild was the brain child of Mrs. Marcelline Brennan and Mrs. Mary Dion, mothers of Sisters Mary Brennan and Julian Dion respectively. The two mothers, friends for years, decided they should do something to help the sisters with their building project. Several conversations later, they had a plan. They would invite the sisters' parents to a meeting at which they would present the idea of organizing a Dominican Parents' Guild to assist the sisters financially in building the chapel and infirmary. They then took their idea to Mother Pius for approval. Mother gave it her blessing and appointed Sister Berchmans Hudson, a councilor, as liaison. In Los Angeles, Mrs. Evelina Stassi, mother of Sister Loretta Stassi, and Mr. William Casper, father of Sisters Dorothy (Mary William) and Evelyn Casper, were appointed as officers of the Guild.

The organizational meeting took place on January 13, 1955. John Connolly, father of Sister Terence (Kathleen) McCarthy, presided; since it was to be a parents' group, the foundresses thought it appropriate to elect a sister's father as president. To familiarize those attending with the idea, they asked Mr. Connolly to do the honors. The first order of business called for a standing vote to determine whether the majority of those present favored having a Dominican Parents' Guild. The result was unanimous, and the

Dominican Guild, Eastbay Division: (l to r) Officers Marcelline Brennan, Mary Dion, Eleanor Fischer, Nora Keane and Angela Cumbelich

meeting proceeded. Elected as officers were the following: Mr. T. F. Keane, president (father of Sister Sheila Keane); Mr. Leo Beck, vice president (brother of Sister Theresa Beck); Mrs. Marcelline Brennan, secretary (mother of Sister Mary Brennan); Mrs. Mary Dion, treasurer (mother of Sister Julian Dion).

A form letter was sent to parents unable to attend the organizational meeting, inviting them to become "auxiliary members," that is, they would pay dues, but need not participate in activities or attend meetings, though welcome to do so.

The group present favored organization by areas; hence the Guild was divided according to the following: San Francisco, Oakland and Los Angeles divisions. Dues were set at $1.00 a year. Each division would elect its own officers and plan its own program of activities. Annually in the spring, the Motherhouse would sponsor a "Guild Day" for all divisions. The day would begin with a Mass of Thanksgiving offered for the Guild, followed by luncheon served the members. A meeting of the three divisions was the highlight of the afternoon at which each division secretary reported the activities of the past year and the president presented a check to the sisters.

Activities varied from division to division, including whist parties, garage sales, bingo luncheons, and candy sales. Members soon found that the activities of the Guild afforded them much social enjoyment. They began looking forward to their monthly meetings and to annual Guild Day when the Los Angeles members would make the trip to Mission San Jose together.

Since that day in January day in 1955 when Mrs. Brennan and Mrs. Dion's ideas were shared with other parents and family members of the sisters, the Guild has been faithful to its purpose and a steady source of financial support for the sisters' ministries. Mrs. Brennan's words written to a prospective division organizer proved true: "Don't be discouraged by a small start. Just keep plugging away, and you will get much satisfaction out of knowing that you are helping the sisters to do their work of educating our youth. All worthwhile things start small."[20]

NOTES

[1] Marbaise, "Kaleidoscopic View of Mexico 1922–1936" (Series of Letters) 4.

[2] Marbaise 22.

[3] Marbaise, Sisters' Remembrance, 1944.

[4] Noel Moholy, O.F.M., Homily, 4 November 1951.

[5] Timothy Manning, letter to Marbaise, 30 January 1950.

[6] Timothy Manning, letter to Marbaise, 7 February 1950.

[7] *The Tidings*, 24 October 1952.

[8] Annals of St. Nicholas Convent entry, 27 October 1953

[9] Annals of St. Nicholas Convent, 1 November 1953.

[10] J. Nuevo, C.M.F., letter to Parishioners, 1945.

[11] Emilia Techtman, O.P. (Personal Interview), 7 February 2002.

[12] Emilia Techtman, O.P. (Personal Interview), 7 February 2002.

[13] Marbaise, Sisters' Remembrance, 1955.

[14] Marbaise, Sisters' Remembrance, 1955.

[15] William E. North, Eulogy for Monsignor Lee, 3 November 1960.

[16] Marbaise, Sisters' Remembrance, 1955.

[17] Marbaise, "Silver Anniversary Booklet," 27 May 1985.

[18] Annals of Sacred Heart Convent, Patterson, 4 September 1962.

[19] Hugh Donohoe O.P., letter to Bonaventure Fritz, O.P., 11 September 1962.

[20] Marcelline Brennan, letter to Guild organizer, n.d.

EPILOGUE

At precisely 10:30 a.m. on the morning of August 1, 1961, the delegates of the Twelfth General Chapter assembled in the chapter room of the Motherhouse for the purpose of electing the fifth Prioress General of the Congregation. In solemn procession they entered the room conscious of their responsibility, but with little foresight of the dramatic events the days ahead would generate. Vatican II was already in the planning stages and would open the following year on October 11, 1962. Closer to home, Oakland, California, would be declared a diocese on January 13, 1962, along with the Dioceses of Santa Rosa and Stockton, and Bishop Floyd L. Begin, auxiliary bishop of Cleveland, Ohio, would be named the first Bishop of the Diocese of Oakland.

More than a century earlier (December 6, 1850) Bishop Joseph Sadoc Alemany, O.P., had come through the Golden Gate to take possession of his Diocese of Monterey, which at the time included all of California. In the short space of three years he would be appointed the first Archbishop of San Francisco and would serve the western Church humbly and faithfully for the next 34 years. Now the Archdiocese of San Francisco had grown to such an extent that Rome had announced that three suffragan dioceses would be formed from it: Oakland, Santa Rosa and Stockton. Bishop Begin was installed as Bishop of Oakland on April 28, 1962, in St. Francis de Sales Cathedral by the Most Reverend Egidio Vagnozzi, apostolic delegate. The story is told that, when the new bishop was informed of his appointment, he asked to have pictures of the priests of his diocese sent to him so that he was able to greet each priest by name when he first met him. Described by his diocesan chancellor, Father Brian Joyce, as having a "canonical mind with a pastoral heart"[1] or, as *The Catholic Voice*, Oakland's diocesan newspaper, put it, "Bishop Begin was first and foremost a Churchman. He loved the Church and God's people....Together with a supportive clergy, religious and laity, a good first chapter in the history of the Oakland Diocese was written." [2]

Second Vatican Council

It must have been something to see! Two thousand mitered bishops, marching six abreast, their white robes billowing in the breeze as they descended Bernini's *Scala Regia* and crossed St. Peter's Square to enter the great Basilica. Behind the bishops walked the scarlet ranks of cardinals and last of all, borne aloft on the *sedia gestatoria* , hand raised in blessing over the throng lining the square, rode His Holiness, John the XXIII!

Within the Basilica, the strains of the ancient hymn, *Veni Creator Spiritus* (Come Creator Spirit) resounded throughout the high-vaulted church, as the prelates invoked the wisdom and the holiness of the Spirit on the event about to take place. The Mass of the Holy Spirit, celebrated by His Eminence, Eugene Cardinal Tisserant, dean of the College of Cardinals, followed. Then singly the cardinals made their ritual obeisance to the Holy Father and the bishops pronounced in unison their profession of faith. The Litany of the Saints and prayers from the Greek Rite recited, a profound hush settled over the huge Basilica as John the XXIII rose to speak. The Second Vatican Council, the twenty-first in the Church's history of nearly 2,000 years, was officially in session. The date was October 11, 1962!

Pope John shared his hopes. The Council would be pastoral in purpose rather than dogmatic. The Church would avail herself of current advances in the fields of biblical, theological, historical, and philosophical knowledge in order to make doctrine more intelligible to contemporary searchers. Lastly, the Holy Father addressed the subject of Christian unity, which, he said, had not yet been achieved. He reminded the Council Fathers that the fullness of charity is the key to brotherly unity among all Christians and, in fact all persons of good will. The Church, he said, must participate in the ecumenical movement and, while preserving the *precious deposit of faith,* work to give these doctrines relevancy for today. Thus the Pope set his seal of approval on the ecumenical movement and the Church's engagement in it. There were some among the Vatican officials to whom John the XXIII was a mystery—simple and humble on the one hand, and revolutionary in outlook on the other.

This Pope would "open the windows" and propel the Church into a new era. He relied on the Holy Spirit to distribute gifts for the well-being of the Church, and the delegates would be charged with responsibility for continuing the story. The Council would succeed better than he knew!

We who by grace and privilege were permitted to live through the conciliar times of Vatican II could not have foreseen changes that would occur in the Church in the ensuing years, although a careful reading of the Pastoral Constitution on *The Church in the Modern World* should alert the reader to such changes as a turning from a spirit of triumphalism to one of greater humility, a recognition in the *Constitution on the Church* of the age of the laity as the "people of God," the use of the vernacular in the liturgy, and the move toward greater Christian unity. The legacy of the Council would be a pastorally focused Church.

For the Congregation it would prove a blessing. From the after-events it would derive a new purpose and energy for mission, would broaden its horizons in a new movement of Dominican preaching and collaboration, would take up the challenge and march with renewed vigor on the ongoing journey.

Mother Mary Dominic Engelhard

It was at this exciting time in the Church that Sister Mary Dominic took office as the fifth Prioress General of the Congregation. A native of Los Angeles, Margaret Engelhard, was born on June 27, 1913, the third daughter and fifth child of Francis Engelhard and Ruby Fitzgerell. A resident of St. Ignatius parish, Margaret was introduced to the Mission San Jose Dominicans when she entered

St. Ignatius Parochial School as a fourth grade student the year the school opened. After graduating from grade school, she received her high school education with the Dominican Sisters as a student at Sacred Heart Academy, Los Angeles. It was a happy association, leading to her entrance to the convent at the Motherhouse, Mission San Jose, in October 1930. She received the habit in June 1931 and pronounced her first vows in June 1932. Her education continued with a B.A. degree from Queen of the Holy Rosary College, Mission San Jose, and M.A. and Ph.D. degrees from Catholic University of America, Washington, D.C.

Mother Mary Dominic Engelhard, Prioress General 1961 - 1973

Sister Mary Dominic's teaching and administrative experience encompassed assignments to Sacred Heart Elementary School, Los Angeles; Holy Rosary School, Portland; Immaculate Heart School, Portland; St. Elizabeth High School, Oakland; and Immaculate Conception Academy, San Francisco.

In 1949 Sister was elected a member of the General Council and appointed Director of Education, an office she held until elected Prioress General in 1961. During the years 1949 to 1961, Sister also served as secretary general and dean of Queen of the Holy Rosary College.

As Prioress General it would be Mother Mary Dominic's responsibility to guide the Congregation through the sometimes troubled years of change following Vatican II, a duty which she discharged with grace, compassion and wisdom. Her contacts with Bishop Begin during this period led to a mutual respect that developed into a friendship that endured until his death. While not within the time frame of this narrative to detail the events of

Sister's administration, the Congregation acknowledges with love and deep gratitude Sister Mary Dominic's years of outstanding service (1961–1973) to the Church and the community.

NOTES

[1] Jeffrey M. Burns and Mary Carmen Batiza. *We are the Church: A History of the Diocese of Oakland*. (Strasbourg: Editions du Signe, 2001) 45.

[2] "The Catholic Voice," Jubilee 87, Vol. 25, No. 13, 15 June 1987 4.

COMMUNITY LORE

Oral Traditions Selected by the Author

Shortly after the sisters' arrival in California, one member of the trio was experiencing frustration. Sister Amanda Bednartz had had her fill of parental comments regarding her youthfulness (17). The parishioners' frequently voiced astonishment at the Motherhouse for sending someone so young across the country became increasingly irksome to her. Returning from school one afternoon after a particularly irritating encounter with the mother of a student, she printed on a piece of paper the number "21" and slipped it in the sole of her shoe. Thereafter, she met all remarks concerning her youth with, "I'm over 21, you know." In consequence, her age gradually ceased to be a matter of parochial concern, and Sister Amanda's serenity returned.

One of Sacred Heart Convent's favorite stories is that of "Mary." Some ten or twelve blocks from Sacred Heart at the far end of Lincoln Park in East Los Angeles was Selig's, a small zoo. One day Mary, a gorilla, managed to escape undetected. Enjoying her new-found freedom, she went strolling down the street undetected. The day was quite warm and Sister Dorothea Frank, Sacred Heart's little cook, had left the door to the street open to let in a little fresh air. While she was busily preparing the resident students' lunch, she suddenly saw a "hand" reach over her shoulder and grab a bun from the pan she had ready to pop into the oven. "You must wait for lunch like the other children," she chided, pushing the "hand" aside—and looked up into the face of a gorilla!

Off the kitchen was a pantry to which Mary retreated with her bun, peering out through an open slide as the little boarders arrived for lunch. Spotting the gorilla, they began to scream hysterically, jumping up and down and waving their arms frantically. At this Mary became greatly amused, thinking the little girls wanted to play. She responded, jumping even higher than the children and making gorilla-like noises. Meantime, other children and sisters arrived to add to the confusion. Someone called the zoo, and the keepers were there in record time. In vain did they try enticing Mary with her favorite foods. She would have nothing of their strategies. "Get Joseph," one of the zoo keepers yelled above the din. Joseph was quickly brought from the zoo, and at sight of her mate, Mary forgot all about the fun she was having with the children and went home with him contentedly. The children, however, needed more persuasion to calm down.

Sister Honora Ehrhart and Sister Benigna Rusting were lifelong friends. They attended school together, entered the Congregation on October 2, 1915 together, received the habit of St. Dominic together, and pronounced vows on May 11, 1917, together. Her health never robust, Sister Honora was the first to succumb to the influenza when the epidemic ravaged the world in 1918. Sister Benigna asked to care for her friend in her illness, which lasted a short week. Sister Honora died peacefully on January 7, 1919. A few days later, Sister Benigna complained of excessive fatigue. By afternoon she was running a high temperature and was diagnosed with the dreaded "flu." One week later she, too, died on January 21, 1919. Friends to the last, they would not be separated in death.

The mortgage on Immaculate Conception Academy was weighing heavily on the community who were weathering the effects of the Great Depression. Meanwhile, the line outside the convent stretched longer every day as hungry men queued up for food at noon. In August 1935 Sister Antonia Callahan, prioress, felt driven to insert an advertisement in the *San Francisco Examiner* and *The*

Chronicle asking for someone willing to lend money at less than six percent. Evidently nothing came of the ads, for in November someone placed an ad in *The Daily News* that read: "For the love of Christ the King, for the love of our Blessed Mother, for the love of all the saints, help the Dominican Sisters pay their debts." This somewhat dramatic appeal reached the notice of Mrs. John J. Murray and Mrs. Patrick Loftus, St. James parishioners and staunch supporters of the Dominican Sisters, who took the ad to Monsignor Patrick Quinn, pastor of St. James, asking what could be done. "Let the Sisters alone," was the reply—whereupon they sent the ad to Archbishop Mitty, hoping to stir up something. It certainly did!

The Archbishop sent Monsignor Connolly to see Sister Antonia and deliver the message that the Archbishop did not like such publicity. She should set up an appointment with Monsignor Ryan. Knowing nothing of the *Daily News* ad, Sister Antonia wondered why the Archbishop was so disturbed and asked, "What are we going to do regarding our debt?" Monsignor Ryan suggested that Monsignor Quinn make an appointment with the Archbishop on the sisters' behalf. That very evening Monsignor Quinn telephoned the sisters that the Archbishop would lend the sisters $80,000 at five percent to clear the mortgage. The Academy was saved, but many faces were red!

Mr. Albert, father of a former Sacred Heart High School student, returned to the school on March 9, 1943, to settle tuition he had been unable to pay when his daughter was enrolled at Sacred Heart—30 years before! To the amount owed, he added $10.00 as interest. Such honesty touched the sisters deeply.

In San Francisco a rash of convent burglaries produced in Mother Pia such uneasiness that she organized the sisters into an all-night watch. Her concern was rewarded when late the first night, three trespassers were observed entering the convent garden. The "vigilantes" were ready for them and lustily blew their only weapon, a police whistle, frightening off the intruders. For three successive nights the sisters kept watch. On the third, the chapel bell rang at one a.m., alerting the community to the intruder seen climbing in a neighbor's window. Alas for the young man who had hoped to make entry into the house without his parents' knowledge!

Undoubtedly for the better, the police now assumed nightly surveillance of the neighborhood, and shortly thereafter the burglars were apprehended. With an eye to future peril, the sisters acquired a watchdog, which Mother Pia, an ardent Democrat, christened "Grover" after President Grover Cleveland.

Sister Thekla Hamacher entered the convent in Moresnet Neutre in 1902. She was one of the sisters who came to the United States as a postulant, receiving the habit in San Francisco on January 7, 1904, and made profession on August 5, 1905. Never of really good health, Sister Thekla was en route to the doctor's office one day as her condition had improved to such a degree that the physician thought she was able to visit him. But, on the way, she suddenly crossed her hands on her chest and breathed her last. Shortly after, the news arrived at the Motherhouse that her beloved mother had died in Germany on the same day.

Born of Protestant parentage, Sister Verona Scheuermann was raised in a staunchly Protestant environment in Germany. In spite of circumstances, however, she felt strongly attracted to the Catholic Church even as a child. In a nearby Catholic village, she had witnessed a Corpus Christi procession and longed to know more about the Church. Hindered by her family who were horrified at her request to become a Catholic, she nevertheless managed to enter the Church on April 12, 1897, at the age of 23. To the family her entrance into the Church was a disgrace, and she was forced to leave the village. She asked admission to the Congregation at Rhondorf and, on being named for America, wished to return to her village once more to take leave of her mother. On hearing of her return, the neighbors peppered the house with rocks. Under cover of darkness, she stole from the house and went to a friend in a neighboring village for shelter for the night.

For several years Mother Pia had corresponded with the Bishop of a Dominican missionary in China. She deeply regretted having to refuse him when he asked for sisters to staff his orphanage and from time to time sent him donations. On one occasion Mother sent the Bishop $20 in gold. With the donation he was able to ransom 50 little Chinese girls and bring them to the orphanage. In gratitude to Mother Pia he had them all named "Pia" at their Baptism. One can imagine the confusion when the sister in charge called "Pia" and 50 little ones came running!

From Immaculate Conception Academy comes this story. During World War I income was not what could be called robust. Sister Pauline Lang, ICA's prioress, asked the sisters to try to collect a little tuition from their high school classes. Sometime later Sister urged the teachers to be conscientious in submitting their reports, as more income was being turned in than the reports warranted!

One afternoon as the anonymous witness of this story was in the treasurer's office making a deposit, Sister Raymunda Wilson, community treasurer, was standing before her desk counting money into a canvas bag. A man, whom she thought a priest, was standing beside Sister watching in silence. He was of medium height, had hair beginning to turn gray and wore a full beard. He was dressed in black with a black overcoat. As Sister Raymunda turned from her desk to get something, he walked behind her and left the room. No one accompanied him down the stairs to the door. At the same time, Sister Raymunda hurried to Sister Pauline's office and said happily, "Sister Prioress, St. Joseph was so good again."

Note to skeptics: It is easier to believe that the visitor was St. Joseph than that a man, be he priest or layman, be allowed to watch a treasurer count the convent funds or wander through the house unescorted!

On one occasion Mother Seraphina brought two small orange trees home with her from Europe; they were slips garnered from trees purportedly planted by St. Dominic himself. One day while Mother was homebound on the ship, she brought the two little pots on the deck to enjoy the sea breeze. Seeing the two pots, a fellow traveler shouted, "Land ho! Land in sight!" The passengers came rushing on deck to see the sight. The only land visible to the eye was the "land" in the pots!

APPENDIX A

Ministry Sites Before 1963

1876–1961	St. Boniface School, San Francisco, CALIFORNIA
1883–	Immaculate Conception Academy, San Francisco, CA (f)
1888–1918	St. Joseph School, Portland, OREGON
1889–1974	Immaculate Heart of Mary School, Portland, OREGON
1889–	St. Catherine's Academy, Anaheim, CA (f)
1890–	Sacred Heart Elementary School, Los Angeles, CA (f)
1891–1910	The Josephinum, Mission San Jose, CA (f)
1892–1907	St. Joseph School, Los Angeles, CA
1893–	St. Elizabeth Elementary School, Oakland, CA
1894–2008	St. Anthony School, San Francisco, CA
1900–1906	St. Thomas School for Boys, San Francisco, CA
1903–1968	The Albertinum, Ukiah, CA
1903–2006	St. Michael Elementary School, Los Angeles, CA
1907–	Sacred Heart Academy (High School), Los Angeles, CA
1907–1930	Dominican Srs. Normal School, Mission San Jose, CA (f)
1909–1921	St. Josef Schule, Altenberg, MORESNET NEUTRE
1910–1967	St. Mary of the Palms (Serra Center) Mission San Jose (f)
1910–1915	St. Aloysius School, Colusa, CA
1910–1913	Academia de Sta. Rosa, Atzcapotzalco, D.F., MEXICO
1911–1973	Immaculata Academy/Marycrest, Portland, OREGON (f)
1912–1955	Holy Rosary School, Portland, OREGON
1912–	Mission San Gabriel Elementary School, San Gabriel CA
1913–1926	Colegio Inmaculada Concepcion, Tlalpam, D.F, MEXICO
1918–1926	Colegio San Rafael, Col. San Rafael, D.F., MEXICO
1920–1924	La Providenza, Cavigliano, SWITZERLAND
1921–	St. Elizabeth High School, Oakland, CA
1922–	St. Ignatius School, Los Angeles, CA
1922–1982	St. Vincent Home and School for Boys, San Rafael, CA
1922–1932	St. Mary's School, Fullerton, CA
1923–1926	Colegio Santa Rosa de Lima, San Felipe, GUANAJUATO
1923–1926	Colegio Madre Santisima de la Luz, San Felipe, GTO
1923–1926	Colegio S. Tomas de Aquino, San Miguel de Allende GTO
1923–	Sts. Peter and Paul Priory, Altenhohenau, BAVARIA (f)

1924–1926	Colegio Nuestra Senora de Loreto, San Angel, D.F.
1924–	St. James Parochial School, San Francisco, CA
1925–1934	Colegio Victoria, Tlalpam, D.F.
1925–1926	Colegio Cristobal Colon, (St. Augustine), Tlalpam, D.F.
1926–1930	St. Therese School, Alhambra, CA
1926–1930	Immaculate Heart of Mary School, San Antonio, TEXAS
1929–1932	Our Lady of Sorrows School, San Antonio, TEXAS
1939–2004	St. Boniface School, Anaheim, CA
1930–2009	Queen of the Holy Rosary College, Mission San Jose, (f)
1931–	Flintridge Sacred Heart Academy, Flintridge, CA
1932–1945	Academia Sor Juana Ines de la Cruz, San Miguel, GTO
1937–1992	School of the Madeleine, Berkeley, CA
1938–	Colegio Sto. Domingo/Instituto Las Casas, San Miguel de Allende, GTO (f)
1932–1962	St. John Seminary, Camarillo, CA
1940–1975	Pax Erholungsheim, Wallgau, BAVARIA
1943–1946	Colegio San Rafael, Col. San Rafael, D.F.
1947–1973	Instituto Lacordaire, Tacubaya, D.F. (f)
1949–	Mission San Gabriel High School, San Gabriel, CA
1950–1970	St. James Boys' School, San Francisco, CA
1950–1906	Santa Teresita School, Los Angeles, CA
1951–2006	St. Frances Cabrini School, Los Angeles, CA
1951–1906	Colegio La Paz, Delicias, CHIHUAHUA (f)
1953–1992	St. Mary of the Angels School, Ukiah, CA
1953–1982	St. Nicholas (St. William) School, Los Altos, CA
1955–1975	St. Joseph the Worker School, Portland, OR
1955–1995	St. Michael High School, Los Angeles, CA
1955–2007	St. Therese School, Portland, OREGON
1956–1978	St. Alfons Seminary for Boys, Ingolstadt, BAVARIA
1957–2008	Immaculate Conception School, San Francisco, CA
1958–2008	St. Anne School, Portland, OREGON
1960–1994	St. Frances Cabrini School, San Jose, CA
1960–	St. Joseph School, Mission San Jose, CA
1962–1972	Sacred Heart School, Patterson, CA

(f) refers to an institution that is owned by the Congregation. In Mexico it was illegal for Religious to own property until well after the years of persecution. Locations were "on loan" from loyal benefactors. Sacred Heart In Los Angeles (1890—) is an anomaly. The elementary school was a parish school although the property and buildings belonged to the Congregation as well as the boarding department which was closed in 1948. The property and the high school became archdiocesan in 1950.

Motherhouse Sites

1876–1888 Holy Cross, Williamsburg, Brooklyn, NEW YORK
1888–1907 Immaculate Conception, San Francisco, CALIFORNIA
1907–   Mission San Jose, CALIFORNIA

Novitiate Sites

In the United States:
1883–1901 Immaculate Conception, San Francisco CALIFORNIA
           (with occasional temporary transfers to Mission San Jose in 1890s)
1901–   Mission San Jose, CALIFORNIA

In Europe:
1901–1923 Nazareth, Altenberg, MORESNET NEUTRE
1923–1965 Sts. Peter and Paul, Altenhohenau, BAVARIA

In Mexiso:
1922–1926 El Rosario, Tlalpam, D.F.
1944–1968 Santo Domingo, San Miguel de Allende, GUANAJUATO

APPENDIX B

Maps

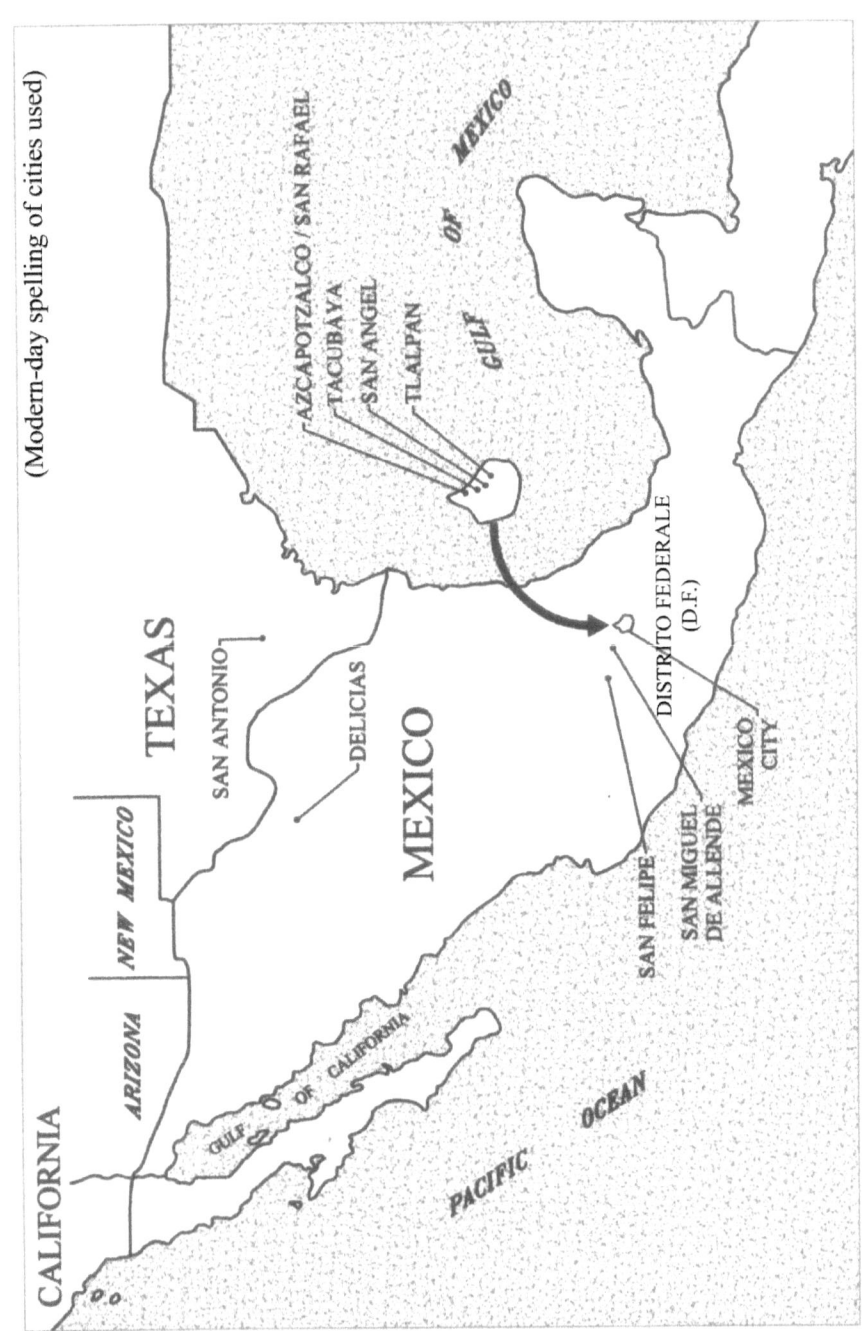

Appendix B / MAPS 635

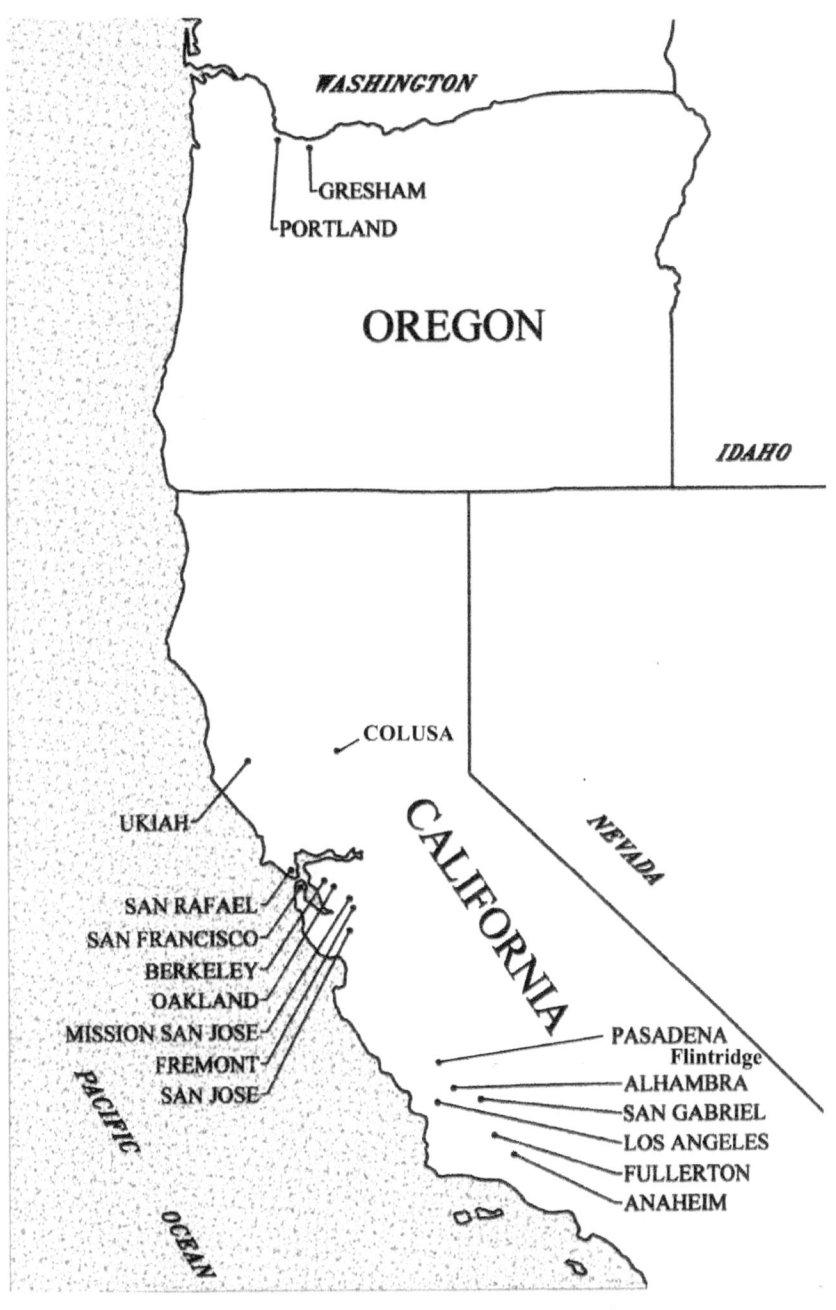

GLOSSARY OF MONASTIC AND CHURCH TERMS

Altar Breads: The bread used at the altar for the celebration of the Eucharist.

C.C.D.: The initials for Confraternity of Christian Doctrine, the official organ for the catechetical instruction of the Catholic laity. In the United States it was established as an independent apostolate in 1935 with a national director and a publishing arm. C.C.D. was seen as the means of instructing youth and their parents who did not have the advantage of Catholic schooling.

C.M.: The initials for the Congregation of the Missions founded by St. Vincent de Paul in 1625 to do missionary work among peasants. Called Vincentians, they form a society of common life. They are secular priests living in community under religious vows.

C.Ss.R: Initials for the Congregation of the Most Holy Redeemer or Redemptorists, founded by St. Alphonsus Ligouri in 1732.

Canon: A member of a cathedral chapter which was a body of clerics assigned there and responsible for the recitation of the Divine Office.

Cardinal Protector: A cardinal in the Roman Curia designated to represent the needs and interests of a religious order or congregation.

Chancery: The administrative branch of a diocese under the authority of the local ordinary such as an archbishop or bishop, vicars or an administrator filling a vacancy.

Chapter: An assembly of members or delegates of a community, province, congregation or the entire Order of Preachers for the purpose of election or legislation. Its membership is determined by election or reason of office and held at intervals as determined by the Constitution. A general chapter refers to a chapter of the whole order of Dominican men or of a congregation of women.

Cistercian: Monks of the Order of Citeaux founded by St. Robert in 1098 to follow a more strict observance of the Rule of St. Benedict.

Cloister: The area of a convent or monastery reserved exclusively for religious. Members of cloistered orders are usually not permitted to live outside the cloister.

Coadjutor Bishop: A special bishop-assistant to a diocesan bishop. He is distinguished from an auxiliary by appointment at the initiative of the Holy See, the right of immediate succession and the manner of taking office.

Coif: A close-fitting headdress, usually white, worn under the veil of a woman religious.

Compline: The official night office that concludes the Liturgy of the Hours, also known as the Divine Office, and signals the end of the day.

Congregatio Episcoporum et Regularium: One of the permanent commissions of cardinals in the Roman Curia which handled the business of bishops and religious orders. Since the period covered in this story, the name has undergone several changes.

Congregation of Rites: One of the permanent commissions of cardinals in the Roman Curia which handled the business of liturgical rites. It is now called the Congregation for Divine Worship and the Discipline of the Sacraments.

Consistory: A meeting of Cardinals convoked and presided over by the Pope.

Council: A governing body, either appointed or elected, of a convent, monastery or congregation to advise the prioress.

Curia: A technical name for a diocesan chancery, which includes a bishop and all the officials who assist him in the administration of the diocese. The Papal Curia is referred to as the Roman Curia.

Dispensation: An act whereby the lawful superiors grants relaxation from an existing law. The law itself is not changed or abrogated but is suspended in a given case.

Divine Office: The public prayer of the Church for praising God and sanctifying the day. It is also known as the Liturgy of the Hours. It consisted of Lauds (morning prayer) daytime prayers (Prime, Terce, Sext and None), Vespers (evening prayer) Compline (last prayer of the day) and Matins (nocturnal prayer.) The number of daytime prayers has since been reduced and Matins is now called the Office of Readings.

Dom: Title placed before the name of professed Benedictine men.

Extern Sister: A member of a cloistered order who lives outside the cloister but within the convent. She is in contact with the outside world and handles any business done outside the convent.

Extraordinary Confessor: One appointed to hear the confessions of men or women over and above their regular confessor to ensure freedom of conscience and broader access to counsel.

Final Vows: Vows of poverty, chastity and obedience pronounced for life. In the enclosed communities of women they were often pronounced as soon as a year after the novitiate; in apostolic congregations temporary vows were pronounced for a specific time and could be repeated. The number of years and times of repetition vary according to the *Constitutions* of the institute before the vows are pronounced for life.

General Council: An elected council to assist the prioress of the congregation. With the prioress general, currently called congregational prioress, they form the executive branch of the congregation.

Generalate: The seat of government of a religious order. For the Dominicans it is in Rome. For the Congregation of the Queen of the Holy Rosary it was first in San Francisco and then in Mission San Jose. The word also applies to the executive body of the community, the prioress and the council.

Grille: In a cloister, the wooden or metal grating which separates the enclosure of cloistered nuns from the visiting room used by the public, also the opening in the chapel wall through which the nuns receive Holy Communion.

Guimps: An outer part of the garment of nuns or sisters which hangs over and around the shoulders to about the waist.

Lay Sister: A sister who serves in a religious order but who is not a choir sister or nun and is not required to recite the Divine Office daily in choir. They devote themselves to the service of the community of which they are real members. Their prayers of obligation are simpler and shorter than those of the choir nuns. In some cloistered communities they are the extern sisters.

Magnificat: The title of a canticle spoken by Mary on the occasion of her visit to Elizabeth. It is part of Vespers, the evening prayer of the Liturgy of the Hours.

Matins: The first of the canonical hours of the Divine Office. It was composed of psalms, scriptural readings, lessons, homilies, antiphons and responses. It was also called the Night Office and dates back to the vigils which preceded the Eucharistic Assembly. It was divided into three divisions as the first, second and third nocturns. Cloistered, contemplative communities of men or women prayed this office during the night; apostolic communities at some time during the day. In some offices Matins consisted of only a single nocturn.

Missa cantata: The Latin name for a sung Mass. In common use it means a sung Mass with one priest as distinguished from a solemn High Mass or *Missa solemnis.*

Motherhouse: The first religious house of an order or society from which other foundations developed. It also refers to the center of a congregation's administration.

Novice: One who undergoes a period of probation and religious training in preparation for the taking of vows as a member of a religious community.

Novitiate: A place for the training of novices or the period of training following the postulancy, lasting at least one year.

Nun: In the strict sense, women in religious life who take solemn vows of poverty, chastity and obedience. Nuns observe the papal cloister and live a life of silence, contemplation and prayer. Until 1888 the subjects of this book were nuns until they became a Congregation of sisters. The terms are commonly misapplied.

Ordo: The annual liturgical calendar, listing the feasts and weekdays with the prayers to be said in the Mass and the Divine Office. The Ordo varies among dioceses and religious orders.

O.C.D.: Order of Discalsed Carmelites, the reformed branch of the Carmelite Order, formed by St. John of the Cross in the 16th century.

O.F.M. Cap.: Order of Friars Minor Capuchins, a branch which broke away from the Franciscans in 1525 in order to restore the literal observance of the Rule of St. Francis.

O.P.: Order of Preachers: The Order founded by St. Dominic de Guzman. Until 1927, the initials O.P. after signatures was reserved for the use of the Priests and Brothers. On December 25, 1927, the Master General extended its use to the enclosed Dominican Nuns and Congregations of Sisters.

O.S.D.: The initials used after the signatures of Dominican nuns and sisters until 1928. Active congregations of sisters were formerly officially named Congregations of the Third Order of the Militia of Jesus Christ, and of the Order of Penance of St. Dominic.

Ordinary: A cleric who exercises ordinary jurisdiction over a specified territory such as a diocese (Bishop), vicariate, prefecture etc.; superiors general, abbots, primate etc.

Postulant: A person in the first period of religious life. The candidate for admission to a religious order or congregation usually spends a year in this stage before entering the novitiate.

Priory: In the Dominican Order the residence of members of the Order as it is defined in its *Constitutions*. The criteria for this designation vary among the men, the nuns and women's congregations.

Prioress: In the Dominican Order, the elected or appointed female superior of a priory. A prioress general is the elected head of a congregation of sisters.

Procurator General: An official with delegated authority to assist the head of the Dominican Order in temporal affairs.

Procuritrix: The person responsible for temporal affairs of a local convent, including the office of treasurer.

Propaganda: The popular title for the Congregation of the Propagation of the Faith, Propaganda Fide, one of the permanent commissions of cardinals for handling the business of the Church. It is now called the Congregation for the Evangelization of Peoples.

Regular Observance: A term used to indicate the faithful following of the *Constitutions*, practices and schedules of the day.

S.J.: The initials for Society of Jesus, better known as Jesuits, a religious order of men, founded by St. Ignatius of Loyola in 1540.

Salve Regina: An ancient hymn to the Blessed Mother; in English: "Hail Holy Queen". Dominicans and some other orders say or sing it daily in procession.

Scapular: A long narrow piece of cloth about the width of the shoulders with in opening in the center so that it can be slipped on over the head and hang in equal lengths in front and back. It is worn over the tunic. It began as a working garment, apron, but later became part of the habit.

Scrutatores: Tabulators and witnesses to an election using secret ballots. In English: Scrutineers.

Simple Vows: In religious institutes the public vows of poverty, chastity and obedience which are pronounced for a specified period of time (temporary vows) or for life (final or perpetual vows). They are distinct from solemn vows in that the person pronouncing them cedes the administration and revenues of her property to the community while retaining the absolute ownership of it. Perpetual vows can be dispensed only by the Vatican Congregation of Institutes of Consecrated Life and any marriage contracted without such a dispensation is in the eyes of the church illicit.

Stole: A liturgical vestment composed of a strip of material, several inches wide, and worn around the neck and hung over both shoulders by priests and bishops; at the left shoulder like a sash by deacons. It is used for the celebration of Mass, administration of the sacraments, and ceremonies of the Blessed Sacrament.

Superior, Religious: The person who governs a religious community. His or her powers are defined in the *Constitutions* of the institute and in the common law of the Church. The community may be a religious institute or a local convent.

Tertiaries: lay persons who are striving after Christian perfection according to the spirit of a religious order to which they are affiliated, and committed to a rule approved for their association by the Apostolic See. They generally do not live in community, but they share in the spirituality and mission of the parent order.

Vespers: Evening Prayer, the Liturgy of the Hours celebrated in the early evening.

Vocal: A sister member of a chapter or assembly who has the right to vote.

WORKS CITED AND CONSULTED

Abbott, Walter M., SJ. Editor. *The Documents of Vatican II.* New York: Herder, 1966.

Antczak, Mary Catherine, OP. "A History of the Schools Staffed by the Dominican Sisters of Mission San Jose, 1945–1982." Thesis. Loyola Marymount University, 1985.

Ashley, Benedict M., OP. *The Dominicans.* Religious Orders. 3. Collegeville: Liturgical Press, 1990.

Atherton, Gertrude Franklin. *Golden Gate Country.* New York: Duell, 1945.

Backes, Pia, OP. *Her Days Unfolded: Woman of the Word.* Trans. and Ed. Bernardina Michel. Ed. Julie Distel. 2nd Ed. Mission San Jose: Dominican Sisters, 1991.

Bedouelle, Guy, OP. *St. Dominic: the Grace of the Word.* Trans: Mary Thomas Noble. San Francisco: Ignatius Press, 1987.

Bellah, Robert N. et. al. *Habits of the Heart: Individualism and Commitment in American Life.* Berkeley: University of California Press, 1985.

Boyle, Edgar. Recommendation. *Cantemus: English and Latin Hymns.* By Gregoria Kratz, OP. Mission San Jose: Dominican Sisters Home Press, 1929.

Breen, Mary Kevin, OP. "The Educational Work of the Sisters of St. Dominic of the Queen of the Holy Rosary." Thesis. Catholic University of America, 1946.

Brown, Rita Marie, OP. "The History of Immaculate Conception Academy, San Francisco, California." Thesis. University of San Francisco, 1953.

Burns, Jeffrey M. *A History of the Archdiocese of San Francisco.* Vol. 1, 1776–1884. Strasbourg: Editions du Signe, n.d.

———. "100 Years of Educational Excellence: the History of St. Elizabeth Elementary School: 1893–1993." Unpublished essay, 1993. Dominican Sisters archives, Mission San Jose.

Burns, Jeffrey M. and Mary Carmen Batiza. *We Are the Church: A History of the Diocese of Oakland*. Strasbourg: Editions du Signe, 2001.
The Centenary: 100 years of the Catholic Church in the Oregon Country, 1889–1939. Portland: Sentinel Press, 1939.
Crawford, Eugene J. *The Daughters of Dominic on Long Island: The History of the Congregation of the Holy Cross, Sisters of the Third Order of Saint Dominic of the Diocese of Brooklyn*. New York: Benziger, 1938.
Dwyer, John T. *One Hundred Years an Orphan*. Fresno: Academy Library Guild, 1955.
"The Establishing and Early Years of San Gabriel Arcángel Mission House and Parochial Grammar School, 1912–1922." Term paper. n.d. Dominican Sisters Archives, Mission San Jose.
Foye, Joseph Francis. *A Treasure of Promises Kept: A Centenary History of Queen of the Most Holy Rosary Priory and Parish, 1894–1994*. Paducah, Kentucky: Turner, 1999.
A Golden Harvest, 1903–1953: The Albertinum. Ukiah: Redwood Journal, 1953.
Golden Jubilee of Holy Cross Convent, Brooklyn, New York. Farmingdale, Long Island: Nazareth Trade School Press, 1903.
Hartman, Irene, OP. *The Dominican Women of the Sunflower State*. Great Bend: Golden Belt Printing, 1997.
———. *Mother Antonina Fischer, O.S.D.: Foundress of the Dominican Sisters of Great Bend, Kansas*. Great Bend: Dominican Sisters, 1977.
Hernandez, Maria Victoria, OP. *Ministry Under Fire: The First Foundations in Mexico (1906–1946)*. Mission San Jose: Dominican Sisters, 1998.
Hinnebusch, William A., OP. *The Dominicans: A Short History*. New York: Alba, 1975.
———. *The History of the Dominican Order: Origins and Growth to 1500*. Vol. 1. New York: Alba, 1966.
Historical Sketch of the Dominican Congregation of the Queen of the Holy Rosary. Golden Jubilee Publication. Mission San Jose: Motherhouse Press, 1926.
History of St. Mary of the Angels, 1887–1997. Ukiah: St. Mary of the Angels Church, 1997.

Holmes, Philip. *Two Centuries at Mission San Jose, 1797–1997*. Fremont: Museum of Local History, 1997.
Kohler, Mary Hortense, OP. *The Life and Work of Mother Benedicta Bauer*. Milwaukee: Bruce, 1937.
———. *Rooted in Hope*. Milwaukee: Bruce, 1962.
Krewitt, H. A. "The Kolping Society." *New Catholic Encyclopedia*. 2nd ed. 2003.
Lavender, David Sievert. *California: Land of New Beginnings*. New York: Harper, 1972.
Lewis, Oscar. *San Francisco: Mission to Metropolis*. Berkeley: Howell-North, 1966.
Liptak, Dolores Ann, RSM. *Immigrants and Their Church*. Makers of the Catholic Community Series 4. New York: Macmillan, 1989.
Marbaise, Pius, OP. "Kaleidoscopic View of Mexico, 1922–1936." Unpublished manuscript. Mission San Jose, 1968.
May, Don. *St. Catherine's Military School, 1889–1964: A Memorial Book Published on the Occasion of the Diamond Jubilee*. Anaheim: St. Catherine's Parents Guild, 1964.
McGloin, John Bernard, SJ. *California's First Archbishop*. New York: Herder, 1966.
———. *San Francisco: the Story of a City*. San Rafael: Presidio Press, 1978.
Marcetteau, B.F. "Recommendation". *Cantemus: English and Latin Hymns*. By Gregoria Kratz, OP. Mission San Jose: Dominican Sisters Home Press, 1929.
Montrose, Donald, et al. *The Story of a Parish: Its Priests and People*. Anaheim: St. Boniface Parish, 1961.
Morrison, Harry B. "Before the Sulpicians: Formation of Priests in Early Diocesan California, 1841–1885." *The Patrician*, Spring, 1992.
Murray, Mary Cecilia, OP. *Other Waters: A History of the Dominican Sisters of Newburgh, New York*. Old Brookville, New York: Brookville Books, 1993.
Parkes, Henry Bamford. *A History of Mexico*. Sentry Editions 61. Boston: Houghton, 1970.
Parmisano, Fabian Stan, OP. *Mission West: The Western Dominican Province 1850–1966*. Oakland: Western Dominican Province, 1995.

Pyne, Donald. "St Thomas Aquinas Seminary." *The Patrician.* Spring, 1952.
Resurrection: St. Joseph Church Dedication Book. Los Angeles: Franciscan Fathers, 1986.
Rudy, Peter. *A Mission That Endures: A History of St. Vincent's School for Boys.* San Rafael: St. Vincent's School for Boys, 2001.
Ryan, Mary Philip, OP. *Amid the Alien Corn: The Early Years of the Sisters of St. Dominic.* Adrian Dominican History 1. St. Charles, Illinois: Jones Wood Press, 1967.
Sandoval, John S. *The History of Washington Township.* Hayward: Mt. Eden Historical Publisher, 1985.
Schutz, Oliver. "Of German Roots: St. Elizabeth's Parish, 1892–1914." *St.Elizabeth Parish, Oakland, California: A Centennial History 1892–1992.* Unpublished collection of essays. 1992.
Shea, Therese Catherine, OP. *An Emerging Woman.* New York: Alba, 1970.
Silva, Carmel Marie, OP. "Presentation." *Silver Anniversary Commemorative Yearbook.* San Jose: St. Frances Cabrini School, 1985.
Tessen, Paula von, OP. *Course of Study and Manual for the Sisters of the Third Order of St. Dominic.* Mission San Jose: Dominican Sisters, 1910.
Traviss, Mary Peter, OP. "The Founding of Anaheim, California." Dissertation. Catholic University of America, 1961.
Tugwell, Simon, OP. *St. Dominic.* Strasbourg: Editions du Signe, 1995.
———.*The Way of the Preacher.* London: Darton, 1979.
Vicaire, Marie Humbert, OP. *The Genius of St. Dominic: A Collection of Study-Essays.* Ed. Peter B. Lobo. Nagpur, India: Dominican Publications, n.d.

Index

A

Academia de Sta. Rosa, Primaria,
    Atzcapotzalco 380–385
Academia Santa Rosa,
    Atzcapotzalco 380–385
Acebes, Diego de 3–5
Adams, George 175–177
Adams, Joachim 166, 167
Aertker, Victor 105, 234, 287, 322, 393
Afflerbaugh, Miriam Joseph 488
Aguerrebere, Rosario 391, 498, 499, 504
Albertinium 289–301
Alemany, Joseph Sadoc 30–32, 34, 36, 43, 47–49, 52–54, 56, 71, 73–74, 79, 84, 87–88, 93, 98–99, 109, 211–213, 215, 456, 458, 478, 617
Almaguer Soto, María 513–515, 517–521, 575
Almanza, Bernarda 515, 517, 519, 521
Alonso, María de Chantal 385, 503
Altenberg, Moresnet Neutre 226, 268–276, 340–341, 346, 413–417, 422, 427, 430, 437–438, 441–443, 484, 579
Altenhohenau 427–452, 526, 571, 608
Althaus, Ancilla 609
Althaus, Flavia 312
Alvarez, Mercedes 385, 512, 522
Amat, Thaddeus 147
Amityville, New York 39, 48, 99, 114, 122, 489, 528
Antczak, Mary Catherine 257, 297
Archdiocese of San Francisco 31, 95, 96, 97, 297, 298, 468, 475, 485, 608, 617
Armstrong, Marie Yvonne 488
Atzcapotzalco 378–386, 526
Aureocochea, Carmelita 503, 505
Ayres, Alan (Allyne) 593, 604

B

Backes, Pia 27–30, 32–33, 36, 37–43, 45–52, 54–57, 61, 63, 65–71, 73–83, 85–88, 93–99, 101–102, 104–107, 109–111, 113, 113–122, 125–126, 129–137, 147–148, 152, 154, 163, 164, 166, 167, 183–191, 193–208, 213–221, 226, 229, 233, 235–242, 244, 249, 252, 254, 263–269, 272–274, 279, 281–285, 287–289, 291, 301, 309, 310, 312–318, 322–327, 329–331, 339–346, 349, 352, 354, 355, 357, 357–359, 364, 365, 367, 368, 377–379, 381, 383, 387, 388, 390, 395, 396, 398, 409, 413, 414, 417–422, 424, 425, 427–436, 443, 446, 459, 461, 473–484, 488, 490–493, 502, 516, 518, 519, 525, 526, 538, 539, 549, 553–556, 558, 564, 580, 625–627
Balde, Evangela 330
Banten, Gregor 274
Barth, Emilia 18, 33, 83, 98, 107, 108
Batiloro, Paul Marie 596, 598
Bauer, Maria Benedicta 10, 18, 24
Bauer, Mary Helen 172, 304, 573, 591
Bay Area Dominican Guild 612–614

Bazzanella, Victor 603
Beata, Gloria 529, 540
Becker, Eugenia 219, 220, 242, 340
Becker, Gerard 105
Becker, Petrina 345, 462
Beck, Theresa 613
Bednartz, Amanda 29, 30, 32, 36, 61, 66, 74, 102, 106, 109, 115, 118, 148, 149, 150, 187, 188, 193, 303, 309, 310, 330, 343, 381, 382, 476, 539, 546, 563, 623
Begin, Bishop Floyd L. 565, 617–618, 620
Behm, Seraphica 137, 139, 592
Benedict XV 418
Berge, Tom 216, 217, 253
Biro, Diana 394, 396
Blake, Patrick 349–368
Blanco, Padre. *See* Dempflin, William
Bleiker, Mauritia 438–440, 443, 469
Boedigheimer, Angela Marie 587
Borgemeister, Aegidia 193
Borgemeister, Hieronyma 288
Borgemeister, Victoria 270
Brandmeier, Celestina 193
Braun, Mary Luke 587
Braun, Michaela 18
Breen, Lawrence 135, 137
Breen, Mary Kevin 252, 549
Breidinger, Coletta 414, 467, 473
Breitenbach, Louise (see Felicitas Weiss)
Bremer, Bartolomeus 266, 467
Brennan, Marcelline 612, 613
Brennan, Mary (David) 613, 614
Breslin, Vincent de Paul 345
Brothers of Mary 331, 333, 366, 587
Browne, Patrick 535
Brown, James N. 369, 603
Brown, Rita Marie 336, 594
Brueggen, Thomasina 193, 269, 269–272, 274, 276, 339

Bruener, Leo 88, 187, 203
Brun, Juana (Guadalupe) 345, 378
Bruttig, Barbara 150, 233
Bucher, Victor 251
Buchmann, Petronilla 462
Buehler, Gonzaga 63–66, 71, 74, 106, 152, 154, 189, 193, 234, 303, 368, 476, 480, 480–481
Buehrle, Mary Ruth 598
Buetler, Harold 609
Burke, Jeremiah 405
Burke, William 468, 469
Busch, Nazaria 443
Bush, Mary Martin 179
Bustamante, Juana (Irene) 391, 576

C

Caballer, Peter 403
Callahan, Antonia (Edocia) 135, 170, 193, 253, 624
Calles, Plutarco Elías 497, 504, 506, 508, 519, 582
Campbell, James 542
Camp Imelda 335–336
Camp St. Albert 296
Canalizo, Carolina 499, 533
Cantwell, John 155, 159, 171, 172, 173, 176, 177, 230, 402, 464, 528, 536, 538–542, 544, 566–568, 583, 588, 608
Carmelites in Herzogenrath 202, 261
Carmody, Mary Raymond 594
Carrancistas 388, 390
Carroll, Aloysa 302
Carroll, Timothy 150, 151
Casper, Dorothy (Mary William) and Evelyn 612
Catechetical Outreach 302–306
Cavalli, Vincent 296
Cavigliano, Switzerland. *See* La Providenza, Cavigliano, Switzerland

Cea, Luis 385
Center, Clarita 573
Cerezo, Agustina 512
Chapel of St. Thomas Aquinas 161–163
Childs, Emeline 238, 239, 240–241
Church of the Most Holy Trinity 13, 44
Claretians 397, 402
Coghlan, Teresita 498, 501, 503, 505
Colegio de Nuestra Señora de Loreto 499
Colegio de Santo Domingo 522, 575
Colegio Fray Bartolomé de las Casas 522
Colegio Inmaculada Concepción, Tlalpam 385–391
Colegio La Paz 576
Colegio San Rafael 497, 575, 581
Colegio Santa Rosa de Lima (San Felipe) 499, 500
Colegio Santo Tomás de Aquino 519
Colusa 312, 313, 314, 316, 317
Conaty, Thomas J. 154, 169, 173, 233, 235–241, 393, 396, 397, 400, 404, 409
Constitutions 21, 187, 189, 190, 191, 194–207, 225, 272, 273, 313, 339–344, 417–426, 429, 475, 483, 490, 492, 493, 499, 517, 525, 554, 555, 557, 558, 560, 580, 639, 641, 642, 643
Convent of Santo Domingo, San Miguel de Allende 512–522
Coon, Clare 223, 224, 406
Cormier, Hyacinth 202, 204, 341–343, 555
Cristeros 507
Cueto, María 386
Cumbelich, Angela 613
Cumbelich, Florence 597

Cunningham, Constantia 340
Curran, John 177–179, 178–180
Curtin, Mary Edmund 601

D

Daly, William A. 135, 144
Daughters of Charity 150, 151, 223, 456
Dávalos, Columba (Mercedes) 391, 499, 532, 586, 594
Dazé, Leo 169
Dazé, Stanislaus (Bernadette) 169, 251
Deckert, Bartholomea 99, 216, 323, 563
Deckert, Bartholomea (Mary) 99
Deisohl, Ermelinda 447, 448
Delahoyde, Charitas 540
Delbrugge, Adelinda 607
Delsman, Jerome 143
Dembowski, Agnes Mary 599
Dempflin, William (Padre Blanco) 49, 215, 288
Densmore, Alacoque 249
Dentlinger, Catherina 312, 313, 315
Derham, Hyacinth 74, 93
Díaz, Beatrice 305
Díaz, María Cecilia 487
Diaz-Martinez, Roberta 568, 569
Díaz, Porfirio 381–382
Dietl, Carola 608
Dietrich, Burchard 244
Diez, María 507, 508, 510, 512
Dignan, Patrick 177, 179, 545, 589, 594
Diones, Irene Mary 482
Dion, Julian 612, 613
Dion, Mary 612–614
Divine Office 47, 201, 203, 254, 282, 324, 325, 341–343, 418, 419, 430, 483, 483–488, 484, 556, 557, 569

Document of Affiliation 186
Doehman, Lioba 409, 487
Domínguez, Adelaida 498, 503
Dominican Collaboration 553–560
Dominican Convent, Marienthal 202, 264, 272–273
Dominican Convent of Dusseldorf 218, 261
Dominican Convent of Nancy 197
Dominican Convent of Speyer 195, 197, 201, 208
Dominican Convent of Stone, England 191, 195, 197, 201, 208, 261, 273, 344, 554
Dominican Convent of Wettenhausen 200, 218
Dominican Convent, San Miguel Allende 512–523
Dominican Fathers 49, 54, 72, 74, 135, 136, 141, 185, 203, 264, 265, 266, 343, 377–380, 386, 474, 478, 485, 489, 506, 534, 571, 580
Dominican Guild 612–614
Dominican Sisters in Cologne 261
Dominican Sisters of Benicia (San Rafael) 30, 50, 458
Dominican Sisters of Great Bend 316
Dominican Sisters of Racine 183, 489
Dominican Sisters of San Rafael 458. *See also* Dominican Sisters of Benicia (San Rafael)
Dominican Sisters of Tacoma 554, 555
Domínquez, Adelaida 305
Donohoe, Patrick 170, 171
Doogan, Mannes 49
Doran, Carmel 406
Doran, Rufina (Mary) 302
Dormann, Euphrasine 225

Dormer, Philomena 273
Dorr, Raphaela 438
Drexel, Katherine 215
Driscoll, Francis Pius 571
Droesch, Valentina 587, 592
Dumoulin, Blandina 225, 303
Dunne, Frances 405, 409, 539, 540
Dwyer, John T. 468, 470
Dyson, Thomas 86, 136

E

Earthquake, Anaheim 156
Earthquake, San Francisco 99, 321–333, 339, 349, 377
Eberl, Germana (Magdalena) 415, 430, 443
Eigenmann, Ceslava 441
Enclosure 9, 14, 54, 184–185, 186, 194, 203, 206, 207, 273, 340
Engelhard, Mary Dominic (Margaret) 170, 369, 549, 619–621
Engelm, Odilia 540
English, Mary Patrick 256
Ensinger, Erharda 568
Erlenheim, Adrian 256
Ertl, Tharcisia 452
Espinosa, Consolata 469, 588
Espinosa, Fidelis 505, 522, 576
Espinosa, Imelda 510, 534
Espinosa, Isabel 306, 468, 505
Esser, Salome 569
Esser, Thomas 273, 418, 492
Essig, Robert 606

F

Falconio, Diomede 313
Faltermeier, Wendelina 289
Farnham, Loyola 469
Fernández, Domingo 386, 501
Fichtner, Salesia (Anna) 29, 30, 32, 36, 55, 65, 66, 73, 105, 106, 109, 152, 188, 190, 193, 200,

220, 229, 230, 289, 330, 339, 476
Fierro, Elías 378, 501
Fischer, Anton 263, 268
Fischer, Antonina 309–318
Fischer, Eleanor 613
Fister, Philomena 312
Fitch, Lillian 540
Flemenco, Eustace 401
Flint, Frank 536
Flintridge Sacred Heart Academy 410, 411, 527, 528, 536–546, 559, 560, 586, 630
Flores, Armella 585
Flores, Luisa de la Soledad 517
Flores, María Luisa 507
Flou, Bertranda de 340
Forgeng, Antoinette 549
Foudy, John 592
Franciscan Fathers 105, 106, 153, 218, 234, 238, 240, 241, 249, 251, 252, 328, 588, 592, 603
Freitas, John 299
Friese, Henrietta 294
Friesinger, Barnaba 443
Friganza, Trixie 542
Fritz, Bonaventure 609
Fruewirth, Andrew 195, 418–420, 442, 492
Fuhr, Raphael 203, 235–236, 254, 282, 283, 396
Fujier, Andre Marie 488

G

Gallagher, Winifred 479
Gantner, Brigitta 443
García-Conde, Doña Concepción (Conchita) 382, 383, 385–386, 389, 501, 502
García de la Cadena, Natalia 519, 520, 540, 575
García, Dolores 401

Gatschene, Marcellina 330, 599
Gatschen, Remigia 328
Gazano, Josefina (Amada) 391, 498
Geidobler, Ursula (Kiliana) 441
General Chapter 124, 135, 168, 177, 181, 182, 193, 225, 292, 316, 339, 340, 344, 398, 413, 493, 525, 541, 554, 558, 560, 563, 567, 572, 579, 583, 617
General Conference. *See* Mothers General Conference
Gerber, Ildephonsa 254, 369
Getz, Canisia 569
Getz, Paulina 447, 570
Ginker, Thomasina 18, 555
Gleason, Richard 405
Glenwood Summer Camp 373–374
Goemaere, Mary 30
González, Angelica 503
González, María del Pilar 503, 507, 512
Governo, [Domingo] 214
Grace, Thomas 313–317
Greb, Leo 413, 503, 506
Gregorian chant 166, 483–485, 590
Griesstaett 439–441
Griffin, Margaretha (Eva Rosa) 261, 263, 267, 269, 270
Grips, Marka 438, 469, 568, 569, 573
Grisez, Celestine 219
Grisez, Evangelista 193, 219, 226–227, 229
Gross, William 101, 125, 130
Guerrero, María Inés (Adda) 576
Guilfoyle, Merlin 248, 296, 337, 607
Gutiérrez, Catalina [Soledad] 305, 379, 383
Guzman, Dominic de 3–8, 12, 514, 641

H

Hagan, Columba 312
Hageman, Rosina 406, 586
Haggerty, John Leo 138
Haltermann, Clare 488
Hanna, Edward J. 255, 458–461, 463, 464, 475, 490, 546, 609
Hanrahan, John 594
Hansen, Ceslaus 202, 205, 264, 274, 341–343, 417–418, 420–422, 432, 492, 493
Harnett, Angela 398
Harnett, Patrick 163
Harth, Christina 122
Haselbeck, Friederick 434–437, 441, 451
Hatanaka, Marie Seraphine 225
Hauber, Joseph 33
Hauer, Aquina 437
Hauer, Febronia 443
Healy, Rosario (Elizabeth) 345, 378
Hebel, Raymond 469
Heim, Simplicia 469
Hengelberger, Julia (Peregrina) 441
Henke, Annunciata 409, 504, 529, 530
Hennessy, James Mary (Rose Marie) 604, 609
Henriques, Frances Marie 300, 603
Henriques, Rosalinda (Linda) 573, 588, 596, 597
Herde, Julius 1, 35, 50
Hernandez, María Luisa 521
Hewelcke, Margaret 601
Hieronyma, Mother 202
Hocker, Alberta (Anne) 80, 130, 131, 169, 172, 190, 193
Holl, Hyacintha 193, 462
Holy Cross Convent, Brooklyn 23, 28, 45, 49, 53, 64, 99, 203, 310, 343, 483
Holy Cross Convent, Ratisbon 8, 10, 23, 436, 437
Holy Rosary Parish, Portland 135–137, 139, 140
Holy Rosary School, Portland 137–143
Holzman, Alma 254
Hornung, Bernarda 193, 234, 328, 333
Howard, Edward D. 135, 595, 597, 599, 601
Huber, Barbara 394
Huber, Rosaria 394, 490, 546, 548
Hudson, Berchmans 225, 345, 612

I

Immaculata Academy / Marycrest High School, Portland 600–602
Immaculata Academy, Portland 143–144
Immaculate Conception Academy, San Francisco 81–85, 89, 246, 328, 332, 333–337, 377, 379, 417, 487, 588, 620, 624, 627
Immaculate Conception Church, San Francisco 602
Immaculate Conception Elementary School, San Francisco 602–604
Immaculate Conception Priory 84, 87, 254, 282, 321–324, 332, 563
Immaculate Heart Elementary School, Portland 135, 143, 601
Immaculate Heart of Mary, Albina 129–130
Immaculate Heart of Mary School, San Antonio 529–534
Indian schools 289, 290
Infanger, Hedwig 394, 569

INDEX 655

Instituto Lacordaire 575
Irish-German conflict (see Chapter 12: Crisis in Community) 279–285
Irving, Innocentia 193, 462, 490, 525, 546
Irwin, Clara 135, 168, 193, 272–273, 275, 342
Isnard, Mr. and Mrs. John 297

J

Jackson, Miriam 540, 605, 606
Jagar, Afra 139
Jesulein 436
Jiménez, Emmanuel 604
John the XXIII 618, 619
Joras, Emygdia 462
Josephinum 216, 217, 219, 223, 225, 237, 239, 289, 327, 372, 629
Juenemann, Perpetua 249, 250

K

Kaffer, Rosemary 529, 544
Kaiserheim (Kaiser Home) 72–73, 75, 78, 93–96
Kaiser, Peter 71, 73–75, 95, 97, 212
Kaiser Property. *See* Kaiserheim
Kassel, Isnarda (Cecilia) 438
Keane, Nora 613
Keane, Sheila 613
Kellerer, Zita 229
Kelly, Geraldine 141, 304, 549, 586
Kelly, Humbert H. 573
Kelly, Mr. and Mrs. John 129
Kena, Victoria. *See* Kine, Victoria (Magdalena)
Kennedy, Isidore 300
Kennedy, John F. 602
Keogh, Carmelita 144, 468
Kept, Thomas 413, 414
Kettlewell, Sophia 592
Kiefer, Thomas 606
Kiesel, Reginalda 219

Kine, Victoria (Magdalena) 44, 66, 165, 220, 340
Klein, Dominica (Frances) 66, 82, 89, 106, 126, 134, 135, 143, 144, 171, 236, 253, 334, 490
Klein, James 82
Klinkenberger, Edmunda 549
Kneusel, Jordana 193
Knights of Columbus 591, 600, 602
Koehl, Josephine 469, 534, 568
Kolezar, Claudia 246
Konigsberger, Regina 193
Konoske, Paul 588, 589
Kozell, Gemma 406
Kratz, Gregoria (Teresa) 437, 446, 484
Kratz, Joseph 437, 439
Kronseder, Alphonsina 441
Kroutsch, Benedicta 193, 287, 300–302
Kroutsch, Scholastica 193
Krug, Mary Benigna 544, 549, 602
Kuhn, Gertrude 222
Kuhn, Mechtilde 234
Ku Klux Klan 138
Kuppers, Elizabeth 302

L

LaCroix, Bonaventura 170, 193
Lafevre, Clementina 487
Laidlaw, John 135
Lamb, Christopher V. 571, 572, 574
Lampe, Seraphin 242–244, 244, 251, 565
Landaverde, Verónica 498
Lang, Pauline 627
La Palmera 349–374
La Providenza, Cavigliano, Switzerland 417, 427–434, 443
Larroca, Joseph Marie 186
La Sta. Escuela de María 522–523
Lasuen, Fermin Francisco de 211

Lawler, Albert 49
Lawrence, Siena 248, 589, 591, 593
Layman, Mary Ignatius (Patricia) 597
Lay Sisters 10, 11, 203–206, 519
Leal, John 474, 610
Leber, Antonia 469
Lee, Michael 396, 397, 605
Lehner, Theophane (Marie) 179
Lehrenfeld, Henrica 221
Leitner, Cornelia 462
Lentz, Dominicus 48–49, 66–67, 74, 86
Lewis, William T. 573
Lillis, Mary Thomas 177–178, 452
Lindner, Florentina 312
Lingelser, Sybillina 409
Linner, Maria (Ruperta) 441
Linneweber, Cecilia 287, 340
Lins, Arsenia 416, 443
Lins, Eusebia 246–247, 257
Lira, Margarita 504–505, 522, 576
Loftus, Gonzaga 599
Lopéz, Margarita 515, 517
Lynch, Patrick 88, 325, 331, 333

M

Maas, Anastasia 462
Maas, Wilhelmina 170
Maciel, Concepta 486–487, 576
Mackey, Annette 248
Madrid, Paz 503, 505, 512, 576
Maerz, Seraphina 43–47, 52, 66, 71, 73, 77, 80, 109, 113–118, 122, 126, 129, 131, 149, 171, 187, 190, 198, 205, 215, 233, 240–243, 261–263, 265–270, 274–275, 283–284, 287, 288, 290, 300, 324, 334, 339, 341, 343, 350, 352–354, 359–366, 368, 377–379, 381, 383, 417–422, 427–430, 430, 435, 437, 446, 462, 476, 487, 489, 493, 497, 502, 505–511, 515, 518–519, 525–530, 533–534, 538–540, 540, 546, 548, 565–567, 571–572, 581, 627
Maeusl, Thecla (Maria) 445, 469
Maguire, William 158–161, 159–162
Mahoney, Dennis 248
Maier, Conrada 221, 222
Manning, Mary Edward 251, 468
Manning, Timothy 174, 177, 408, 584–585, 594
Marbaise, Pius 224, 345, 371, 490, 497, 501–512, 522, 549, 579–589, 592, 595, 599, 603, 604, 605, 607–610, 612
Marianists. *See* Brothers of Mary
Marini, Frank 590
Martin, Charles C. 373, 374
Martin, Mara 606
Martin, Mary Jordan 469
Martin, W. G. 574
Marycrest High School, Portland 595, 600–602
Mater Dei Press 225, 231
May, Michael 33, 38–39, 43, 49, 53, 58, 63, 71, 76, 78–80, 86, 93, 95, 98, 110, 114–115, 118
Maza, Ancilla de la 534
McAuliffe, Michael 169–170
McCarthy, Brigitta 219
McCarthy, Francisca 126, 131
McCarthy, Gabriel 607
McCarthy, Raphael 304, 396
McElroy, Francis P. 461–468
McEnnis, Frances 456
McGovern, Benedict 49, 54, 132, 137
McGrath, Father 314
McGucken, Joseph T. 176–177, 539
McIntyre, James Francis 160–161, 178, 179, 404, 408, 544, 583–584, 587, 594–595, 605

McKenna, Clement 468–470
McMahon, Lawrence 474
McNeil, Benedict 406, 530, 574
McSweeney, Aloysia 135, 137, 487
McSweeney, Patricia 168, 193, 282
Meade, Richard 593
Medrano, Benita 501, 503
Meehan, John 223
Mendoza, Marguerite 330, 585–587
Menéndez, Juan 514
Meuer, Leonarda 430, 431, 443, 445
Meyer, Amanda 137, 139, 249, 587
Meyer, Imelda 193
Meyers, Amanda 573
Meyer, Teresa 149, 217, 378, 382, 383, 387, 390, 400, 487, 497, 498, 504, 515, 576, 581
Michael Montoya 404
Michel, Bernardina 35, 174, 176, 177, 189, 190, 193, 217, 247, 249, 253, 292, 345, 438, 449, 489, 490, 522, 525, 527, 543, 546, 548, 549, 559, 560, 563–569, 574–576
Michel, Maria Bernardina 189
Miller, Mary Hilary 545, 593
Missionary Sons of the Immaculate Heart of Mary 397
Mission San Gabriel Arcangel 397, 398, 402
Mission San Gabriel Elementary School 397–404
Mission San Gabriel High School 593–595
Mission San Jose 211–213, 221, 474
Mission San Jose, Motherhouse 100, 220–231, 302, 312–316, 333, 339, 352, 368, 468, 487, 546, 583
Mission San Jose, the Town 71, 189, 213–220, 227, 231, 303, 331, 339, 350, 368, 565, 604, 610

Mission San Rafael Arcangel 455, 457
Mitty, John J. 256, 257–259, 296, 298, 371, 470, 573, 590–591, 593, 603, 609, 625
Moholy, Noel 583
Monaghan, Rosalia 303–306, 469
Monotti, Liberata 417, 419, 421, 428, 430, 433
Montgomery, Archbishop 220, 329
Montgomery, Bishop 169
Montgomery, George 95, 169, 220, 329, 339
Montgomery, Mrs. J. B. 130
Montoya, Michael 404
Moore, Emilia 130–131, 148–149, 233, 253
Mora del Rio, José 383
Mora, Francis 147, 149–150, 166, 183
Moran, Brice 256
Morris, Amata 137, 139
Moser, Ildephonse 245, 249
Most Holy Trinity Church 13, 44
Motherhouse Chapel and Infirmary 610–612
Motherhouse, Mission San Jose 220
Mothers General Conference 527, 528, 557–560
Mullally, Ignatia 135, 227
Muller, Maria 443
Muller, Seraphin 251, 565
Muller, Walburga 233
Mulligan, Agnes (Maggie) 66, 89, 131, 135, 165, 193
Murphy, Captain W.A. 159
Murphy, Maureen 594
Murphy, Pius 49, 52, 137, 188, 283, 284
Murphy, Timoteo 455–457
Murphy, W.A. 159
Murray, James M. 372

N

Narváez, Francisca 383
Nazareth Novitiate, Altenberg 272, 414–416, 427, 442
Nelson, Karen 607
Neumann, Maximilian 220
Niedermeyer, Ambrosia 153, 189
Niemierski, Justina 225–227, 574
Nolan, Louis 205, 422, 424, 492, 493, 542, 557, 558
Normal School, Mission San Jose 345–346, 580
Norton, William 574, 611
Nuevo, J. 593, 594
Nuñez, Joaquina 499

O

Oberbrunner, Hyacintha 183–186, 198, 204
O'Brien, Daniel 571
Ochoa, Dominica 386, 519, 532, 575
O'Connell, Eugene 212
O'Connor, Augustina (Maggie) 149, 165, 171, 193, 312, 546
O'Donaghue, Patrick Joseph 405–407
O'Dowd, James T. 609
Oehlke, Alberta 256, 487, 595
Okos, Mechtildis 447–449, 570
Olive Oil 229–231, 396
Olsen, Stanislaus 139, 424
Olvera, Francisca 515, 517, 519
Onate, Miguel 398–401
O'Neill, James 604
O'Reilly, Charles 132–134
Ortega, Albertina 512
Ortíz, Señora 509–511
O'Shea, Matthew (Mary Alice) 587
Osuna, Luciano 287
Our Lady of Sorrows School, San Antonio 534–535
Our Lady of the Visitation, Verboort 101–104, 102

P

Panhaus, Fabiana 430
Papal Approval
 A Dream Fulfilled 417–426
 Dominican Support in Rome 341–344
 The Journey Begins 190–202
 The Journey Continues 272–276
Pascal, Concepción (María) 391, 498, 503
Patterson, California 306, 608–610
Pax Erholungsheim (Pax Heim) 569–571
Pellettieri, Imelda 488
Peralta, Sister Rosa María (Francisca) 242, 576
Pérez, Angelina 469
Pérez, Joaquin 504
Pérez, Ma. de los Angeles 517
Peri, Edwina 427, 434
Perochena, Inés 386, 390, 498
Pfeffer, Louise 177, 545–546, 548, 564
Philipp, Pudentia 221, 223, 230–231
Phipps, Mary Michael 179
Pidgeon, Robertina 302
Piernikarczyk, Bertranda 345
Pons, María Lourdes 503
Portland, Oregon 49, 80, 101, 102, 104, 125–127, 129–140, 142, 143, 189, 203, 219, 275, 487, 548, 595, 597–600, 602, 620, 629
Poschmann, Cyrilla 139, 487
Possberg, Thoma 413, 416, 430, 443, 445, 446
Powers, Vincentia (Catherine) 80, 102, 148, 193, 242–243
Preciado, José María 509, 529–530

Prendergast, Very Rev. (John Joseph) 188
Preun, Wilhelmina 462
Prose, Redempta 141, 548–549, 594, 599–601

Q

Queen of the Holy Rosary College 346, 526, 546–549, 564, 576, 620
Queen of the Holy Rosary Convent 35, 44, 49, 54, 55, 65–67, 80, 83
Quinlan, Celestine 299
Quinn, Patrick J. 587, 625

R

Raffeiner, Stephan 12–14, 17, 24
Ratisbon 18–19, 21–23, 57, 61, 90, 149, 190, 342, 434, 436, 437, 556
Rauw, James 132
Reams, Cecile Marie (Mary) 605–607
Regalado, Vincenta 503
Regensberg. *See* Ratisbon
Rehers, Mary Bertha 48– 487, 536, 612
Rehers, Thomasina 536, 545
Reichert, Ignatia 436
Reichert, Pulcheria 276, 323, 394, 436, 487
Reilly, Father J. 132–134, 590–593, 612
Rentfle, Jacobina 254
Reyes, María Victoria 503
Rhoendorf-on-the-Rhine 264–268
Rielly, Patricia 605, 606
Rimpau family 148, 149
Riordan, Patrick William 83, 87, 88, 93–99, 117–119, 121, 187–188, 191, 194–195, 197, 205, 213, 215, 217–218, 236, 237, 239, 242–243, 252–253, 282–285, 287, 289, 292, 301, 326, 329, 343–344, 352, 354, 368, 458, 553
Rivera, Magdalena 515, 517
Rodríguez, Joaquín 377, 378, 380
Rolland, Ludgera 254
Romkowski Wilson, Clara 80. *See also* Wilson, Raymunda
Ruegg, Frank and Mary 61, 62, 77, 78, 85
Rusting, Bernadine 479
Rusting, Vincentia 306
Ryder, Mrs. Leo 594

S

Sacred Heart Academy/High School, Los Angeles 172–179, 225, 620
Sacred Heart Convent 164, 168, 170, 177–179, 181, 233, 396, 398, 399, 400, 405, 406, 526, 529, 536, 541, 585, 623
Sacred Heart Elementary School, Los Angeles 163–172
Sacred Heart Priory 168, 177
Sacred Heart School, Patterson, Calif. 608–610
Sacred Heart School, Ukiah 287
Sailer, Josepha 216
Salas, Bertrand 469
Salus Infirmorum 565, 612
Samaha, John Dominic 172, 595
Sánchez, Dominga 515
Sandoval, Elisa 406
San Francisco Archdiocese 31, 95, 96, 97, 297, 298, 456, 468, 475, 485, 608, 617
San Francisco Earthquake. *See* Earthquake, San Francisco
San Gabriel Convent 402
San Gabriel (Town) 397–398, 400

San Lucas Catechism Center, Atzcapotzalco 380
San Miguel de Allende 512, 514–516, 575
Santa Rosa Academy, Atzcapotzalco. *See* Academia Santa Rosa, Atzcapotzalco
Santa Teresita School, Los Angeles 584–587
Santo Domingo Convent. *See* Convent of Santo Domingo
Santo Domingo Novitiate 575, 576
Savant, Mariella 487
Schafer, Loretto 138, 345, 379, 400
Schallwig, Balbina 229
Scheer, Dominicus 197, 199, 200, 201–204, 206, 263, 265–266, 268, 270, 272–274, 281, 477, 478, 492, 554, 556
Schell, Cunigunda 18, 33, 68, 83, 90, 102, 107–110, 115, 122, 191
Scheuermann, Verona 626
Schinstock, Mary Francesca 316
Schlickenrieder, Armella 381, 383, 386–387
Schmidbauer, Walburgis 469
Schmidbauer, Wunibalda 469
Schmidt, Delfina 608
Schmidt, Mary Catherine 486, 490
Schmitt, Charles A. 157, 159, 162–163
Schmitt, Delphina 441
Schmitz, Jerome 595–600
Schneider, Hyacintha 102, 126, 128, 130, 131, 147, 219, 220
Schoeffler, Hans 450
Schoenstein, Louis 255, 546
Schoenstein, Mary Mark 255, 546
Schonborn, Gertrudis 437, 469

School of the Madeleine, Berkeley 571–574
Schreiber, Josephina 269, 272, 275, 416
Schreiber, Sebastiana 206, 462, 463
Schrickler, Lambertina 437
Schriever, Marcolina 394
Schumacher, Ludovika 193
Schwarzenback, Nemesia 374, 568
Schwarz, Peter 33, 53, 107
Second Order 9, 71–73, 93, 95, 96, 183–187, 190, 194, 199, 435
Second Vatican Council 618–619
Seghers, Charles 101
Serra Center 372, 629
Serranía, Carlotta 503, 505
Serranía, Magdalena 386
Sewald, Ludovica 447
Sewald, Ludovika 448
Sharkey, Laurentia 385, 386, 546, 548
Siena Studio 223–224
Sinseder, Stilla 447, 571, 608
Sisters of Tacoma. *See* Dominican Sisters of Tacoma
Sisters of the Holy Family 50, 609
Sisters of the Holy Names 50, 138, 169
Smith, Raymond 296
Solís, Refugio 517, 519
Sommers, Alois 125
Soyer, Katarina 437
Spada, Emily 249
Spagl, Manessa 469
St. Aloysius School 312–317
St. Alphons Seminar, Ingolstadt, Bavaria 608
St. Anne School, Gresham 598–599
St. Anthony School, San Francisco 252–259, 323, 325–326, 546, 563
St. Boniface Church, Anaheim 147–148, 153, 158, 162, 535

St. Boniface Church, San Francisco 1, 27, 35, 50, 54, 71, 105, 148, 158, 220, 328, 563
St. Boniface School, Anaheim 529, 535–536
St. Boniface School, San Francisco 35, 45, 61–63, 65, 79, 83, 106, 110, 274, 328–331, 336
St. Catherine's Academy, Anaheim 148–151
St. Catherine's Military Academy 155–164, 535
St. Catherine's Orphanage 151–154, 409
St. Dominic's Convent, Portland 135, 137, 138, 139, 143
St. Dominic's Priory, San Francisco 54
St. Elizabeth Elementary School 241–249
St. Elizabeth High School 249–252
St. Elizabeth Parish 241–242, 245, 250, 251
St. Frances Cabrini School, Los Angeles 588–590
St. Frances Cabrini School, San Jose 606–607
St. Ignatius School, Los Angeles 404–409, 619
St. James Boys' School, San Francisco 587–588
St. James Parish 88, 331, 333, 588, 606, 612
St. James Parochial School for Girls 333
St. John Seminary, Camarillo 565–569
St. Josef Schule, Altenberg 413, 414, 416–417
St. Joseph Church, Mission San Jose, 71
St. Joseph Elementary School, Mission San Jose 233–235
St. Joseph Parish, Portland 125–126
St. Joseph School, Los Angeles 233
St. Joseph School, Mission San Jose 604–605, 630
St. Joseph School, Portland, Oregon 126–132, 134–136
St. Joseph's Church, Portland 126
St. Joseph's, Los Angeles 233
St. Joseph the Worker Parish, Portland 596
St. Joseph the Worker School, Portland 595–597
St. Lucy's Mission, Los Angeles 587
St. Martin's Residence (see Salus Infirmorum) 612
St. Mary Magdalen Parish 201, 571, 573, 611
St. Mary of the Angels Parish 287, 299
St. Mary of the Angels School 299–300
St. Mary of the Palms 227, 334, 367–374, 474, 604, 629
St. Mary's Elementary School, Fullerton 409–411
St. Michael Elementary School 393–397
St. Michael High School, Los Angeles 605–606
St. Michael's Convent 395
St. Nicholas / St. William School, Los Altos 590–593
Sts. Peter and Paul Convent (Priory), Altenhohenau 434–452, 608
Sts. Peter and Paul School, Altenhohenau 631

St. Therese School, Alhambra 528–529
St. Therese School, Alhambra, California 630
St. Therese School, Portland 597–598
St. Thomas Aquinas Chapel 160
St. Thomas Aquinas Seminary (see Saint Thomas Aquinas Seminary) 213, 214
St. Thomas School for Boys 331–333
St. Vincent Orphanage 456–461
St. Vincent's Abbey 11
St. Vincent's School for Boys 629
Stabel, Bonifacia 63, 414, 437–441, 443
Staimer, Seraphina 18, 31–33, 37, 39–41, 43, 45, 46, 48–57, 61, 63, 64, 67–71, 73–83, 85–87, 93–95, 98, 101–111, 108, 113–117, 120–122, 147–148, 165, 311
Steer, Geralda 570
Steinberger, Florentina 469
Stein, Johanna 540
Stellner, Katharina 441
Stiebritz, Celestine 609
Stoetters, Peter 147, 148
Stolz, Clothilda 340
Stopper, Callista 141, 400, 487
Stopper, Dolores 139, 177, 403, 406, 585
Strauss, Clara 233
Struett, Placida 221
Struffert, Polycarp 225, 502–503
Sturz, Gerarda 441, 469
Stute, Theodora 416, 430, 443, 545
Suárez-Peredo, Amalia (Rosita) 222, 381, 385, 498, 512
Sullivan, Charles 548
Sunderer, Abbie 216
Sunderer, Joseph and Rosa 214
Sunderer, Rose (see Whiteside, Rose) 213

T

Tessen, Paula von 224, 345, 346, 487
Theissling, Ludwig 417
Thielen, Martin 141
Third Order 10, 183–187, 190, 191, 194, 203, 204, 311, 378, 418, 419, 420, 421, 425, 428, 483, 514, 516, 517, 554, 557, 558, 641
Thoren, Anna 413, 414, 430, 431, 443
Thuente, Clement M. 555
Thyk, Magdalena 223
Tiffany, Agnes Mary 406
Torres, Angel Sebastian 377, 379, 380
Torres, Guadalupe 345, 385
Trapp, Albertus 201, 263, 265–267, 270, 271, 273
Traviss, Mary Peter 452, 536, 588
Trippe, Ancilla 608
Tschirner, Antonina 169, 193
Twenty-first Street School 77–78, 85

U

Ukiah, California 223, 287–306
Ukiah Home Missions 300–302
Uriarte-Healy, Auxilia 512

V

Valverde, Emeterio Téllez 514
Van Lin, Gerard 129, 130
Vásquez-Dávila, María de la Cruz (Sara) 520, 532, 533
Vásquez-Dávila, Soledad 391, 530
Veloz, Josefina 379, 383, 487, 498, 504

INDEX   663

Verboort, Oregon 101–104, 109, 122, 125, 147
Vilarrasa, Francis Sadoc 30, 49, 136
Voggenauer, Ludwig Maria 570
Vordermayer, Bonifatius 434, 436, 441

W

Waechter, Magdalena (Maria Rosa) 51, 66
Wagner, John 393, 396
Wagner, Roger 540, 545
Wagner, Vibiana 393
Wallrath, Dolorosa 155, 156, 168, 180, 190, 193, 224, 274, 275, 312, 413, 489, 536, 538–546
Wallrath, Michael 224, 275, 312, 314, 316, 317
Walsh, Cabrini (Patricia Marie) 589
Walsh, John 336, 337
Watts, Agatha 193, 287, 288, 300
Weber, Amalia 276, 585
Weber, Juliana 404
Weber, Osanna 462
Weigl, Columba 434–436, 453
Weimar, Adam 505
Weisenberg, Seraphine 312
Weiss, Casimira 607
Weiss, Felicitas 63–66, 71, 89, 150, 151, 164, 165, 188, 190, 193, 214, 216–218, 220, 222, 229, 243, 312, 334, 339, 476, 553
Westmark, Felicia 462
Whiteside, Rose (nee Sunderer) 213, 217
Wiemand, Petrina 193, 340
Wildenauer, Karl 451
Wilhelm, Jeanette 300
Williamsburg 12–17, 20–22, 32, 310, 631
Wilson, Catharina 148
Wilson, Damian 592

Wilson, Raymunda 153, 190, 203, 293, 339, 481, 627
Wimmer, Boniface 11–13, 17, 24, 34
Wimmer, Guala 469
Winschuh, Fidelis 609
Wittemann, Cortona 540
Wittenzellner, Verona 160, 330, 404
Wittmann, Marietta 608
World War I 415, 427, 459, 627
World War II 140, 157, 173, 222, 230, 247, 257, 403, 446–449, 467, 570, 576, 590

Z

Zapata, Emiliano 382
Zapatistas 382, 386–390
Ziesche, Cesla 400
Zimbrón, Rosa María 501
Zimmerman, Stella 487
Zircus, Mathia 586
Zobelein, Michael Marie (Giulii) 225

www.ingramcontent.com/pod-product-compliance
Lightning Source LLC
Chambersburg PA
CBHW021822220426
43663CB00005B/99